Analyze Your ACT

Winni van Gessel

Published by van Gessel, Inc

2017

Second Edition

Acknowledgements

Thanks to those who helped at home: Corrie van Gessel, Veronica van Gessel, Ania van Gessel, Matt Vassil, and Hunter Carter. They helped me write and edit and rewrite and then write some more. They gave me honest feedback throughout the project and during the final days when finishing this book seemed almost impossible.

Thanks to those who helped in the office and across the USA: Austin Jones, Ian Hafley, and Joel Parker for their numerous contributions. Mary Brenzel, Donna Hill, Hazem Khazbak, Elise Mandel, and Baily Ogger for their precise editing and Sheri Woods for her design of the cover. Thanks also to Tom Pabin, Betsy Filchak, Annie Griggs, and my colleagues from Class 101 across the country who helped to create ideas, formulate questions, correct my grammar, and inspire me to aim higher.

Creating an ACT book is a daunting task, but I was determined to be student-oriented as well as curriculum-oriented. I wanted to provide feedback instead of just presenting a score. Furthermore, I wanted to provide 1-page handouts and 1-page quizzes to keep students motivated and to keep the material manageable. I wholeheartedly believe that a student who follows the instructions in this book can tackle the areas of the ACT in which he or she had previously struggled.

I want to dedicate this book to my family and to all my students who have worked hard on their ACT to make their education count. Their feedback, their willingness, and even their mistakes helped to make this book what it is today. This second edition is much improved, thanks to the requests, insights, and comments of all who worked with the book over the last year.

Winni van Gessel

May 2017

About the Author: Winni van Gessel

Originally from the Netherlands, Winni has taught students of all ages in Lexington, KY, from Pre-K to graduate students. He has been a Montessori guide and headmaster, a soccer coach, and a motivational speaker. He has also taught study skills to hundreds of students across the United States. Winni is an owner and college planner at Class101. He helps families and students save tens of thousands of dollars of college tuition by analyzing standardized tests, scrutinizing essays, and pursuing the best colleges and scholarships.

Winni has an M.Ed. in Educational Policies and Evaluation from the University of Kentucky, where he continued his doctoral studies in Instructional Design. His passion for education and his boundless energy enable Winni to focus on the unique needs of his scholars who have inspired him to create individualized tools for their success.

Winni lives in Lexington with his wife, Ania, and their two daughters, Corrie and Veronica. The girls were the reason that Winni became interested in the conundrums of the ACT, and they have both been willing pioneers of Winni's worksheets and exercises. The whole family has been an essential ingredient in the creation of this book.

CONTENTS

How To Use This Book

1) Take a test provided by the ACT. Download 1267C or 1572C from the web. The ACT has made those tests available for free, although it does NOT do a very good job of helping you to figure out what you are doing wrong.

2) Mark the wrong answers on the trendsheets. (page 7-17) Count your mistakes to find your score.

   (For additional trendsheets, see our website www.analyzeyouract.com. Our website has numerous trendsheets from tests in popular books as well as from many official ACTs in the past.)

3) Analyze your ACT by finding areas in which you made several mistakes. These are your *trends*. Determine how many areas you need to address to increase your score by three points, an achievable goal for a motivated student.

4) Study the handouts on the pages as indicated under each box on the trendsheet.

5) Practice with the quizzes that are provided after each handout. Aim for mastery.

6) Revisit the test questions that you missed previously in this area. Did you spot the correct answer this time? Having newly-developed skills can help.

7) Repeat steps 3-6 with any other subject from the trendsheet. Work top to bottom.

8) Finally, once you have mastered several new concepts, take another test. (See the end of each chapter.) Analyze that test with the provided trendsheet. Are you still making the same mistakes? If you followed the above steps closely, you should have "increased your score like never before."

TRENDSHEETS

The trendsheets in this book give you very precise feedback about your skills and your weaknesses. Use the trendsheets to help you set a goal. Find out how many errors you need to address to improve three points on your next test. Then, find the areas of your choice on the trendsheet that add up to the number of errors you want to address, and work on the pages in the book as indicated.

If you use your trendsheets as a guideline, you will find out where you went wrong and how to avoid those mistakes during your next test.

1) Mark your score on the right side of the trendsheet.
2) Circle the questions you missed.
3) Find your trends (categories with the most mistakes.)
4) Set a goal: How many mastered categories will lead to a 3-point improvement?
5) Study the pages in this book that will help you master the required skills.
6) Review your missed questions.

SAMPLE TRENDSHEET

Conventions of Standard English

Fragment	Modifier	Pronoun	Punctuation		Other
			Comma		
25	11	9	2	52	1
38	(42)	21	(7)	(61)	10
59	51	(47)	19	64	(17)
	66	(54)	26	72	20
	73		31	(75)	32
			36		41
Page 18	Page 48	Page 64	Page 22	Page 26	P. 32

Knowledge of language

Idioms	Verb use			Redundancy	Word choice
	Tense	Agree	Parallel		
22	3	(16)	23	34	40
	12	62	57	43	44
	33	74	71	55	46
	63			68	49
					(60)
					67
Page 58	Page 81	Page 76	Page 87	Page 72	P. 92

Production of Writing

Clarity	Transition	Order	Redundancy	Purpose	
53	6	14	4	(13)	45
69	8	27	5	(18)	48
	15			24	(50)
	39			28	56
	58			(30)	
	65			35	**Tone**
	70			37	29
Page 104	Page 108		Page 115	Page 119	P. 357

#mistakes	ACT Score
46-48	13
44-46	14
41-43	15
38-40	16
36-37	17
34-35	18
31-33	19
29-30	20
26-28	21
24-25	22
21-23	23
19-20	24
17-18	25
14-16	26
12-13	27
11	28
9-10	29
7-8	30
6	31
5	32
3-4	33
2	34
1	35
0	36

Setting a goal of increasing your score by three points is a good short-term objective. Focusing on just **two areas** will help you to achieve this. Going from a 26 to a 32? That is possible when you master three concepts: **commas, pronouns, and purpose questions.** This book will help you to overcome your trends.

SAMPLE TRENDSHEET

Conventions of Standard English

Fragment	Modifier	Pronoun	Punctuation		Other
			Comma		
25	11	(9)		(52)	1
38	(42)	(21)	2	(61)	10
59	51	(47)	(7)	(64)	(17)
	(66)	(54)	19	72	20
	73		(26)	(75)	(32)
			31		(41)
			(36)		
Page 18	Page 48	Page 64	Page 22	Page 26	Page 32

Knowledge of language

Idioms	Verb use			Redundancy	Word choice
	Tense	Agree	Parallel	(34)	40
22	3	(16)	23	43	44
	12	62	57	(55)	46
	(33)	74	71	68	49
	63				(60)
					67
Page 58	Page 81	Page 76	Page 87	Page 72	Page 92

Production of Writing

Clarity	Transition	Order	Redundancy	Purpose	
53	6	14	4	13	45
(69)	8	(27)	5	18	48
	(15)			24	(50)
	39			28	56
	58			(30)	
	(65)			(35)	Tone
	70			37	29
Page 104	Page 108		Page 115	Page 119	Page 357

#mistakes	ACT Score
46-48	13
44-46	14
41-43	15
38-40	16
36-37	17
34-35	18
31-33	19
29-30	20
26-28	21
24-25	22
21-23	23
19-20	24
17-18	25
14-16	26
12-13	27
11	28
9-10	29
7-8	30
6	31
5	32
3-4	33
2	34
1	35
0	36

Setting a goal of increasing your score by three points is a good short-term objective. Focusing on just **two areas** will help you to achieve this. Going from a 21 to a 26? That is possible when you master three concepts: **Commas, other punctuation, and pronouns.** This book will help you to overcome your trends.

English - ACT *1572CPRE (ACT 2015 – 2016)*

Name: _____ Date: _____

Mistakes: _____ ACT Score: _____

Conventions of Standard English

Fragment	Modifier	Pronoun	Punctuation			
			Comma		Other	
39	4	42	1	32	9	
	19	43	5	33	12	
	21	46	10	47	24	
	61	74	16	49	25	
			20	53	50	
			22	64	62	
			31	67	66	
					69 72	
Page 18	Page 48	Page 64	Page 22		Page 32	

# mistakes	ACT Score
53-55	10
51-52	11
49-50	12
47-48	13
44-46	14
40-43	15
37-39	16
35-36	17
33-34	18
31-32	19
28-30	20
25-27	21
23-24	22
20-22	23
18-19	24
16-17	25
14-15	26
13	27
11-12	28
10	29
9	30
8	31
6-7	32
5	33
4	34
1-3	35
0	36

Knowledge of language

Idioms	Verb use			Redundancy	Word choice
	Tense	Agree	Parallel		
11	3	54	14	18	28
	6	63	29	40	
	8		44	52	
	17			59	
	35		51		
	37		52		
Page 58	Page 81	Page 76	Page 87	Page 72	Page 92

Production of Writing

Clarity	Transition	Order	Purpose		
			Detail		Summary
23	2	14	7	68	15
28	27	29	13	70	30
38	34	44	26	71	45
55	48	Redundancy	36		57
Page 104	58	51	41		60
Tone	65	52	56		75
	73				
Page 357	Page 108	Page 115	Page 119		Page 121

1) Mark your score on the right. Circle the questions you missed. **2)** Find your trends (categories with the most mistakes.) Set a goal: How many mastered categories will lead to a 3-point improvement? **3)** Study the pages in this book that will help you master the required skills. **4)** Review your missed questions.

English - ACT   *1267C (ACT 2013 / 2014)*

Name: _____ Date: _____

Mistakes: _____ ACT Score: _____

Conventions of Standard English

Modifier	Pronoun	Punctuation			
		Comma			Other
	3				
23	8	1	16	45	4
31	11	2	22	47	13
32	21	6	25	63	14
56	26	9	38	71	17
62	49	10	40	72	36
	50	12	43	74	46
Page 48	Page 64	Page 22			Page 32

Knowledge of language

Idioms	Verb use			Redundancy	Word choice
	Tense	Agree	Parallel		
34	37	35		24	57
55	41	70		33	58
61	53			52	66
					73
Page 58	Page 81	Page 76	Page 87	Page 72	Page 92

Production of Writing

Clarity	Transition	Order	Redundancy	Purpose	
	27	29	19	Detail	
Read the question	44	51		5	42
7	69	60		18	54
48				20	64
65		Tone		28	Summary
67		68		30	15
75				39	59
Page 104	Page 108	Page 357	Page 115	Page 119	Page 121

#mistakes	ACT Score
47-48	12
46	13
43-45	14
41-42	15
38-40	16
36-37	17
34-35	18
31-33	19
28-30	20
25-27	21
23-24	22
20-22	23
18-19	24
16-17	25
14-15	26
12-13	27
10-11	28
9	29
8	30
7	31
6	32
5	33
3-4	34
1-2	35
0	36

1) Mark your score on the right. Circle the questions you missed. **2)** Find your trends (categories with the most mistakes.) Set a goal: How many mastered categories will lead to a 3-point improvement? **3)** Study the pages in this book that will help you master the required skills. **4)** Review your missed questions.

Math-ACT

1267CPRE (ACT 2013 – 2014)

Name: _____ Date: _____

\# Mistakes: _____ ACT Score: _____

Essential Skills Number & Quantity

Fractions, %	Average	Ratio	Irrational Imaginary	Roots & Exponents	Sequence	Factoring
46	4	27			58	16
51		35		15		
				19		
				25		
P. 164, 170	Page 174	Page 182	Page 198	Page 194	Page 190	Page 186

Algebra Geometry

Simple Equations	Quadratic Equation	Translation	Coordinates	Polygons	Circles	Triangles
				10	18	11
2 49	9	1	30	17	36	31
7 54	59	3	34	20	37	47
21 55		5		23	45	
26 60		6		38	48	
29		8		40		
		13		44		
Page 202	Page 206	Page 218	Page 252	Page 248	Page 240	Page 222

Functions Stats and Probability

Logic	Trig	Functions	Linear Equations	Tables & Graphs	Matrix	Probability
	22	14				
	42		24	50	53	12
	56		28	52		32
	57		33			43
			39			
			41			
Page 274	Page 262	Page 254	Page 258	Page 286	Page 278	Page 282

# of mistakes	ACT Score
49-50	13
46-48	14
42-45	15
37-41	16
34-36	17
32-33	18
30-31	19
28-29	20
27	21
25-26	22
23-24	23
20-22	24
18-19	25
16-17	26
14-15	27
12-13	28
11	29
9-10	30
8	31
7	32
6	33
4-5	34
2-3	35
0-1	36

1) Mark your score on the right. Circle the questions you missed. **2)** Find your trends (categories with the most mistakes.) Set a goal: How many mastered categories will lead to a 3-point improvement? **3)** Study the pages in this book that will help you master the required skills. **4)** Review your missed questions.

Math-ACT *1572CPRE (ACT 2015 – 2016)*

Name: _____ Date: _____

Mistakes: _____ ACT Score: _____

Essential Skills   Number & Quantity

Fractions, %	Average	Ratio	Irrational Imaginary	Roots & Exponents	Sequence	Factoring
6						
18	2	3	29	19	7	
21	10	33		22	16	
25	37	51		48		
32						
43						
56						
P. 164, 170	Page 174	Page 182	Page 198	Page 194	Page 190	Page 186

Algebra   Geometry

Simple Equations	Quadratic Equation	Translation	Coordinates	Polygons	Circles	Triangles
4	24	15	40	9	14	13
23		35	44	12	49	17
52		54		34		20
58				41		26
				46		27
				50		
				53		
Page 202	Page 206	Page 218	Page 252	Page 248	Page 240	Page 222

Functions   Stats and Probability

Logic	Trig	Functions	Linear Equations	Tables & Graphs	Matrix	Probability
55	30	5	39	8	45	1
	57	11		28		31
	60	42		36		43
				38		47
						55
						59
Page 274	Page 262	Page 254	Page 258	Page 286	Page278	Page 282

# of mistakes	ACT Score
50-52	13
48-49	14
41-43	15
38-40	16
37-39	17
34-36	18
32-33	19
31	20
29-30	21
27-28	22
25-26	23
23-24	24
21-22	25
14-16	26
12-13	27
13-15	28
11-12	29
9-10	30
7-8	31
6	32
4-5	33
3	34
1-2	35
0	36

1) Mark your score on the right. Circle the questions you missed. **2)** Find your trends (categories with the most mistakes.) Set a goal: How many mastered categories will lead to a 3-point improvement? **3)** Study the pages in this book that will help you master the required skills. **4)** Review your missed questions.

Reading - ACT

1267C (ACT 2013 / 2014)

Name: _____ Date: _____

Mistakes: _____ ACT Score: _____

Prose Fiction			Time:		
Purpose	Reference	Vocab	Except	Infer	Tone / View
1	6		2	4	
	7		3	8	
	9		5		
	10				
Pg. 363	Pg. 342, 365	Pg. 358	-	Pg. 353	Pg. 361

Social Science			Time:		
Purpose	Reference	Vocab	Except	Infer	Tone / View
14	17	20	16	11	
15	18		19	12	
				13	
Pg. 363	Pg. 342, 365	Pg. 358	-	Pg. 353	Pg. 361

Humanities			Time:		
Purpose	Reference	Vocab	Except	Infer	Tone / View
23	22		30	21	
25	24			27	
29	26				
	28				
Pg. 363	Pg. 342, 365	Pg. 358	-	Pg. 353	Pg. 361

Natural Science			Time:		
Purpose	Reference	Vocab	Except	Infer	Tone / View
31	34	36		32	32
33	35	37			
	38				
	39 40				
Pg. 363	Pg. 342, 365	Pg. 358	-	Pg. 353	Pg. 361

# mistakes	ACT Score
30-31	11
28-29	12
27	13
25-26	14
23-24	15
22	16
21	17
19–20	18
18	19
16-17	20
16	21
14	22
12-13	23
11	24
10	25
9	26
8	27
7	28
6	29
5	30
4	31
3	32
2	34
1	35
0	36

1) Mark your score on the right. Circle the questions you missed. **2)** Find your trends (categories with the most mistakes.) Set a goal: How many mastered categories will lead to a 3-point improvement? **3)** Study the pages in this book that will help you master the required skills. **4)** Review your missed questions.

Reading - ACT   *1572CPRE (ACT 2015 – 2016)*

Name: _____ Date: _____

Mistakes: _____   ACT Score: _____

Prose Fiction			Time:		
Purpose	Reference	Vocab	Except	Infer	Tone / View
1	2	6			4
7	3	9			8
10	5				
Pg. 363	Pg. 342, 365	Pg. 358	-	Pg. 353	Pg. 361

Social Science			Time:		
Purpose	Reference	Vocab	Except	Infer	Tone / View
13	12	18			11
15	14				
16	17				
	19 20				
Pg. 363	Pg. 342, 365	Pg. 358	-	Pg. 353	Pg. 361

Humanities			Time:		
Purpose	Reference	Vocab	Except	Infer	Tone / View
27	21			23	26
	22			29	
	24			30	
	25 28				
Pg. 363	Pg. 342, 365	Pg. 358	-	Pg. 353	Pg. 361

Natural Science			Time:		
Purpose	Reference	Vocab	Except	Infer	Tone / View
31	34	33		35	32
	36	37			
	38				
	39 40				
Pg. 363	Pg. 342, 365	Pg. 358	-	Pg. 353	Pg. 361

# mistakes	ACT Score
30-31	12
29	13
27-28	14
26	15
24-25	16
23	17
22	18
20-21	19
19	20
17-18	21
16	22
14-15	23
13	24
12	25
11	26
10	27
9	28
8	29
7	30
6	31
4-5	32
3	33
2	34
1	35
0	36

1) Mark your score on the right. Circle the questions you missed. **2)** Find your trends (categories with the most mistakes.) Set a goal: How many mastered categories will lead to a 3-point improvement? **3)** Study the pages in this book that will help you master the required skills. **4)** Review your missed questions.

Science - ACT

1267C (ACT 2013 / 2014)

Name: _____ Date: _____

\# Mistakes: _____ ACT Score: _____

Charts and Graphs

	Lookup				What if?	Why?
Graph	1 2 13 16		36 37 38 40		16 39	15 17
Table					14 23	
Other	3 / 5		6			4
	Tables: Page 412 Graphs: Page 430					

Experiments

	Lookup				What if?		Why?	
Graph	7 8	11 19	18 33		9 20	31 32	 35	
Table								
Other	21				10		12 22	34
	Tables: Page 412 Graphs: Page 430 Experiments: Page 446							

Opposing Viewpoints

	Lookup		What if?		Why?
Graph					
Table					
Other	24 29	25	26	27	28
	Conflicting Viewpoints: Page 454				

# Mistakes	ACT Score
31	12
30	13
29	14
28	15
27	16
25-26	17
24	18
22-23	19
20-21	20
18-19	21
17	22
15-16	23
13-14	24
11-12	25
10	26
8-9	27
7	28
6	29
5	30
4	31
3	33
2	34
1	35
0	36

1) Mark your score on the right. Circle the questions you missed. **2)** Find your trends (categories with the most mistakes.) Set a goal: How many mastered categories will lead to a 3-point improvement? **3)** Study the pages in this book that will help you master the required skills. **4)** Review your missed questions.

Science - ACT   *1572 ACT 2013 / 2014)*

Name: _____ Date: _____

\# Mistakes: _____ ACT Score: _____

Charts and Graphs

	Lookup		What if?		Why?	
Graph	15 18	36 39 40	16 17	19	38	
Table						
Other	37				20 34	35

Tables: Page 412   Graphs: Page 430

Experiments

	Lookup		What if?		Why?	
Graph	1 22	23 25	26		2 24	
Table	29 32	33	4 30	31	5 6	
Other	3 27				7 21	28

Tables: Page 412   Graphs: Page 430   Experiments: Page 446

Opposing Viewpoints

	Lookup		What if?	Why?
Graph	10			
Table				
Other	8 9	13	11 12	14

Conflicting Viewpoints: Page 454

# Mistakes	ACT Score
31	12
30	13
29	14
28	15
27	16
25-26	17
24	18
22-23	19
20-21	20
19	21
17-18	22
15-16	23
13-14	24
11-12	25
9-10	26
8	27
7	28
6	29
5	30
4	31
3	33
2	34
1	35
0	36

1) Mark your score on the right. Circle the questions you missed. **2)** Find your trends (categories with the most mistakes.) Set a goal: How many mastered categories will lead to a 3-point improvement? **3)** Study the pages in this book that will help you master the required skills. **4)** Review your missed questions.

ENGLISH

CONTENTS

ENGLISH

Conventions of Standard English

SENTENCE STRUCTURE

Make sure you can identify the following patterns in the ACT:

The Sentence

The Fragment

The Run-On Sentence

The Comma Splice

Sentence Structure

It is important that you know how to recognize the following sentence structures:

The Sentence

Each full sentence needs to have a subject and verb. The following phrase is the shortest sentence in the English language that has both:

"I do."

The Fragment

Although a fragment has a subject and a verb, it is not a complete thought. The sentence is not finished.
Example:

"When I do."

 Tip: Here is a quick test: run into a crowded room and yell your sentence. If it does not make any sense, it is most likely a fragment. "Because the girl with the pink hair!" See? That is a good test for a fragment.

 Tip: If an action word ends on "–ing", it is only a verb if it is accompanied by a helping verb such as is, are, am, was, were, etc.

"I <u>am</u> running across the fields behind my house."   This is a full sentence.
"Running across the fields behind my house."   This is a fragment.
"Don't run across the field behind my house!"   There is no subject, but it is a full sentence.
    Commands always have the subject of "you".

The Run-On Sentence

Two full sentences <u>cannot</u> be written back to back without a conjunction or a punctuation mark. Watch for sentences with two subjects and two verbs.

"I like chocolate I eat it every day." (Incorrect)

The Comma Splice

Two full sentences <u>cannot</u> be written back to back with a simple comma to "splice" them. (See comma rules on page 22.)

"I like chocolate, I eat it every day." (Incorrect)

 Tip: A popular punctuation question on the ACT is: Which punctuation mark is <u>not</u> correct between two full sentences?

A. _____. _____.   Sure, you can always put a period between two sentences.
B. _____; _____.   No problem. (See the punctuation rules on page 32.)
C. _____, and _____.   Yes, this is allowed. (See the comma rules on page 22.)
D. _____, _____.   The comma splice! This is never a good option.

Fragments - Quiz 1

Find the full sentences. For many of the following exercises, it is important to know how to spot a fragment or how to identify a full sentence (a.k.a. a complete thought or an independent clause.)

1.
    A. Mrs. Blanco gone to visit her mother at the hospital.
    B. Finding a parking space there is usually easy during the week.
    C. Driving in the city during the evening rush hour.

2.
    A. To apply for a job at the new store in the mall.
    B. Asking the interviewer how often she would have to work on weekends.
    C. Shaking his new boss's hand, Tony knew he would like working there.

3.
    A. By the time Frances found out how expensive the wallpapering job would be.
    B. After getting estimates from five contractors, she decided to do the work herself.
    C. Before picking out an interesting wallpaper pattern that went well with her furniture.

4.
    A. Who borrowed Stefanie's car Saturday night.
    B. The nineteen-year-old car looked out of place next to the new models.
    C. Which the salesman was surprised to find in such good shape.

5.
    A. While waiting for her neighbor to move the car that blocked the driveway.
    B. To avoid hitting the other car, Michael had to back across the corner of the lawn.
    C. By making sure that no one will park across the driveway again.

6.
    A. Because Manuel was sure he had heard the same strange story many months ago.
    B. Although I will never forget how cold we were when we lost our heat last winter.
    C. Since Anna wasn't at the meeting, I took notes so that she wouldn't miss anything.

7.
    A. When my cousin moved to Troy, New York, after he finished school.
    B. After he went to all the trouble of fixing up his apartment.
    C. While living there, he made very few friends.

8.
    A. My sister has been running a charter fishing boat for five years.
    B. Many of her customers coming back three or four times over the summer.
    C. Her business been so busy that she has very little time for anything else.

9.
    A. In the hiding place that Carl had been using for years to get away from the noisy house.
    B. By the time that everyone had quieted down, my favorite television show was over.
    C. Before planning another family get-together at the already crowded park.

10.
    A. Although I knew she might wear something outrageous, I was still shocked by her dress.
    B. Because she didn't want to tell me where she had bought the strange outfit.
    C. When we finally heard that she had made the dress herself.

---

1) **B.** A=fragment C=fragment 2) **C.** A=fragment B=fragment 3) **B.** A=fragment C=fragment 4) **B.** A would need a question mark to be a sentence. C=fragment 5) **B.** A=fragment C=fragment 6) **C.** A=fragment B=fragment 7) **C.** A=fragment B=fragment 8) **A.** The other choices would be correct if the verbs were "came back" and "had been so busy." 9) **B.** A=fragment C=fragment 10) **A.** B=fragment C=fragment.

Fragments & Run-Ons - Quiz 2

1. Although he had often been a straight-A student and had volunteered often to improve his resume.
    A. NO CHANGE.
    B. Run-on: put a comma after *student*.
    C. Fragment: put a comma after *resume*, and finish the sentence.

2. This is going to be the most important game of your career, you had better start practicing for it.
    A. NO CHANGE.
    B. Fragment: put a comma after *it*, and finish the sentence.
    C. Run-on: replace the comma with a semicolon.

3. Knowing better than anyone else how the financially strapped families ignored the needs of her students and realizing that someone had to do something about the situation or the children would not be able to move on to higher education, Mrs. Roberta Lopez began to implement a program that would help financially challenged children achieve better grades and participate in more after-school activities.
    A. NO CHANGE.
    B. This sentence is too long; it must be a run-on.
    C. Even though this sentence is very long, it is actually a fragment.

4. Mr. Walker really wants this job with NASA, it is his dream to invent something useful.
    A. NO CHANGE.
    B. Fragment: put a comma after *useful*, and finish the sentence.
    C. Run-on: change the comma to a period and start a new sentence by capitalizing *it*.

5. During fall break and Thanksgiving when the students get a chance to go home from college.
    A. NO CHANGE.
    B. Fragment: put a comma after *college* and finish the sentence.
    C. Run-on: put a comma after *Thanksgiving*

6. He cried.
    A. NO CHANGE.
    B. Fragment: the sentence is too short and needs more details to be grammatically correct.
    C. Fragment: the sentence does not have the required components of subject, verb, and object.

7. Confused by what his professor said in class and worried by his most recent chemistry grade.
    A. NO CHANGE.
    B. Run-on: put a comma after *class*.
    C. Fragment: put a comma after *grade* and finish the sentence.

8. James understands the consequences of his actions, I guess, but he will probably do it anyway.
    A. NO CHANGE.
    B. Fragment: the sentence is missing part of a verb.
    C. Run-on: change the comma after *actions* to a semicolon.

9. Michael likes to play games, however, his work does not allow him any time to relax.
    A. NO CHANGE.
    B. Run-on: remove the verb from the second part of the sentence.
    C Run-on: change the comma after *games* to a semicolon.

1)C 2)C 3)A 4)C 5)B 6)A 7)C 8)A 9)C

COMMAS

Each ACT has on average 10 comma-placement questions. This is an area where many students make mistakes. Practice makes perfect.

Here are the most important rules:

Use ONE comma
- between **two equal adjectives**
- after an **introduction** followed by a full sentence
- before one of the "**FANBOYS**" conjunctions when they connect two full sentences
- between two parts that emphasize a distinct **contrast**

Use TWO commas
- to highlight **added information**
- to separate items in a list using **serial commas**
- to combine any of the **one-comma rules** mentioned above

Comma Usage - One Comma

Commas can save lives!	
Let's eat Grandpa!	Let's eat, Grandpa!

If there is ONE comma in a sentence, the sentence structure most often follows one of the following rules:

Two Equal Adjectives

If a sentence has two adjectives of equal status describing the same noun, **use a comma** in between the adjectives. (Equal status means you can put "and" in between the adjectives or you can reverse the order.)

We had a nice, relaxing vacation.   - You can say "a nice and relaxing vacation."
We had a wonderful winter break.   - You cannot say "a winter wonderful break."

 Tip: Do not use a comma between the final adjective and the noun.

Introduction (Time, Place, and How)

Some sentences start with an introduction that describes the time, place, or manner in which a sentence takes place.

Always **use a comma** after the introduction. Introductions <u>can be left out entirely</u>, leaving a complete sentence.
<u>Yesterday</u>, I went to the mall.   - Comma after the time introduction
<u>In my hometown</u>, we have only three traffic lights.   - Comma after the place introduction
<u>Growing up in the South</u>, I ended up with a distinct accent.   - Comma after the how introduction

 Tip: Do not use a comma if the introduction is not at the beginning of the sentence.

FANBOYS

Two complete sentences can be combined with a conjunction, but you **ONLY use a comma** before the conjunction if you use one of the "**FANBOYS**" conjunctions (For, And, Nor, But, Or, Yet, So).

<u>Melissa</u> studied for her test and got an A in English.   **No comma:** not two complete sentences
<u>Melissa</u> studied for her test, and <u>she</u> got an A in English. **Comma:** two complete sentences plus fanboys
<u>Jerry</u> went to the restaurant, for <u>he</u> was hungry.   **Comma:** two complete sentences plus fanboys
<u>Jerry</u> went to the restaurant because <u>he</u> was hungry.   **No comma:** two complete sentences – no fanboys

 Tip: With other conjunctions, or when the part after the FANBOYS does not have a subject, do not use a comma.
Arnold organized his office and finally cleaned out his files.   **No comma:** not two complete sentences
Clemens visited an art fair since he wanted to buy a sculpture.   **No comma:** Two sentences - no fanboys
René wanted to save money; thus he did the work himself.   **No comma:** Two sentences - no fanboys

Contrast

If there is a contrast between two concepts in one sentence, **use a comma** to emphasize the dissimilarity.

I like peanuts, not peanut butter.
You like cream in your coffee, don't you?
Anna has a great artistic skill, unlike her husband.

Commas - Quiz 1 (FANBOYS)

1. **A.** She ate her sandwich, and then took a nap.
   B. She ate her sandwich, then took a nap.
   C. She ate her sandwich and then took a nap.
   D. She ate her sandwich and then, took a nap.

2. **A.** Jennifer read the information carefully and she put the bed frame together quickly.
   B. Jennifer read the information carefully, and she put the bed frame together quickly.
   C. Jennifer read the information carefully and, she put the bed frame together quickly.
   D. Jennifer read the information carefully and she put the bed frame together, quickly.

3. **A.** Laura did not read the information carefully and could not put the bed frame together well.
   B. Laura did not read the information carefully, and could not put the bed frame together well.
   C. Laura did not read the information carefully and, could not put the bed frame together well.
   D. Laura, did not read the information carefully, and could not put the bed frame together well.

4. **A.** I do not like lifting weights nor do I, enjoy running on the treadmill.
   B. I do not like lifting weights nor do I enjoy running, on the treadmill.
   C. I do not like lifting weights, nor do I enjoy running on the treadmill.
   D. I do not like lifting weights nor, do I enjoy running on the treadmill.

5. **A.** Maya received 20% off when she purchased a computer but she could not use her coupon as well.
   B. Maya received 20% off when she purchased a computer, but she could not use her coupon as well.
   C. Maya received 20% off when she purchased a computer but, she could not use her coupon as well.
   D. Maya received 20% off, when she purchased a computer but she could not use her coupon as well.

6. **A.** We will help you improve your grades, if you come to our tutoring sessions each Friday.
   B. We will help you improve your grades if you come, to our tutoring sessions each Friday.
   C. We will help you improve your grades if you come to our tutoring sessions, each Friday.
   D. We will help you improve your grades if you come to our tutoring sessions each Friday.

7. **A.** Ed got an excellent price when he purchased a new computer for he did a lot of research.
   B. Ed got an excellent price, when he purchased a new computer for he did a lot of research.
   C. Ed got an excellent price when he purchased a new computer for, he did a lot of research.
   D. Ed got an excellent price when he purchased a new computer, for he did a lot of research.

8. **A.** Would you like to see a movie, or would you rather go bowling downtown?
   B. Would you like to see a movie or, would you rather go bowling downtown?
   C. Would you like to see a movie or would you rather go bowling downtown?
   D. Would you like to see a movie or would you rather go bowling, downtown?

9. **A.** She did not save enough money so she could not buy the latest iPhone, when I bought mine.
   B. She did not save enough money so, she could not buy the latest iPhone when I bought mine.
   C. She did not save enough money so she could not buy the latest iPhone when I bought mine.
   D. She did not save enough money, so she could not buy the latest iPhone when I bought mine.

10. **A.** She wanted to stay after school, because she had organized a study group with her friends.
    B. She wanted to stay after school because she had organized a study group with her friends.
    C. She wanted to stay after school because, she had organized a study group with her friends.
    D. She wanted to stay after school because she had organized a study group, with her friends.

1) C no commas: just two actions by one person 2) B Fanboys 3) A no commas 4) C Fanboys 5) B Fanboys 6) D no commas and no introduction 7) D fanboys 8) A fanboys 9) D fanboys 10) B no commas: no fanboys.

Commas - Quiz 2 (Mixed)

1. **A.** I want to speak to the owner of the restaurant, not the manager.
   B. I want to speak to the owner of the restaurant not the manager.
   C. I want to speak to the owner, of the restaurant not the manager.
   D. I want to speak, to the owner of the restaurant not the manager.

2. **A.** Although, they may be safe I will not ride rollercoasters.
   B. Although they may be safe, and I will not ride rollercoasters.
   C. Although they may be safe I will not ride rollercoasters.
   D. Although they may be safe, I will not ride rollercoasters.

3. **A.** To help students with their, new environment the school has printed a very, special map.
   B. To help students with their new environment, the school has printed a very special map.
   C. To help students with their new environment the school has printed a very special map.
   D. To help students, with their new environment the school has printed a very special map.

4. **A.** The three, old men were fishing for large, rainbow trout.
   B. The three old men were fishing for large rainbow trout.
   C. The three old men, were fishing for large, rainbow trout.
   D. The three, old men were fishing for large rainbow trout.

5. **A.** At several times throughout, the day she likes to go on long walks.
   B. At several times, throughout the day she likes to go on long walks.
   C. At several times throughout the day, she likes to go on long walks.
   D. At several times throughout the day she likes to go on long walks.

6. **A.** My parents believed in a very open, hands-on education.
   B. My parents believed in a very open hands, on education.
   C. My parents believed in a very open hands on education.
   D. My parents believed in a very open, hands-on, education.

7. **A.** By the time, a Great Dane is mature it can weigh as much as 200 pounds.
   B. By the time a Great Dane is mature it can weigh, as much as 200 pounds.
   C. By the time a Great Dane is mature, it can weigh as much as 200 pounds.
   D. By the time a Great Dane is mature it can weigh as much as 200 pounds.

8. **A.** If necessary, hamsters can contort their bodies to fit into tight spaces.
   B. If necessary hamsters can contort, their bodies to fit into tight spaces.
   C. If necessary hamsters can contort their bodies to fit into tight spaces.
   D. If necessary hamsters can contort their bodies, to fit into tight spaces.

9. **A.** I hated the ugly lawn furniture, they used during the warm summer months.
   B. I hated the ugly, lawn furniture they used during the warm, summer months.
   C. I hated the ugly lawn furniture they used during the warm, summer months.
   D. I hated the ugly lawn furniture they used during the warm summer months.

10. **A.** On lakes and oceans speedboats have the freedom, to go as fast as they please.
    B. On lakes and oceans, speedboats have the freedom to go as fast as they please.
    C. On lakes and oceans speedboats have the freedom to go, as fast as they please.
    D. On lakes, and oceans, speedboats have the freedom to go as fast as they please.

Commas - Quiz 3 (Mixed)

1. **A.** Yesterday, I read three chapters of my book, before I got out of bed.
    B. Yesterday I read three chapters of my book before I got out of bed.
    C. Yesterday I read three chapters of my book, before I got out of bed.
    D. Yesterday, I read three chapters of my book before I got out of bed.

2. **A.** Although I like France, Italy is still my favorite country in the world.
    B. Although, I like France, Italy is still my favorite country in the world.
    C. Although I like France, Italy is still my favorite country, in the world.
    D. Although I like France Italy is still my favorite country in the world.

3. **A.** If you are looking for a good winter coat you will find that down is warmer than cotton.
    B. If you are looking for a good winter coat, you will find that down is warmer than cotton.
    C. If you are looking for a good winter coat you will find that down is warmer, than cotton.
    D. If you are looking for a good winter coat, you will find that down is warmer, than cotton.

4. **A.** The couple placed high expectations, on their eldest teenage daughter.
    B. The couple placed high, expectations on their eldest, teenage daughter.
    C. The couple placed high expectations on their eldest teenage daughter.
    D. The couple placed high, expectations on their eldest teenage daughter.

5. **A.** Despite Robert's broken arm, his track record remains unchanged.
    B. Despite Robert's broken arm his track record remains, unchanged.
    C. Despite Robert's broken arm, his track record, remains unchanged.
    D. Despite Rober.'s broken arm his track record, remains unchanged.

6   **A.** Before she went, to college in 2002, Louise was in the marching band.
    B. Before she went to college in 2002 Louise, was in the marching band.
    C. Before she went to college in 2002, Louise was in the marching band.
    D. Before she went to college, in 2002 Louise was in the marching band.

7. **A.** The fat, grumpy, man wore the same pair of clothes day in and day out.
    B. The fat grumpy man wore the same pair of clothes, day in and day out.
    C. The fat, grumpy man wore the same pair of clothes day in and day out.
    D. The fat, grumpy man wore the same pair of clothes, day in and day out.

8. **A.** Jack could finally see the welcoming water fountain over the next hill.
    B. Jack could, finally, see the welcoming water fountain over the next hill.
    C. Jack could finally see the welcoming, water fountain over the next hill.
    D. Jack could finally see the welcoming water fountain, over the next hill.

9. **A.** Corrie scored high on her math GRE, not on the verbal section with the complicated sentences.
    B. Corrie scored high, on her math GRE not on the verbal section with the complicated sentences.
    C. Corrie scored high on her math GRE not on the verbal section with the complicated sentences.
    D. Corrie scored high on her math GRE, not on the verbal section, with the complicated sentences.

10. **A.** Growing up, in Tunisia taught her how to deal with the heat.
    B. Growing up in Tunisia taught her how to deal with the heat.
    C. Growing up in Tunisia, taught her how to deal with the heat.
    D. Growing up in Tunisia, taught her, how to deal with the heat.

Comma Usage - Two Commas

If there are TWO commas in a sentence, the sentence structure most often follows one of the following rules:

Added Information

Put two commas around information that <u>can be left out entirely</u> without changing the meaning of the text. The remaining sentence needs to have a subject and a verb.

> Judge Bill Clinton, who is not related to our former President, retired last month.
> My 85-year-old mother, who lives in Holland, still walks several miles each day.
> The wedding ceremony, which lasted only five minutes, surprised most of the guests.
> The intern, in his efforts to impress the boss, analyzed 500 files in one week.

Use a comma before and after a noun or phrase that renames another noun right beside it.

> My husband, <u>Jeff</u>, went to the store.
> My husband, <u>the most devoted man I know</u>, always does the laundry.

Tip: If the added information is necessary (a restrictive clause,) do not use commas. Ask, "Do I need the information to identify which subject we are talking about?"

> All students <u>who have an F in English</u> need to stay after school.
> The attorney <u>Dean Hunt</u> is famous for his in-depth research and detailed reports.
> My friend <u>Harold</u> is going on vacation with me next year.

Tip: Added information can appear at the end or at the beginning of a sentence as well. However, it is always placed between two punctuation marks (a comma and a period, a comma and a semicolon, etc.)

> I love my husband, <u>the most devoted man I have ever met</u>.
> <u>A most devoted man</u>, my husband buys me flowers every week.

The Serial Comma

If a sentence has a series of two items (subjects or objects) **do NOT use a comma** in between them.
If a sentence has a series of three or more items, **use a comma** after all but the last item in the series.

> I went to the store and to the doctor.   Two items in the series – no comma
> I went to the store, to the pharmacy, and to the doctor. Three items in the series – commas

Tip: Rules are different in England and in the United States. However, the ACT is an American test, so follow the American rule: place a comma before the word "and" in the last item of a series.

A Combination of One-Comma Rules

Two commas can appear when a sentence has two introductions, or an intro and two equal adjectives.

> <u>This morning</u>, <u>before I got out of bed</u>, I read three chapters of my book.
> <u>In my hometown pharmacy</u>, we still have a <u>working, old-fashioned</u> soda fountain.

Commas - Quiz 4 (Added Information)

1 **A.** For example Great Danes, the world's tallest living dogs, can be over three feet tall.
   B. For example, Great Danes, the world's tallest living dogs, can be over three feet tall.
   C. For example, Great Danes, the world's tallest, living dogs can be over three feet tall.
   D. For example, Great Danes, the world's tallest, living, dogs, can be over three feet tall.

2 **A.** I prefer not to go out for lunch, on Wednesday the busiest day of the week.
   B. I prefer not to go out for lunch on Wednesday, the busiest day of the week.
   C. I prefer not to go out, for lunch, on Wednesday the busiest day of the week.
   D. I prefer not to go out for lunch on Wednesday the busiest day of the week.

3. **A.** Universities have trained counselors and advisors to help troubled students.
   B. Universities have trained, counselors and advisors to help troubled students.
   C. Universities have trained counselors, and advisors to help troubled students.
   D. Universities have trained counselors, and advisors, to help troubled students.

4 **A.** "Well, if you don't like milk, do you still eat, cereal?" Dale asked Leslie.
   B. "Well, if you don't like milk do you still eat cereal?" Dale asked Leslie.
   C. "Well if you don't like milk do you still eat cereal?" Dale asked Leslie.
   D. "Well, if you don't like milk, do you still eat cereal?" Dale asked Leslie.

5 **A.** If you listen closely, boys, and girls you can in fact, hear its heartbeat.
   B. If you listen closely, boys and girls, you can, in fact hear its heartbeat.
   C. If you listen closely, boys and girls, you can, in fact, hear its heartbeat.
   D. If you listen closely, boys, and girls, you can, in fact, hear its heartbeat.

6 **A.** I am worried that my midterms, mainly chemistry and Spanish are going to ruin my GPA.
   B. I am worried that my midterms, mainly chemistry and Spanish, are going to ruin my GPA.
   C. I am worried, that my midterms, mainly chemistry and Spanish, are going to ruin my GPA.
   D. I am worried that my midterms, mainly chemistry and Spanish, are going to ruin, my GPA.

7 **A.** James, my older brother is a kind, generous and thoughtful person.
   B. James, my older brother, is a kind, generous, and thoughtful person.
   C. James my older brother, is a kind, generous, and thoughtful person.
   D. James, my older brother, is a kind generous and thoughtful person.

8 **A.** My hardest class math, has a passing rate of about, 80%.
   B. My hardest class, math, has a passing rate of, about, 80%.
   C. My hardest class, math, has a passing rate of about 80%.
   D. My hardest class math, has a passing rate of, about, 80%.

9 **A.** My dorm room comes with two beds two desks and a sink.
   B. My dorm room comes with, two beds two desks, and a sink.
   C. My dorm room comes with two beds, two desks and a sink.
   D. My dorm room comes with two beds, two desks, and a sink.

10 **A.** Martha, the busiest girl in the class, has the highest grades.
   B. Martha the busiest girl in the class, has the highest grades.
   C. Martha, the busiest girl in the class has the highest grades.
   D. Martha the busiest girl in the class has the highest grades.

1) **B** intro and added information 2) **B** "the busiest day of the week." is added information 3) **A** "and advisors." is not added information 4) **D** intro, intro, full sentence 5) **C** "Boys and girls." is added information (you are already talking to them) "in fact" is added information: you can leave it out. 6) **B** "mainly chemistry and Spanish." is added information: you can leave it out. 7) **B** "My older brother." is added information. Three equal adjectives in a list. 8) **C** "math." is added information. "about." is NOT added information: leaving it out changes the sentence. 9) **D** a list of three items 10) **A** "the busiest girl in the class." is added information.

Copyright 2017 Winni van Gessel

Commas - Quiz 5 (Mixed)

1. **A.** I need, envelopes, paper, and stamps from the post office.
    B. I need envelopes, paper, and stamps, from the post office.
    C. I need envelopes, paper and stamps, from the post office.
    D. I need envelopes, paper, and stamps from the post office.

2. **A.** I asked Louise, the girl who never goes out to the prom yesterday.
    B. I asked Louise, the girl who never goes out, to the prom last night.
    C. I asked Louise the girl who never goes out, to the prom last night.
    D. I asked Louise, the girl who never goes out, to the prom, last night.

3. **A.** David, and I, have a great friendship.
    B. David and I, have a great friendship.
    C. David and I have a great friendship.
    D. David and I have, a great friendship.

4. **A.** Kentucky is known for its horse farms, natural parks and Kentucky Fried Chicken.
    B. Kentucky is known for its horse farms, natural parks, and Kentucky Fried Chicken.
    C. Kentucky is known for its horse, farms, natural, parks and Kentucky, Fried Chicken.
    D. Kentucky is known for its horse farms natural parks and Kentucky Fried Chicken.

5. **A.** You are I think, telling me a lie.
    B. You are, I think, telling me a lie.
    C. You are I think telling, me a lie.
    D. You are, I think telling me a lie.

6. **A.** She left Philadelphia, Pennsylvania, on January 18 last year.
    B. She left Philadelphia, Pennsylvania on January 18, last year.
    C. She left Philadelphia Pennsylvania, on January 18 last year.
    D. She left, Philadelphia Pennsylvania, on January 18 last year.

7. **A.** Haiti's culture shows traces of European, African, and Indian heritage.
    B. Haiti's culture shows traces of European, African and Indian heritage.
    C. Haiti's culture shows traces of European African and Indian heritage.
    D. Haiti's culture shows traces, of European, African, and Indian heritage.

8. **A.** Please Rebecca, finish your homework as soon as you can.
    B. Please, Rebecca, finish your homework as soon as you can.
    C. Please, Rebecca finish your homework as soon as you can.
    D. Please Rebecca, finish your homework, as soon as you can.

9. **A.** Students who like foreign languages recently started a club at the local high school.
    B. Students, who like foreign languages recently started a club at the local high school.
    C. Students who like foreign languages, recently started a club at the local high school.
    D. Students, who like foreign languages, recently started a club at the local high school.

10. **A.** The Willis Tower, which is over 100 stories tall used to be the tallest building in the world.
    B. The Willis Tower which is over 100 stories tall, used to be the tallest building in the world.
    C. The Willis Tower which is over 100 stories tall used to be the tallest building in the world.
    D. The Willis Tower, which is over 100 stories tall, used to be the tallest building in the world.

Commas - Quiz 6 (Challenge)

1. **A.** He says that he can't imagine receiving an A in that class.
   B. He says, that he can't imagine receiving an A in that class.
   C. He says, that, he can't imagine receiving an A in that class.
   D. He says that, he can't imagine receiving an A in that class.

2. **A.** Holding down the "CTRL," and the "I" keys, on your computer will italicize your font.
   B. Holding down the "CTRL" and the "I" keys, on your computer will italicize your font.
   C. Holding down the "CTRL" and the "I" keys on your computer will italicize your font.
   D. Holding down the "CTRL" and the "I" keys on your computer, will italicize your font.

3. **A.** She wants to incorporate some hip hop, into her routine, a contemporary piece.
   B. She wants to incorporate some hip hop into her routine, a contemporary piece.
   C. She wants to incorporate some hip hop, into her routine a contemporary piece.
   D. She wants to incorporate some hip hop into her routine a contemporary piece.

4. **A.** Tom's positive attitude gained him popularity, in many groups at his school.
   B. Tom's positive attitude gained him popularity in many groups at his school.
   C. Tom's positive attitude gained him popularity, in many groups, at his school.
   D. Tom's positive attitude gained him popularity in many groups, at his school.

5. **A.** Violet, who moved, to Mexico for a year is bilingual.
   B. Violet, who moved to Mexico for a year is bilingual.
   C. Violet, who moved, to Mexico for a year, is bilingual.
   D. Violet, who moved to Mexico for a year, is bilingual.

6. **A.** Next to the restaurant, I love, is a pet store.
   B. Next to the restaurant, I love is a pet store.
   C. Next to the restaurant I love, is a pet store.
   D. Next to the restaurant I love is a pet store.

7. **A.** Apple's CEO and cofounder, Steve Jobs, is considered a genius.
   B. Apple's CEO, and cofounder Steve Jobs is considered a genius.
   C. Apple's CEO and cofounder Steve Jobs, is considered a genius.
   D. Apple's CEO and cofounder Steve Jobs is considered a genius.

8. **A.** Sometimes a friend you thought was gone, will come back into your life.
   B. Sometimes a friend you thought was gone will come back into your life.
   C. Sometimes a friend you thought was gone, will, come back into your life.
   D. Sometimes a friend you thought was gone will, come back into your life.

9. **A.** Sometimes the programs, on my new computer, will freeze and close unexpectedly.
   B. Sometimes, the programs on my new computer will freeze and close, unexpectedly.
   C. Sometimes the programs on my new computer, will freeze and close unexpectedly.
   D. Sometimes, the programs on my new computer will freeze and close unexpectedly.

10. **A.** The Greek goddess, Aphrodite, was known as the goddess of love, beauty and pleasure.
    B. The Greek goddess, Aphrodite, was known as the goddess of love, beauty, and pleasure.
    C. The Greek goddess Aphrodite was known as the goddess of love, beauty and pleasure.
    D. The Greek goddess Aphrodite was known as the goddess of love, beauty, and pleasure.

1) A B, C, and D do not follow the comma rules 2) C A, B, and D do not follow the comma rules 3) B "a contemporary piece." is added information at the end of the sentence. 4) B an "intro." at the end of a sentence does not need a comma. 5) D "who moved to Mexico for a year." is added information: you need it to ID which restaurant you are talking about. 7) A You do not need "Steve Jobs" to ID the CEO of Apple. It is added information. 8) B A, C, and D do not follow the comma rules. 9) D Intro. Full sentence. 10) D "Aphrodite" is NOT added information; you cannot leave it out. + List of three.

Commas - Quiz 7 (Challenge)

1. **A.** I appreciate those, who walked with me, at the relay.
   B. I appreciate those who, walked with me at the relay.
   C. I appreciate those, who walked, with me at the relay.
   D. I appreciate those who walked with me at the relay.

2. **A.** The most extroverted or, outgoing, person usually leads the group.
   B. The most extroverted, or outgoing, person usually leads the group.
   C. The most extroverted or outgoing person, usually leads the group.
   D. The most extroverted or, outgoing person usually leads the group.

3. **A.** What's clear, is that you will need to work harder now.
   B. What's clear is that, you will need to work harder now.
   C. What's clear is, that you will need to work harder now.
   D. What's clear is that you will need to work harder now.

4. **A.** My planner is full of homework that I must complete, study, and turn in.
   B. My planner is full of homework, that I must complete, study, and turn in.
   C. My planner is full of homework, that I have to complete, study, and turn in.
   D. My planner is full of homework, I must complete it, study it, and turn it in.

5. **A.** After, I fill out the paperwork, the real work begins.
   B. After I fill out the paperwork the real work begins.
   C. After I fill out the paperwork, I begin, the real work.
   D. After I fill out the paperwork, the real work begins.

6. **A.** Joe was thinking of the correct answer when he noticed a hint, clear as day, in the question.
   B. Joe was thinking of the correct answer when noticing a hint, clear as day, in the question.
   C. Joe was thinking of the correct answer, when a hint, clear as day, in the question.
   D. Joe was thinking of the correct answer, when seeing a hint, clear as day, in the question.

7. **A.** Even though she supposedly studied all night, Susie failed her test.
   B. Even though she, supposedly studied all night, Susie failed her test.
   C. Even though she supposedly, studied all night, Susie failed her test.
   D. Even though she supposedly studied all night Susie failed her test.

8. **A.** Finally, Jared decided, to take his own temperature.
   B. Finally, Jared decided to take his own temperature.
   C. Finally Jared decided, to take his own temperature.
   D. Finally Jared, decided to take his own temperature.

9. **A.** The parents talk daily on Skype, with their oldest daughter who has recently moved to England.
   B. The parents talk daily on Skype, with their oldest daughter, who has recently moved to England.
   C. The parents talk daily on Skype with their oldest daughter, who has recently moved to England.
   D. The parents talk daily on Skype with their oldest daughter who has recently moved to England.

10. **A.** The suspect, in the lineup, who has burn marks on his fingers, is the arsonist.
    B. The suspect, in the lineup who has burn marks on his fingers, is the arsonist.
    C. The suspect in the lineup, who has burn marks on his fingers, is the arsonist.
    D. The suspect in the lineup who has burn marks on his fingers is the arsonist.

1) **D** "who cheered with me," is NOT added information; you cannot leave it out 2) **B** "or outgoing" is added information: it redefines the word "outgoing". 3) **D** A, B, and C do not follow the comma rules. 4) **A** a list of three: "that I need to complete ..." is NOT added information. D contains a comma splice. 5) **D** intro, full sentence. 6) **A** "clear as day," is added information: you can leave it out. "when" is not a FANBOYS, so you do not need a comma. 7) **A** intro, full sentence. 8) **B** intro, full sentence. 9) **C** "who has recently moved to England" is not needed to ID the oldest daughter. 10) **D** "who has burn marks on his fingers," is NOT added information: you need it to ID the suspect.

OTHER PUNCTUATION MARKS

Along with the commas, the following punctuation marks are a big part of the ACT. Each test has six or seven questions that will test your knowledge of the rules in this section.

Colon   A colon is placed after a full sentence before a list or an explanation.

Semicolon   A semicolon is placed after a full sentence before another full sentence that offers further detail or a contrast.

Dash   Can informally be used in place of a comma, two commas, a colon, or a semicolon. It can also be used for an interruption.

Hyphen   Used between two words that together describe a noun when they are placed before the noun.

Apostrophe   Indicates possession or a contraction.

Note: the ACT does not make you choose between colons and semicolons or between hyphens and dashes.

Punctuation - Semicolons & Colons

The Semicolon

A semicolon can separate two full sentences (independent clauses) <u>without a conjunction</u>.
The second part of the sentence needs to relate to the first part in one of the following two ways:

By <u>further detail:</u>

Mary went to Europe this summer; she visited at least six countries.

By <u>contrast:</u>

John loves to eat cereal for breakfast; I, however, prefer pancakes.

Tip: The ACT tries to trick you by using a semicolon with two unrelated sentences.

I love to eat ice cream; I also love to bike.

Review: The second sentence expresses neither further detail nor contrast.

Revision: I love to eat ice cream. I also like to bike.

A sentence that can be separated by a semicolon can also be separated by a comma with one of the FANBOYS conjunctions (For, And, Nor, But, Or, Yet, So) but not both.

Tip: Another typical ACT trap uses a semicolon AND a conjunction.

I am exhausted; so I want to go straight to bed.

Review: Because there are two full sentences on each side of the semicolon, you must use either a semicolon <u>or</u> a conjunction, but you can never use both.

Revision: I am exhausted; I want to go straight to bed.

A semicolon can be used as a super comma to distinguish between items that contain commas.

This is John, our secretary, Mary, our treasurer, and James, our director.

Review: Are there six people here or three? Use a semicolon for clarity.

Revision: This is John, our secretary; Mary, our treasurer; and James, our director.

The Colon

Colons are used <u>after a complete sentence</u> to <u>introduce a list of items.</u>

Tip: A typical ACT trap is not using a complete sentence before the colon.

To make an apple pie, I need: flower, sugar, milk, butter, and apples.

Review: The fragment, "To make an apple pie, I need," is not a full sentence.

Revision 1: To make an apple pie, I need flower, sugar, milk, butter, and apples.

Revision 2: I need five things to make an apple pie: flower, sugar, milk, butter, and apples.

Colons are used <u>after a complete sentence</u> when the second sentence <u>explains</u> or illustrates the first sentence.

Tip: An additional ACT trap uses a colon after "such as" or "for example."

I need some basic tools, such as: a hammer, a drill, and a screwdriver.

Review: "I need some basic tools, such as" is not a full sentence.

Revision 1: I need some basic tools, such as a hammer, a drill, and a screwdriver.

Revision 2: I need some basic tools: a hammer, a drill, and a screwdriver.

Tip: Use this diagram to remember when to use the colon and the semicolon.

_____ : ____ explains / lists____ .

_____ ; ____ further detail _____ .

Punctuation - Quiz 1 (Colons & Semicolons)

1.   **A.** When I am sick, I cannot; eat, study, or exercise.
    B. When I am sick, I cannot: eat, study, or exercise.
    C. When I am sick; I cannot eat, study, or exercise.
    D. When I am sick, I cannot eat, study, or exercise.

2.   **A.** Don't forget to bring these to the game; cleats, shin guards, water, socks, etc.
    B. Don't forget to bring these to the game: cleats, shin guards, water, socks, etc.
    C. Don't forget to bring these to the game, cleats, shin guards, water, socks, etc.
    D. Don't forget to bring these: to the game, cleats, shin guards, water, socks, etc.

3.   **A.** Try making notecards, they make the subject easier to study.
    B. Try making notecards they make the subject easier to study.
    C. Try making notecards, they make the subject easier to study!
    D. Try making notecards: they make the subject easier to study.

4.   **A.** To book a room, contact Roger Newman in our business office.
    B. To book a room, contact: Roger Newman in our business office.
    C. To book a room; contact Roger Newman in our business office.
    D. To book a room contact Roger Newman, in our business office.

5.   **A.** Hedgehogs look like porcupines: but they are related to moles.
    B. Hedgehogs look like porcupines, but they are related to moles.
    C. Hedgehogs look like porcupines but they are related to moles.
    D. Hedgehogs look like porcupines; but they are related to moles.

6.   **A.** Here are my favorite countries (1) Italy; (2) Spain; (3) Portugal; and (4) Greece.
    B. Here are my favorite countries; (1) Italy; (2) Spain; (3) Portugal; and (4) Greece.
    C. Here are my favorite countries: (1) Italy; (2) Spain; (3) Portugal; and (4) Greece.
    D. Here are my favorite countries, (1) Italy; (2) Spain; (3) Portugal; and (4) Greece.

7.   **A.** Liza prefers biology to chemistry because it contains less math.
    B. Liza prefers biology to chemistry; because it contains less math.
    C. Liza prefers biology to chemistry, because it contains less math.
    D. Liza prefers biology to chemistry: because it contains less math.

8.   **A.** Beau got a high ACT score; hence he will get a good scholarship.
    B. Beau got a high ACT score, hence he will get a good scholarship.
    C. Beau got a high ACT score hence he will get a good scholarship.
    D. Beau got a high ACT score: hence he will get a good scholarship.

9.   **A.** She loves dogs, she has never lived without one.
    B. She loves dogs she has never lived without one.
    C. She loves dogs; she has never lived without one.
    D. She loves dogs (she has never lived without one)

10. **A.** He asked her to repeat the following words; blue, house, egg, and bicycle.
    B. He asked her to repeat the following words. Blue, house, egg, and bicycle.
    C. He asked her to repeat the following words: blue, house, egg, and bicycle.
    D. He asked her to repeat the following words, blue, house, egg, and bicycle.

1) D. A, B, and C have a (semi)colon after a fragment. 2) B. A full sentence, followed by a list. 3) D. A full sentence, followed by an explanation. 4) A. Follow the comma rule: intro, full sentence. B, and C have a (semi)colon after a fragment. 5) B. Use the FANBOYS rule to separate two full sentences with a conjunction. 6) C. A full sentence, followed by a list. (The semicolon can be used as a super comma.) 7) A. Use the FANBOYS rule to separate two full sentences with a conjunction. 8) A. B does not follow the FANBOYS rule, C is a run-on sentence, and D does not have a list or an explanation. 9) C. A contains a comma splice, B is a run-on sentence, and D does not have a period at the end. 10) C. Use a colon after a full sentence, followed by a list.

Punctuation - Quiz 2 (Mixed)

1. **A.** My favorite Disney heroines are; Mulan, Rapunzel, and Ariel.
   B. My favorite Disney heroines are Mulan, Rapunzel, and Ariel.
   C. My favorite Disney heroines are, Mulan, Rapunzel, and Ariel.
   D. My favorite Disney heroines are: Mulan, Rapunzel, and Ariel.

2. **A.** I am nervous about getting a cat and it requires a lot of responsibility.
   B. I am nervous about getting a cat; because it requires a lot of responsibility.
   C. I am nervous about getting a cat: it requires a lot of responsibility.
   D. I am nervous about getting a cat, it requires a lot of responsibility.

3. **A.** Our furnace broke; we kept warm with blankets and played games by candlelight.
   B. Our furnace broke, we kept warm with blankets, and played games, by candlelight.
   C. Our furnace broke we kept warm with blankets, and we played games by candlelight.
   D. Our furnace broke; we kept warm with blankets, and played games by candlelight.

4. A. I know why I passed the test, I studied, practiced, and slept a lot.
   B. I know why I passed the test: I studied, practiced, and slept a lot.
   C. I know why I passed the test; I studied, practiced and slept a lot.
   D. I know why I passed the test. I studied, practiced and slept a lot.

5. **A.** The medalists are: Usain Bolt, 9.58 sec.; Tyson Gay, 9.69 sec.; and Yohan Blake, 9.69 sec.
   B. The medalists are Usain Bolt, 9.58 sec.; Tyson Gay, 9.69 sec.; and Yohan Blake, 9.69 sec.
   C. The medalists are Usain Bolt, 9.58 sec., Tyson Gay, 9.69 sec., and Yohan Blake, 9.69 sec.
   D. The medalists are: Usain Bolt, 9.58 sec., Tyson Gay, 9.69 sec., and Yohan Blake, 9.69 sec.

6. **A.** When she traveled, she never forgot to bring socks, tickets, or a water bottle.
   B. When she traveled she never forgot to bring socks, tickets, or a water bottle.
   C. When she traveled she never forgot to bring: socks, tickets, or a water bottle.
   D. When she traveled, she never forgot to bring: socks, tickets, or a water bottle.

7. **A.** I would like several of the items freshly delivered, such as: flowers, meat, and vegetables.
   B. I would like several of the items freshly delivered: such as flowers, meat, and vegetables.
   C. I would like several of the items freshly delivered such as flowers, meat, and vegetables.
   D. I would like several of the items freshly delivered, such as flowers, meat, and vegetables.

8. **A.** You can take classes of different types, to broaden the level of your education.
   B. You can take classes of different types: to broaden the level of your education.
   C. You can take classes of different types to broaden the level of your education.
   D. You can take classes of different types; to broaden the level of your education.

9. **A.** The fact that he had a mooses' antlers on the wall made me uncomfortable.
   B. The fact that he had a moose's antlers on the wall made me uncomfortable.
   C. The fact that he had a mooses antlers on the wall made me uncomfortable.
   D. The fact that he had a moos's antlers on the wall made me uncomfortable.

10. **A.** I would trust my best friend, Lizzie – with my life.
    B. I would trust my best friend – Lizzie – with my life.
    C. I would trust my best friend – Lizzie with my life.
    D. I would trust my best friend, Lizzie with my life.

Punctuation - Quiz 3 (Mixed)

1. **A.** Don't forget to bring these things: tennis shoes, water, and headphones.
   B. Don't forget to bring these things; tennis shoes, water, and headphones.
   C. Don't forget to bring these things, tennis shoes, water, and headphones.
   D. Don't forget to bring these things tennis shoes, water, and headphones.

2. **A.** I always go to school with: a notebook, a pen, and a snack.
   B. I always go to school with; a notebook, a pen, and a snack.
   C. I always go to school with, a notebook, a pen, and a snack.
   D. I always go to school with a notebook, a pen, and a snack.

3. **A.** I bought a bag of sparkly, colorful streamers; two boxes of balloons, and a huge, tasty birthday cake.
   B. I bought a bag of sparkly, colorful streamers; two boxes of balloons; and a huge, tasty birthday cake.
   C. I bought a bag of sparkly, colorful streamers, two boxes of balloons; and a huge, tasty birthday cake.
   D. I bought a bag of sparkly, colorful streamers, two boxes of balloons, and a huge, tasty birthday cake.

4. **A.** The doctor suggested that I stop eating: chips, hamburgers, and ice cream.
   B. The doctor suggested that I stop eating; chips, hamburgers, and ice cream.
   C. The doctor suggested that I stop eating, chips, hamburgers, and ice cream.
   D. The doctor suggested that I stop eating chips, hamburgers, and ice cream.

5. **A.** You are the girl – the only girl with whom I want to go to prom.
   B. You are the girl – the only girl, with whom I want to go to prom.
   C. You are the girl – the only girl; with whom I want to go to prom.
   D. You are the girl – the only girl – with whom I want to go to prom.

6. **A.** I like to eat all kinds of foods, however, there are three exceptions: meat, veggies, and wheat products.
   B. I like to eat all kinds of foods: however, there are three exceptions; meat, veggies, and wheat products.
   C. I like to eat all kinds of foods; however, there are three exceptions - meat, veggies, and wheat products.
   D. I like to eat all kinds of foods; however, there are three exceptions meat, veggies, and wheat products.

7. **A.** My sister is a great student, in fact, she has never received a C in a class.
   B. My sister is a great student in fact she has never received a C in a class.
   C. My sister is a great student; in fact, she has never received a C in a class.
   D. My sister is a great student in fact, she has never received a C in a class.

8. **A.** History was her toughest subject, hence she never skipped a class.
   B. History was her toughest subject: hence she never skipped a class.
   C. History was her toughest subject; hence she never skipped a class.
   D. History was her toughest subject hence she never skipped a class.

9. **A.** The beach was empty, not one person showed up all day.
   B. The beach was empty: not one person showed up all day.
   C. The beach was empty; not one person showed up all day.
   D. The beach was empty not one person showed up all day.

10. **A.** The beach was empty, it was cold, and the dark clouds gathered on the horizon.
    B. The beach was empty: it was cold, and the dark clouds gathered on the horizon.
    C. The beach was empty, it was cold and the dark clouds gathered on the horizon.
    D. The beach was empty it was cold and the dark clouds gathered on the horizon.

1) **A.** A full sentence, followed by a list. 2) **D.** Don't use a (semi)colon after a fragment. 3) **B.** The semicolon needs to be used to separate items in a list that contains commas. 4) **D.** Don't use a (semi)colon after a fragment. 5) **D.** With added information, always use two commas, two dashes, or two parentheses. 6) **C.** A is a run-on sentence. The semicolon in C and D correctly separate two full contrasting sentences. D does not follow the comma rules of a list. The dash can be used as a colon. 7) **C.** Use a semicolon before *in fact* (a conjunctive adverb.) 8) **C.** Use a semicolon before *hence* (a conjunctive adverb.) 9) **C.** A contains a comma splice, and D is a run-on sentence. C provides further information after a full sentence. 10) **B.** A and C contain a comma splice, and D is a run-on sentence. B contains an explanation after the colon.

Punctuation - Quiz 4 (Challenge)

1. **A.** I hate snakes, I don't like to walk in the grass after it rains.
   B. I hate snakes: I don't like to walk in the grass after it rains.
   C. I hate snakes; I don't like to walk in the grass after it rains.
   D. I hate snakes I don't like to walk in the grass after it rains.

2. **A.** They wanted to see a horror movie, I did not.
   B. They wanted to see a horror movie: I did not.
   C. They wanted to see a horror movie; I did not.
   D. They wanted to see a horror movie I did not.

3. **A.** Here are three tips for finals week: get a good night's sleep, review your notes, and quiz one another.
   B. Here are three tips for finals week; get a good night's sleep, review your notes, and quiz one another.
   C. Here are three tips for finals week, get a good night's sleep, review your notes, and quiz one another.
   D. Here are three tips for finals week get a good night's sleep, review your notes, and quiz one another.

4. **A.** This semester I am taking, Spanish, photography, English, and history.
   B. This semester I am taking: Spanish, photography, English, and history.
   C. This semester I am taking; Spanish, photography, English, and history.
   D. This semester I am taking Spanish, photography, English, and history.

5. **A.** A good friend is, open, trustworthy, and caring.
   B. A good friend is: open, trustworthy, and caring.
   C. A good friend is; open, trustworthy, and caring.
   D. A good friend is open, trustworthy, and caring.

6. **A.** Jeff told me that the job was still available and that the manager wanted to interview me
   B. Jeff told me that the job was still available, and, that the manager wanted to interview me
   C. Jeff told me that the job was still available, and that the manager wanted to interview me
   D. Jeff told me, that the job was still available and, that the manager wanted to interview me

7. **A.** Nate always carries a compass; which will be helpful when he gets lost in the woods.
   B. Nate always carries a compass, which will be helpful when he gets lost in the woods.
   C. Nate always carries a compass which will be helpful, when he gets lost in the woods.
   D. Nate always carries a compass, which will be helpful, when he gets lost in the woods.

8. **A.** She was a good student, if she tried hard, she knew she could succeed.
   B. She was a good student; if she tried hard, she knew she could succeed.
   C. She was a good student, if she tried hard she knew she could succeed.
   D. She was a good student if she tried hard, she knew she could succeed.

9. **A.** He doesn't often admit he is wrong, especially not in front of his colleagues; and coworkers.
   B. He doesn't often admit he is wrong; especially not in front of his colleagues and coworkers.
   C. He doesn't often admit he is wrong, especially not in front of his colleagues and coworkers.
   D. He doesn't often admit he is wrong especially not in front of his colleagues and coworkers.

10. **A.** I bought bananas, apples, grapes, watermelon, etc so I could make a fruit salad.
    B. I bought bananas, apples, grapes, watermelon, etc. so I could make a fruit salad.
    C. I bought bananas, apples, grapes, watermelon, etc, so I could make a fruit salad.
    D. I bought bananas, apples, grapes, watermelon, etc., so I could make a fruit salad.

1) C. A contains a comma splice, and D is a run-on sentence. C provides further information after a full sentence. 2) C. The semicolon in C correctly separates two full contrasting sentences. followed by a list. 4) D. Don't use a (semi)colon after a fragment. 3) A. A full sentence. 5) D. Don't use a (semi)colon after a fragment. 6) A. Jeff told me two things. Don't use the FANBOYS rule because the second part is not a full sentence. 7) B. The added information (*which ... woods*) can be left out. 8) B, A, C, and D contain a comma splice. 9) C. A and B contain a fragment after the semicolon. 10) D. The abbreviation etc. is always followed by a comma unless it occurs at the end of a sentence.

Hyphens, Dashes and Apostrophes

The Hyphen

The hyphen is used when an adjective is <u>used in front of the noun</u> and is made up of <u>two or more words.</u>

The melody was well known.	It was a well-known melody.
You can do this project yourself.	This is a do-it-yourself project.

Hey, look at the people eating snakes.	*You are looking at people.*
Hey, look at the people-eating snakes.	*You are looking at snakes.*

The Dash

In informal writing, a dash may replace a comma, a semicolon, a colon, or a parenthesis.
to indicate added emphasis, an interruption, or an abrupt change of thought.

I studied all night – she went to the party.	(semicolon)
Please tell my teacher – Mrs. Johnson – that I was sick today.	(comma)
I need to remember to bring these items – ice cream, sprinkles, and spoons.	(colon)
I used to give everyone a second chance – before I met him.	
I really want to – oh, forget it.	

The Apostrophe

The apostrophe is used in contractions, certain plurals, and possessive cases.

Contractions:

You can't, he won't, and I shouldn't.
Please, ma'am, let's dance?

👀 *Tip: Every ACT has an it's / its / its' question in it. <u>It's</u> means "<u>it is</u>" or "<u>it has</u>".*

👀 *Tip: The word <u>its'</u> does not exist.*

Plurals (to avoid misreading):

In the 1960s, I received A's and B's.
Now, I mind my p's and q's.

Possessive cases:

The dog's tail is long.	**Correct**: possessive is indicated by an apostrophe and an s.
The dog wags <u>it's</u> tail.	**Incorrect**: "it's" always means "it is" or "it has".
The dog wags its tail.	**Correct**: possessive pronouns do not need an apostrophe.

👀 *Tip: Her tail (no apostrophe); his tail (no apostrophe); <u>its</u> tail (no apostrophe)*

👀 *Tip: If a word already ends in an "s", you add the apostrophe, but not the possessive "s."*
Don't worry: This is not a question in the ACT.

Punctuation - Quiz 5 (Other)

1. **A.** Mr. Taylor's grandmother was born in the early 1950s.
   B. Mr. Taylors grandmother was born in the early 1950s.
   C. Mr. Taylor's grandmother was born in the early 1950's.
   D. Mr. Taylors' grandmother was born in the early 1950's.

2. **A.** The stewardess's seats were located at the back of the airplane.
   B. The stewardesses seats were located at the back of the airplane.
   C. The stewardesses' seats were located at the back of the airplane.
   D. The stewardess seats were located at the back of the airplane.

3. **A.** Lisa showered before her next class in the girl's locker room.
   B. Lisa showered before her next class in the girls locker room.
   C. Lisa showered before her next class in the girlses locker room.
   D. Lisa showered before her next class in the girls' locker room.

4. **A.** The sophomores final scores are posted in the principal's office.
   B. The sophomores' final scores are posted in the principal's office.
   C. The sophomore's final scores are posted in the principals office.
   D. The sophomores' final scores are posted in the principals office.

5. **A.** Mr. Jones car is bigger than the garage of the Jones'.
   B. Mr. Jones car is bigger than the garage of the Jones'.
   C. Mr. Jones' car is bigger than the garage of the Joneses.
   D. Mr. Jone's car is bigger than the garage of the Joneses.

6. **A.** Her history, teacher was a grey-haired, needle-nosed crone.
   B. Her history teacher was a grey haired, needle nosed crone.
   C. Her history teacher, was a grey-haired needle-nosed crone.
   D. Her history teacher was a grey-haired, needle-nosed crone.

7. **A.** I really enjoy the newly-released chocolate chip Girl Scout cookies.
   B. I really enjoy the newly-released, chocolate chip Girl Scout cookies.
   C. I really enjoy the newly-released, chocolate chip, Girl Scout cookies.
   D. I really enjoy the newly-released, chocolate chip, Girl Scout, cookies.

8. **A.** My grandpa gave me a tough, long-winded speech about a son's duties.
   B. My grandpa gave me a tough long winded speech about a sons duties.
   C. My grandpa gave me a tough, long-winded, speech about a sons' duties.
   D. My grandpa gave me a tough long-winded speech about a sons' duties.

9. **A.** I adopted a new, short tailed, golden retriever from the pound.
   B. I adopted a new, short, tailed golden retriever from the pound.
   C. I adopted a new short-tailed-golden retriever from the pound.
   D. I adopted a new short-tailed golden retriever from the pound.

10. **A** Though Elvis died in 1977, his legacy: rock 'n' roll lives on.
    B. Though Elvis died in 1977, his legacy, rock 'n' roll – lives on.
    C. Though Elvis died in 1977, his legacy – rock 'n' roll – lives on.
    D. Though Elvis died in 1977, his legacy rock 'n' roll – lives on.

Read possessive cases backwards. 1) **A.** the grandmother of Mr. Taylor 2) **C.** the seats of the stewardesses 3) **D.** the locker room of the girls 4) **B.** the final scores of the sophomores: the office of the principal 5) **C.** the car of Mr. Jones 6) **D.** The crone has two equal adjectives (they can be switched), so use a comma. Two-worded adjectives before the noun need a hyphen. 7) **A.** The adjectives cannot be switched. 8) **A.** Tough and long-winded are two equal adjectives that can be switched 9) **D.** *new, short-tailed,* and *golden* are not equal adjectives. 10) **C.** With added information, always use two commas, two dashes, or two parentheses.

The Apostrophe

Possessive Cases

Tip: Read it backwards. Instead of the apostrophe (') - or the apostrophe and the s ('s) - read "of."

With a pronoun: her eye (no apostrophe) his eye (no apostrophe) its eye (no apostrophe)
With a noun:

Bob's eye	Read it backwards: the eye *of* Bob
Mary's dog	Read it backwards: the dog *of* Mary

With a noun that ends in an s:

Jesus' disciples	Read it backwards: the disciples *of* Jesus
Tess' homework	Read it backwards: the homework *of* Tess

Without the apostrophe, there are simply two nouns in a row. (no apostrophe= no "*of*")

The dogs collar	Incorrect. Read it backwards: the collar dogs
The peoples republic	Incorrect. Read it backwards: the republic peoples

Plural and Possessive

Plural words get an s at the end, so plural possessive words get just an apostrophe at the end.

The dogs' collars	Read it backwards: the collars *of* the dogs
The maidens' voyage	Read it backwards: the voyage *of* the maidens

Female and Possessive

Female words often get an added "es" or "ess", so female possessive words just add an apostrophe.

The stewardess' warning	Read it backwards: the warning *of* the stewardess
The tigress' meal	Read it backwards: the meal *of* the tigress

Female, Plural, and Possessive

Be very careful when the rules above when two or three rules apply.

The lionesses' tails wagged	Read it backwards: the tails *of* the lionesses
The actresses' voices	Read it backwards: the voices *of* the actresses

Tricky Possessive Cases

When two nouns share one item, only the second has an apostrophe.

My mom and dad's bank account	The bank account *of* mom and dad
Laurel and Hardy's movie	The movie *of* Laurel and Hardy

When two nouns share *different* items, both possessives have an apostrophe.

My mom's and dad's clothes	The clothes *of* my mom and the clothes *of* my dad
Our friends' and neighbors' pets	The pets *of* our friends and the pets *of* our neighbors

The 90's or the 90s?

The term is a plural amount of 10 years. It is not possessive. "The 90s were a fun decade."

It's & Who's

These words mean "it is" and "who is" or sometimes "it has" or "who has".

Could've & Would've

These words mean "could have" and "would have". Never write "could of" or "would of".

Apostrophes - Quiz 1

1. Evan stopped when he noticed the <u>pennys</u> glimmer at the bottom of the pond.

    A.   NO CHANGE
    B.   pennys'
    C.   penny's
    D.   pennys's

2. The lawyer proved that his <u>clients'</u> rights were violated and won a $10,000 settlement for him.

    A.   NO CHANGE
    B.   clients's
    C.   clients
    D.   client's

3. By the end of the experiment, the <u>fungis</u> smell was unbearable.

    A.   NO CHANGE
    B.   fungis's
    C.   fungi's
    D.   fungis'

4. The <u>stairs</u> steep angle made them difficult to climb.

    A.   NO CHANGE
    B.   stair's
    C.   stairs's
    D.   stairs'

5. The <u>professors</u> notes are available on his web site.

    A.   NO CHANGE
    B.   professors'
    C.   professors's
    D.   professor's

6. I had to laugh when I saw <u>Maria's</u> new shoes.

    A.   NO CHANGE
    B.   Marias's
    C.   Marias'
    D.   Marias

7. The <u>emails's</u> origin was very clear: all messages came from the same IP address.

    A.   NO CHANGE
    B.   emails'
    C.   emails
    D.   email's

8. The <u>club's</u> budget is posted on the web.

    A.   NO CHANGE
    B.   clubs'
    C.   clubs's
    D.   clubs

9. All of the <u>nations's</u> leaders were present, but each country had its own agenda.

    A.   NO CHANGE
    B.   nations'
    C.   nations
    D.   nation's

10. My <u>dog's</u> bark is worse than his bite.

    A.   NO CHANGE
    B.   dogs
    C.   dogs's
    D.   dogs'

Apostrophes - Quiz 2

1. My <u>apartment's</u> walls are so thin that I can hear the neighbors talking.

   A. NO CHANGE
   B. apartments's
   C. apartments'
   D. apartments

2. During our break, you can find the <u>man's</u> room down the hall and to the left of the cafeteria.

   A. NO CHANGE
   B. mens
   C. men's
   D. mens'

3. All of the <u>cars</u> license plates are made in our state penitentiary.

   A. NO CHANGE
   B. car's
   C. cars'
   D. cars's

4. The <u>oceans'</u> waves crashed upon the beach.

   A. NO CHANGE
   B. oceans
   C. oceans's
   D. ocean's

5. Use the nice stationery for any letters to our <u>companys's</u> customers.

   A. NO CHANGE
   B. company's
   C. companys
   D. companys'

6. But my <u>friends</u> parents let him stay up late!

   A. NO CHANGE
   B. friends'
   C. friends's
   D. friend's

7. She found last <u>months'</u> phone bill in the drawer.

   A. NO CHANGE
   B. months
   C. month's
   D. months's

8. The <u>windows</u> glass was shattered by the storm. Not even one was unbroken.

   A. NO CHANGE
   B. window's
   C. windows'
   D. windows's

9. This <u>pencils'</u> eraser is missing.

   A. NO CHANGE
   B. pencil's
   C. pencils
   D. pencils's

10. You also need to paint the <u>front doors</u> frame.

   A. NO CHANGE
   B. front doors'
   C. front door's
   D. front doors's

Apostrophes - Quiz 3

1.   **A.**   Her husbands wallet was full of curious items.
       B.   Her husband's wallet was full of curious items.
       C.   Her husbands' wallet was full of curious items.

2.   **A.**   I went to the editor-in-chief house for dinner last night.
       B.   I went to the editor-in-chief's house for dinner last night.
       C.   I went to the editor-in-chiefs' house for dinner last night.

3.   **A.**   You may not enter Mr. Harris' office without his permission.
       B.   You may not enter Mr. Harris office without his permission.
       C.   You may not enter Mr. Harrises office without his permission.

4.   **A.**   What are your childrens names?
       B.   What are your childrens' names?
       C.   What are your children's names?

5.   **A.**   The women's dresses are on the second floor.
       B.   The womans' dresses are on the second floor.
       C.   The womens' dresses are on the second floor.

6.   **A.**   It's a shame that that's not happening today.
       B.   Its a shame that that's not happening today.
       C.   It's a shame that thats not happening today.

7.   **A.**   It's a dog wagging it's tail.
       B.   It's a dog wagging its tail.
       C.   Its a dog wagging its tail.

8.   **A.**   The two city's weather is always warm.
       B.   The two cities weather is always warm.
       C.   The two cities' weather is always warm.

9.   **A.**   The elephants' routine was different every day. The animals knew a variety of tricks.
       B.   The elephant's routine was different every day. The animals knew a variety of tricks.
       C.   The elephants routine was different every day. The animals knew a variety of tricks.

10.   **A.**   The seamstress's do great work.
       B.   The seamstresses do great work.
       C.   The seamstresses' do great work.

Read possessive cases backwards. 1) **B.** the wallet of your husband 2) **B.** the house of the editor in chief. 3) **A.** the office of Mr. Harris 4) **C.** the names of your children 5) **A.** the dresses of the women 6 **A.** *it's* always means "it is"; *that's* always means "that is." 7) **B.** *it's* always means "it is"; *its* is the pronoun that indicates possession. 8) **C.** the weather of the two cities 9) **A.** the routine of the elephants (note that it talks about the animals) 10) **B.** There is no possessive noun in this sentence. It just talks about more than one seamstress who do great work.

Conjunctive Adverbs

A conjunctive adverb acts like a conjunction and can connect two sentences.

Accordingly, additionally, again, almost, anyway, as a result, besides, certainly, comparatively, consequently, contrarily, conversely, elsewhere, equally, finally, further, furthermore, <u>hence</u>, henceforth, however, in addition, in comparison, in contrast, in fact, incidentally, indeed, instead, just as, likewise, meanwhile, moreover, namely, nevertheless, <u>next</u>, nonetheless, notably, <u>now</u>, otherwise, rather, similarly, <u>still</u>, subsequently, that is, <u>then</u>, thereafter, therefore, <u>thus</u>, undoubtedly, uniquely.

In ONE full sentence, the conjunctive adverbs are set off by two commas.

I do not, however, want you to repeat that risky behavior again.   **Correct**

My mother, meanwhile, was working on another project in her office.   **Correct**

However, TWO full sentences can only be joined with a comma if you use one of the FANBOYS conjunctions. (for, and, nor, but, or, yet, so.) (See comma rules in the last chapter.)

I like to take risks, however, I do not want to climb that mountain again.   **Incorrect**: no FANBOYS

My mother was in her office, meanwhile, my dad worked in the yard   **Incorrect**: no FANBOYS

Tip: The words on top of this page are <u>not</u> FANBOYS. Therefore, you cannot use one OR two commas if a conjunctive adverb is used to join two full sentences. Use a semicolon instead.

Punctuation with Conjunctive Adverbs

Use a semicolon or period BEFORE the conjunctive adverb to separate two full sentences joined by a conjunctive adverb.

Use a comma AFTER the conjunctive adverb when it appears at the beginning of the second clause unless the adverb has <u>one syllable</u> (hence, next, now, still, then, and thus.)

Alternatively, you can use a period INSTEAD OF a semicolon.

Lisa wants to be a veterinarian; however, she does not like animals.

Lisa wants to be a veterinarian. However, she does not like animals.

Using a Conjunctive Adverb in a Sentence

In the BEGINNING of a sentence, it is capitalized and followed by a comma.

If they appear in the MIDDLE of the sentence, it is normally enclosed in commas.

When they appear at the END of the sentence, it is preceded by a comma.

When it appears in the MIDDLE OF TWO FULL SENTENCES, it is preceded by a semicolon, and followed by a comma.

---, _____.

_____, ---, _____.

_____, ---.

_____;---,_____.

Punctuation- Quiz 6 (Conjunctive Adverbs)

1. **A.** She wants a new phone; however she spent all of her money on her car.
   B. She wants a new phone; However she spent all of her money on her car.
   C. She wants a new phone; however, she spent all of her money on her car.
   D. She wants a new phone; However, she spent all of her money on her car.

2. **A.** My mother is a baker consequently, I am always well fed.
   B. My mother is a baker, consequently I am always well fed.
   C. My mother is a baker; consequently; I am always well fed.
   D. My mother is a baker; consequently, I am always well fed.

3. **A.** Beau is afraid of planes and therefore, does not like to travel.
   B. Beau is afraid of planes, and therefore does not like to travel.
   C. Beau is afraid of planes and, therefore, does not like to travel.
   D. Beau is afraid of planes; and, therefore, does not like to travel.

4. **A.** I needed to take a long nap yet, I went to my friend's house.
   B. I needed to take a long nap, yet, I went to my friend's house.
   C. I needed to take a long nap, yet I went to my friend's house.
   D. I needed to take a long nap; yet I went to my friend's house.

5. **A.** Nelly ate ice cream before bed, therefore she could not sleep at night.
   B. Nelly ate ice cream before bed; therefore, she could not sleep at night.
   C. Nelly ate ice cream before bed: therefore she could not sleep at night.
   D. Nelly ate ice cream before bed, therefore, she could not sleep at night.

6. **A.** Victoria wanted to eat healthier, but her parents, in contrast, liked to eat fast food.
   B. Victoria wanted to eat healthier, but her parents in contrast, liked to eat fast food.
   C. Victoria wanted to eat healthier; but her parents, in contrast liked to eat fast food.
   D. Victoria wanted to eat healthier; but her parents, in contrast, liked to eat fast food.

7. **A.** Rome is the most fascinating place in the world, I have, however never left the USA.
   B. Rome is the most fascinating place in the world. I have however never left the USA.
   C. Rome is the most fascinating place in the world; I have, however, never left the USA.
   D. Rome is the most fascinating place in the world: I have, however, never left the USA.

8. **A.** I always worked late nights, and received the promotion I, finally, deserved.
   B. I always worked late nights, and finally, received the promotion I deserved.
   C. I always worked late nights and, finally, received the promotion I deserved.
   D. I always worked late nights; and finally I received the promotion I deserved.

9. **A.** In comparison, to Algebra, Calculus undoubtedly is a lot harder.
   B. In comparison to Algebra, Calculus, undoubtedly is a lot harder.
   C. In comparison to Algebra, Calculus, undoubtedly, is a lot harder.
   D. In comparison, to Algebra Calculus undoubtedly is a lot harder.

1) C. Use a semicolon two full sentences without a FANBOYS conjunction. Use a comma after the conjunctive adverb. 2) D. Use a semicolon two full sentences without a FANBOYS conjunction. Use a comma after the adverb. 3) C. These are NOT two full sentences. 4) C. Use a comma with a FANBOYS conjunction and two full sentences. 5) B. Use a semicolon two separate two full sentences without a FANBOYS conjunction. Use a comma after the conjunctive adverb. 6) A. Use a comma with a FANBOYS conjunction and two full sentences. Set off the conjunctive adverbs by commas. 7) C. Use a semicolon between two contrasting full sentences. Set off the conjunctive adverbs by commas. 8) C, only one full sentence with a conjunctive adverb 9) C. Intro, full sentence. Set off the conjunctive adverbs by commas.

Punctuation - Quiz 7 (Challenge)

1. The magician bowed gracefully before the <u>audience, many</u> people gave a standing ovation, letting the performer know how much they appreciated the show.
   - A. NO CHANGE
   - B. audience many
   - C. audience. Many
   - D. audience. While many

2. The governor bought the finest lab equipment and hired the best instructors to instruct his son <u>in: physical</u> and chemical sciences.
   - A. NO CHANGE
   - B. in, physical
   - C. in physical,
   - D. in physical

3. He understood that his <u>countrys</u> language was influenced by Portuguese, Spanish, Taíno, and several West African languages.
   - A. NO CHANGE
   - B. countrys'
   - C. country's
   - D. countries

4. I write and draw all my own stories. I also enjoy illustrating someone <u>else's</u> work.
   - A. NO CHANGE
   - B. elses'
   - C. elses
   - D. else

5. This is not a special <u>function, which</u> I just happen to contribute to local charities.
   - A. NO CHANGE
   - B. function, that
   - C. function
   - D. function.

6. The U.S. Army made <u>it's</u> most important decisions just before the end of the war.
   - A. NO CHANGE
   - B. its
   - C. their
   - D. its'

7. The weather forecasts have become more accurate since the invention of the Doppler <u>radar, a</u> specialized radar that makes use of the Doppler effect to produce velocity data about objects at a distance.
   - A. NO CHANGE
   - B. radar: A
   - C. radar; a
   - D. radar a

8. Those who followed the <u>teachers directions</u> met the state standards and earned several awards.
   - A. NO CHANGE
   - B. teacher's directions
   - C. teacher's directions,
   - D. teachers directions,

9. An excellent administrator and <u>headmaster:</u> he is most remembered for his daily one-on-one lunch meetings with students.
   - A. NO CHANGE
   - B. headmaster;
   - C. headmaster,
   - D. headmaster

10. On September 11, 2001, the day of the terrorist attack on the Twin <u>Towers. U.S.</u> citizens were shaken in their sense of safety and security.
    - A. NO CHANGE
    - B. Towers U.S.
    - C. Towers, U.S.
    - D. Towers; U.S.

11. The innovative additions to the robot made it impossible to <u>beat the</u> multi-player control panel that allowed several operators to steer its motions, the 360-degree optical field that did not leave one detail unnoticed, and, most importantly, its capability to advance regardless of which of its eight sides was up.
    - A. NO CHANGE
    - B. beat: the
    - C. beat. The
    - D. beat, the

---

1) C. The sentence has a comma splice. 2) D. Only use a colon after a full sentence. Only use commas in lists of three or more items. 3) C. Read it backwards: the language of the country. 4) A. Read it backwards: the work of someone else. 5) D. The best way is to split the two statements up into two separate sentences. 6) B. Use the singular possessive pronoun "its"; there is only one U.S. Army. 7) A. the part after the comma is added information. B has a capital after the colon. C does not have two full sentences. D is a run-on sentence. 8) B. The directions of the teacher. NOT and intro and a full sentence. 9) C. the added information sits at the beginning of the sentence. 10) C. "the day .... Twin Towers" is added information. 11) B. Use a colon between a full sentence and a list.

MODIFIERS

Modifiers:

    1) A modifier describes only the word closest to it.

    2) Everything before the comma refers to the first (pro)noun after the comma.

Learn to spot the issues:

Misplaced Modifiers

Dangling Modifiers

Which & That modifiers

Ambiguous Modifiers

The good news is that modifiers often make you smile if they are used incorrectly. ☺

Modifiers

A modifier is a word or phrase that adds a detail or a description to a sentence. In the next sentence, the modifiers are underlined.

Feeling creative, I decorated several stores in the mall of my town.

While modifiers are great for adding detail and interest to sentences, they must be used carefully so that the reader clearly understands which detail describes which noun.

Modifiers

Tip: A modifier describes only the word CLOSEST TO IT.

Look at the sentences below. The same sentence ("I am decorating in the mall") is written four times. See how the word *Washington* affects only the word next to it.

I am decorating in the Washington Mall.	*(The name of the mall is Washington.)*
I, Washington, am decorating in the mall.	*(My name is Washington.)*
Washington, I am decorating in the mall.	*(I am talking to Washington.)*
I am decorating Washington in the mall.	*(I am decorating Washington.)*

Misplaced Modifiers

Misplaced modifiers are not placed directly before or after the noun or verb they describe.
In the sentence below, the placement of one of the modifiers is awkward. This often happens when there are two or more modifiers in one sentence.

I gave a diamond to my girlfriend in a beautiful box.

Review: *"In a beautiful box"* modifies the closest noun to it. Is my girlfriend in a box?

Revision: I gave a diamond in a beautiful box to my girlfriend.

The ACT questions will be worded like this: Where should the following sentence fragment be placed?
Tip: Ask yourself what the underlined fragment describes (what it modifies) and place it right next to it.

Dangling Modifiers

Dangling modifier occur when there is no subject **before** the comma. According to the rules above, the first part of the sentence modifies the closest word to it, which is the first (pro)noun **after** the comma.

Tip: Everything before the comma refers to the first (pro)noun after the comma.

Topped with pepperoni, my mother served pizza to all my friends.

Review: *Who is topped with pepperoni? The first noun after the comma (closest to it) is "my mother."*

Revision 1: Topped with pepperoni, pizza was served to all my friends by my mother.

Revision 2: After she topped it with pepperoni, my mother served pizza to all my friends.

The ACT loves dangling modifiers! It often gives you three incorrect solutions for the modifier.
Tip: Look at the sentence structure, not at the content.

Modifiers - Quiz 1

 Tip: If you follow the English grammar rules, misplaced and dangling modifiers will always make you smile.

Find the misplaced modifiers. (Pay attention to the rules!)

1. My mother wrote thank-you notes to her guests on homemade stationery.

2. She was skyping with her boyfriend on her laptop.

3. In my backyard, I shot the squirrel with my dart gun after missing numerous times.

4. We saw elephants and giraffes on a 3-day safari trip through Kenya.

5. The professor observed the cells growing through his microscope.

6. Before you give the sausage to the dog, make sure you cut it in small pieces.

7. The fashion model walked her dog in 6-inch heels and a see-through raincoat.

8. The family waited behind the door with gifts and balloons to surprise the graduate student.

Find the dangling modifiers:

9. Even after putting on sunscreen, the sun was too strong, and I became sunburned.

10. Exploring the back roads of Florida, my car broke down.

11. Running to class, the bell rang before I got there.

12. Being slightly damaged, I bought the couch for 50% off the original price.

13. After eating all of the pizza, Andy's stomach began to hurt.

14. Trying to complete my homework, the cat lay on top of my papers all the time.

15. While repairing the roof, a squirrel jumped out from behind the chimney and scared the roofer.

16. After driving through Death Valley for hours, the hotel pool was a nice place to cool off.

17. Flying low over the stadium, we could see the pilots in the old warplanes waving at us.

18. Trying not to disturb my parents, they woke up anyway and scolded me for coming home at 4:00 a.m.

1) Are her guests on homemade stationery? No, she wrote thank-you notes on homemade stationary to her guests.
2) Is her boyfriend on the laptop? That might crack the screen! No, she is skyping on her laptop to her boyfriend.
3) This is dangerous: "a squirrel with my dart gun." How did the squirrel get my dart gun in the first place?
4) The elephants and giraffes were on a safari trip? How did they fit in a Jeep?
5) The cells were growing through his microscope. Yikes. I hope he has another one.
6) According to the modifier rules, your instructions are to cut the dog in small pieces before you feed him.
7) I have never seen a dog wearing 6-inch heels and a raincoat, have you?
8) If it was a door with a double lock, sure. But a door with gifts and balloons? I have never seen one.
9) The sun was not putting on sunscreen. I was! However, the sentence does not make that clear.
10) That is why I could not find my car this morning! It was exploring the backroads of Florida.
11) Imagine the bell running to class. Maybe it will be on time for a "bell ringer" in math class?
12) "I" was not slightly damaged. Would that really help me to get a discount?
13) Andy's stomach did not eat the pizza. That would be gross.
14) I love having a cat that completes my homework. At least it tries!
15) I hope the squirrel that repairs roofs is insured and licensed.
16) So, the hotel pool drove through Death Valley. Was it full of water the whole time?
17) What a thrill: we were flying over the stadium that was filled pilots in warplanes. I wonder whom they were playing that day!
18) In this case, my parents were trying not to disturb my parents. Then they scolded me. Next time, I'll try not to disturb them.

Modifiers 2 (For Better Insight)

Why are modifiers so hard to spot? (Read this out loud)

Mdfioriers are wrods or desciorptins taht pvroide frtuher dtaeil aoubt athnoer wrod. Hwoveer, yuor bairn desraepetly wntas to mkae snese of the irmnftioaon, and thrfoeere it wlil logllaicy cocennt the seprteeaed patrs of a sncenete, eevn if the Eisnlgh rlue stetas taht mdioefirs afefct olny the wrod rghit nxet to it.

To rcoeignze danligng mifoiedr mstikeas, reebemmr: evthinerg boerfe the cmoma olny rerefs to the fsirt sbjucet atefr the cmmoa.

Trehfoere: Fuocs on the rlues, not on the inftioroman.

Notice how you cannot trust your brain. It will put words and letters in the order that makes sense.

My friend just ran ten miles in the park.	(He just ran, he did not walk.)
Just my friend ran ten miles in the park.	(Nobody else ran, just my friend.)
My friend ran just ten miles in the park.	(Normally he runs 20 miles, today just 10.)
My friend ran ten miles just in the park.	(He stayed in the park for all 10 miles.)

 Watch out for words like **almost, just, merely, nearly**, **barely, even, hardly, exactly, simply,** and **only**.

Tip: Remember to focus on the word right next to the modifier.

Which & That

The part of a sentence that begins with *"that"* or *"which"* should immediately follow the word that it modifies.

Example: The helpful farmer gave me directions to the corn maze on the other side of the river, which was famous for its creepy design.

Although your brain might tell you otherwise, in the sentence above the <u>river</u> is famous for its creepy design. Remember, a modifier describes only the word closest to it.

 *Tip: **Don't** use a comma before adding a modifier that starts with "that." It is a restrictive clause. You need it to identify the noun.*
The wallet <u>that was lying on the table</u> was green.

 *Tip: **Do** use a comma before adding a modifier that starts with "which." It is added information.*
The wallet, <u>which was lying on the table</u>, was green.

Ambiguous Modifiers

If a modifier sits between two words that it could equally affect, move it for the sake of clarity.

I observed him <u>silently</u> watering his plants.	**Review:** Did I observe him silently, or did he water his plants without a sound? **Revision:** *I observed him watering his plants silently.*
Students who talk <u>rarely</u> will be asked to leave.	**Review:** Do the students talk rarely, or will they rarely be asked to leave? **Revision:** *Students who talk will rarely be asked to leave.*
I told her <u>at 3:00 p.m.</u> I would stop working.	**Review:** Did you tell her at 3:00 p.m., or would you stop working then? **Revision:** *At 3:00 p.m., I told her that I would stop working.*

Modifiers - Quiz 2

Find the misplaced modifiers in the following sentences.

1. I did not have much cash on me. I only gave the waiter a $2.00 tip.
2. David only had to study for one more exam before he could start his summer vacation.
3. After a slow start, the vendor almost sold all of his pottery items before packing up at 5:00 PM.
4. The rotten bag of potatoes under the kitchen sink made me almost gag.
5. I just need two more dollars to buy the guitar for which I have been saving.
6. We nearly raised four thousand dollars towards chemistry lab items with our dance marathon!
7. Although we had great hopes for our new kicker, he barely kicked the football 20 yards.
8. The pilot located the landing strip looking at the map that he had almost memorized.

 Did you find them already? If not, it is very comforting to know that the ACT is always multiple choice.
Tip: Read the whole sentence several times, each time with the modifier in its new place.

1. The word "only" should be placed
   - **A.** Where it is now
   - **B.** After the word "tip"
   - **C.** After the word "gave"
   - **D.** After the word "waiter"

2. The word "only" should be placed
   - **A.** Where it is now
   - **B.** After the word "study"
   - **C.** After the word "could"
   - **D.** After the word "for"

3. The word "almost" should be placed
   - **A.** Where it is now
   - **B.** After the word "before"
   - **C.** After the word "sold"
   - **D.** After the word "items"

4. The word "rotten" should be placed
   - **A.** Where it is now
   - **B.** After the word "of"
   - **C.** Before the word "kitchen"
   - **D.** After the word "potatoes"

The word "just" should be placed
   - **A.** Where it is now
   - **B.** After the word "two"
   - **C.** After the word "have"
   - **D.** After the word "need"

6. The word "nearly" should be placed
   - **A.** Where it is now
   - **B.** After the word "raised"
   - **C.** Before the word "we"
   - **D.** After the word "items"

7. The word "barely" should be placed
   - **A.** Where it is now
   - **B.** After the word "we"
   - **C.** After the word "new"
   - **D.** After the word "football"

8. The words "located the landing strip" should be placed
   - **A.** Where they are now
   - **B.** Before the word "pilot"
   - **C.** After the word "memorized"
   - **D.** Before the word "map"

1. You *only gave* it to him? I gave the waiter only a $2.00 tip.
2. He *only had* to study? David had to study for only one more exam …
3. He *almost sold* them? The vendor sold almost all of his pottery items …
4. *Was* it a *rotten bag*? The bag of rotten potatoes under the kitchen sink …
5. *You just need* it? I need just two more dollars to buy …
6. *You nearly raised* that much? We raised nearly four thousand dollars.
7. He *barely kicked* the ball? He kicked the football barely 20 yards.
8. *Was* the landing strip looking at the map? The pilot looking at the map that he had almost memorized located the landing strip.

1) D. 2) D. 3) C. 4) B. 5) D. 6) B. 7) D. 8) C.

Modifiers - Quiz 3

Tip: Remember why modifiers are so hard to spot.

Mdfioriers are wrods or desriopctins taht pvroide frtuher dtaeil aoubt athnoer wrod. Hwoveer, yuor bairn desraepetly wntas to mkae snese of the irmnftioaon, and thrfoeere it wlil logllaicy ceconnt the seprteeaed patrs of a sencente, eevn if the Eisnlgh rlue stetas taht <u>mdioefirs afefct olny the wrod rghit nxet to it.</u>
To rcoeignze danligng mifoiedr mstikeas, reebemmr: <u>evthinerg boerfe the cmoma olny rerefs to the fsirt sbjucet atefr the cmmoa.</u>
Trehfoere: Fuocs on the rlues, not on the inftioroman.

Write the two modifier rules one more time in plain English:
1) _____
2) _____

Find the misplaced and dangling modifiers in the following sentences:

1) I gave the award certificate to the essay winner with a thousand-dollar check.
2) Decorated with 94 burning candles, the director brought a cake to his oldest resident on her birthday.
3) Standing 16 feet tall, the giraffe's eating habits were easy to observe.
4) While dancing at the party, my phone fell out my pocket and broke.
5) Although the snow had turned to ice and made the highway slippery, it had melted before the morning rush hour.
6) After Amy used her phone to find the hotel, its battery died.
7) Cassidy wore a dress to the party with hundreds of tiny polka dots.
8) Although funny at times, I did not enjoy the play in the community theater.
9) The three students stood behind the gym smoking cigarettes.
10) The detective observed an object behind the door that was left behind.

Tip: Look at the sentence structure, not at the content.

1) It is not an essay winner with a thousand-dollar check, but the "award with a thousand-dollars check"!
2) The director is not decorated with candles, the cake is.
3) The eating habits are not 16 feet tall, the giraffe is.
4) The phone was not dancing at your party, you were.
5) What does "it" stand for? The highway? Consider the revisions "the snow had melted" or "the highways".
6) Did the hotel's battery die? Do not use "it" if the pronoun can refer to two separate single nouns in a sentence.
7) The sentence indicates that there was a "party with hundreds of tiny polka dots".
8) This sentence indicates that I am funny at times. Revise: Although the play in the community theater was funny at times, I did not enjoy it.
9) Was the gym smoking cigarettes? Revise: Smoking cigarettes, the three students stood behind the gym.
10) Was the door left behind? Revise: an object that was left behind the door.

Modifiers - Quiz 4

1. Sorry, there is a rule at the library: <u>I will only let you check out three books</u>.
   A. NO CHANGE
   B. I will let you only check out three books.
   C. I will let you check out only three books.
   D. I only will let you check out three books.

2. Hopefully, we will complete the project before the deadline.
   A. NO CHANGE
   B. We will hopefully complete the project before the deadline.
   C. We hope to complete the project before the deadline.
   D. We will complete the project before the hopeful deadline.

3. Having completed the project plan, <u>it seemed to include all necessary actions.</u>
   A. NO CHANGE
   B. all necessary actions seemed to be included.
   C. included were all the necessary actions.
   D. she seemed to have included all the necessary actions.

4. Bob found a letter <u>on his desk that did not belong to him</u>.
   A. NO CHANGE
   B. on his desk to him that did not belong.
   C. that did not belong to him on his desk.
   D. on his desk which did not belong to him.

5. Working always in the absence of his supervisor, <u>the custodian only cleaned one office per day</u>.
   A. NO CHANGE
   B. only one office was cleaned each day by the custodian.
   C. daily cleaning by the custodian only included one office.
   D. the custodian cleaned only one office per day.

6. A woman needs time to recover after childbirth, which can take many weeks.
   A. NO CHANGE
   B. A woman needs time to recover, which can take many weeks, after childbirth.
   C. A woman needs time, which can take many weeks, to recover after childbirth.
   D. A woman, which can take many weeks to recover after childbirth, needs time.

Modifiers - Quiz 5

1. A. Telling Tina I was going to Spain, excitedly, she taught me some common Spanish phrases.
    B. Teaching me some common Spanish phrases, I told Tina I was going to Spain, excitedly.
    C. Telling I was going to Spain, excitedly, I was taught by Tina some common Spanish phrases.
    D. I excitedly told Tina I was going to Spain, and she taught me some common Spanish phrases.

2. A. I loved the enthusiastically wisdom of the professors at my school.
    B. I loved the enthusiastic wisdom of the professors at my school.
    C. I loved the wisdomly enthusiasm of the professors at my school.
    D. I loved the wisdom enthusiasm of the professors at my school.

3. A. He improved his ACT score by discovering what his common mistakes were.
    B. His ACT score was improved by discovering what his common mistakes were.
    C. His score on the ACT was improved by discovering what his common mistakes were.
    D. The improvement of his ACT score occurred by discovering what his common mistakes were.

4. A. In 2014, she finished graduate school, a time that had a limited job market.
    B. She finished graduate school in 2014, a time that had a limited job market.
    C. She finished in 2014, graduate school, a time that had a limited job market.
    D. It was in 2014 that she finished graduate school, a time that had a limited job market.

5. A. If you wash your hands, as I do, you are less likely to get often sick.
    B. If you wash your hands, as I do, you are less often likely to get sick.
    C. If you wash often, as I do, your hands, you are less likely to get sick.
    D. If you wash your hands, as I do often, you are less likely to get sick.

6. A. If that vase is broken, you had hope that it better costs less than your allowance.
    B. If that vase is broken, better you had hope that it costs less than your allowance.
    C. If that vase is broken, you had better hope that it costs less than your allowance.
    D. If that vase is broken, you had hope that it costs less than your better allowance.

7. A. She put the bags with the baby clothes into her new Mercedes, which she planned to bring to Goodwill later that day.
    B. Later that day, she put the bags that she planned to bring to Goodwill into her new Mercedes with the baby clothes.
    C. She put the bags with the baby clothes that she planned to bring to Goodwill later that day into her new Mercedes.
    D. She put the bags with the baby clothes, which she planned later that day to bring to Goodwill into her new Mercedes.

8. A. Orangutans are already understood to be solo creatures by Goodall.
    B. As Goodall understood, orangutans are already solo creatures.
    C. Goodall already understood that orangutans are solo creatures.
    D. Being solo creatures, Goodall already understood that orangutans live alone.

---

1) D. A and B have dangling modifiers: Telling Tina ... she taught me. Teaching me ... Tina taught me. C is a passive-voice sentence. Avoid those when possible. D is clear and correct. 2) B. A and C use adverbs to describe a noun! D uses a noun to describe a noun. 3) A. Ask yourself, "Who did the discovering?" Not his score! 4) B. "a time that ..." modifies the word right before it. 5) D. What does the word *often* modify? Washing hands! Eliminate A and B. C is awkward. 6 C. Does it "better cost?" something? No. Is it about a "better allowance"? No. She does not want to bring her Mercedes to Goodwill (A). She does not have a "Mercedes with the baby clothes" (B). "Which" is used for added information, and "that" is used for necessary information. Answer D is wrong because the part before the comma is not a full sentence. 8) C Answer A contains passive voice. B misplaces the word already, and D implies that Goodall is a solo creature.

Copyright 2017 Winni van Gessel

Modifiers - Quiz 6

Find the misplaced and dangling modifiers before looking at the answers. Did you spot them already?
If not, it is very comforting to know that the ACT is always multiple choice.

1. After proving that I had already completed the form, <u>my advisor let me sign up for the course.</u>
   A. NO CHANGE
   B. the course I wanted was finally permitted by my advisor.
   C. it was finally possible for me to sign up for the course.
   D. I finally received permission from my advisor to sign up for the course.

2. Located behind large hedges and trees, <u>it was hard to find the hotel at night.</u>
   A. NO CHANGE
   B. the hotel was hard to find at night.
   C. I could hardly find the hotel at night.
   D. the hotel at night was hard to find.

3. I asked the dealer to replace the seatbelt in my car that gets stuck all the time.
   A. NO CHANGE.
   B. To replace the seatbelt, I asked the dealer in my car that gets stuck all the time.
   C. I asked the dealer to replace the seatbelt that gets stuck all the time in my car.
   D. I asked the dealer in my car to replace the seatbelt that gets stuck all the time.

4. Anna could not stand the dog in her neighborhood that continually barked all night.
   The words <u>"in her neighborhood"</u> should be placed
   A. where they are now.
   B. after the word "Anna".
   C. before the word "Anna" (changing the capitalization accordingly.)
   D. after the word "night", before the period.

"Talking louder occasionally solves the problem." Which would NOT be a possible placement for the word "<u>occasionally</u>"?
   A. Where it is now
   B. Before the word "talking" (changing the capitalization accordingly)
   C. After the word "problem"
   D. After the word "talking"

6. <u>After cleaning the floor and making the bed,</u> my bedroom looked almost respectable again.
   A. NO CHANGE
   B. After making the bed and cleaning the floor,
   C. I cleaned the floor, and after making the bed,
   D. After I cleaned the floor and made the bed,

7. <u>At the age of two,</u> I taught my youngest child how to play the piano.
   A. NO CHANGE
   B. At just two years old,
   C. When she was two years old,
   D. As a two-year old,

8. <u>The professor forgot to hand out a study guide, which caused me to fail my exam.</u>
   A. NO CHANGE
   B. The professor forgot to hand out a study guide that caused me to fail time.
   C. The professor that caused me to fail my exam forgot to hand out a study guide.
   D. The fact that my professor forgot to hand out a study guide caused me to fail my exam.

---

1) **D.** Who is proving that I already completed my form? Not my advisor, not the course, and not "it". 2) **B.** What was located behind the hedges and trees? Not "it" and not "I". What does "at night" modify? Not the hotel (D) but finding it. 3) **C.** It was not the car that got stuck (A), nor was there a dealer in my car (B and D) 4) **D.** In the current sentence, it looks like the neighborhood barked all night. Anna dislikes "The dog that continually barked all night in her neighborhood." 5) **A.** Currently, the word "occasionally" is ambiguous. Does it modify talking louder, or does it modify solving the problem? All other solutions are clear and correct. 6) **D.** The information before the comma needs to talk about the bedroom. Without the word "I", it looks like the bedroom cleaned the floor and made the bed. A, B and C all have dangling modifiers. 7) **C.** Only when you add the word "I", to the modifier can you avoid saying that you were two years old when you taught your daughter how to play piano. 8) **D.** It was not the study guide that made you fail the exam, nor was it the professor. It was the fact that he forgot to hand out a study guide

IDIOMS

The idiom questions in the ACT are mostly combinations between verbs and prepositions.

If you made mistakes in this category, practice with the quizzes on the next few pages. Although there are many idioms, you will learn that there are rules that guide the use of each idiom.

Idioms

In English, we do not say, "It is raining cats and puppies." We say, "It is raining cats and dogs." This is called an idiomatic expression. A native speaker knows that we do not wish each other Happy Christmas and Merry New Year, but Merry Christmas and Happy New Year. There is just one way to say these expressions correctly.

The types of idioms on the ACT are mostly about combinations between verbs, nouns, and prepositions. We do not say, "I was happy **at** the Christmas present." You can say, however, "I had my eyes **on** the present," "I was looking **at** the present," or "I was happy **with** the present."

The ACT often mixes two idiomatic expressions that both sound familiar.

Tip: Using the same verb, construct a new sentence with a different subject and object. It will help you to determine which preposition to use.

Idioms - Quiz 1

Find the idioms that are incorrect and correct them.

1. The boy is able of speaking up for himself.
2. The janitor has access in all the offices.
3. Picasso is acclaimed to be a famous painter.
4. The singer is accompanied with guitars and violins.
5. This is according with the contract you signed.
6. The student is accused about cheating for his test.
7. The contractor is acquainted about the specific requirements.
8. The book is adapted to a younger audience.
9. My mother is afraid for spiders.
10. The two parties agree about these terms.
11. The two opponents agree on be nice to each other.
12. I am allergic of poison ivy.
13. This portion of the budget is allocated for educational materials.
14. This proposal is an alternative for the other plan to save money.
15. A budget cut will amount for unhappy employees.

1) The boy is able to speak **up** 2) The janitor has access **to** 3) Picasso is acclaimed **as a** 4) The singer is accompanied **by** 5) This is according **to** 6) The student is accused **of** 7) The contractor is acquainted **with** 8) The book is adapted **for** 9) My mother is afraid **of** 10) The two parties agree **on** these terms (noun) 11) The two opponents agree **to** be nice 12) I am allergic **to** 13) This portion of the budget is allocated **to** 14) This proposal is an alternative **to** 15) A budget cut will amount **to**

Idioms - Quiz 2

Find the idioms that are incorrect and correct them.

1. The boy blamed his dog with making the mess.
2. Jessica approved on making the change to the paper.
3. The mom was afraid to leave her young child alone.
4. The teacher was getting very tired with the students' misbehavior.
5. The moral of the story sounded similar to one she had heard of before.
6. Even though several things had gone wrong, they had to proceed by the show.
7. I am currently occupied with this movie. Can you get the door for me?
8. Martin was in the habit on listening to audiobooks.
9. The teenager was finally independent of her parents when she went to college.
10. I am concerned about your failing grade in history.
11. You need to stay accountable for the people who have hired you.
12. I'm really grateful, from the bottom of my heart, to Miranda's help this week.
13. You should congratulate your sister for her accomplishments.
14. I cannot begin to compete against Emily: she is just too good at what she does.
15. The dad was very satisfied by how everything turned out.

1. The boy blamed his dog **for**
2. Jessica approved **of**
3. The mom was afraid **of** leaving
4. The teacher was getting very tired **of**
5. Correct
6. They had to proceed **with** the show
7. I am currently occupied **by** this movie
8. Martin was in the habit **of**
9. Correct
10. I am concerned **with** your failing grade
11. You need to stay accountable **for**
12. I am really grateful **for** Miranda's help
13. You should congratulate your sister **on**
14. I cannot begin to compete **with**
15. The dad was very satisfied **with**

Idioms - Quiz 3

Find the idioms that are incorrect and correct them.

1. The young girl was upset that she had to adhere with the rules.

2. Mary wished she could go to the movies, but she was engaged with helping her mom do the dishes.

3. We need to show respect to your mom; let's wait for her to finish eating.

4. Is Josh even conscious of some of his actions?

5. Interestingly, the twins' preferences were opposite to each other.

6. I am very interested to learn about the new documentary.

7. Her actions turned out to be very inconsistent of her words.

8. Judi's mom told her that she had to stay accountable for her parents.

9. The contract prohibited the trapeze artists to try anything too dangerous.

10. Josh usually leaves the forms next, or sometimes behind, the fax machine.

11. Prior to the lecture, Miranda had no knowledge of how responsible humans are to their environment.

12. I could of probably eaten one more banana, but I was concerned about getting sick.

13. It gets aggravating when younger children keep complaining about not getting what they want.

14. Mom served me a lunch composed with my favorite foods: an apple, some chips, and a ham sandwich.

15. George never got his homework done because he was always occupied by talking on the phone.

1. She had to adhere to the rules
2. She was engaged in helping
3. To show respect for
4. Correct
5. Were opposite of each other.
6. I am very interested in learning
7. Inconsistent with her words
8. Stay accountable to her parents
9. Prohibited the artists from trying
10. Put the forms next to the machine
11. Humans are for their environment
12. I could've (or could have) probably
13. Correct
14. Mom served me a lunch composed of
15. He was always occupied with talking

Idioms - Quiz 4

Find the idioms that are incorrect and correct them.

1. I cannot say I really approve completely with those actions of yours.

2. The CEO was insistent on getting to the yearly report.

3. Justin found out that he was actually related, although twice removed, with Abraham Lincoln.

4. My father keeps telling me that I should be more concerned in my choice of friends.

5. Grace was a soccer player prior before being a basketball player.

6. Kristan glanced at the glass of the store's window to see a fancy purse on sale.

7. Xavier gets very bored of listening to the same song repeatedly.

8. Don't talk to Margaret or Alex; they are currently on conflict with each other.

9. There are only eight planets in our solar system, according with a recent study of NASA.

10. Jack felt quite grateful for his many close friends.

1. I really approve **of**
2. Correct
3. He was actually related **to**
4. I should be more concerned **with**
5. A soccer player prior **to** being
6. Christen glanced **through** the glass
7. Xavier gets very bored **with**
8. They are currently **in** conflict with
9. According **to** a recent study
10. Correct

PRONOUNS

Do not trust pronouns!

Always check what pronouns stand for.

Checking what the pronouns stand for helps you to understand a difficult text segment.

Pronouns must replace a noun in the same sentence or in the sentence before.

Every ACT has a who / whom question!

Every ACT has an its / it's question!

Pronouns - Types

Subject Pronoun

Subjects <u>do</u> an action: "Veronica studies all day."
You can replace the name with a pronoun.
Instead of "Veronica studies all day," you can say, "**She** studies all day."

He made a birthday cake.
She is a great listener.
We enjoy Chinese food.

"Who" is a Subject Pronoun

"Who" is a subject pronoun like "he," "she" and "we" in the examples on the left.
Use "who" to ask <u>which person does the action</u>.

Who made the birthday cake?
Who is a great listener?
Who enjoys Chinese food?

Object Pronoun

Objects <u>receive</u> an action:

The neighbors invited **him**.
Thomas blamed **her** for the accident.
The boss hired **us** to do the job.

"Whom" is an Object Pronoun

Use "whom" to ask <u>which person receives an action</u>.

Whom are you going to invite?
Whom did he blame for the accident?
Whom did he hire to do the job?

Possessive Pronoun

Possessive forms tell us the person something <u>belongs to</u>:

His phone is expensive.
I like **her** new dress.
The teacher graded **our** test.

"Whose" is a Possessive Pronoun

Use "whose" to find out <u>which person something belongs to</u>.

Whose phone is this?
Whose dress is the nicest?
Whose test did he grade?
Note. "*Who's*" means "*who is*" or "*who has.*"

Pronouns	Singular	Plural	Both
Subject pronouns:	**I, you , he, she, it**	**we, you, they**	**who**
Object pronouns:	**me, you, him, her, it**	**us, you, them**	**whom**
Possessive pronouns:	**my, your, his, hers, its**	**our, your, their**	**whose**

 Tip: Do not use "they're" (which means "they are") or "there" (which refers to a place) as a possessive pronoun. These words may sound the same as "their", but the ACT wants you to know the difference.

 Tip: The word "there" has the word "here" in it. Both here and there are places.

Pronouns - Tips

Pronouns refer to a NOUN in the sentence (or in the sentence before). Never trust a pronoun. Be suspicious! Double check what each pronoun stands for.

 Tip: Always ask, "What does this pronoun stand for?"

WEATHER AND TIME

When you say, "It is four o'clock" or "It is cold outside," the pronoun *it* does not stand for anything. In this case, "it" is called a dummy pronoun.

Its / It's

Tip: Every ACT has an it's / its question.

Remember: "*it's*" means "*it is*" or "*it has.*" "*Its'* " is never correct.
Tip: Even if "it's" looks possessive and sounds possessive, it still means "it is" or "it has."

Tip: Possessive pronouns do not have an apostrophe: mine, your, his, hers, its, our, your and their.

Who's / Whose

Similarly, "*who's*" means "*who is* or "*who has.*" "*Whose*" is a possessive pronoun.
> *Whose* car is this? It is the car of the senator, *who's* talking to the mayor right now.

*Tip: If you answer the question with **HIS**, you should have used **WHOSE***

Who / That

Use "*who*" when you talk about people. Use "*that*" when you talk about objects.
> The person *who* gave you the package is a friend of mine.
> The package *that* my friend gave to you comes from England.

Use the word "whose" for both objects and people.
> The person *whose* car is in the driveway is my uncle.
> The car, *whose* interior is bright red, is an antique Bentley.

Who / Whom

Most people never use "whom." Each ACT, however, has a who/whom question.
Remember: Both "who" and "whom" are question words. Just **answer the question**:

*Tip: If you answer the question with **HE**, you should have used **WHO**.*
> *If you answer the question with **HIM**, you should have used **WHOM**.*

<u>Who</u> is our president? <u>He</u> is our president. ➔ "Who" is used correctly.
<u>Who</u> did you vote for? I voted for <u>him</u>. ➔ You should have use <u>whom</u>. **Revision**: <u>Whom</u> did you vote for?
<u>Who</u> is coming to your party? <u>He</u> is coming to your party. ➔ "Who" is used correctly.
<u>Who</u> did you invite? I invited <u>him</u>. ➔ You should have use <u>whom</u>. **Revision**: <u>Whom</u> did you invite?

Everybody / Everyone

These indefinite pronouns are SINGULAR. Do not use these words with "their." Use them with "his or her."
Other tricky singular pronouns are *anyone, anybody, somebody, someone, no one*, and *nobody*.
> Nobody forgot his or her homework today.
> Everybody on the football team remembered to bring his helmet.

Pronoun - Quiz 1 (Who Whom Who's Whose)

Tip: After a preposition, you almost always use WHOM.

With WHOM are you going to the prom (I am going with HIM)

To WHOM did you gave that package? (I gave it to HIM)

For WHOM are you running this errand? (I run it for HIM)

1. _____ that guy across the hall? Is he the man _____ wife just left him?

2. I would rather vote for Bob, _____ record is exemplary, than for Paul, _____ always late.

3. _____ are you going to support?

4. _____ coffee mug is on the table?

5. It doesn't look like this is the right place. _____ did you ask for directions?

6. We have two extra tickets for the game. _____ wants to go with us?

7. I have no idea _____ in charge of the reservations nor _____ I should talk to.

8. _____ car is parked in the no-parking zone? It will be towed!

9. The detectives have called in an expert to identify _____ handwriting is on the ransom letter.

10. Do you remember _____ received the Emmy Award for best actor last year?

11. I can't remember the name of the student _____ project won last year.

12. I know exactly _____ I'm going to support in the next presidential election.

13. _____ the professor _____ spent nine years in the Sahara studying sandstorms?

14. She's the singer _____ he sang a duet with last year.

15. Can you list the people _____ helped organize the prom last year?

16. The park is being renamed in honor of our old mayor, _____ environmental efforts helped create lots of green space in our city.

1) **Who's** (Who is.) **whose** (Whose wife? His wife.) 2) **whose** (Whose record? His record.) **who's** (Who is late? He is late.) 3) **Whom** (You are going to support him.) 4) **whose** (Whose mug? His mug.) 5) **whom** (You asked him.) 6) **who** (Who wants to go? He wants to go.) 7) **who's** (Who is in charge? He is in charge.) **whom** (I should talk to him.) 8) **Whose** (Whose car? His car.) 9) **whose** (Whose handwriting? His handwriting.) 10) **who** (Who received the award? He received the award.) 11) **whose** (Whose project? His project.) 12) **whom** (I am going to support him.) 13) **Who's** (Who is? He is.) **who** (Who spent nine years? He spent nine years.) 14) **whom** (He sang a duet with him.) 15) **Who** (Who helped? He helped.) 16) **whose** (Whose environmental efforts? His environmental efforts.)

Pronoun - Quiz 2

Are these pronouns correct? Check what the pronouns stand for. Change all sentences that are incorrect.

1. Everybody loves their mother.

2. I do not like these kind of movies.

3. Last year, our soccer team had a goalie that came from Lima, Peru. His name was Julio Gonzalez.

4. You have to give credit to someone who's life motto is "There's always room to improve."

5. The farmer announced that while he knows that his foods do not have an organic certification, it

   is all grown locally.

6. Each of the boys on the football team played their best.

7. Darius met his sister and her friend at the movies, and he insisted on buying her a ticket.

8. I forgot my calculator. Can I borrow your's?

9. There's a lot of good reasons to join at least one club at school.

10. Children like snack machines in school. They like to have options during lunch, and they provide

    funding for needed equipment.

1. Everybody loves **his or her** mother. (Everybody is a singular pronoun)
2. I do not like these **kinds** of movies. (or this kind of movie)
3. …**who** came from Lima (use "that" only with objects)
4. …credit to someone **whose** life motto… (Who's always means "who is.")
5. … **they (the foods)** are all grown locally. (Always ask, "What does this pronoun stand for?")
6. Each (one) of the boys played **his best.**
7. …buying **her friend** a ticket (Whom did he want to buy the ticket for: his sister or her friend?)
8. Can I borrow **yours?**
9. **There are** a lot of good reasons.
10. **The children** like to have more options and **the machines provide**… (Who is "**they**"? The children or the snack machines? You cannot use a pronoun if it is not clear which noun it replaces.)

Pronoun - Quiz 3

Choose the correct pronoun.

1. Can Frank and (me/I) go see the concert tonight?

2. My dad gave great presents to my brother and (me/I).

3. Either the middle school or the preschool needs to have (its/their) gymnasium renovated.

4. After two hours of deliberation, the board did arrive at (its/their) decision.

5. The teacher said the awards needed to be distributed by (he/him) and (me/I).

6. (Us/we) soldiers must remember the importance of discipline in combat.

7. After winning big, I decided to divide the spoils between my mother and (I/me/myself), but later ended gifting the lot entirely to (I/me/myself).

8. I'm so slow! A tortoise could move faster than (I/me).

9. The textbook company reserves special books for (it's / its / their) school board customers.

10. My father was a person (that / who) drew strength from his faith.

11. Do you like (these / these ones)?

12. Each person on the academic team needs to do (his or her / their) best to win the state title.

13. (They're / There / Their) are too many variables in this experiment.

---

1) Both "Frank" and "I" are subjects of the sentence, so "I" should be in the subjective case. A strategy is to leave "Frank" out of the sentence.

2) The speaker is receiving, not giving, the gift, so the answer should be in the objective case (me).

3) The possessive pronoun needs to refer to the subject of the verb (which), because it is closer to the verb, is "preschool").

4) While multiple people make up a board, the noun itself is singular and takes the singular possessive pronoun "its".

5) Both pronouns are objects of the preposition "by", so should be in the objective case. (by him; by me)

6) The pronoun must agree with the subject "soldiers", so the subjective form "we" is necessary. Alternatively, leave out the word soldiers: we must remember. ...

7) In the first clause, the speaker is the object (receiving the action), so the objective case "me" should be used. In the second clause, the speaker is giving the money to himself, so the reflexive "myself" is necessary.

8) A tortoise could move faster than I [could move]—the subjective case is necessary.

9) Company is singular, so do not use "their." "It's" always means "it is." The sentence talks about its (the company's) customers.

10) Use "that" for objects, use "who" for people.

11) "These ones" is too wordy. "These" already implies you are talking about several objects.

12) Each (one) person is a singular subject. It needs a singular pronoun: his or her.

13) "They're" means "they are." "Their" is a possessive pronoun. "There" is correct.

1) I 2) me 3) it 4) its 5) him and me 6) we 7) me and myself 8) I 9) its 10) who 11) these 12) his or her 13) There

---

Copyright 2017 Winni van Gessel

Pronoun - Quiz 4

Choose the correct pronoun.

1. It's clear that the administration doesn't consider the needs of (we/us) students.

2. I love him so much! He's a man (who/whom) I think is very affectionate.

3. (Who/whom) should I give my money to?

4. I can't remember (who/whom) the movie was about.

5. My dad will complain about my mom to (whoever/whomever) asks him.

6. (Hers/her's) was the fastest car on the racetrack.

7. Did you forget that it was (he/him) who got the highest score on the test?

8. My school is very proud of (it's/its) new computer lab.

9. Every dragon in the cave guards (its/their) gold carefully.

10. (Whose / Who's) going to let me copy their homework?

11. Most people aren't bothered by (it's / its) origin in the halls of the Capitol.

12. I am taller than (him / he).

---

1) Students is the object of the sentence, so the pronoun should be in the objective case ("us").

2) Who/whom is not the object of "I think". If you manipulate the order of the sentence to "He's a man (who/whom) is very intelligent, I think," it is clear that the objective "who" is correct.

3) The person receiving the money is the object of the sentence, so use the objective case "whom."

4) The person in the movie is the object, so use the objective case "whom."

5) There are two clauses in this sentence. Each verb needs a subject. My dad will complain. Dad is the subject. So, who is doing the asking? The verb asking needs a subject as well: Whoever asks him. "Whoever" is the subject, and "him" is the object. Note: "whoever asks him" is a prepositional phrase that is the object of the first part of the sentence. It would have been correct to say, "My dad will complain about my mom to whomever." In this case, whomever is the object of the sentence.

6) "Hers" is the third person female singular possessive pronoun and is correct in this case. Despite the familiar use of apostrophe + s to denote possession, "her's" is not a word.

7) He got the highest score vs. him got the highest score—the objective "he" is correct.

8) "It's" is a shortened form of "it is", while "its" is the third person singular possessive pronoun. As the school has ownership of the computer lab, "its" is correct.

9) "Every dragon" is singular, so use the third person singular possessive "its."

10) "Who's" always means "who is". That makes sense in this sentence.

11) "It's" always means "it is." That would not make sense in this sentence.

12) I am taller than he (is). In a comparison, use two object pronouns or two subject pronouns.

1) us 2) who 3) whom 4) whom 5) whoever 6) Hers 7) he 8) its 9) its 10) who's 11) its 12) he

---

ENGLISH

Knowledge of

Language

REDUNDANCY

The ACT is very meticulous about wordiness.

In sentences:

The ACT avoids sentences in which words can be omitted without loss of meaning. The ACT prefers a similar sentence with fewer words.

A sentence that uses too many words is considered wrong.

If several answers have the same meaning, pick the answer with the most concise answer.

In paragraphs (see page 115):

Paragraphs can also contain redundant elements. Although the sentence can be grammatically correct, the information in it might have been previously stated.

Redundancy in Sentences

Redundancy = Repeated Information

Often, we have two expressions in English for the same statement.

You can say "at 10 a.m.," or you can say "at 10 in the morning." Both options tell us about the correct time. However, if you say, "Let's meet at 10 a.m. in the morning," you are really saying: "Let's meet at 10 in the morning in the morning." One of those time references is redundant.

Why do we not catch this? Because our brains love redundancy.

When our brains hear "at 10 a.m. in the morning," they get a double message about the time, and they are happy with the confirmation about the correctness of the statement.

Here are some other examples of redundant statements:

absolutely necessary	to fill in the empty blanks	other alternatives
the ACT test	a free gift	past history
an added bonus	a handwritten manuscript	a PIN number
an ATM Machine	to hang down	to postpone until later
bare naked	knowledgeable experts	a round circle
begin to proceed	live audience	a safe haven
to circulate around	mental thought	a specific example
a closed fist	money-saving coupon	to surround on all sides
a complete monopoly	new innovations	a terrible tragedy
to descend down	new discovery	an unmarried bachelor

The good news is, in the ACT, you do not have to spot the redundancies; the multiple-choice questions will almost give them away to you. (see example 1.)

 Tip: You can often spot this type of question when three out of four answers have redundant words in them.

Question: Should you use "the person that lives next to me" or "my neighbor"?
Answer: Both are appropriate English expressions, but in the ACT, "my neighbor" is preferred.

 Tip: The ACT likes conciseness, so PICK THE SHORTEST ANSWER; it is often the best one.

Question: Should I use "a complete monopoly" or just "monopoly"?
Answer: If you are not sure if answers have the same meaning, choose the shortest answer: "monopoly".

 Tip: When in doubt, leave it out.

Generally, the answer "delete the underlined portion" creates a shorter sentence. Make sure, however, that you do not omit any important information.
(See example 2)

 Tip: Don't just count words when you look for the shortest answer.

THIS BOOK WILL NOT ALLOW REDUNDANCY IN THIS BOOK!

1) The manager presented the first 20 customers with <u>a free gift.</u>
   A. NO CHANGE
   B. a complimentary gift.
   C. a gift that they did not need to pay for.
   D. a gift.

2) The pollution in our town was a problem <u>that needed to be solved</u>.
   A. NO CHANGE
   B. That needed a solution.
   C. that needed to be dealt with.
   D. Delete the underlined portion of the sentence.

1) D 2) D

Redundancy - Practice

Exercise 1: **Count the redundancies in the following paragraph**.

I have two female daughters who often have great ideas and never give me advanced warning about their plans. They know that I like to read written material from many different writers, so they brought me an unexpected surprise last week. It was a book about all the basic fundamentals of police research. I immediately commenced to begin reading the first chapter. In the beginning, I was initially surprised by all the specific examples that the author used, but I quickly came to realize that the unsolved mysteries in each chapter were based on true facts. I thought to myself that it was the best gift that I had ever received.

See? Your brain does not mind redundancies. Did you know that there are 11 redundant statements in the paragraph above?

Exercise 2: **Cross out the portion of the sentence that is redundant.**

1) After the presidents' faces were cut out in Mt. Rushmore, they were immortalized forever.

2) This Third World Gift Store specializes in foreign imports from East Africa.

3) I did not understand you. Can you repeat that again?

4) In my opinion, I think that is an impossible task.

5) Mr. Wilson is the original founder of our company.

6) Please do not unbuckle your seatbelt until the car comes to a complete stop.

7) My grandma is eighty-seven years old.

---

1) Delete *forever* 2) Delete *foreign* 3) Delete *again* 4) Delete *In my opinion* or *I think* 5) Delete *original* 6) Delete *complete* 7) Delete *years old*

I have two female daughters who often have great ideas and never give me advanced warning about their plans. They know that I like to read written material from many different writers, so they brought me an unexpected surprise last week. It was a book about all the basic fundamentals of police research. I immediately commenced to begin reading the first chapter. In the beginning, I was initially surprised by all the specific examples that the author used, but I quickly came to realize that the unsolved mysteries in each chapter were based on true facts. I thought to myself that it was the best gift that I had ever received.

Redundancy in Sentences - Quiz 1

1) <u>The advertisements that you can see</u> on the side of buildings often tell a lot about the history of a town.
   A. NO CHANGE.
   B. The visible advertisements that you can see
   C. The advertisements
   D. The advertisements that are visible

2) The instructions <u>were repeated again.</u>
   A. NO CHANGE
   B. were once more repeated.
   C. were repeated again another time.
   D. were repeated.

3) The quills of a porcupine <u>have the function to protect the animal defensively</u>.
   A. NO CHANGE
   B. have the function to provide defensive protection.
   C. protect the animal.
   D. have the function to provide protection.

4) We wanted to eat the soup, but we had to wait until it <u>cooled to a lower temperature.</u>
   A. NO CHANGE
   B. cooled.
   C. lowered its temperature to cool.
   D. cooled down its temperature.

5) The Irish rock group recorded its latest album <u>in front of a live audience.</u>
   A. NO CHANGE
   B. in front of a live audience, not in a recording studio.
   C. in front of a lively audience.
   D. in front of an audience.

6) His idea, <u>that he came up with,</u> was well regarded by his colleagues
   A. NO CHANGE
   B. His idea
   C. His idea, that was his own,
   D. His own idea

7) <u>The house in which he lived was very unique.</u>
   A. NO CHANGE
   B. He lived in a very unique house.
   C. His house was unique.
   D. His house was very unique.

8) His <u>two female daughters, both girls,</u> were very gifted piano players.
   A. NO CHANGE
   B. two daughters
   C. two female daughters
   D. two female daughters, none of them a boy,

9) To illustrate his lecture on pre-colonial art, the professor talked about the Olmec heads <u>to give a specific example</u>.
   A. NO CHANGE
   B. to give an example
   C. as an example
   D. OMIT the underlined portion of the text.

10) In the 1920s, various groups worked towards a society in which men and women would be <u>equal to one another.</u>
   A. NO CHANGE
   B. equal to each other.
   C. equal and the same.
   D. equal.

1) C. By definition, advertisements are visible, which means you can see them. **2) D. To repeat** means to say it again. You don't have to mention "one more time", or "another time". **3) C.** The words "have the function" sound academic, but without them, the sentence has the same meaning. **4) B.** If something gets cooler, its temperature goes down. **5) D. A "live"** recording means in front of an audience. **6) B. If it was** *his* idea, then the sentence does not need to repeat that it was "his own", or "that he came up with". **7) C. Unique** means that there is only one of them. Something cannot be very unique. Between answer C and D, remember the rule, "when in doubt, leave it out." **8) B. Daughters** are always considered female. **9) D. You can** explain a general subject (e.g. pre-colonial art) by *illustrating* it, giving an *example*. These elements are more *specific* and help others to understand the subject. **10) D. All four** answers provide the same information. Choose the one that is most concise.

VERBS

There are three types of verb questions in the ACT:

Verb Agreement
Verb Tense
Parallel Verbs

Learn to recognize these three different types and find out which traps the ACT has in store for you.

1) Be aware of indefinite pronouns such as everybody.
2) Learn the rules about the use of the different tenses.
3) Review the tenses of some common irregular verbs.

Verb-Subject Agreement

"The <u>boys run</u>" and "one of the <u>boys runs</u>"

Singular subjects go with singular verbs; plural subjects go with plural verbs.
However, both underlined sections above are correct. The trick is not to look at the plural noun but to spot the real subject. When it says, ".. of the boys", something else must be the subject, not the boys.
"<u>One</u> of the boys…." The subject is <u>one</u> (of them). "<u>One</u> (boy)….." The subject is a singular noun.

1) The value of the numbers on these spreadsheets is/are important.
2) The treatment with several types of medicines is/are essential for a quick recovery.

Sentences with either, neither, or none (of)

3) "Either of the flowers is/are red."
4) "Neither of the boys is/are coming."
5) "None of my friends is/are on my soccer team."

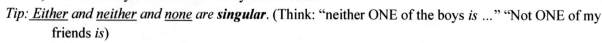 *Tip: <u>Either</u> and <u>neither</u> and <u>none</u> are **singular**.* (Think: "neither ONE of the boys *is* ..." "Not ONE of my friends *is*)

Sentences with <u>each</u>

6) Each of my brothers have/has bought a car.
7) Each of my parents is/are against my going to the prom with Jake.

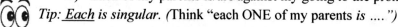 *Tip: <u>Each</u> is singular. (*Think "each ONE of my parents *is* ....")

Sentences with <u>everybody</u>

8) Should I say "Everybody loves their teacher" or "Everybody loves his or her teacher"?

Tip: "<u>Everybody</u>" and "<u>Everyone</u>" are singular words! Do not use these words with "they" or "their".
Other words that are always singular: <u>Somebody</u>, <u>Anybody</u>, <u>Nobody</u>, <u>Everybody</u>, <u>Someone</u>, <u>Anyone</u>, <u>No one</u>, <u>Everyone</u>, <u>Something</u>, <u>Anything</u>, <u>Nothing</u>, <u>Everything and None</u>,

Sentences with a group word (a collective noun)

The team, the committee, the family, the group, the herd, the audience, the majority: All singular words.

9) The group of boys is/are coming to my house.
10) The herd of wild and dangerous buffaloes is/are crossing the river.

Tip: Go to the beginning of the sentence. It is about a group (ONE group, ONE herd.) The subject is singular.

Sentences with added information between the subject and verb

11) The opinion of the politicians, who are just like kings and rulers of the past, is/are not subjective.
12) The group of boys, that caused many problems during numerous parties, is/are coming to my house.
13) Anthony Davis, along with all the other UK basketball players, is/are celebrating the victory.

Tip: Ignore all information between two commas.
This added information makes you think about plural nouns and distracts you from the actual singular subject: the group.

---

1) is 2) is 3) is 4) is 5) is (None - not one - is singular) 6) has 7) is 8) his or her 9) is 10) is 11) is 12) is 13) is

Verb-Subject Agreement II

Words that are sometimes plural, sometimes singular

My pants are lying on the couch. (Pants is a plural noun.)
My pair of pants is lying on the couch. (Singular: There is only one pair.)

Watch out for the word <u>number</u>. It is not always plural.
The number of students taking the ACT varies from year to year. *(One number: Singular)*
A number of people taking the SAT wish they had taken the ACT. *(Several people: Plural)*

Watch out for the word <u>half</u>. It is not always singular.
Half of the country is against the new law. (*There is only one country: Singular*)
Half of the people are against the new law. (*This half indicates many people: Plural*)

Verbs that are placed between singular and plural nouns. Which verb is correct?

1. The biggest problem of our football team is/are the defensive players.
2. The best part of our school is/are the teachers.
3. The worst offenders of the school policies was/were the staff.

Tip: The verb needs to agree with the subject.
Do not pay attention to the last part of the sentences (the predicate noun).

Verbs that are placed AFTER singular and plural nouns

4. The mayor or the council members is/are against the proposal.
5. The council members or the mayor is/are against the proposal.

Tip: The verb needs to agree with the subject that is closest.
Note: Of course, if the council members **and** the mayor are against it, then you are just dealing with a compound subject. John and the mayor are having lunch (plural)

Sentences where the subject is placed after the verb

Tip: Whenever you see a verb question in the ACT, especially those with answers that have singular and plural versions, find the subject of the sentence to match.

6. Here is/are a piece of paper and a pen.
7. In the middle of the shop sit/sits metal crates with a lot of junk.

Sentences that start on one page, but end on the next page

When I descended into my uncle's basement, I did not know how many treasures there were in store for me. Hundreds of inventions lined the walls. I was surprised by the amount of fascinating devices in front of me. Each of the colorful

machines <u>was</u>[8] standing against a wall full of wires and flashing lights. Machines filled the floor, the walls and even hung from the ceiling. They were labeled and color-coded.

8. A. NO CHANGE
   B. are
   C. were
   D. have been

Answer: 1) is 2) is 3) were 4) are 5) is 6) are 7) sit 8) was

Verb-Subject Agreement - Quiz 1

If a sentence is incorrect, find the error:

1. A pound of oranges, just like peaches and strawberries, are getting more expensive each week.

2. The donuts look great, and the batch of cookies on the counter smell delicious as well.

3. The display of 542 different colors in the paint store appear overwhelming.

4. One of the motives for his volunteer work are that he has too much free time.

5. The crowd of boys, who have created havoc at many parties, are coming to my house tonight.

6. Be careful with that pair of scissors. I just sharpened them.

7. A majority of the students has not studied for the test.

8. Here is your coat, but where is your scarf and your hat?

9. In the second paragraph of your paper is a spelling mistake and a missing quotation mark.

10. My mom, as well as my dad, are against the mayor's proposal.

11. All the players of the volleyball team and the coach has received an award.

12. The hardest part of our English test were the multiple-choice questions.

13. I need a new pair of glasses. I will call the optician to ask about their price.

14. The swimmer had a nice set of abs. He told me he trained daily to condition it.

15. I like to thank my coaches and teachers. Each were an important part of my success.

16. Geometric patterns are a characteristic of art forms in Moroccan architecture.

17. Too many injuries gives football a bad reputation among college sports.

Answers: 1) a pound is getting 2) the batch smells 3) the display appears 4) one of the motives is 5) the crowd is coming 6) I sharpened it (the pair) 7) correct: The majority has 8) Your scarf and your hat are here 9) Two mistakes are found in your paragraph 10) My mom is against it. 11) All the players and the coach have received 12) The hardest part was 13) I called to ask about its price. (the pair) 14) correct as written 15) Each one of them was an important part. 16) Correct as written 17) Injuries give football a bad reputation.

Verb-Subject Agreement - Quiz 2

Rudyard Kipling was a famous British author who wrote extensively about colonial India. One[1] of his works are written from the perspective of a foreigner who makes clear the difference between British and Indian culture. *The Man Who Would Be King*, for example, is about a pair of British adventurers who unexpectedly become the kings of Kafiristan.

While his works can be found on the bookshelves of many children, some argue that the same works has[2] long portrayed the British

as advocates for, instead of subjugators of, their colonial subjects. Post-colonial academics has[3]

labeled his works as racist, while each and every devotee and relative of Kipling works[4] tirelessly to clear his name. Some say that while modern-day critics judge Kipling to be racist, his works

are a product of his time. What was once a belief commonly held by Britons are[5] now reviled by our racially-conscious society. Amidst all the

debate, one thing is clear: as time progresses, a shift in values changes[6] the way we view famous literary works.

1. **A.** NO CHANGE
   B. Each
   C. Many
   D. Any one

2. **A.** NO CHANGE
   B. have
   C. often has
   D. could of

3. **A.** NO CHANGE
   B. have been
   C. would have
   D. have

4. **A.** NO CHANGE
   B. have
   C. have been
   D. were working

5. **A.** NO CHANGE
   B. have become
   C. is
   D. were

6. **A.** NO CHANGE
   B. change
   C. as a change of
   D. changing

1) **C.** ... of his works are written. This sentence needs a plural subject. ("Each" and "any one" are singular.) 2) **B.** The works have long portrayed. A plural subject needs a plural verb. 3) **D.** Academics have labeled his work. A plural subject needs a plural verb. 4) **A.** Each and every relative of Kipling works tirelessly. A singular subject needs a singular verb. 5) **C.** A belief was once common. That belief is now reviled. 6) **A.** A shift changes the way we view things.

Verb-Subject Agreement - Quiz 3

The modern Summer and Winter Olympic Games—which began in 1894 and occur every two years— <u>is</u>[1] the premier international sporting event of our day and age. Not only the Summer Games, with sports such as swimming and running, but also the Winter Games, which <u>features</u>[2] more unusual sports

such as curling and the biathlon, <u>draw</u>[3] a large television audience from across the globe.

<u>Each</u>[4] of the sports originate in a different part of the world but are nonetheless watched by a global audience, which makes the Olympics a wonderful showcase of regional cultures and traditions. Handball, for example, <u>is</u>[5] played mostly in Europe, but is closely followed by viewers in Africa, and water sports,

such as sailing, <u>is</u>[6] popular among viewers in landlocked countries of Central Asia.

Olympic athletes can be awarded gold, silver, or bronze medals based on their performances. While over a hundred countries participate in the Olympic Games, only one of the nations <u>are</u>[7] able to end the Olympics with the largest medal count. However, when a very small country with only one or two athletes <u>snatch</u>[8] a space on the podium, the whole world smiles in appreciation of this individual effort.

1. **A.** NO CHANGE
   B. had been
   C. were
   D. are

2. **A.** NO CHANGE
   B. feature
   C. is featuring
   D. has featured

3. **A.** NO CHANGE
   B. draws
   C. have been drawing
   D. are drawing

4. **A.** NO CHANGE
   B. A majority
   C. Many
   D. One

5. **A.** NO CHANGE
   B. is being
   C. for the most part is
   D. are

6. **A.** NO CHANGE
   B. was
   C. are
   D. is being

7. **A.** NO CHANGE
   B. is
   C. Is being
   D. have been

8. **A.** NO CHANGE
   B. have snatched
   C. snatching
   D. snatches

1) **D.** The Olympic Games are the premier event. A plural subject needs a plural verb. (The words "of our day" indicates a present tense.) 2) **B.** The Winter Games feature unusual sports. A plural subject needs a plural verb. 3) **A.** The Games draw a large audience. A plural subject needs a plural verb. Answer C and D are not parallel to the rest of the verbs. 4) **C.** The words "originate" and "are watched" are plural verbs, so we need a plural subject. Answer A, B, and D are all singular. 5) **A.** Handball is played. The sentence is correct, concise, and parallel with the verbs in other sentences. 6) **C.** Water sports are popular. A plural subject needs a plural verb. 7) **B.** One of the nations is able to end it. A singular subject needs a singular verb. 8) **D.** A very small country snatches a space. A singular subject needs a singular verb.

Verb Tense

Regular verbs have three forms:

Present Tense	Past Tense	Past Participle
I *walk*	I *walked*	I have *walked*
I *work*	I *worked*	I had *worked*

Verb Tense Rules

To find out which of these three verbs forms should be used, look carefully at the rest of the sentence and at other sentences in the paragraph. (See parallel structure on page 87.)

Verb tenses need to stay consistent and follow certain rules.

Present Tense:	when something is happening right now.
	I walk or *I am walking*
	I work or *I am working*
Past Tense	when something started and finished in the past.
	I walked or *I was walking*
	I work or *I was working*
Present Perfect	when something happened in the past (unspecified time) or still continues.
	I have walked or *I have been walking*
	I have worked or *I have been working*
Past Perfect	when something happened in the past before something else happened in the past.
	I had walked or *I had been walking*
	I had worked or *I had been working*

Irregular Verbs

Irregular verbs are tricky, because they do not follow a regular pattern like the ones above.
Most importantly, the past participle is different from the simple past tense, creating three different forms.

Present	Past Tense	Past Participle
I *go*	I *went*	I have *gone*
I *write*	I *wrote*	I have *written*
I *speak*	I *spoke*	I have *spoken*

 Tip: Learn the three forms of the most common irregular verbs (see page 83) and combine that knowledge with the rules described above.

Verb Tense - Quiz 1

1. **A.** Last fall, one of my teachers being Mr. Fox, who had came from England.
   B. Last fall, one of my teachers was Mr. Fox, who had come from England.
   C. Last fall, one of my teachers, named Mr. Fox, who came from England.
   D. Last fall, one of my teachers, Mr. Fox, who had come from England.

2. **A.** I remember the time before technology taken over the world.
   B. I remember the time before technology took over the world.
   C. I remember the time before technology had took over the world.
   D. I remember the time before technology begun to take over the world.

3. **A.** Four years ago, I had gone back to Africa to volunteer with the hospital.
   B. Four years ago, I will have gone back to Africa to volunteer with the hospital.
   C. Four years ago, I went back to Africa to volunteer with the hospital.
   D. Four years ago, I go back to Africa to volunteer with the hospital.

4. **A.** Since they are in charge of the foundation, the Tripps were sponsors of Mary's mission trip.
   B. Since they are in charge of the foundation, the Tripps had been sponsors of Mary's mission trip.
   C. Since they are in charge of the foundation, the Tripps have been sponsors of Mary's mission trip.
   D. Since they are in charge of the foundation, the Tripps are sponsors of Mary's mission trip.

5. **A.** When she has gone to find a tutor, the office told her that no one was available.
   B. When she had gone to find a tutor, the office had told her that no one was available.
   C. When she went to find a tutor, the office told her that no one was available.
   D. When she goes to find a tutor, the office told her that no one was available.

6. **A.** Mom demands to know where I have been, and I ashamedly tell her the truth.
   B. Mom demanding to know where I have been, and I ashamedly tell her the truth.
   C. Mom having demanded to know where I have been, and I ashamedly told her the truth.
   D. Mom had demanded to know where I have been, and I had ashamedly told her the truth.

7. **A.** The clouds in the sky indicated that the nice weather might not last.
   B. The clouds in the sky had been indicated that the nice weather might not last.
   C. The clouds in the sky will have indicated that the nice weather might not last.
   D. The clouds in the sky indicates that the nice weather might not last.

8. **A.** We used this cleaning service since 2005.
   B. We were using this cleaning service since 2005.
   C. We had been using this cleaning service since 2005.
   D. We have been using this cleaning service since 2005.

Irregular Verbs List

The three forms represent the present, the past, and the past participle
Example: Today I **break** a record. I just **broke** a record. I **have** just **broken** the record.
(Note: the past participle always need a helping verb with it)

beat	beat, beaten	put	put, put
begin	began, begun	ring	rang, rung
bite	bit, bitten	rise	rose, risen
break	broke, broken	run	ran, run
bring	brought, brought	set	set, set
burst	burst, burst	shut	shut, shut
catch	caught, caught	show	showed, shown
choose	chose, chosen	sing	sang, sung
come	came, come	sink	sank, sunk
drink	drank, drunk	sit	sat, sat
draw	drew, drawn	slay	slew, slain
drown	drowned, drowned	speak	spoke, spoken
fight	fought, fought	spring	sprang, sprung
flee	fled, fled	sting	stung, stung
fling	flung, flung	swear	swore, sworn
get	got, gotten	swim	swam, swum
hang (a person)	hanged, hanged	swing	swung, swung
hang (an item)	hung, hung	take	took, taken
lead	led, led	tear	tore, torn
lend	lent, lent	wear	wore, worn

 Tip: Memorize the tenses for lie and lay.

lay (to place)	laid, laid	I **laid** the object on my desk yesterday
lie (recline)	lay, lain	The object **lay** on my desk yesterday
lie (untruth)	lied, lied	The subject **lied** to the police yesterday

Exercise:
The ACT likes to mix up a verb's tenses. Correct the wrong tense in the following sentences:
1) We had *began* the test.
2) They had already *swam* in the pool.
3) He would have *drank* the whole bottle.
4) He *sunk* the ship.
5) The bell had *rang* three times.

1) We had *begun.* 2) They had already *swum* .... 3) He would have *drunk* .... 4) He *sank* .... 5) The bell had *rung* ....

Irregular Verbs - Quiz 1

The three forms represent the present, the past, and the past participle
Example: Today I **drink** my tea. I just **drank** my tea. I have **drunk** two cups of tea.
      (Note: the past participle always need a helping verb with it)

<u>Exercise</u>: Write the past tense and the past participle of each verb:

beat	_____	_____	lie (untruth)	_____	_____
begin	_____	_____	put	_____	_____
bite	_____	_____	ring	_____	_____
break	_____	_____	rise	_____	_____
bring	_____	_____	run	_____	_____
burst	_____	_____	set	_____	_____
catch	_____	_____	shut	_____	_____
choose	_____	_____	show	_____	_____
come	_____	_____	sing	_____	_____
drink	_____	_____	sink	_____	_____
draw	_____	_____	sit	_____	_____
drown	_____	_____	slay	_____	_____
fight	_____	_____	speak	_____	_____
flee	_____	_____	spring	_____	_____
fling	_____	_____	sting	_____	_____
get	_____	_____	swear	_____	_____
go	_____	_____	swim	_____	_____
hang (a person)	_____	_____	swing	_____	_____
hang (an item)	_____	_____	take	_____	_____
lay	_____	_____	tear	_____	_____
lead	_____	_____	wear	_____	_____
lend	_____	_____	write	_____	_____
lie (recline)	_____	_____	(answers on page 83)		

Verb Tense - Quiz 2

1. **A.** Laura thought she might have made a mistake.
    B. Laura thought she might of made a mistake.
    C. Laura thought she could of made a mistake.
    D. Laura thought she could made a mistake.

2. **A.** If you are confused, IKEA's instructions explain exactly how to put your desk together.
    B. If you are confused, IKEA's instructions explained exactly how to put your desk together.
    C. If you are confused, IKEA's instructions had explained exactly how to put your desk together.
    D. If you are confused, IKEA's instructions in explaining exactly how to put your desk together.

3. **A.** I loved my cat. I care for it as if it were my child.
    B. I have love my cat. I care for it as if it were my child.
    C. I loved my cat. I cared for it as if it were my child.
    D. I have loved my cat. I have care for it as if it were my child.

4. **A.** I will not sleep tonight. The mattress being as hard as a rock and has bed bugs.
    B. I will not sleep tonight. The mattress was as hard as a rock and has bed bugs.
    C. I will not sleep tonight. The mattress is as hard as a rock and has bed bugs.
    D. I will not sleep tonight. The mattress as hard as a rock and has bed bugs.

5. **A.** I spend last week shopping and visiting friends.
    B. I spent last week shopping and visiting friends.
    C. I have spend last week shopping and visiting friends.
    D. I have spended last week shopping and visiting friends.

6. **A.** He had began the test on time, but could not finish it within the required 45 minutes.
    B. He had beginned the test on time, but could not finish it within the required 45 minutes.
    C. He had beganned the test on time, but could not finish it within the required 45 minutes.
    D. He had begun the test on time, but could not finish it within the required 45 minutes.

7. **A.** Where is my watch? It lay on the table just an hour ago!
    B. Where is my watch? It lied on the table just an hour ago!
    C. Where is my watch? It laid on the table just an hour ago!
    D. Where is my watch? It layed on the table just an hour ago!

8. **A.** I have been to the pool three times since Monday, and I have swimmed over 20 miles this week.
    B. I have been to the pool three times since Monday, and I have swam over 20 miles this week.
    C. I have been to the pool three times since Monday, and I have swum over 20 miles this week.
    D. I have been to the pool three times since Monday, and I have swammed over 20 miles this week.

1) **A.** Don't use "could of" or "might of". The correct form is "could have" and "might have". Answer D should say, "she could *make* a mistake. 2) **A.** The present tense in the first part of the sentence calls for the present tense in the second part as well. Answer D is a fragment. 3) **C.** Answer C correctly uses the past tense in both sentences. Make sure you use "have loved" and "have cared" for the perfect tense. 4) **C.** Use present tense when something is happening right now. The mattress *is* hard. 5) **B.** (spend, spent, have spent) Only answer B uses the correct word for the past tense. 6) **D.** (begin, began, have begun) Only answer D uses the correct word for the past participle. 7) **A.** (lie, lay, have lain) Lied is the past tense for lying, and laid is the past tense for laying. 8) **C.** (swim, swam, have swum). Only answer C uses the correct word for the past participle.

The Conditional

"I would have" is a conditional statement: it did not happen, it is not possible to fulfill it, and it is too late now. Other parts of a sentence that are conditional are
"I could have", "I should have", "I wish I had", "if I had done it", "if I had known it", etc.

The word **"IF"** makes something conditional. Do not combine it with another conditional statement in the same sentence.

Example: You learn that your friend went fishing yesterday. You would have liked to go fishing too, but you never knew he was going.

Example: If **would have known** you were going fishing, I **would have** gone too.
Review: There are two conditional statements in the same sentence.
Revision: If I **had known** you were going fishing, [then] I **would have** gone too.

 Tip: Never put "IF" and "would have" in the same sentence.

 Tip: An "if" statement is already conditional.

 Tip: Wishing for something to happen creates a conditional statement.

Exercise: Are the following conditional sentences correct? If not, correct the mistake.

1. He could have gotten more money if he would have paid attention to the stock.

2. I wish I would have known about your condition.

3. If I had received my passport on time, we could have traveled together.

4. If I would have known you were going to the mall, I would have gone too.

5. I could have prevented the problem if I had only listened to the rumors.

6. I could have helped you if you would have asked me,

7. If you would have been older, you could have gone to the party.

8. My girlfriend wishes you would not have told me her secret.

9. We all wish they would have been more honest about their company's finances.

10. We would not have to hurry now if we would have started earlier.

---

1) ... *if he had paid* attention. 2) I wish I *had known*. 3) Correct 4) If I *had known*... 5) Correct 6) ... *if you had asked* me. 7) If you *had been* older. 8) ... *you had not told* me. 9) ... *they had been* more honest. 10) ... *if we had started earlier.*

Parallel Structure

It is important that two sentences (or two parts of one sentence) are parallel (similar) to each other, especially in paragraphs, in lists, and in comparisons.

Parallelism in Paragraphs

In a paragraph, the verb tense needs to stay consistent.

Example: Peter went to the store to buy some candy. He takes a long time to look at all the choices. Peter left with a mixed bag that contained all his favorites.

Review: In the example above, "*He takes a long time to look at all the choices*" is not a bad sentence by itself. However, because the rest of the paragraph is written in the past tense, this sentence also should be in the past tense.

Revision: He *took a long time to look at all the choices.*

Tip: Always read the sentences that come before and after the one you need to correct.

Parallelism in a List

Example: I like eating, drinking, and to watch TV.

Review: I do like "*to watch TV*", but in this case, I have to keep my verb parallel to the others in my list.

Revision: *I like eating, drinking, and watching TV.*

Example: Grandpa likes reading the newspaper daily, playing cards at home with his friends during the cold winter months, and to work in the garden when the weather is warm.

Revision: *and working in the garden when the weather is warm.*

Tip: The ACT likes to put the third part of a list after a long description in the second listed item.

Example: I studied hard for the ACT, SAT, and the PSAT exams.

Review: Either all three words need the article "the," or only the first item in the list.

Revision: *I studied hard for the ACT, SAT, and PSAT exams.* **or**
I studied hard for the ACT, the SAT, and the PSAT exams."

Parallelism in Comparisons and Choices

Example: I enjoy canoeing more than I like to kayak.

Review: To better show that we are comparing two activities, the two verbs should be parallel.

Revision: *I enjoy canoeing more than I like kayaking.*

Tip: Do not just look at the verbs. The items that you compare also have to be similar to each other.

Example: I like Beethoven's music better than I like Mozart.

Review: In this case, Beethoven's music is compared with another composer: Mozart.

Revision: *I like Beethoven's music better than I like Mozart's music.*

Parallelism in Prepositions.

Tip: Watch for consistent use of prepositions in parallelism.

Example: Always check the amount whether people pay you in cash or checks.

Review: ...people pay you in cash or people pay you checks? or people pay you *in* checks?

Revision: The correct ending should be, "*.. whether people pay you in cash or with checks.*"

Tip: To discover consistency, repeat the sentence with a different ending.

Paralellism - Quiz 1

1. Before going to class, Jason had done his homework, brushed his teeth, and ate breakfast.
   A. NO CHANGE.
   B. Before going to class, Jason done his homework, brushed his teeth, and eaten breakfast.
   C. Before going to class, Jason had done his homework, brushed his teeth, and eaten breakfast.
   D. Before going to class, Jason had done his homework, had brushed his teeth, and eaten breakfast.

2. I want to run fast, win, and to set a state record.
   A. NO CHANGE.
   B. I want to run fast, win, and set a state record.
   C. I want to run fast, to win, and set a state record.
   D. I want run fast, to win, and to set a state record.

3. You love me—that's a fact—and wanting me to be rich.
   A. NO CHANGE.
   B. You love me—that's a fact—and wanted me to be rich.
   C. You love me—that's a fact—but had wanted me to be rich.
   D. You love me –that's a fact—and want me to be rich.

4. In the Art Institute, patrons look at paintings, and docents had provided the background information.
   A. NO CHANGE.
   B. In the Art Institute, patrons look at paintings, and docents provided the background information.

   C. In the Art Institute, patrons look at paintings, and docents provide the background information.
   D. In the Art Institute, patrons look at paintings, and docents could have provided the background information.

5. First, the oven is set to 350°, and then the butter is melted.
   A. NO CHANGE.
   B. First, the oven is set to 350°, and then the butter was melted.
   C. First, the oven is set to 350°, and then the butter has been melted.
   D. First, the oven is set to 350°, and then the butter melts.

6. First, the baby will explore his environment by picking up some toys, and then go to sleep.
   A. NO CHANGE.
   B. First, the baby will explore his environment by picking up some toys and then will go to sleep.
   C. First, the baby will explore his environment by picking up some toys and going to sleep.
   D. First, the baby will explore his environment by picking up some toys, and then by going to sleep.

7. The artist became accomplished at painting abstracts and landscapes and being a talented sculptor.
   A. NO CHANGE.
   B. The artist became accomplished at painting abstracts and landscapes, and he also became a talented sculptor.
   C. The artist became accomplished at painting abstracts and landscapes and a sculptor.
   D. The artist became an accomplished abstract and landscape painter and a talented sculptor.

1) C. Use consistent verb tenses in a list: He had done, he (had) brushed, and he (had) eaten) Also correct would have been: He did, he brushed, and he ate. 2) B. Stay consistent with the word "to". Use it only once at the beginning, or use it for all the verbs. 3) D. Only D uses parallelism by using the present tense in both parts of the sentence. 4) C. Stay parallel in your verb tenses: patrons *look* and docents *provide*. 5) A. Because the present perfect is used in the first part of the sentence, it should also be used in the second part: *it is set*, and then *it is melted*. 6) B. Look at the verb in the first part. The baby *will explore*. Match this in the correct answer: the baby *will go to sleep*. 7) D. There is a false parallelism in answer A. You can become accomplished at *painting*, but not at *being*. Answer B and C mix verbs and nouns in the comparison. Answer D uses parallelism: painter and sculptor.

Paralellism - Quiz 2

As a child, I lived in my family's palace in Udaipur, India. Every day, I saw my tutors, took polo lessons, and would swim[1] in Lake Pichola. I was friends with the servant's child, Babu. Though he was no older than twelve, he helped his family earn their keep both by cleaning my room and through walking[2] my father's many dogs. My family never condoned our friendship—they put far too much stock in the concept of caste—but I occasionally snuck out[3] of my chambers to see Babu. Whenever my manservant wasn't watching, I would crawl out of my window onto the roof. The pitch of the roof is [4] treacherous, but I always managed to make it down safely. My life was one of comfort and affluence, but in retrospect I now see that there were certain downsides to being the son of the maharaja. I had to worship the gods properly, which was always difficult, and a maharaja's son must spend[5] lots of time in fancy clothes. Babu and I wanted to escape Udaipur, move to Peru, and to start[6] a llama farm. What dreamers we were. My friend died of tuberculosis on his 13th birthday.

1. **A.** NO CHANGE
   B. swam
   C. had swum
   D. swim

2. **A.** NO CHANGE
   B. he walked
   C. by walking
   D. walk

3. **A.** NO CHANGE
   B. sneak out
   C. was sneaking out
   D. had sneaked

4. **A.** NO CHANGE
   B. could have been
   C. being
   D. was

5. **A.** NO CHANGE
   B. I must spend
   C. I had to spend
   D. one must spend

6. **A.** NO CHANGE
   B. start
   C. we would start
   D. started

---

1) B. The list uses past tense: I *saw*, I *took*, and I *swam*. **2) C.** Stay parallel in expressions: by *cleaning* and by *walking* **3) A.** Stay parallel in the past tense: They *condoned*, and I *snuck* out. (sneak, snuck, have snuck) **4) D.** Stay parallel with the past tense throughout the story: I *managed* to make it down although the roof *was* treacherous. **5) C.** Stay parallel to the subject and the tense. I *had to* worship, and I *had to* spend time in fancy clothes. **6) B.** Stay consistent with the word "to". Use it only once at the beginning, or use it for all the verbs in a list. I wanted *to escape, move* to Peru, and *start* a farm.

Parallelism - Quiz 3

Find the incorrect use of parallelism and correct the sentence without looking at multiple-choice answers.

1) Martha Graham's ballet company was notable for its creativity, technical skill, and that they could dance in many different ways.

2) Lucy's desire to be accepted into Magdalen College seemed to be greater than her brother Edmund.

3) Three of the greatest civilizations in the history of India are the Indus Valley, the Maruya, and Mughal.

4) The high school has money for new tennis courts, but not new computers.

5) The requirements for this essay are first, that you must use three academic sources; second, you must cite these sources; and third, you have to double-space it.

6) I squandered my tuition money by studying too little and hanging out a lot.

7) Jenny is proud of her mother's knowledge and interest in estate planning.

8) The birds went looking for worms, they built their nests, they preened their young, and tried to escape the hungry eye of Mittens, the cat.

---

1. Martha Graham's ballet company was notable for its creativity, technical ability, and **versatility.**

2. Lucy's desire to be accepted into Magdalen College seemed to be greater than her brother **Edmund's** (We have to compare Lucy's desire to her brother's desire, not to her brother.)

3. Three of the greatest civilizations in the history of India are the Indus Valley, **the** Maruya, and **the Mughal.**

4. The high school has money for new tennis courts but not **for** new computers.

5. The requirements for this essay are first, **that** you must use three academic sources; second, **that you must** cite these sources; and third, **that** you must double-space it.

6. I squandered my tuition money by studying too little and hanging out **too much.**

7. Jenny is proud of her mother's knowledge **of** and interest **in** estate planning.

8. The birds went looking for worms, **they** built their nests, **they** preened their young, and **they** tried to escape the hungry eye of Mittens, the cat.

WORD CHOICES

Sometimes it takes finesse to choose the right word in a sentence. Other times you simply have to know the rules.

Practice on the next pages might help you gain insight before your next test. It will certainly help you to make ~~less~~ *fewer* mistakes.

Word Choices

There are many word choices that can appear in the ACT, such as the choice between *passed* and *past*. The choice always depends on the context. Here are a few sets that have simple rules:

It's means *"it is"* or *"it has"* **Its** is possessive **THIS QUESTION APPEARS IN EVERY ACT**	**Who** or **Whom**? He -> who Him -> whom Use "whom" after a preposition **THIS QUESTION APPEARS IN EVERY ACT**
Because = for the reason that **Due to** = caused by Don't use: <u>the reason</u> was <u>because</u> …	If you can count it If you cannot **Fewer** (cookies) **Less** (milk) **Number** (of movies) **Amount** (of time spent) **Many** (cups of coffee) **Much** (sugar)
Lie – lay – lain (to recline) **Lay – laid – laid** (to place) (+ object) Note: the past tense of lie is lay.	ALWAYS USE IN PAIRS: **either** and **or** **neither** and **nor** **not only** and **but also**
Between one-on-one **each other** **Among** groups **one another**	**A is the action word.** **Affect** = verb **Accept** = verb **Effect** = noun **Except** = preposition
If: needs a condition **Whether:** needs two alternatives	**Than** for comparisons **Then** for time
There A place **They're** They are **Their** Possessive	**Where** A place **We're** We are **Were** past tense of *"are"* **Wear** clothing / carrying
You're you are **Your** possessive	**Farther** for physical distance ("far") **Further** for time, amount, or process

Word Choices - Quiz 1

Choose the correct word:

1. (Preventive / Preventative) medicine has the potential to reduce healthcare costs greatly.

2. "You've reached the front desk. How (can / may) I help you?"

3. After the team was crushed by its opponent, player (moral / morale) reached a new low.

4. As we build the new school, we must keep in mind the six major (tenets / tenants) of architectural beauty.

5. Don't be afraid to (loose / lose) yourself in the music.

6. Grace isn't going on vacation to Iraq this year (since / because) the State Department has declared the country unsafe.

7. He usually arrives at school later (than / then) Julie.

8. I am running the race tomorrow (regardless / irregardless) of my knee pain.

9. I feel great now that I've changed to a (healthier / more healthful) lifestyle.

10. I should find the (number / amount) of CFC particles in the river to check for pollution.

11. I was admitted to a Ph.D. program. My future excites me, and I am (eager / anxious) to start school.

12. I'm not sure (if / whether) he'll go or not.

13. I've had famous teachers (like / such as) Milton Friedman, John Mearsheimer, and Junot Diaz.

14. I've never found the mortuary to be a particularly (quite / quiet / quit) place.

15. It was difficult to determine (whether / weather) he was drunk or not.

1) Preventive 2) may 3) morale 4) tenets 5) lose 6) because 7) than 8) regardless 9) healthier 10) number 11) eager 12) whether 13) such as 14) quiet 15) whether

Word Choices - Quiz 2

Choose the correct word:

1. It has proven difficult to find a new (cite / sight / site) for the state housing complex.

2. It is really a challenge to (accept / except) your decision to end our relationship.

3. Jim is less (oriented / orientated) toward social justice issues than he is toward financial issues.

4. The king and the queen argued with (one another/ each other.)

5. Most college students spend weekend mornings (lieing / laying / lying) in their beds.

6. My talents (complement / compliment) yours nicely.

7. Rebecca has been struggling with her diet and weight gain seems (eminent / imminent).

8. Samantha needs to choose from (among / between) six possible prom dresses.

9. Sipping the potion had a strange (effect / affect) on Peter.

10. Great Britain is without a doubt (uninterested / disinterested) in being a member of the European Union.

11. The Ebola outbreak has made me more risk (adverse / averse).

12. There were (fewer / less) cases of homicide in Chicago than in Ciudad Juarez.

13. There were (less / fewer) than 20 people at the party.

14. When deciding to admit a new student, the dean is not dwelling on a single (criteria / criterion).

15. When the physicist finished her experiment, the data (where / were) incontrovertible.

1) site 2) accept 3) oriented 4) each other 5) lying 6) complement 7) imminent 8) among 9) effect 10) uninterested 11) averse 12) fewer 13) fewer 14) criterion 15) were

GRAMMAR QUIZZES

Once you have mastered all the concepts of the last few chapters, the following quizzes are a great way to test yourself.

The quizzes also include a few additional small rules that did not receive their own chapter in this book.

See if you can spot the errors in the next few quizzes.

Grammar - Quiz 1

This is a collection of sentences that contain errors that are discussed in the previous chapters and a few more that sporadically appear on the ACT.

Find the mistakes (if any):

1. My family is from the north.

2. I begged mom to buy me a new skateboard.

3. The crowd applauded chancellor Angela Merkel.

4. Hyde Park is on the south side of Chicago.

5. I'm enrolled in calculus I and Roman historiography.

6. I started crying when Sophie said, "I'm dumping you"!

7. My wife Beatrice is sick today.

8. My pair of shoes are missing.

9. All the boys wore a tuxedo to the prom.

10. Please don't throw trash in the river.

11. I did really good on the test.

12. His new sneakers are to-die-for!

13. I saw two bird's building a nest in that tall tree.

14. Can I order off the kids menu?

1. Capitalize **North**. Regions are capitalized, directions are not.
2. **Mom** is always capitalized, except when the word "my" is in front of it.
3. Capitalize **Chancellor**. Capitalize words when they are part of a title or of a person's name.
4. Correct as is.
5. **Calculus** and **Roman Historiography** should be capitalized.
6. I started crying when Sophie said, "I'm dumping you!" (Use punctuation inside the quote.)
7. There should be **commas** before and after **Beatrice** (it is an appositive: a restatement of the same subject. Added information should be placed between two commas.)
8. Use **is** instead of **are** when talking about a single noun like "pair".
9. All the boys wore **tuxedos** to the prom.
10. Please, don't throw trash **into** the river. "In" is used with place; "into" is used with direction.
11. Use **well** instead of **good**. (Adverbs talk about verbs and adjectives; adjectives talk about nouns.)
12. If a compound adjective comes after the noun, don't use **hyphens**. (Do it if it comes before the noun.)
13. I saw two **birds** building a nest in that tall tree. (Plural, not possessive.)
14. Can I order off the **kids'** menu? (Are we talking about the menu of the kid or the menu of the kids?)

Grammar - Quiz 2

This is a collection of sentences that contain errors that are discussed in the previous chapters and a few more that sporadically appear on the ACT.

Find the mistakes (if any):

1. The car is their's.

2. Bastian is the captain of the German mens' soccer team.

3. She was born in the 1980's.

4. If I was you, I would sell that musty house.

5. Sarah complains a lot about me eating lots of junk food.

6. Frank only drank three liters of soda.

7. The man who's coat is made of alpaca wool cannot find a good repair shop.

8. You have a real nice smile.

9. Eva and Milou are relatives of me.

10. Before you rent property, you should understand do it yourself repairs.

11. I like Timothy better than Austin.

12. I should buy me a new pink dress.

13. Every student gave it their best shot on the test.

14. Glen followed his grandmother's cake recipe exactly, but his cake tasted differently.

---

1. The car is **theirs**. (**Their** is already possessive) (There's always means "there is".)
2. Bastian is the captain of the German **men's** soccer team. The apostrophe comes after the noun.
3. The 80s are a collection of plural items: 1980, 1981, 1982, etc. Use **1980s** in this sentence.
4. If I **were** you, I would ... (This is an odd grammar rule: use "if I were", "if you were", "if he were", and "if we were".)
5. Sarah complains a lot about **my** eating lots of junk food. (look up *gerunds* for this rule. "Eating" is a noun)
6. Frank **drank only** three liters of soda. (The word "only" modifies just the word next to it, he did not only drink it.)
7. The man **whose** coat is made of alpaca wool cannot find a good repair shop. Who's always means "who is" or "who has."
8. The adverb **really** is needed in place of real. Adverbs describe adjectives, adjectives describe nouns.
9. Hank is a comrade of Miranda's and **mine**.
10. You should understand **do-it-yourself** repairs. If a compound adjective comes before the noun, use hyphens.
11. I like Timothy better than I like Austin (Ambiguous sentence: who likes whom? The ACT likes clarity!)
12. I should buy **myself** a new pink dress.
13. Every student gave **his/her** best shot on the test.
14. "...but the cake tasted differently **different**. A descriptive word that follows a linking verb modifies the subject and should be an adjective.

Grammar - Quiz 3

This is a collection of sentences that contain errors that are discussed in the previous chapters and a few more that sporadically appear on the ACT.

Find the mistakes (if any):

1. The presentation had a very strange affect on me.

2. The tigresses cubs watched as their mothers raced after the zebra.

3. Your father makes more tastier pizzas than mine does.

4. Jim's dog has a habit of biting it's tail.

5. The moment the soccer player played the pass, his teammate starts running.

6. I plan on getting an internship before graduation.

7. Who did you inform about the meeting tomorrow?

8. We used this landscaper since we moved into this neighborhood in 1974. We can certainly recommend her services.

9. Harry Potter is not really a person, but most people have heard of him.

10. Please take the car to the gas station, and fill it up with gasoline.

11. Because I pay attention in class, I do not need to refer back to my notes.

---

1. a very strange **affect** **effect** on me. "Affect" means "to influence." The word needed here is the noun "effect," which means "a result."

2. The **tigresses'** **tigress's** cubs. To form the possessive of a plural noun that ends in -s, we add an apostrophe after the -s. Watch out for plurals and possessives together!

3. Your grandma makes **more** tastier pies than my mine. Use "more" for some two- and all three-syllable adjectives; add -er to most other adjectives. Don't use both of them at the same time.

4. Jim's dog has a habit of biting it's **its** tail. "It's" is always a contraction of "it is." The sentence needs the possessive pronoun "its," which has no apostrophe. Every ACT/SAT test has an it's or its question.

5. his teammate **starts** **started** running. Use the same tense for verbs that name actions happening at the same time. (parallel action need parallel tenses)

6. I plan **on getting** **to get** an internship before graduation. Idioms: "to plan to do something", not "to plan on doing something"

7. **Who** **Whom** did you inform about the meeting tomorrow? The subject is you. "You" performs the action (invite). "Who" is the object, so change it to "whom". You only use "who" when it is the subject of a sentence, and performs the action. Him, them ← whom. He, they ← who

8. We used **have been using** this landscaper. We can certainly recommend his services. The action began in the past and continuing in the present. Don't use past tense in that case.

9. Harry Potter is not really a **real** person, but most people have heard of him. The meaning of the sentence is unclear. As written, it implies that Harry Potter is not a human being. It should say he is fictional, that is, not a living or real person.

10. Please take the car to the gas station, and fill it up **the tank / the car** with gasoline. Who does "it" refer to? We might guess it is the car, or the tank, but in this sentence it could well refer to the gas station.

11. Because I pay attention in class, I do not need to refer **back** to my notes. Redundancy. The ACT/SAT likes to take two items: "to refer to" and "look back on" and mix them up as one: "to refer back to".

Grammar - Quiz 4

This is a collection of sentences that contain errors that are discussed in the previous chapters and a few more that sporadically appear on the ACT.

Find the mistakes (if any):

1. If you like to write and to act, please join our local drama group.

2. Here is a pen and a piece of paper to write a thank-you note.

3. Entering the school, the office will be on your right.

4. The use of vitamin supplements and herbs, especially those without added artificial ingredients, are becoming increasingly popular.

5. Beer is the world's best-selling alcohol drink.

6. Sorry, he speaks neither English or Spanish.

7. The storm prevented us to play baseball this weekend.

8. A man's concept of romance is different from a woman.

9. The girl, who's mother is a famous scientist, won the first prize at the science fair.

10. The teacher told them to not forget the important assignment over the weekend.

11. She barely finished reading the two first chapters of the book on time.

12. If he is right or wrong does not matter in this case. He should have told us.

---

1. If you like to write and to act, please join our local drama group. (no error/ parallelism)

2. Here is **are** a pen and a piece of paper to write a letter to your grandmother. Verb noun agreement. Use reverse strategy: a pen and a piece of paper **are** laying on the table.

3. Entering the school, **you will** ~~will be~~ see the office on your right. Dangling modifier. It is not clear who is entering the school. It certainly is not the office, as indicated in this sentence. Everything before the comma refers to the first noun or pronoun after the comma. (Rule of proximity)

4. The use of vitamin supplements and herbs, especially those without added artificial ingredients, ~~are~~ **is** becoming increasingly popular. Verb noun agreement. It is not about supplements (plural), herbs (plural), or ingredients (plural) but about the use (singular) of them. The ACT/SAT likes group words like team, bunch, etc. to confuse the reader. They often separate the verb and the subject by added information between two commas.

5. Beer is the world's best-selling ~~alcohol~~ **alcoholic** drink. A word that describes a noun (drink) is an adjective. Alcohol is another noun.

6. Sorry, he speaks neither English ~~or~~ **nor** Spanish. Idioms: Always use "neither ... nor ... and "not only, ... but also" ...

7. The storm prevented us ~~to play~~ **from playing** baseball this weekend. Idioms: to prevent you *from* doing something.

8. A man's concept of romance is different from a ~~woman~~ **woman's**. Compare the man with the woman; compare the man's behavior with the woman's behavior.

9. The boy, ~~who's~~ **whose** father is a famous scientist, won the prize of the fair at school. "Who's" is always a contraction of "who is." The sentence needs the possessive pronoun "whose," which has no apostrophe. Every ACT/SAT test has a who/whom's.who/whom question.

10. The teacher told them ~~to not~~ **not to** forget the important assignment over the weekend. (a case of split infinitives)

11. She barely finished reading the ~~two first~~ **first two** chapters of the book on time. This sounds good but is impossible. There cannot be two chapters that are both the first one in the book.

12. If **whether** he is right or wrong does not matter in this case. He should have told us. If he is right, he should ha've told us. This is a conditional phrase. If he is wrong, he should keep his mouth shut. This stipulates a condition (if ....) and a solution. When a sentence considers two alternatives, the word "whether" is used. (whether you like it or not 😊)

Grammar - Quiz 5

This is a collection of sentences that contain errors that are discussed in the previous chapters and a few more that sporadically appear on the ACT.

Find the mistakes (if any):

1. My grandfather purchased a 12 foot ladder.

2. I saw you Sarah in the back of a police car.

3. I confess that yes I did forget to feed the dog today.

4. Did every one on the track team pass everyone of his midterms?

5. My new high heels are very different than Rebecca's

6. We ordered pizza to be delivered at seventy-one Linden Street.

7. I found the babie's blankets that were needed in the prenatal unit.

8. Neither Clementine or Dominique was at school today.

9. Everybody is worried about their final test.

10. I wrote an essay for my creative writing class, and a poem.

11. When the rain continued to pour down, the family begun to worry about the boxes in the basement.

12. Grandma made sandwiches for my friends with ham and pickles.

13. You got a package for me?

---

1. **12-foot ladder. If** a compound adjective comes before the noun, use hyphens.
2. When talking to someone, you use **commas** before and after the name. (*appositive for you = Ashley*)
3. I confess that, **yes,** I did forget to feed the dog today. "Yes" is added information.
4. Did **everyone** (all of them) on the track team pass **every (single) one** of the midterms?
5. Use **different from.** Only use "than" for superlative forms (higher or lower level)
6. We ordered pizza to 71 Linden Street. Never spell out numbers in addresses.
7. I found the **babies'** blankets.
8. Neither Franklin **nor** Teddy was at school today. (Some words always come in pairs: either...or, neither...nor, not only...but also.)
9. Everybody is worried about **his or her** final test. (Every is singular while there is plural so have to use his/her)
10. Only two items are listed. There is no reason for a comma.
11. When the rain continued to pour down, the family **began** to worry about their basement. Remember your conjugations of irregular verbs. Begin, began, had begun. This sentence uses the wrong tense. The ACT/SAT likes to do this with irregular verbs. "To begin" is one of their favorites.
12. Grandma made sandwiches with ham and pickles for my friends. "With ham and pickles" modifies just the word next to it.
13. The ACT and SAT use formal language. Say "**Do you have a** package for me?"

English Grammar Overview

who or whom?
he➜who   him➜whom
Use "whom" after a preposition

because – for the reason that ..
due to – caused by
Don't use: *the reason was because*

fewer   if you can count it
less   if you can't
number   if you can count it
amount   if you can't

it's means "*it is*" or "*it has*"
its   is possessive

lie – lay – lain (to recline)
lay – laid – laid (to place) (+ object)

Always use in pairs:
either   **or**
neither   **nor**
not only   **but also**

between   one-on-one   **each other**
among   groups   **one another**

affect = verb
effect = noun

Comma Rules
1) Intro**,** full sentence
1) Full sentence**,** FANBOYS full sentence
2) Full .... **,** __added information__**,** ... sentence
    No commas around restricted information
3) Commas in between items (3 or more) in a list
Also: A comma between contrasts in a sentence

Colon and semicolon
:
- Full sentence: list or explanation
- ⇨ Do not use if the list has "for example" or "such as".

;
Full sentence; full sentence
⇨ Use for elaboration or contrast
Use the semicolon as a super comma in lists that contain other commas.

Redundancy
If in doubt, leave it out. Shorter is better …...
(if it does not change the meaning of the sentence.)

Modifier
Rule of proximity: a modifier describes only the word closest to it.
Dangling rule: words before the comma refer to the first noun/pronoun after the comma.
Make sure that "it", and "he" are not ambiguous.

Subject-verb agreement
Either & neither & none➜ singular
Each & everybody ➜ singular (Don't use with "their")
Watch out for the word "of"

Parallel – paragraph, list, or comparisons
All verbs in a paragraph should have the same tense.
Compare two items very logically (e.g. don't compare Beethoven's music with Mozart.)
When comparing *two* people, don't use "best" or "tallest"; use "better" and "taller."

Verb tense
If an event in the past takes place before another event in the past, use the past perfect (had + verb)
If the event happened in the past and is still going on, use the present perfect. *(have + verb)*

Conditional
Do not put "if" and "would have" in the same clause
If I would have known … ➜ If I had known …

Gerund
Watch out for words that end on -ING.
Without the helping verb, they are often NOUNS!
I am painting. (v) ↔ Painting is fun! (n)
I am cleaning. (v) ↔ She did not like my cleaning. (n)

Pronouns. Pronouns refer to a noun in the same sentence or the one before. ●Do NOT trust pronouns: always check what 'it' or 'they' stands for. ● Use parallel pronouns: *I* am taller than *he* (is). ● Don't use 'they' in a general way (*They* should do something about it. Who is "*they*"?) ● Do not use a pronoun when it can refer to two subjects: *Diego asked if Glen brought his book. (Whose book?)*

English Grammar Overview Worksheet

who or whom?
→   →
Use "whom" after a ____

because –
due to –

fewer   -
less   -
number   -
amount   -

it's
its

lie – _____ - _____
lay – _____ - _____

Always use in pairs:
either   _____
neither   _____
not only   _____

between   **each other**
among   **one another**

affect =
effect =

The four comma rules
1)
1)
2)
3)
One more rule:

Colon and semicolon
•
• _____
;
,

Redundancy
If in doubt, _____
Pick the _____ answer.

Modifier
A modifier describes only _____
_____
Dangling rule: everything before the comma refers to _____

Subject-verb agreement
Either & neither & none →
Each and Everybody →   (don't use with ….)
Watch out for the word _____

Parallelism
Use in _____, _____ and _____
Make sure all _____ have the same ____
Compare two items very _____
When comparing *two* people, don't use ___ or ____

Verb tense
If an event in the past takes place before another event in the past, use _____ + _____
If the event happened in the past and is still going on, use _____ + _____

Conditional
Do not put _____ and _____ in the same clause.

Gerund
Watch out for words that end on _____
Without the _____, it is often a _____!

Pronouns. • Pronouns refer to _____ in the _____. • Do not ____ pronouns.
• Check the meaning of words such as _____ and _____. • Use _____ pronouns: I am taller than ___ .
• Don't use _____ in a general way • Do not use a pronoun when _____ .

ENGLISH

Production of Writing

CLARITY

Some questions in the ACT evaluate your knowledge of the English grammar rules. Others evaluate how well you pay attention.

If you read the question very carefully, it is often <u>clear</u> that only one answer actually answers what the question is asking for.

This test-taking technique will come handy throughout all portions of the ACT.

Clarity

Many questions in the English ACT have four alternate options from which to choose.
About a third of all questions **start with a question**, after which the four answers are provided.
Often, the answer can be found by reading the question VERY PRECISELY.
Practicing this skill will help you throughout the ACT in English, Reading, Science, and even Math.

 Tip: Make it a habit to underline the most important part of the question.

Example: Based on the number of questions, which part of the ACT takes the most effort to complete?
  A. Math, because you have to read questions, memorize formulas, and calculate several steps to arrive to the answer.
  B. Reading, because there is a lot of information in the stories, and there is not enough time to process all the details.
  C. Science, because you have to understand the materials, the experiments, and the information in the tables and the graphs.
  D. English, because it has the most questions, and not everybody is a native speaker.

Review: When you read the question for content, you might feel drawn to answer A, B, or C. However, if you read the question very precisely, there is an element in the way it is phrased that is only addressed by answer D.
Based on the number of questions, which part of the ACT takes the most effort to complete?
If you read the underlined portion carefully, the answer needs to show a reason that addresses the number of questions in the ACT sections. Only one answer does that.

 Tip: Read the questions like a lawyer! Every word adds a detail that needs to be considered.

Often, students skim the question and then bite their nails when more than one answer seems to be correct. You can save yourself a lot of time if you underline the essence of the questions in the first place.

 Tip: If you end up with two (or more) answers that seem correct, re-read the question.

Example: What does Jolene always do at the end of her high-intensity exercises in the gym?
  A. She bows to her teacher to thank him and rolls up her new yoga mat.
  B. She slows down and takes a couple of breaths.
  C. She takes a shower, changes into her jeans and red blouse, and then goes straight home.
  D. She pays her monthly fees, so she can continue her membership.

Review: If you followed the directions, you would have underlined the word "always" in the question and concluded that only the second answer has to be correct. **(B)**

 Tip: Often, students make mistakes when the question reads, "Which one is NOT correct," or "All statements are correct, EXCEPT which one?" The techniques on this page also help with those questions

Clarity - Quiz 1

1. Which of the following gives the most vivid depiction of a school classroom?
   - A. The room was filled with desks and a whiteboard stood in front on a podium.
   - B. The whiteboard was full of children's drawings and the instructions for homework assignments were clearly displayed in a corner of the board.
   - C. The classroom is right next to the hallway bathrooms, opposite of the cafeteria, and adjacent to the principal's office.
   - D. There were numerous cracks in the walls and in one place you could actually see the electric wiring behind the plaster.

2. Given that all choices are true, which of the following descriptions shows how the hair salon is different from any other?
   - A. The salon has many different hair styles and color treatments from which to choose.
   - B. The salon has five different stylists from which to choose.
   - C. Once a year, the salon offers a day for clients to bring their pets for a haircut.
   - D. Numerous magazines are located on a coffee table, so people can enjoy reading articles while waiting for a haircut.

3. Which of the following most clearly expresses the relationship between a husband and wife?
   - A. They fell in love in high school and the got married right after graduation.
   - B. The wife cooked a different meal each day.
   - C. The husband performed numerous chores around the house every day.
   - D. Their children were amazed how their parents always did everything together and never had a fight.

4. Which example best depicts how Jessica thought her mother felt after the fight?
   - A. Her mother paced the kitchen floor for several minutes before she addressed Jessica in a sad voice.
   - B. Her mother did not look sad as much as hurt.
   - C. Her mother felt around in the cabinet for a tissue because she felt sad.
   - D. Her mother felt sad as she sat on the sofa.

5. Which of the following incidents best shows why Sarah thought that Andrew was rude?
   - A. Andrew yelled at the cashier for giving him the wrong change.
   - B. Andrew forgot to tip the server at the pub.
   - C. Andrew accidentally bumped into someone on the sidewalk.
   - D. Andrew had been stuck in traffic and was late to the event.

6. Given that all choices are true, which statement shows people's negative attitude towards the future of automobiles?
   - A. Automobiles will improve the speed of transportation in the coming years.
   - B. Automobiles have caused many deaths in the past few years.
   - C. Automobiles will only increase pollution in next decade.
   - D. Automobiles have revolutionized the transportation industry.

7. Last year, Matt set a record.
   Which of the following gives the most specific account of this event?
   - A. NO CHANGE
   - B. This month
   - C. A long time ago
   - D. On his birthday

---

1) A. Only A answers the questions and describes the room. B talks about the whiteboard. C tells you where the room is, and D describes the walls. 2) C. Answer A, B, and D all describe a hair salon that you can find in any city. Only B answers the question, but not their relationship. D talks about their relationship the past. B and C describe the tasks of each spouse, but not their relationship. D talks about their relationship through their children's description. 4) B. Answers A, C, and D, describe how the mother felt, but not (as specified in the questions) what Jessica thought her mother felt. The clue lies in the words "she looked sad" and "she looked annoyed" of Answer B. This is how her mother appears to someone else, in this case to Jessica. 5) A. Underline *why* and underline *rude* in the question. Only answer A describes a rude behavior. (yelling at the waiter) and only Answer A gives a reason for this behavior. (giving the wrong change.) Answer B talks about forgetfulness, C talks about clumsiness, and D talks about tardiness. 6) C. Underline *negative attitude* and *future* in the question. Answer B and D talk about the past. Answer A is a positive attitude. 7) D. Underline the words most specific. "Last year," "this month," and "a long time ago" are not very specific time frames. Answer D states that Matt set a record on his birthday, which helps us to pinpoint the exact date.

Copyright 2017 Winni van Gessel

CONJUNCTIONS
and
TRANSITIONS

There are a few rules that determine how to put two parts of a sentence together. Other rules determine how a sentence connects to the one before.

You need to put your thinking cap on, and ask yourself, "How are the two parts related?"

Most transitions can be placed in the following two categories:

Changing Direction   Oppose the previous statement

Maintaining Direction   Support the previous statement

Conjunctions

Coordinating Conjunctions

FANBOYS are conjunctions that join two or more items (such as words, main clauses, or sentences) of equal importance.

For, and, nor, but, or, yet, and so.

They are always preceded by a comma when they separate two full sentences.

Subordinating Conjunctions

All conjunctions that are NOT Fanboys are *subordinating conjunctions*. When they separate two parts of a sentence, no comma is required.

after, although, as, as far as, as if, as long as, as soon as, as though, because, before, even if, even though, every time, if, in order that, since, so, so that, than, though, unless, until, when, whenever, where, whereas, wherever, and while.

Paired Conjunctions

Some conjunctions always come in pairs. Memorize the following combinations:

Both (this)	**and**	(that)
Either (this)	**or**	(that)
Neither (this)	**nor**	(that)
no sooner (did this happen)	**than**	(something else happened)
not only (did I do this)	**but also**	(did I do something else)
rather (this)	**than**	(that)
whether (you do this)	**or**	(you do that)

 Tip: All conjunctions can be split up in two groups according to their function. Look at the two parts of the sentence and determine what type of conjunction you need.

Supporting Conjunctions

Continuing thought: additionally, also, again, as well as, besides, correspondingly, by the same token, for the same reason, furthermore, identically, in addition, likewise, moreover, similarly, together with.

Cause and effect: accordingly, as a result, consequently, due to, ergo, for this reason, for this purpose, hence, otherwise, so, so then, since, subsequently, therefore, thus, thereupon, when.

Further detail: above all, chiefly, coupled with, especially, for example, for instance, in fact, including, in this case, namely, particularly, singularly, specifically, such as, with attention to.

Generalizing: as a rule, as usual, briefly, for the most part, generally, generally speaking, in brief, in essence, in other words, in short, ordinarily, usually, to put it differently.

Summarizing: after all, all in all, all things considered, anyhow, by and large, in any case, in any event, in conclusion, in short, in summary, in the final analysis, in the long run, finally, to sum up, to summarize.

Opposing Conjunctions

Contrast: although, but, conversely, comparatively, despite, even so, however, in contrast, instead, in spite of, ironically, nevertheless, notwithstanding, on the other hand, on the contrary, rather, regardless, still, unfortunately, while, yet.

Exclusion: aside from, barring, beside, except, excluding, other than, outside of, save.

Conjunctions - Quiz 1

1. My brother moved to college in the fall. We had a room to spare, <u>yet</u> we wanted someone to take up the empty space.
   A. NO CHANGE
   B. but
   C. and
   D. however

2. We wanted to buy mangos, cherries, and pears, along with some paper plates, <u>which</u> we didn't have enough money for it all.
   A. NO CHANGE
   B. and
   C. for
   D. but

3. I was grounded on Saturday, and I could not go to the movies, <u>if</u> my mother found out that I had an F in English.
   A. NO CHANGE
   B. movies because
   C. movies, but
   D. movies, while

4. Morgan and John considered trying to climb the ledge, and they would have gone through with their plan, <u>unless</u> their parents told them not to.
   A. NO CHANGE
   B. and
   C. if
   D. but

5. Since Susan wanted to make things right between her two sons, <u>and</u> she took them out for ice cream after dinner.
   A. NO CHANGE
   B. but
   C. still
   D. Delete the underlined portion.

6. Maya is extremely involved in <u>lacrosse, but</u> she goes to the practice three times a week.
   A. NO CHANGE
   B. lacrosse,
   C. lacrosse, so
   D. lacrosse, then

7. The snake may seem like a sneaky, cunning predator, considering its diligent patience and speedy movements, <u>but</u> it fears the owl that swoops down from above.
   A. NO CHANGE
   B. and
   C. so
   D. until

8. Many farmers will tell you that their hard work on the farm has led them to be better parents, <u>while</u> it taught them how to be patient.
   A. NO CHANGE
   B. but
   C. because
   D. for

---

1) C. There is no contrast between the two parts of the sentence. 2) D. We need a contrast between the cost of the many items and our funds. 3) B. The words "if" and "while" are not FANBOYS and do not need a comma. The word "but" in answer C would indicate a contrast, but there is none. 4) D. The words "if," and "unless" are not FANBOYS and do not need a comma. There is a contrast between the two parts of the sentence. 5) D. Watch out for the word "Since" at the beginning of the sentence. The first part is a fragment, and we do not need a FANBOYS conjunction. 6) C. Eliminate answer A because the sentence lacks contrast. Eliminate B because of the comma splice. Eliminate D because "then" is not a Fanboys conjunction. 7) A. We need an opposing conjunction between the two parts of the sentence. 8) D. Look at the comma. Eliminate A and C. There is no contrast between the two parts. Eliminate B.

Transitions

Transition words can be split into two categories:

Transition words that change direction and **oppose another statement**

Although	Nevertheless	Still
But	Nonetheless	Though
Despite	Notwithstanding	Unfortunately
Even so	On the contrary	While
However	On the other hand	Yet
In spite of	Rather than	; (the semicolon*)
Ironically	Regardless	

Transition words that maintain direction and **support another statement**

: (the colon)	Because	In fact
; (the semicolon*)	Besides	Moreover
Accordingly	Consequently	Since
Additionally	Due to	So
After all	Ergo	Therefore
And	Furthermore	Thus
Anyhow	Hence	When

*The semicolon can show either an explanation or a contrast.

 Tip: On the ACT, transition words often appear without any reason. Grammatically, nothing is wrong with the sentence. However, it would make more sense to OMIT the underlined transition word. This happens especially in the beginning of new paragraphs.

Examples:

1) She wanted to buy new clothes. <u>However,</u> she parked her car at the mall and spent the afternoon shopping.

2) In her town, there were not many opportunities for entertainment. <u>Furthermore,</u> besides movies at the church on Wednesdays, the only other place to go with friends was the local restaurant that featured karaoke.

3) My desk is an antique and fragile piece of furniture. <u>Besides,</u> I inherited it from my grandfather.

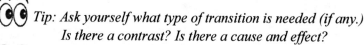 *Tip: Ask yourself what type of transition is needed (if any.)*
      Is there a contrast? Is there a cause and effect?

Tip: Look at the placement of the commas when you see a multiple choice question; certain transitions need a comma while others do not.

Tip: In the beginning of a new paragraph, a transition word is rarely needed.

Transitions - Quiz 1

Place the following words into the transitions category in which they belong.

above all, accordingly, additionally, after all, again, all in all, all things considered, also, although, and, anyhow, as a result, as a rule, as usual, as well as, at the same time, aside from, barring, beside, besides, briefly, but, by and large, by the same token, by the way, by the way, chiefly, comparatively, consequently, conversely, correspondingly, coupled with, despite, due to, ergo, especially, even so, except, excluding, finally, for example, for instance, for the most part, for the same reason, for this purpose, for this reason, furthermore, generally, generally speaking, hence, however, identically, in addition, in any case, in any event, in brief, in conclusion, in contrast, in essence, in fact, in other words, in short, in spite of, in summary, in the final analysis, in the long run, in this case, incidentally, including, instead, ironically, likewise, moreover, namely, nevertheless, notwithstanding, on the contrary, on the other hand, ordinarily, other than, otherwise, outside of, particularly, rather, regardless, save, similarly, since, singularly, so, so then, specifically, still, subsequently, such as, therefore, thereupon, thus, to put it differently, to sum up, to summarize, together with, unfortunately, usually, when, while, with attention to, yet.

Supporting

Cause and Effect

Continuing Thought

Further detail

Generalizing

Summarizing

Opposing

Contrast

Exclusion

Departure

Transitions - Quiz 1 (Answers)

Transitions show a relationship between two parts of a sentence, between two sentences, or between two parts of a paragraph. They can be split into two categories: supporting and opposing. Before you use any transition word, determine the relationship between the two parts that you are trying to connect.

Supporting

Continuing Thought

additionally, again, also, and, as well as, besides, correspondingly, by the same token, for the same reason, furthermore, identically, in addition, likewise, moreover, similarly, subsequently, together with

Cause and Effect

accordingly, as a result, consequently, due to, ergo, for this reason, for this purpose, hence, so, so then, since, therefore, thus, thereupon, when

Further detail

above all, chiefly, coupled with, especially, for example, for instance, in fact, including, in this case, namely, particularly, singularly, specifically, such as, with attention to

Generalizing

as a rule, as usual, briefly, for the most part, generally, generally speaking, in brief, in essence, in other words, in short, ordinarily, usually, to put it differently

Summarizing

after all, all in all, all things considered, anyhow, by and large, in any case, in any event, in conclusion, in short, in summary, in the final analysis, in the long run, finally, to sum up, to summarize

Opposing

Contrast

although, at the same time, but, conversely, comparatively, despite, even so, however, in contrast, instead, in spite of, ironically, nevertheless, notwithstanding, on the other hand, on the contrary, rather, regardless, still, unfortunately, while, yet

Exclusion

aside from, barring, beside, except, excluding, other than, otherwise, outside of, save

Departure

by the way, incidentally

Transitions - Quiz 2

1. Jim did not want to eat any cake today, but, <u>in contrast,</u> I am not going to bake it until tomorrow.
   - A. NO CHANGE
   - B. in any case,
   - C. accordingly,
   - D. particularly,

2. The painting had a very modern style but <u>as a result</u> included a classical theme.
   - A. NO CHANGE
   - B. in spite of
   - C. at the same time
   - D. therefore

3. The school had a no-smoking policy. <u>That is to say,</u> the administration tried to influence the students and faculty to adapt healthier lifestyles.
   - A. NO CHANGE
   - B. Conversely
   - C. Besides
   - D. On the other hand

4. The lyrics to the song were sung rapidly and aggressively although they were <u>likewise</u> a peaceful and emotional message.
   - A. NO CHANGE
   - B. usually
   - C. therefore
   - D. coupled with

5. The professor presented many difficult theories and equations. <u>Even so,</u> he provided easy-to-read charts and graphs.
   - A. NO CHANGE
   - B. In essence,
   - C. Unfortunately,
   - D. As a result,

6. <u>In fact,</u> there were very few A's on the midterm, the students were only concerned with getting a passing grade in the class.
   - A. NO CHANGE
   - B. Although
   - C. After all,
   - D. Subsequently,

7. Johnathan studied medicine <u>and to</u> satisfy his parents' expectations.
   - A. NO CHANGE
   - B. despite of
   - C. mostly to
   - D. in other words to

8. Every student in the algebra class agreed on ending class early <u>such as</u> the students who loved learning mathematics.
   - A. NO CHANGE
   - B. on the other hand
   - C. except for
   - D. inclusive of

9. The jurors assembled in the jury room <u>therefore</u> to determine the subject's sentence.
   - A. NO CHANGE
   - B. for example
   - C. in order to
   - D. delete the underlined word

10. Veronica was the fastest runner. <u>Therefore,</u> she did not win the race.
    - A. NO CHANGE
    - B. Finally,
    - C. In fact,
    - D. However,

1) **B.** There is no contrast in between the two parts of the sentence. There is neither cause and effect nor further detail either. 2) **C.** There is a contrast between the classic theme and the modern style. 3) **A.** The two sentences do not oppose each other. Eliminate answer B, C, and D. 4) **D.** There is a contrast aggressive and peaceful. The word "although," already does a good job of indicating that fact. The next transition word needs to keep that same message, not contradict it. Eliminate answer A, B, and C. 5) **A.** There is a contrast between the difficult theories and the easy-to-read explanations, but it was not "unfortunate". 6) **B.** Look at the commas in this question. Answer A, C, and D all cause a comma splice. 7) **C.** Answer A is not parallel. B is idiomatically incorrect ("despite of satisfy,") and D has a misplaced modifier. (He studied medicine in other words.) They all sound awkward when you read the whole sentence aloud. 8) **C.** The class could be including excluding the math-loving students. Inclusive of is idiomatically incorrect. 9) **D.** No transition is needed. Watch out for C. The extra words are redundant, but when placed in the sentence they also cause an error. ("in order to to determine.") 10) **D.** There is a contrast between fastest runner and not winning the race.

Transitions - Quiz 3

1. Rachel broke her leg <u>as usual</u> on the same day that her best friend, Brittany, was working in the Emergency Room.
   - **A.** NO CHANGE
   - **B.** regardless
   - **C.** coincidentally
   - **D.** conversely

2. Otis ate too much turkey on Thanksgiving. <u>Ironically,</u> he had a stomachache for hours.
   - **A.** NO CHANGE
   - **B.** However
   - **C.** Consequently
   - **D.** For this purpose

3. Julia is a hard-working waitress and just makes enough money to pay the bills. <u>Particularly,</u> Sally is a lazy manager, but makes more money.
   - **A.** NO CHANGE
   - **B.** On the other hand
   - **C.** As usual
   - **D.** Therefore

4. Amanda became very fit <u>instead</u> of her daily workout routine.
   - **A.** NO CHANGE
   - **B.** aside from
   - **C.** as a result
   - **D.** because of

5. The temperatures have been declining over the last few days. <u>Unfortunately,</u> Allie put on a sweater and a scarf.
   - **A.** NO CHANGE
   - **B.** After all,
   - **C.** For this purpose,
   - **D.** consequently,

6. My cat Oliver has long fur that grows <u>quickly; thus</u> he requires a daily brushing.
   - **A.** NO CHANGE
   - **B.** quickly and
   - **C.** quickly, for this reason
   - **D.** quickly, while

7. Jennifer travels long distances for her job. <u>In contrast,</u> she flew to Hong Kong for a meeting last week.
   - **A.** NO CHANGE
   - **B.** For instance
   - **C.** Regardless
   - **D.** Usually

8. <u>Although</u> the tree fell on the school, there will be no class on Monday.
   - **A.** NO CHANGE
   - **B.** Incidentally,
   - **C.** Delete the underlined word
   - **D.** Since

9. Lisa spent her spare time practicing the oboe, going to soccer practice, volunteering at the shelter, and painting her mom's pottery. <u>In summary,</u> Lisa is a well-rounded individual.
   - **A.** NO CHANGE
   - **B.** Ironically
   - **C.** Similarly
   - **D.** Additionally

10. <u>Furthermore,</u> the Eiffel Tower used to be the tallest man-made structure in the world for 41 years. It was finally surpassed in height by the New York Chrysler Building in 1930.
    - **A.** No Change
    - **B.** Although,
    - **C.** Since,
    - **D.** Delete the underlined portion of the text and capitalize "The".

1) C. There is no relationship between the two parts; it was coincidence. 2) C. We need a cause and effect transition. 3) B. There is a contrast between the two sentences. 4) C. Find a transition that indicates cause and effect. Be aware of the double "of" in answer D. 5) D. Answer C and D both have a cause-and-effect transition. However, there is no *purpose* mentioned in the first sentence. 6) A. Watch out for the comma placement in these answers. FANBOYS need a comma while other conjunctions do not. Eliminate B, C, and D. 7) B. There is no contrast in these sentences. Eliminate answer A and C. Her trip to Hong Kong is not a generalization, but a specific detail. 8) D. Answer B and C cause a comma splice. Answer D shows cause and effect. There is no contrast. 9) A. We need a summarizing transition her. 10) D. No transition is needed.

Redundancy in Paragraphs

For most students, the English part of the ACT does not have the time pressure that is a problem for many in the Math, Science, and Reading parts. Instead of skipping from question to question, you actually have time to read the rest of the passage, and you should!

Redundancy = Repeated Information (see page 72)

The ACT likes to hide redundant information in a paragraph. The sentence with the underlined part may be grammatically correct, but the information is repeated.

 Tip: Don't skip from question to question; read the whole text.

Example: Kneeling in church, Amy prayed for her mother, who was in the hospital. Her mom was undergoing a critical operation, and the doctors had warned about possible complications. Worried, Amy had crossed the street to the small church in front of the hospital. Now she was keeping her eyes closed, praying <u>on her knees,</u> and asking for a small miracle.

If you have a habit of only reading the underlined part of the test, you might not have caught the redundant part in the paragraph above: If you are kneeling, then you are already on your knees.

Example: Winni was born and raised in the Netherlands. He learned English in his foreign-language classes during high school. Afterwards, he used his English when he traveled. His knowledge of English was crucial when Winni wanted to attend university classes in the USA. It is ironic that Winni, <u>who is from the Netherlands,</u> now teaches English grammar to native speakers.

Luckily, the ACT often gives its secrets away in its answers: "What should the author do with the underlined part of the sentence?"

    A. Keep it, because it adds an interesting detail to the paragraph.
    B. Keep it, because only people from the Netherlands learn English as a foreign language.
    C. Remove it, because it has nothing to do with the main idea of the paragraph.
    D. Remove it, because the information has already been mentioned in the paragraph.

 Tip: Whenever you see an answer that is similar to answer D above, check the earlier sentences.
Or, as suggested before, make it a habit to read all information in the English test. You probably have enough time, and reading every detail will help you with your rhetorical skills.

Example: Originally, Betsy had wanted to retire after 33 years in the classroom. She was looking forward to reading good books and taking long walks. She did not have plans to start a second career <u>initially</u>. However, when she was offered an exciting position as a Director of Franchise Relations in a growing company, she could not refuse.

The ACT is notorious for is emphasis on concise language. Whenever you have a chance to "delete the underlined portion of the text," pay attention! If the sentence or the meaning of the text does not change significantly, leave it out. If the information is already stated elsewhere (*originally* means the same thing as *initially*) leave it out.

 Tip: When in doubt, leave it out.

Redundancy in Paragraphs - Quiz 1

1. Savanah had waited weeks for the big event. She had stood in the first row during the whole concert. The lead singer had actually reached out and touched her. After the last song, Savanah had waited in vain for an hour to get a glimpse of the group at the backdoor of the theater. <u>Being unsuccessful,</u> she finally called her dad around midnight to come and pick her up. It had not broken her spirit though; she was still humming all the tunes when she walked through her front door.

   A. NO CHANGE
   B. Before heading home,
   C. In the end,
   D. Delete the underlined portion of the text, starting the sentence with She and capitalizing accordingly.

2. "Occasionally, we get large swarms of locusts on our farm," said Jim Trout, an organic farmer. He refused to spray pesticides, even though animals would sporadically eat a significant percentage of his crop. <u>"It does not happen frequently."</u> His wife concurred: "We have tried to discourage the locusts by keeping soil covers, but there is no effective way to keep them away. I guess it is just nature's way."

   A. NO CHANGE
   B. "They do not visit often."
   C. "It occurs sometimes, but not regularly."
   D. Delete the underlined portion of the text.

3. The office party was a success. The director had wanted to reward his staff with some great entertainment and some excellent food. Almost everybody had shown up and most of them had danced to the tunes of the live band. Long after the band had left, he had to remind people that the building was closing because the security and maintenance people needed to go home as well. Therefore, he took the microphone and started to sing a lullaby<u> to remind people that the building was closing</u>.

   A. NO CHANGE
   B. To remind people that the band had left.
   C. To remind people that the office party had been a success.
   D. Delete the underlined portion of the text.

4. During her dad's absence, Alexandra had to put in a lot of extra hours at her small store. She had to open the backdoor by six o'clock each morning, so the delivery van could unload its goods. She had to restock the shelves and haul the large boxes from the storage room to the front by herself <u>because her dad was not there</u>. She was used to closing the store and keeping the books, but the extra physical labor in the morning caused her to collapse into bed each night before eight o'clock.

   A. NO CHANGE
   B. because she had to restock the shelves
   C. although she was only a small woman
   D. Delete the underlined portion of the text

---

1) D It already said that she waited in vain, which means without success. 2) D Occasionally means that it does not happen frequently. 3) D The paragraph already stated elsewhere that the building was closing. 4) D The paragraphs starts with the words: During her dad's absence. This means her dad is not there.

Purpose Questions - Detail

Redundancy = Unnecessary Information
(Information that can be left out because it does not fit in the main focus of the paragraph.)

Example: During my recent trip to Rome, I saw many museums. These museums had a wide variety of art. Many artistic artifacts were paintings by famous artists. Some of those canvases were created by Rembrandt. Rembrandt is a painter from Holland. I really enjoyed my trip to Rome.[1]

1. Which sentence does not belong?
First, determine the main topic of the paragraph. The main topic is "Art in Rome."
Ask yourself, "Which sentence does not talk about the main topic?"
The answer is "Rembrandt is a painter from Holland." The author got off topic here.

Tip: In the ACT, this question is often stated as: "At this place in the text, the author is considering adding / deleting the following statement. Should (s)he?"

Example: In undertaking a study of insects, it is important to know something about what they are, their general nature, appearance, habits, and development. Insects comprise the largest group of animals on the globe.[2] There are about four times as many different kinds of insects as all other kinds of animals combined. Insects vary greatly in size. <u>Some are as large as small birds, while others are so small that a thousand placed in one pile would not equal the size of a pea.</u>[3]

2. At this point in the text, the author wants to add the following sentence: <u>The second largest group is mollusks.</u> Should he?
First, determine the main topic of the paragraph. The main topic is "Insects."
Ask yourself, "Does this sentence talk about the main topic?"
Answer: No. Take it out. The information is unnecessary and distracts from the main topic.

3. The author is considering deleting the underlined sentence because he already talked about size. Should he?
First, determine the main topic of the paragraph. The main topic is "Insects."
Ask yourself, "Does this sentence talk about the main topic?" It does.
The information adds additional details to the main topic. It does not merely repeat a fact.
Answer: Keep it in.

Tip: Each time, ask yourself, "What is the main topic of the paragraph?"

Tip: If the sentence adds a <u>detail about the main topic</u>, keep it! It adds an interesting element.

Tip: If the sentence adds a <u>detail about a detail</u> of the paragraph, take it out. It distracts from the main idea.

Purpose - Quiz 1

Insects are commonly spoken of as "bugs." This term, however, is properly used only when referring to the one order of insects that includes the sap and blood-sucking insects such as the chinch bug, bedbug, squash bug, and the like. <u>The bed bug even has its own expression: don't let the bedbugs bite[1]</u> Then, too, there are many so-called "bugs" that are not insects at all. Spiders, thousand-legs, crawfishes and even earth-worms are often spoken of as bugs<u>, but people often confuse the term "bug" with the proper terminology of other creatures[2]</u>.

1. The author is considering deleting the underlined sentence. Should he?
   A. Yes, because the sentence distracts from the main topic of the paragraph.
   B. Yes, because other bugs also have expressions, like "busy as a bee."
   C. No, because the sentence adds an interesting detail to the paragraph.
   D. No, because there is no similar expression for squash bugs or chinch bugs.

2. The author is considering deleting the underlined part of the sentence. Should he?
   A. Yes, because most people do not care about the correct terminology.
   B. Yes, because that part of the sentence is redundant, as it is already stated elsewhere.
   C. No, because it adds an interesting detail to the main topic.
   D. No, because it is important to know that an earthworm is not a bug.

What must a great singer have? There must be a good vocal basis. There must be a voice capable of development through a sufficient range to encompass the great works written for such a voice.[3] It must be capable of development into sufficient "size" and "power," so that it may fill large auditoriums. <u>Some auditoriums can fill up to 5000 people![4]</u> It must be sweet, true to pitch, clear, and, above all, it must have that kind of an individual quality that seems to draw the musical interest of the average person to it. [5]

3. At this point in the text, the author is considering adding the following sentence:
   Some singers can span a range of four octaves.
   Should he?
   A. No, because the sentence distracts from the main topic of the paragraph.
   B. No, because no singer can actually span four octaves.
   C. Yes, because the sentence adds an interesting detail to the paragraph.
   D. Yes, because it explains how important it is to sing in more than three octaves.

4. The author is considering deleting the underlined sentence. Should he?
   A. Yes, because the sentence distracts from the main topic of the paragraph.
   B. Yes, because most singers sing with microphones these days.

   C. No, because the sentence adds an interesting detail to the paragraph.
   D. No, because size and power are the most important element in the paragraph and the size of the auditorium helps to illustrate this.

5. Feeling that the paragraph is incomplete, the author is considering adding the following detail here:
   Finally, great singers must have a wide vocal range to sing a variety of songs.
   Should he add this sentence?
   A. No, because the sentence distracts from the main topic of the paragraph.
   B. No, because that part of the sentence is redundant as it is already stated elsewhere.
   C. Yes, because it adds an interesting detail to the main topic.
   D. Yes, because range is more important than sweetness and pitch.

1) A This is a detail about a bedbug, which is an example in the paragraph, not the main topic. Take it out.
2) B This information is already stated earlier in the paragraph. It is redundant.   3) C   4) A   5) B

Purpose Questions - Main Idea

Most students consider only the test as a whole or look only at specific sentences. Looking at the formatting of the paragraphs can provide additional insights that help with rhetorical questions.

 Tip: Notice how the English sections are split up in paragraphs.

The tip above might sound obvious, but it is a crucial skill to "think in paragraphs."
In the purpose questions of the previous pages, you might have discovered that …
All the sentences **in a paragraph** are organized along a central theme.

The same is true for the story as a whole:
All the paragraphs in a story have a central theme (the main idea.)

 *Tip: To find the central theme of a story, ask yourself, "What do all **the paragraphs** have in common?"*

Summarize the Paragraph

Summarize the paragraph in **one word** that includes the gist of all sentences.
Review: Are all (or most) sentences about this main idea?
If a sentence of a paragraph focuses on another idea, that sentence is often redundant.

Summarize the Passage

Summarize the passage in **one sentence** that includes the gist of all main topics.
Review: Are all (or most) paragraphs about this main idea?

Students often make two mistakes when answering this type of question.

1. Thinking too small: just because the author mentions something once does not mean it is the **main** theme.
2. Thinking too big: just because the author talked about a detail does not mean he covered the **whole** area.

Look for Repetition of Ideas

If you read through a paragraph and you have no idea how to summarize it because there is so much information, start looking for repeated words, phrases, or similar ideas.

Example: If the author of this book, *Analyze the ACT*, had wanted to write a chapter about the English language, did he do a good job?

A. No, because he did not talk about the English language at all. *(Obviously incorrect)*
B. Yes, because the talked about all kind of different English rules. *(This might be true. However, if you reverse the question, would it still be true? If the author wanted to write a book on the English language, he would have included Beowulf, dialects, England, Shakespeare, etc. This book is more about the English grammar so far.)*
C. No, because he only talks about the English grammar rules that apply to the ACT. *(Correct answer)*
D. Yes, because the book is written in the English language. *(True, but it does not answer the question.)*

Purpose - Quiz 2

Lately, groups of wolves have been spotted in various areas of Eastern Kentucky. Wolves are social animals that hunt in packs. Their leader is called the Alpha wolf. Wolves can be recognized by their large stature and their grey fur. Fur is a popular fashion item these days. Many local citizens are worried about wolves, but these predators are very beneficial to the Eastern Kentucky mountains; they help balance the wildlife ecological cycle and prevent overpopulation of deer and small game. Residents of Eastern Kentucky should be proud of their wolves.

1. This article is mainly about:
   A. Alpha wolves
   B. Eastern Kentucky
   C. Overpopulation of deer
   D. Wild animals

2. The author wanted to write an article about the social interaction of wolves. Would this essay successfully fulfill that purpose?
   A. Yes, because he describes their status in the group and their interaction.
   B. Yes, because he gives a distinct example about the status of the Alpha wolf.
   C. No, because he does not mention social interaction at all.
   D. No, because he writes mostly about the interaction of wolves with their environment.

3. What is the purpose of mentioning the "balancing of the ecological cycle"?
   A. It helps prevent overpopulation of deer and small game.
   B. It shows why wolves have been spotted in various areas of Eastern Kentucky.
   C. It is an example why residents should appreciate wolves.
   D. It is an example why residents are worried about wolves.

4. The author has decided that one sentence is not needed for the intention of this article. Which one should he delete?
   A. Their leader is called the Alfa wolf.
   B. Wolves are social animals that hunt in packs.
   C. Fur is a popular fashion item these days.
   D. Eastern Kentucky residents should be proud of their wolves.

ENGLISH TEST 1

45 Minutes - 75 Questions

The texts in this test are adapted from:

Harpsichords*
      Cynthia A. Hoover

Monopoly
      Ittai Eres

The Hunter
      Arsenio Benitez Jr.

The Hike
      Winni van Gessel

Black Holes
      Hunter Carter

English Test 1

HARPSICHORDS

    The harpsichord, the grandfather of the piano, was an important keyboard instrument in Europe from the 15th through the 18th centuries. The harpsichord and its smaller relatives, the virginal and the spinet, <u>have</u>[1] strings that are plucked. The harpsichord is <u>wing-shaped, most</u>[2] virginals and spinets are either rectangular or polygonal.

    When the harpsichord key is pressed, a wooden jack is raised so that a quill or leather plectrum <u>is inserted</u>[3] into the jack plucks the string. When the key is released, the jack falls back into place, the pivoted tongue allowing the plectrum to pass the string without plucking <u>them.</u>[4] A felt damper (inserted in a slit at the top of the jack) touches the string to stop the sound. [5]

    The design <u>in</u>[6] the harpsichord limits dynamic nuance. Because of <u>its</u>[7] plucking mechanism, the sound of a harpsichord is not

1. **A.** NO CHANGE
    B. has
    C. used to have
    D. had

2. **A.** NO CHANGE
    B. wing-shaped; most
    C. wing-shaped but most
    D. wing-shaped and most

3. **A.** NO CHANGE
    B. inserted
    C. inserts
    D. has inserted

4. **A.** NO CHANGE
    B. those.
    C. these.
    D. it.

5. The writer is thinking of adding the following phrase to the end of the paragraph
    The sound of the harpsichord is sometimes described as "rich and powerful."
    Should the writer make this addition there?
    A. Yes, it is a relevant detail in the history of the harpsichord.
    B. Yes, because it explains how the plucking of the strings causes the desired effect.
    C. No, because it digresses from the main point of the paragraph.
    D. No, because not everybody agrees with that description.

6. **A.** NO CHANGE
    B. from
    C. of
    D. that

7. **A.** NO CHANGE
    B. it's
    C. its'
    D. their

GO ON TO THE NEXT PAGE

greatly altered by <u>increasing, or lessening the</u>

<u>impact</u>[8] of fingers on the keys.

For instance,[9] the tone of a keyboard

instrument is affected by its general outline, the

material and thickness of the soundboard, <u>the</u>

<u>length and material of the strings,</u>[10] and the type of

case construction. The case must be strong enough

to counteract the tension of the strings <u>and</u>

<u>withstand the impact of the hands of the player.</u>[11]

The smaller members of the harpsichord

family, the virginals and spinets, were commonly

found in homes of modest means, as well as in

royal courts. <u>The spinet, a member of the</u>

<u>harpsichord family,</u>[12] was a popular domestic

keyboard instrument in England and America

during the 18th <u>century and was mentioned</u>[13] in

many American diaries and inventories of that

time.

8. **A.** NO CHANGE
    B. increasing or lessening the impact
    C. increasing: or lessening the impact
    D. increasing; or lessening the impact

9. **A.** NO CHANGE
    B. Specifically
    C. Especially
    D. Delete the underlined portion of
    the text, starting the sentence
    with "The tone…

10. **A.** NO CHANGE
    B. the length, and material of the strings
    C. the length and material of the strings;
    D. the length, and material of the strings,

11. Which choice would most logically and
    effectively emphasize the contrast that affects
    the case?
    A. NO CHANGE
    B. yet light enough to allow the sound to
    resonate
    C. and the strength of the material is very
    important
    D. but should not affect the tone of the
    instrument.

12. **A.** NO CHANGE
    B. The spinet, a musical instrument,
    C. The popular spinet
    D. The spinet

13. Which of the following alternatives of the
    underlined text is NOT acceptable?
    A. century. It was mentioned
    B. century; it was mentioned
    C. century, it was mentioned
    D. century, and it was mentioned

GO ON TO THE NEXT PAGE

The spinet had often served[14] as the keyboard instrument for the household that could not afford or did not have room for the harpsichord or organ. [15]

MONOPOLY

In many ways, life is like a game of Monopoly. Not only in its absurd length, but also in its available options and the events that occur.[16] Before even beginning true play, the game requires me to select a piece.[17] Should I be the dog, obedient and humble? Should I choose the car—a fast and reckless beast—in lieu of the moronic thimble?

However,[18] I prefer to use the top hat. While it does convey an aura of serious 1930s' business and determination, it also manages to come across as somewhat droll and comical[19]— just like me.

By the time the banker has finished doling out the Benjamins, everyone, including myself, is reviewing their strategy.[20] Should I aim to get a monopoly on Park Place and Boardwalk? Should I establish my monopoly on the corners of the

14. **A.** NO CHANGE
    B. often would serve
    C. often could serve
    D. often served

15. Suppose the writer's goal had been to write an essay about 18th century instruments. Would this essay accomplish that goal?
    A. Yes, because it discusses several instruments that were played in the 18th century.
    B. Yes, because it focuses on an instrument of the 18th century.
    C. No, because it focuses primarily on keyboard instruments.
    D. No, because only the spinet was played in the 18th century.

16. **A.** NO CHANGE
    B. the events that happen throughout.
    C. its dynamics.
    D. how dynamic it is.

17. **A.** NO CHANGE
    B. the choice of a game piece faces me next.
    C. a piece needs to be selected.
    D. I have to choose a piece.

18. **A.** NO CHANGE
    B. Therefore
    C. Nevertheless
    D. Delete the underlined portion of the text.

19. **A.** NO CHANGE
    B. funny and comical
    C. humorous and comical
    D. comical

20. **A.** NO CHANGE
    B. thinking about their strategy
    C. strategizing
    D. developing their strategy

GO ON TO THE NEXT PAGE

board[21] that will create inescapable gauntlets for my opponents? Perhaps I should not even buy properties this consciously choosing[22] instead to purchase on impulse everyplace on which I land. I find that some combination of careful planning and thoughtless purchasing is best. [23] After all, I can only plan for the future to a certain extent—who knows when I will land on Chance or Community Chest.

The pieces have been picked and the bills were handed out by the banker,[24] but the game cannot commence; the order of play still has to be chosen. Just like in life, each family has its own separate customs and rituals. I have heard people purport[25] that the only fair way to decide is to have everyone roll the dice, and I have heard others swear by playing in order from youngest to oldest in age.[26] I am a staunch supporter of letting the youngest begin and then continuing from there in a clockwise manner. If[27] it was the sneaking suspicion that my parents were in cahoots with each other or my difficulty pronouncing all the railroads (I still had trouble with my R's,) I will never know. Therefore, I feel that it is more than

21. **A.** NO CHANGE
    B. Should I use the corners of the board to establish my monopoly
    C. Should I use the board to use my monopoly on the corners
    D. Should I use the corners of my monopoly to establish the board

22. **A.** NO CHANGE
    B. consciously; choosing
    C. consciously and choosing
    D. consciously, choosing

23. If the author were to delete the previous sentence, the essay would primarily lose
    A. a reflection that reveals the author's strategy.
    B. an example of how conscious the author plays monopoly.
    C. a contrast with the previous sentence.
    D. a description that illustrates the impulsiveness of the author.

24. Given that all the choices are true, which one best describes the players' attitude towards the money in this game?
    A. NO CHANGE
    B. the money was dispersed,
    C. the money has all but been drooled over,
    D. the money was organized in colorful stack around the board,

25. Which of the following alternatives to the underlined word would be LEAST acceptable?
    A. say
    B. claim
    C. pretend
    D. propose

26. **A.** NO CHANGE
    B. according to birthday.
    C. in age, starting with the youngest.
    D. Delete the underlined portion of the text.

27. **A.** NO CHANGE
    B. When
    C. Weather
    D. Whether

GO ON TO THE NEXT PAGE

fitting to cut the "kid" some slack. <u>As for the</u>[28]

clockwise order—well, that is just common sense.

(1) All the preparation to play the actual

bulk of the game—I am still in that section of life.

(2) Unfortunately, I am not sure I can expand this

metaphor any further. (3) The beginning of

Monopoly does not correlate to the beginning of

life. (4) Now, at long last, the game can start. I am

sheltered, and I am still organizing the quick,

tactical thoughts while the money is being passed

out. I am sure, though, that once I leave college

and head off to "the real world," I will run into

plenty of Chance and maybe some Free Parking

here and there. I know I will trade properties with

other players and drag on late into the night.

For now, however, rolling the dice is but a dream.

THE HUNTER

Four months out of the year, my mind is

swarmed with images of tall trees and old enemies.

<u>You see an animal</u>[31] lives inside me. He is

awakened by the smell of competition and

<u>adversity, he</u>[32] loves being tested, so when he

introduced me to the crossbow and a tree stand, I

was instantly hooked.

<u>I have always embraced challenges,</u>[33] and

28. **A.** NO CHANGE
   B. Because of the
   C. Due to the
   D. As the

29. For the sake of logic and coherence, the correct order of the sentences should be
   A. NO CHANGE
   B. 4,2,3,1
   C. 3,2,4,1
   D. 3,2,1,4

30. Suppose the author had wanted to write an essay to explain the general outline of the monopoly game to a person who never played the game before. Would this essay successfully fulfill the writer's goal?
   A. Yes, because the author introduces the game board, the pieces, the street names, the railroads, and many more details.
   B. Yes, because he provides insights about the intention of the game and how it relates to life.
   C. No, because he uses terms that would only be recognized by someone who had played Monopoly before.
   D. No, because he only focuses on the beginning of the game and the rituals.

31. **A.** NO CHANGE
   B. You see, an animal,
   C. You see, an animal
   D. You see an animal,

32. **A.** NO CHANGE
   B. adversity, because he
   C. adversity, therefore he
   D. adversity; he

33. Which of the following statements would provide the best transition to the next paragraph?
   A. NO CHANGE
   B. I had hunted with a gun before, but it was too easy,
   C. I had never used a crossbow before,
   D. The crossbow tested my patience and perseverance,

GO ON TO THE NEXT PAGE

I had learned early on that hunting is the ultimate setting in which <u>natures elements</u>[34] test me physically and mentally. Hunting with a bow and arrow <u>tests</u>[35] my patience and perseverance. The animal and I are continually forced to make decisions that are crucial to our success and <u>finding</u>[36] alternatives to certain situations.

At first, the beast was furious at our inability to succeed in the field. Most things had come naturally to me, so the bitter taste of failure was hard to <u>swallow, however, it</u>[37] motivated me to continue trying. Failure has taught me lessons essential to my success in the field, including <u>hunting and hiking.</u>[38] More <u>importantly, though failure</u>[39] has taught me the importance of self-discipline and perseverance. [40]

34. **A.** NO CHANGE
    B. natures' element's
    C. natures element's
    D. nature's elements

35. **A.** NO CHANGE
    B. test's
    C. test
    D. testing

36. **A.** NO CHANGE
    B. are finding
    C. is finding
    D. to find

37. **A.** NO CHANGE
    B. swallow. however it
    C. swallow, however it
    D. swallow; however, it

38. Given that all the choices are true, which one would give the most specific example of the lessons in the essay?
    A. NO CHANGE
    B. playing the winds and moving stealthily through the woods.
    C. staying on a tree stand and spotting a deer.
    D. self-discipline and perseverance.

39. **A.** NO CHANGE
    B. importantly though, failure
    C. importantly, though failure,
    D. importantly though failure

40. At this place, the author is considering adding the following true statement.
    These lessons have been crucial to my success in other situations.
    Should the author add this sentence here?
    A. Yes, it provides important information about his hunting experience.
    B. Yes, it explains that self-discipline and perseverance lead to success.
    C. No, because it distracts the reader from the main point of this paragraph.
    D. No, because the author already has made this point elsewhere in the essay.

GO ON TO THE NEXT PAGE

Now, each time I head for the <u>woods, that old battlefield at 5 a.m.,</u>[41] I do so with the stealth of a wolf, and my motions flow with the swaying of the trees. Every detail of the forest is an essential clue to <u>me and the animal.</u>[42]

The necessary attributes for a successful hunt have allowed me <u>with success</u>[43] in many other aspects of life. On the soccer field, I practice observation and anticipation. <u>But</u>[44] in the classroom, I persevere through any problem. I am never sure what is waiting for me, but I am ready to <u>work and play.</u>[45]

THE HIKE

During our vacation, we visited a national park and enjoyed a tour with a very knowledgeable guide. He had met us in front of the hotel and we had learned more about the local <u>flora, including the trees and the plants,</u>[46] in the first five minutes than we had picked up in the last two weeks. There were edible plants, carnivorous ones, and even fluorescent mosses throughout the forest. [47]

41. **A.** NO CHANGE
    B. woods that old battlefield at 5 a.m.
    C. woods that old battlefield at 5 a.m.,
    D. woods, that old battlefield, at 5 a.m.,

42. **A.** NO CHANGE
    B. me, and the animal.
    C. I and the animal.
    D. the animal and I.

43. **A.** NO CHANGE
    B. for success
    C. to success
    D. to succeed

44. **A.** NO CHANGE
    B. However,
    C. Although
    D. Delete the underlined word and start the sentence with "In," capitalizing accordingly.

45. Given that all the choices are true, which one would best end the story as a whole?
    A. NO CHANGE
    B. study, work, and play.
    C. pounce, pursue and overcome.
    D. to hunt for it.

46. **A.** NO CHANGE
    B. flora, including the vegetation,
    C. flora, the plant life especially,
    D. flora

47. At this moment, the author is considering adding the following true statement.
    Our guide knew the specifics of every plant and animal we encountered.
    Should the writer add this sentence here?
    A. Yes, it adds an interesting detail to this paragraph.
    B. Yes, it explains why our guide knew so much about nature.
    C. No, because it distracts the reader from the main point of this paragraph.
    D. No, because the author has already made this point elsewhere in the essay.

GO ON TO THE NEXT PAGE

After leading us through the woods for about four miles, our tour guide consulted a map. He explained that he was trying a slightly new route through the forest[48] that was suggested by a colleague. Over the next two hours, he consulted his map with increasing frequency[49] as we hiked along the narrow forest paths.

Finally, we came to a fork in the road, and by the look of confusion on our leader's face, it was clear he was not as sure of the route because he hesitated too much.[50] "I think we need to go left here," he said without conviction. As the sun begun[51] to set, the rest of the hiking party continued to follow because they[52] knew they did not have any better sense of direction themselves. As we rounded a bend that led to a daunting and imposing[53] cliff face, the trek became more difficult with each step.

When we reached level ground again, in the light of the sunset,[54] we found ourselves staring up a large rock wall. Our leader gathered us around and said, "The good news is, that I know exactly where we are now. However, we are

48. **A.** NO CHANGE
 B. on the map
 C. to add to his experience
 D. Delete the underlined portion of the text.

49. **A.** NO CHANGE
 B. with increasingly frequency
 C. with increased frequently
 D. with increasing frequently

50. **A.** NO CHANGE
 B. as he had let on.
 C. that he had wanted to portray.
 D. as he really was.

51. **A.** NO CHANGE
 B. had began
 C. was beginning
 D. began

52. Which of the following alternatives to the underlined words is NOT acceptable?
 A. follow since they
 B. follow as they
 C. follow for they
 D. follow - they

53. **A.** NO CHANGE
 B. daunting, imposing
 C. daunting, imposing,
 D. daunting

54. Which choice provides the most detail about the condition of the hikers during this part of the trail?
 A. NO CHANGE
 B. as we followed our guide,
 C. huffing and puffing,
 D. not looking back,

55. **A.** NO CHANGE
 B. is: that
 C. is that
 D. is that,

GO ON TO THE NEXT PAGE

on the other side of the mountain, and it will take

us a few more hours to get back to the hotel." [A]

We were shocked at his incompetence and

worried about hiking in the dark. [B] We were

certainly going to miss our dinner reservations,

and some people were already exhausted from

what was advertised as <u>a four-hour adventure in</u>

<u>the woods.</u>[56] [C]

   "We should take a small rest before the

long trek back," our tour guide suggested. <u>I</u>

<u>listened</u>[57] to the whispered complaints and hushed

expressions of disbelief, our guide simply stared at

the ground. [D] A few minutes later, he led us

westwards around the cliff and, <u>to our disbelief,</u>[58]

we found ourselves back at the parking lot of our

hotel at six o'clock sharp. The guide could not

stop grinning as he shook hands with the relieved

hikers and collected handsome tips from several

group members <u>that</u>[59] he had tricked, but who

would never again doubt his skills. [60]

56. To highlight the mocking tone of the author, quotations marks can be used
   A. Before and after "four-hour"
   B. Before and after "adventure"
   C. Before and after "in the woods."
   D. Before and after "adventure in the woods.'

57. A. NO CHANGE
   B. I had listened
   C. Because I listened
   D. As I listened

58. Given that all the choices are true, which one would best illustrate how cunning the tour guide had been?
   A. NO CHANGE
   B. as we hiked for another two hours,
   C. as we reversed our steps on the route,
   D. as our guide knew a lot about nature,

59. A. NO CHANGE
   B. which
   C. who
   D. whom

60. The author wants to add the sentence:
   However, there was nothing we could do to change our situation.
   The best placement for this sentence is at Point
   A. A.
   B. B.
   C. C.
   D. D.

GO ON TO THE NEXT PAGE

BLACK HOLES

Black holes are some of the <u>most strange</u> <u>and intriguing</u>[61] phenomena in the universe, and have continued to mystify scientists ever since <u>they</u>[62] were first imagined centuries ago. The first concept of the existence of black holes <u>were</u>[63] posed by physicists and mathematicians in the late 1700s, when scientists predicted <u>through</u> <u>calculation</u>[64] that there could be something in space so dense that not even light would be able to escape its pull.

Back then, black holes were known as "dark stars," a concept <u>which drew</u>[65] the attention of many experts. <u>Even Albert Einstein, as he</u> <u>constructed his theories of general relativity, came</u> <u>across the possibility that gravity could have an</u> <u>effect on light.</u>[66] His insights on gravity and density lead to the belief that, if dense enough, a spherical mass could actually trap light itself. As science progressed, so did the theories of black holes, and soon the speculations solidified into what we know <u>today; a concept</u>[67] that has a mixture of many different theories.

61. **A.** NO CHANGE
B. most strange and most intriguing,
C. strangest and most intriguing
D. strangest and intriguinest

62. **A.** NO CHANGE
B. it
C. those
D. these occurrences

63. **A.** NO CHANGE
B. was
C. would have been.
D. could have been.

64. If the author were to delete the words "through calculation," the essay would primarily lose
A. a description that indicates scientists knew about the size of the black holes
B. an interpretation that describes how scientists knew where the black holes were.
C. nothing, because the author already stated that the scientists were physicists and mathematicians.
D. an indication that the scientist based their prediction on scientific data.

65. **A.** NO CHANGE
B. that drew
C. drawing
D. which draws

66. The author is considering deleting the previous sentence. Should the author do this?
A. No, because Einstein was the first one to conceptualize the black holes.
B. No, because the sentence is needed for the logic and coherence of rest of the paragraph.
C. Yes, because the sentence distracts from the main idea of this paragraph.
D. Yes, because Albert Einstein was a scientist, and this sentence merely repeats information elsewhere in the essay.

67. **A.** NO CHANGE
B. today a concept
C. today: a concept
D. today. A concept

GO ON TO THE NEXT PAGE

Todays' scientists[68] conclude that black holes are the product of collapsed stars and form at the end of a powerful and violent process.[69] When a star begins to collapse on itself, it first expands and becomes denser as it grows. Then, in a process that is famously known as a supernova, it collapses inward. The super-dense core of the star remains and forms the black hole hanging in space[70] about which we speculate today. No scientist has ever seen a black hole, but all the evidence and observations point to the fact that they are for real.[71]

Although we are still gaining information of these[72] cosmic anomalies, the common misconception that they are giant vacuum cleaners that suck up all that surrounds them, continues[73] to persist. Although early scientists were wrong,[74] the simple answer is only partially true. Although black holes do pull in very small amounts of matter that reach them, the vast majority of matter is actually just stuck spinning around its own super-dense center.

Regardless of new information, black holes are still a mystery to most modern scientists and will remain just a theory until we can actually visit them.[75]

68. **A. NO CHANGE**
    B. To day's scientists
    C. Todays scientists
    D. Today's scientists

69. Given that all the choices are true, which one most effectively describes the energetic origin of black holes
    A. NO CHANGE
    B. a long and extensive development.
    C. a progression of unknown proportion.
    D. a mysterious arrays of activities.

70. The best place for the underlined portion of the text is
    A. where it is now.
    B. after the word core.
    C. after the word remains.
    D. after the word speculate.

71. **A. NO CHANGE**
    B. real and they are present.
    C. real and factual.
    D. real.

72. **A. NO CHANGE**
    B. gained from these
    C. about these
    D. for these

73. **A. NO CHANGE**
    B. them continues
    C. them continues,
    D. them; continues

74. Which choice best indicates that this is not the only misconception in this field?
    A. NO CHANGE
    B. Because nobody really knows for sure,
    C. As with many statements in astronomy,
    D. As the truth must be told,

75. Which choice best concludes this essay by providing information that is relevant to the essay as a whole?
    A. NO CHANGE
    B. are now part of every astronomy textbook.
    C. most people actually believe they exist.
    D. early scientists were definitely wrong.

GO ON TO THE NEXT PAGE

END OF THIS TEST
STOP! DO NOT TURN THE
PAGE UNTIL TOLD TO DO SO.

English Test 1 - Answer Key

1. A	16. C	31. C	46. D	61. C
2. B	17. D	32. D	47. A	62. D
3. B	18. D	33. A	48. D	63. B
4. D	19. D	34. D	49. A	64. D
5. C	20. C	35. A	50. B	65. B
6. C	21. B	36. D	51. D	66. B
7. A	22. D	37. D	52. C	67. C
8. B	23. A	38. B	53. D	68. D
9. D	24. C	39. B	54. C	69. A
10. A	25. C	40. D	55. C	70. C
11. B	26. D	41. D	56. A	71. D
12. D	27. D	42. A	57. D	72. C
13. C	28. A	43. D	58. A	73. B
14. D	29. B	44. D	59. D	74. C
15. C	30. C	45. C	60. C	75. A

English – Test 1

Analyze Your ACT, Page 122

Name: _____ Date: _____

Mistakes: _____ ACT Score: _____

Conventions of Standard English

Fragment	Modifier	Pronoun	Punctuation		Other
			Comma		
3	17	4	2	41	32
22	21	7	8	52	34
	48	20	10	55	37
	61	42	13	73	67
	65	59	31		68
	70	62	39		
Page 18	Page 48	Page 64	Page 22		Page 32

Knowledge of language

Idioms	Verb use			Redundancy	Word choice
6	Tense	Agree	Parallel	12	25
28	14	1	16	19	27
43	51	35	36	26	49
50	63			46	
72				53	
				71	
Page 58	Page 81	Page 76	Page 87	Page 72	Page 92

Production of Writing

Clarity	Transition	Order	Purpose		Summary
11	9	29	Detail		
24	18	60	5	58	15
54	33		23	64	30
69	44		38	66	75
74	57	Redundancy	45		
Page 104		40	47		
Tone					
56					
Page 357	Page 108	Page 115	Page 117		Page 119

# mistakes	ACT Score*
58-60	10
55-57	11
52-54	12
49-51	13
46-48	14
43-45	15
40-42	16
38-39	17
36-37	18
34-35	19
32-33	20
30-31	21
28-29	22
26-27	23
24-25	24
22-23	25
20-21	26
18-19	27
16-17	28
14-15	29
12-13	30
10-11	31
8-9	32
6-7	33
4-5	34
1-3	35
0	36

*approximate score

1) Mark your score on the right. Circle the questions you missed. 2) Find your trends (categories with the most mistakes.) Set a goal: How many mastered categories will lead to a 3-point improvement? 3) Study the pages in this book that will help you master the required skills. 4) Review your missed questions.

English Test 1 - Explanations

HARPSICHORDS

1. Answer A is correct because the author is talking about multiple instruments, so the plural form is used. Although the beginning of the passage is written in past tense, the present tense should be used when describing the instruments themselves because they still exist today. Therefore, no change is needed. **(Answer A)**

2. A comma cannot separate two complete sentences (a.k.a. the comma splice). Using the word "but" is incorrect because the second part of the sentence does not contradict the first half. Answer D is incorrect because there is no comma after the word "wing-shaped." A semi-colon is needed because it separates the two complete sentences and also shows that they are related. **(Answer B)**

3. In three choices, the word insert is used as a verb, creating an awkward sentence with two verbs: the quill <u>is inserted</u> in the jack <u>plucks</u> the string. Using *inserted* as an adjective solves the problem: the quill - inserted in the jack - <u>plucks</u> the string **(Answer B)**

4. Answer D is correct because the pronoun in question is referring to the *string* that the plectrum is passing. Therefore, the singular form *it* should be used. **(Answer D)**

5. The paragraph, up to this point, has been focusing on the structure and design of the harpsichord. Adding a sentence about the harpsichord's sound to end the paragraph digresses from the main point. **(Answer C)**

6. Answer C is correct because the words *design* and *of* go together idiomatically. (A design *in* the harpsichord would be an engraving.) **(Answer C)**

7. When you use the possessive form of "it," an apostrophe is not used. An apostrophe is only used when a contraction is needed, such as "it is." **(Answer A)**

8. The semicolon and the colon would need a complete sentence in front of them. The word "or" does not separate two full sentences and does not need a comma in front of it. There is no punctuation needed to separate the parts of the sentence. **(Answer B)**

9. When starting a new paragraph, an author begins a new story. Seldom is there a transition needed from the paragraph before. Words like *specifically* and *especially* indicate that we are still talking about the same subject and therefore these words should appear within the last paragraph. **(Answer D)**

10. This sentence has a list of four items, and some of them have multiple aspects. Normally, you would expect a comma before "and" in a list, but in this case, that serial comma can be found after the word strings. The segment "the length and material of the strings" is the third item of this list and does not need any additional commas. C is incorrect because a semicolon needs to separate two full sentences. When a semicolon is used as a "supercomma, all the items in the list need to be followed by a supercomma, except for the last item. **(Answer A)**

11. Underline the word <u>*contrast*</u> in the question. Answer B is correct because the lightness of the case is contrasted with the strength of the case. The word "yet" also puts emphasis on the contrasting aspects of the statement. **(Answer B)**

12. The paragraph already stated that the spinet is part of the harpsichord family. The fact that the spinet is a popular musical instrument can also be found in the following sentence. Therefore, none of these details needs to be repeated in this sentence. **(Answer D)**

13. A comma, without the word "and" after it, is not an acceptable alternative in this case because a comma cannot separate two complete sentences. **(Answer C)**

14. Only use "had served" is something happened in the past *before* another event happened in the past. In this case, the regular past tense continues the style of the essay. **(Answer D)**

15. Answer C is correct because the essay did not discuss other types of instruments used in the 18th century. Therefore, it cannot be established that this essay covered 18th century instruments in general. **(Answer C)**

MONOPOLY

16. When listing items or when providing a contrast, it is important that the words are used in a parallel form. *Its* absurd length parallels *its* available options, which should be used parallel to *its* dynamics **(Answer C)**

17. In the answer, it looks like *the game* is beginning to play. (dangling modifiers) The only answer that fixes this problem is D, which starts with the person who actually begins to play. **(Answer D)**

18. The underlined portion should be deleted because the start of the paragraph does not contradict or explain the previous paragraph; it merely discusses the writer's choice of game piece. **(Answer D)**

19. *Funny, humorous, droll,* and *comical* all have similar meanings. It is not necessary to have additional adjectives when one adjective can be used to convey the same message. **(Answer D)**

20. The word *everyone* is singular. It cannot be used with the plural pronoun *their.* **(Answer C)**

21. Is it the board that will create inescapable gauntlets? No, and neither are the corners doing this. Modifiers need to be close to the word they describe, so the only correct placement of the words *that will create inescapable gauntlets* is next to the word monopolies. **(Answer B)**

22. Eliminate the wrong answers. Answer A is confusing. It appears that the word *consciously* describes the verb choosing instead of the action of buying properties. Answer B does not provide a full sentence after the semicolon, C provides the wrong tense of the verb choosing. Answer D correctly splits the statement into a full sentence followed by added information after the comma. **(Answer D)**

23. The author poses several questions about possible strategies in this paragraph. The to-be-deleted sentence functions as a detail that provides a possible answer. **(Answer A)**

24. Underline the words *players' attitude towards the money* in the question. All answers provide information about the money, but only answer C describes the behavior (and feelings) of the players: they almost drooled over the money. **(Answer C)**

25. Answer C is the LEAST acceptable alternative to the word "purport" because if the other three options were placed in the underlined portion, the sentence would have the same meaning. **(Answer C)**

26. The underlined portion should be deleted because adding any of the other three options would be redundant. The words "youngest to oldest" already convey the message that the order is based on age. **(Answer D)**

27. Use the word *if* when you provide a solution to a conditional statement. Use the word *whether* when you provide several options. **(Answer D)**

28. Answer B. C and D create awkward sentences. The idiom *As for the* can be translated as *concerning.* **(Answer A)**

29. Sentence 2 and 3 are logically connected in the text. Keep those sentences in that order. The only transition to the rest of the paragraph that makes sense is when sentence 1 is the last statement of the four mixed-up sentences. **(Answer B)**

30. If the purpose of the essay were to explain the game of monopoly to a first-time player, the writer would need to provide a more detailed explanation of the game. There is no further description of terminology, such as "Free Parking," "Community chest," or "Boardwalk" to help a beginner player understand the rules of the game. **(Answer C)**

THE HUNTER

31. There needs to be a comma after "you see" but not after "an animal." "You see" is an intro, used to speak to the reader, and the sentence would still make sense if the section was taken out. "An animal" is not an intro, nor is it added information. Without it, the sentence would no longer make sense. **(Answer C)**

32. The section before the underlined portion is a complete sentence, and the section after the comma is a complete sentence. This is an example of a comma splice. Both B and C use a conjunction with a comma, but neither of them uses a FANBOYS conjunction, A period or a semicolon is needed, as in answer D. **(Answer D)**

33. The next paragraph is about testing the writer's skills. Therefore, "I have always embraced challenges" is a good introduction into this topic. No change is needed. **(Answer A)**

34. Nature, in this sense, is a singular word. There is only one nature being described. Therefore, it needs an apostrophe before the s. Elements is in a plural form because more than one element is being discussed. Therefore, it does not need an apostrophe. **(Answer D)**

35. When the ACT asks you to choose between "test" and "tests", look for the subject-verb agreement. The subject is "hunting," a singular noun that needs a singular verb: tests. Answer B incorrectly uses the possessive case, while answer D creates a fragment. **(Answer A)**

36. Make sure to look at the entire sentence. Since there is an "and" in the sentence, it is split up into two parts. Look at the other parts of the sentence to find the correct tense to use. This sentence is about the speaker and the animal being forced "to make" and forced "to find". Because these two actions need to be parallel, only answer D is correct. **(Answer D)**

37. As written, the word "however" is situated between two commas, but when removed it leaves a run-on sentence. Answer B is incorrect because the first word after the period is not capitalized. Answer C is incorrect because "however" is not a FANBOYS. The only option that separates both parts of the sentence correctly is the semicolon. **(Answer D)**

38. Answer B is correct because the question asks for the most specific lesson, and the other choices are bland and general. **(Answer B)**

39. "More importantly" can sometimes function as an intro, but in this case, the rest of the sentence would be a fragment. A comma needs to be placed after "though." If you remove the intro, "More importantly though," it leaves a complete sentence. This is the only option where this is achieved. **(Answer A)**

40. This essay is all about the failures and challenges of the speaker. The speaker has already mentioned that his failures have led to success in different situations. The statement is not needed in the essay. **(Answer D)**

41. The battlefield and the time of the departure are two separate elements of "added information." Both need separated by commas. The only option that gives a separation of the battlefield <u>and</u> the time is Answer D. Without the added comma, it would appear that *the woods at 5 A.M.* is the battle field. **(Answer D)**

42. Answer A is correct because me is the object in this case. It is clear to me. Not: it is clear to I. The comma in answer B is incorrect. **(Answer A)**

43. Answer D is correct because it is idiomatically correct. You do not say, "This has allowed me for doing something," or "This has allowed me with doing something." The correct idiom is, "this has allowed me <u>to</u> do something." **(Answer D)**

44. The underlined portion is not needed in the sentence because it is not a comparison. Instead, this is a continuation of the same theme of the sentence prior to this one. **(Answer D)**

45. This essay has been about overcoming obstacles and learning from failures. Answer C provides the best description of the overall theme of the essay. Answers A and B are true, but do not describe the theme of the entire essay. Answer D repeats the word "to". **(Answer C)**

THE HIKE

46. Answer D is concise and not redundant. Flora means "plant life." **(Answer D)**
47. The statement adds a new description to the hike and the tour guide that was not previously mentioned. It helps with the flow of the essay, and it follows the theme of the current paragraph. **(Answer A)**
48. It is already stated in the text that the group is traveling through the forest. Since this was already stated, it would be redundant to have the underlined portion in the text. **(Answer D)**
49. Frequency means the number of times something happens. Frequently means that something is happening often. The best choice here is the word "frequency", a noun. A word that described a noun is an adjective (increased), not an adverb (increasingly). **(Answer A)**
50. Watch out for the little word "as". If the guide was *sure*, fine. But in this sentence, it states that he was not *as sure*...... We need an ending that will complete this thought in a parallel manner: "as sure as …" is the correct idiom. (Answer B or D) D is confusing: He was not as sure as he was? Only answer B is correct. **(Answer B)**
51. Begin, began, begun. Do not use the word begun in the simple past tense. **(Answer D)**
52. Answer C is correct because it provides the only conjunction that needs a comma (FANBOYS,) which is not provided in this sentence. **(Answer C)**
53. This is a typical ACT trick. The ACT is looking for the most concise answer that is still correct. In this question, using the word" daunting" for the underlined portion would not change the message of the sentence, and it is grammatically correct. **(Answer D)**
54. Underline the words *condition of the hikers* in the question. Only answer C provides this information. **(Answer C)**
55. Answer A, B and D break all the punctuation rules that are discussed in this book, leaving only answer C as an option. **(Answer C)**
56. The part of the tour that is being ridiculed is the length of the hike. Already four hours had passed, and the hikers were just told it might take another few hours to get back. The adventure takes place in the woods, so nobody can mock those facts, However, since the hikers are frustrated with the time of the hike, "four-hour" should be in quotation marks. **(Answer A)**
57. Watch out for the comma later on in this sentence: answers A and B result in a comma splice. Answer C suggests that the guide stared to the ground *because* I listened. Only answer D creates a grammatically-correct and logic sentence. **(Answer D)**
58. *To our disbelief* indicates that nobody expected this outcome. It indicates that each hiker had been tricked, which proves the craftiness of the guide. **(Answer A)**
59. For who and whom questions, answer the question. "Who" had he tricked? He had tricked HIM. You should have used WHOM. Never use *which* and *that* with people. **(Answer D)**
60. This added sentence needs to go after a sentence that describes the bad situation. The only logical location for this is Location 3. This would conclude the paragraph's message as a whole. **(Answer C)**

BLACK HOLES

61. "Most strange" is a grammatically incorrect; use "strangest" instead. However, this is different for the word "intriguing." There is no superlative such as "the intriguingest"; use "most intriguing" instead. **(Answer C)**

62. The underlined portion is plural, so Answer B is automatically eliminated. Because the sentence could be about multiple topics (black holes, phenomena), the underlined portion needs to be specific. It is not clear whether black holes or phenomena were imagined centuries ago. **(Answer D)**

63. Even though the subject looks plural, it is not. The subject that we need to match with the verb is "the concept", not "the black holes". Answers C and D are wrong because of the incorrect use of the conditional tense. Answer B provides the past tense in the singular form needed. **(Answer B)**

64. Without the underlined portion, it is unclear why the scientists made this prediction. Although the underlined portion is not completely necessary, it adds that the prediction that was made due to scientific data. **(Answer D)**

65. This sentence is written in the past tense. Therefore, eliminate answers C and D. Modifiers that start with the word "which" provide added information and can be deleted. Modifiers that start with the word "that" provide a restricted clause that cannot be deleted from the sentence. **(Answer B)**

66. This question is asking about the sentence before the underlined portion since the word "previous" was used. The previous sentence is a good introduction to the message of the paragraph. If the sentence was deleted, the underlined sentence would not make sense. The first sentence makes the paragraph easy to follow. **(Answer B)**

67. This is a complex sentence. Try to eliminate the wrong answers. A semicolon (A) is incorrect because the second portion is not a complete sentence. Answer D creates a fragment and B creates a run-on sentence. A colon is used for lists and explanations. The last part is indeed an explanation about what we know today. **(Answer C)**

68. An apostrophe after an "s" is used to show that something is possessive. The word 'today" is singular, so it does need an apostrophe before the "s". Read it backwards: the scientists of today. **(Answer D)**

69. The original answer is the most dramatic explanation for the origin of black holes. It is energetic, which is what the question is asking for. **(Answer A)**

70. What hangs in space? Not us, as we speculate (Answer D) nor the core (Answer B) A modifier describes only the word closest to it. The underlined portion is describing the core of the star. And needs to be placed right after it. Currently, the words "about which we speculate today" incorrectly modify the word "space"; they should modify the words "black hole". **(Answer C)**

71. The ACT likes to be as concise as possible. The word "for" is not needed in the sentence because it does not add value. Answers B and C may be true, but they are not as concise as Answer D. Because Answer D does not change the message of the sentence and it is the most concise option, it is the best option. **(Answer D)**

72. The ACT asks here for the correct idiom: which preposition should be used after the words "gain information"? You gain information *about* something, gain information *of* something, or gain information *from* somebody. A and D are idiomatically incorrect. B uses the word gain twice. **(Answer C)**

73. Commas and semicolons would create an incomplete sentence on either side of the punctuation mark. No punctuation is necessary. **(Answer B)**

74. Underline *not the only misconception* in the question. Only answer C provides proof that there are *other statements that are partially true* in astronomy as well. **(Answer C)**

75. The essay talks about the black holes as a theory, which is answered by A **(Answer A)**

ENGLISH TEST 2

45 Minutes - 75 Questions

The texts in this test are adapted from:

The Glue Gun
        Sarah Jeoung

The Museum
        Hunter Carter

Classic Rock
        Hunter Carter

To Wash or Not to Wash
        Joel Parker

Adélie Penguins*
        George Murray Levick

English Test 2

THE GLUE GUN

My glue gun allows me to become a

creator, a designer, an inventor,[1] and a destroyer. I

have been able to piece together a full functioning[2]

arm, to glue beads into

delicate jewelry pieces, to create a tree from

scratch, and fix bathroom tiling.[3]

Because[4] being a creator gives me

opportunities to transform materials packed with

potential into never-before-seen constructions, I

find myself transitioning from an inventor to a

demolisher in a flash. As a destroyer, I have

melted counter tops; deformed[5] my sister's plastic

figurines, and severed my parents' trust[6] for a

period of time. Each destruction was caused by

idleness and curiosity, which, at one time, cost me

not only my pride, but also the use of my hands

for five minutes.

I was home alone for a couple of

hours when a "brilliant"[7] question came into

1. **A.** NO CHANGE
    B. a creator, who designs and invents things,
    C. a creator, who makes things,
    D. a creator

2. **A.** NO CHANGE
    B. fully function
    C. fully functioning
    D. full function

3. **A.** NO CHANGE
    B. fixing bathroom tiling.
    C. to fix bathroom tiling.
    D. I fix bathroom tiling.

4. **A.** NO CHANGE
    B. While
    C. Therefore,
    D. However,

5. **A.** NO CHANGE
    B. tops, and deformed
    C. tops, deformed
    D. tops, and I deformed

6. **A.** NO CHANGE
    B. parent's trust
    C. parents's trust
    D. parents trust

7. If the writer were to remove the underlined
    portion of the text, the passage would lose
    information that
    A. indicates how intelligent the question was.
    B. clarifies that the type of question was
    unusual for the author.
    C. indicates an irony that unfolds later in the
    story.
    D. provides evidence of the intelligence of the
    author.

GO ON TO THE NEXT PAGE

142

my mind. Rushing up the stairs, <u>my glue gun</u>

<u>was ready on my desk,</u>[8] and I packed glue

sticks into the end. Once the glue oozed out

<u>onto my palms; I slapped</u>[9] my hands together. I

held my breath in anticipation of pain as I stared at

my glued hands. Instead of pulling my hands apart

as a normal person would, I decided to <u>wait:</u>[10] glue

needs time to dry, and this particular experiment

was no exception.[11]

However,[12] when I could not wait any

longer and tried to pull them apart, my hands

would not budge. Panic settled in, and I began to

shake as my palms started to tingle. As time

passed, the prickling and aching sensation

worsened, and I felt the blood rush to my head.

Flustered and frantic, I stumbled to the bathroom,

twisted the knob with my elbows, and <u>I drenched</u>[13]

my hands with hot water.

8. **A.** NO CHANGE
   B. I quickly grabbed my glue gun,
   C. my desk displayed the glue gun,
   D. the idea of using my glue gun became more detailed,

9. **A.** NO CHANGE
   B. onto my palms, I slapped
   C. onto my palms, and I slapped
   D. onto my palms. I slapped

10. **A.** NO CHANGE
    B. wait and not pull my hands apart
    C. wait, unlike a normal person
    D. wait because this was an experiment

11. At this moment, the author wants to add the following sentence:
    All glues have different dry times, which can vary from seconds to minutes.
    Should she?
    A. Yes, the drying time of glue is important in this story, and it adds an interesting detail to the paragraph.
    B. Yes, because without this information the reader would not know why the author is waiting to pull her hands apart.
    C. No, because it digresses from the main point in the paragraph.
    D. No, because the dry time of glue has already been discussed.

12. **A.** NO CHANGE
    B. Although,
    C. Therefore,
    D. Delete the underlined portion of the text, capitalizing "When" accordingly.

13. **A.** NO CHANGE
    B. drenched
    C. then I drenched
    D. I commenced to drench

GO ON TO THE NEXT PAGE

When I realized that water had absolutely no effect on the glue, I decided that I had nothing to lose and deliberately peeled my hands apart. I clenched my jaw and slowly separated my palms, ripping layers of skin from both sides.

Who knew that gluing your hands together would later make your parents wary to leaving[14] you alone?

THE MUSEUM

"Art is not simply what you see on the canvas, art[16] is what it makes you feel." The curator tried to inspire the clearly unimpressed teens as he waded into the middle of the group. "Art is an expression across the mediums[17] of the emotions of the artists who dared stroke their pens, brushes, or pencils," the curator lectured. "It is something to appreciate, to[18] find your own meaning within - rather than to take at face value." The teenagers continued to look unimpressed; they were more involved with their cell phones then[19] with the millions of dollars of inspiration that surrounded them. A few students were a bit more involved, taking[20] pictures of works from various well-known artists, such as:[21] Monet, Degas, and Raphael. But at the back of the tour, I was taking it

14. **A.** NO CHANGE
    B. of leaving
    C. for leaving
    D. leaving

15. The main purpose of the story was
    A. to inform people not to leave their children home alone.
    B. to discuss the properties of glue.
    C. to discuss the details of a science experiment.
    D. to tell people not to glue their hands together.

16. **A.** NO CHANGE
    B. canvas, and art
    C. canvas, however art
    D. canvas; art

17. The best placement for the underlined portion of the sentence would be
    A. where it is now.
    B. after the word emotions.
    C. after the word artists.
    D. after the word pencils.

18. **A.** NO CHANGE
    B. appreciate; to
    C. appreciate - to
    D. appreciate to

19. **A.** NO CHANGE
    B. there cell phones than
    C. their cell phones than
    D. there cell phones then

20. **A.** NO CHANGE
    B. involved, they took
    C. involved; taking
    D. involved, because they were taking

21. **A.** NO CHANGE
    B. artists: such as
    C. artists, such as
    D. artists, such as,

GO ON TO THE NEXT PAGE

all in; I reveled[22] in the history and beauty of such a collection.

The tour of the Louvre had more than one implication for an experienced[23] art student such as myself. It was not as if I had not studied many of these works before, but I had seen most of them in books or on my computer screen. Actually being here was a completely different experience. The images felt so much more alive than a textbook page or an image search. [24] I especially felt this as we stopped at the statues. Handcrafted by the finest artists in history,[25] it was a surreal experience to walk around them and taken[26] in every perfection and every flaw, both equally amazing.

The tour was a special treat in itself, as there were hardly any people in the museum at the time. Our educational tour had began[27] just before the crowds started to flood the gilded halls. Our headmaster was a good friend of the curator, who's[28] expertise in the field was well known as a consultant for various organizations that grew with his every word of advice. Because of this special friendship, our school has had more visiting artists, lectures, and art electives than any other institute in our state.

22. Which alternative to the underlined words is NOT acceptable?
   A. all in because I reveled
   B. all in, I reveled
   C. all in. I reveled
   D. all in as I reveled

23. Which choice would best reflect the desires of the author?
   A. NO CHANGE
   B. aspiring
   C. inspiring
   D. diligent

24. At this point, the author is considering to add the following sentence:
   The art in the books was of much better quality than the images on my computer.
   Should the author add this sentence here?
   A. No, because the art in the museum was even better than in the pictures.
   B. No, because the sentence distracts from the main point of this paragraph.
   C. Yes, because the quality of art in books and on screen is obviously very important.
   D. Yes, because the sentence adds an important detail to the story.

25. A. NO CHANGE
   B. Surrounded by all the masterpieces,
   C. As I looked at the paintings,
   D. Awed by the inspiring artwork,

26. A. NO CHANGE
   B. taking
   C. have taken
   D. to take

27. A. NO CHANGE
   B. had begun
   C. began
   D. was beginning

28. A. NO CHANGE
   B. whom
   C. whose
   D. who

GO ON TO THE NEXT PAGE

I myself aspire to be an expert one day. However, I want to apply my skills in a more modern <u>field, because</u>[29] slowly but surely pencils and brushes have been surpassed by styluses and touchscreens. While some may weep for the nostalgia of older ways, new technology has let me take my designs and my applications to a completely new level. This trip to the Louvre, courtesy of our headmaster and tutor, was bound to be <u>remembered by all students for a long time</u>.[30]

CLASSIC ROCK

As a newly-graduated student of music, I did not want to be a starving artist, and my first attempts at making a living after college <u>was less exciting</u>[31] than I had imagined. I played at weddings, champagne parties, wine tastings, and a host of <u>other black tie and invitation only events</u>,[32] which resulted in financial gains <u>at the cost to</u>[33] my spirit and my dignity. On the bright side, I had assembled a small ensemble to accompany me on certain occasions, and some of <u>its</u>[34] members were bright, creative musicians, who <u>nevertheless</u>[35] played all the classical pieces in a flawless manner. However, everything changed when my brother got married.

29. **A.** NO CHANGE
    B. field because
    C. field: because
    D. field; because

30. Which choice would best end the essay and connect to the main idea?
    A. NO CHANGE
    B. a source of inspiration for my upcoming projects.
    C. a wonderful experience, because the expertise of the curator.
    D. inspiring, because of the wonderful details in the canvases and the statues.

31. **A.** NO CHANGE
    B. had not been exciting
    C. were less exciting
    D. is less exciting

32. **A.** NO CHANGE
    B. other black-tie and invitation-only events,
    C. other black-tie-and-invitation only events,
    D. other blacktie and invitationonly events,

33. **A.** NO CHANGE
    B. at the cost for
    C. at the cost of
    D. the cost of

34. **A.** NO CHANGE
    B. it's
    C. its'
    D. their

35. If the author were to leave out the underlined word in this sentence, the essay would primarily lose
    A. the author's contrast with the creativity and the brightness of the musicians.
    B. the author's contrast between the author and the other musicians.
    C. the author's contrast between playing music and accompanying others.
    D. the author's contrast between creativity and playing classical music.

GO ON TO THE NEXT PAGE

146

My brother was a much different person than I, in practice and profession. An architect by trade, his skill with ink and chalk was comparable[36] to my craft of beat and note. Recently, his designs had landed him an impressive contract with a different[37] firm in New York. He decided that was a perfect time to propose to his long-time sweetheart, and I did[38] not take much convincing to get me to sign on as the musical event of the reception. The bride-to-be had a soft spot for the classics, however, my brother[39] and I shared more than blood and a last name: we shared an obsession with rock and roll. He asked me if I could compose something "Just for us," and his wink meant to me that he was not referring to[40] the soon-to-be-wed couple.

On the day of the wedding, the ceremony passed without a hitch under the beautiful decorations of the chapel. My older brother said, "I do" and began his new life with his dearly beloved. The band and I played popular tunes such as the *Peer Gynt Suite*[41] *No. 1*, the *Ride of the Valkyries* and *Beethoven's 5th*. I even managed to try out a classical composition, that I had composed[42] in my senior year, and it was well received by the posh crowd.

36. **A.** NO CHANGE
    B. my brother had a skill with ink and chalk that was comparable
    C. my brother's skill with ink and chalk was comparable
    D. with ink and chalk, his skill was comparable

37. Which choice would most logically and effectively emphasize the status of the New York firm?
    A. NO CHANGE
    B. reputable
    C. architectural
    D. designing

38. **A.** NO CHANGE
    B. they did
    C. it did
    D. he did

39. **A.** NO CHANGE
    B. classics; however, my brother
    C. classics however, my brother
    D. classics, however my brother

40. Which of the following alternatives to the underlined portion would NOT be acceptable?
    A. talking about
    B. referring
    C. alluding to
    D. mentioning

41. **A.** NO CHANGE
    B. tunes such: as the Peer Gynt Suite
    C. tunes such as: the Peer Gynt Suite
    D. tunes, such: as the Peer Gynt Suite

42. **A.** NO CHANGE
    B. composition that I had composed
    C. composition, which I had composed
    D. composition which I had composed

GO ON TO THE NEXT PAGE

When it was time for the <u>newlyweds first dance</u>,[43] I bid homage to my sibling with a raised glass [A]. Then, my cellist began to play the opening notes of AC/DC's heavy metal classic *Thunderstruck* [B]. We then flurried through a montage of hits by Queen, Metallica, Meatloaf and Bon Jovi, all played on string instruments and piano [C]. The crowd was visibly <u>taken</u>,[44] [D] but my brother could not have looked happier, and that was all that mattered. [45] After the performance, a few guests who had also reveled in the combination of classic and modern music approached me, and my career as a classic-rock musician took its first steps.

TO WASH OR NOT TO WASH

It seems preposterous to think of <u>eggs, displayed</u>[46] in outdoor markets for people to buy, but in many parts of the world that's exactly how they are sold. Outside of the United States, many countries do not refrigerate their eggs, but how is that possible? In America, eggs that aren't refrigerated quickly become <u>rotten and unpleasant</u>,[47] but that doesn't seem to be the <u>case</u>[48] abroad. <u>Eggs</u>[49] are kept for many weeks outside the fridge without an issue. In a supermarket in

43. **A.** NO CHANGE
    B. the newlyweds' first dance
    C. the newly weds' first dance
    D. the newlywed's first dance

44. **A.** NO CHANGE
    B. taken aback,
    C. taken in,
    D. taken up,

45. Upon review, the author realizes that the following information has been left out of the paragraph.

    followed in kind by the rest of the band

    These words would most logically be placed at point
    A. A.
    B. B.
    C. C.
    D. D.

46. **A.** NO CHANGE
    B. eggs; displayed
    C. eggs displayed
    D. eggs - displayed

47. **A.** NO CHANGE
    B. rotten and bad
    C. rotten and decaying
    D. rotten

48. Which of the following alternatives to the underlined portion would NOT be acceptable?
    A. situation
    B. circumstance
    C. location
    D. problem

49. **A.** NO CHANGE
    B. There, eggs
    C. Many eggs
    D. All eggs

GO ON TO THE NEXT PAGE

Great Britain you can find them next to the bread while in India they can be found <u>in outdoor markets,</u>[50] and nobody seems to get sick from eating these eggs. So why are American eggs so finicky <u>about their location?</u> [51]

The answer <u>lies</u>[52] in the cleanliness of the eggs, believe it or not. When eggs are harvested on farms, they are often fairly dirty. They could have debris or feces stuck to them, and this idea is unsettling to American consumers. In order to solve this problem, American egg producers thoroughly wash their eggs so that they are clean and safe for the American public to consume. <u>A hot, soapy shower</u>[53] that leaves the eggs squeaky clean, but stripped of something that each of the unwashed eggs <u>have:</u>[54] a slight luster that covers them. While this seems like nothing major, it compromises the integrity of the egg dramatically.

The lustrous coating of unwashed eggs <u>serve</u>[55] not only to make them shine in the light, but also to protect them from harmful bacteria that can seep in through micro-cracks in washed egg shells. The coating fills in these <u>cracks acts</u>[56] as a shield to anything harmful that might want to spoil the eggs. Because of this coating, unwashed eggs w<u>ould</u>[57] be kept in most any environment without too much

50. Considering that all choices are true, which choice would provide new information to this essay?
   A. NO CHANGE
   B. outside the fridge,
   C. outdoors,
   D. displayed on a peddler's cart,

51. Which choice provides the best ending for this paragraph?
   A. NO CHANGE
   B. about their temperature?
   C. about their taste?
   D. about their status?

52. A. NO CHANGE
   B. lays
   C. is lieing
   D. is laying

53. A. NO CHANGE
   B. They take a hot, soapy shower
   C. A disinfecting shower
   D. Companies use a hot, soapy shower

54. A. NO CHANGE
   B. are having:
   C. were having:
   D. has:

55. A. NO CHANGE
   B. serves
   C. serving
   D. served

56. A. NO CHANGE
   B. cracks, acts
   C. cracks and acts
   D. cracks, and acts

57. A. NO CHANGE
   B. are
   C. could have been
   D. can

GO ON TO THE NEXT PAGE

worry, though they do not have a very long shelf-

life. The washed eggs, on the other hand, are

<u>incredibly</u>[58] susceptible to bacterial contamination.

In order to prevent any consequences of

contamination, these washed eggs must be

refrigerated from the time <u>their</u>[59] washed until they

go into the skillet.

A positive aspect of washing eggs is that the

refrigeration that comes as a consequence can more

than double their shelf life. Refrigeration comes

with a cost, though. The fact that the eggs must be

completely refrigerated from farm to store means

that the monetary cost of moving them is incredibly

high. The cost is so high that most countries

wouldn't have the ability to sustain the practice—

hence the unwashed eggs. All things considered,

the practice of washing or not washing eggs seems

mostly subjective and both methods work for their

individual markets. [60]

ADÉLIE PENGUINS

(1) The penguins of the Antarctic <u>regions,</u>

<u>very rightly</u>[61] have been termed the true

inhabitants of that country. (2) Its proficiency in

the water has been gained at the expense <u>over</u>[62] its

power of flight, but this is a matter of small

58. Which choice maintains the essay's tone of wonder and inquiry and provides detail about the level of contamination?
A. NO CHANGE
B. hardly
C. vulnerable and
D. Delete the underlined portion of the text.

59. A. NO CHANGE
B. there
C. they're
D. their'

60. Suppose the writer's primary purpose had been to stop the practice of washing eggs in the United States. Would this essay accomplish that purpose?
A. Yes, because it describes how the process is flawed and makes the eggs susceptible to contamination.
B. Yes, because it describes how the rest of the world does not wash their eggs at all.
C. No, because it provides arguments both for and against washing eggs.
D. No, because American laws require the eggs to be washed.

61. A. NO CHANGE
B. regions very rightly
C. regions, very rightly,
D. regions very rightly,

62. A. NO CHANGE
B. for
C. to
D. of

GO ON TO THE NEXT PAGE

concern. (3) To a degree far in advance of any other bird, the penguin has adapted itself to the sea to such a means of livelihood that it rivals the fish. (4) The species is of great <u>antiquity; fossil remains</u>[63] of their ancestors having been found that showed they flourished as far back as the Eocene epoch. [64]

In few other regions could such an animal as the penguin rear its young; when on land, its short legs offer no advantage as a means of moving around, and, as it cannot fly, it would become an easy prey to any of the carnivores <u>that abound in other parts of the globe.</u>[65] Here, there are none of the bears and foxes that inhabit the North Polar <u>regions, so,</u>[66] once ashore, the penguin is safe.

The reason for this state of affairs is that there is no food of any description to be found inland. Ages back, a different situation existed: tropical forests abounded, and at one time, the seals ran around on the shore like dogs. As conditions <u>changed and became different,</u>[67] these latter had to take to the sea for food, with the result that their four legs, in course of time, gave place to wide paddles or "flippers," as the penguins' wings have done, <u>so that at length</u>[68] they became true

63. **A.** NO CHANGE
    B. antiquity, fossil remains
    C. antiquity and fossil remains
    D. antiquity, because fossil remains

64. For the sake of logic and consistency, the order of the numbered sentences in this paragraph should be:
    A. 1, 2, 4, 3
    B. 1, 3, 4, 2
    C. 1, 4, 2, 3
    D. 1, 4, 3, 2

65. Given that all the choices are true, which one would provide the most detail about the number of carnivorous animals that might prey on penguins?
    A. NO CHANGE
    B. that share their territory with the Adélie penguins.
    C. that attack the penguins because penguins cannot fly.
    D. that could wipe out a colony of 50 penguins within weeks.

66. Which of the following alternatives of the underlined text is NOT acceptable?
    A. regions, and,
    B. regions, therefore,
    C. regions, and so,
    D. regions, so, therefore,

67. **A.** NO CHANGED
    B. changed into new conditions,
    C. changed and altered,
    D. changed,

GO ON TO THE NEXT PAGE

inhabitants of the sea.

Was[69] the sea-leopards (the Adélies'

worst enemy) to take to the land again, there

would be a speedy end to all the southern penguin

colonies. As only[70] these, however, are inhabited

during four and a half months of the year, the

advantage to the seals in growing legs again would

not be great enough to influence evolution in that

direction. At the same time, I wonder why the sea-

leopards, who can move along at a fair pace on

land, have not crawled up the few yards of ice that

stands[71] between the water and some of the

colonies. Even if they could not catch the old

birds, the sea-leopards would reap a rich harvest

among the chicks, the hatchlings, and the baby

penguins[72] when these are hatched. Fortunately,

however, they never do this.

When you look at the bird through your

binoculars from the boat,[73] the Adélie penguin

gives you the impression of a smart little man in

an evening dress suit, so absolutely immaculate is

he, with his shimmering white front and black

back and shoulders. His carriage is confident as he

approaches you over the snow, curiosity in his

68. **A.** NO CHANGE
    B. because at length
    C. but at length
    D. additionally, at length

69. **A.** NO CHANGE
    B. Were
    C. Had
    D. Delete the underlined portion of the text.

70. For the sake of logic and clarity, the word *only* in this sentence should be placed
    A. where it is now.
    B. after the word during.
    C. before the word growing.
    D. after the word evolution.

71. **A.** NO CHANGE
    B. stand
    C. is standing
    D. has been standing

72. **A.** NO CHANGE
    B. the chicks and the baby penguins
    C. the chicks and the hatchlings
    D. the chicks

73. **A.** NO CHANGE
    B. When you look through your binoculars at the bird from the boat,
    C. When you look from the boat through your binoculars at the bird,
    D. When you look through your binoculars from the boat at the bird,

GO ON TO THE NEXT PAGE

every movement. When within a yard or two of

you, as you stand silently watching him, he halts,

poking his head forward with little jerky

movements, first to one side, then to the other,

using his right and left eye alternately during his

inspection. [74]

After a careful inspection, he may

suddenly lose all interest in you, and, ruffling up

his feathers, sink into a doze. Stand still for a

minute till he has settled himself to sleep. Then,

make just enough sound to wake him up without

startling him, and he opens his eyes, stretching

himself, yawns, then finally walks off, caring no

more about you.

74. At this point, the author is considering adding the following sentence:
   His demeanor reveals confidence and curiosity.
   Should the author add this sentence here?
   A. No, because his eyes show that the penguin is not sure of himself.
   B. No, because the information has already been stated in the essay.
   C. Yes, because the paragraph is about the demeanor of the Adélie penguin and this fact provides an interesting detail.
   D. Yes, Because the word *inspection* reveals that the penguin is fully in charge.

75. Suppose the author had wanted to write an essay about the social interactions of Adélie penguins. Would this essay successfully fulfill the writer's goal?
   A. Yes, because the author provides details about the birds, the environment, its predators and its demeanor.
   B. Yes, because the author notes how the birds interact in families and how they raise their chicks in colonies.
   C. No, because he writes mostly about the interactions between the penguins and their harsh environment.
   D. No, because he does not mention any social interactions at all.

END OF THIS TEST
STOP! DO NOT TURN THE
PAGE UNTIL TOLD TO DO SO.

English Test 2 - Answer Key

1. **D**	16. **D**	31. **C**	46. **C**	61. **B**
2. **C**	17. **D**	32. **B**	47. **D**	62. **D**
3. **C**	18. **C**	33. **C**	48. **C**	63. **A**
4. **B**	19. **C**	34. **A**	49. **B**	64. **D**
5. **C**	20. **A**	35. **D**	50. **D**	65. **A**
6. **A**	21. **C**	36. **B**	51. **B**	66. **B**
7. **C**	22. **B**	37. **B**	52. **A**	67. **D**
8. **B**	23. **B**	38. **C**	53. **D**	68. **A**
9. **B**	24. **B**	39. **B**	54. **D**	69. **B**
10. **A**	25. **C**	40. **B**	55. **B**	70. **B**
11. **C**	26. **D**	41. **A**	56. **C**	71. **B**
12. **D**	27. **B**	42. **B**	57. **D**	72. **D**
13. **B**	28. **C**	43. **B**	58. **A**	73. **C**
14. **B**	29. **B**	44. **B**	59. **C**	74. **B**
15. **C**	30. **B**	45. **B**	60. **C**	75. **C**

English Test 2

Name: _____ Date: _____

Mistakes: _____ ACT Score: _____

Conventions of Standard English

Fragment	Modifier	Pronoun	Punctuation		
			Comma		Other
53	8	28	9	46	5
	17	34	16	56	6
	25	38	20	61	18
	36	59	21	63	32
	70		22	66	39
	72		29		41
	73				43
Page 18	Page 48	Page 64	Page 22		Page 32

Knowledge of language

Idioms	Verb use			Redundancy	Word choice
	Tense	Agree	Parallel	1	2
14	27	31	3	10	19
33	57	54	13	47	40
62	69	55	26	67	42
	71				44
					48
					52
Page 58	Page 81	Page 76	Page 87	Page 72	Page 92

Production of Writing

Clarity	Transition	Order	Purpose	
			Detail	Summary
23	4	45		
37	12	64	7	15
65	49		24	30
	68	Redundancy	35	60
Page 104		11	51	75
Tone		50	74	
58				
Page 357	Page 108	Page 115	Page 117	Page 119

# mistakes	ACT Score*
53-55	10
51-52	11
49-50	12
48	13
46-47	14
44-45	15
41-43	16
39-40	17
37-38	18
35-36	19
33-34	20
30-32	21
28-29	22
26-27	23
24-25	24
22-23	25
20-21	26
18-19	27
16-17	28
14-15	29
12-13	30
10-11	31
9	32
6-8	33
4-5	34
1-3	35
0	36

*approximate score

1) Mark your score on the right. Circle the questions you missed. 2) Find your trends (categories with the most mistakes.) Set a goal: How many mastered categories will lead to a 3-point improvement? 3) Study the pages in this book that will help you master the required skills. 4) Review your missed questions.

English Test 2 - Explanations

THE GLUE GUN

1. All three words (creator, designer, and inventor) have similar meanings. The ACT likes to be as concise as possible, so using all three words is not necessary for the sentence. **(Answer D)**
2. The first word of the underlined portion needs to be "fully" because it is describing the function of the arm. The second word of the underlined portion needs to be "functioning" because it is describing the arm itself. **(Answer C)**
3. In a list, maintain parallel structure. Each action begins with the word "to", so the underlined portion should also start this way. **(Answer C)**
4. Answers C and D are incorrect because nothing in the previous sentence causes a contrast or explanation. A new paragraph seldom starts with a transition. In this sentence, the author is comparing her role as a creator and as a demolisher. "Because" creates a cause and effect relationship. Answer B offers the correct wording for a comparison. **(Answer B)**
5. The underlined portion separates ideas that are part of a list. There are more items in the list after the comma, therefore "and" is not necessary. Eliminate answer B and D. If a semicolon separates the parts of a list (as a supercomma) it needs to separate *all* parts, not just two of them. Eliminate answer A. Option C has the correct punctuation. **(Answer C)**
6. There are multiple parents being discussed in this underlined portion. Therefore, the form of parents needs to be plural. This eliminates Answer B. Answer C is incorrect because "parents's" is not a correct form of a possessive noun. Answer D is incorrect because the underlined portion lacks the possessive apostrophe. Read it backwards: the trust of my parents. No change is needed. **(Answer A)**
7. The use of quotations provides the clue for the answer to this question. Answers A and D are incorrect because there would be no use for quotations if the word "brilliant" was used without irony. Answer B is incorrect because it has nothing to do with the type of question the author is mentioning. Answer C is the only possible answer, even without reading the rest of the story. **(Answer C)**
8. Who is rushing up the stairs? Not my glue gun! This is a problem with a dangling modifier. Modifiers need to be placed close to the word they describe. Only Answer C starts with the pronoun of the person who performs the action. **(Answer B)**
9. Because the word "once" was used in a way that signifies a break in the sentence, a comma is needed between "palms" and "I". Otherwise there would be an incomplete or run-on sentence. **Answer B)**
10. Look for the answer that is the most concise. Answer B, C and D all have redundant elements that are mentioned elsewhere in this paragraph. The original option is concise, and does not leave out any additional information. **(Answer A)**
11. The point of this paragraph is to explain how glue got on the author's hands. It is not to explain the different drying times of glue. Therefore, this sentence should not be added because it distracts from the main idea of the paragraph. **(Answer C)**
12. This sentence is not contradicting the previous thought. It is the start of a new paragraph; therefore, it is the beginning of a new thought. The underlined portion is not needed in the sentence because of this. **(Answer D)**
13. This underlined portion is part of a list of actions. The action right before the underlined portion does not use the word "I", so this one should not either. Whenever there is a list, maintain parallel structure in all parts of the list. **(Answer B)**
14. The correct idiom is *to be wary of something*. Only Answer B has the correct preposition. **(Answer B)**
15. Answer A is incorrect because the purpose was not to tell a terrible story about a child being left alone. Answer B is incorrect because the properties of glue were not discussed at length. Answer D is incorrect because this was not a story teaching people what not to do. Answer C is the best answer because it is about the details of a science experiment the author conducted. **(Answer C)**

THE MUSEUM

16. These are two complete sentences that are related. Therefore, a semicolon is the best option for the punctuation needed. **(Answer D)**
17. Place the words "across the mediums" at all four alternative points in the sentence. Does it talk about the artists, the emotions, or the expressions? No. The word "medium" refers to the pieces of art that require pens, brushes, and pencils. Therefore, placing the underlined portion after the word "pencils" is the best option. "stroke their pens, brushes, and pencils across the mediums". **(Answer D)**
18. Dashes can be used as a separation of thought. Just like two commas, two dashes signify a portion of the sentence that could be deleted (and the sentence still makes sense), but adds value to the sentence. **(Answer C)**
19. "Their" signifies ownership. "There" is a direction. "Then" is part of a sequence of events. "Than" is a word used for comparison. **(Answer C)**
20. This underlined portion does not need a change. Answer B is incorrect because it would create two complete sentences. Therefore, a period or semicolon is needed. Answer C is incorrect because semicolons separate two complete sentences, and there are not two complete sentences. Answer D is incorrect because the word *because* is not one of the FANBOYS and therefore does not need a comma. **(Answer A)**
21. If a colon is used, the words "such as" are not necessary. A colon needs to be proceeded by a full sentence and followed by a list or explanation. Two commas around "such as" would incorrectly indicate you could leave that segment out without any other punctuation. The sentence does need a comma between "artists" and "such as" (added information). **(Answer C)**
22. These two complete sentences are related to each other. This means that a semicolon or a period is acceptable. If the sentences were to be combined, there is no comma needed because there is no change in subject. Instead, other words such as "because" or "as" provide a transition into the next part of the sentence. **(Answer B)**
23. The author has made it clear that he/she is an aspiring artist. He/she is fascinated by the Louvre and is insulted by other students not appreciating the art in it. Answer B describes the author's desire to be an artist. **(Answer B)**
24. The author made the point that seeing the art in-person is much better than reading about it or viewing it on the internet. Therefore, the underlined portion is not needed because this was already stated. This is not the main point of the paragraph. **(Answer B)**
25. Answer A, B and D all have dangling modifier mistakes. It is not clear who performs the action. Surely *it* was not handcrafted, awed or surrounded; *I* was. Answer C is the only one that correctly identifies who performs the action. **(Answer C)**
26. The same tense needs to be used in this sentence in a parallel fashion. There are two actions described (walk and take in). "Walk" was preceded with "to", therefore "take in" also needs to be preceded with "to". **(Answer D)**
27. Begin began begun. Use *began* for the simple past tense. Use *had begun* when an action in the past took place before another action in the past. **(Answer B)**
28. *Who's* means *who is* or *who has*. In this case, we need the possessive pronoun *whose*. (Answers C)
29. There is no punctuation needed in this underlined portion because there is no need to separate the thoughts of the sentence. The second part of the sentence is describing the first, but since the word "because" is used, no punctuation is necessary. **(Answer B)**
30. The entire essay is about the author's feelings towards the trip. It was not about the other students enjoying the trip. The author also mentions multiple times that viewing the art is large source of his inspiration. **(Answer B)**

CLASSIC ROCK

31. The underlined portion is describing the multiple attempts made by the author in the past. Therefore, a plural form is needed. "Were" is the plural form of "was" and should be placed into the underlined portion. **(Answer C)**

32. There needs to be a hyphen between "black" and "tie" and also between "invitation" and "only". Both of these descriptive adjective pairs come before the noun, in which case they need to be hyphenated. **(Answer ...**

33. The correct idiom is *at the cost of* ... **(Answer C)**

34. No change is needed to the underlined portion. "Its" is used when a possessive form of "it" is needed. **(Answer A)**

35. The underlined portion creates a contrast between the creativity of the musicians and the classical music the... play. If it were to be deleted, this contrast would also be taken away. **(Answer D)**

36. His skill is not an architect by trade. This is a case of a dangling modifier. Only B correctly places *my broth...* next to the modifier *an architect by trade.* **(Answer B)**

37. The question asks for the word that beset emphasizes the status of the New York firm. In other words, the question is asking for the word that makes the firm sound as good as possible. The word "reputable" makes the firm sound sophisticated and well-known. **(Answer B)**

38. The correct idiom is *I did not need* much convincing, or *it did not take* much convincing. **(Answer C)**

39. The underlined portion divides two complete sentences. "However" is not one of the FANBOYS. The two sentences are related by contrast; therefore, a semicolon is the only suitable option to divide them. **(Answer B)**

40. *Referring to* a person means to talk about or to mention him or her. *Referring* a person means to give him or... her a good reference. **(Answer B)**

41. A *colon* only comes after a full sentence. **(Answer A)**

42. Do not use a comma before a restrictive clause that starts with *that.* The words *that I had composed in my senior year* are needed to identify which classical peace the author writes about. **(Answer B)**

43. The word "newlyweds" describes two people. It is a plural word. Therefore, it needs to have an apostrophe after the "s". **(Answer B)**

44. The underlined portion is meant to show that the audience is shocked by the type of music being played. The only answer that shows this is Answer B. **(Answer B)**

45. The portion being added describes a single person or instrument being played. The only place in the paragraph that describes a single person or instrument is at position 2. **(Answer B)**

TO WASH OR NOT TO WASH

46. No punctuation is necessary between the words "eggs" and "displayed" because they are part of one continuous sentence. Keeping the comma would create added information, which always can be left out. However, we need the words *displayed for people to buy in outdoor markets* to identify which eggs the author is writing about. There should therefore be no commas around this restrictive clause. **(Answer C)**

47. It is unnecessary to have multiple adjectives to describe something if they all have similar meanings. In this case, just the word "rotten" conveys the desired message. **(Answer D)**

48. Answer C is an unacceptable alternative to the word "case" because it is the only option that would change the meaning of the sentence. **(Answer C)**

49. Answer B is correct because the word is "there" lets the reader know that the author is referring to the previous sentence and describing the process of egg treatment outside of the United States. **(Answer B)**

50. Answer D is correct because all of the other options describe an outdoor location, which has previously been discussed in the passage. A peddler's cart has not been mentioned before and is therefore the only answer that provides new information. **(Answer D)**

51. The theme of the paragraph is the refrigeration of eggs. Only Answer B uses that fact (the temperature) to close the line of thought. **(Answer B)**

52. Answer A is correct because C is misspelled, and B and D use the wrong verb. To lay means to put something down. **(Answer A)**

53. Currently, this is not a sentence but a fragment. We need a subject. We cannot use *they* because that might refer to the American public. Using *companies* as the subject provides clarity. **(Answer D)**

54. Even though the word *eggs* is in plural form, it is important to pay attention to the words "each of the" used earlier in the sentence. Since the word "each" refers to a single egg, the singular form of the verb ("has) should be used. **(Answer D)**

55. The underlined verb is referring to the coating of the egg and not the unwashed eggs themselves. Therefore, the singular form of the verb should be used. **(Answer B)**

56. The subject of the sentences is *the coating*, not *the fills*. The word *fills* is a verb in this sentence. The coating fills the cracks and acts as a shield. **(Answer C)**

57. This is not a conditional sentence about what could happen or what should happen. Answer A makes an awkward sentence. ("are be kept?") Use *can*. **(Answer D)**

58. Answer A is correct because the word "incredibly" demonstrates the high level of susceptibility to contamination, continuing the author's main view on the issue. Answer B is incorrect because the word "hardly" portrays a low level of susceptibility, which does not match previous statements in the essay. Answer C is incorrect because the word "vulnerable" has a similar meaning to "susceptible" and therefore does not add any information about the level of contamination. Deleting the underlined portion would also add no information about the degree of contamination the washed eggs are susceptible to. **(Answer A)**

59. "Their" is used to describe a group of people. "There" is used to describe a direction. "They're" is a contraction of the words "they are". "Their" should never have an apostrophe after it. In this sentence, "they're" is needed because it replaces the words "they are". **(Answer C)**

60. This essay was not persuasive because it provided both sides of the argument without discrediting one of them. This essay was written to inform the reader about different processes of getting eggs ready for consumption. **(Answer C)**

ADÉLIE PENGUINS

61. There is no comma necessary in the current sentence because the second part is not a full sentence. The words *very rightly* are not added information, and they modify the words *have been termed.* **(Answer B)**

62. The correct idiom is *at the expense of.* **(Answer D)**

63. A semicolon is necessary because it separates the two complete sentences while also showing that they are related to each other. **(Answer A)**

64. Sentence 2 starts with the word *Its.* However, the sentence before talks about *penguins (plural) and inhabitants (plural).* Therefore, it cannot be the next sentence. Similarly, this sentence cannot be placed after sentence 4, which talks about *The species.* Sentence 2 needs to follow sentence 3, which talks about *the penguin.* **(Answer D)**

65. The first portion of the sentence is stating that there are not many predators close to the penguins. Therefore, Answers B and C are incorrect. Answer D gives an example of what could happen, but is not a detail about the <u>number</u> of carnivorous animals that might prey on the penguins. **(Answer A)**

66. *So* and *and* are FANBOYS conjunctions. They need a comma if a full sentence follows. *Therefore* is not a FANBOYS conjunction. **(Answer B)**

67. Answer D is correct because the other options are redundant. *Became different, new conditions, altered* and *changed* all have similar meanings. There is no need for extra descriptive words if they do not provide new information. **(Answer D)**

68. Find the relationship between the two sentences. There is no contrast or explanation. **(Answer A)**

69. Because Sea-Leopards are plural, the beginning of the sentence also needs to be plural. "Were" is the plural form of "was." This is because of the comma later on in the sentence. **(Answer B)**

70. The word "only" is describing the amount of time the land is inhabited. By placing the word right before the amount of time, the sentence would make logical sense because it is clear what the word is describing. **(Answer B)**

71. The underlined verb is referring to the "yards of ice." Since the word "yards" is plural, the correct verb is "stand." **(Answer B)**

72. *Hatchlings, baby penguins,* and *chicks* all have the same meaning. Therefore, only one of these words is needed. **(Answer D)**

73. Is it a bird from your boat? Is it a bird through your binoculars? Read the sentence precisely; the modifier needs to be right next to the word it modifies. **(Answer C)**

74. Answer B is correct because this information has already been stated earlier in the passage when the author wrote, "his carriage is confident as he approaches you over the snow, curiosity in his every movement." **(Answer B)**

75. The passage only discusses how the penguins interact with their environment and humans. The author rarely mentions any social interactions among penguins themselves or in between penguins and other living creatures. However, answer D states that he does not mention any social interactions AT ALL, which is incorrect; he mentions that they live in colonies, for example. **(Answer C)**

Math

MATH
Essential Skills

Fractions

Fractions

$\frac{1}{2}$ is a fraction. The top part is called the *numerator* and the bottom part the *denominator*.

Addition and Subtraction

You **CAN** add and subtract two fractions with the same denominator. $\quad \frac{3}{8} + \frac{2}{8} = \frac{5}{8}$

You **CANNOT** add or subtract two fractions with different denominators. $\quad \frac{1}{3} + \frac{1}{6} = ?$

You can **change** a fraction by *multiplying* the top AND the bottom by the same number. $\qquad \frac{2*1}{2*3} + \frac{1}{6} = \frac{2}{6} + \frac{1}{6} = \frac{3}{6}$

 *Tip: **Simplify** each fraction by dividing the top and bottom by the same number.* $\qquad \frac{3}{6} = \frac{3 \div 3}{6 \div 3} = \frac{1}{2}$

Multiplying

You can multiply fractions straight across.

$$\frac{3}{8} * \frac{1}{3} \quad = \quad \frac{3*1}{8*3} \quad = \quad \frac{3}{24} \quad \text{simplify} \quad \frac{3 \div 3}{24 \div 3} \quad = \quad \frac{1}{8}$$

 *Tip: Watch out! This is different from **cross-multiplying**, which is used in equations:* $\frac{a}{b} = \frac{c}{d} \rightarrow ad = bc.$

Dividing

Dividing by a fraction is the same as multiplying by its reciprocal (= 1 divided by that number.)

Remember KFC. (**K**eep the first, **F**lip the second, **C**hange the sign.) Sometimes it is easier to write 4 as $\frac{4}{1}$.

$$\frac{3}{8} \div \frac{1}{3} = \frac{3}{8} * \frac{3}{1} = \frac{3*3}{8*1} = \frac{9}{8}$$

Multiplying and Dividing

A fraction with factors already contains the elements of multiplication and division.
You can cancel out the parts of multiplications that are called factors.

$$\frac{5*3*4}{5} = \frac{\cancel{5}*3*4}{\cancel{5}} = 3*4 = 12 \qquad \frac{3}{8} * \frac{1}{3} * \frac{4}{8} * \frac{1}{4} = \frac{\cancel{3}}{8} * \frac{1}{\cancel{3}} * \frac{\cancel{4}}{8} * \frac{1}{\cancel{4}} = \frac{1}{8*8} = \frac{1}{64}$$

Do NOT cancel out subtractions or additions.

WRONG: $\frac{8-\cancel{4}}{\cancel{4}} = 8$ RIGHT: $\frac{-\cancel{4}(-2+1)}{-\cancel{4}} = -1$

Fractions and Algebra

Use the same rules as above with unknown quantities.

$$\frac{6x+3}{3} = \frac{\cancel{3}(2x+1)}{\cancel{3}} = 2x + 1$$

$$\frac{x}{\frac{1}{k}} = \frac{x}{1} * \frac{k}{1} = xk$$

$$\frac{1}{4} + \frac{2}{x} = \frac{11}{12} \rightarrow \frac{3}{12} + \frac{2}{x} = \frac{11}{12} \rightarrow \frac{2}{x} = \frac{8}{12} \rightarrow 8x = 24$$

$$\rightarrow x = 3$$

Memorize common fractions and decimals.			
1/2	5/10	0.5	50%
1/3	333.3/1000	0.333	33.3%
1/4	25/100	0.25	25%
1/5	2/10	0.2	20%
1/8	125/1000	0.125	12.5%
1/9	111.1/1000	0.1111	11.1%
1/10	1/10	0.1	10%
=======================================			
2/3	666.6/1000	0.666	66.6%
3/4	75/100	0.75	75%
2/5	4/10	0.4	40%
3/8	375/1000	0.375	37.5%

Fractions - Quiz 1

1. How much is 4 divided by $\frac{1}{2}$?

   A. $4\frac{1}{2}$

   B. $3\frac{1}{2}$

   C. 8

   D. 2

2. How much is $\frac{2}{3}$ times $\frac{4}{5}$?

   A. $\frac{7}{10}$

   B. $\frac{10}{7}$

   C. $\frac{6}{8}$

   D. $\frac{8}{15}$

3. How much is $\frac{4}{5} + \frac{7}{8}$?

   A. $\frac{11}{13}$

   B. $\frac{11}{40}$

   C. $\frac{67}{40}$

   D. $\frac{28}{40}$

4. For what value of x is the equation
   $\frac{12}{x} = \frac{8}{6}$ true?

   A. 10

   B. 9

   C. 8

   D. 6

5. For what value of x is the equation
   $\frac{x}{51} = \frac{12}{9}$ true?

   A. 68

   B. 63

   C. 60

   D. 54

6. What is $\frac{4}{x}$ divided by $\frac{10}{3}$ when x = 7?

   A. $\frac{3}{14}$

   B. $\frac{6}{7}$

   C. $\frac{6}{35}$

   D. $\frac{3}{70}$

7. For what value of z is the equation
   $\frac{52}{z} = \frac{26}{40}$ true?

   A. 40

   B. 63

   C. 72

   D. 80

8. What is $\frac{x}{7}$ divided by $\frac{12}{z}$
   when $x = 9$ and $z = 14$?

   A. $\frac{4}{9}$

   B. $\frac{7}{9}$

   C. $\frac{2}{3}$

   D. $\frac{3}{2}$

9. Mary owns a quarter of all the books in her house. One third of those books are spy novels. If there are 240 books in the house, how many of Mary's books are NOT spy novels?

   A. 40

   B. 20

   C. $\frac{1}{12}$

   D. $\frac{1}{6}$

1) C 2) D 3) C 4) B 5) A 6) C 7) D 8) D 9) A

Fractions - Quiz 1 (Answers)

1. How much is 4 divided by $\frac{1}{2}$?
   A. Dividing by a fraction is the same as multiplying by its reciprocal. Write 4 as $\frac{4}{1}$.
   B. $\frac{4}{1} * \frac{2}{1} = \frac{8}{1} = 8$ **(Answer C)**

2. How much is $\frac{2}{3}$ times $\frac{4}{5}$?
   A. You can multiply fractions straight across.
   B. $\frac{2}{3} * \frac{4}{5} = \frac{8}{15}$ **(Answer D)**

3. How much is $\frac{4}{5} + \frac{7}{8}$?
   A. You **CANNOT** add or subtract two fractions with different denominators.
   B. In order to add the two fractions, they need to have the same denominator. The smallest number that has a factor of five AND a factor of eight is 40. $(8 * 5 = 40)$
   C. You can **change** a fraction by *multiplying* the top AND the bottom by the same number.
   D. Multiply both sides of the first fraction by 8.
   E. Multiply the second fraction by $\frac{5}{5}$.
   F. $\frac{8}{8} * \frac{4}{5} = \frac{32}{40}$.   and $\frac{7}{8} * \frac{5}{5} = \frac{35}{40}$
   G. $\frac{32}{40} + \frac{35}{40} = \frac{67}{40}$ **(Answer C)**

4. For what value of x is the equation $\frac{12}{x} = \frac{8}{6}$ true?
   A. Cross multiply for the same results:
      $8x = 72 \quad \rightarrow \quad x = 9$ **(Answer B)**

5. For what value of x is the equation $\frac{x}{51} = \frac{12}{9}$ true?
   A. Cross multiply for the same results:
      $9x = 612 \rightarrow x = 68$ **(Answer A)**

6. What is $\frac{4}{x}$ divided by $\frac{10}{3}$ when $x = 7$?
   A. When $x = 7$, the question reads $\frac{4}{7}$ divided by $\frac{10}{3}$.
   B. Dividing by a fraction is the same as multiplying by its reciprocal.
   C. Rewrite as $\frac{4}{7} * \frac{3}{10}$.
   D. You can multiply fractions straight across.
      $\frac{4}{7} * \frac{3}{10} = \frac{12}{70} = \frac{6}{35}$ **(Answer C)**

7. For what value of z is the equation $\frac{52}{z} = \frac{26}{40}$ true?
   A. Cross multiply to solve for z:
      $26z = 2080 \rightarrow z = 80$ **(Answer D)**

8. What is $\frac{x}{7}$ divided by $\frac{12}{z}$ when $x = 9$ and $z = 14$?
   A. When $x = 9$ and $z = 14$, the question reads $\frac{9}{7}$ divided by $\frac{12}{14}$.
      Rewrite as $\frac{9}{7} * \frac{14}{12}$.
   B. You can multiply fractions straight across.
      $\frac{9}{7} * \frac{14}{12} = \frac{126}{84} = \frac{3}{2}$ **(Answer D)**
   C. Alternate method: cancel factors first.
      $\frac{9}{7} * \frac{14^2}{12} = \frac{9}{1} * \frac{2}{12} = \frac{18}{12} = \frac{3}{2}$ **(Answer D)**

9. Mary owns a quarter of 240 the books in her house. $= \frac{1}{4} * 240 = 60$
   A. One third of those books are spy novels. $\frac{1}{3} * 60 = 20$ are spy novels.
   B. How many of Mary's books are NOT spy novels?
   C. $60 - 20 = 40$ **(Answer A)**

Fractions - Quiz 2

1. What is the sum of the solutions of this equation? $\frac{x+4}{3} = \frac{3}{x-4}$
   A. $x = 12$
   B. $x = 7$
   C. $x = 4$
   D. $x = 0$
   E. $x = -1$

2. Solve for x. $\frac{x^2}{27} = \frac{3}{x^2}$
   A. $x = 3$
   B. $x = -3$
   C. $x = -3 \ or \ x = 3$
   D. $x = 9 \ or \ x = -9$
   E. $x = 9$

3. What is the product of the two solutions of this equation? $\frac{x+4}{2} = \frac{1}{x+3}$
   A. $x = 10$
   B. $x = 7$
   C. $x = 4$
   D. $x = 1$
   E. $x = -10$

4. Solve for x. $\frac{x^2}{16} - \frac{4}{x} = 0$
   A. $x = 64$
   B. $x = 16$
   C. $x = 4$
   D. $x = -4$
   E. $x = 4 \ or \ x = -4$

5. Solve for x. $2\frac{1}{8} + 1\frac{1}{5} = x$
   A. $x = \frac{121}{40}$
   B. $x = \frac{133}{40}$
   C. $x = \frac{31}{40}$
   D. $x = \frac{29}{13}$
   E. $x = \frac{51}{20}$

6. Solve for x. $1\frac{1}{3} * 2\frac{1}{4} = x$
   A. $x = 1\frac{3}{4}$
   B. $x = 2\frac{1}{2}$
   C. $x = 2\frac{1}{12}$
   D. $x = 3\frac{7}{12}$
   E. $x = 3$

7. Solve for x. $\frac{4}{5} * \frac{9}{2} * \frac{5}{4} * \frac{x}{5} * \frac{10}{9} = 4$
   A. $x = 1$
   B. $x = 2$
   C. $x = 3$
   D. $x = 4$
   E. $x = 5$

8. Solve for x. $\frac{2}{5} - \frac{1}{x} = \frac{3}{20}$
   A. $x = 1$
   B. $x = 2$
   C. $x = 3$
   D. $x = 4$
   E. $x = 5$

9. Solve for x. $\frac{2}{3} - \frac{1}{x} = \frac{3}{5}$
   A. $x = 15$
   B. $x = 10$
   C. $x = 9$
   D. $x = 8$
   E. $x = 6$

10. A car drives $3\frac{1}{10} \ mile$ in $\frac{1}{5}$ of a minute. How far does the car drive in 10 minutes?
    A. 31 miles
    B. 31.1 miles
    C. 31.5 miles
    D. 155 miles
    E. 310 miles

1)D 2)C 3)A 4)C 5)B 6)E 7)D 8)D 9)A 10)D

Fractions - Quiz 2 (Answers)

1. $\frac{x+4}{3} = \frac{3}{x-4}$ ➔ $(x+4)(x-4) = 9$ ➔ $x^2 - 16 = 9$ ➔ $x^2 = 25$ $x = 5 \ or \ x = -5$

   The sum of the two solutions is $-5 + 5 = 0$ **(Answer D)**

2. $\frac{x^2}{27} = \frac{3}{x^2}$ ➔ $x^4 = 81$ ➔ $x = 3 \ \ or \ x = -3$ **(Answer C)**

3. $\frac{x+4}{2} = \frac{1}{x+3}$ ➔ $x^2+7x + 12 = 2$ ➔ $x^2 + 7x + 10 = 0$ ➔ $(x+2)(x+5) = 0$

   ➔ $x = -2 \ or \ x = -5$

   The product of the two solutions is $(-5) * (-2) = 10$ **(Answer A)**

4. $\frac{x^2}{16} - \frac{4}{x} = 0$ ➔ $\frac{x^2}{16} = \frac{4}{x}$ ➔ $x^3 = 64$ ➔ $x = 4$ **(Answer C)**

   Note: $(-4)^3 = -64$, so -4 is not a solution.

5. $2\frac{1}{8} + 1\frac{1}{5} = x$ ➔ $\frac{17}{8} + \frac{6}{5} = x$ ➔ $\frac{5*17}{5*8} + \frac{8*6}{8*5} = x$ ➔ $\frac{85}{40} + \frac{48}{40} = x$ ➔ $\frac{133}{40} = x$ **(Answer B)**

6. $1\frac{1}{3} * 2\frac{1}{4} = x$ ➔ $\frac{4}{3} * \frac{9}{4} = x$ ➔ $\frac{36}{12} = x$ ➔ $3 = x$ **(Answer E)**

7. $\frac{4}{5} * \frac{9}{2} * \frac{5}{4} * \frac{x}{5} * \frac{10}{9} = 4$ ➔ $\frac{\cancel{4}}{\cancel{5}} * \frac{\cancel{9}}{\cancel{2}} * \frac{\cancel{5}}{\cancel{4}} * \frac{x}{\cancel{5}} * \frac{\cancel{10}^{2*5}}{\cancel{9}} = 4$ ➔ $\frac{x}{1} = 4$ ➔ $x = 4$ **(Answer D)**

8. $\frac{2}{5} - \frac{1}{x} = \frac{3}{20}$ ➔ $\frac{2}{5} - \frac{3}{20} = \frac{1}{x}$ ➔ $\frac{4*2}{4*5} - \frac{3}{20} = \frac{1}{x}$ ➔ $\frac{8}{20} - \frac{3}{20} = \frac{1}{x}$ ➔ $\frac{5}{20} = \frac{1}{x}$ ➔ $x = 4$

   (Answer D)

9. $\frac{2}{3} - \frac{1}{x} = \frac{3}{5}$ ➔ $\frac{2}{3} - \frac{3}{5} = \frac{1}{x}$ ➔ $\frac{5*2}{5*3} - \frac{3*3}{3*5} = \frac{1}{x}$ ➔ $\frac{10}{15} - \frac{9}{15} = \frac{1}{x}$ ➔ $\frac{1}{15} = \frac{1}{x}$ ➔ $x = 15$

   (Answer A)

10. The car drives $3\frac{1}{10}$ miles in $\frac{1}{5}$ of a minute. To get rid of fractions, multiply each side by 10:

    The car drives $3\frac{1}{10}$ x 10 miles in $\frac{1}{5}$ x 10 of a minute.

    The car drives $30\frac{10}{10}$ miles in $\frac{10}{5}$ of a minute.

    The car drives   31   miles in 2   minutes.

    How far does the car drive in 10 minutes? Multiply each side by 5.
    The car drives   31 * 5   miles   in 2 * 5   minutes.
    The car drives   155   miles   in   10   minutes. **(Answer D)**

PERCENTAGES

Percentages

Percent means "per hundred." You can write a percentage as a fraction and then use it in an equation.

Twenty percent of fifty is the same as $\frac{20}{100} * 50$ (= 10)

IS over OF

Tip: Commit to memory that <u>percent over hundred equals "is" over "of"</u>. Then cross-multiply.

$$\frac{\%}{100} = \frac{is}{of} \qquad or \qquad \frac{\%}{100} = \frac{part}{whole}$$

The number with the percent is always placed over the hundred. The number with the word "of" always indicates the whole. The number with the word "is" represents the part and goes on top of the whole. Examples.

20 is 40% of what number? $\qquad \frac{\%}{100} = \frac{is}{of} \rightarrow \frac{40}{100} = \frac{20}{x} \rightarrow 40x = 2000 \rightarrow x = 50$

What is 15% of 60? $\qquad \frac{\%}{100} = \frac{is}{of} \rightarrow \frac{15}{100} = \frac{x}{60} \rightarrow 100x = 900 \rightarrow x = 9$

20 is what percent of 80? $\qquad \frac{\%}{100} = \frac{is}{of} \rightarrow \frac{x}{100} = \frac{20}{80} \rightarrow 80x = 2000 \rightarrow x = 25$

What percent of 60 is 42? $\qquad \frac{\%}{100} = \frac{is}{of} \rightarrow \frac{x}{100} = \frac{42}{60} \rightarrow 60x = 4200 \rightarrow x = 70$

Tip: Do not trust percentages! They look like real numbers but they are not. Do the math.

Example: Johnny bought a watch that was priced at $100.00. He had a coupon for 10% off. However, he also needed to pay 10% sales tax. How much did he pay?
It looks easy: The watch costs one hundred dollars, add 10 percent and subtract 10 percent. He pays one hundred dollars, right?

Review: Do not trust percentages. Always calculate each step:
10% off of $100.00 is $\frac{10}{100} = \frac{x}{100} = \$10.00$. The price after the coupon is $90.00.

Revision: **Now** we need to add 10 percent tax.
10% added to $90.00 is $\frac{10}{100} = \frac{x}{90} = \$9.00$. The price after tax is $99.00.

Tip: The percentage can change even if the number stays the same!

Example: There are 3 girls and 3 boys in a classroom. What is the percentage of boys?
The percentage of boys is $\frac{x}{100} = \frac{3}{6}$ Answer: 50%.
Now two girls leave. What is the percentage of boys?
The number of boys has not changed. 50%?

Review: Although there is still the same **number** of boys in the room, the percent can change. A percentage is always ratio of the part to the whole. And in this case, the whole (class) has changed.
Remember: do not trust percentages. Do the math.

Revision: The percentage of boys is $\frac{x}{100} = \frac{3}{4}$. Answer: 75%.

Tip: If the ACT mentions a percentage, such as 15%, look for the NUMBER. 15% of what?

Percentages - Quiz 1

1. What is 15% of 520?
   A. 64
   B. 72
   C. 78
   D. 82

2. What is 45% of 680?
   A. 294
   B. 300
   C. 306
   D. 312

3. An investor makes a 50 percent profit the first year, but loses 50 percent the next. What is the percentage of the original investment that he has left after two years?
   A. 50 %
   B. 75 %
   C. 100 %
   D. 125 %

4. A business owner decides to stop buying products, and she sells 20 % of her inventory each year. After 3 years, what percent of her inventory does she still own?
   A. 60 %
   B. 51.2 %
   C. 40 %
   D. 23 %

5. After a 20% discount, a product costs 100 dollars. What is the original price?
   A. $125.00
   B. $120.00
   C. $110.20
   D. $80.00

Use the following information to answer questions 6-8.

The workers at J&J's Ice Cream Shop are having a competition to determine who scoops the most ice cream from July to October in a certain year. Numbers are measurements of scoops per month.

	Month			
	July	August	Sept	Oct
Jane	380	460	290	150
Jack	540	440	350	120
Jill	330	410	400	260
Justin	460	280	480	130

6. Which of the following is the closest to the percent decrease in Jane's scoops from August to September?
   A. 20%
   B. 37%
   C. 38.6%
   D. 41%

7. Which worker had the greatest percent decrease from September to October?
   A. Jane
   B. Jack
   C. Jill
   D. Justin

8. If each worker had a 10 percent decrease from October to November, what was the total number of scoops in November?
   A. 726
   B. 660
   C. 594
   D. 66

1)C 2)C 3)B 4)B 5)A 6)B 7)D 8)C

Percentages - Quiz 1 (Answers)

1. $\frac{\%}{100} = \frac{is}{of}$ $\frac{15}{100} = \frac{X}{520}$ Cross-multiply to get $520 * 15 = 100X$. $X = 78$

   (Answer C)

2. $\frac{\%}{100} = \frac{is}{of}$ $\frac{45}{100} = \frac{X}{680}$ Cross-multiply to get $680 * 45 = 100X$.   X=306

   (Answer C)

3. Use the variable x to represent the original investment.
   a. The investor initially made a $\frac{50}{100}$ X or 0.5X profit, so after the first year, he has 1.5X.
   b. He loses 50% or $\frac{50}{100}$ of 1.5X the following year: $1.5X * \frac{1}{2} = .75X$ or $\frac{75}{100}X$.
      Answer: He has 75% of the original investment remaining.   **(Answer B)**

4. Use the variable x to represent her original inventory.
   a. She sells 20% of her inventory each year for three years, leaving 80% of that year's inventory remaining; write this as $x * \frac{80}{100} * \frac{80}{100} * \frac{80}{100}$ *or* $x * 0.8 * 0.8 * 0.8 = .512x$
   b. She has 51.2% of her original inventory remaining.   **(Answer B)**

5. 20 % discount means 100% − 20%. You will pay 80% of the original price. This 80% is $100.00
   $\frac{\%}{100} = \frac{is}{of}$ $\frac{80}{100} = \frac{100}{x}$ Cross-multiply to get   X=125   **(Answer A)**

6. To find the percent decrease, first divide Jane's September scoop count by her August scoop count.
   a. $\frac{\%}{100} = \frac{is}{of}$ $\frac{x}{100} = \frac{290}{460}$ Cross-multiply to get $460X = 29000 = 63\%$,
   b. Be careful! You just learned that her September count is 63% of her August count, but that is not what the questions asks you to calculate.
   c. To find the percent *decrease*, subtract 63 from 100; $100\% - 63\% = 37\%$ decrease.
   (Answer B)

7. To solve this, you need to do the calculation for each worker.
   a. First find how many scoops each worker had in October. Divide that number by the September number of scoops to find the percentage.
      For Jane: $\frac{150}{290} = \frac{51.7}{100}$ For Jack: $\frac{120}{350} = \frac{34.3}{100}$ For Jill: $\frac{260}{400} = \frac{65}{100}$ For Justin: $\frac{130}{480} = \frac{27.1}{100}$

   b. The worker whose October count is the lowest percent of his or her September count had the greatest percent decrease—Justin is the correct answer.   **(Answer D)**

8. First, find the total number of scoops in October.
   a. $150 + 120 + 260 + 130 = 660$.
   b. If each worker had a decrease in productivity of 10%, then the total number of scoops in November decreased by 10%.
   c. $660 * 0.9 = 594$ scoops in November   **(Answer C)**

AVERAGES

Averages

Calculating an Average

1) Add up all the numbers. Get the TOTAL.
2) Divide the total by HOW MANY NUMBERS there are.
3) Voila! You found the AVERAGE.

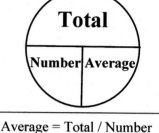

Total

| Number | Average |

What makes ACT average questions so difficult?
In the difficult average questions, they never tell you the TOTAL.
Tip: Find the TOTAL and finding the average will be much easier.
   Draw the circle with averages, numbers, and totals for each question.

Average = Total / Number
Number = Total / Average
Total = Number ∗ Average

Average Terms

Mean = average (see method above)
Mode = the value that appears *most* often
        (There can be two or more numbers that are the mode.)
Median = the middle value in a sorted list. (Sometimes you have to put the numbers in order.)
        = the number that separates the high numbers from the low ones.
          (In a list with an even amount of numbers, take the average of the two middle numbers.)
Range = the difference between the smallest number and the largest number.

Weighted Average

Add the values of each occurrence, then divide the total by the total number of occurrences.
If 4 people in your class have a 60, and the other 26 have a hundred, the average is NOT 80.
$4 ∗ 60 = 240$. $26 ∗ 100 = 2600$
The total in the class is 2840. Divide by 30 students = 94.66 average.

2840

| 30 | 94.66 |

Shortcuts

Short Series

How much is the average of the following five numbers? 1,2,3,4,5
Tip: In a series of numbers with equal distance (=arithmetic sequence), the middle number is the average.
Examples:

2; 4; 6; 8; 10	$2 + 4 + 6 + 8 + 10 = 30$	$30/5 = 6$
0; 5; 10; 15; 20	$0 + 5 + 10 + 15 + 20 = 50$	$50/5 = 10$
$x - 2; x - 1; x; x + 1; x + 2$	$(x - 2) + (x - 1) + (x) + (x + 1) + (x + 2) = 5x$	$5x/5 = x$

Long Series

Example: How much is the average of all numbers $0 - 100$?
        You could enter all the values in your calculator and get the answer.
Review: The distance between each number is the same.
        Take the average of the first and last number. $(100 + 0)/2 = 50$
        Repeat this with other pairs $(99 + 1)/2 = 50$ and $(98 + 2)/2 = 50$, etc.
Revision: The average = 50

Averages - Quiz 1

Use the following information to answer
questions 1-4.

Eight students in Ms. McKinney's class took a test, and she recorded their scores as follows:				
Girls:	79	96	88	83
Boys:	88	85	92	93

1. What is the mode of all test scores?

   A. 21
   B. 96
   C. 79
   D. 88
   E. 86

2. What is the median of all test scores?

   A. 85
   B. 88
   C. 93
   D. 92
   E. 96

3. What is the range of all test scores?

   A. 4
   B. 8
   C. 9
   D. 11
   E. 17

4. What is the mean of all test scores?

   A. 88
   B. 92
   C. 86
   D. 85.25
   E. 86.5

5. A math professor asks his class, "If you take the multiples of ten from 0 to 200 inclusive, what is the arithmetic mean of those numbers?"

   A. 70
   B. 75
   C. 100
   D. 105
   E. 110

6. In late October in Anchorage, Alaska, the temperatures for each of seven consecutive days were 13°C, 4°C, 6°C, 0°C, −3°C, 1°C, and −7°C. What was the average temperature for these days?

   A. 1°C
   B. 2°C
   C. 2.85°C
   D. 4°C
   E. 4.85°C

7. A family consists of two grandparents whose average age is 86, two parents whose average age is 39, and three grandchildren whose average age is 10 years old. What is the average age of the whole family?

   A. 31
   B. 40
   C. 45
   D. 55.25
   E. 73.7

8. What is the average of 7/8 and 3/4?

   A. $\frac{7}{4}$

   B. $\frac{13}{8}$

   C. $\frac{21}{32}$

   D. $\frac{13}{4}$

   E. $\frac{13}{16}$

1) D 2) B 3) E 4) A 5) C 6) B 7) B 8) E

Average - Quiz 1 (Answers)

1. Remember mode = most

   79   83   85   <u>88</u>   <u>88</u>   92   93   96

   The number 88 appears twice. Every other number is only mentioned once. **(Answer D)**

2. The median is the middle number when all numbers are lined up in order.

   79   83   85   <u>88</u>   <u>88</u>   92   93   96

   There are two numbers in the middle. Take the average between the two: $\frac{88+88}{2} = 88$

   (Answer B)

3. The range is the difference between the lowest and the highest number.

   $96 - 79 = 17$ **(Answer E)**

4. The mean is the arithmetic average. Add up all the numbers (=704) and divide them by the number of students (= 8)   704 / 8 = 88 **(Answer A)**

   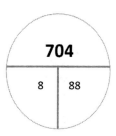

5. In an arithmetic series, take the average of the first item and the last item.

   The average of the first and last number is $\frac{200+0}{2} = 100$

   You can quickly check this for the rest of the items: $\frac{199+1}{2} = 100$ and $\frac{198+2}{2} = 100$. Yep, every pair has an average of 100 . **(Answer C)**

   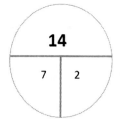

6. Watch the negative numbers. Also, make sure you count seven days even if you don't add anything (zero) for day four.

   Add up all the numbers (=13 + 4 + 6 + 0 + −3 + 1 + −7 = 14)

   and divide them by the number of days (seven)   14/7 = 2 **(Answer B)**

7. This is an example of a weighted average.

   DO NOT take the average of 86, 39 and 10 (= $\frac{135}{3}$ = 45. Incorrect!)

   Although you see only three numbers, there are seven people.
   You need to add up all the numbers:
   86 + 86 + 39 + 39 + 10 + 10 + 10 = 280

   Divide the total by 7. ($\frac{280}{7}$ = 40) **(Answer B)**

   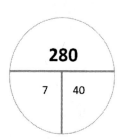

   Alternative approach: Add 2 x 86, 2 x 39, and 3 x 10 to get the total, and then divide by 7.

8. $\frac{\frac{7}{8}+\frac{3}{4}}{2}$ ➔ $\frac{\frac{7}{8}+\frac{6}{8}}{2}$ ➔ $\frac{\frac{13}{8}}{2}$ ➔ $\frac{13}{8} * \frac{1}{2}$ $= \frac{13}{16}$ **(Answer E)**

   To get the average of two numbers, add them up and divide the result by two. Remember your rules about fractions. You can only add and subtract two fractions with the same denominator. Dividing by two is the same as multiplying by ½.

Averages - Quiz 2

Use the following information to answer questions 1-3.

A recent exit poll of a popular movie asked moviegoers to rate the film they had seen based on characters, plot, and special effects on a scale of 0-10. Researchers realized not all of the information had come in when they began to construct a chart:

	Characters	Plot	Special Effects
Person 1	5	6	8
Person 2	7	5	6
Person 3	3	4	3
Person 4	8	7	5
Person 5	7	6	X

1. What was the mean of the characters rating among the five people polled?
   A. 5.5
   B. 5.6
   C. 6
   D. 6.4
   E. 6.7

2. What is the lowest score Person 5 could give to get an average special-effects rating of 6.5 or more?
   A. 6
   B. 7
   C. 9
   D. 10
   E. The average will always be less than 6.5

3. If four more outsiders all rated the plot as a 7, the new average plot rating would be
   A. 5.8
   B. 6.2
   C. 6.5
   D. 6.8
   E. 7.2

4. Three consecutive integers add up to 381. Which of the following is the correct set of numbers?
   A. 127, 128, 129
   B. 126, 127, 128
   C. 125, 126, 127
   D. 128, 129, 130
   E. 125, 127, 129

5. Each of the six players in a game received a score between 0 and 100 inclusive. If their average score was 85, what is the greatest possible number of players who could have received a score of 50?
   A. 1
   B. 2
   C. 3
   D. 4
   E. 5

6. Seven consecutive numbers have an average of 25. What is the difference between the median and the mean of those seven numbers?
   A. 0
   B. 1
   C. 2
   D. 3
   E. 4

1) C   2) E   3) B   4) B   5) A   6) A

Averages - Quiz 2 (Answers)

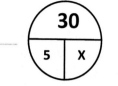

1. (Remember average = mean)
    To get the average, add up all values and divide by the number of
    (3+5+7+7+8)/5 =   30/5   = 6   **(Answer C)**

2. For the average of 5 people to be 6.5, the total would need to be $5 * 6.5 = 32.5$.
    The current total of the other four people polled is 22. Each person was asked to rate the film on a
    scale of 0-10. In order to achieve a total of 32.5, person 5 would need to rate the special effects
    with a 10.5. Therefore, the average of 6.5 is not obtainable. **(Answer E)**

3. The current plot value has five votes. The average is (4+5+6+6+7)/5 = 5.6
            The new plot average will have nine votes. The average is
    (4+5+6+6+7+7+7+7+7)/9 = 6.22. **(Answer B)**

4. **Method 1:** The average of a consecutive series is always the middle number.
    Divide 381 into 3 to get 127. This must be the middle number. **(Answer B)**

    Method 2: Three consecutive numbers add up to 381.
    The first unknown number is x, the next one $x + 1$, and the third one $x + 2$.
    Solve for x.
    $(x) + (x + 1) + (x + 2) = 381$ → $3x + 3 = 381$ → $3x = 378$ → $x = 126$

5. An average score of 85 among six means the total was 510.
    Tip: Draw an average pie chart.

    For each person that could score 50, subtract 50 from the total and redraw
    the pie chart. If one person scores 50, the remaining total is 460, which
    divided by 5 leaves an average of 92. That is possible. The average for all six people
    would still be 85.

    If two people get a 50, the remaining total for the other four is 410. This means
    that their average needs to be 102.5. However, the maximum score is 100. It is
    impossible for two people to get a 50. **(Answer A)**

6. In a sequence of seven consecutive numbers, the middle number is always the mean.

    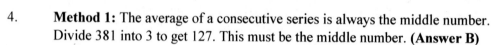

    $(x) + (x + 1) + (x + 2)) + (x + 3) + (x + 4) + (x + 5) + (x + 6) = (7x + 21)$
            Find the mean (= average): $(7x + 21)/7 = x + 3$
            $x + 3 = 25$ Therefore $x = 22$, which is the first number of the sequence.
    The sequence is 22, 23, 24, 25, 26, 27, 28

    The middle number (25) is also the median. What is the difference between
    the mean (25) and the median (25) of those seven numbers?
    $25 - 25 = 0$
    (Answer A)

    Tip: In an arithmetic sequence of numbers, the mean is always equal to the median.

Averages - Examples

We do not do "average" questions; we prefer "total" questions.
(See page 174)

Example 1

Three numbers have an average of 20.
By adding another number (X) the average increases to 40.
How much is X?

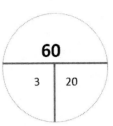

Solution: 1) Draw the circle with the averages and the numbers.

2) Find the totals.

3) Restate the question by using the word "total".

Three numbers have a TOTAL of 60.

By adding another number (X)

the TOTAL increases to 160.

4) Find the answer. (See the bottom of this page.)

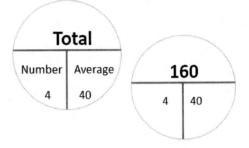

Example 2

Winni was a car salesman before he had his current job. During his first month, he sold three cars. During his second month, he sold four of them. During his third month, he sold five cars, and in month four, he sold six cars. Winni thought he was quite getting the hang of it, but his manager was less pleased. She told Winni that by his next month, he needed to have sold an AVERAGE of six cars per month, or else she would fire him.
How many cars does Winni need to sell in month five to keep his job?

Solution: 1) Draw the circle with the averages and the numbers.

2) Find the total.

3) Restate the question by using the word "total".

   "He needs to sell a TOTAL of 30 cars in five months.

   How many cars does he need to sell to keep his job?"

4) Find the answer (See the bottom of this page.)

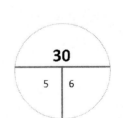

Example 1: From a total of 60 to a total of 160? The number added is 100.
Example 2: He sold 3+4+5+6 cars = 18 cars. He needs to sell 30 cars, which is 12 more in month five.

RATIOS

Ratios

Comparing Two Proportions

Example 1: One pound of sugar costs one dollar, how much do 20 pounds cost?

        That one is easy. One dollar **times** twenty = $20.00

Example 2: Three pounds of salt cost 60 cents, how much do 10 pounds cost?

        You could solve this by **dividing** the price by three, to get $0.20 for one pound.

        Then **multiplying** $0.20 by 10 to get the answer $2.00

        Alternatively, you can **cross multiply** to find the answer, because both proportions have the

        same relationship. $\frac{3}{60} = \frac{10}{x}$ = 200 cents = $2.00

 *Tip: Ratio problems can be solved by **cross multiplying** the proportions.*

How to Write a Ratio

Ratios can be written as fractions, as a comparison with a colon, or by using the word "to."

The ratio of hands to fingers is	2:10	two to ten	or $\frac{2}{10}$
This ratio can be simplified (like a fraction)	1:5	one to five	or $\frac{1}{5}$

Compare the Totals

In difficult ratio questions, they never tell you the TOTAL.

The proportions in the ratio from 2:3 are *two out of five* and *three out of five*. (2/5 and 3/5)

Example 3: The proportions of the angles in a triangle are 2:3:4.   Add the terms to get a total of 9.

        Compare this to the total degree of angles in the triangle.   All angles add up to a total of 180.

Example 4: In a 1:3 boy to girl ratio, there are FOUR parts. The boys consist of 25% (of the TOTAL): one out

        of four, and the girls make up 75% (of the TOTAL): three out of four.

 Tip: Don't confuse 1:3 with 1 out of every 3 people. (That would be 33%.)

 Tip: Remember that 2:1 is NOT the same as 1:2! The ACT likes to trick you with this.

        $\sqrt{3}$:1 can also be written as $1{:}\frac{\sqrt{3}}{3}$

Ratio Trap

Example: A trophy is 12" tall, and the base on which is stands is 9" tall.

        Which one is the correct ratio of the height of the trophy to the height of the base?

                A. 16 : 12

                B. 9 : 12

Review: Do not pick B! Notice how the statue is taller than its base. The correct proportion is 12:9,

        which is NOT one of the given answers.

Revision: Multiply both part by $\frac{4}{3}$ to see that 16:12 is identical to 12:9. **(Answer A)**

 Tip: Use common sense with ratio questions. Draw a picture to get a sense of the proportions and the

        TOTAL.

Ratio - Quiz 1

1. An 8-foot spruce tree has a shadow of 10 feet long in the afternoon. A six-foot man nearby has a shadow that is how long?
   - **A.** 5
   - **B.** 7.5
   - **C.** 12.5
   - **D.** 18
   - **E.** 33

2. In a certain rectangle, the ratio of width to length is 2:3. If the perimeter of the rectangle is 30", what is the area?
   - **A.** 6"
   - **B.** 24"
   - **C.** 45"
   - **D.** 48"
   - **E.** 54"

3. To build 5 patios, a crew needed exactly 12 bags of cement. How many bags do they need to buy to build 8 patios?
   - **A.** 15
   - **B.** 19
   - **C.** 20
   - **D.** 40
   - **E.** 84

4. Mom has twice as many books as Dad. They have 30 books together. How many does Dad have?
   - **A.** 10
   - **B.** 12
   - **C.** 15
   - **D.** 20
   - **E.** 45

5. In a bag of candy, the ratio of red sweets to green sweets is 3:4. If the bag contains 140 green sweets, how many red sweets are there?
   - **A.** 40
   - **B.** 80
   - **C.** 90
   - **D.** 105
   - **E.** 187

6. ∠ AOC is a right angle and the ratio ∠ AOB : ∠ BOC = 2 : 3 What is the size of ∠ BOC?
   - **A.** 27
   - **B.** 30
   - **C.** 36
   - **D.** 54
   - **E.** 72

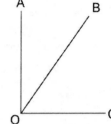

7. A police car is travelling down the highway at a high speed for a call. The distance it covers in 1 second is 132 ft. Given that there are 5280 feet in a mile, what is the police car's speed, in miles per hour?
   - **A.** 30
   - **B.** 45
   - **C.** 60
   - **D.** 75
   - **E.** 90

8. One match releases approximately 1,100 joules of heat energy when it is lit. If 1 kilojoule equals 239 calories, how many matches must be lit to produce at least 5,600 calories of heat energy?
   - **A.** 5
   - **B.** 21
   - **C.** 21.3
   - **D.** 22
   - **E.** 23

1)B 2)E 3)C 4)A 5)D 6)D 7)E 8)D

Ratio - Quiz 1 (Answers)

1. When you work with proportions, draw figures. There are two triangles:

The relationship between 8 and 10 is the same as the relationship between 6 and x.

Mathematically, you can say that $\frac{8}{10} = \frac{6}{x}$

Cross-multiply: 8x = 60 ➔ $x = \frac{60}{8} = 7.5$

(Answer B)

2. For every 2 units in the width, there are 3 units in the length.
   a. This makes the perimeter 2 units + 3 units + 2 units + 3 units long. (= 10 units)
   b. If 10 units make 30 inches, each unit must be 3 inches (10 * 3 = 30)
   c. Therefore, the width is 3 * 2 = 6" and the length is 3 * 3 = 9"
   d. The area of the rectangle is 6 * 9 = 54"

(Answer E)

3. The 12 and the 5 have the same relationship as the X and the 8.

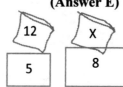

$$\frac{12}{5} = \frac{x}{8}$$

Cross-multiply: $5x = 96$ ➔ $x = 19.2$

But the answer is not B! 19 bags would not be enough to build 8 patios. Beware of these tricky round-off answers. They need more cement, but they cannot buy 1/5 of a bag. ➔ They need to buy 20 bags.   **(Answer C)**

4. Method 1: Draw pictures. Then divide the books into two groups in which one of the groups has twice as many books as the other group:

Answer: The bigger group has 20 books, the smaller one has 10 books. Dad has 10 books.

(Answer A)

Method 2: The proportion of books is 1:2 (Total 3)

Cross-multiply: $\frac{1}{3} = \frac{x}{30}$ ➔ x = 10 **(Answer A)**

5. How many are there **total** in the ratio?

Answer:7

What part is green?   Four out of seven = 4/7
What part is red?   Three out of seven = 3/7

Method 1: Cross-mutiply:
$\frac{140}{4} = \frac{x}{3}$ ➔ 4x = 420 ➔ x = 105 **(Answer D)**

Method 2: Cross-mutiply:
$\frac{3}{4} = \frac{x}{140}$ ➔ 4x = 420 ➔ x = 105   **(Answer D)**

6. AOC is a right angle. Therefore, the two smaller angles will have a total of 90 degrees together.

We need to consider the **total** of the two ratios: the 2 and the 3 in the proportion make a total of 5, and the two angles make a total of 90.

The ratio from 5 to 90 is identical to the ratio from 2 to x. $\frac{5}{90} = \frac{3}{x}$ ➔ 5x = 270 ➔ x = 54

(Answer D)

7. When you solve ratios, always change one measurement at a time. (Go from seconds to hours, then go from feet to miles.)

Always simplify to single units: 1 mile, 1 minute, 1 hour, etc.).

$\frac{1\ sec}{132\ ft} = \frac{1\ min}{60*132\ ft} = \frac{1\ hour}{60.60*132\ ft} = \frac{1\ hour}{475200\ ft} =$

$\frac{1\ hour}{\frac{475200}{5280}\ miles} = \frac{1\ hr}{90\ miles}$ **(Answer E)**

8. Cross multiply

For 1 match: $\frac{1000}{239} = \frac{1100}{x}$ x = 262.9 calories

For the total $\frac{1}{262.9} = \frac{x}{5600}$ x=21.3 matches

You cannot light .3 of a match, so you need to light 22 matches. (21 would not be enough) **(Answer D)**

Read the question. It states, "how many matches must be lit to produce **at least** 5,600 calories."

MATH
NUMBER &
QUANTITY

FACTORING

Factoring

The ACT expects you to know your **multiplication tables**.

The test also expects you to know your **prime numbers**.

A prime number has only two factors: 1 and itself.

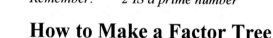

Remember: *0 is not a prime number!*
Remember: *1 is not a prime number!*
Remember: *2 IS a prime number*

How to Make a Factor Tree

Split the number into factors until you only have prime numbers left.

First start by splitting into 2's, then 3's, then 5's and 7's, etc.

Example: The factors of 42 are 2, 3, and 7. $(2 * 3 * 7 = 42)$
The factors of 180 are $2^2, 3^2$ and 5. $(2 * 2 * 3 * 3 * 5 = 180)$
Circle the factors for clarity.

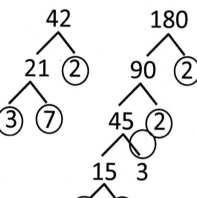

Factoring helps to see hidden patterns.

1) What do these numbers have in common?

> The number 42 and 180 both have a single 2 and 3 in common.
> The **Greatest Common Divisor (GCD)** (also called the GCF) is 6 $(2 * 3 = 6)$.
> **The GCD is the largest positive integer that divides the numbers without a remainder.**

2) What is the next number that is divisible by these numbers?

> A multiple of 42 and 180 has to have the factors of all three numbers in it, without overlap.
> It needs to have **at least** two 2's, two 3's, and a 7 to make it a multiple of 180, but it needs to have another 7 to make it a multiple of 42 AS WELL. (A multiple of 180 already has a 2 and a 3 in it by definition)
> The **Least Common Multiple (LCM)** is 1260 $(2 * 2 * 3 * 3 * 5 * 7 = 1260)$
> **The LCM is the smallest positive integer that is divisible by both numbers.**
> *Tip: The LCM and the GCD do not have to be prime numbers.*

Division rules:

> Divisible by 2:   if the last digit is a 2, 4, 6, 8, or 0 (all even numbers.)
> Divisible by 3:   if the sum of its digits is divisible by 3.
> Divisible by 5:   if the last digit is a 0 or 5.

Factoring - Quiz 1

1. What is the sum of the first four prime numbers?
   - A. 6
   - B. 10
   - C. 14
   - D. 17
   - E. 26

2. What is the least common multiple of 42, 27, and 54?
   - A. 123
   - B. 378
   - C. 1134
   - D. 2,268
   - E. 61,236

3. What is the greatest common denominator of 336, 51, and 612?
   - A. 1
   - B. 2
   - C. 3
   - D. 6
   - E. There is no greatest common denominator.

4. How many prime numbers are there between 15 and 25?
   - A. 1
   - B. 2
   - C. 3
   - D. 4
   - E. 5

5. What is the greatest common denominator of 412, 328, and 64?
   - A. 2
   - B. 4
   - C. 8
   - D. 16
   - E. There is no greatest common denominator.

6. If x and y are integers and $x^2 y^4 = 400$, what is x?
   - A. 2
   - B. 3
   - C. 4
   - D. 5
   - E. 6

7. If x and y are integers and $x^3 y^2 = 500$, How much is $2x + y$?
   - A. 7
   - B. 8
   - C. 9
   - D. 12
   - E. 14

8. What is the sum of the two largest factors of 24?
   - A. 36
   - B. 20
   - C. 14
   - D. 11
   - E. 10

1)D 2)B 3)C 4)C 5)B 6)D 7)D 8)A

Factoring - Quiz 1 (Answers)

1. 2 is the smallest prime number. 3 is also prime. 4 is not, 5 is a prime number, 6 is not a prime, 7 is a prime number: The smallest primes added up are $2 + 3 + 5 + 7 = 17$ **(Answer D)**

2. Create a factor tree to determine the build-up of each number.
   $42 = 2 * 21 \quad = 2 * 3 * 7$ Stop. All primes
   $27 = 3 * 9 \quad = 3 * 3 * 3$ Stop. All primes
   $54 = 2 * 27 \quad = 2 * 3 * 9 = 2 * 3 * 3 * 3$ Stop. All primes
   A multiple of these numbers has to have the factors of all three numbers in it.
   It needs to have three 3s to make it a multiple of 27, it needs to have a 2 to make it even, and it needs to have a seven in it as well. The number needs to have the factors 2, 3, 3, 3, and 7 to satisfy all numbers. (It does not need another three or another two.) The least common multiple is $2 * 3 * 3 * 3 * 7 = 378$ **(Answer B)**

3. Create a factor tree to determine the build-up of each number.
   $336 \quad = 2 * 2 * 2 * 2 * 3 * 7$ (the sum of its digits is divisible by 3)
   $51 \quad = 3 * 17$ (the sum of its digits is divisible by 3)
   $612 \quad = 2 * 2 * 3 * 3 * 17$ (the sum of its digits is divisible by 3)
   What number do they all have in common? 3   **(Answer C)**

4. You can write out 10 numbers fairly quickly to get an overview.
   For a faster process, simply leave out all even numbers, because they cannot be prime numbers.
   17, 19, 21, and 23
   From memory: are any of these numbers part of a familiar times table?
   By analysis: are any of these numbers divisible by 3 (add up the digits,) 5, 7, 11, 13, or 17?
   Only 21 is. This leaves three prime numbers.   **(Answer C)**

5. Create a factor tree to determine the build-up of each number.
   $412 = 2 * 2 * 103$
   $328 = 2 * 2 * 2 * 41$
   $64 = 2 * 2 * 2 * 2 * 2 * 2$
   What number do they all have in common? Two 2's. The GCD is 4.   **(Answer B)**

6. $x^2 y^4 = 400$. Create a factor tree to determine the build-up of the number 400.
   $400 = 2 * 2 * 2 * 2 * 5 * 5 = 2^4 * 5^2$
   Compare this to the variables in the question to determine that $x = 5$.   **(Answer D)**

7. $x^3 y^2 = 392$. Create a factor tree to determine the build-up of the number 392.
   $392 = 2 * 2 * 2 * 7 * 7 = 2^3 * 7^2$
   The question states that $392 = x^3 y^2$. Therefore $x = 2$ and $y = 7$. $2x + y = 11$ **(Answer D)**

8. The factors of 24 are 1, 2, 3, 4, 6, 8, 12 and 24. (These do not have to be prime factors.)
   (You could factor 24 out as $1 * 24$ or $2 * 12$ or $3 * 8$ or $4 * 6$.) All of these numbers are factors.
   The sum of the two largest factors is $12 + 24 = 36$ **(Answer A)**

SEQUENCES

Sequences

There are different types of mathematical sequences:

Arithmetic Sequence - Equal distances between each term

Examples: 1, 3, 5, 7, 9, 11, etc.
6, 12, 18, 24, 30, 36, etc.
4, 9, 14, 19, 24, 29, 34, etc.
x, (x+4), (x+4)+4, (x+4+4)+4, (x+4+4+4)+4, etc.

In arithmetic sequences, you use **adding and subtracting** a *constant* to get to the next term.

 Tip: If the ACT gives you the first term and the fourth term only, **draw lines** *for the unknown quantities.* (Think on paper.) Despite the fact that there are TWO open spots and there are FOUR numbers, you will need to split the difference of those two terms into THREE equal quantities. Draw it: 8 __ __ 20

Geometric Sequence - Different distances between each term

Examples: 2, 4, 8, 16, 32, 64, etc.
1, 4, 9, 16, 25, 36, etc.
$10, 10^2, 10^3, 10^4, 10^5, 10^6$, etc.
x, 2(x), 2(2x), 2(4x), 2(8x), etc.

In geometric sequences, you use **multiplication and division** of a *constant* to get to the next term.

Other Sequences

Sometimes you have to find a pattern in questions such as "Find the nth term in this sequence."

Example: $\frac{1}{7} = 0.1428571428571428571....$ What is the value of the 200th digit?

Note: the pattern repeats every six numbers. Every **sixth** number is a seven. The **sixtieth** digit will be a seven. The **hundred-and-twentieth** and the **hundred-and-eightieth** will be a seven. The **hundred-and-ninety-eighth** number will be a seven. The 200th digit will therefore be a 4.

Example: i^{100} = ?

Note: the exponents of *i* repeat in patterns of **four**:
$i^1 = $ ***i***, $i^2 = $ **−1**, $i^3 = $ **−*i***, $i^4 = $ **1**, $i^5 = $ ***i***, $i^6 = $ **−1**, $i^7 = $ **−*i***, $i^8 = $ **1**, $i^9 = $ ***i***, etc.
Each **fourth** term is a 1. Therefore, $i^{40} = 1$, $1^{80} = 1$, and $i^{100} = 1$ (100 is divisible by **four**.)
(See page 198 for imaginary numbers. Remember that they form a sequence.)

Example: January 1 falls on a Monday. What day of the week does the 70th day of the year fall?

Days of the week repeat in a cycle of **seven**. Each seventh day is a **Sunday**.
70 is divisible by seven, so the seventieth day falls on a Sunday.

 Tip: Don't fall for the mentioning of the first term in the test. Find the cycle of the repetition.

Sequences - Quiz 1

1. What is the next number in the sequence
   2, 5, 8, 11, …?
   A. 2
   B. 13
   C. 14
   D. 17
   E. 21

2. What is the next number in the sequence
   1, 1, 2, 3, 5, 8, … ?
   A. 9
   B. 11
   C. 13
   D. 17
   E. 19

3. What is the next number in the sequence
   1, 2, 4, 7, 11, 16, … ?
   A. 18
   B. 19
   C. 20
   D. 21
   E. 22

4. Let x, y, and z be distinct positive
   integers. What is the next term in the
   following sequence?
   $3xy$, $3xy^2 z$, $3xy^3z^2$, $3xy^4z^3$, …
   A. $3xy^2z$
   B. $3x^2yz^2$
   C. $3xy^5z^3$
   D. $3xy^4z^5$
   E. $3xy^5z^4$

5. Let x, y, and z be distinct positive
   integers. What is the next term in the
   following sequence?
   $2x^4y^2$, $4x^3y^3z^2$, $8x^2y^4z^4$, …
   A. $8xy^5z^5$
   B. $8x^2y^4z^2$
   C. $16xy^6z^5$
   D. $16xy^5z^6$
   E. $32xy^6z^8$

6. What is the 100th digit after the decimal
   point of the digital notation of $\frac{11}{13}$?
   ($\frac{11}{13}$ *is* 0.846153846153846153846153461)
   A. 1
   B. 3
   C. 4
   D. 5
   E. 6

7. If the first day of the year falls on a
   Monday, then the 200th day will fall on
   which day of the week?
   A. Monday
   B. Tuesday
   C. Wednesday
   D. Thursday
   E. Friday

8. How much is $i^{19} * i^{52}$?
   A. i
   B. -1
   C. $-i$
   D. 1
   E. $-i^2$

Sequences - Quiz 1 (Answers)

1) This problem asks about a simple arithmetic sequence.
   a) First, find the difference between any two terms:
      The difference $= 5 - 2 = \mathbf{3}$; $8 - 5 = \mathbf{3}$, etc.
   b) Add the difference (3) to the last given term of the sequence (11) to find the next term
   c) $11 + 3 = 14$ **(Answer C)**

2) This is the Fibonacci Sequence.
   a) Any term in the Fibonacci Sequence is the sum of the previous two terms.
   b) $8 + 5 = 13$ **(Answer C)**

3) In this sequence, the gap increases by one between each number.   **(Answer E)**

4) This problem requires is a little critical thinking. The 3 stays the same throughout the sequence, and so does the x, however, each next term gets an extra y and z.
   a) What is the pattern? Each term is multiplied by yz to yield the next term.
   b) $3xy^4z^3 * yz = 3xy^5z^4$ **(Answer E)**

5) This problem is very similar to no. 4.
   a) Divide any term by the previous term to find the common difference: $\dfrac{4x^3y^3z^2}{2x^4y^2} = \dfrac{2yz^2}{x}$
   b) $\dfrac{2yz^2}{x} * 8x^2y^4z^4 = 16xy^6z^8$ **(Answer D)**
   c) Alternatively, look for the pattern of each component: 2, 4, 8, ➔ 16
      x^4, x^3, x^2 ➔ x^1 y^2, y^3, y^4 ➔ y^5 z^0, z^2, z^4 ➔ z^6

6) $\dfrac{11}{13}$ can be written as 0.846153846153846153846153846153385 (say it out loud)
   a) This number repeats every **six** digits (8,4,6,1,5,3)
   b) This means that the 6th, the 12th, the 18th, the 24th digits are all going to be a 3.
   c) Every number that is divisible by **six** will be a three.
   d) The nearest number to the desired 100th term that is divisible by **six** is 96.
   e) Count **four** more spaces to determine that the 100th digit must be a 1.   **(Answer A)**

7) This is about the days of the week, which repeat in a cycle of **seven.**
   a) The **seventh** day of the week will be on a Sunday; and so will the 14th, the 21st and the 28th day.
   b) Each day that can be divided by **seven** will be a Sunday.
   c) 196 is divisible by **seven** and therefore falls on a Sunday.
   d) Count 4 more days to determine that day 200 falls on a Thursday.   **(Answer D)**

8) How much is $i^{19}*i^{52}$?
   a) First solve this by adding the exponents. $i^{19} * i^{52} = i^{71}$
   b) The patterns of the imaginary numbers repeat every **four** terms
   c) $i^1 = i$; $i^2 = -1$; $i^3 = -i$; $i^4 = 1$; .....$i^5 = i$; $i^6 = -1$; $i^7 = -i$; $i^8 = 1$; etc.
   d) Each term that can be divided by **four** will be a 1.
   e) 68 is divisible by **four** and therefore will be **1**
   f) Count three more spaces to determine that i^{71} must be $-i$.   **(Answer C)**

EXPONENTS
AND
ROOTS

Exponents and Roots

Exponents

$A^5 = A*A*A*A*A$ — The exponent tells you how many times to multiply a factor.
Example: $3^4 = 3*3*3*3 = 81$

$A^1 = A$ — Any number to the first power is itself.

$A^0 = 1$ — Every number to the zero power is 0.

$(A+4)^2 \neq A^2 + 4^2$ — Watch out: Distributing an exponent only works on multiplications and divisions.
Write this problem out and FOIL: $(A+4)(A+4) = A^2 + 8A + 4^2$

$(4A)^2 \neq 4A^2$ — $(4A)^2 = 4A*4A = 4^2*A^2 = 16A^2$ The exponent affects both factors.

$(2AB)^2 = 4*A^2*B^2$ — Distribute the exponent over each factor.

$A^m A^n = A^{m+n}$ — $2^2*2^3 = 2*2 * 2*2*2 = 2^5 = 3^{(2+3)}$

$(A^m)^n = A^{mn}$ — $(2^3)^2 = 2*2*2 * 2*2*2 = 2^6 = 3^{(3*2)}$

$\dfrac{A^m}{A^n} = A^{m-n}$ — $\dfrac{2^5}{2^3} = \dfrac{2*2*2*2*2}{2*2*2} = \dfrac{\cancel{2*2*2}2*2}{\cancel{2*2*2}} = 2*2 = 2^2 = 2^{5-3}$

$\dfrac{2^3}{2^5} = \dfrac{2*2*2*}{2*2*2*2*2} = \dfrac{\cancel{2*2*2}}{\cancel{2*2*2}*2*2} = \dfrac{1}{2*2} = 2^{-2} = 2^{3-5}$

$A^{-m} \neq -A^m$ — 2^{-3} is **not** a negative number (see the equation above.)
(Note: remember your lessons in science: the size of a water molecule is $275*10^{-12}$ cm.
That is not a negative number; it is just very small.)

$A^{-m} = \dfrac{1}{A^m}$ — 2^{-3} simply means $\dfrac{1}{2^3} = \dfrac{1}{2*2*2} = \dfrac{1}{8}$ (Think small; think fractions.)

$A^{\frac{1}{2}} = \sqrt{A}$ — Use fractions just like natural numbers: $3^{\frac{1}{2}} * 3^{\frac{1}{2}} = 3^{\frac{1}{2}+\frac{1}{2}} = 3^1 = 3$
Note: What number times itself is 3? That number must be $\sqrt{3}$: $3^{\frac{1}{2}} = \sqrt{3}$

$A^{\frac{3}{4}} = \sqrt[4]{A^3}$ — It's complicated. Just memorize where the parts of the fraction go.

$2^3 * 8^3 = ?$ — You **cannot** add, subtract, or multiply exponents with different bases.
Therefore, first express 8^3 in a base-2 form: $8^3 = (2^3)^3 = 2^9$
Now you can solve the problem: $2^3 * 2^9 = 2^{12}$

Square Roots

$\sqrt{A^2} = A$ — Remember that a square root is the opposite of squaring. $(\sqrt{3})^2 = \sqrt{3^2} = 3$

$\sqrt{A}\sqrt{B} = \sqrt{AB}$ — You **can** multiply different square roots. $\sqrt{2} * \sqrt{8} = \sqrt{2*8} = \sqrt{16} = 4$

$\sqrt{A} + \sqrt{B} \neq \sqrt{A+B}$ — You **cannot** add or subtract different square roots. $\sqrt{16} + \sqrt{9} \neq \sqrt{25}$ $(4+3 \neq 5)$

$\sqrt{AB} = \sqrt{A}\sqrt{B}$ — You can distribute a square root over two factors: $\sqrt{75} = \sqrt{25*3} = \sqrt{25}*\sqrt{3} = 5\sqrt{3}$

$\sqrt{\dfrac{A}{B}} = \dfrac{\sqrt{A}}{\sqrt{B}}$ — You can distribute square roots in a fraction as well. $\sqrt{\dfrac{9}{16}} = \dfrac{\sqrt{9}}{\sqrt{16}} = \dfrac{3}{4}$

Exponent and Roots - Quiz 1

1. If $x = a + 2$, then $(a - x)^3 = ?$
   A. 8
   B. 6
   C. 2
   D. −2
   E. −8

2. $(n^5)^6$ is equivalent to:
   A. n^{11}
   B. n^{30}
   C. $5n^6$
   D. $6n^5$
   E. $30n$

3. If $n = 8$ and $16 * 2^m = 4^{n-8}$, then m = ?
   A. 8
   B. 1
   C. 0
   D. -4
   E. -8

4. If $n^x n^6 = n^{30}$ and $(n^4)^y = n^{20}$, what is the value of $x + y$?
   A. 10
   B. 21
   C. 25
   D. 29
   E. 40

5. $\dfrac{(a^{-2})^3 a^2}{a^0} = ?$
   A. a^0
   B. a^3
   C. 0
   D. $\dfrac{1}{a^2}$
   E. $\dfrac{1}{a^4}$

6. For all x ≠ 0 and y ≠ 0, $\dfrac{(4x^3 y^3)^2}{(2x^2 y)^2} = ?$
   A. $2xy^3$
   B. $2x^2 y^4$
   C. $12x^2 y^3$
   D. $4x^2 y^4$
   E. $4xy^3$

7. If 0.00047291 is expressed in the form $4.7291 * 10^n$, what is the value of n?
   A. −5
   B. −4
   C. 4
   D. 5
   E. 8

8. $\dfrac{2(2^3)^0}{(2^0)2^3} = ?$
   A. 0
   B. 1
   C. 1/2
   D. 1/4
   E. 1/8

9. $\sqrt{75} * \sqrt{27} = ?$
   A. 135
   B. 45
   C. $15\sqrt{3}$
   D. $\sqrt{102}$
   E. $\sqrt{48}$

10. How much is n if $(2^n)(8) = 16^3$?
    A. 3
    B. 4
    C. 6
    D. 9
    E. 12

1)E 2)B 3)D 4)D 5)E 6)D 7)B 8)D 9)B 10)D

Exponent and Roots - Quiz 1 (Answers)

1) For this one, just plug in the given value for x. The equation now becomes $(a - (a + 2))^3$, or $(a - a - 2)^3$ or $(-2)^3$, which is -8. **(Answer E)**

2) $(A^m)^n = A^{mn}$ When an exponent is raised to another exponent, the two exponents are multiplied. This means $(n^5)^6$ is the same as n^{5*6} or n^{30}. **(Answer B)**

3) When $n = 8$, then $4^{n-8} = 4^{8-8} = 4^0 = 1$.
$16 \cdot 2^m$ can be written as $2^4 * 2^m = 2^{4+m}$.
According to the directions, $2^{4+m} = 1$.
Any number to the zero power is 1, so $4 + m = 0$, and $m = -4$. **(Answer D)**

4) $A^m A^n = A^{m+n}$ When two equal values are both raised to a power and multiplied, it is equal to that value raised to the two powers added together. In this case,
$n^x n^6 = n^{x+6} = n^{30}$ so $x = 24$.
When one exponent is raised to another one, the two exponents are multiplied by each other. In this case,
$(n^4)^y = n^{4*y} = n^{20}$, so y = 5.
X + Y is $24 + 5 = 29$. **(Answer D)**

5) Much like problem #4, we have one exponent raised to another, and then two equal values both raised to a power and multiplied. This means $(a^{-2})^3 * a^2 = a^{-6} * a^2 = a^{-4}$. This is divided by a^0, and any number raised to the zero power is 1. Therefore, the equation becomes $\frac{a^{-4}}{1}$ or simply a^{-4}.
$A^{-m} = \frac{1}{A^m}$ Whenever a value is raised to a negative exponent, it is the same as 1 over that value raised to a positive exponent. Therefore, our answer is $\frac{1}{a^4}$. **(Answer E)**

6) First, distribute the exponent on the outside of the parentheses over all the values inside the parentheses. This leaves us with $\frac{4^2 x^6 y^6}{2^2 x^4 y^2}$.
$\frac{A^m}{A^n} = A^{m-n}$
The three parts of the equation become
$\frac{16}{4} = 4$, $\frac{x^6}{x^4} = x^{6-4}$ and $\frac{y^6}{y^2} = y^{6-2}$.
The final value therefore is $4x^2 y^4$. **(Answer D)**

7) Each time you move the decimal point one place to the right, you have gone to another 10^{-1}. Since it takes 4 shifts to reach 4.7291 from 0.00047291, it must be multiplied by 10^{-4}. **(Answer B)**

8) For the numerator, follow PEMDAS rules.
First solve parentheses $2^3 = 8$ and $2^0 = 1$
$\frac{2(8)^0}{(1)2^3}$
Then solve exponents $(8)^0 = 1$ and $2^3 = 8$
$\frac{2*(1)}{(1)*8}$
Then solve multiplications.
$\frac{2}{8} = \frac{1}{4}$ **(Answer D)**

9) When we break the two radicals into their factors, we find $\sqrt{25} * \sqrt{3} * \sqrt{9} * \sqrt{3}$
25 and 9 are both perfect squares, so simplify to $5 * 3 * \sqrt{3} * \sqrt{3}$. These last two square roots multiplied equal 3, so we end up with $5 * 3 * 3 = 45$. **(Answer B)**

10) You cannot compare components of different bases. Make each part the same base to find the solution. 8 is the same as 2^3, and 16 is the same as 2^4. When the equation is rewritten as such, we have $2^n * 2^3 = (2^4)^3$ This simplifies to $2^{n+3} = 2^{12}$.
Therefore, n must equal 9. **(Answer D)**

IRRATIONAL
AND
IMAGINARY
NUMBERS

Irrational/Imaginary Numbers

Integers - all whole numbers, positive or negative, including 0.

Examples: −4, −3, −2, −1, 0, 1, 2, 3, 4, etc.

Rational Numbers - numbers that can be expressed as a fraction (or as the ratio of two integers.)

Examples: ¼, ½, 1, 2.3, 0.001, etc.

Irrational Numbers - any number that cannot be expressed as a fraction of two integers. When written as a decimal, they do not have a repeating pattern.

Examples: $\sqrt{2}$, $\sqrt{3}$, $\sqrt{5}$, $\sqrt{11}$, π, e

Real Numbers - the combined set of rational numbers and irrational numbers.

Imaginary Numbers - the product of a real number and an imaginary unit i.

i has the property so that $i^2 = -1$

Therefore, $i^3 = i^1 * i^2 = i * -1 = -i$

and thus $i^4 = i^2 * i^2 = -1 * -1 = 1$

i	i^1	i^5	i^9	i^{13}
−1	i^2	i^6	i^{10}	i^{14}
−i	i^3	i^7	i^{11}	i^{15}
1	i^4	i^8	i^{12}	i^{16}

Notice how this pattern repeats in series of four. If the exponent of i can be divided by 4, we know the answer is 1.

Example: What is the value of $(i)^{43} * (i)^{38}$?

We learned that we can add the exponents when we multiply two factors with the same base. $(i)^{43} * (i)^{38} = (i)^{81}$

From the table above we learned that if the exponent of i can be divided by 4, the answer is 1. $(i)^{81} = (i)^{80} * (i)^1 = 1 * (i)^1 = 1 * i = i$

You can also use the pattern by counting backwards into negative numbers:

i^{-3}	**i**	i^1
i^{-2}	**−1**	i^2
i^{-1}	**−i**	i^3
i^0	**1**	i^4

Example: What is the square of the imaginary number $5i$?

$(5i)^2 = (5)^2(i)^2 = 25(i)^2 = 25 * -1 = -25$

Example: What is $\sqrt{-16}$?

$\sqrt{-16} = \sqrt{-1 * 16} = \sqrt{-1} * \sqrt{16} = \sqrt{-1} * 4 = 4i$

198

Irrational/Imaginary Numbers - Quiz 1

1) How much is i^0?
   - A. 1
   - B. i
   - C. -1
   - D. 0
   - E. The answer does not exist

2) How much is i^2?
   - A. $-i$
   - B. -1
   - C. 1
   - D. 0
   - E. i

3) How much is i^4?
   - A. -1
   - B. 0
   - C. $-i$
   - D. i
   - E. 1

4) How much is i^3?
   - A. i
   - B. $-i$
   - C. 0
   - D. 1
   - E. -1

5) What is the smallest possible value for the product of two real numbers that differ by 8?
   - A. -16
   - B. -7
   - C. 0
   - D. 8
   - E. 9

6) Which is not an irrational number?
   - A. $\sqrt{2}$
   - B. $\sqrt{3}$
   - C. $\sqrt{4}$
   - D. $\sqrt{5}$
   - E. $\sqrt{6}$

7) All of the following statements about rational and/or irrational numbers must be true EXCEPT:
   - A. The sum of any two rational numbers is rational.
   - B. The product of any two rational numbers is rational.
   - C. The sum of any two irrational numbers is irrational.
   - D. The product of a rational and an irrational number may be rational or irrational.
   - E. The product of any two irrational numbers is irrational.

8) For the imaginary number i, which of the following is a possible value of i^n if n is an integer less than 8?
   - A. 0
   - B. 1
   - C. 2
   - D. 3
   - E. 4

9) How much is $i^7 * i^9$?
   - A. $16i$
   - B. $63i$
   - C. 1
   - D. -1
   - E. $-i$

10) $i^n = -i$ for what value of n?
   - A. $n = 0$
   - B. $n = -1$
   - C. $n = 8$
   - D. $n = 16$
   - E. $n = i$

1)A 2)B 3)E 4)B 5)A 6)C 7)E 8)B 9)C 10)B

Irrational/Imaginary - Quiz 1 (Answers)

1) Anything—even i—raised to the power of 0 is 1; the answer is $i^0 = 1$. **(Answer A)**

2) The definition of i states: $i^2 = -1$. **(Answer B)**

3) Method 1:
   - First, rewrite i⁴ as $(i^2)^2$.
   - $i^2 = -1$, so $(i^2)^2 = (-1)^2 = 1$ **(Answer E)**

   Method 2: Memorize the sequence about the consecutive exponents of i:
   - $i^1 = i;$ $i^2 = -1;$ $i^3 = -i;$ $i^4 = 1;$
   - $i^5 = i;$ $i^6 = -1;$ $i^7 = -i;$ $i^8 = 1;$

   The sequence follows a pattern of $i, -1, -i, 1$ and repeats indefinitely.

4) Solution:
   - First rewrite i³ as $i * i^2$.
   - $i * i^2 = i * -1 = -i$ **(Answer B)**

5) Method 1. Define the two numbers as x and $(x + 8)$
   - Solve for the equation $y = x(x + 8)$ or $y = x^2 + 8x + 0$
   - Solve for x when y is 0: $0 = (x + 0)(x + 8)$
   - $x = 0 \; or \; x = -8$
   - These are the Y intercepts of the graph: $x = -8 \; and \; x = 0$
   - The lowest value should be right in between these two values.
   - The lowest value is $x = -4, x + 8 = 4$
   - The product of 4 and -4 is -16 **(Answer A)**

   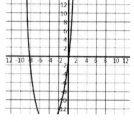

   Method 2. Test quickly how the two numbers behave by making a grid.
   You can test 10 pairs of numbers fairly easy in one minute. **(Answer A)**

x	$x + 8$	$x(x + 8)$
0	8	0
1	9	9
2	10	20 (Too big. Reverse your numbers,)
-1	7	-7
-2	6	-12
-3	5	-15
-4	4	-16
-5	3	-15 (Stop)

6) Any positive number under a square root sign is irrational unless it is itself a perfect square. $\sqrt{4}$ is the only answer choice with a perfect square under the radical, $\sqrt{4} = 2$ **(Answer C)**

7) Go through each answer choice to find the one which is not true.
   a. must be true (you can add fractions)
   b. must be true (you can multiply fractions)
   c. $\sqrt{3} + \sqrt{3} = 2\sqrt{3}$ This number is still irrational. The statement is true.
   d. True for $5 * \sqrt{3} = 5\sqrt{3}$ (irrational) Also true for $0 * \sqrt{3} = 0$ (rational)
   e. True for $\sqrt{3} * \sqrt{5} = \sqrt{15}$ (irrational) NOT TRUE for $\sqrt{3} * \sqrt{3} = 3$ (rational) **(Answer E)**

8) There are only four possible results when i is raised to an exponent $i, -1, -i, and \; 1$ **(Answer B)**

9) First, write $i^7 * i^9$ as i^{16}. ➜ Write i^{16} as $(i^2)^4$. $(i^2)^4 = -1^4 = 1$ **(Answer C)**

10) Eliminate answer a ($i^0 = 1$), c ($i^8 = 1$), and d ($i^{16} = 1$). You have memorized the sequence; if the exponent can be divided by 4, we know the answer is 1. Now either use the sequence backwards to find ($i^{-1} = -i$) or solve for i: $i^{-1} = \frac{1}{i^1} = \frac{1}{i} * \frac{i}{i} = \frac{i}{i^2} = \frac{i}{-1} = -i$ **(Answer B)**

MATH

Algebra

SIMPLE EQUATIONS

Simple Equations

Think on Paper

What do TOP students do? They **T**hink **O**n **P**aper.

Many ACT math problems take two or three steps to solve.

If you do those steps in your head, you are bound to make small mistakes. Be a TOP student! (Think On Paper)

Writing down the steps only takes seconds, but it will help you to avoid simple mistakes.

 One way to get a better score in the math portion is to get better in math.

*Tip: The other way to get a better score is to **MAKE FEWER MISTAKES.***

Distribution Rules

$$A(x + y) = ax + ay$$

$$(x + 2)b^2 = xb^2 + 2b^2$$

$$(4x)^2 = 4^2 * x^2$$

$$\frac{x + 2}{3} = \frac{x}{3} + \frac{2}{3}$$

Understand Patterns

Positive and Negative Numbers

$$Positive \ times \ negative \ = negative$$
$$Positive \ times \ positive \ = positive$$
$$Negative \ times \ negative \ = positive$$

Odd and Even Numbers

$$odd \ + odd \ = even \qquad odd \ times \ odd \ = odd$$
$$even + even \ = even \qquad even \ times \ even \ = even$$
$$odd \ + even \ = odd \qquad odd \ times \ even \ = even$$

Negative Signs

Too often, students make mistakes by not "carrying" the negative sign to the next step in their equations.

Refer to the "Think on Paper" strategy to avoid making mistakes in this area. Be a TOP student.

$$-(x + 4) = -x - 4$$
$$-2(x - 4) = -2x + 8$$

PEMDAS

Remember "Please excuse my dear aunt Sally."

Solve complex equations in the following order:

Parentheses, then **E**xponents, then **M**ultiplications and **D**ivisions, and lastly **A**dditions and **S**ubtractions.

Simple Equations - Quiz 1

1. If $y = -14$, what is the value of $\frac{4-y^2}{y+2}$?

   A. -16

   B. -12

   C. 8

   D. 12

   E. 16

2. If $-4(x - 13) = 17$, then $x = ?$

   A. $\frac{-35}{4}$

   B. -1

   C. 1

   D. $\frac{30}{4}$

   E. $\frac{35}{4}$

3. Which of the following values of x is a solution to the equation
   $$\frac{7}{9}(x - 8) = 14$$

   A. 2

   B. 18

   C. $22\frac{9}{7}$

   D. 26

   E. 52

4. The expression
   $$7(y - 3) + (-12)(-y + 2)$$
   is equivalent to:

   A. $19y - 45$

   B. $19y + 3$

   C. $-5y + 3$

   D. $-5y - 45$

   E. $5y - 3$

5. The expression $4(x + 3) - 3(6 - x)$
   is equivalent to:

   A. $x - 12$

   B. $x + 30$

   C. $7x + 6$

   D. $-x - 12$

   E. $7x - 6$

6. If $2a + 3b = 17$, and $2a - 3b = -13$,
   then $2b = ?$

   A. 2.5

   B. 5

   C. 10

   D. 15

   E. 20

7. What is the solution to the equation
   $$12x = -8(10 - x)$$

   A. 20

   B. 4

   C. $\frac{-4}{5}$

   D. -4

   E. -20

8. Which of the following values of x is a solution to the equation $x - 10 = 2(x + 5)$

   A. -20

   B. -15

   C. -5

   D. 0

   E. 5

1)E 2)E 3)D 4)A 5)E 6)C 7)E 8)A

Simple Equations - Quiz 1 (Answers)

1. To find the value of this equation, insert -14 in for y.
    $$\frac{4-(-14)^2}{(-14)+2} = \frac{4-196}{-12} = \frac{-192}{-12} = 16.$$
    Alternatively, remember that the difference between two squares can be written as
    $$\frac{4-y^2}{y+2} = \frac{(2-y)(2+y)}{y+2} = 2-y \quad \text{(substitute } -14 \text{ for } y) = 2-(-14) = 16 \quad \textbf{(Answer E)}$$

2. To solve

    $-4(x-13) = 17$

    Distribute the factor -4. $-4x + 52 = 17$

    Subtract 52 from each side: $-4x = -35$

    Multiply both sides by -1: $4x = 35.$

    Divide both sides by 4 $x = \frac{35}{4}$ **(Answer E)**

3. To solve $\frac{7}{9}(x-8) = 14$

    Multiply both sides by 9: $7(x-8) = 126$

    Divide both sides by 7 $x-8 = 18$

    Add 8 to both sides for the solution $x = 26$ **(Answer D)**

4. To solve $7(y-3) - 12(-y+2)$

    Distribute the factors 4 and 3 $7y - 21 + 12y - 24$

    Add: $7y + 12y = 19y$ and $-21 - 24 = -45$ $19y - 45$ **(Answer A)**

5. To solve, $4(x+3) - 3(6-x)$

    Distribute the factors 4 and 3 $4x + 12 - 18 + 3x$

    Add: $4x + 3x = 7x$ and $12 - 18 = -6$ $7x - 6$ **(Answer E)**

6. Remember, you can subtract or add the two equations.
    Because the question asks to calculate *2b*, we will *subtract* to eliminate a.

    $$\begin{array}{r} 2a + 3b = 17 \\ - \quad (2a - 3b = -13) \\ \hline 6b = 30 \end{array}$$

    To find the value of 2b, divide both sides of the resulting equation by 3.
    $$\frac{6b}{3} = \frac{30}{3} \rightarrow 2b = 10 \quad \textbf{(Answer C)}$$

7. To solve $12x = -8(10-x)$

    First distribute the factor -8: $12x = -80 + 8x)$

    Subtract $8x$ from each side: $4x = -80$

    Divide each side by 4: $x = -20$ **(Answer E)**

8. To solve $x - 10 = 2(x+5)$

    Distribute the factor two: $x - 10 = 2x + 10$

    Subtract x from each side: $-10 = x + 10$

    Then, subtract 10 from each side: $-20 = x$ **(Answer A)**

ABSOLUTE VALUE

Absolute Value

Basic Variations:

$|4| = x$ This means $x = 4$ The absolute value of 4 is always 4.

$|-4| = x$ This means $x = 4$ The absolute value of -4 is always 4.

$|x| = -4$ This does not exist. An absolute value is never negative.

$-|x| = 4$ Don't be fooled. $|x|$ is always positive. $-|x|$ is therefore always negative. There are therefore NO solutions for x to satisfy this equation.

$|4| = -x$ This is possible for $x = -4$. x can be negative, $|x|$ cannot be negative.

$|-4| = -x$ This is possible for $x = -4$. x can be negative, $|x|$ cannot be negative.

$|x| = 4$ Make two equations $x = 4$ **or** $x = -4$

$|-x| = 4$ Make two equations $-x = 4$ **or** $-x = -4$

👀 *Tip: Most ACT absolute value questions are variations of the examples above. You have to know your math and you have to do some thinking about what absolute value actually means.*

Complicated variations:

$|x - 4| = Z$ Simply means $x - 4 = Z$ **or** $x - 4 = -Z$
The equation inside the absolute values can be positive or negative.

👀 *Tip: Always **make two equations** when you see an absolute value equation.*

$|x - 4| = -4$ This looks like $x = 0$, but don't forget: Absolute values are always positive! There is no possible value of x that would solve this equation.

$|x - 4| = x$ A number minus 4 equals that same number? That looks impossible. But the absolute value indicates that the number can also be negative.

Make two equations: $x - 4 = x$ (impossible) **or** $x - 4 = -x$ ➔ $2x = 4$ ➔ $x = 2$

$|x - 4| = -x$ Make two equations: $x - 4 = -x$ or $x - 4 = -(-x)$ (impossible) ➔ $x = 2$
However, you need plug this solution into the equation: $|-2| = -2$ (impossible)

👀 *Tip: What if the absolute value is **part** of an equation? Treat it like a variable and move all other parts of the equation to the other side of the equal sign.*

$6 - |x - 4| = 4$ Change to $-|x - 4| = -2$ => $|x - 4| = 2$
Make two equations: $x - 4 = 2$ **or** $x - 4 = -2$ ➔ $x = 2$ *or* $x = 6$

Inequalities

👀 *Tip: Make sure to flip the sign for the negative value of the absolute value.*

$|x - 4| > 10$ Make two equations: $x - 4 > 10$ **or** $x - 4 < -10$ ➔ $x > 14$ or $x < -6$

$|4 - x| \leq 2$ Make two equations: $4 - x \leq 2$ **or** $4 - x \geq -2$ ➔ $x \geq 2$ and $x \leq 6$

206

Absolute Value - Quiz 1

1. Find a possible solution for x.

$|x + 2| = 4$

A. $x = -6$
B. $x = -2$
C. $x = 2$
D. $x = 2 \, or \, x = -6$
E. There are no possible solutions for x.

2. Find a possible solution for x.

$-|x + 4| = 2$

A. $x = 1$
B. $x = -7$
C. $x = -1$
D. $x = 7$
E. There are no possible solutions for x.

3. Find a possible solution for x.

$-|3| + |2 - 6| = X$

A. $x = 1$
B. $x = -7$
C. $x = -1$
D. $x = 7$
E. There are no possible solutions for x.

4. Find a possible solution for x.

$|-6| - |-8| * -|-x| = -34$

A. $x = 48$
B. $x = -5$
C. $x = 17$
D. $x = -17$
E. There are no possible solutions for x.

5. Find the smallest possible value for x.

$-|3| * |6 - x| = -12$

A. $x = -10$
B. $x = -2$
C. $x = 2$
D. $x = 10$
E. $x = 2 \, or \, 10$

6. Find a possible solution for x.

$\dfrac{|-16|}{8} + \dfrac{|-x|}{6} - |-3 * 4| = -4$

A. $x = -36$
B. $x = -14$
C. $x = -6$
D. $x = 6$
E. $x = 14$

7. Find a possible solution for a.

$|2a + 1| + 5 = |-2 + 6|$

A. -5
B. -1
C. -1 and -5
D. 1 and 5
E. There are no possible solutions for a.

8. Find a possible solution for a.

$|2a + 5| = a + 4$

A. -3
B. -1
C. -3 and -1
D. ½
E. 4.5

9. Find a possible solution for x.

$|x - 2| = 2x - 3$

A. 1
B. $\dfrac{3}{5}$
C. $\dfrac{5}{3}$
D. $\dfrac{3}{5}$ and $\dfrac{5}{3}$
E. 1 and $\dfrac{5}{3}$

Absolute Values - Quiz 1 (Answers)

1. $|x + 2| = 4$ The equation inside the absolute values can be positive or negative. Solve for both options.

   $x + 2 = 4$ or $x + 2 = -4$

   $x \quad = 2$ or $x \quad = -6$ **(Answer D)**

2. $-|x + 4| = 2$ To solve absolute values, treat it like a variable and move all other parts of the equation to the other side of the equal sign. In this case, multiply both sides by -1 so that only the absolute value is on the left side of the equation.

   $|x + 4| = -2$ An absolute value can never be negative.   **(Answer E)**

3. $-|3| + |2 - 6| = X$ If absolute values only contain numbers solve them first.
   (Similar to using PEMDAS and first solving parentheses)

   $-3 + |-4| = x$ ➜ $-3 + 4 = x$ ➜ $x = 1$ **(Answer A)**

4. $|-6| - |-8| * -|-x| = -34$ If absolute values only contain numbers solve them first.

   $6 - 8 * -|-x| = -34$

   $-8 * -|-x| = -40$ ➜ $-|-x| = 5$ ➜ $|-x| = -5$

   An absolute value can never be negative.   **(Answer E)**

5. $-|3| * |6 - x| = -12$ If absolute values only contain numbers solve them first.

   $-3 * |6 - x| = -12$ ➜ $|6 - x| = 4$

   The equation inside the absolute values can be positive or negative. Solve for both options.

   $6 - x = 4$ or $6 - x = -4$ ➜

   $x = 2$ or $x = 10$

   The question asks for the smallest possible value: $x = 2$ **(Answer C)**

6. $\frac{|-16|}{8} + \frac{|-x|}{6} - |-3 * 4| = -4$ If absolute values only contain numbers, solve them first.

   $2 + \frac{|-x|}{6} - 12 = -4$ ➜ $\frac{|-x|}{6} = 6$ ➜ $|-x| = 36$ ➜ $x = 36 \: or \: x = -36$ **(Answer A)**

7. $|2a + 1| + 5 = |-2 + 6|$ If absolute values only contain numbers, solve them first.

   $|2a + 1| + 5 = 4$

   $|2a + 1| = -1$ Absolute values can't be negative.   **(Answer E)**

8. $|2a + 5| = a + 4$ The equation inside the absolute values can be positive or negative.

   $2a + 5 = a + 4$ or $2a + 5 = -(a + 4)$ (Watch out for the negative sign!)

   $a = -1$ or $a = -3$)   **(Answer C)**

9. $|x - 2| = 2x - 3$ The equation inside the absolute values can be positive or negative.

   $x - 2 = 2x - 3$ or $x - 2 = -(2x - 3)$

   $-x = -1$ or $3x \quad = 5$

   $x = 1$ or $x = \frac{5}{3}$

   Substituting 1 and $\frac{5}{3}$ in the question gives $|1| = -1$ (impossible) and $\left|-\frac{1}{3}\right| = \frac{1}{3}$ **(Answer C)**

QUADRATIC EQUATIONS

Quadratic Equations

A quadratic expression is as simple as the area of a square.
To find the area, you square each side.   Area = 4^2 which is equal to 16.
Vice versa, if you only have the area, you need to think backwards.
You need to take the "square" root of the area.   Each side is $\sqrt{25} = 5$

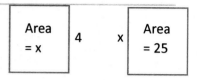

Binomial Squares

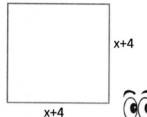

What does it mean when each side of a square is (x+4)? Perform the same actions as above: square each side. $(x + 4)^2 = x^2 + 8x + 16$
If you draw the square, you can see that there is
one block of x^2, one block of 4^2, and two blocks of 4x.
In algebra form this is written as $x^2 + 2(4x) + 4^2$
or $x^2 + 8x + 16$.
Tip: Compare the squares on the left and right to understand the formula.

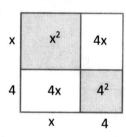

FOIL

In algebra, you most likely learned the term FOIL. Here are the steps you need to remember:
First terms multiplied: $x * x = x^2$
Outer terms multiplied: $x * 4 = 4x$
Inner terms multiplied: $4 * x = 4x$
Last terms multiplied: $4 * 4 = 4^2$
Add them up: $x^2 + 2(4x) + 16$

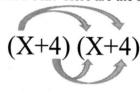

(X+4) (X+4)

FOIL and un-FOIL

Tip: Memorize the following common patterns backwards and forwards.

1. $(a + b)^2$ $= a^2 + 2ab + b^2$
2. $(a - b)^2$ $= a^2 - 2ab + b^2$
3. $(a + b + c)^2$ $= a^2 + b^2 + c^2 + 2(ab + bc + ca)$
4. $a^2 - b^2$ $= (a + b)(a - b)$ = difference of two squares ("DOTS")
5. $a^2 + b^2$ $= (a + b)^2 - 2ab$ *or* $(a - b)^2 + 2ab$ (See patterns 1 and 2)

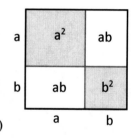

Factor

Consider the equation $x^2 + 8x + 15$. What are the factors (sides) of that square?
*Tip: There are two numbers that are important. The 8 indicates that if you **add the two factors** you will get 8, and the 15 indicates that if you **multiply the two factors** you get 15.*

Factors of 15	
1	15
3	5
−1	−15
−3	−5

The best strategy is to first to determine the factors of 15. With integers, these can only be a combination of four sets of numbers. Write them in a table. (See table on the left) Then, find out which set of two factors add up to 8. The two factors that add up to 8 must be 3 and 5. The answer is $(x + 3)(x + 5)$ = $x^2 + 3x + 5x + 15 = x^2 + 8x + 15$

Quadratic Formula $x = \dfrac{-b \pm \sqrt{b^2 - 4ac}}{2a}$

Quadratic Equations - Quiz 1

1) Which of the following is a factor of the polynomial $2x^2 - 3x - 5$?
   A. $x - 1$
   B. $2x - 3$
   C. $2x - 5$
   D. $2x + 5$
   E. $3x + 5$

2) For $Y = 4$, $(Y - 2)^2 + (Y + 3)^2 = $?
   A. 53
   B. 45
   C. 37
   D. 27
   E. 5

3) What is the x-intercept of the graph of $y = x^2 - 4x + 4$?
   A. 2
   B. 1
   C. 0
   D. -1
   E. -2

4) Each side of the smaller square in the figure below is x inches long, and each side of the larger square is c inches longer than a side of the smaller square. The area of the larger square is how many square inches greater than the area of the smaller square?

   A. c^2
   B. xc
   C. $4c$
   D. $(x + c)^2$
   E. $2xc + c^2$

5) Solve for x. $\frac{x^2 - 81}{x + 9} = 5$
   A. $X = -4$
   B. $X = 4$
   C. $X = -14$
   D. $X = 14$
   E. $X = 77$

6) $(3x + 4)^2$ is equivalent to:
   A. $X = 3x^2 + 4$
   B. $X = 9x^2 + 16$
   C. $X = 9x^2 + 4$
   D. $X = 9x^2 + 12x + 16$
   E. $X = 9x^2 + 24x + 16$

7) What are the factors of $8x^2 - 46x - 12$?
   A. $(X + 2)(8x - 23)$
   B. $(x - 2)(8x - 23)$
   C. $(X - 6)(8x + 2)$
   D. $(4x - 2)(x + 6)$
   E. $(4x + 2)(x - 6)$

8) $\frac{x^2 - 196}{x + 14}$ is equal to
   A. $\frac{x - 196}{14}$
   B. $\frac{x^2 - 182}{x}$
   C. $x - 172$
   D. $X - 14$
   E. $X + 14$

1)C 2)A 3)A 4)E 5)D 6)E 7)C 8)D

Quadratic Equations - Quiz 1 (Answers)

1. $2x^2 - 3x - 5 = (x + 1)(2x - 5)$.   **(Answer C)**

2.   Plug 4 in for y, and then use PEMDAS to solve inside the parentheses first.
$(4 - 2)^2 + (4 + 3)^2 =$
$(2)^2 + (7)^2 =$
$4 + 49 = 53$.   **(Answer A)**

3.   To find the *x*-intercept, replace *y* with 0, and solve for *x*. If $x^2 - 4x + 4 = 0$, then $(x - 2)^2 = 0$.
Therefore, $x - 2 = 0$ ➔ $x = 2$.   **(Answer A)**

4.   The area of the larger square is $(x + c)^2$ and the area of the smaller square is x^2.
So $(x + c)^2 - x^2 \quad = \quad x^2 + 2xc + c^2 - x^2 \quad = \quad 2xc + c^2$ **(Answer E)**

5)   This is a problem that involves the difference of two squares.
$\frac{x^2 - 81}{x + 9} = 5$ can be rewritten as $\frac{(x+9)(x-9)}{x+9} = 5$ which simplifies to $x - 9 = 5$.
Hence, $x = 14$.   **(Answer D)**

6) $(3x + 4)^2$ Follow the formula $(a + b)^2 = a^2 + 2ab + b^2$, or use the FOIL method.
$(3x)^2 + 2(4 * 3x) + 4^2 = 9x^2 + 24x + 16^2$ **(Answer E)**

7) $8x^2 - 46x - 12$

First, we have to find the factors of 96 $(8 * -12)$ that add up to -46

2	−48
−2	48
4	−24
−4	24
6	−16
−6	16
8	−12
−8	12

Make a table. (see right) Only the first pair (2 and −48) add up to −46, which is the number we need for the middle. This means our two factors should be
$8x^2 - 48x + 2x - 12$

Now we can factor out the number that the two pairs have in common
$8x(x - 6) + 2(x - 6)$

Simplified, this can be written as $(8x + 2)(X - 6)$.   **(Answer C)**

8)   This is an example of the problem known as "the difference between two squares."
$(a^2 - b^2) = (a + b)(a - b)$
Once you recognize that 196 is a perfect square, you will see the pattern emerge:

$\frac{x^2 - 196}{x + 14} = \frac{x^2 - 14^2}{x + 14} = \frac{(x+14)(x-14)}{x+14} = x - 14$ **(Answer D)**

👀 *Tip: Memorize the squares over 10, because the ACT likes to use them.*
$11^2 = 121$ $12^2 = 144$ $13^2 = 169$ $14^2 = 196$ $15^2 = 225$ and $16^2 = 256$

Quadratic Equations - Quiz 2

1) When $(3x - 7)^2$ is written in the format $ax^2 + bx + c$, where a, b, and c are integers, what is the value of $a - b + c$?
   A. -82
   B. -4
   C. 9
   D. 10
   E. 16

2) What is the sum of the two solutions to the equation $x^2 - 18x - 40 = 0$?
   A. -18
   B. -8
   C. 0
   D. 18
   E. 58

3) When $(4x + 5)^2$ is written in the format $ax^2 + bx + c$, where a, b, and c are integers, what is the value of $a + b - c$?
   A. 1
   B. 9
   C. 31
   D. 56
   E. 81

4) Which of the following equations has the roots $\frac{4}{7}$, and -2?
   A. $X^2 + \frac{10}{7}x - \frac{8}{7}$
   B. $X^2 - \frac{10}{7}x - \frac{8}{7}$
   C. $X^2 + \frac{10}{7}x + \frac{8}{7}$
   D. $X^2 + \frac{18}{7}x + \frac{8}{7}$
   E. $X^2 - \frac{18}{7}x - \frac{8}{7}$

5) What is the product of $4x^3$ and $16x^8$?
   A. $64x^{11}$
   B. $64x^{24}$
   C. $20x^{11}$
   D. $20x^{24}$

6) Which of the following is a possible graph for $3x^2 - 4x + 2$?

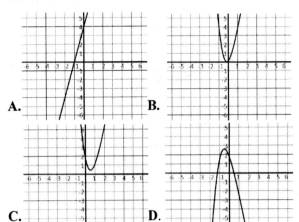

A.   B.

C.   D.

7) Which of the following equations is a possible match for this graph?

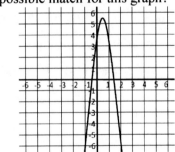

   A. $y = 2x^2 + 2x - 5$
   B. $y = -4x^2 - 5x - 2$
   C. $y = -5x^2 + 5x + 4$
   D. $y = -3x^2 - 2x + 7$
   E. $(y - 0.5) = (x - 5.5)^2$

1)E 2)D 3)C 4)A 5)A 6)C 7)C

Quadratic Equations - Quiz 2 (Answers)

1) To solve this problem, you must know how to expand the squared binomial using FOIL.
   1. $(3x - 7)^2 = 9x^2 - 21x - 21x + 49 = 9x^2 - 42x + 49$
   2. Written as ax^2+bx+c, a = 9, b = -48 and c = 49.
   3. Solve for $a - b + c$ $= 9 - 42 + 49 = 16$ **(Answer E)**

2) This problem requires you to know how to factor.
   1. The factors of 40 are 1 and 40; 2 and 20; 4 and 10; 5 and 8.
   2. Because is the equation has -40, one of the factors must be negative.
   3. One of these combinations needs to add up to the other number in our equation: -18
   4. A quick review of all possibilities gives us the numbers -20 and 2
   5. $x^2 - 18x - 40 = 0$ factors to $(x - 20)(x + 2) = 0$
   6. Solving for X means either $x - 20 = 0$ or $x + 2 = 0$. Therefore, $x = 20$ or $x = -2$
   7. Read the question: Add the two solutions. $20 + (-2) = 18$ **(Answer D)**

3) This problem is very similar to the first problem.
   1. First, expand: $(4x + 5)^2 = 16x^2 + 20x + 20x + 25 = 16x^2 + 40x = 25$
   2. Written as $ax^2+bx + c$, $a = 16, b = 40$ and $c = 25$.
   3. Solve for $a + b - c$: $16 + 40 - 25 = 31$ **(Answer C)**

4) If the roots are $\frac{4}{7}$ and -2, then the binomial must be $(x - \frac{4}{7})(x + 2)$.

   1. By using the FOIL method, $\frac{4}{7}$ and -2 are respectively multiplied by x and then added.

   2. Multiplication gives $\frac{4}{7} * -2 = -\frac{8}{7}$ (eliminate answer c and d)

   3. Now add 2 and $-\frac{4}{7}$, (the coefficient b of the form ax^2+bx+c) $b = -\frac{4}{7} + \frac{14}{7} = \frac{10}{7}$,
   (Answer A)

   4. Alternatively, you could also use FOIL to expand the binomial.
   5. $x^2 + 2x - \frac{4}{7}x - \frac{8}{7}$ ➔ $x^2 + \frac{10}{7}x - \frac{8}{7}$

5) Remember the exponent rules: For multiplication, add the exponents. (Careful, do not multiply!)
   1. $4x^3$ and $16x^8$ can be written as $4*16*x^3*x^8$
   2. This can be written very simply as $4*16*(x*x*x)(x*x*x*x*x*x*x*x)$
   3. Counting the x's will give you 11 x's or x^{11}
   4. Or remember the rule $x^a*x^b=x^{a+b}$ $x^3*x^8=x^{3+8}$
   5. $4*16 = 64$, so the answer is $64x^{11}$ **(Answer A)**

6) Solve this problem using the process of elimination.
   1. This is a quadratic, not linear, equation. Ignore choice A.
   2. Since the coefficient of x^2 is positive, the parabola opens upwards. Ignore choice D.
   3. Find the y-intercept.
   4. In the formula, when $x = 0$, what is y? $y = 3(0) - 4(0) + 2$ ➔ $y = 2$
   In the graph, when $x = 0$, we are looking at the y intercept. It needs to be 2. **(Answer C)**

7) Solve this problem using your knowledge of y-intercepts.
   1. When $x = 0, y = 4$. In other words, the y-intercept is 4.
   2. Of all the answers, only C contains +4. **(Answer C)**

Quadratic Equation - Quiz 3

1) The expression $(z - 3y^2)(z + 3y^2)$ is equivalent to:
   A. $z^2 - 9y^4$
   B. $z^2 - 6y^4$
   C. $z^2 + 9y^4$
   D. $2z^2 - 9y^4$
   E. $2z^2 - 6y^4$

2) If $4^x = 75$, then which of the following must be true?
   A. $1 < x < 2$
   B. $2 < x < 3$
   C. $3 < x < 4$
   D. $4 < x < 5$
   E. $5 < x$

3) A school of fish grows in number as described by the equation $y = 12(2^t)$, where t represents the number of days and y represents the number of fish. According to this formula, how many fish will be in the school at the end of the first 3 days?
   A. 60
   B. 72
   C. 96
   D. 144
   E. 1382

4) In the equation $ax^2 + bx + c = 0$, b and c are integers. If the *only* possible value for x is -4, what is the value of b?
   A. -8
   B. 8
   C. 12
   D. -16
   E. 16

5) The expression $-6x^2(12x^5 - 2x^7)$ is equivalent to:
   A. $-72x^7 + 12x^9$
   B. $-72x^7 - 12x^9$
   C. $-72x^{10} + 12x^{14}$
   D. $-72x^{10} - 12x^{14}$
   E. $-85x^{16}$

6) Which of the following equations has solutions $x = 2z$ and $x = -7q$?
   A. $x^2 - 14zq$
   B. $x^2 - x(7q - 2z) - 14q$
   C. $x^2 - x(7q - 2z) + 14q$
   D. $x^2 + x(7q - 2z) - 14q$
   E. $x^2 + x(7q - 2z) + 14q$

7) Which of the following equations expresses z in terms of x for all real numbers x, y, and z such that
   $$x^4 = y \text{ and } y^{\frac{1}{3}} = z?$$
   A. $z = x^{\frac{4}{3}}$
   B. $z = x^{\frac{1}{12}}$
   C. $z = x^{\frac{13}{3}}$
   D. $z = 4x^{\frac{1}{12}}$
   E. $z = x$

8) What are the factors of $x^2 + 2x\sqrt{8} + 8$?
   A. $(x + 2)(x + \sqrt{8})$
   B. $(2x + \sqrt{8})(x + 2)$
   C. $(x + 8)(x + \sqrt{2})$
   D. $(x + \sqrt{8})(x + \sqrt{8})$
   E. $((x + 8)(x + 2\sqrt{8})$

Quadratic Equation - Quiz 3 (Answers)

1) Use FOIL to multiply the binomials. You can skip the middle step if you realize it is a difference of two squares.

$(z - 3y^2)(z + 3y^2)$ $= z^2 + 3y^2z - 3y^2z - 9y^4$ $= z^2 - 9y^4$ **(Answer A)**

2) Since 4 raised to any whole-number exponent cannot be 75, we need to find the range of the two consecutive values of x: one that provides an answer to 4^x below 75, and the other that provides an answer to 4^x larger than 75.
   - Begin by building up the powers: $4^1 = 4, 4^2 = 16, 4^3 = 64, 4^4 = 256$.
   - 4^3, or 64, is the last power before 75, so the lower value is 3. $x > 3$
   - 4^4, or 256, is the next power after 75, so the upper value must be 4. $x < 4$ **(Answer C)**

3) Solve the equation where $t = 3$.
   - $y = 12(2^3)$ $= 12(8)$ $= 96$.
   - There will be 96 fish in the school after 3 days. **(Answer C)**

4) Since the only possible value of x is −4, the binomial is a perfect square.
   - The binomial is $(x + 4)^2$, which expands to $x^2 + 8x + 16$.
   - b is the coefficient of the term with x, so b is 8. **(Answer B)**

5) To answer this question, distribute the first term over BOTH terms in parentheses.

$6x^2(12x^5 - 2x^7)$ $= (-6x^2 * 12x^5) + (-6x^2 * -2x^7)$ $= -72x^7 + 12x^9$ **(Answer A)**

6) You already know the solution. ("The equation has the solutions $x = 2z$ and $x = -7q$")
   Work backwards from there.
   - Use the solution to create the factors: $(x - 2z)(x + 7q)$
   - Foil this factors to get a quadratic equation: $(x - 2z)(x + 7q) = x^2 + 7qx - 2zx - 14q$
   - Now factor the term x out of the two elements in the middle.
   - $= x^2 + x(7q - 2z) - 14q$ **(Answer D)**

7) Given is $x^4 = y$, $y^{\frac{1}{3}} = z$
   i. Substituting x^4 for y gives us: $Z = (x^{4)\frac{1}{3}}$
   ii. Remember your exponent rules: $(a^{b)^C} = a^{b*c}$. Therefore $z = x^{4*\frac{1}{3}}$
   iii. $z = x^{4*\frac{1}{3}}$ is simplified to $z = x^{\frac{4}{3}}$. **(Answer A)**

8) Recognize this problem as a variant of $(a + b)^2 = a^2 + 2ab + b^2$
   in which $a^2 = x^2, 2ab = 2x\sqrt{8}$ and $b^2 = 8$
   It follows that the two factors are $(x + \sqrt{8})(x + \sqrt{8})$. **(Answer D)**

TRANSLATIONS

Translations (Word Problems)

If a mathematical problem is written in English, you have to "translate" it into another language: math!

1) Split the problem into simple steps

Almost all steps in word problems refer to the four basic functions: add, subtract, multiply and divide.

increased by more than combined	sum of added to	together and	**Add** +
decreased by minus	fewer (than)	less (than) difference between/of	**Subtract** −
of times	increased by a <u>factor</u> of	multiplied by product of	**Multiply** *
per out of	percent (divide by 100) decreased by a <u>factor</u> of	ratio of quotient of	**Divide** /
is are was	yields sold for total of	were will be gives	**Equals** =

 Tip: Watch out for subtractions in word problems.

"Seven less than a number x" does **not** mean $\qquad$ $7 - x$

It is properly translated as $\qquad$ $x - 7$

2) Find the quantity you know and then start your math with that quantity

Example: Ken is twice as old as Brian. Brian is three years younger than Loni. Loni is 16. How old is Ken?

Solution: Start with the quantity you know. Loni is 16. Then work from there. Brian is 13. Ken is 26.

3) If no quantities are given, name one of the unknown quantities "x"

Example: Three brothers are each born two years apart. Together, their age is 66. How old is the youngest brother?

Solution: Name the youngest brother "x". The other two brothers will then be $x + 2$, and $x + 4$. Now, go to the next step: "Together, their age is 66." Translated, this can be written as: $x + (x + 2) + (x + 4) = 66$ ➜ $x = 20$

4) Underline what they ask for

Too often, the answers show solutions for totals and solutions that are not part of the question.

5) Think on paper!

Don't do word problems in your head. Write down each step. Be precise.

Translations - Quiz 1

2. An integer, x, is added to 5. That sum is then multiplied by 4. This product is 20 more than one-third the original integer. Which of the following equations represents the relationship?

   A. $4(x + 5) = \frac{x}{3} + 20$

   B. $4(x + 5) + 20 = \frac{x}{3}$

   C. $4(x + 5) = \frac{x+20}{3}$

   D. $4x + 5 = \frac{x}{3} + 20$

   E. $4x + 5 = \frac{x+20}{3}$

3. If you square an integer, x, then add five-eighths of x, you get 266. What is x?

   A. 10
   B. 12
   C. 16
   D. 18
   E. 21

4. An integer, y, is subtracted from 12. That difference is then divided by 3. This quotient is 2 times the sum of 7 and three-fourths of the original integer. Which of the following is the correct equation?

   A. $\frac{12-y}{3} = 2(7 + \frac{3}{4}y)$

   B. $3(y - 12) = 2(\frac{3}{4})(7 + y)$

   C. $Y - \frac{12}{3} = 2((7 + y)(\frac{3}{4}))$

   D. $2(\frac{y-12}{3}) = 7 + (\frac{3}{4})$

   E. $\frac{12-y}{3} = (7 + (\frac{3}{4}) + y)(2)$

5. If you take the square root of an integer, z, then multiply that number by four-thirds of z, you get 288. What is z?

   A. 16
   B. 25
   C. 36
   D. 54
   E. 81

6. If John has two more dollars than Cindy, and Frank has twice as much money as Jack, and Jack has two thirds as much money as Cindy, and Frank has 12 dollars, how much money does John have?

   A. $9
   B. $11
   C. $14
   D. $18
   E. $26

7. Two trains, which are 320 miles apart, are travelling towards each other. Their speeds differ by 20 miles per hour. They pass each other after 4 hours. Find their speeds.

   A. 20 and 40 mph
   B. 30 and 50 mph
   C. 35 and 55 mph
   D. 40 and 60 mph
   E. 50 and 70 mph

1)A 2)C 3)A 4)C 5)B 6)B

219

Translations - Quiz 1 (Answers)

1. An integer, x, is added to 5. $(5 + x)\ or\ (x + 5)$

   That sum is then multiplied by 4. $4(5 + x)\ or\ 20 + 4x$

   This product is 20 more than $4(5 + x) - 20$ (if it is 20 more than a number, subtract 20)

   one-third the original integer. $x/3$

   Write out each step to get: $4(5 + x) - 20 = \frac{x}{3}$ or $4(5 + x) = \frac{x}{3} + 20$ **(Answer A)**

2. If you square an integer, x, x^2

   then add five-eighths of x, $+\frac{5}{8}x$ 👀 *(Tip: the answers must be divisible by 8.)*

   you get 266. $x^2 + \frac{5}{8}x = 266$

   Plug in the answers. $10^2 + \frac{5}{8}10 = 100 + 6.25\ =\ 106.25$

   Tip: Memorize your squares. $12^2 + \frac{5}{8}12 = 144 + 6.25\ =\ 151.5$

   Tip: Always start in the middle. $16^2 + \frac{5}{8}16 = 156 + 10\ \ \ = 266$ **(Answer C)**

3. An integer, y, is subtracted from 12. $12 - y$

   That difference is then divided by 3. $\frac{12-y}{3}$

   This quotient is 2 times $= 2 *$

   the sum of 7 and three-fourths of y. $(7 + \frac{3}{4}y)$

   Write out each step $\frac{12-y}{3} = 2 * (7 + \frac{3}{4}y)$ **(Answer A)**

4. Take the square root of an integer Z. $\sqrt{z}$ (Tip: the answer must be a square.)

   Multiply that number by four-thirds of z. $\sqrt{z} * \frac{4}{3}z$ (Tip: the answer must be divisible by 3.)

   You get 288. $\sqrt{z} * \frac{4}{3}z = 288$ **(Answer C)**

   Plug in the answers. (Try the middle one first) $6 * 48 = 288$ Bingo!

5. What do we know? Frank has 12 dollars. $(F = 12)$

   Frank has twice as much money as Jack. Jack has six dollars. $(F = 2J$ ➜ $J = 6)$

   Jack has two thirds as much money as Cindy. $J = \frac{2}{3} * C$ ➜ $6 = \frac{2}{3}C$ ➜ Cindy has 9 dollars.

   John has two more dollars than Cindy. John has $(9 + 2 = 11)$ dollars. **(Answer B)**

6. Train 1 travels x miles per hour. Call unknown quantities "x".

   Train 2 travels $x + 20$ miles per hour. $x + 20$

   They pass each other after 4 hours. Translate: After 4 hours, they have traveled 320 miles.

   After 4 hours, they have traveled 320 miles. $4(x) + 4(x + 20) = 320$

   $8x + 80 = 320$ ➜ $8x = 240$ ➜ $x = 30$

   Train 1 goes 30 miles per hour. Train 2 goes $(c + 20 = 50)$ miles per hour.

   (Answer B)

MATH

Geometry

BASIC SHAPES

Basic Shapes

Calculate the areas and perimeters of the shapes below.

1) Square

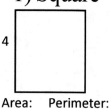

Area: Perimeter:

2) Rectangle

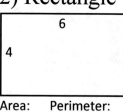

Area: Perimeter:

3) Parallelogram

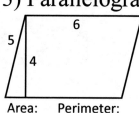

Area: Perimeter:

4) Trapezoid

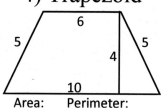

Area: Perimeter:

5) Triangle

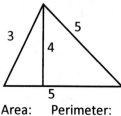

Area: Perimeter:

6) Right triangle

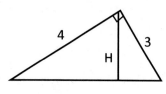

Area: Perimeter:

7) Equilateral Triangle

Area: Perimeter:

8) Circle

Area: Circumference:

9) Cube

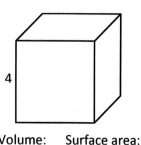

Volume: Surface area:

10) Prism

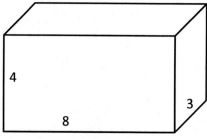

Volume: Surface area:

11) Cylinder

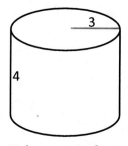

Volume: Surface area:

 Tip: Memorize the formulas for all shapes on this page.

Memorize your formulas!

Square: Area: S^2 Perimeter: $4S$ **Rectangle:** Area: L*W Perimeter: 2L+2W **Parallelogram:** Area: b*h
Perimeter: 2L+2W **Trapezoid:** Area: $(L_1+L_2)/2*h$ Perimeter: $L_1+L_2+S_1+S_2$ **Triangle:** Area: ½*b*h
Perimeter: $b+S_1+S_2$ **Right triangle:** Are: ½*S_1*S_2 **Equilateral Triangle:**
Area: ¼*S*¼* $\sqrt{3}$ Perimeter: 3*S **Ci cle:** Area: πr Circumference: $2\pi r$ **Cube:** Volume: S^3 Surface area: $6*S^2$
Prism: Volume: L*W*H Surface area: ? $H*L+2*L*V$ +2*W*H **Cylinder:** Volume: $h*\pi r^2$ Surface area: $2\pi r^2 + 2\pi r*h$

1) 16, 16 **2)** 24, 20 **3)** 24, 22 **4)** 32, 26 **5)** 10, 13 **6)** 6, 12 **7)** $4\sqrt{3}$ 12 **8)** 9π, 6π **9)** 64, 96
10) 96, 136 **11)** 36π, 42π

Basic Shapes - Quiz 1

1. Find the area of the triangle.

   A. 64
   B. $64\sqrt{3}$
   C. 128
   D. $128\sqrt{2}$

2. If a bicycle wheel with a radius of 4 units rolls a full 50 times, how much distance was traveled?
   A. 200 units
   B. 200π units
   C. 400 units
   D. 400π units

3. If you triple each side of a cube, how much greater is the surface area?
   A. 3
   B. $3\sqrt{2}$
   C. 6
   D. 9

4. If a cylinder that has a height of 5 feet and a radius of 3 feet is filled with water to the two-thirds mark, how much water is in the cylinder?
   A. 10π feet^2
   B. 15π feet^2
   C. 30π feet^2
   D. 45π feet^2

5. What is the area of this quadrilateral?
   A. 624 units^2
   B. 390 units^2
   C. 75 units^2
   D. 65 units^2
   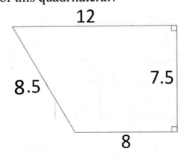

6. A company recently purchased a rundown apartment complex. The roof is fine, but the outside walls need to be completely repainted. If the complex is 140 units long, 50 units high, and 40 units wide, how much surface area needs to be painted?
   A. 280,000 units^2
   B. 30,200 units^2
   C. 18,000 units^2
   D. 9,000 units^2

7. The area for the following triangle is 30 units^2. What is the perimeter?
   A. 17 units
   B. 24 units
   C. 30 units
   D. 42 units
   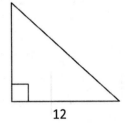

8. What is the area of the following parallelogram?
   A. 6 units
   B. 12 units
   C. 18 units
   D. 36 units
   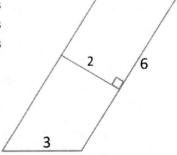

1)B 2)D 3)D 4)C 5)C 6)C 7)C 8)B

Basic Shapes - Quiz 1 (Answers)

1) This is an equilateral triangle. Use the formula for area of an equilateral triangle ($A = \frac{1}{2}s * \frac{1}{2}s\sqrt{3}$).

   1. $\frac{1}{2}16 * \frac{1}{2}16\sqrt{3}$ $=$ $8 * 8\sqrt{3}$ $=$ $64\sqrt{3}$ **(Answer B)**

2) This problem requires an understanding of the circumference of a circle.
   1. Circumference $= 2\pi r = 2\pi 4 = 8\pi$
   2. If the wheel rolls a full 50 times, then the distance it rolls is 50 times its circumference of 8π.
   3. $50 * 8\pi = 400\pi$ **(Answer D)**

3) One way to solve this problem is to first plug in any initial side length.
   1. Let the initial side length $= 2$. It follows that the initial surface area is 24 (6 sides of a cube $= 6 * (2*2)$.
   2. Triple the side length to equal 6. The new surface area $= 6 * (6 * 6) = 216$.
   3. $\frac{216}{24} = 9$ The new surface area is 9 times greater than the original. **(Answer D)**

   Another way to solve this problem is by using algebra.
   1. The side is unknown; we will call it x.
   2. It follows that the initial surface area is 6x^2 (6 sides of a cube $= 6 * (x*x)$.
   3. Triple the side length to equal 3X. The new surface area $= 6 * (3x * 3x) = 54x^2$
   4. $\frac{54x}{6x} = 9$ The new surface area is 9 times greater than the original. (

4) To solve this problem, first use the formula for the volume of a cylinder.
   1. *Volume $= \pi r^2 h$, so the volume of this cylinder $= 45\pi$* units^3
   2. Multiply the volume of the full cylinder times how much water is in the cylinder
   3. $(\frac{2}{3} * 45\pi) = 30\pi$ **(Answer C)**

5) Any quadrilateral with parallel lines can be calculated by $\frac{1}{2}$ *(base ₁ + base ₂) * h*

   (also known as a*verage of the bases * height*) $\frac{1}{2}(8 + 12) * 7.5 = 10 * 7.5 = 75$ **(Answer C)**

6) Don't immediately calculate the entire surface area. Think instead about what is actually being painted.
   1. Only the exterior walls are being painted, not the roof or the part on the ground. The area to be painted $= 2(140 * 50) + 2(40 * 50) = 18,000$ units^2 **(Answer C)**

7) This problem requires knowledge of the area formula for triangles and the Pythagorean formula. (See page 240)
   1. First, find the height of the triangle. Area$=\frac{1}{2}bh$, so $30 = \left(\frac{1}{2}\right)12h$. $h = 5$.
   2. If two of the triangle's sides are 5 and 12, then the third side must be 13 (Pythagorean triple)
   3. Add the sides to find the perimeter. $5 + 12 + 13 = 30$ **(Answer C)**

8) Sometimes you need to redraw or turn a figure. Then use the formula:
   Area $= $ b $*$ h $= 6 * 2 = 12$ **(Answer B)**

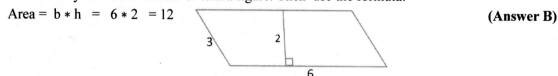

Basic Shapes - Quiz 2

1. The width of a pool is 10 feet less than half its length. How can you express the perimeter of the pool in terms of its length?
   A. $4L - 10$
   B. $10L - 4$
   C. $3L - 10$
   D. $3L - 20$
   E. $2L + 20$

2. The volume of the box below is 40 cm³. What is its surface area?

   A. 160 cm²
   B. 72 cm²
   C. 64 cm²
   D. 36 cm²
   E. 16 cm²

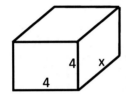

3. The length of a driveway is 10 times half its width. If the width is 8 feet, what is the total area of the driveway in square feet?
   A. 320
   B. 160
   C. 80
   D. 40
   E. 18

4. A trapezoid has a height of 12 inches, a bottom base of 15 and an area of 120. What is the perimeter of the trapezoid?
   A. 56 inches
   B. 54 inches
   C. 46 inches
   D. 44.4 inches
   E. 44 inches

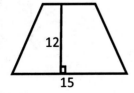

5. The surface area of the prism below is 164 square inches. What is x in inches?
   A. 3
   B. 4
   C. 5
   D. 6
   E. 7

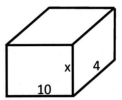

6. A cylinder has a height of 6 inches and a volume of 96π inches³. What is the volume in cubic inches of a second cylinder with half the height and half the radius?
   A. 12π
   B. 18π
   C. 24π
   D. 36π
   E. 48π

7. A soccer field measures 110 by 70 yards. Around the whole field is a 10-yard-wide area for track. The school is planning to build a fence to enclose the soccer field and the track area. What will be the perimeter of that fence?
   A. 200 yards
   B. 220 yards
   C. 300 yards
   D. 400 yards
   E. 440 yards

1) D 2) B 3) A 4) C 5) C 6) A 7) E

Basic Shapes - Quiz 2 (Answers)

1) The perimeter of a rectangle is 2L + 2W. We know the width W is 1/2 L − 10, so we can substitute that into the equation. Now the perimeter is 2L + 2(1/2L − 10), or 2L + L − 20. This simplifies to 3L − 20.

(Answer D)

2) The volume is $L * W * H = 40 \text{ cm}^3$, $L = 4$, and $H = 4$. Therefore $4 * 4 * x = 40$. Solve for x to get $x = 2.5$. The surface area of a prism is $2 * H * L + 2 * L * W + 2 * W * H$. Filling in the numbers for the sides gives $(2 * 4 * 2.5) + (2 * 4 * 4) + (2 * 4 * 2.5) = 72$

(Answer B)

3) First find the length of the driveway. It is given that the width is 8 feet. Therefore, half the width is 4 feet, and 10 times half the width is 40 feet, which is the length of the driveway. The area of the driveway is length ∗ width. 8 ∗ 40 = 320

(Answer A)

4) To find the area of a trapezoid, we must take the average of the two base lengths times the height. $Area = \frac{L_1+L_2}{2} * H$. Solve for x. $\frac{15+x}{2} * 12 = 120$. ➔ $\frac{15+x}{2} = 10$ ➔ $15 + x = 20$ ➔ $x = 5$
Now we can draw the proper trapezoid:

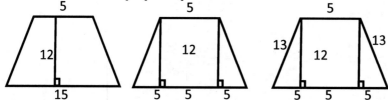

To determine the sides, first split the area up into rectangles and triangles. The width of the rectangle is 5. Subtract this number from the original base and split the remainder into two equal quantities to determine that the base of each triangle is 5 as well. If you drawing these quantities into the figure, you can see that each triangle is a 5-12-13 triangle. (Alternatively, you could use the Pythagorean Theorem to calculate each side: $5^2 + 12^2 = x^2$ ➔ $x = \sqrt{169}$ ➔ $x = 13$
Now we can measure the perimeter. $5 + 13 + 15 + 13 = 46$

(Answer C)

5) The top and bottom rectangles equal 40 square inches apiece = 80 square inches. The remaining four rectangles total 84 square inches. $10x + 4x + 10x + 4x = 84$ ➔ $28x = 84$ ➔ $x = 3$ **(Answer A)**

6) Think on paper! Draw the cylinders. Then use the formulas.
Volume $96\pi = h * \pi r^2$ ➔ $96 = 6 * r^2$ ➔ $r = 4$
A cylinder with half the height and half the radius
has a volume of $h * \pi r^2$ ➔ $3 * \pi 2^2$ ➔ 12π

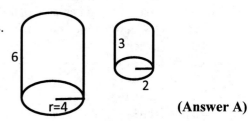

(Answer A)

7)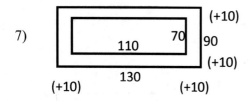

Think **On Paper**. Draw the field and the track. Notice that the track extends the length and width 10 yards ON EACH SIDE. The new perimeter is
130 + 90 + 130 + 90 = 440 **(Answer E)**

ANGLES
and
TRIANGLES

Angles and Triangles

All angles in a triangle add up to 180°.

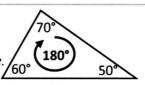

👀 *Tip: The longest side is always across from the largest angle.*

<u>Supplementary</u> angles add up to 180°.

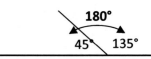

<u>Complementary</u> angles add up to 90°.

<u>Vertical angles</u> are equal. They are opposite when two lines cross.

**If a line crosses two parallel lines,
then the <u>corresponding angles</u> are equal.**

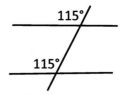

 Tip: In any figure with parallel lines, look for zigzag patterns like the ones below or U-turns of 180°.

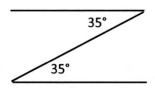

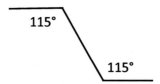

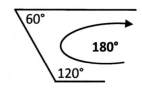

Inequality Theorem

The sum of the lengths of any two sides must be greater than the length of the remaining side

Example: How can you quickly determine the length of the third side of a triangle?

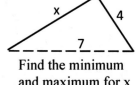

Find the minimum
and maximum for x

Solution: Think of the two known sides of the triangle as hinges. If side 4 points to the left, x has to be at least $(7 - 4) = 3$ and cannot be less. If side 4 points to the right, x has to be almost $(7 + 4) = 11$ and cannot be more.

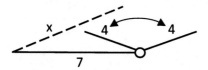

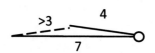

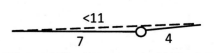

Angles and Triangles - Quiz 1

1. How big is angle a?
   A. 40^0
   B. 60^0
   C. 80^0
   D. 100^0

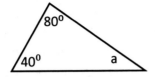

2. How big is angle b?
   A. 35^0
   B. 45^0
   C. 125^0
   D. 135^0

3. What is the value of x?
   A. 5
   B. 10
   C. 18
   D. 36

4. How big is angle c?
   A. 36^0
   B. 46^0
   C. 54^0
   D. 126^0

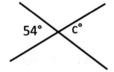

5. The two horizontal lines are parallel.
   How big is angle d?
   A. 15^0
   B. 75^0
   C. 105^0
   D. 255^0

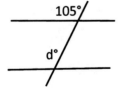

6. The two horizontal lines are parallel.
   How big is angle e?
   A. 25^0
   B. 55^0
   C. 65^0
   D. 155^0

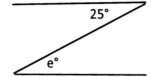

7. The two horizontal lines are parallel.
   How big is angle f?
   A. 60^0
   B. 80^0
   C. 100^0
   D. 120^0

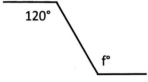

8. The two horizontal lines are parallel.
   How big is angle g?
   A. 35^0
   B. 55^0
   C. 125^0
   D. 145^0

9. What is a possible value of y?
   A. 12
   B. 14
   C. 22
   D. 23

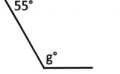

1)B 2)C 3)C 4)C 5)C 6)A 7)D 8)C 9)B

Angles and Triangles - Quiz 1 (Answers)

1. All angles in a triangle add up to 180.
   Therefore, angle a is
   180 – 80 – 40 = 60
   degrees **(Answer B)**

   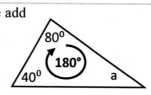

2. Supplementary angles add up to 180°.
   Therefore, angle b is
   $180 - 55 = 125$ degrees
   (Answer C)

   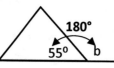

3. Complementary angles add up to 90°.
   Therefore, $2x + 3x = 90$ ➔ $5x = 90$
   ➔ $x = 18$
   (Answer C)

   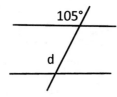

4. Vertical angles are equal.
   Therefore, angle c is 54 degrees.
   (Answer C)

   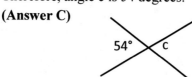

5. Corresponding angles are equal.
   Therefore, angle d is 105 degrees.
   (Answer C)

6. Draw. Extend the three lines to reveal vertical and corresponding angles.
   Corresponding and vertical angles are equal. Therefore, angle e is 25 degrees.
   (Answer A)

   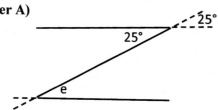

7. Draw. Extend the three lines to reveal vertical and corresponding angles. Corresponding and vertical angles are equal.
   Therefore, angle f is 120 degrees. **(Answer D)**

8. Draw. Extend the three lines to reveal vertical and corresponding angles. Corresponding and vertical angles are equal.
   Therefore, angle g is
   $180 - 55 = 125$ degrees.
   (Answer C)

9. The *Inequality Theorem* states that the sum of the lengths of any two sides must be greater than the length of the remaining side.
   $y + 5$ must be greater than 17
   $y + 17$ must be greater than 5
   $17 + 5$ must be greater than y
   Only 14 is a value that complies with all three conditions. **(Answer B)**
   Alternatively, using the idea of hinges from page 228, you find that the value of y has to be between, but not including, 12 and 22.
   $(17 - 5$ and $17 + 5)$ **(Answer B)**

   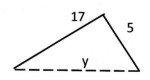

Special Triangles

An Isosceles Triangle has **two** sides of equal length and **two** angles of equal size. The third angle x can be found by the formula: $180 - 2x$.

 Tip: Triangles made of radii in circles are isosceles.

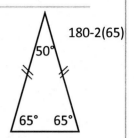

180-2(65)

50°

65°   65°

A right Isosceles Triangle (45°, 45° and 90°)

has two equal sides (so it is isosceles) and has dimensions of S, S, and $S\sqrt{2}$.

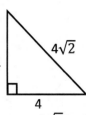

4

$4\sqrt{2}$

4

The *diagonal of a square* follows the same rule as the right
       isosceles triangle: S, S, and $S\sqrt{2}$
       The angles are 45, 45, and 90 degrees.
       (The diagonal is $\sqrt{2}$ times the side)

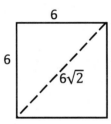

6

6

$6\sqrt{2}$

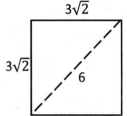

$3\sqrt{2}$

$3\sqrt{2}$

6

A triangle with angles of 30°, 60° and 90° has the dimensions of S, 2S and $S\sqrt{3}$.

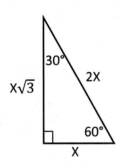

30°

2X

$X\sqrt{3}$

60°

X

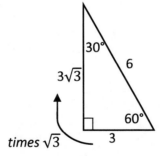

30°

6

$3\sqrt{3}$

60°

times $\sqrt{3}$ 3

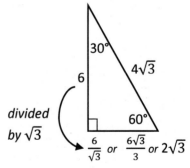

30°

$4\sqrt{3}$

6

divided by $\sqrt{3}$

60°

$\frac{6}{\sqrt{3}}$ *or* $\frac{6\sqrt{3}}{3}$ *or* $2\sqrt{3}$

An Equilateral Triangle has 3 equal sides, 3 equal corners of 60° each, and an area of

     $\frac{1}{2} S * \frac{1}{2} S * \sqrt{3}$.

 Tip: For better insight, think of the equilateral triangle as two 30-60-90 triangles back to back.

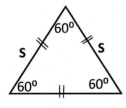

60°

S   S

60°   60°

Area = ½ S ½ S $\sqrt{3}$

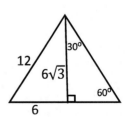

30°

12   $6\sqrt{3}$

60°

6

Area = ½ *b*h = $36\sqrt{3}$

Area = ½ 12 ½ 12 $\sqrt{3}$ = $36\sqrt{3}$

Special Triangles - Quiz 1

Solve the unknown quantities in the triangles on this sheet.

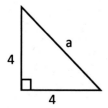

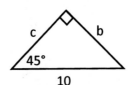

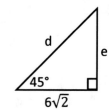

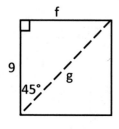

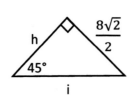

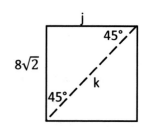

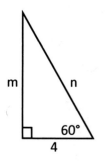

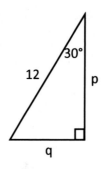

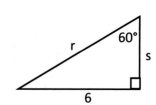

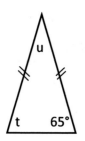

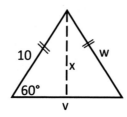

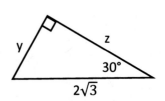

A) $4\sqrt{2}$ B) $5\sqrt{2}$ C) $5\sqrt{2}$ D) 12 E) $6\sqrt{2}$ F) 9 G) $9\sqrt{2}$ H) $4\sqrt{2}$ I) 8 J) $8\sqrt{2}$ K) 16 L) $4\sqrt{3}$ N) 8
P) $6\sqrt{3}$ Q) 6 R) $4\sqrt{3}$ S) $2\sqrt{3}$ T) 65° U) 50° V) 10 W) 10 X) $5\sqrt{3}$ Y) $5\sqrt{3}$ Z) $\sqrt{3}$

Special Triangles - Quiz 2

1) Ximena shoots a firework rocket from her house at a 45⁰ angle. When the rocket reaches an altitude of 100 feet, it explodes and falls straight down to earth. How far from Ximena's house does the extinguished rocket land?

   A. 50 feet
   B. $50\sqrt{2}$ feet
   C. $50\sqrt{3}$ feet
   D. 100 feet
   E. $100\sqrt{2}$ feet

2) In the figure below, A, D and C are collinear. $AD = BC$ and $BC = BD$ If $\angle CAB$ is 40⁰, what is the degree of $\angle ABC$?

   A. 70⁰
   B. 60⁰
   C. 50⁰
   D. 40⁰
   E. 20⁰

   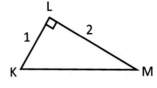

3) In the rectangle ABCD below, side BC = 6 and AE = 4.
   The line CE bisects ∠BCD.
   What is the area of ABCD?

   A. 36
   B. 40
   C. 48
   D. 54
   E. 60

   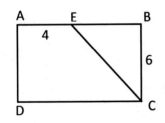

4) In the figure below, A, D and C are collinear and $AD = BD$. What is the value of 2x?

   A. 50⁰
   B. 65⁰
   C. 75⁰
   D. 100⁰
   E. 130⁰

   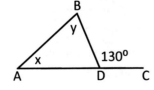

5) What is the length of the hypotenuse in triangle KLM below?

   A. $\sqrt{2}$
   B. $\sqrt{3}$
   C. $\sqrt{4}$
   D. $\sqrt{5}$
   E. $\sqrt{6}$

   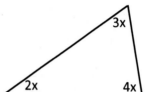

6) The ratio of the angles in the triangle below is 2:3:4. What is the measure of the smallest angle?

   A. 20⁰
   B. 30⁰
   C. 40⁰
   D. 50⁰
   E. 60⁰

   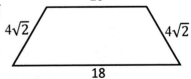

7) A truck driver drives 100 miles from his warehouse to customer A. He then turns 120 degrees to his left and drives 50 miles to customer B. He then turns 90 degrees to his left and drives straight back to the warehouse. Approximately, how far is it between customer B and the warehouse??

   A. 50 miles
   B. 60 miles
   C. 72 miles
   D. 87 miles
   E. 173 miles

8) What is the area of the trapezoid below?

   A. $28 + 8\sqrt{3}$
   B. $180 + 8\sqrt{3}$
   C. 56
   D. 72
   E. It cannot be determined with the information provided.

1)D 2)B 3)E 4)E 5)D 6)C 7)D 8)C

233

Special Triangles - Quiz 2 (Answers)

1) Ximena shoots a firework rocket from his house in a 45⁰ angle. Combined with the 90⁰ drop to earth, this forms a 45-45-90 triangle, which is isosceles and has two equal sides. Knowing that one side (not the hypotenuse) is 100 feet, it is clear that the other side, the distance from her house, is also 100 feet. **(Answer D)**

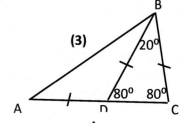

2) The notation $AD = BC$ and $BC = BD$ means we are talking about two isosceles triangles. Think On Paper and mark the identical lines in your figure.

Next, mark the given component. If ∠CAB is 40⁰, you can complete all angles of triangle ABD (1)

Next, note that supplementary angles ADB and CDB add up to 180°. (2)

Last, fill in the remaining angles of triangle BCD, to find that the other half of ∠ABC is 20°. (3)

The two parts of ∠ABC are 40⁰ and 20⁰ which together make 60⁰. **(Answer B)**

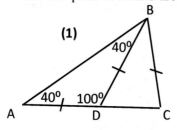
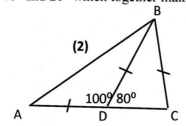

3) ABCD is a rectangle, which means each corner is 90⁰. The line CE *bisects* ∠BCD, which means it splits the corner into two angles of 45⁰. From this, we can conclude that EBC is a 45-45-90 triangle, and $BC = EB$. In conclusion, $AB = 10$ and the *Area of ABCD = 60* **(Answer E)**

4) $AD = BD$ means the triangle ABD is isosceles. Mark the equal sides on your figure. Also note that supplementary angles ADB and CDB add up to 180°, which make angle ADB 50⁰ and angles x and y each 65⁰. However, do not mark answer B as correct. Read the question. The value for 2x is 130⁰. **(Answer E)**

5) Use the Pythagorean Theorem. The hypotenuse is $\sqrt{5}$. **(Answer D)**

6) All angles add up to 180⁰. $2x + 3x + 4x = 180$. ➜ $9x = 180$ ➜ $x = 20$

However, do not mark answer B as correct. Read the question. The value for **2x** is 40⁰. **(Answer C)**

7) Draw the route. The truck driver makes a triangle with a 60-degree turn and a 90 degree turn. Once you know you are dealing with a 30-60-90 triangle, you can plug in the distance of the third leg as $50\sqrt{3}$, which is a little less than 87 miles **(Answer D)**

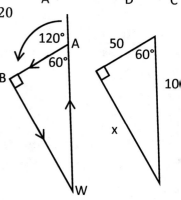

8) The trapezoid has a top base of 10, so we can draw a rectangle that has a bottom base of 10 inside the trapezoid. This leaves two segments of 4 each for the bases of the two triangles. Because it is given that the hypotenuse of the triangle is $4\sqrt{2}$, we can determine that we are dealing with a 45-45-90 triangle and the height of the triangle (and of the trapezoid) is 4. The area of the trapezoid is the sum of the areas of the rectangle (40) and the two triangles (8 each) **(Answer C)**

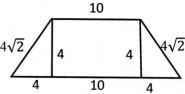

Triangles and Circles - Quiz 3 - Challenge

1. AB is the diameter of a circle with midpoint D and the base of Triangle ABC; What is the height DC of the triangle ABC?
    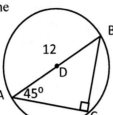
    A. 5
    B. 6
    C. 8
    D. $6\sqrt{2}$
    E. 13

2. What is the diameter of the following circle?
    A. $3\sqrt{2}$
    B. 6
    C. 7
    D. 8
    E. $6\sqrt{2}$

3. In this equilateral triangle with sides 6, what is the radius of the inscribed circle?
    A. $\frac{1}{3}\sqrt{2}$
    B. $\sqrt{2}$
    C. $\frac{1}{3}\sqrt{3}$
    D. $\sqrt{3}$
    E. 3

4. If $AB = 4$, and $BD = 2$, and $BC = 5$, then $DE = ?$
    A. 6
    B. 6.5
    C. 7
    D. 7.5
    E. 8

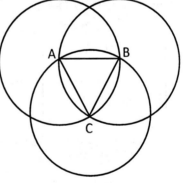

5. What is the size of the shaded area in square inches in the figure above?
    A. 38
    B. 40
    C. 42
    D. 44
    E. 46

6. Three identical circles with midpoint A, B, and C each have an area of 16π. What is the area of triangle ABC?
    A. $2\sqrt{3}$
    B. 8
    C. $4\sqrt{3}$
    D. 12
    E. 16

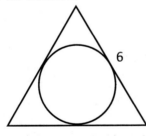

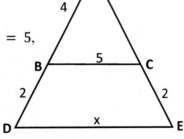

1) B 2) E 3) D 4) D 5) A 6) C

Triangle and Circles - Quiz 3 - Answers

1) **What is the length of segment DC?**
The height is always perpendicular (90⁰) to the base. It was already given that ∠DAC is 45⁰, making triangle ADC a 45-45-90 triangle, with two equal sides. AD is half of the diameter = 6, and so is DC.
(Answer B)
Visually, you can determine that both AD and DC are radii of the same circle with a diameter of 12, and it follows that DC = 6. **(Answer B)**

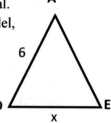

2) **What is the diameter of the circle?**
Draw a diagonal diameter. This diagonal creates a 45-45-90 triangle with a hypotenuse of $6\sqrt{2}$. **(Answer E)**

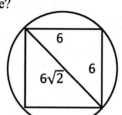

3) Draw the radius and complete the inside 30-60-90 triangle. The hypothenuse bisects the previous 60° angle. The long side is 3, which is $\sqrt{3}$ times the short side. The short side is the radius of the circle.

$$\frac{3}{\sqrt{3}} = \frac{3*\sqrt{3}}{\sqrt{3}*\sqrt{3}} = \frac{3\sqrt{3}}{3} = \sqrt{3}$$

(Answer D)

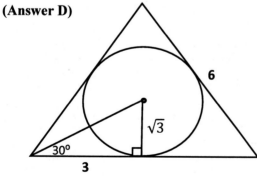

4) **If AB = 4, AD = 6, and BC = 5, Then DE= ?**
When two figures overlap, draw them seperately for clarity. The triangles are similar because ∠BAC and ∠DAE are identical. Because BC and DE are parallel, ∠ABC and ∠ADE are identical. Therefore, this problem can be solved with ratios.

$$\frac{AB}{BC} = \frac{AD}{DE} \rightarrow \frac{4}{5} = \frac{4+2}{x}$$

$\rightarrow 4x = 30 \rightarrow x = 7.5$ **(Answer D)**

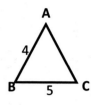

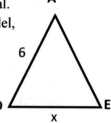

5) **What is the shaded area in square inches?**
Determine the area of each part of this shape:
- Large rectangle = 7 * (6 + 4) = 70
- Triangle A = ½ * 7 * 6 = 21
- Triangle B = ½ * 4 * 4 = 8
- Triangle C = ½ * 2 * 3 = 3
- Rectangle − all triangles = grey area
= 70 − (21 + 8 + 3) = 38 **(Answer A)**

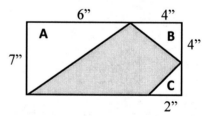

6) Three identical circles with midpoint A, B, and C each have an area of 16π inch².

The area $= \pi r^2 = 16\pi \rightarrow r^2 = 16 \rightarrow r = 4$

The radius of each circle goes from their midpoint to the outside of the circle. Each side of the triangle, therefore, is identical to the radius and measures 4 inches.

The area of this equilateral triangle is $\frac{1}{2}S * \frac{1}{2}S\sqrt{3}$

The area of the triangle is $2 * 2 * \sqrt{3} = 4\sqrt{3}$
(Answer C)

THE COORDINATE PLANE

The Coordinate Plane

Distance Formula

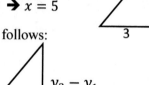

Tip: The distance between two points in a coordinate plane is a variation of the Pythagorean Theorem.

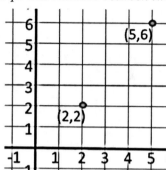

1) Count the difference of the points on the x-axis from 2 *to* 5 = 3
2) Count the difference of the points on the y-axis from 2 *to* 6 = 4
3) Use the Pythagorean Theorem: $3^2 + 4^2 = x^2$ ➔ $x = 5$

In Math terms, these three steps can be written as follows:

1) $(x_2 - x_1)$
2) $(y_2 - y_1)$
3) $(x_2 - x_1)^2 + (y_2 - y_1)^2 = x^2$

However, we want to know the value of x, not of x^2. Therefore, we need to take the square root of the final result. **The Distance Formula is** $d = \sqrt{(x_2 - x_1)^2 + (y_2 - y_1)^2}$

In the example above, $\sqrt{(5 - 2)^2 + (6 - 2)^2} = \sqrt{25} = 5$

The distance between any two points can be determined by plugging in the coordinates in the distance formula. Watch out for negative values.

Example: The distance between $(-2, 5)$ and $(3, -7)$ is

$$\sqrt{(-2 - 3)^2 + (5 - (-7))^2} = \sqrt{(-5)^2 + (12)^2} = \sqrt{169} = 13$$

Midpoint Formula

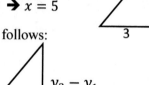

Tip: the midpoint between two point can be found by averaging the x values and the y values.

The distance between two points in a coordinate plane can be determined by finding the midpoint between the x coordinates and the midpoint of the y coordinates. The midpoint of two numbers can be found by adding them up and dividing them by 2. (See averages, page 174)

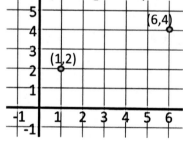

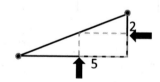

The Midpoint Formula is $\left(\dfrac{x_1 + x_2}{2}, \dfrac{y_1 + y_2}{2}\right)$

In the example above, use the coordinates and plug them into the formula to find the midpoint.

$\left(\dfrac{1+6}{2}, \dfrac{2+4}{2}\right) = (3\frac{1}{2}, 3)$

Example: The midpoint between $(-2, 5)$ and $(3, -7)$ is $\left(\dfrac{-2+3}{2}, \dfrac{5+ -7}{2}\right) = (\frac{1}{2}, 1)$

The Coordinate Plane - Quiz

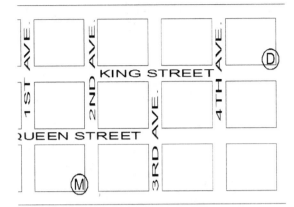

1. On the map above, each intersection is exactly 500 meters from the next one. Martha (M) and Dominique (D) live several blocks apart. As the crow flies, how far is it approximately between the two houses?
   A. 1200 meters
   B. 1500 meters
   C. 1800 meters
   D. 2500 meters
   E. 3800 meters

2. In a coordinate plane, what is the distance between the points $(-3, -12)$ and $(4, 12)$?
   A. 12
   B. 15
   C. 17
   D. 24
   E. 25

3. In a coordinate plane with 1 inch units, the distance between (-2, 5) and (3, -7) is …
   A. 10 inches
   B. 11 inches
   C. 12 inches
   D. 13 inches
   E. 14 inches

4. What is the distance and the midpoint between the two points in the graph below?

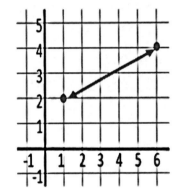

Distance	Midpoint
A. 5	$(3, 3.5)$
B. $\sqrt{7}$	$(3.5, 3)$
C. $\sqrt{29}$	$(3.5, 3)$
D. $\sqrt{29}$	$(3, 3.5)$
E. $\sqrt{7}$	$(3, 3.5)$

4. Use the distance formula $\sqrt{(1-6)^2 + (2-4)^2} = \sqrt{5^2 + 2^2} = \sqrt{29}$ Then, use the midpoint formula. $\frac{(1+6)}{2}, \frac{2+4}{2} \rightarrow (3.5, 3)$ (Answer C)

3. Use the distance formula $\sqrt{(-2-3)^2 + (5-(-7))^2} = \sqrt{5^2 + 12^2} = \sqrt{169} = 13$ (Alternatively, you might spot the 5-12-13 Pythagorean triple. (Answer D)

2. Use the distance formula $\sqrt{(-3-4)^2 + (-12-12)^2} = \sqrt{7^2 + 24^2} = \sqrt{225} = 25$ (Alternatively, you might spot the 7-24-25 Pythagorean triple. (Answer E)

1. Three blocks to the right and two blocks up, gives us a distance of $\sqrt{3^2 + 2^2} = \sqrt{13}$. However, the units on this map are 500 meters each. $\sqrt{13} * 500 = 1802$ (Answer C)

Pythagorean Theorem

The ACT loves the Pythagorean Theorem. The same triplets appear in many of the problems, from simple geometry to trigonometry. Only use the Pythagorean Theorem in right triangles. Use the formula (side 1)^2 + (side 2)^2 = hypotenuse^2, more commonly known as $a^2 + b^2 = c^2$

 Tip: It will be worth it to memorize the following triplets:

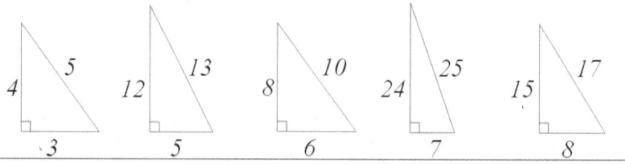

After memorizing the five triples above, solve the following problems without a calculator. Try to solve all problems in less than 1 minute.

1) A ladder is standing 5 feet away from a wall and it reaches 12 feet high. How long is the ladder?

2) A rectangle of 8" x 15" is inscribed in a circle. What is the diameter of that circle?

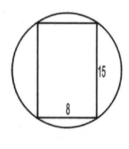

3) The 13-foot ramp of a truck touches the ground 12 feet behind the truck. How far is the top of the ramp from the floor?

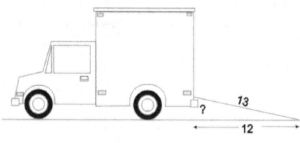

4) A handicap ramp of 25 feet leads to a door that is 7 feet of the ground. How far is the bottom of the ramp away from the house?

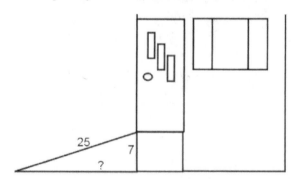

5) A small circle with a radius of 8" sits within a larger circle. A bar of 12" fits in between the circles, as displayed. What is the radius of the larger circle?

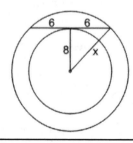

1) 13 ft. 2) 17" 3) 5 feet 4) 24 feet 5) 10".

CIRCLES

Circles

Area and Distance

Diameter	=	**D = 2r**
Circumference	=	**2πr** or **πD**

 Tip: A rolling wheel moves a distance of
1 circumference for every full rotation.

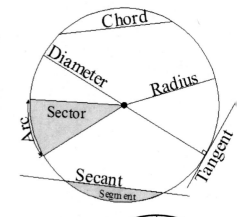

Area	=	**πr²**

 Tip: A circle with TWICE the radius has FOUR times the
area. $\pi(2r)^2 = \pi 4r^2$

Standard Form Equation

Formula:	*if centered on (0,0)*	$x^2 + y^2 = r^2$
or	*if centered on (a,b)*	$(x-a)^2 + (y-b)^2 = r^2$
or:		$\cos\theta^2 + \sin\theta^2 = r^2$

Every point on a circle can be defined with the Pythagorean Theorem:
Its *x-coordinate-squared* plus its *y-coordinate-squared* equals its
hypotenuse-squared.

 Tip: Look at the two numbers in parentheses. Use the <u>opposites</u> of these two
numbers to find the midpoint. Take the <u>square root</u> of the number after the equal sign to
find the radius.

Example: If the formula is $(X-2)^2 + (Y+3)^2 = 16$, then the midpoint is $(2, -3)$ and the radius is 4.

Angles and Degrees

Degrees in a circle: 360°
The central angle = angle of the arc = A
The length of the arc = $\frac{angle}{360} * circumference$
The inscribed angle = B = half of the central angle

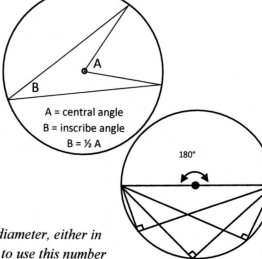

A = central angle
B = inscribe angle
B = ½ A

 Tip: A right triangle that is inscribed in a circle
has an inscribed angle of 90° and a central angle of
180°, which makes the hypotenuse the diameter.

 Tip: Questions about circles in the ACT often give the diameter, either in
the description or in the figure. It is a common mistake to use this number
when calculating the area or the circumference. Be aware of this trap and always convert the
Diameter into the Radius. (D = 2R)

242

Circles - Quiz 1 (Area and Distance)

1) A wheel rotates with a speed of 15 rotations per minute. After 20 seconds, it has traveled 30 feet. What is the diameter of the wheel?

   A. 6π feet

   B. $\frac{6}{\pi}$ feet

   C. 12π feet

   D. $\frac{12}{\pi}$ feet

   E. 30π feet

2) The area of circle B is twice that of circle A. The area of circle C is twice that of circle B. The diameter of circle B is 4. What is the area of all three circles together?

   A. $7\pi\ in^2$

   B. $12\pi\ in^2$

   C. $14\pi\ in^2$

   D. $21\pi\ in^2$

   E. $56\pi\ in^2$

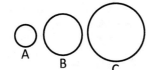

3) Two circles have the same midpoint. The radius of circle A is 3, and the Radius of circle B is 7. What is the area of the shaded portion that is in-between circle A and circle B?

   A. $9\pi\ in^2$

   B. $16\pi\ in^2$

   C. $40\pi\ in^2$

   D. $49\pi\ in^2$

   E. $100\pi\ in^2$

4) The numbers on the face of a clock are evenly spaced around the outside of a circle. The length of the minor arc between the 1 and the 4 is 10 inches. What is the approximate diameter of that clock?

   A. 1.06"

   B. 4.77"

   C. 6.36"

   D. 9.54"

   E. 12.73"

5) What is the measure of ∠DAB?

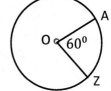

   A. less than 86^0

   B. 86^0

   C. between 86^0 and 94^0

   D. 94^0

   E. the answer cannot be determined

6) O is the center of a circle with a diameter of 12 feet and ∠ AOZ = 60^0. What is the length of minor arc AZ?

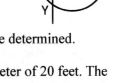

   A. $\pi\ feet$

   B. $2\pi\ feet$

   C. $3\pi\ feet$

   D. $4\pi\ feet$

   E. $6\pi\ feet$

7) Point O on the circle with a radius of 4 inches below lies on the origin of the XY coordinate system. What is the distance between the X intercept and the Y intercept of that circle?

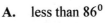

   A. 4 inches

   B. 6 inches

   C. 8 inches

   D. 4π inches

   E. The answer cannot be determined.

8) A circular pool has a diameter of 20 feet. The owner wants a concrete area around the pool that is 5 feet wide. What is the area of the concrete surface?

   A. 25π square feet

   B. 75π square feet

   C. 100π square feet

   D. 125π square feet

   E. 225π square feet

1)B 2)C 3)C 4)E 5)D 6)B 7)C 8)D

Circles - Quiz 1 (Answers)

1) A wheel rotates with a speed of 15 rotations per minute.
   i. After 20 seconds, it has traveled 30 feet.
   ii. 20 seconds is 1/3 of a minute, which means it has rotated 5 times in 20 seconds
   iii. In those 5 rotations, it travels 30 feet
   iv. In 1 rotation, therefore, it travels 6 feet, which must be the circumference of the circle
   v. The circumference is π∗diameter   6 feet = πD
   vi. $D = \frac{6}{\pi}$ feet   **(Answer B)**

2) The Diameter of circle B is 4. Which makes its radius 2.
   i. Therefore, the area of circle B is $\pi r^2 = 4\pi$
   ii. It follows that circle A has an area of 2π and circle C has an area of 8π
   iii. Add all three areas = $2\pi + 4\pi + 8\pi = 14\pi$ **(Answer C)**

3) The radius of circle A is 3, its area is 9π.
   i. the radius of circle B is 7. Its area is 49π.
   ii. the shaded portion that is in between circle A and circle B is $49\pi - 9\pi = 40\pi$.
                                                                                   (Answer C)

4) The length of the minor arc between the 1 and the 4 is 10 inches.
   i. The span of three numbers is ¼ of the total span of 12 numbers.
   ii. Therefore, the total span around the clock is 4 x 10 = 40 inches
   iii. The circumference is π times the diameter.
   iv. The diameter is $\frac{40}{\pi} = 40$ = 12.73 inches   **(Answer E)**

5) C is an inscribed angle of 86^0. Therefore, the minor arc DAB is 86 x 2 = 172 degrees.
   i. The circumference is 360 degrees, therefore the arc DCB must be 188 degrees.
   ii. The ∠DAB is an inscribed angle with an arc of 188 degrees
   iii. Therefore ∠DAB = 94^0 **(Answer D)**

6) The circle has a diameter of 12, and circumference of 12π
   i. Central angle ∠ AOZ = 60^0, which creates an arc of 60^0 (= minor arc AZ).
   ii. That arc is 1/6 of the total circumference of 360^0.
   iii. 1/6 of $12\pi = 2\pi$ **(Answer B)**

7) Look careful at point O. It creates an inscribed angle of 90^0 inside the circle.
   i. Therefore, the arc from the x-intercept to the y-intercept must be 180^0.
   ii. In other words, the x-intercept and the y-intercept lie on opposite sides of the diameter of the circle.
   iii. The radius is 4, therefore the diameter is 8, therefore the distance between the x-intercept to the y-intercept is also 8 inches   **(Answer C)**

8) The pool has a diameter of 20 feet, which equals a radius of 10 feet and an area of 100π ft^2.
   i. The concrete area makes a circle with a radius of (10+5) = 15 feet, with an area of 225π ft^2.
   ii. Of this larger circle, the inner 100π ft^2 (the pool) is filled with water, leaving 125π ft^2 of concrete area   **(Answer D)**

Circles - Quiz 2 (Formulas)

1) The square has two sides that are tangent to the circle. The area of the circle is 4π m², what is the area of the square?
   A. 1m^2
   B. 2m^2
   C. 4m^2
   D. 16m^2
   E. 32m^2

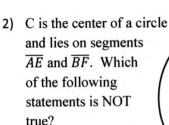

2) C is the center of a circle and lies on segments $\overline{AE}$ and $\overline{BF}$. Which of the following statements is NOT true?

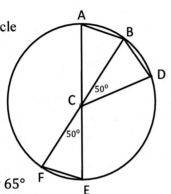

   A. $\overline{AB} \cong \overline{BD}$
   B. $\angle BAC$ measures $65°$
   C. $\overline{AB}$ is parallel to $\overline{EF}$
   D. $\angle BCE \cong \ < DCF$
   E. $\overline{CF} \cong \overline{EF}$

3) The diameter of a circle with center O is 7 and the measure of angle XOY is 100. What is closest to the length of minor arc XY ?

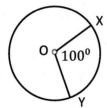

   A. 1.94
   B. 6.1
   C. 12.2
   D. 100
   E. 260

4) Which of the following is the circle formula of a circle with midpoint of (h,k) and a radius of r?
   A. $(x-h)^2 - (y-k)^2 = r^2$
   B. $(x-h)^2 + (y-k)^2 = r^2$
   C. $(x+h)^2 - (y+k)^2 = r^2$
   D. $(x+h)^2 + (y+k)^2 = r$
   E. $(x+h)^2 + (y-k)^2 = r^2$

5) The endpoints of the diameter of a circle O are B and D. In the standard (x,y) coordinate plane, B is at $(5, -2)$ and D is at $(-7,6)$. What is the y-coordinate of the center of the circle?
   A. -1
   B. 0
   C. 2
   D. 4
   E. 14.42

6) If the formula for a circle is $(x+4)^2 + (y+3)^2 = 16$, what are the coordinates of the center, and what is the radius?
   A. $(4,\ 3);\quad r = 16$
   B. $(-4, -3);\ r = 256$
   C. $(-4,\ 3);\quad r = 16$
   D. $(-4, -3);\ r = 4$
   E. $(4, 3);\qquad r = 4$

7) Knowing that a circle has the midpoint of $(-4, -2)$, and a radius of 9, which of the following is the correct equation for the circle?
   A. $(x+4)^2 + (y+2)^2 = 9$
   B. $(x+4)^2 + (y+2)^2 = 81$
   C. $(x-4)^2 + (y-2)^2 = 9$
   D. $(x-4)^2 - (y-2)^2 = 81$
   E. $(x+4)^2 + (y+2)^2 = 3$

8) A 3 by 4 rectangle is inscribed in circle ABC. What is the circumference of the circle ABC? (polygon)
   A. 2.5π
   B. 3π
   C. 5π
   D. 4π
   E. 10π

1)D 2)E 3)B 4)B 5)C 6)D 7)B 8)C

Circles - Quiz 2 (Answers)

1) If two sides of the square are tangent to the circle, then the length of any of the square's sides must be equal to the length of the circumference of the circle.
   a.   Use the formula $A = \pi r^2$
   b.   Fill in the numbers: $\pi(2m)^2$ to determine that circle's radius is 2m.
       NOTE: It is not $4\pi m^2$ but $\pi r^2 = \pi 4m^2$ or $\pi 2^2 m^2$ or $\pi(2m)^2$
   c.   Diameter= 2m*2 = side of the square
   d.   Area of the square= side^2=(4m)^2=16m^2 **(Answer D)**

2) Which answers ARE correct?
   a.   Because the X in FCE and the vertical angle in ACB are equal,
       there are three similar sections with an angle of x.
   b.   Because each long side of the three triangles are all equal to the
       radius, all three displayed triangles are isosceles, with angles 50°, 65° and 65°.
   c.   ABC and CFE are both 65°, making AB and EF parallel
   d.   BCE and DCF are identical, just 50° rotated.
   e.   IF CF was identical to EF, CFE would be an equilateral triangle with 60°angles **(Answer E)**

3) Think about this question as asking what percentage of the circle's circumference is between points A and B.
   a.   First, find the circumference. Circumference = $\pi d = 7\pi$.
   b.   A circle has 360 degrees. What percentage of 360 degrees is 100 degrees between A and B?
       $$\frac{100}{360} = \frac{x}{7\pi}$$
       Cross-multiply to find $x = 6.1$ **(Answer B)**

4) The formula is $(x-a)^2 + (y-b)^2 = r^2$ where the midpoint is (a,b) and the radius is r.
   Remember that it is a variation on the Pythagorean Theorem.   **(Answer B)**

5) Use the midpoint formula to find the y-coordinate of the center $\frac{-2+6}{2} = \frac{4}{2} = 2$ **(Answer C)**

6) Use your knowledge of the formula of a circle.
   $(x-a)^2 + (y-b)^2 = r^2$ where the midpoint is (a,b) and the radius is r
   a.   In this question, $x = -4\ and\ y = -3$; therefore, the center is located at $(-4, -3)$
   b. $r = \sqrt{16} = 4$
   c.   It is helpful to determine the length of the radius first.   **(Answer D)**

7) Use your knowledge of the formula of a circle. (see question 4)
   If the midpoint of the circle is $(-4, -2)$, then $x + 4 = 0\ and\ y + 2 = 0$, so the first part of the
       equation must be $(x + 4)^2 + (y + 2)^2$.
   If the radius is 9, then the second part of the equation must be $9^2 = 81$.   **(Answer B)**

8) In problems like these, it is crucial to draw a picture.
   a.   Remember your facts about inscribed angles (= half of the central angle)
       You can derive from this, that each inscribed angle of 90° in a circle will
       end up in the diameter of that circle, which has a central angle of 180°.
   b.   If you draw the rectangle inscribed in a circle, then it is immediately
       apparent that the diagonal of the rectangle is also the diameter of the circle.
   c.   Use Pythagorean triples to find the diameter. If one side is 3 and the
       other is 4, then the diameter must be 5.
   d.   Circumference = πd $= 5\pi$ **(Answer C)**

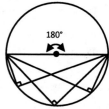

Circles - Quiz 3 (Polygons)

Use your knowledge about triangles to solve these questions.

1) A right triangle with sides 3, 4, and 5 is inscribed in a circle, what is the circumference of that circle?
   - **A.** 3π
   - **B.** 4π
   - **C.** 5π
   - **D.** $16\pi^2$
   - **E.** $25\pi^2$

2) A right triangle with a short side of 6 inches is inscribed in a circle with a circumference of 10π. What is the area of the triangle?
   - **A.** 16π square inches
   - **B.** 24π square inches
   - **C.** 25π square inches
   - **D.** 24 square inches
   - **E.** 25 square inches

3) A rectangle of 5 x 12 is inscribed in a circle. What is the radius of the circle?
   - **A.** 2.5
   - **B.** 5
   - **C.** 6
   - **D.** 6.5
   - **E.** 8.5

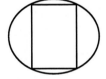

4) A square with sides 4 is inscribed in a circle. What is the area of the circle?
   - **A.** $2\pi^2$
   - **B.** $4\pi^2$
   - **C.** $8\pi^2$
   - **D.** $16\pi^2$
   - **E.** $32\pi^2$

5) A circle with a diameter of 26", sits on top of a box with a width of 24". How far is the center of the circle above the top side of the box?
   - **A.** 5"
   - **B.** 6"
   - **C.** 7"
   - **D.** 8"
   - **E.** 9"

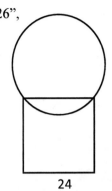

24

6) Three circles with a radius of 4 lie tangent to each other across the diameter of a larger circle. What is the area of the larger circle?
   - **A.** 4π
   - **B.** 16π
   - **C.** 32π
   - **D.** 144π
   - **E.** 256π

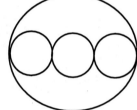

7) A square has two sides that are tangent to circle A. The area of the square is 4 m², what is the area of the circle?
   - **A.** 1π m²
   - **B.** 2π m²
   - **C.** 3.14π m²
   - **D.** 4π m²
   - **E.** 16π m²

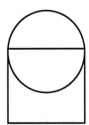

1)C 2)D 3)D 4)C 5)A 6)D 7)A

Circles - Quiz 3 (Answers)

1) a. Remember your facts about inscribed angles (= half of the central angle.)
    You can derive from this, that each inscribed angle of 90° in a circle will
    end up in the diameter of that circle, which has a central angle of 180°.

   a. If you draw a tight triangle inscribed in a circle, the diagonal of that right triangle
    has to be the diameter of that circle.

   b. The diameter D is 5, the circumference is $\pi D = 5\pi$ **(Answer C)**

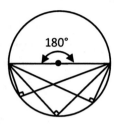

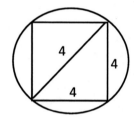

2) a. The circumference = $\pi D = 10\pi$
   b. Therefore, the diameter D = 10
   c. This is a 6-8-10 tight triangle (memorize or use Pythagorean Theorem)
   d. The area is ½ * b * h = ½ * 6 * 8 = 24   **(Answer D)**

3) a. All four corners of the rectangle touch the circle
   b. The diagonal of the rectangle = the diameter of the circle
   c. Use the Pythagorean Theorem to find D=13
   d. The radius is half the diameter. R=6.5   **(Answer D)**

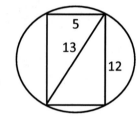

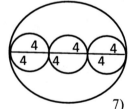

4) a. The diagonal of the square is $4\sqrt{2}$, which equals the diameter
   b. Therefore, the radius of the circle is $2\sqrt{2}$,
   c. The area of the circle is $\pi r^2 = \pi(2\sqrt{2})^2 = 8\pi$
                                 (Answer C)

5) a. Most circle questions center around the radius.
   b. Draw the radius = 13 and connect it to a corner of the box
   c. Make a triangle with a right angle, by drawing another radius straight down
   d. The last line bisects the box, revealing a 5-12-13 triangle.
   e. The distance from the center the top of the box is 5.   **(Answer A)**

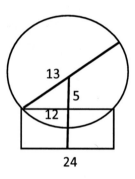

6) a. Draw the picture! The larger circle has a diameter of 6 x 4 = 24
   b. Therefore, the radius of the circle is 12
   c. The area = $\pi r^2 = \pi 12^2 = 144\pi$ **(Answer D)**

7)   If two sides of the square are tangent to the circle, then the
    length of any of the square's sides must be equal to the length of the
    diameter of the circle.

   a. Use the formula $A = s^2$
   b. Fill in the numbers: $4 = s^2$ to determine that square's side is 2 m.
    The diameter of the circle is also 2m, Hence the radius is 1m
   c. Area of the circle is $\pi r^2 = \pi 1^2 = \pi = 3.14$ m^2 **(Answer A)**

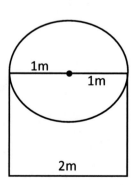

POLYGONS

Polygons

(see also page 222)

Angles in a Regular Polygon

The first polygon has THREE sides, and the angles add up to ONE times 180^0.
The next polygon has FOUR sides, and the angles add up to TWO times 180^0.
The next polygon has FIVE sides, and the angles add up to THREE times 180^0.
For a polygon with N sides, the angles add up to $(N-2)*180^0$, and each angle is $\frac{N-2}{N}$ *times* 180^0.

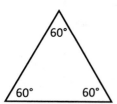
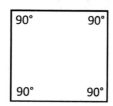
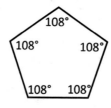
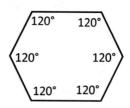

Diagonals in a Regular Polygon

The number of diagonals can be determined by counting the corners or vertices (N). Each vertex has $N-3$ diagonals originating from it. (There are no diagonals to its neighbors or to itself, thus $N-3$). However, each diagonal is counted twice this way, because it originates and ends in a vertex.

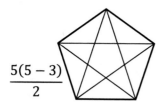
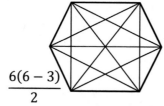

$$\frac{5(5-3)}{2} \qquad \frac{6(6-3)}{2} \qquad \frac{8(8-3)}{2} \qquad \frac{N(N-3)}{2} \text{ diagonals}$$

Exterior Angles of a Regular Polygon

Each exterior angle is 360°/N

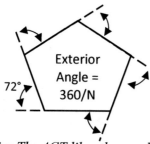

Exterior Angle = 360/N

72°

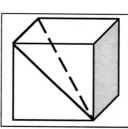

The diagonal of a cube can be determined by the Pythagorean Theorem. A quicker way is to remember that the diagonal of a cube is its **side times $\sqrt{3}$.**

👀 *Tip: The ACT likes the regular hexagon.* Its exterior angles are 60^0, its interior angles are 120^0, and the hexagon can be split up in six equilateral triangles that have the same side as one of the sides of the hexagon.

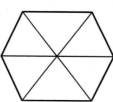

Perimeter of a Rectangular Polygon

Note that all dark segments on **top** (4.5+4.5+4.5+4.5)
    equal the distance of the segment on the **bottom** (18).
Note that the segments on the **right side**, (3+3+3+3)
    equal the distance of the segment on the **left side** (12).

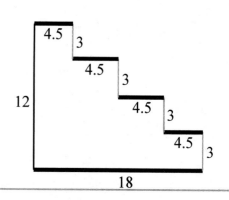

250

Polygons - Quiz 1

1) What is the perimeter of a rectangle that has a side of 12 inches, and an area of 48 inches?
   A. 4"
   B. 16"
   C. 32"
   D. 36"

2) What is the area, in square feet, of the figure below?
   A. 32
   B. 40
   C. 46
   D. 58

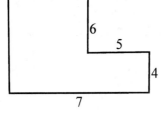

3) A trapezoid has two parallel sides, one that is 6 inches and one that is 14 inches. If the trapezoid is 7 inches tall, what is the area, in square inches, of the trapezoid?
   A. 42
   B. 98
   C. 70
   D. 140

4) Regular polygon X has 9 sides. What is the degree measure of each angle inside the polygon?
   A. 80
   B. 110
   C. 120
   D. 140

5) A pentagon has 5 diagonals. How many diagonals are there in a decagon?
   A. 9
   B. 10
   C. 28
   D. 35

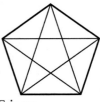

6) ABCD is a square, and ADE is an isosceles right triangle. What is the area of polygon ABCDE?
   A. 56
   B. 73.5
   C. 98
   D. 122.5

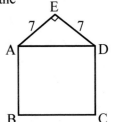

7) A shaded square ABCD is inscribed in a larger square. JKLM. $\overline{BL}$ is twice the size of $\overline{CL}$. If $\overline{JK}$ is 6 inches long, what is the area, in square inches, of the shaded region?
   A. 30
   B. 24
   C. 20
   D. 18

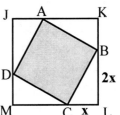

8) What is the perimeter of the area below?
   A. 14(6x) +18(2y+4)
   B. 32+6x + 2y
   C. 36
   D. 64

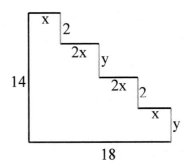

Polygons - Quiz 1 (Answers)

1) Always draw a picture. The area of the rectangle is: $B * H = 48$ ➔ $48 = 12 * X$.
$X = 48/12 = 4$ inches.
Do not mark answer A! Underline the question.
How much is the perimeter?
$4 + 12 + 4 + 12 = 32$ inches. **(Answer C)**

2) T.O.P. students think on paper.
Underline the questions and put all facts on the figure. Complete the rest of the measurements before answering the question. The two right sides should equal the left side 6+4=10 feet. The top and bottom sides should equal the same length.
$7 - 5 = 2$ feet.
Now we can answer the question about the area. There are two ways to do that.

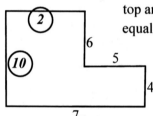

Method 1) <u>Subtract</u>. The large rectangle is $10 * 7 = 70$ square feet. The small rectangle is $6 * 5 = 30$ square feet. The shape is therefore $70 - 30 = 40$ square feet.

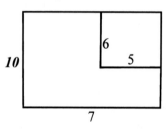

Method 2) <u>Add.</u>
The large rectangle is $10 * 2 = 20$ square feet. The small rectangle is $4 * 5 = 20$ square feet.

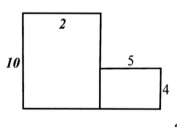

The shape is therefore $20 + 20 = 40$ square feet. **(Answer B)**

3) Use the formula for the area of a trapezoid:
$(B_1 + B_2)/2 * H$ ➔ $\frac{6+14}{2} * 7 = 70$ square inches.
(Answer C)

4) Use the formula of angles in a polygon.
$\frac{N-2}{N} 180^0$. ➔ $\frac{9-2}{9} 180^0 = 140$
Alternatively, use the outside angle information.
Outside angle is $360/9 = 40$ degrees. Inside angle is supplementary:
$180-40=140$ degrees **(Answer D)**

5) Use the formula for diagonals in a polygon:
$\frac{N(N-3)}{2}$ ➔ $\frac{10(10-3)}{2} = 35$ diagonals. **(Answer D)**

6) The triangle on top is isosceles. Therefore, it has two angles of 45 degrees. The dimensions in a 45-45-90 triangle have a ratio of $1:1:\sqrt{2}$.
The hypotenuse of the triangle is therefore $7\sqrt{2}$.
This hypotenuse is also the side of the square. The area of the square is $7\sqrt{2} * 7\sqrt{2} = 98$.
The area of the right triangle is ½*side*side = 24.5.
(You can rotate the triangle and use $½ * b * h = 24.5$)
Add the shapes together to get
$98 + 24.5 = 122.5$ **(Answer D)**

7) $CL = BK,$ so we can deduce *that* $x + 2x = 6$
Therefore $x = 2$ *and* $2x = 4$
Use the Pythagorean Theorem to determine the hypotenuse of the triangle CLB $2^2 + 4^2 = h^2$
➔ $h = \sqrt{20}$. A square with sides $\sqrt{20}$ has an area of 20. **(Answer C)**

8) The four sides on the right equal the left side. (=14
The four sides on top equal the bottom side. (=18)
The perimeter is 14+18+14+18 = 64 **(Answer D)**

MATH
Functions

SIMPLE FUNCTIONS

Simple Functions

 A function is a series of inputs that result in a series of outputs.
Tip: Each input can only result in exactly one output.

A function can be reflected in a **table**:

Function: $y = 2x$				
Input (x)	1	2	3	4
Output (y)	2	4	6	8

Or it can be reflected in a **graph**:

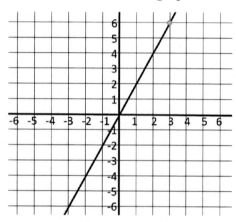

You can find the input and output in the **formula**.
For the value $x = 3$ $y = 2 * (3)$ $y = 6$

You can find the input and output in the **table**.
Under the value $x = 3$, you can see that $y = 6$

You can find the input and output in the **graph**.
For the value $x = 3$, you can see that $y = 6$

How to Read a Function

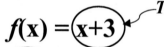 —*This is the function.*

$f(x) =$ (x+3)

(f(2)) = 2+3 — *This is the input*
simply replace the x with a 3

$f(2) =$ (5) — *This is the output.*

 Tip: *Most ACT questions about functions are set up like this.*

 Tip: *In a graph, the terms x and y are used, instead of x and f(x)*

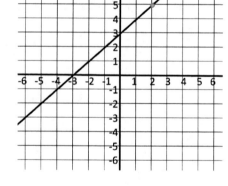

Variations of Functions.

For the function $f(x) = x + 3$, solve for the following:

$f(p + 2)$	➔ Replace the x with $p + 2$	➔ $(p + 2) + 3$ ➔ $f(p + 2) = p + 5$	
$f(-2)$	➔ Replace the x with -2	➔ $(-2) + 3$ ➔ $f(-2) = 1$	
$-f(3)$	➔ Multiply each side by -1, then replace the x with 3:		

$$f(3) = -x - 3 \qquad ➔ -3 - 3 \qquad ➔ -f(3) = -6$$

$f^{-1}(3)$ ➔ This is the inverse function; now the ***answer*** to $x + 3$ needs to be 3.

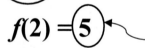   *(Tip: switch the x and the y)*   ➔ $x + 3 = 3$ ➔ $f^{-1}(3) = 0$

Simple Functions - Quiz 1

For all following equations:
$$f(x) = 4x - 6,$$
$$g(x) = 2x^2 + 4x - 2$$
$$h(x) = 3x + 2.$$

1) What is $h(3)$?
   - A. 6
   - B. 9
   - C. 11
   - D. 28

2) What is $g(-3)$?
   - A. 28
   - B. 4
   - C. −18
   - D. −32

3) What is (are) the possible value(s) for x when $g(x) = 28$?
   - A. 5 and −3
   - B. 3 and −5
   - C. 3 and −3
   - D. 8.5

4) What is $f(-x)$?
   - A. $-4x - 6$
   - B. −4x+6
   - C. $\frac{x}{4} + 6$
   - D. $\frac{-x}{4} + 6$

5) What is $-h(x)$?
   - A. $-3x - 2$
   - B. $-3x + 2$
   - C. $\frac{-x}{3} - 2$
   - D. $\frac{x}{3} - 2$

6) What is $h(4x - 6)$?
   - A. $\frac{4x}{3} - 3$
   - B. $-x - 8$
   - C. $12x - 16$
   - D. 7x - 4

7) What is $h(f(x))$?
   - A. $\frac{4x}{3} - 3$
   - B. $-x - 8$
   - C. $12x - 16$
   - D. 7x − 4

8) What is $f(h(x))$?
   - A. $\frac{3x}{4} - \frac{1}{3}$
   - B. $7x - 4$
   - C. $-x - 8$
   - D. $12x + 2$

9) What is $g(f(x))$?
   - A. $2(x^2 + 4x - 4)$
   - B. $2(x^2 + 2)$
   - C. $2(4x^3 - 13)$
   - D. $2(16x^2 - 40x + 23)$

10) What is $h(g(x))$?
   - A. $6x^2 + 12x - 4$
   - B. $6x^2 + 12x - 6$
   - C. $18x^2 + 30x + 14$
   - D. $6x^3 + 12x^2 + 2x - 4$

11) What value of $h(x) = g(-4)$?
   - A. $h(-4)$
   - B. $h(4)$
   - C. $h(6)$
   - D. $h(14)$

Simple Functions - Quiz 1 (Answers)

For all following equations:

$$f(x) = 4x - 6,$$
$$g(x) = 2x^2 + 4x - 2$$
$$h(x) = 3x + 2$$

1) $h(3)$ signifies that 3 should be plugged in for x in the function of h(x).
⇨ $h(3) = 3(3) + 2 = 11$. **(Answer C)**

2) $g(-3)$ signifies that −3 should be plugged in for x on both places in the function of $g(x)$.
Be careful with the negative.
$$g(-3) = 2(-3)^2 + 4(-3) - 2$$
$$= 2(9) - 12 - 2$$
$$= 18 - 14 = 4 \quad \text{(Answer B)}$$

3) $g(x) = 28$ signifies that the answer of this function needs to be 28. Read as $28 = 2x^2 + 4x - 2$
   a. First, turn the equation: $2x^2 + 4x - 2 = 28$ into $2x^2 + 4x - 30 = 0$.
   b. Factor out the number 2 ➔ $2(x^2 + 2x - 15) = 0$
      a. Look for two numbers that add up to 2 and have a product of −15)
   c. Factor the polynomial: $2(x + 5)(x - 3) = 0$ (Note: Don't fall for x = 5 or x = −3)
   d. To make this correct, one of the factors needs to be 0.
   e. This is true when x = −5, or when x = 3 **(Answer B)**

4) To answer the problem, replace x with −x in the original equation. (Don't be confused—you are NOT finding the inverse, written as f⁻¹(x)
   a. $f(x) = 4(-x) - 6 = -4x - 6$ **(Answer A)**

5) This differs slightly from the above question. Instead of plugging −x into the equation, you are moving around a negative sign.
   a. If one side of the equation (h(x)) is multiplied by −1, then the other side must be as well.
   b. Multiply 3x+2 by −1 to find the answer.
   c. $-1(3x + 2) = -3x - 2$ **(Answer A)**

6) To solve this problem, plug in 4x−6 for x in the original equation.
   a. $h(4x - 6) = 3(4x - 6) + 2 = 12x - 16$ **(Answer C)**

7) This is a composition function. Read it as "h of f of x".
   a. The f of x is the first function: $f(x) = 4x - 6$
   b. Next, plug in $4x - 6$ for x in h(x):
   c. $h(f(x)) = h(4x - 6) = 3(4x - 6) + 2 = 12x - 16$. **(Answer C)**
   d. Compare this with question 6 for additional insight.

8) This is a composition function. Read it as "f of h of x".
   a. First solve the "h of x", then plug in the answer into the "f of x"
   b. $h(x) = 3x + 2$ Plug in $3x = 2$ for x in f(x):
   c. $f(h(x)) = 4(3x + 2) - 6 = 12x + 2$ **(Answer D)**

9) This composition is slightly more difficult, as it is necessary to expand a binomial.
   a. First, factor out 2 in the equation for g(x): $2x^2 + 4x - 2 = 2(x^2 + 2x - 1)$
   b. Now plug in $4x - 6$ for x in the factored form of $g(x)$ and use FOIL to expand.
   c. $2((4x - 6)^2 + 2(4x - 6) - 1) = 2(16x^2 - 40x + 23)$ **(Answer D)**

10) In this problem, you are finding a composition where the inner component is a polynomial.
   $h(g(x)) = 3(2x^2 + 4x - 2) + 2 = 6x^2 + 12x - 4$ **(Answer A)**

11) This problem requires you both to evaluate and to solve a function.
   a. First, find g(−4): $g(-4) = 2(-4^2) + (4 * -4) - 2 = 32 - 16 - 2 = 14$
   b. Now, set 14 equal to the equation for h(x): $14 = 3x + 2$
   c. Solve for x. $3x = 12$, so x = 4 **(Answer B)**

LINEAR
EQUATIONS

Linear Equations

A straight line in the coordinate plane can be defined as:

$$y = mx + b$$

 Tip: m is the slope and b is the y intercept ONLY when the equation is written this way!

When x is zero, b is the **y intercept**, (where the line crosses the y-axis) $y = 0x + b$

When y is zero, the **x intercept** is determined by $x = \dfrac{-b}{m}$ $0 = mx + b$

When two lines cross, the intersection is defined as the point where the equations are equal.

Example: Line 1 $y = 4x + 1$
          Line 2 $y = 2x + 3$
          The lines cross where $4x + 1 = 2x + 3$
                                      $2x = 2$
                                      $x = 1$

You can "add" or "subtract" lines in order to eliminate one of the two variables.

$4y - 2x = 16$	$2y - 2x = 11$	$2y + 5x = 1$	$6y + 15x = 3$
$2y + 2x = 8$	$2y + 3x = 6$	$6y - 3x = 6$	$6y - 3x = 6$
========== +	========== −	======== ? ⟶	========== −
$6y \quad = 24$	$-5x = 5$	????	$-18x = 9$
$y \quad = 4$	$x = -1$	*(multiply line 1 times 3)*	$x = -2$

Slope

The **slope** is $m = \dfrac{rise}{run} = \dfrac{y_2 - y_1}{x_2 - x_1}$ between any two points (x_1, y_1) and $x_2, y_2)$ on the line.

A **positive** slope m goes from bottom left to top right; a **negative** slope m goes from top left to bottom right.

A **horizontal** line has a slope m of 0.   (The rise is 0 since $y_2 - y_1 = 0$)

A **vertical** line has a slope m that is undefined. (Since $x_2 = x_1$, there is no run.) (You cannot divide by 0)

A line that makes a **45°** with the axis has a slope m of 1 or -1. (The rise is equal to the run.)

A second line with the same slope m is **parallel** to the first one.

A second line with a **perpendicular** slope has an opposite reciprocal of m: $-\dfrac{1}{m}$.

Original line: $y = 2x + 4$
Parallel: $y = 2x - 6$ (Only the slope matters, not the y-intercept.)
Parallel: $2y = 4x + 12$ (Note that the slope is still 2 if written as $y = mx + b$.)
Perpendicular: $y = -\dfrac{1}{2}x + 13$ (The new slope is the opposite reciprocal of the old one.
                                    The y-intercept does not matter)

 Tip: To find the Y intercept if you only have a slope (5) and one point on the line (2,3), plug this information into the equation $y = mx + b$ ➔ $3 = (5)2 + b$ Then, solve for b ➔ $b = -7$

Linear Equations - Quiz 1

1. Line p has a slope of zero and a y-intercept of 5. Line q has a slope that is undefined and an x-intercept of 2. What is the distance between the origin and the point of intersection between these two lines?

   A. $3\sqrt{2}$

   B. $4\sqrt{5}$

   C. $\sqrt{29}$

   D. 6

2. Line v passes through points (6,7) and (8,13). Line w is defined by the equation $y = -2x - 6$. What is the point of intersection of line v and w?

   A. (1 , 8)

   B. (1, −8)

   C. (−1, 8)

   D. (−1, −8)

3. If the expression $2x^3 + 4dx - 7$ is equal to -1 when $x = 3$, what is the value of d?

   A. −5

   B. −4

   C. 0

   D. 2

4. What is the slope of the line given by the equation $7x - 12y + 24 = 0$?

   A. −12

   B. $\frac{-12}{7}$

   C. $\frac{-7}{12}$

   D. $\frac{7}{12}$

5. In 1997, the cost of food for a certain family was $10,000. In 2002, the cost of food for this family was $13,500. Assuming the cost increases linearly, what will be the cost of this family's food in 2013?

   A. $19,800

   B. $20,700

   C. $21,200

   D. $23,600

6. The table below gives some (x,y) pairs that fit a linear relationship. What does k equal?

X	F(x)
-3	-5
3	7
0	1
6	13
4.5	k

   A. 8.5

   B. 9

   C. 10

   D. 11.5

7. If $3x - 2y = 12$, and $-x + 5y = 9$, solve for (x,y).

   A. (3,5)

   B. (5,6)

   C. (5,5)

   D. (6,3)

8. Which of the following lines has the same slope as the line $3y + 7x = 36$?

   A. $-3y - 7x = -4$

   B. $3x + 7y = 36$

   C. $9y + 49x = 36$

   D. $3y = 7x + 18$

Linear Equations - Quiz 1 (Answers)

1) A slope of zero means the line is horizontal. A slope that is undefined is vertical.
The lines intercept in the coordinate (2,5). Using the Pythagorean Theorem (or the distance formula) you can figure out that the distance is $\sqrt{2^2 + 5^2} = \sqrt{29}$. **(Answer C)**

2) First find the slope of line v. $\frac{Rise}{run} = \frac{6}{2} = 3$
Then find the y intercept of line v. You already know the slope and one point (6,7) so plug this information into the equation
$y = mx + b$➜ $7 = (3)6 + b$ ➜ $b = -11$
Now write the formula of line v: $y = 3x - 11$
The two lines intersect at the point where the formulas are equal. Substitute $3x - 11$ for the y-value in line w to get $3x - 11 = -2x - 6$
Now, solve for x. ➜ $5x = 5$ ➜ $x = 1$
To find the Y-value of the intersection, simply use -1 for the x value in one of the equations.
$3(1) - 11 = -8$ or $-2(-1) - 6 = -8$
The intercept is $(1, -8)$ **(Answer B)**

3) The expression $2x^3 + 4dx - 7$ is equal to -1 when x = 3
Plug the known quantities into the equation:
$2(3)^3 + 4d(3) - 7 = -1$ ➜ $54 + 12d = 6$
➜ $12d = -48$ ➜ $d = -4$
(Answer B)

4) What is the slope of the line given by the equation $7x - 12y + 24 = 0$?
Rewrite the equations in the form $y = mx + b$, where m is the slope.
$7x - 12y + 24 = 0$ ➜ $-12y = -7x - 24$
➜ $y = \frac{7}{12} + 2$ ➜ The slope of this line is $\frac{7}{12}$.
(Answer D)

5) You can solve this problem by using the x coordinates (1997, and 2002) and y coordinates (10,000 and 13,500), finding the slope ($\frac{rise}{run}$), the y-intercept (by using one coordinate and the slope) and then plug in the new x-value (2013).
$(\frac{rise}{run}) = (\frac{3,500}{5}) = 700$. What does this mean? For every year added, the cost of food goes up $700. You can go straight to the answer because 11 years after 2002, the cost of food must have risen 11*700 or $7,700 = $21,200. **(Answer C)**

6) The table shows x coordinates and y coordinate ($F(x)$).
Taking the difference between two points will give you the slope. $\frac{rise}{run} = \frac{y_2-y_1}{x_2-x_1} = \frac{7-1}{3-0} = 2$
Using the slope (2) with one coordinate pair (0,1) will give us the y-intercept (b) of $y = mx + b$.
$1 = 2(0) + b$ the y-intercept is 1.
Now we can put the latest x-value of 4.5 into this equation to find k.
$k = 2(4.5) + 1$ ➜ $k = 10$ **(Answer C)**

7) The lines can be added and subtracted.
For the second equation, multiply both sides by three so it matches the first equation. Substitute $y = 3$ in either equation to find $x = 6$.
(Answer D)

$3x - 2y = 12$
$-3x + 15y = 27$
========== +
$13y = 39$
$y = 3$

8) Rewrite the equations in the form $y = mx + b$. Only A has the same slope as the original equation. $(-\frac{7}{3})$ **(Answer A)**

TRIGONOMETRY

Trigonometry Review

SOH-CAH-TOA (only use SOHCAHTOA for right triangles.)

 Tip: Three out of four ACT trig questions can be answered with SOHCAHTOA.

$$\text{Sin } \theta = \frac{Opp}{Hyp} \qquad \text{Csc } \theta = \frac{Hyp}{Opp} = \frac{1}{Sin} \qquad \tan \theta = \frac{sin\,\theta}{cos\,\theta}$$

$$\text{Cos } \theta = \frac{Adj}{Hyp} \qquad \text{Sec } \theta = \frac{Hyp}{Adj} = \frac{1}{Cos}$$

$$\text{Tan } \theta = \frac{Opp}{Adj} \qquad \text{Cot } \theta = \frac{Adj}{Opp} = \frac{1}{Tan}$$

To find the angle, use the inverse function.
$\sin(30°) = 0.5$
$\sin^{-1}(0.5) = 30°$

Commonly Used Values

 Tip: Study this diagram; quizzes will often use one of these values.

Degrees	0	30°	45°	60°	90°
Radians	0	π/6	π/4	π/3	π/2
Sin θ	0	$\frac{1}{2}$	$\frac{\sqrt{2}}{2}$	$\frac{\sqrt{3}}{2}$	1
Cos θ	1	$\frac{\sqrt{3}}{2}$	$\frac{\sqrt{2}}{2}$	$\frac{1}{2}$	0
Tan θ	0	$\frac{\sqrt{3}}{3}$	1	$\sqrt{3}$	Undefined

Angles Over 90 Degrees

Quadrant II
sin θ : +
cos θ : −
tan θ : −

Quadrant I
sin θ : +
cos θ : +
tan θ : +

Quadrant III
sin θ : −
cos θ : −
tan θ : +

Quadrant II
sin θ : −
cos θ : +
tan θ : −

or:

Students — *Sin positive*
All — *All positive*
Take — *Tan positive*
Calculus — *Cos positive*

Law of Sines: $\dfrac{\sin A}{a} = \dfrac{\sin B}{b} = \dfrac{\sin C}{c}$

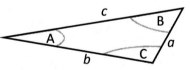

Practice:

Degrees	0	30°	45°	60°	90°
Radians					
Sin Θ					
Cos Θ					
Tan Θ					

SOHCAHTOA - Quiz 1

1) Based on the below right triangle, select the equation which is true.

   A. $\sin\theta = \frac{9}{13}$

   B. $\sin\theta = \frac{13}{9}$

   C. $\cos\theta = \frac{9}{13}$

   D. $\cos\theta = \frac{13}{9}$

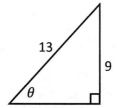

2) In reference to the below right triangle, which of the following is the value of $\tan\theta$?

   A. $\frac{a}{b}$

   B. $\frac{b}{a}$

   C. $\frac{b}{c}$

   D. $\frac{c}{b}$

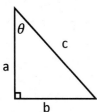

3) An eagle is flying toward a mouse at a height of 40 feet above level ground. The mouse stares up at the eagle at an angle of 30°. What is the eagle's horizontal distance from the mouse in feet?

   A. $\frac{40}{\sin 30°}$

   B. $\frac{\sin 30°}{40}$

   C. $\frac{40}{\tan 30°}$

   D. $\frac{\tan 30°}{40}$

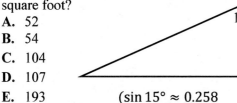

4) The right triangle shown below has a leg of 20 feet and an angle of 15°. What is the triangle's area, measured to the closest square foot?

   A. 52

   B. 54

   C. 104

   D. 107

   E. 193

   ($\sin 15° \approx 0.258$
   $\cos 15° \approx 0.965$
   $\tan 15° \approx 0.268$)

5) A kite is attached to a stake in the ground by a 40-foot length of cord. The angle between the cord and the ground is 50°. About how many feet above the ground is the kite when the rope is taut? (Note: $\sin 50° \approx 0.766$
$\cos 50° \approx 0.643$
$\tan 50° \approx 1.192$)

   A. 26

   B. 31

   C. 48

   D. 52

   E. 62

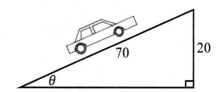

6) A 70-foot-long ramp leads from level ground to the entrance of a parking garage, which is 20 feet above the ground. At what angle, measured in degrees, does the ramp meet the ground?

   A. $\sin^{-1}\frac{2}{7}$

   B. $\cos^{-1}\frac{2}{7}$

   C. $\tan^{-1}\frac{2}{7}$

   D. $\sin^{-1}\frac{7}{2}$

   E. $\cos^{-1}\frac{7}{2}$

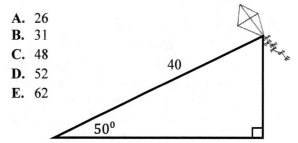

1)A 2)B 3)C 4)B 5)B 6)A

SOHCAHTOA - Quiz 1 (Answers)

1. Use SOHCAHTOA to determine quickly which option is the correct one for each equation against the picture. Answer A is sine (opposite over hypotenuse) is 9/13. When looking at the picture, we see that this answer is true. **(Answer A)**

2. Watch out: θ is located on the top. Therefore, SOHCAHTOA needs to be calculated from the perspective of θ. Tangent is opposite over adjacent. Looking at the triangle, the opposite side is b, and the adjacent is a. (It is important to know the hypotenuse will always be dictated as such; the adjacent side is never the hypotenuse). This means tangent is b over a. **(Answer B)**

3. We are given an angle and its opposite side, and we need to find the adjacent side x. (Note: x is the horizontal distance) The equation that makes use of opposite and adjacent is tangent: the tangent of an angle equals opposite over adjacent. $\tan 30° = \frac{40}{x}$
Now you need to solve for x.
$x * \tan 30° = 40$ or $x = \frac{40}{\tan 30°}$

(Answer C)

4. To find the triangle's area ($\frac{1}{2} * b * h$), you need the length of the base (x). Before using SOHCAHTOA, watch out: you need to determine the opposite and adjacent from the top! We already know the adjacent, (20) and we will have to use the tangent equation to solve for the opposite side. $\tan 15° = \frac{x}{20}$
Rearranged to solve for the opposite, we get $20 * \tan 15° = x$. 20 times the tangent of

15 degrees = 20*0.268= 5.36 feet. To then find the area, we take half of the base times the height, or $\frac{1}{2} * 5.36 * 20 \approx 53.6$ which comes closest to 54. **(Answer B)**
Alternatively, you can follow these steps:
Area $= \frac{1}{2} * 20 * (20 \, tan15°)$
Area $= 10 * (20 \, tan15°)$
Area $= 200 \, tan15°$
Area $= 53.6$

5. We have to find the distance between the kite and the ground, which is the opposite side from the angle. That means we will be working with the sine function, where the sine of an angle equals the opposite over the hypotenuse. $\sin 50° = \frac{x}{40}$ This can be rearranged to solve for the opposite, $\sin 50° * 40 = x$ or $0.766 * 40 = x$
$x \approx 31 \, feet.$ **(Answer B)**

6. We are looking for the angle (θ) where the ramp meets the ground, or the bottom left angle of the triangle. Since we are given the opposite and the hypotenuse lengths relative to that angle, we know we are working with the sine function, and the answer is
$\sin \theta = \frac{20}{70}$ or $\sin \theta = \frac{2}{7}$. However, **this is not one of the answer options.** We don't need the sine; we need to find the angle θ. You need to refer to the <u>inverse</u> of sine to find the angle.
$sin^{-1} \left(\frac{20}{70}\right) = \theta$ or $\theta = sin^{-1}(\frac{2}{7})$.

(Answer A)

SOHCAHTOA - Quiz 2

1. A child is riding her bike when she notices an RC helicopter hovering 120 feet above the ground. At first, the angle at which she looks at the helicopter is 15°, but after biking for an additional 15 seconds, that angle has changed to 30°. At around what speed, measured in feet per second, is the child biking?

   A. 1
   B. 15
   C. 16
   D. 20
   E. 24

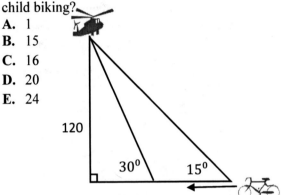

2. Jane is staring up at a moored blimp; she is 160 feet away from the base of the blimp's mooring tower, which is 300 feet tall, as shown in the below illustration. At about what angle does the blimp's pilot stare back at Jane? (At what angle out does he look at Jane compared to his view straight down)

   A. 28°
   B. 32°
   C. 44°
   D. 58°
   E. 62°

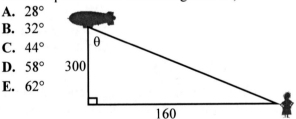

3. The two legs of a right triangle measure 34 centimeters and 61 centimeters, respectively. What is the sine of the triangle's smallest interior angle?

   A. $\frac{34}{\sqrt{34+61}}$

   B. $\frac{61}{\sqrt{34+61}}$

   C. $\frac{34}{\sqrt{34^2+61^2}}$

   D. $\frac{61}{\sqrt{34^2+61^2}}$

   E. $\frac{34}{61}$

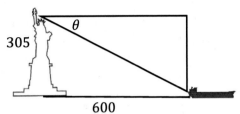

4. While standing on top of the Statue of Liberty, Ian sees a ship—currently 600 feet from the base of the statue—bringing tourists to Ellis Island, as shown below. The angle of depression, θ, can be found using which of the following equations?

   A. $\sin\theta = \frac{305}{600}$

   B. $\sin\theta = \frac{600}{305}$

   C. $\cos\theta = \frac{305}{600}$

   D. $\tan\theta = \frac{305}{600}$

   E. $\tan\theta = \frac{600}{305}$

5. A 13-foot ladder stands against a wall as shown below. The bottom of the ladder is 5 feet from the wall. How can you calculate the angle that the ladder makes with the ground?

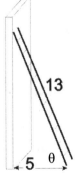

   A. $\sin\theta^0 = \frac{5}{13}$

   B. $\cos\theta^0 = \frac{13}{5}$

   C. $\cot\theta^0 = \frac{5}{13}$

   D. $\tan\theta^0 = \frac{5}{13}$

   E. $\sec\theta^0 = \frac{13}{5}$

1) C 2) A 3) C 4) D 5) E

SOHCAHTOA - Quiz 2 (Answers)

1. We need to find the distance the child covered in the 15 seconds in order to determine her speed in feet per second. To do this, we first need to find the distance on the ground between the right angle and the bike. Since we are given the angle and the opposite and need to find the adjacent, we will be using the tangent function.

$$\tan 15° = \frac{120}{x} \quad \text{or} \quad x = \frac{120}{\tan 15°} \approx 447.85$$

We now need to solve for the 30-degree portion, which will be accomplished in the same way as before. The distance on the ground is

$$\tan 30° = \frac{120}{x} \quad \text{or} \quad x = \frac{120}{\tan 30°} \approx 207.85$$

The difference in the two distances found is 240. If over 15 seconds, 240 feet were travelled, then the child is travelling at 16 feet per second.

(Answer C)

2. Since we know the opposite and the adjacent relative to the angle, we will be using the tangent function.

$$\tan \theta° = \frac{160}{300}$$

You need to refer to the <u>inverse</u> of the tangent to find the angle.

$$tan^{-1}\left(\frac{160}{300}\right) = \theta \quad \text{or} \quad \theta = tan^{-1}(\tfrac{8}{15}).$$

This results in 28 degrees. **(Answer A)**

3. When a picture is not given, draw one!

The smallest angle will be opposite the smallest side, or in this case, the 34 centimeters.

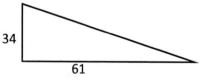

To find the sine, we need to take the opposite (34) over the hypotenuse (c). The hypotenuse can be calculated using the Pythagorean theorem, or $a^2 + b^2 = c^2$. In this case, the hypotenuse will be the square root of $a^2 + b^2$, in this case $c = \sqrt{34^2 + 61^2}$.

Therefore, the sin of the smallest angle will be

$$\frac{Opp}{Hyp} = \frac{34}{c} = \frac{34}{\sqrt{34^2 + 61^2}}. \qquad \textbf{(Answer C)}$$

4. The angle of depression from one side is the same as the angle of elevation from the other side, or the angle that the boat looks up at Ian.

This means we have the opposite and the

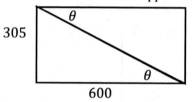

adjacent sides relative to that angle, and we will be using the tangent function. This limits our options to answers D and E. The tangent of an angle equals the opposite over the adjacent.

(Answer D)

5. To find the angle, we need to use the inverse function.

We already have the hypotenuse (13) and the adjacent (5), so we could find the angle of θ by the formula: $\cos \theta° = \frac{Adj}{Hyp} = \frac{5}{13}$. This is, however, NOT one of the options. (Do not fall for Answer B) By using the Pythagorean Theorem, we can figure out that the height of the wall at the top of the ladder is 12 feet. However, no viable options are given with 12/13 or 5/12 either.

We then need to look at the reciprocals of the sin, cos and tan functions: the sec, the csc, and the cot. Because we already have the hypotenuse (13) and the adjacent (5), we can find the angle of θ by the formula: $\sec \theta° = \frac{Hyp}{Adj} = \frac{13}{5}$.

(Answer E)

Trigonometry - Quiz 1

1) For α, an angle whose measure is between 270° and 360°, $\sin \alpha = \frac{-7}{25}$. Which of the following equals $\tan \alpha$?

A. $\frac{-12}{25}$

B. $\frac{12}{25}$

C. $\frac{7}{24}$

D. $\frac{-7}{24}$

2) The hypotenuse of the right triangle RST shown below is 10 feet long. The cosine of ∠ R is $\frac{4}{5}$. About how many feet long is line RS?

A. 5 feet

B. 6 feet

C. 7 feet

D. 8 feet

3) The hypotenuse of the right triangle WXY shown below is 15 feet long. The sine of ∠ W is $\frac{4}{5}$. About how many feet long is line XY?

A. 9 feet

B. 10 feet

C. 12 feet

D. 14 feet

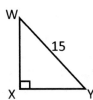

4) If the cosine of ∠ c in triangle ABC is $\frac{24}{25}$, how much is the tangent of ∠ C?

A. $\frac{7}{24}$

B. $\frac{24}{7}$

C. $\frac{25}{24}$

D. $\frac{25}{7}$

5) In the right triangle shown below, which of the following statements is true about ∠ L?

A. $\cos L = \frac{4}{5}$

B. $\sin L = \frac{5}{4}$

C. $\tan L = \frac{4}{3}$

D. $\sin L = \frac{3}{5}$

E. $\tan L = \frac{3}{4}$

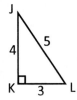

6) The lengths, in feet, of the sides of right triangle ABC are as shown in the diagram below, with x > 0. What is the cosecant of ∠ A, in terms of x?

A. $\frac{3}{x}$

B. $\frac{x}{3}$

C. $\frac{\sqrt{9-x^2}}{3}$

D. $\frac{3}{\sqrt{9-x^2}}$

E. $\frac{\sqrt{9-x^2}}{x}$

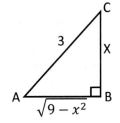

7) If the value, to the nearest thousandth, of sin θ is 0.485, which of the following could be the measure of θ?

A. 29°

B. −29°

C. 119°

D. −151°

Trigonometry - Quiz 1 (Answers)

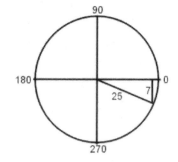

1) You should draw a picture to help visualize the question. This angle lies in quadrant IV, so the y-value is negative and the x-value is positive. The triangle is a Pythagorean triple, so its length along the x-axis must be 24. $(7^2 + x^2 = 25^2)$ Use SOHCAHTOA to find that the tangent $= \frac{opp}{adj}$, so by definition, $\tan \alpha = \frac{-7}{24}$.   **(Answer D)**

2) This problem requires knowledge both of trig functions and ratios. Use SOHCAHTOA: Cosine $= \frac{adj}{hyp}$. We know the length of the hypotenuse and are trying to find the length of the adjacent side. Since we know the value of $\cos R$, and the length of the hypotenuse, we can set up the equation as a ratio: $\frac{4}{5} = \frac{x}{10}$. Cross multiply and solve to find that $x = 8$ feet.   **(Answer D)**

3) Use SOHCAHTOA: $Sine = \frac{opp}{hyp}$. We know the length of the hypotenuse and are trying to find the length of the opposite side. Since we the value of $\sin W$ and the length of the hypotenuse, we can set up the equation: $\frac{4}{5} = \frac{x}{15}$. Cross multiply and solve to find that $x = 12$ feet.

(Answer C)

4) You should draw a triangle to help solve this problem. Use SOHCAHTOA: insert the opposite and adjacent values. Then, find the length of the opposite side. The triangle is a Pythagorean triple, so the opposite side must be 7. Tangent $= \frac{opp}{adj}$, and we know that the adjacent side is 24, and the opposite side is 7 so $\tan C = \frac{7}{24}$.

(Answer A)

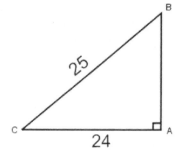

5) Use SOHCAHTOA to go through each answer choice and check if it is true. The only correct one is choice C.   **(Answer C)**

6) Don't be distracted by the square root sign. Just treat it like any other variable. The Cosecant $= \frac{1}{sin} = \frac{hyp}{opp}$. The side **opposite** $\angle$ A is x, and the **hypotenuse** is 3, so $\csc A = \frac{3}{x}$.

(Answer A)

7) Visualize the unit circle. If $\sin \theta = .485$, then the angle must lie in the first two quadrants of the unit circle, where sine is positive. Sin 29° is less than .50, while sin 119° is greater than .50, so answer choice A is the only acceptable choice.   **(Answer A)** Alternatively, you can use the inverse sine function of your calculator (make sure you are in degree mode.) to approximate the corresponding angle.

The Unit Circle

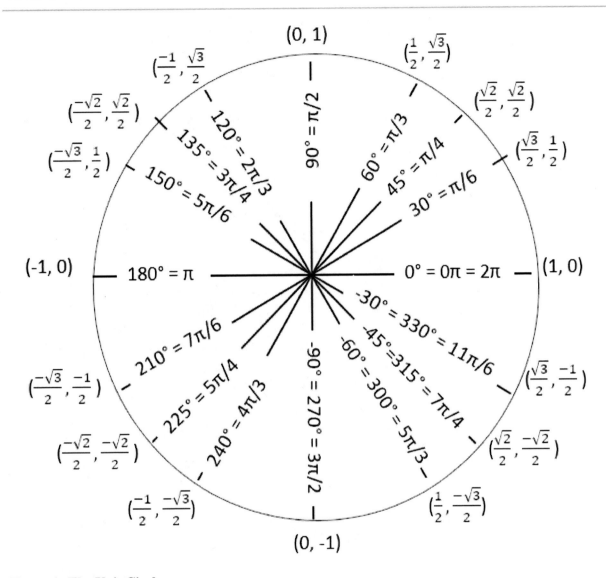

Figure 1: The Unit Circle.
  Inside: Angle in degrees and radians. **Outside**: <u>Cosine</u> of the angle, <u>Sine</u> of the angle.

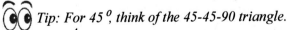 *Tip: For 30°, think of the 30-60-90 triangle.*

at 30°, the hypotenuse is 1 ➜ the short side is ½ ➜ the sine = ½

at 60°, the hypotenuse is 1 ➜ the short side is ½ ➜ the long side is $\frac{\sqrt{3}}{2}$ ➜ the sine = $\frac{\sqrt{3}}{2}$

Tip: For 45°, think of the 45-45-90 triangle.

At 45 degrees, the hypotenuse is 1 ➜ both sides are $\frac{\sqrt{2}}{2}$ ➜ the sine = $\frac{\sqrt{2}}{2}$

The Unit Circle - Exercise

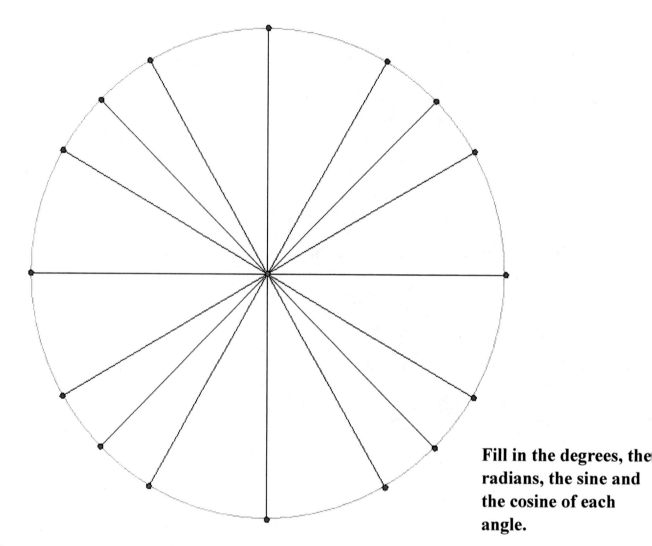

Fill in the degrees, the radians, the sine and the cosine of each angle.

Tip: You can solve all sine and cosine values in the unit circle with the Pythagorean Theorem.

Remember: The sine is the value of Y.   Sin of 30° is ½.

The cosine is the value of X.   Cos of 60° is ½.

All radii (= hypotenuse) are 1.

*Tip: Once you know **one** quadrant, you can transpose the values across the x-axes and the y-axes.*

Look for patterns in the sine:

90°	60°	45°	30°	0°
$\dfrac{\sqrt{4}}{2}$	$\dfrac{\sqrt{3}}{2}$	$\dfrac{\sqrt{2}}{2}$	$\dfrac{\sqrt{1}}{2}$	$\dfrac{\sqrt{0}}{2}$

The Unit Circle - Quiz 1

1) What is the degree measure of an angle that measures $\frac{5\pi}{4}$ radians?

   A. 180°
   B. 210°
   C. 225°
   D. 240°
   E. 300°

2) What is an equivalent radian measure of an angle that measures −120°?

   A. $\frac{4\pi}{3}$
   B. $-\frac{3\pi}{4}$
   C. $\frac{3\pi}{4}$
   D. $-\frac{\pi}{4}$
   E. $-\frac{\pi}{3}$

3) What is the sine of an angle with a radian measure of $\frac{\pi}{4}$?

   A. $\frac{1}{2}$
   B. $-\frac{1}{2}$
   C. $\frac{\sqrt{2}}{2}$
   D. $-\frac{\sqrt{2}}{2}$
   E. $\frac{\sqrt{3}}{2}$

4) What is the tangent of an angle that measures −30°?

   A. $-\frac{1}{2}$
   B. $\frac{\sqrt{3}}{2}$
   C. $\frac{\sqrt{3}}{3}$
   D. $-\frac{\sqrt{3}}{3}$
   E. $\sqrt{3}$

5) $\frac{\pi}{2} < \theta < \frac{3\pi}{2}$ and $\cos\theta = -\frac{1}{2}$. What is θ?

   A. 150°
   B. 210°
   C. 240°
   D. 300°
   E. 330°

6) In trigonometry, an angle of $-\frac{2\pi}{3}$ radians has the same sine and cosine as an angle that has which of the following degree measure?

   A. 60°
   B. 120°
   C. 240°
   D. 300°
   E. 330°

7) If $\sin\theta = -\frac{5}{13}$ and $\frac{3\pi}{2} < \theta < 2\pi$, then $\cos\theta =$?

   A. $\frac{12}{13}$
   B. $-\frac{12}{13}$
   C. $\frac{5}{12}$
   D. $-\frac{5}{12}$
   E. $\frac{13}{12}$

8) If $\tan\theta = \frac{3}{4}$ and $\pi < \theta < \frac{3\pi}{2}$, then $\sin\theta =$?

   A. $\frac{3}{5}$
   B. $-\frac{3}{5}$
   C. $\frac{4}{5}$
   D. $-\frac{4}{5}$
   E. $\frac{5}{3}$

1)C 2)A 3)C 4)D 5)C 6)C 7)A 8)B

Unit Circle - Quiz 1 (Answers)

1) What is degree measure of an angle that measures $\frac{5\pi}{4}$ radians?
A. $4\pi/4$ radians is 1π radian = 180 degrees (2π radians is the circumference)
B. $\frac{1}{4}\pi$ radian more would be another 45 degrees. ($\frac{1}{2}\pi$ radian = 90 degrees)
C. $180 + 45 = 225$ degrees

2) What is an equivalent radian measure of an angle that measures $-120°$?
A. 120 degrees is exactly 1/3 of the whole circumference (which is 2π radian all around)
B. The answer we are looking for is $-\frac{2}{3} *$ $2\pi = -\frac{2\pi}{3}$, which is not an answer option.
C. Going in a positive direction, the same angle can be notated as $\frac{2}{3} * 2\pi = \frac{4\pi}{3}$

3) What is the sine of an angle with a radian measure of $\frac{\pi}{2}$?
A. The whole circle (360^0) measures 2π radians. Half a circle (180^0) measures π radians, a quarter circle (90^0) measures $\frac{\pi}{2}$ radians, and, consequently, $\frac{\pi}{4}$ radians indicates and angle of 45^0.
B. The sine of 45^0 derives from the 45-45-90 triangle proportions.
C. If the hypotenuse of the unit circle is 1 (= the radius) each side must be $\frac{\sqrt{2}}{2}$

4) What is the tangent of an angle which measures $-30°$?
A. The tangent of an angle with 30 degrees can be derived from the 30-60-90 triangle proportions. ($1 - 2 - \sqrt{3}$)
B. In the unit circle, the hypotenuse is 1, the short side is $\frac{1}{2}$ and the long side is $\frac{\sqrt{3}}{2}$
C. The tangent $= \frac{opp}{adj} = \frac{\sqrt{3}}{3}$

D. Looking back of the question, we need the tangent of $-30°$ which is $\frac{-\sqrt{3}}{3}$

5) $\frac{\pi}{2} < \theta < \frac{3\pi}{2}$ and $\cos\theta = -\frac{1}{2}$. What is θ?
A. Cos = $\frac{1}{2}$ means the angle is 60^0, it can also be -60^0
B. For the cosine to be $-\frac{1}{2}$, the cosine must be reflected on the Y axis: 120^0 or -120^0
C. Looking at the answer options, neither is there. However, -120^0 equals 240^0.

6) In trigonometry, an angle of $-\frac{2\pi}{3}$ radians has the same sine and cosine as an angle that has which of the following degree measure?
A. $-\frac{2\pi}{3}$ means one third of the whole circumference (which is 2π) clockwise
B. -120^0 degrees (or 240^0 counterclockwise) is exactly 1/3 of the whole circumference.

7) If $\sin\theta = -\frac{5}{13}$ and $\frac{3\pi}{2} < \theta < 2\pi$, then $\cos\theta =$?
a. Draw a picture: Sine is in the fourth quadrant. Sine $= \frac{opp}{hyp}$
b. Find the length of the adjacent side; the triangle is a Pythagorean triple, so the adjacent side must be 12.
c. Cosine $= \frac{adj}{hyp} = \frac{12}{13}$ The cosine in the fourth quadrant is always positive.

8) If $\tan\theta = \frac{3}{4}$ and $\pi < \theta < \frac{3\pi}{2}$ then $\sin\theta =$?
A. θ is in between 180^0 and 270^0
B. tangent $= \frac{opp}{adj} = \frac{3}{4}$
C. Use Pythagorean triples: the adjacent side = 5.
D. Sine $= \frac{opp}{hyp} = \frac{3}{5}$
E. Sine in the third quadrant is always negative

LOGIC

Logic

Several problems in the ACT just have letters such as "a" and "b", and you have to determine their relationship based on certain rules.

Strategy: Students are taught to *plug in* numbers to find the solution.

Problem: Students tend to plug in the counting numbers for which the rule apparently will work.
They do **NOT** verify the rules for the number zero, for negative numbers, for fractions, etc.

Solution: Use ZONE-F for all the logic questions. Plug in the numbers that do not always behave like the natural numbers.

Tip: Plug in zero, one, a negative number, a fraction, a big number, or a small number.
*You only need **one** exception to proof that the rule is invalid.*
Try combinations as well, such as −1 and negative fractions.

ZONE-F
<u>Z</u>ero – <u>O</u>ne – <u>N</u>egative – <u>E</u>xtremes – <u>F</u>ractions

Example: Given A > B. Does it follow that $A^2 > B^2$?
It works with lots of numbers $(3 > 2 \rightarrow 9 > 4$ ☑$)$ $(5 > 4 \rightarrow 25 > 16$ ☑$)$
But does it work for ALL numbers? Use ZONE-F!

ZERO	$(4 > 0 \rightarrow 16 > 0$ ☑$)$ $(0 > -4 \rightarrow 0 > 16$ ☒$)$	Incorrect
ONE	$(5 > 1 \rightarrow 25 > 1$ ☑$)$ $(1 > -1 \rightarrow 1 > 1$ ☒$)$	Incorrect
NEGATIVE NUMBERS	$(-2 > -3 \rightarrow 4 > 9$ ☒$)$	Incorrect
EXTREME	Big: $(10^6 > 10^3 \rightarrow 10^{12} > 10^6$ ☑$)$	Correct
	Small: $(10^{-3} > 10^{-6} \rightarrow 10^{-9} > 10^{-12}$ ☑$)$	Correct
FRACTIONS	$(\frac{1}{2} > \frac{1}{3} \rightarrow \frac{1}{4} > \frac{1}{9}$ ☑$)$ $(\frac{1}{3} > \frac{-1}{2} \rightarrow \frac{1}{9} > \frac{1}{4}$ ☒$)$	Incorrect

Words to Know:

Natural numbers	The counting numbers	(1, 2, 3, 4, etc.)
Whole numbers	The set of numbers that includes zero and all of the natural numbers	(0, 1, 2, 3, etc.)
Integers	The set of numbers containing 0, the natural numbers, and all the negatives of the natural numbers	(..... −2, −1, 0, 1, 2, etc.)
Rational numbers	Numbers that can be expressed as the ratio of two integers	$(\frac{1}{2}, \frac{11}{12}, \frac{15}{11},$ etc)
Irrational numbers	Numbers that cannot be expressed as the ratio of two integers	$(\pi, \sqrt{2},$ etc.)
Real numbers	The combined set of rational numbers and irrational numbers	$(0, \sqrt{2}, 2, \pi,$ etc.)
Mixed numbers	Numbers written as a whole number and a fraction	$(1\frac{3}{4}, 2\frac{1}{2}\, 3\frac{1}{3},$ etc.)

Logic - Quiz 1

1. Given A>B: does it always follow that A∗B > A?
   - **A.** Yes, for all real numbers
   - **B.** Yes, for all positive real numbers
   - **C.** Yes, unless A or B is negative
   - **D.** Yes, for all integers
   - **E.** No.

2. Challenge: For which numbers do the number, the square and the cube lie in the following order?

   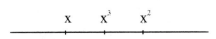

   - **A.** $X > 1$
   - **B.** $X < -1$
   - **C.** $-1 < X > 1$
   - **D.** $0 < X < 1$
   - **E.** $-1 < X < 0$

3. If x is a real number, which of the following statements can be true for X?
   - I. $X^2 = x$
   - II. $X^2 > x$
   - III. $X^2 < x$
   - **A.** I only
   - **B.** I and II only
   - **C.** I and II and III
   - **D.** II only
   - **E.** II and III only

4. If $ab < 0$ and $bc > 0$, which of the following statements must be true?
   - **A.** $ac < 0$
   - **B.** $ac > 0$
   - **C.** $ac = 0$
   - **D.** $ac = bc$
   - **E.** $a = c$

5. $\frac{10}{x} = z$ and $x \neq 0$. If X is getting bigger, what will happen to the value of z?
   - **A.** z gets bigger
   - **B.** z gets smaller
   - **C.** z stays the same
   - **D.** z is the opposite reciprocal of x
   - **E.** It cannot be determined if z gets bigger or smaller.

6. X is an integer and $x^2 + 4 > 20$, Which statement must be true?
   - **A.** $X = 4$
   - **B.** $X > 4$
   - **C.** $X < 4$
   - **D.** $-4 < x < 4$
   - **E.** $-5 \geq x \ or \ x \geq 5$

7. Which graph represents the equation $y = x^5 + 3x^2 - 2x + 3$?

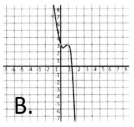

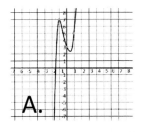

A.

B.

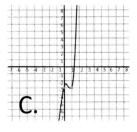

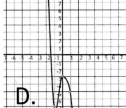

C.

D.

Logic - Quiz 1 (Answers)

1) Use ZONE F when you are faced with unknown quantities.

First try Z for ZERO: If $A = 0$, that would make B a negative number. However, $A * B$ would still be zero, and the product of $A * B$ is NOT bigger than A.

Then try O for ONE: For the sake of argument, let's pretend A and B had to be positive. If $A = 1$, that would make B a fraction between 0 and 1. A*B would NOT be bigger than A   **(Answer E)**

2) Use ZONE F:

	x	x^3	x^2	
Zero	0	0	0	no
One	1	1	1	no
−2	−2	−8	4	no
−1	−1	−1	1	no
100	10^2	10^6	10^4	no
$\frac{1}{2}$	$\frac{1}{2}$	$\frac{1}{8}$	$\frac{1}{4}$	no

We have not tried negative fractions.

$-\frac{1}{2}$	$-\frac{1}{2}$	$-\frac{1}{8}$	$\frac{1}{4}$	yes!

(Answer E)

3) Use ZONE F: I. is true for $X = 0$ and $X = 1$. II is true for all numbers when $x < 0 \ and \ X > 1$. III is true for all fractions when $0 < x < 1$ **(Answer C)**

4) Plug in numbers from ZONE F. ZERO: you cannot use zero because the product is not zero. ONE: If $B = 1$, A has to be negative and C has to be positive. NEGATIVE NUMBERS: If $B = -1$, then A has to be positive and C has to be negative. We cannot determine if A or C are positive or negative, but we can conclude that if one is positive, the other must be negative. A positive times a negative number will ALWAYS be negative.   **(Answer A)**.

5) Use ZONE F: ZERO: you cannot divide by zero. ONE: If X is getting bigger (2,3,4,5, etc.) Z will get smaller (0.5, 0.33, 0.25, 0.2, etc.)NEGATIVE NUMBERS: IF X is negative 3, Z will be −0.33. If X is getting bigger $(-2, -1, 1, 2, 3, etc)$, Z will first get smaller, than bigger $(-0.5, -1, 1, 0.5, 0.33, etc.)$ **(Answer E)**

6) Solve for x. $x^2 > 16$. Your brain tells you that X must be bigger than 4. ZONE F tells you to weigh all your options. Zero? Nope. One? Nope. Negative numbers? Aha! X can be $-5, -6, etc$.   **(Answer E)**

7) Use ZONE F with all graphs and functions.

First plug in $X = 0. = (0)^5 + 3(0)^2 - 2(0) + 3 = 3$ The coordinate (0,3) must be on the graph.
Then plug in $X = 1. = (1)^5 + 3(1)^2 - 2(1) + 3 = -1$ The coordinate $(1, 3)$ must be on the graph.
Then plug in $X = -1. = (-1)^5 + 3(-1)^2 - 2(-1) + 3 =$ The coordinate $(-1, 7)$ must be on the graph.   **(Answer A)**

THE MATRIX

The Matrix

A matrix is a quick, systematic way of writing information in rows and columns.

Example. The functions $2x + 14y$

$$-x + 2y$$ can be written like this $\begin{bmatrix} 2 & 14 \\ -1 & 2 \\ 4 & -3 \end{bmatrix}$.

$$4x - 3y$$

Terminology

A matrix is defined by its *rows* and *columns,* in that order.

A **3 x 2** matrix looks like this: $\begin{bmatrix} 4 & 0 \\ 1 & 12 \\ -4 & -5 \end{bmatrix}$! **x 3** matric looks like this: $\begin{bmatrix} -7 & 4 & 6 \\ 2 & 8 & 1 \end{bmatrix}$

The numbers in the matrix are called *elements* or *entries*.

The *determinant* of the matrix $\begin{bmatrix} a & b \\ c & d \end{bmatrix}$ equals $ad - cb$.

Adding and Subtracting Matrices.

 Tip: You can ONLY **add** and **subtract** matrices with the same dimensions: $A = \begin{bmatrix} 1 & 2 \\ 3 & 4 \end{bmatrix}$ $B = \begin{bmatrix} 5 & 6 \\ 7 & 8 \end{bmatrix}$

$A + B =$ $\begin{bmatrix} 1 & 2 \\ 3 & 4 \end{bmatrix}$ $\begin{bmatrix} 5 & 6 \\ 7 & 8 \end{bmatrix}$ $\begin{bmatrix} 6 & 8 \\ 10 & 12 \end{bmatrix}$ add the elements.

Multiplying a Matrix by a Number.

Just like $2(3x + 14) = 6x + 28$ and $2(-4x + 5) = -8x + 10$,

so is $2 * \begin{bmatrix} 3 & 14 \\ -4 & 5 \end{bmatrix} = \begin{bmatrix} 6 & 28 \\ -8 & 10 \end{bmatrix}$ Simply multiply each element in the matrix by 2.

In the example above, the number 2 is called the *scalar*.
The multiplication above is called a *scalar multiplication*.

Multiplying Two Matrices.

 Tip: $\begin{bmatrix} 1 & 2 \\ 3 & 4 \end{bmatrix} * \begin{bmatrix} 5 & 6 \\ 7 & 8 \end{bmatrix} \neq \begin{bmatrix} 5 & 12 \\ 21 & 32 \end{bmatrix}$ *You **cannot** simply multiply the entries!*

To multiply two matrices, you have to multiply the **paired entries of each row of the first matrix** by the **entries of each column in the second matrix.** A * B =

$\begin{bmatrix} 1 & 2 \\ 3 & 4 \end{bmatrix} * \begin{bmatrix} 5 & 6 \\ 7 & 8 \end{bmatrix} = \begin{bmatrix} first\ row\ A * first\ column\ B & first\ row\ A * second\ column\ B \\ second\ row\ A * first\ column\ B & second\ row\ A * seond\ column\ B \end{bmatrix} =$

Then, add the multiplied elements $\begin{bmatrix} 1*5 + 2*7 & 1*6 + 2*8 \\ 3*5 + 4*7 & 3*6 + 4*8 \end{bmatrix} = \begin{bmatrix} 19 & 22 \\ 43 & 50 \end{bmatrix}$

 *Tip: You can only multiply two matrices if the **number of columns** in the first one equals the **number of rows** in the second one.*

 Tip: Order matters in matrix multiplications. Therefore A * B **is not the same as** B * A.

The Matrix - Quiz 1

1. The *determinant* of a matrix $\begin{bmatrix} c & d \\ e & f \end{bmatrix}$ equals $cf - ed$.
   What must be the value of x for the matrix $\begin{bmatrix} x & 4 \\ x & x \end{bmatrix}$ to have a determinant of -4 ?
   A. -4
   B. -2
   C. x
   D. 2
   E. 4

2. What is the determinant of the matrix shown below?
   $$\begin{bmatrix} 12 & 3 \\ -6 & -2 \end{bmatrix}$$
   A. -42
   B. -6
   C. 4
   D. 6
   E. 7

3. Which of the following matrices is equal to the matrix product
   $$\begin{bmatrix} 5 & -2 \\ -3 & 4 \end{bmatrix} * \begin{bmatrix} 1 \\ -2 \end{bmatrix}?$$
   A. $\begin{bmatrix} 5 & -2 \\ -6 & 8 \end{bmatrix}$
   B. $\begin{bmatrix} 5 & -2 \\ 6 & -8 \end{bmatrix}$
   C. $\begin{bmatrix} 5 & -2 \\ 6 & 4 \end{bmatrix}$
   D. $\begin{bmatrix} 1 \\ 5 \end{bmatrix}$
   E. $\begin{bmatrix} 9 \\ -11 \end{bmatrix}$

4. Solve for x: $\begin{bmatrix} 1 & 2 \\ 3 & 4 \end{bmatrix} * \begin{bmatrix} 5 \\ 6 \end{bmatrix} = \begin{bmatrix} 17 \\ x \end{bmatrix}$
   A. 18
   B. 24
   C. 39
   D. 49
   E. 360

5. Four matrices are given below.
   $A = \begin{bmatrix} a & b \\ c & d \end{bmatrix}$ $B = \begin{bmatrix} e \\ f \end{bmatrix}$ $C = \begin{bmatrix} g & h & i \\ j & k & l \end{bmatrix}$
   and $D = \begin{bmatrix} m & n \\ o & p \\ q & r \end{bmatrix}$
   Which of the following matrix products is undefined?
   A. AB
   B. AC
   C. AD
   D. CD
   E. DC

6. Solve for A when
   $$A + \begin{bmatrix} 12 & 3 \\ -6 & -2 \end{bmatrix} = \begin{bmatrix} 12 & 3 \\ -6 & -2 \end{bmatrix}$$
   A. $A = 1$
   B. $A = 0$
   C. $A = \begin{bmatrix} -12 & -3 \\ 6 & 2 \end{bmatrix}$
   D. $A = \begin{bmatrix} 0 & 0 \\ 0 & 0 \end{bmatrix}$
   E. $A = \begin{bmatrix} 0 \\ 0 \end{bmatrix}$

7. What is the matrix product $[0,1,2] \begin{bmatrix} x \\ 2x \\ 3x \end{bmatrix}$
   A. $\begin{bmatrix} 0 & x & 2x \\ 0 & 2x & 4x \\ 0 & 3x & 6x \end{bmatrix}$
   B. $\begin{bmatrix} 0 & 0 & 0 \\ x & 2x & 3x \\ 2x & 3x & 6x \end{bmatrix}$
   C. $[0 \quad 2x \quad 4x]$
   D. $[0 \quad 6x \quad 12x]$
   E. $[8x]$

The Matrix - Quiz 1 (Answers)

1. If we follow the directions about the definition of the determinant,
    we get $x * x - x * 4 = -4$ ➔ $x^2 - 4x = -4$ ➔ $x^2 - 4x + 4 = 0$
    We now have a quadratic equation to solve: $(x - 2)(x - 2) = 0$ ➔ $x = 2$ **(Answer D)**

2. The determinant of a matrix $\begin{bmatrix} c & d \\ e & f \end{bmatrix}$ equals $cf - ed$. In this problem, the determinant is
    $(12 * (-2)) - (-6 * 3) = -24 - (-18) = -6$ **(Answer B)**

3. First, we multiply the set of numbers of the first row of the first matrix, with the first column of the
    second matrix: $5 * 1 + -2 * -2. = 5 + 4 = 9$. Then, we multiply the set of numbers of the second
    row of the first matrix with the first column of the second matrix.
    $-3 * 1 + 4 * -2 = -11$. The solution is a matrix with two entries. $\begin{bmatrix} 9 \\ -11 \end{bmatrix}$ **(Answer E)**

4. First, we multiply the set of numbers of the first row of the first matrix, with the first column of the
    second matrix: $1 * 5 + 2 * 6. = 17$. Then, we multiply the set of numbers of the second row of the first
    matrix with the first column of the second matrix.
    $3 * 5 + 4 * 6 = 39$. **(Answer C)**

5. You can only multiply two matrices if the **number of columns** in the first one
    equals the **number of rows** in the second one. This works in all products, except for AD: the first
    matrix (A) has two columns, but the second matrix (D) has three rows. **(Answer C)**

6. When adding two matrices, add the entries that are in the same position. Alternatively, we can use
    algebra to determine that if $A + B = C$, then $A = B - C$
    $A + \begin{bmatrix} 12 & 3 \\ -6 & -2 \end{bmatrix} = \begin{bmatrix} 12 & 3 \\ -6 & -2 \end{bmatrix}$ ➔ $A = \begin{bmatrix} 12 & 3 \\ -6 & -2 \end{bmatrix} - \begin{bmatrix} 12 & 3 \\ -6 & -2 \end{bmatrix}$ ➔ $A = \begin{bmatrix} 0 & 0 \\ -0 & 0 \end{bmatrix}$
    Answer B is incorrect because you cannot add a matrix and an integer. Answer E is incorrect, because
    you can only add and subtract two matrices with the same dimensions. Answer A would be correct if
    this had been a scalar multiplication. **(Answer D)**

7. To multiply these two matrices, multiply the first row of the first matrix times the first column of the
    second matrix. (There is only one row in the first matrix, and only one column in the second matrix.
    You should end up with two entries.) Add the paired products of these rows and columns. $0 * x + 1 *$
    $2x + 2 * 3x = 0 + 2x + 6x = [8x]$. **(Answer E)**

MATH

Statistics

PROBABILITY

Probability

$$\text{Probability} = \frac{\text{the number of desired outcomes}}{\text{the number of possible outcomes}}$$

Picking One Object

Example: The chance of picking ONE white circle $= \frac{1\ white}{4\ possible} = \frac{1}{4}$

The chance of picking ONE non-black circle $= \frac{4-2\ black}{4\ possible} = \frac{2}{4} = \frac{1}{2}$

For two mutually exclusive events, add of the probability of each event.

 *Tip: For exclusive events, **add** your chances.*

Example: The chance of picking ONE black **or** ONE gray circle

$$= \frac{2\ black}{4\ possible} + \frac{1\ gray}{4\ possible} = \frac{1}{2} + \frac{1}{4} = \frac{3}{4}$$

If the events overlap, subtract the chance of the outcomes that are part of both events so you will not count them twice.

 *Tip: For overlapping events, **subtract** your chances.*

Example: The chance of picking ONE gray object **or** ONE circle:

$$\frac{2\ gray}{4\ possible} + \frac{2\ circles}{4\ possible} - \frac{1\ (gray+circle)}{4\ possible} = \frac{1}{2} + \frac{1}{2} - \frac{1}{4} = \frac{3}{4}$$

Picking Two Objects - Independent events

Independent means that the second outcome does not depend on the outcome of the first outcome.

Rolling two dice (the second die does not depend on the first die), tossing a coin twice, or winning the lottery AND winning a bingo game are all examples of independent events.

 *Tip: For multiple objects from independent events, **multiply** your chances.*

Example: Rolling two fours with a die $= \frac{1\ four}{6\ possible} * \frac{1\ four}{6\ possible} = \frac{1}{6} * \frac{1}{6} = \frac{1}{36}$

Picking Two Objects - Dependent events

Adjust the chances of the second event AFTER the occurrence of the first event.

Example: Picking two circles from the group.

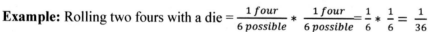

The first circle has a chance of $\frac{2\ circles}{4\ possible} = \frac{1}{2}$

Now the group has changed! The chance of the second circle is $\frac{1\ circle}{3\ possible} = \frac{1}{3}$

The chance of picking **two** circles is therefore $\frac{1}{2} * \frac{1}{3} = \frac{1}{6}$

Permutations

How many different ways can you wear 4 pants, 2 shirts, and 3 hats? $\quad 4 * 2 * 3 = 12$

How many 2-topping pancakes can you make with five different toppings? $\frac{5*4}{1*2}$

 Tip: If the order does not matter, divide the total by the amount of identical sets.

Probability - Quiz 1

For Questions 1-3: A jar contains 12 marbles: three red, two white, and seven blue. The marbles are not replaced after they are drawn.

1. What are the chances of drawing one blue marble followed by one red marble?
   A. $\frac{2}{12}$
   B. $\frac{1}{21}$
   C. $\frac{7}{48}$
   D. $\frac{7}{44}$

2. What is the most likely order to draw the first three marbles?
   A. Red, Blue, White
   B. Blue, Blue, Red
   C. Blue, Red, Blue
   D. Blue, Blue, Blue

3. What is the probability of drawing all seven blue marbles in a row?
   A. $\frac{7}{12}$
   B. $\frac{1}{792}$
   C. $\frac{1}{94}$
   D. $\frac{49}{144}$

==============================

4. There are 14 girls and 18 boys in Ms. Johnson's class. For a project, Ms. Johnson is drawing names out of a hat to pair two students together: a boy and a girl. If Claire and Clark are friends and want to work together, what are the chances that, after one team is selected, they will be drawn next?
   A. $\frac{1}{221}$
   B. $\frac{1}{252}$
   C. $\frac{1}{992}$
   D. $\frac{1}{870}$

5. A number is chosen at random from 1 to 50. What are the odds that the number chosen is NOT a multiple of 2 or 3?
   A. $\frac{17}{50}$
   B. $\frac{12}{50}$
   C. $\frac{38}{50}$
   D. $\frac{33}{50}$

6. A number is chosen at random from 1 to 50. What are the odds that the number chosen is a factor of 36?
   A. $\frac{6}{50}$
   B. $\frac{8}{50}$
   C. $\frac{9}{50}$
   D. $\frac{12}{50}$

7. You draw two cards from a standard deck of 52 cards. What is the probability of drawing two aces? (The cards are not replaced in the deck.)
   A. $\frac{2}{52}$
   B. $\frac{1}{221}$
   C. $\frac{12}{51}$
   D. $\frac{12}{52}$

8. If you flip three coins, what is the probability of getting at most two heads?
   A. $\frac{3}{4}$
   B. $\frac{1}{4}$
   C. $\frac{3}{8}$
   D. $\frac{7}{8}$

1)D 2)D 3)B 4)A 5)A 6)C 7)B 8)D

Probability - Quiz 1 (Answers)

1) Note that the marbles are drawn without replacement, so if one marble is drawn, the second marble to be drawn is 1 of 11 in the jar. First, find the probability of drawing a blue marble, which is $\frac{7}{12}$.

   Now, find the probability of drawing a red marble after drawing a blue, which is $\frac{3}{11}$.

   Multiply to find the chances of drawing them in that order: $\frac{7}{12} * \frac{3}{11} = \frac{21}{132} = \frac{7}{44}$. **(Answer D)**

2) First, find the most likely initial draw. Since there are more blue marbles than any other color, it is most likely that blue will be drawn first.
   If a blue marble is drawn first, there are still 6 remaining blue marbles in a pool of 11, so blue is also the most likely second draw.
   Even if two blue marbles are drawn, there are still five blue marbles remaining, more than any other color:
   The most likely order is blue, blue, blue.
   (Answer D)

3) To answer, multiply the probability of drawing a blue marble without replacement 7 times.
   $$\frac{7}{12} * \frac{6}{11} * \frac{5}{10} * \frac{4}{9} * \frac{3}{8} * \frac{2}{7} * \frac{1}{6} = \frac{5040}{3991680} = \frac{1}{792}$$

   Alternatively, you can cancel out factors
   Start with crossing off a seven from the top and from the bottom, then a six, etc.

   $$\frac{\cancel{7}}{\cancel{12}} * \frac{\cancel{6}}{11} * \frac{\cancel{5}}{\cancel{10}} * \frac{\cancel{4}}{9} * \frac{\cancel{3}}{8} * \frac{\cancel{2}}{\cancel{7}} * \frac{1}{\cancel{6}} = \frac{1}{11*9*8} = \frac{1}{792}$$

   (Answer B)

4) To solve, multiple the probability of drawing a specific girl (Claire) by the probability of drawing a specific boy (Clark).
   One team has already been drawn, so subtract 1 boy and girl from the pool from which to draw. $\frac{1}{13} * \frac{1}{17} = \frac{1}{221}$
   (Answer A)

5) Half of the numbers from 1 to 50 are even (divisible by 2). This leaves 25 numbers: 1, 3, 5, 7, 9, 11, 13, 15, etc. One-third of those 25 odd numbers from 1 to 49 are divisible by 3. This leaves 17 numbers: 1, 5, 7, 12, 13, 17, 19, etc.

   (Answer A)

6) The desired outcomes are the factors of 36: 1, 2, 3, 4, 6, 9, 12, 18 and 36 (a total of 9 possibilities)
   The possible outcomes are numbers 1-50
   The chance is $\frac{9}{50}$ **(Answer C)**

7) There are 4 aces in a deck, so the probability of drawing the first ace is $\frac{4}{52}$ or $\frac{1}{13}$.
   Now, there are only three aces left, and, in total, there are 51 cards left in the deck. Therefore, the probability of drawing this second ace is $\frac{3}{51} \; or \; \frac{1}{17}$.
   The chance of drawing two aces is
   $\frac{4}{52} * \frac{3}{51} = \frac{1}{13} * \frac{1}{17} = \frac{1}{221}$ **(Answer B)**

8) The probability of getting at most two heads is the same as 1 minus the probability of three heads.
   $$1 - \left(\frac{1}{2}\right)^3 = 1 - \frac{1}{8} = \frac{7}{8}$$
   Alternatively, you can think this out: There are $2 * 2 * 2 = 8$ options. There are three chances of getting one head, three chances of getting two heads, and one chance of getting zero heads. Seven out of eight possibilities satisfy the demand.

H	T	T
T	H	T
T	T	H
H	H	T
T	H	H
H	T	H
T	T	T

   (Answer D)

GRAPHS

Graphs

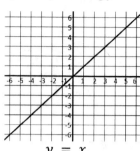 *Tip: The following four basic graphs often appear in the ACT. Memorize the shapes and the functions.*

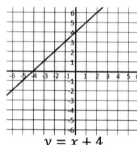
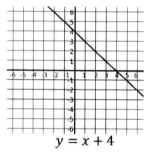
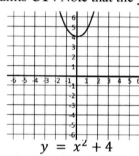
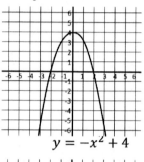

$$y = x \qquad\qquad y = -x \qquad\qquad y = x^2 \qquad\qquad y = -x^2$$

Adding 4 **to the functions** above moves the graph 4 units **UP**: Note that the y-intercept is 4 when $x = 0$.

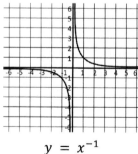
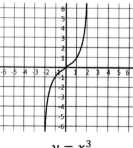
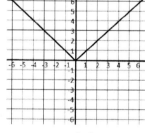
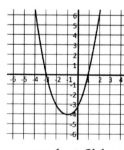

$$y = x + 4 \qquad\qquad y = x + 4 \qquad\qquad y = x^2 + 4 \qquad\qquad y = -x^2 + 4$$

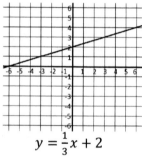
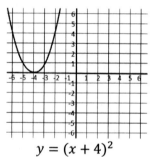
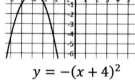

$$y = \tfrac{1}{3}x + 2 \qquad\qquad\qquad y = (x + 4)^2 \qquad\qquad y = -(x + 4)^2$$

The graph above shows the slope $\left(\tfrac{1}{3}\right)$ and the y-intercept (2)

Adding 4 **to the x-value** in the functions above moves the graph 4 to the **left**.

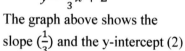 *Tip: Memorize some other basic graphs:*

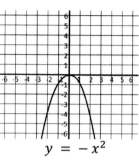

$$y = x^{-1} \qquad\qquad y = x^3 \qquad\qquad y = |x| \qquad\qquad y = (x + 3)(x - 1)$$

 Tip: Notice the intercepts on the X-axis: $x = -3$ and $x = 1$

286

Graphs - Quiz 1

Use the following information to answer questions 1 and 2.

Veronica makes and sells hand-crafted coffee mugs in 2 sizes. It takes her 2 hours to make a small mug and 3 hours to make a large mug.

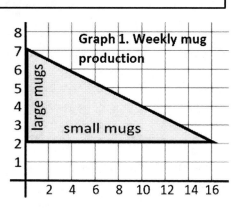

Graph 1. Weekly mug production

small mugs

mug. She makes a variety of sizes, but never more than 7 large mugs or 16 small mugs. (All possible combinations are plotted in the grey area of graph 1. Veronica makes a profit of 8 dollars per small mug and 12 dollars per large mug.

1) The weekly constraint represented by the horizontal line segment containing (8,2) means that each week Veronica makes a minimum of:

   A. 8 large mugs per week
   B. 8 small mugs per week
   C. 2 small mugs per week
   D. 2 large mugs per week

2) What is the maximum profit Veronica can earn from the mugs she makes in one week?
   A. 32.00
   B. $84.00
   C. $128.00
   D. $152.00

3) Which of the following graphs can be of the equation $y = x^2 + 2x + 4$?

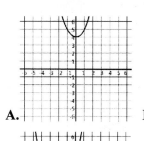
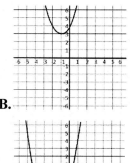

A.   B.

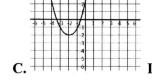
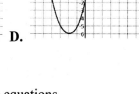

C.   D.

4) The graph of the equations $y = x - 1$ and $y = (x - 1)^2$ are shown on the standard (x,y) coordinate plane below. Which real values, if any, satisfy the inequality $(x - 1)^2 < (x - 1)$?

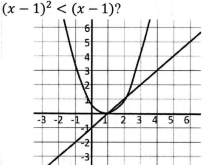

   A. No real values
   B. $1 < x < 2$
   C. $0 < x < 1$
   D. $0 < x < 2$

287   Copyright 2017 Winni van Gessel

Graphs - Quiz 1 (Answers)

1) The horizontal line segment represents the y-value of a coordinate.
   The minimum y-value at every possible x value in the triangle is 2, so each week Veronica must make a minimum of 2 large mugs. **(Answer D)**

2) The maximum number of large mugs is 7, in which case she makes no small mugs.
   $7 * 12 = \$84.00$.
   The maximum number of small mugs is 16, which is a profit of $16 * 8 = \$128.00$.
   However, every week she makes a minimum of 2 large mugs (=$24.00).
   $128 + 24 = \$152.00$ **(Answer D)**

3) The easiest way to solve this problem is to plug in simple x values such as 0 and 1
   An x value of 0 helps you to find the y-intercept of the given equation and match it to the graphs.
   Find the y-intercept by plugging in 0 for x.
   $0^2 + (2 * 0) + 4 = 4$
   Only two graphs have a y-intercept of 4. (A and B)
   Next, plug in an x-value of 1.
   $1^2 + (2 * 1) + 4 = 7$
   This eliminates graph A. **(Answer B)**

4) Look at the intercepts of the graph to find the values for which $y = x - 1$ is greater than $y = (x - 1)^2$.
   $y = (x - 1)^2$ is **the same as** $y = (x - 1)$ at $x = 1$ and $x = 2$,
   $y = x - 1$ is **smaller than** $y = (x - 1)^2$ between 1 and 2. **(Answer B)**

   Alternatively, use algebra to solve the equation:

   $(x - 1)^2 < (x - 1)$
   $x^2 - 2x + 1 < x - 1$
   $x^2 - 3x + 2 < 0$
   $(x - 1)(x - 2) < 0$
   This last statement is valid for $x < 1$ and $x < 2$.
   To make sense of this, you can simply say $x < 2$.

LOGARITHMS

Logarithms

When dealing with logarithm questions, it is important to **count the exponents.**

$5*5*5*5 = 5^4 = 625$

Therefore: $\log_5(625) = 4$

5 is called the **base**. This is the number that is multiplied 4 times.
4 is called the **exponent**. This is the part that a logarithm counts.
The **log** indicates those exponents by only mentioning the base and the product: $\log_5(625)$, translates as "This is the exponent of 5 to get 625."

Example: $\log_4(16) = \log_4(4^2) = 2$
Example: $\log_{10}(1,000) = \log_{10}(10^3) = 3$
Example: $\log_3(81) = \log_3(3^4) = 4$

A logarithm is an expression that counts the **exponents** of a number.
It is important to review your rules about exponents. (See box on right)
Tip: Most logarithm problems in the ACT are variants of the following exponent rules:

Multiplication

$\log_a(xy) = \log_a x + \log_a y$

The log of a multiplication is the sum of the logs of each factor.
Example: $\log_2(32) = \log_2(4) + \log_2(8)$
Example: $\log_3(9x) = \log_3(9) + \log_3(x)$

Division

$\log_a\left(\dfrac{x}{y}\right) = \log_a x - \log_a y$

The log of a division is the difference of the logs of each factor.
Example: $\log_2\left(\dfrac{32}{8}\right) =$
$\qquad \log_2(32) - \log_2(8) = 5 - 3 = 2$
Example: $\log_2\left(\dfrac{1}{16}\right) =$
$\qquad \log_2(1) - \log_2(16) = 0 - 4 = -4$

 Tip: If no base is mentioned, such as in log(9x+9), then it is assumed that we talk about base 10: $\log(9x + 9) = \log_{10}(9x + 9)$

Remember:

$$\log_a(a^x) = x$$

In logarithms, you count the exponents of base *a*.
The exponent of a is x.

Therefore the answer is x

$(\log_2(8) = \log_2(2^3) = 3)$

A^0	$= 1$
A^1	$= A$
$\sqrt{\dfrac{a}{b}}$	$= \dfrac{\sqrt{a}}{\sqrt{b}}$
$\sqrt{ab}$	$= \sqrt{a}\sqrt{b}$
$A^m A^n$	$= A^{m+n}$
$(A^m)^n$	$= A^{mn}$
$\dfrac{A^m}{A^n}$	$= A^{m-n}$
A^{-m}	$= \dfrac{1}{A^m}$
$A^{\frac{m}{n}}$	$= \sqrt[n]{A^m}$

Shortcut 1

$$\log_a(a^x) = x * \log_a(a) = x$$

Example: $\log_3(3^4) = 4 * \log_3(3) = 4$
Example: $\log_2(4^3) = 3 * \log_2(4) = 3 * 2 = 6$

Shortcut 2

if $\qquad \log_x(a) = y$
then $\quad x^y = a$

Example: $\log_4(64) = 3$ then $4^3 = 64$

Logarithms - Quiz 1

1) If $\log_3(27) = x$, then x is
   A. 3
   B. 9
   C. 24
   D. 30
   E. $\frac{1}{9}$

2) If $\log_6(x) = 3$, then x is
   A. $\frac{6}{3}$
   B. $6 * 3$
   C. $6x^3$
   D. 36
   E. 6^3

3) If $\log_5 x = \frac{2}{3}$, then x is
   A. $\frac{10}{3}$
   B. 25
   C. $\sqrt[3]{25}$
   D. $\sqrt[2]{25}$
   E. 125

4) If $\log_x 36 = 2$, then x is
   A. $\frac{1}{18}$
   B. 4
   C. 6
   D. 18
   E. 38

5) $\log_2 10 + \log_2 5 = ?$
   A. 5
   B. 15
   C. $\log_2 2$
   D. $\log_2 15$
   E. $\log_2 50$

6) $\log_6 18 - \log_6 9 = ?$
   A. $\log_6(\frac{9}{18})$
   B. $6^{\frac{9}{18}}$
   C. $\log_6(\frac{18}{9})$
   D. $6^{\frac{18}{9}}$
   E. $\log_6(18 - 9)$

7) If $\log_4(2^6) = x$, then x is
   A. 2
   B. 3
   C. 4
   D. 5
   E. 6

8) What is equivalent to $\log_5(x^{\frac{1}{5}})$?
   A. $\frac{1}{5}\log_5(x)$
   B. $\sqrt[5]{\log_5(x)}$
   C. $5\log_x(\frac{x}{5})$
   D. $log(x)$
   E. -1

9) If $\log_{16}(4) = x$, then x is
   A. $\sqrt{2}$
   B. ½
   C. 2
   D. 2^2
   E. -2

10) If $\log_8(1) = x$, then x is
   A. -8
   B. 0
   C. $\frac{1}{8}$
   D. 1
   E. 8

11) If $\log_9(0.11\bar{1}) = x$, then x is
   A. -1
   B. $\frac{1}{81}$
   C. $\frac{1}{9}$
   D. 1
   E. 9

12) If $log_x(4^3) = 3$, then x is
   A. 1
   B. 3
   C. 12
   D. ¾
   E. 4

291

Logarithms - Quiz 1 (Answers)

1) Logarithms are about counting the <u>exponents</u> <u>of the base</u>. What <u>exponent</u> do you need to put on the base (in this case 3) to get the log (in this case 27)?
$3^x = 27$ ➜ $3^3 = 27$ ➜ $x = 3$.   **(Answer B)**

2) The answer (3) is the exponent of the base. The exponent of the base (in this case 6) is 3. This equation can be rewritten as $6^3 = x$ or $\log_6(6^3) = 3$.   **(Answer E)**

3) The answer (3) is the exponent of the base. The exponent of the base (in this case 5) is $\frac{2}{3}$. This equation can be rewritten as $5^{2/3} = x$. Now solve for x.
(You have to know your exponent rules.)
$5^{2/3} = x$. ➜ $X = \sqrt[3]{5^2}$ ➜ $X = \sqrt[3]{25}$.

   (Answer C)

4) Logarithms are about counting the <u>exponents</u> <u>of the base</u>. This question asks, "What number squared makes 36?" $x^2 = 36$, ➜ x is 6 or −6.   **(Answer C)**

5) Because we work with the exponents of a similar base, log rules follow the exponents rule $A^m * A^n = A^{m+n}$
When log equations with a similar base are **added** together, they can be combined as one log with the two values **multiplied** by each other. The correct answer is $\log_2 50$.

   (Answer E)

6) Because we work with the exponents of a base, log rules follow the exponents rule $\frac{A^m}{A^n} = A^{m-n}$ In much the same way, if two log equations with similar bases are **subtracted** from one another, it is equivalent to one log equation where the two values are **divided**. The correct answer then is $\log_6 \frac{18}{9}$, or $\log_6 2$.

   (Answer C)

7) $2^6 = (2^2)^3 = 4^3$
Rewritten as a base 4, the equation is now $\log_4(4^3) = x$. ➜ $x = 3$ **(Answer B)**

8) (see shortcut 1 on handout)
Whenever something inside a log function is raised to a power, it is the same as multiplying the whole function by whatever that value is. In this case, the correct answer is $\frac{1}{5}\log_5(x)$.   **(Answer A)**

9) If $\log_{16}(4) = x$, x is the exponent of the base (in this case 16) to get 4. By using an exponent, we need to get a smaller number. (Therefore, x must be smaller than 1)
Remember the exponent rule $A^{\frac{m}{n}} = \sqrt[n]{A^m}$?
A solid rule to remember is $A^{\frac{1}{2}} = \sqrt{A}$. $16^x = 4$
➜($\sqrt{16} = 4$)➜$16^{\frac{1}{2}} = 4$ ➜ $x = \frac{1}{2}$
   (Answer B)

10) Logarithms are about counting the <u>exponents</u> <u>of the base</u>. What <u>exponent</u> do you need to put on the base (in this case 8) to get the log (in this case 1)?
$8^x = 1$ ➜ $8^0 = 1$ ➜ $x = 0$.   **(Answer B)**

11) For equations with a log smaller than 1, you need to use negative exponents. Remember $A^{-m} = \frac{1}{A^m}$?
What <u>exponent</u> do you need to put on the base (in this case 9) to get the log (in this case 0.1111 or $\frac{1}{9}$)? $9^{-1} = \frac{1}{9}$ ➜ x= −1
   (Answer A)

12) Logarithms are about counting the <u>exponents</u> <u>of the base</u>. This question asks, "What number cubed makes 4^3?" $x^3 = 4^3$, ➜ x is 4.   **(Answer E)**

Logarithms - Quiz 2 (Challenge)

1) If $\log_b d = r$ and $\log_b z = t$, then
$\log_b(dz)^2 = ?$
A. $r + t$
B. $2rt$
C. $4rt$
D. $(r + t)^2$
E. $2(r + t)$

2) Which of the following is a value of x that satisfies $\log_x 64 = 3$?
A. 2
B. 4
C. 8
D. 16
E. 32

3) The value of $\log_{13}(13^{\frac{27}{12}})$ is between which of the following pairs of consecutive integers?
A. 0 and 1
B. 1 and 2
C. 2 and 3
D. 4 and 5
E. 6 and 7

4) Whenever q is an integer greater than 1,
$\log_q \frac{q^3}{q^9} = ?$
A. -6
B. -3
C. $-\frac{1}{3}$
D. $\frac{1}{3}$
E. 9

5) For all $x > 3$,
$\log(2x - 6) + \log x = ?$
A. $\log(-6)$
B. $\log(3x - 6)$
C. $\log(2x^2 - 6x)$
D. $\log(\frac{2x-6}{x})$
E. $\log(\frac{x}{2x-6})$

6) $\log_2 24 - \log_2 3 =$
A. 1
B. 2
C. 3
D. $\log_2 21$
E. 27

7) For all $x > 0$, which of the following expressions is equal to $\log(3x)^{\frac{1}{3}}$?
A. $\log x$
B. $\log 3 + \frac{1}{3}\log x$
C. $\log 1 + \log\frac{x}{3}$
D. $\frac{1}{3}\log 3 + \frac{1}{3}\log x$
E. $\frac{1}{3}(\log 3)(\log x)$

8) Which of the following is a value of x that satisfies $\log_4(2) + \log_4(x) = -3$
A. $\frac{1}{6}$
B. 6
C. $\frac{1}{64}$
D. -6
E. $\frac{1}{128}$

9) Express $15\log_9 r + 3\log_9 p - 6\log_9 z$ as a single logarithm.
A. $12\log_9 rpz$
B. $\frac{45\log_9 rp}{6\log_9 z}$
C. $\log_9(\frac{r^{15}p^3}{z^6})$
D. $\log_9(r^{15} + p^3 - z^6)$
E. $\log_9((\frac{rp}{z})^{\frac{18}{6}})$

1)E 2)B 3)C 4)A 5)C 6)C 7)D 8)E 9)C

Logarithms - Quiz 2 (Answers)

1) Since both d and z are squared, when they are broken up into two log functions, each of the log functions will be multiplied by two.
$\log_b(dz)^2 = 2 * \log_b(dz)$
$2 * \log_b(dz) = 2 * \log_b(d) + 2 * \log_b(z)$
This simplifies to 2(r) + 2(t), or 2(r + t),
(Answer E)

2) This log function can be rewritten as x³=64, or x = 4. **(Answer B)**

3) (See shortcut 1 on the handout.) We can start by pulling the $\frac{27}{12}$ to the front of the equation since it is a power inside of a log, leaving us with $\log_{13} 13$, which equals 1. The value is therefore $\frac{27}{12}$, which falls between $\left(\frac{24}{12}\right)$ and $\left(\frac{36}{12}\right)$ or in between the integers 2 and 3.
(Answer C)

4) Rewrite $\log_q(\frac{q^3}{q^9})$ as
$\log_q(q^3) - \log_q(q^9)$.
$\log_q(q^3) = 3$ and $\log_q(q^9) = 9$
$3 - 9 = -6$ **(Answer A)**

Alternatively, rewrite $(\frac{q^3}{q^9})$ as q^{-6}
$\log_q(q^{-6}) = -6$

5) $\log_a(xy) = \log_a x + \log_a y$

Since we are adding two logs with the same base, we can multiply the values and make one log function. We get $\log(x(2x - 6))$ or $\log(2x^2 - 6x)$. **(Answer B)**

6) Logarithms follow the rules of exponents. Remember $\frac{A^5}{A^3} = A^{5-3}$ In much the same way, if two log equations are **subtracted** from one another and the bases are the same, it is equivalent to one log equation where the two values are **divided**.
$\log_2 24 - \log_2 3 = \log_2 \frac{24}{3} = \log_2 8 = 3$
(Answer C)

7) **Shortcut**: $\mathbf{\log_a(a^x) = x * \log_a(a) = x}$
$\log((3x)^{\frac{1}{3}}) = \frac{1}{3}\log(3x)$
Rewrite $log(3x)$ as $log(3) + log(x)$
We can now separate the equation into two logarithms, where each is multiplied by $\frac{1}{3}$, We are left with

$\frac{1}{3}\log(3x) = \frac{1}{3}\log 3 + \frac{1}{3}\log x.$ **(Answer D)**

8) Negative logarithms ask the question, "How many times do I need to **divide** a number to get the answer?" (Remember $A^{-m} = \frac{1}{A^m}$.)
Therefore 4^{-5} means $1 \div 4 \div 4 \div 4 \div 4 \div 4$
   a) Combine the logs with the same base:
      $\log_4(2X) = -3$
   b) $4^{-3} = 2X \rightarrow \frac{1}{4^3} = 2X \rightarrow X = \frac{1}{2*4^3}$
   c) $X = \frac{1}{128}$ **(Answer E)**

Alternatively, you can reason that $2x = \frac{1}{4^3} \rightarrow$
$2x = \frac{1}{64} \rightarrow x = \frac{1}{64} * \frac{1}{2} = \frac{1}{128}$

9) Since all of the bases are the same, we know we can combine the terms. The first step is to change all of the multiplications into powers within the function, so we get
$\log_9 r^{15} + \log_9 p^3 - \log_9 z^6$.
Now we combine them into one function, where those added together are multiplied and those subtracted are divided. This leaves us with an answer of $\log_9(\frac{r^{15}p^3}{z^6})$. **(Answer C)**

THE BEAST:
All the math you need to memorize on one page!

Study these terms and formulas one group at a time.
They are the building blocks of the Math ACT.

For interactive formulas visit **www.analyzeyouract.com**
© Winni van Gessel

TERMINOLOGY

Absolute value	The distance of a number from zero; the positive value of a number.
Acute angle	A positive angle measuring less than 90°.
Acute triangle	A triangle in which all angles measure less than 90°. (An *obtuse* triangle has one angle larger than 90°. A right triangle has exactly on angle of 90°.)
Adjacent angles	Two angles that share both a side and a vertex.
Axis of symmetry	A line that passes through a figure in such a way that the part of the figure on one side of the line is a mirror reflection of the part on the other side of the line.
Bisect	To divide into two similar parts.
Central angle	An angle that has its vertex at the center of a circle.
Coefficient	A constant that multiplies a variable. In $ax^2 + bx + c$, "x" is a *variable*, and "a" and "b" are coefficients.
Complementary angles	Two angles whose sum is 90°.
Composite number	A whole number that can be divided evenly by numbers other than 1 and itself. (All whole numbers that are not prime.)
Congruent figures	Figures that have the same size and same shape. $\cong$
Dependent events	Two events in which the outcome of the second is influenced by the outcome of the first, such as pulling two cards from a deck.
Difference	The result of subtracting two numbers.
Dividend	In $8:4 = 2$, **8** is the dividend. In a fraction $\frac{8}{4} = 2$, 8 this is called the numerator.
Divisor	In $12:3 = 4$, **3** is the divisor. In a fraction $\frac{12}{3} = 4$, this is called the denominator.
Greatest common factor	The GFC is the largest number that divides two or more numbers evenly. The common factors of 12 and 18 are 1, 2, 3 and 6, so 6 is the GFC.
Inscribed angle	An angle placed inside a circle with its vertex on the circle.
Integers	The set of numbers containing 0, the natural numbers, and their negatives: (… -2, -1, 0, 1, 2, 3, ...)
Inverse	Inverse means opposite. In *additions*, -3 is the inverse of 3. In *multiplications*, 1/3 is the inverse of 3.
Irrational number	A number that cannot be expressed as the ratio of two integers, such as π or $\sqrt{2}$.
Isosceles triangle	A triangle with at least two equal sides.
Least common denominator	The smallest multiple of the denominators of two or more fractions.
Least common multiple	The smallest nonzero number that is a multiple of two or more numbers. Common multiples of 5 and 8 are 20, 40, 60, etc., so 20 is the LCM.
Mean	Same as the average. The sum of all entries, divided by the number of entries.
Median	The middle number in a data set when the data is put in order.
Mixed number	A number written as a whole number and a fraction.
Mode	A type of average; the number(s) that occurs most often in a set of data.
Natural numbers	The counting numbers. (1, 2, 3, etc.)
Prime number	A number whose only factors are 1 and itself. (2, 3, 5, 7, 11, etc.) (Not 1.)
Quotient	The answer to a division problem.
Range	The difference between the highest and lowest number in a set of data.
Rational number	A number that can be expressed as the ratio of two integers.
Real numbers	The combined set of rational numbers and irrational numbers.
Reciprocal number	1 divided by that number. The reciprocal of 12 is 1/12.
Similar figures	Figures that have the same shape, but not necessarily the same size. ~
Supplementary angles	Two angles whose sum is 180°.
Vertex	The point on an angle where the two sides intersect.
Whole numbers	The set of numbers that includes zero and the natural numbers. (0, 1, 2, etc.)

THE BEAST: All the math formulas that matter on the ACT

Exponents

$A^0 = 1$ $\qquad A^1 = A$

$A^{\frac{1}{2}} = \sqrt{A}$

$\sqrt{\dfrac{a}{b}} = \dfrac{\sqrt{a}}{\sqrt{b}}$

$\sqrt{ab} = \sqrt{a}\sqrt{b}$

$A^m A^n = A^{m+n}$

$(A^m)^n = A^{mn}$

$\dfrac{A^m}{A^n} = A^{m-n}$

$A^{-m} = \dfrac{1}{A^m}$

Quadratic Equations

$(a+b)^2 = a^2 + 2ab + b^2$

$(a-b)^2 = a^2 - 2ab + b^2$

$(a+b)(a-b) = a^2 - b^2$

Quadratic Formula

$Ax^2 + bx + c = 0$

➔ $x = \dfrac{-b \pm \sqrt{b^2 - 4ac}}{2a}$

Distance-Time Formula

$Speed\ (v) = \dfrac{Distance\ (d)}{Time\ (t)}$ $\qquad t = \dfrac{d}{v}$

Linear Equations

$y = mx + b$

The y intercept is b (x=0)

The slope is $m = \dfrac{rise}{run} = \dfrac{y_2 - y_1}{x_2 - x_1}$

A perpendicular line has a slope of $-\dfrac{1}{m}$

Distance Formula

$d = \sqrt{(x_2 - x_1)^2 + (y_2 - y_1)^2}$

Midpoint Formula =

$\left(\dfrac{x_1 + x_2}{2}, \dfrac{y_1 + y_2}{2}\right)$

Perfect Squares

$11^2 = \mathbf{121}$; $12^2 = \mathbf{144}$; $13^2 = \mathbf{169}$;

$14^2 = \mathbf{196}$; $15^2 = \mathbf{225}$; $16^2 = \mathbf{256}$;

Percent

$\dfrac{\%}{100} = \dfrac{is}{of} = \dfrac{part}{whole}$

Triangles

Triangle Area

$\dfrac{1}{2} * b * h$

Equilateral Triangle Area

$\dfrac{1}{2}S * \dfrac{1}{2}S * \sqrt{3}$

Pythagorean Theorem

$a^2 + b^2 = c^2$

3, 4, 5
5, 12, 13
6, 8, 10
7, 24, 25
8, 15, 17

Probability

desired outcomes

possible outcomes

Imaginary Numbers

When squared, i gives a negative result

$i * i = -1$ $\quad i = \sqrt{-1}$ $\quad \sqrt{(-x)} = i\sqrt{x}$

$i^1 = i; i^2 = -1; i^3 = -i; i^4 = 1; i^5 = i^1$

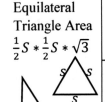

$180 - 2\alpha$

$\dfrac{180 - \beta}{2}$

Isosceles Triangle

Logarithms

$\log_a a^x = x$

$\log_a(xy) = \log_a x + \log_a y$

$\log_a\left(\dfrac{x}{y}\right) = \log_a x - \log_a y$

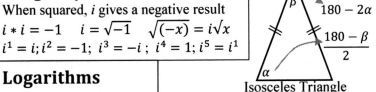

Area = $L * H$ $\qquad$ Area = $\dfrac{(B_1 + B_2)}{2} * H$

$x\sqrt{3}$ $\quad$ $2x$ $\quad$ 30° $\quad$ 60° $\quad$ x

Circles

Area = πr^2

Circumference = $2\pi r$

Formula: $x^2 + y^2 = r^2$

For $(x-a)^2 + (y-b)^2 = r^2$

➔ Midpoint = (a, b)

➔ Radius = r

Cylinders

Area: $2(\pi r^2) + h * 2\pi r$

Volume: $\pi r^2 * h$

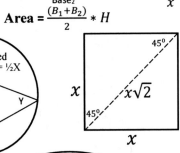

Y = inscribed angle = ½X

X = central angle = arc

x $\quad x\sqrt{2}$ $\quad$ 45° $\quad$ 45°

Sum of angles in a regular polygon with n sides: **180(n-2)**

# of diagonals = $\dfrac{1}{2} * n(n-3)$

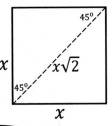

Ellipse $\quad \dfrac{x^2}{a^2} + \dfrac{y^2}{b^2} = 1$

Major axis = 2a; minor axis = 2b

Trig: SOHCAHTOA

$Sin\ \theta = \dfrac{Opp}{Hyp}$ $\quad Csc\ \theta = \dfrac{1}{Sin}$

$Cos\ \theta = \dfrac{Adj}{Hyp}$ $\quad Sec\ \theta = \dfrac{1}{Cos}$

$Tan\ \theta = \dfrac{Opp}{Adj}$ $\quad Cot\ \theta = \dfrac{1}{Tan}$

$tan\ \theta = \dfrac{sin\ \theta}{cos\ \theta}$

Averages

Average = Total/number

Weighted Average = dd the values for each occurrence; divide by total occurrences.

Total

Number | Average

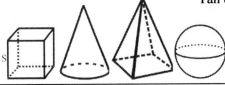

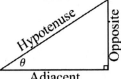

Hypotenuse $\quad$ Opposite $\quad$ Adjacent $\quad \theta$

$\cong$ Congruent (shape and size)

~ Similar (shape)

Volume: Cube: $V = s^3$ Cone: $V = 1/3\ \pi r^2 h$

Pyramid: $V = 1/3\ lwh$ $\quad$ Sphere: $V = 4/3\ \pi r^3$

THE BEAST: All the math formulas that matter on the ACT

Exponents

$A^0 =$ $A^1 =$

$A^{\frac{1}{2}} =$

$\sqrt{\dfrac{a}{b}} =$

$\sqrt{ab} =$

$A^m A^n =$

$(A^m)^n =$

$\dfrac{A^m}{A^n} =$

$A^{-m} =$

Quadratic Equations

$(a + b)^2 =$

$(a - b)^2 =$

$(a + b)(a - b) =$

Quadratic Formula

$Ax^2 + bx + c = 0$

➔ $x =$

Distance Time Formula

$Speed\ (v) = -$ $t = -$

Linear Equations

$y = mx + b$

The y intercept is _____

The slope is _____

A perpendicular line has a slope of _____

Distance Formula

$d =$

Midpoint Formula =

Perfect Squares

Commonly used on the ACT:

$11^2 =$ $12^2 =$ $13^2 =$

$14^2 =$ $15^2 =$ $16^2 =$

Percent

___ = ___ = ___

Triangles

Triangle Area

Equilateral Triangle Area _____

Pythagorean Theorem

$a^2 + b^2 = c^2$

3, ___, ___

5, ___, ___

6, ___, ___

7, ___, ___

8, ___, ___

Imaginary Numbers

When squared, i gives a negative result

$i * i =$ $i = \sqrt{\ }$ $\sqrt{(-x)} =$

$i^1 =$; $i^2 =$; $i^3 =$; $i^4 =$; $i^5 =$

Logarithms

$\log_a a^x =$

$\log_a(xy) =$

$\log_a\left(\dfrac{x}{y}\right) =$

Probability

_____

Isosceles Triangle

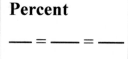

Circles

Area =

Circumference =

Formula:

For $(x-a)^2 + (y-b)^2 = r^2$

➔Midpoint =

➔Radius =

Cylinders

Area:

Volume:

Area =

Area =

Base₁

W

H

H

Base₂

L

30°

60°

x

Sum of angles in a regular polygon with n sides:

# of diagonals =

x 45°

45°

x

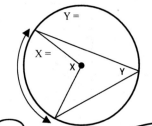

$Y =$

$X =$

X

Y

Ellipse

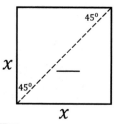

___ + ___ =

Major axis =   ; minor axis =

Trig: SOHCAHTOA

$\sin \theta = ---$ $\csc \theta = ---$

$\cos \theta = ---$ $\sec \theta = ---$

$\tan \theta = ---$ $\cot \theta = ---$

$\tan \theta = ---$

Averages

Average =

Weighted Average =

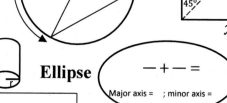

$\cong$

$\sim$

Volume: Cube: V =   Cone: V =

Pyramid: V =   Sphere: V =

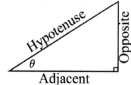

Hypotenuse

Opposite

θ

Adjacent

MATH TEST 1

60 minutes - 60 questions

Math Test 1

1. The second term of an arithmetic sequence is 14, and the third term is 10. What is the first term?
   A. 4
   B. 6
   C. 12
   D. 14
   E. 18

2. The cost of a pool membership is a onetime fee of $220, plus a monthly fee of $20. Cornelius wrote a $360 check to pay his pool membership for a certain number of months, including the onetime fee. How many months did he pay for?
   A. 6
   B. 7
   C. 8
   D. 14
   E. 18

3. Let $f(x) = \dfrac{x^2 - 25}{x - 5}$.
   What is the value of $f(15)$?
   A. 200
   B. 120
   C. 20
   D. 2
   E. −1

4. If $x = 7, y = 3, z = -6$, what does $(x - y + z)(y - x)$ equal?
   A. −114
   B. −64
   C. −12
   D. 8
   E. 32

5. The area of a square cement foundation of a garage is 36 square yards. What is the length, in yards, of one side of the foundation?
   A. 2
   B. 4
   C. 6
   D. 9
   E. 12

6. In $\triangle JKL$, $\angle J$ and $\angle L$ are congruent, and the measure of $\angle K$ is 32°. What is the measure of $\angle L$?
   A. 37°
   B. 58°
   C. 74°
   D. 111°
   E. 148°

7. Sarah will pick 1 marble at random out of a bag containing 34 marbles that are in the colors and quantities shown below.

Color	Red	Black	White	Green	Blue	Gray
Quantity	4	7	5	3	6	9

What is the probability that Sarah will pick a red or blue marble?
   A. $\dfrac{2}{17}$
   B. $\dfrac{11}{34}$
   C. $\dfrac{2}{3}$
   D. $\dfrac{3}{17}$
   E. $\dfrac{5}{17}$

GO ON TO THE NEXT PAGE

8. In the figure below, $\overline{BC}$ and $\overline{AD}$ intersect at E. What is the measurement of ∠C?

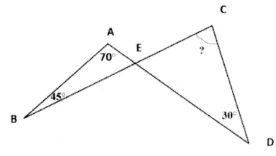

A. 55°
B. 70°
C. 85°
D. 110°
E. 125°

9. What value of p will make the equation $\frac{8+p}{18+p} = \frac{2}{3}$ true?

A. −16
B. 4
C. 6
D. 9
E. 12

10. If $3x + 24 = -9$, then $4x + 12 = $?
A. −40
B. −32
C. −12
D. 16
E. 56

11. The expression $\dfrac{7 + \frac{5}{6}}{4 - \frac{1}{12}}$ is equal to:

A. $\frac{1}{2}$

B. $\frac{3}{4}$

C. 2

D. 3

E. $\frac{2209}{72}$

12. Barrel 1, Barrel 2, and Barrel 3 when full each hold the same amount of water. At the current time, Barrel 1 is $\frac{11}{12}$ full, Barrel 2 is $\frac{1}{6}$ full, and Barrel 3 is $\frac{7}{24}$ full. Water will be transferred between the barrels so that each of the 3 barrels contains the same amount of water. After the transfer, each of the 3 barrels will be what fraction full?

A. $\frac{5}{6}$

B. $\frac{5}{12}$

C. $\frac{7}{24}$

D. $\frac{11}{24}$

E. $\frac{13}{24}$

13. In the standard (x,y) coordinate plane, what is the midpoint of the line segment with endpoints $(2, -7)$ and $(-8, 5)$?
A. $(-3, -2)$
B. $(-4, -1)$
C. $(-6, -2)$
D. $(-3, -1)$
E. $(-4, -4)$

14. The decimal representation of 4.8×10^{-84} is:
A. a decimal point, followed by 83 zeros, then the digits 4 and 8.
B. a decimal point, followed by 84 zeros, then the digits 4 and 8.
C. a negative sign, followed by the digits 4 and 8, then 83 zeros, then a decimal point.
D. a negative sign, followed by a decimal point, then 84 zeros, then the digits 4 and 8.
E. a negative sign, followed by the digits 4 and 8, then 84 zeroes, then a decimal point.

GO ON TO THE NEXT PAGE

15. A square and a triangle have the same area. The width of the square is 22 inches and the base of the triangle is 6 inches. What is the height of the triangle?

A. 17.5 inches

B. 40.33 inches

C. 80.67 inches

D. 144.33 inches

E. 161.33 inches

16. Which of the following proportions, when solved for n, gives the correct answer to the following problem?

n = 48% of 73.

A. $\dfrac{48}{100} = \dfrac{73}{n}$

B. $\dfrac{48}{100} = \dfrac{n}{73}$

C. $\dfrac{48}{73} = \dfrac{n}{100}$

D. $\dfrac{n}{100} = \dfrac{73}{48}$

E. $\dfrac{73}{100} = \dfrac{48}{n}$

17. Which of the following graphs shows the solution set for the inequality $x + 5 \le 7$?

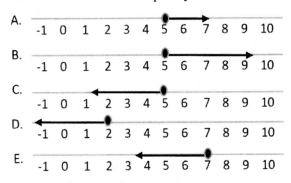

18. Whenever $6x + 6 = 3x - k$, which of the following expressions must be equal to x?

A. $\dfrac{-k-6}{3}$

B. $\dfrac{-k+6}{3}$

C. $\dfrac{-k+6}{9}$

D. $\dfrac{2}{k}$

E. -1

19. In the diagram below, lines y and z are cut by a transversal x. Lines y and z are NOT parallel. Which of the following statements must be true?

A. $\angle 1 \cong \angle 2$

B. $\angle 1 \cong \angle 3$

C. $\angle 1 \cong \angle 5$

D. $\angle 2 \cong \angle 8$

E. $\angle 3 \cong \angle 5$

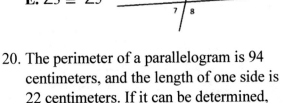

20. The perimeter of a parallelogram is 94 centimeters, and the length of one side is 22 centimeters. If it can be determined, what are the lengths, in centimeters, of the other 3 sides?

A. 22, 19, 19

B. 22, 22, 28

C. 22, 36, 36

D. 22, 25, 25

E. Cannot be determined from the given information.

21. For the function $g(x) = 5x^2 - 4x + 2$, what is the value of $g(-3)$?

A. -31

B. -15

C. -1

D. 59

E. 74

22. The sum of $(5x^3 - 2x^2 + x - 4)$ and which of the following polynomials results in the polynomial $(3x^3 + x^2 - 4x - 1)$?

A. $-2x^3 - 5x^2 + 7x - 5$

B. $-2x^3 + 3x^2 - 5x + 3$

C. $8x^3 - 3x^2 + 7x + 3$

D. $2x^3 - x^2 - 3x - 5$

E. $8x^3 - x - 3x - 5$

GO ON TO THE NEXT PAGE

23. In the figure below, $\triangle ABC$ has an area of 96 square inches, $\overline{BC}$ is 12 inches long, and $\angle B$ is a right angle. What is the length, in inches, of $\overline{AC}$?

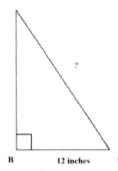

  A. 8 inches
  B. 14 inches
  C. 16 inches
  D. 20 inches
  E. 25 inches

24. As part of a physics lesson on motion, students observed a ball rolling at a constant rate along a straight line. As shown in the chart below, they recorded the distance (y feet) of the ball from a reference point at 1 second intervals from $t = 0$ seconds to $t = 5$ seconds.

t	0	1	2	3	4	5
y	17	26	35	44	53	62

  Which of the following equations represents this data?
  A. $y = t + 17$
  B. $y = 9t + 9$
  C. $y = 9t + 17$
  D. $y = 17t + 9$
  E. $y = 26t$

25. Which of the following sets of 3 numbers could be the side lengths, in inches, of a right triangle?
  A. 1, 1, 1
  B. 2, 3, 4
  C. 4, 5, 7
  D. 5, 9, 12
  E. 6, 8, 10

26. Jonathon's 8-hour drive to his cousins' house was 412 miles long. He averaged 55 miles per hour for the first 2 hours. Which of the following is closest to his average speed, in miles per hour, for the remainder of his drive?
  A. 38
  B. 43.5
  C. 47
  D. 50
  E. 51.5

27. What is the sum of the 2 solutions of the equation $x^2 + x - 30 = 0$?
  A. -30
  B. -12
  C. -5
  D. -1
  E. 6

28. To win the student council election, a candidate must receive over 60% of the votes cast. There were 1200 votes cast. Which of the following expressions is true about x, the number of votes that a candidate must have received to win the election?
  A. $x > 720$
  B. $x = 720$
  C. $x \geq 720$
  D. $x < 721$
  E. $x = 721$

29. The inequality $5(x + 3) < 6(x - 12)$ is equivalent to which of the following inequalities?
  A. $x > 87$
  B. $x > 72$
  C. $x < -87$
  D. $x < -57$
  E. $x > 30$

GO ON TO THE NEXT PAGE

30. For a certain plant, the recommended daytime temperature range in degrees Fahrenheit is $77° \leq F \leq 95°$. Given the formula $C = \frac{5}{9}(F-32)$, where C is the temperature in degrees Celsius and F is the temperature in degrees Fahrenheit, what is the corresponding daytime temperature range in degrees Celsius for the plant?
    A. $15° \leq C \leq 25°$
    B. $15° \leq C \leq 35°$
    C. $25° \leq C \leq 30°$
    D. $25° \leq C \leq 35°$
    E. $25° \leq C \leq 40°$

31. The diameter of a given circle is 32 yards. What is the circumference of the circle in feet?
    A. 16π
    B. 32π
    C. 64π
    D. 96π
    E. 256π

32. What fraction of $4\frac{2}{3}$ is $1\frac{10}{18}$?
    A. $\frac{2}{9}$
    B. $\frac{1}{3}$
    C. $\frac{4}{9}$
    D. $\frac{1}{2}$
    E. $\frac{2}{3}$

USE THE FOLLOWING INFORMATION TO ANSWER QUESTIONS 33-35.

In the figure below, point E lies on side $\overline{AB}$ of rectangle ABCD. Line segments $\overline{AC}$ and $\overline{EC}$ are also drawn. The given lengths are in centimeters. (Figure not drawn to scale)

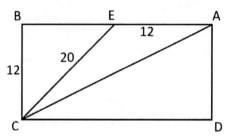

33. How many centimeters long is $\overline{AB}$?
    A. 16 centimeters
    B. 24 centimeters
    C. 28 centimeters
    D. 32 centimeters
    E. 41 centimeters

34. Which of the following is an expression for cos ∠BCA?
    A. $\frac{AB}{AC}$
    B. $\frac{AB}{BC}$
    C. $\frac{AC}{BC}$
    D. $\frac{BC}{AC}$
    E. $\frac{BC}{AB}$

35. Point E is reflected across the line (not shown) that connects the midpoints of $\overline{AD}$ and $\overline{BC}$. This reflection of E is labeled F. How many centimeters from $\overline{AB}$ is the intersection of $\overline{BF}$ and $\overline{CE}$?
    A. 4 centimeters
    B. 6 centimeters
    C. 8.5 centimeters
    D. 10 centimeters
    E. 12.5 centimeters

GO ON TO THE NEXT PAGE

36. A 17-foot ladder stands against a wall as shown below. The bottom of the ladder is 8 feet away from the wall. How can you calculate the angle, θ, that the ladder makes with the ground?

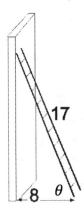

A. $\sin \theta^0 = \frac{8}{17}$

B. $\cos \theta^0 = \frac{17}{8}$

C. $\cot \theta^0 = \frac{8}{17}$

D. $\tan \theta^0 = \frac{15}{8}$

E. $\sin \theta^0 = \frac{17}{15}$

37. A test rocket for a school project is launched from ground level. Its height, h meters above the ground, t seconds after it is launched, is given by the equation $h = -12t^2 + 36t$.
During the rocket's ascent, at what value of t is the rocket 24 meters off the ground?

A. $\frac{1}{2}$

B. $\frac{2}{3}$

C. 1

D. 2

E. 3

38. In the figure below, the measures of four angles of pentagon ABCDE are given. What is the measure of $\angle C$?

A. 80°

B. 100°

C. 110°

D. 120°

E. 140°

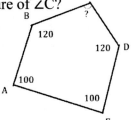

39. In the standard (x,y) coordinate plane, which of the following lines is perpendicular to the line $y = 3x + 5$?

A. $y = -3x + 5$

B. $y = \frac{1}{3}x + 5$

C. $y = 3x - \frac{1}{5}$

D. $y = -3x + \frac{1}{5}$

E. $-3y = x + 8$

40. If $\frac{2x-y}{x+y} = \frac{7}{8}$, then $\frac{x}{y} = ?$

A. $\frac{1}{3}$

B. $\frac{3}{5}$

C. $\frac{12}{17}$

D. $\frac{5}{3}$

E. $\frac{17}{12}$

41. Which of the following equations shows a correct use of the quadratic formula to solve $x^2 - 4x + 7 = 0$?

A. $x = \frac{4 \pm \sqrt{16-(4)(1)(7)}}{2(1)}$

B. $x = \frac{4 \pm \sqrt{16+(4)(1)(7)}}{2(1)}$

C. $x = \frac{-4 \pm \sqrt{16-(4)(1)(7)}}{2(1)}$

D. $x = \frac{-4 \pm \sqrt{16-(4)(1)(-7)}}{2(1)}$

E. $x = \frac{-4 \pm \sqrt{16+(4)(1)(7)}}{2(1)}$

GO ON TO THE NEXT PAGE

42. A club has only freshman and senior band members. To raise money for new club materials, the members sold cookies. Cookie sales averaged $45 for each freshman and $59 for each senior. If the ratio of freshman to seniors in the club was 4:3, cookie sales averaged how many dollars per club member?
   A. $47
   B. $48
   C. $50
   D. $51
   E. $53

43. What is the largest 2-digit integer that is divisible by 6 and a multiple of 7?
   A. 42
   B. 63
   C. 84
   D. 98
   E. 126

44. The difference (larger minus smaller) between 2 numbers is 19. If n represents the larger number, which expression below represents the average of the 2 numbers?
   A. 9.5
   B. n + 9.5
   C. n – 19
   D. n + 19
   E. n – 9.5

45. Circles A, B, and C have diameters of x inches, $3x$ inches, and $9x$ inches, respectively. What is the ratio of the radius of circle B to the diameter of circle A?
   A. 1:1
   B. 2:3
   C. 1:3
   D. 3:2
   E. 2:145

46. If n is a positive integer, which of the following expressions must be an odd integer?
   A. n^3
   B. 3^n
   C. $3n$
   D. $\frac{n}{3}$
   E. 3+n

47. A regular pyramid with a square base is shown in the figure below. The slant height is $2\sqrt{3}$ and the length of the base edge is 4 units. What is the total length, in units, of all 8 edges of the pyramid?

   A. $8\sqrt{7}$
   B. $8\sqrt{7} + 16$
   C. 16
   D. 28
   E. 32

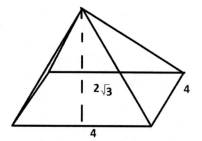

48. When using the quadratic formula, Martha found that an equation had solutions
   $x = 4 \pm \sqrt{-16a^2}$, where a is a positive real number. Which of the following expressions gives Martha's solutions as complex numbers?
   A. $x = 4 \pm 2ai$
   B. $x = 4 \pm 4ai$
   C. $x = 4 \pm 8ai$
   D. $x = 4 \pm 16ai$
   E. $x = 4 \pm 64ai$

GO ON TO THE NEXT PAGE

49. If k is a positive number such that $\log_k \frac{1}{256} = -4$, then k = ?

   A. 4
   B. 8
   C. 64
   D. $\frac{1}{4}$
   E. $\frac{1}{8}$

50. Charlie found $16.50 in pennies, nickels, dimes, and quarters while walking home from the movies one week. When he deposited this money in his piggy bank, he noticed that he had twice as many nickels as pennies, 2 fewer dimes than nickels, and 2 more quarters than nickels. How many quarters did Charlie find that week?

   A. 6
   B. 9
   C. 18
   D. 31
   E. 42

51. A line segment has endpoints (a, b) and (c, d) in the standard (x, y) coordinate plane, where a, b, c, and d are distinct positive integers. The segment is reflected across the y axis. After this reflection, what are the coordinates of the endpoints of the image?

   A. $(-a, b)$ and $(-c, d)$
   B. $(a, -b)$ and $(c, -d)$
   C. $(-a, -b)$ and $(-c, -d)$
   D. (a, b) and (c, d)
   E. $(0, b)$ and $(0, d)$

52. The perimeter of a rectangle is P units and the length is L units. The width of the rectangle is x units shorter than the length. Which of the following equations expresses x in terms of P and L?

   A. $x = -\frac{P}{2} + L$
   B. $x = -\frac{P}{2} + 2L$
   C. $x = -\frac{P}{2} + 4L$
   D. $x = -P + 2L$
   E. $x = -2P + 4L$

53. In ΔXYZ, the measure of $\angle X$ is 36°, the measure of $\angle Y$ is 82°, and the length of $\overline{YZ}$ is 14 centimeters. Which of the following is an expression for the length, in cm, of $\overline{XZ}$?
   (Note: The law of sines states that for any triangle, the ratios of the lengths of the sides to the sines of the angles opposite those sides are equal.)

   A. $\frac{\sin 36°}{14 \sin 82°}$
   B. $\frac{\sin 82°}{14 \sin 36°}$
   C. $\frac{14 \sin 36°}{\sin 82°}$
   D. $\frac{14 \sin 82°}{\sin 36°}$
   E. $\frac{(\sin 36°)(\sin 82°)}{14}$

54. Which of the following is an irrational number that is a solution to the equation $|x^2 - 6| - 3 = 0$?

   A. 3
   B. $\sqrt{3}$
   C. $2\sqrt{2}$
   D. $2\sqrt{3}$
   E. $3\sqrt{2}$

GO ON TO THE NEXT PAGE

55. William has 35 collectible bottle caps. He paid $23.25 for each bottle cap 5 years ago. The bottle caps are currently valued at $41.90 each. How much *more* must the average value per bottle cap rise for the combined value of these 35 bottle caps to be exactly $850 more than William paid for them?

    A. $3.78
    B. $4.31
    C. $5.65
    D. $6.12
    E. $6.83

56. Whenever w is an integer greater than 1, $\log_w \frac{w^3}{w^9} = ?$

    A. -6
    B. -3
    C. $-1/3$
    D. $1/3$
    E. 3

57. If $f(x) = 4x + 7$, then $f(f(x)) = ?$

    A. $16x^2 + 14x + 49$
    B. $16x + 14$
    C. $4x + 35$
    D. $8x + 11$
    E. $16x + 35$

58. Which of the following is equivalent to $|x - 4| < Z$?

    A. $x - 4 < Z$ and $4 - x < Z$
    B. $x - 4 < Z$ and $4 - x > Z$
    C. $x - 4 > Z$ and $4 - x < Z$
    D. $x + 4 < Z$ and $4 - x < Z$
    E. $x + 4 < Z$ and $4 - x > Z$

59. Water is considered contaminated when the level of arsenic in the water reaches 6 parts of arsenic per 1 million parts of water. What is this level of arsenic contamination written in scientific notation?

    A. 6.0×10^{-9}
    B. 6.0×10^{-6}
    C. 6.0×10^{-3}
    D. 6.0×10^{6}
    E. 6.0×10^{9}

60. In a regular nonagon, all 9 interior angles are congruent. What is the measure of each interior angle of a regular nonagon?

    A. 90°
    B. 120°
    C. 140°
    D. 160°
    E. 225°

GO ON TO THE NEXT PAGE

END OF THIS TEST
STOP! DO NOT TURN THE
PAGE UNTIL TOLD TO DO SO.

Math Test 1 – Answer Key

1. **E**	21. **D**	41. **A**
2. **B**	22. **B**	42. **D**
3. **C**	23. **D**	43. **C**
4. **D**	24. **C**	44. **E**
5. **C**	25. **E**	45. **D**
6. **C**	26. **D**	46. **B**
7. **E**	27. **D**	47. **E**
8. **C**	28. **A**	48. **B**
9. **E**	29. **A**	49. **A**
10. **B**	30. **D**	50. **E**
11. **C**	31. **D**	51. **A**
12. **D**	32. **B**	52. **B**
13. **D**	33. **C**	53. **D**
14. **A**	34. **D**	54. **B**
15. **E**	35. **B**	55. **C**
16. **B**	36. **D**	56. **A**
17. **D**	37. **C**	57. **E**
18. **A**	38. **B**	58. **A**
19. **B**	39. **E**	59. **B**
20. **D**	40. **D**	60. **C**

Math Test 1

Analyze Your ACT, Page 300

Name: _____   Date: _____

Mistakes: _____   ACT Score: _____

Essential Skills   ## Number & Quantity

Fractions	Average	Ratio	Irrational & Imaginary	Roots & Exponents	Sequence	Factoring
11	26	9	48	14	1	
12	44	40	54	59	43	
32		42				
Percent						
16						
28						
P. 164, 170	Page 174	Page 182	Page 198	Page 194	Page 190	Page 186

Algebra   ## Geometry

Simple Equations	Quadratic Equation	Translation	Coordinates	Polygons	Circles	Triangles
		2	13	5	31	6
4	22	30	51	15	45	8
10	27	37		20		19
18	41	50		35		23
29		55		38		25
58				52		33
				60		47
Page 202	Page 206	Page 218	Page 252	Page 248	Page 240	Page 222

Functions   ## Stats and Probability

Logic	Trig	Functions	Linear Equations	Tables & Graphs	Logarithm	Probability
46	34	3	39	17	49	7
	36	21			56	
	53	24				
		57				
Page 274	Page 262	Page 254	Page 258	Page 286	Page 290	Page 282

# of mistakes	ACT Score*
49-50	13
46-48	14
42-45	15
37-41	16
34-36	17
32-33	18
30-31	19
28-29	20
27	21
25-26	22
23-24	23
20-22	24
18-19	25
16-17	26
14-15	27
12-13	28
11	29
9-10	30
8	31
7	32
6	33
4-5	34
2-3	35
0-1	36

*approximate score

1) Mark your score on the right. Circle the questions you missed. **2)** Find your trends (categories with the most mistakes.) Set a goal: How many mastered categories will lead to a 3-point improvement? **3)** Study the pages in this book that will help you master the required skills. **4)** Review your missed questions.

Math Test 1 - Explanations

1. This is an arithmetic sequence problem, which means the relationship between the numbers can be found by adding or subtracting the same amount each time. If the second and third terms are 14 and 10, respectively, then the entire sequence can be written out x, 14, 10. To go from 10 to 14, 4 is added, so it follows that adding another 4 to 14 would give 18, making 18 the first term. **(Answer E)**

2. To begin, write out the problem as an equation. The total $360 needs to equal the $220 onetime fee plus <u>a certain number of</u> $20 monthly fees. Therefore, 360 = 220 +20x, where x is the number of months. Subtract 220 from both sides to get 140 = 20x, then divide by 20 to find x. The number of months is 7. **(Answer B)**

3. Plug in 15 for all of the x's in the given equation.
   This results in $\frac{225-25}{15-5}$, which simplifies down to $\frac{200}{10}$, or 20.
   Alternatively, recognize that $x^2 - 25$ breaks down into $(x-5)(x+5)$, so the equation becomes $\frac{(x-5)(x+5)}{(x-5)}$. The $(x-5)$ cancels out on the bottom and top, leaving $(x+5)$. Plugging in 15 for x gives 20. **(Answer C)**

4. The best way to solve this problem is to plug the values into the equation. You obtain $(7-3-6) * (3-7)$. Use PEMDAS and solve the part in parentheses first. Once simplified, the equation becomes $(-2)*(-4)$, or 8. **(Answer D)**

5. Reading the problem is key on this problem. Since it states the area of a **square** foundation, you know that both length and width will be equal to each other, and the area of a square is s^2. Taking the square root of 36 means each side would be 6 yards. **(Answer C)**

6. This is question involves the 3 inner angles of an isosceles triangle, which all add up to 180°. When two angles are congruent, they are equal to each other. A way to represent this in an equation would be $2x + 32 = 180$, where x is either of the two congruent angles; for our purposes, angle L. Once solved, $2x = 148$ ➔ $x = 74$. **(Answer C)**

7. This is a probability problem. Since the questions states a red **or** blue marble, both options are valid, which means the chances of each are added together. $\frac{6}{34}$ for blue $+ \frac{4}{34}$ for red equals $\frac{10}{34}$ for either blue or red. When simplified, the chance is $\frac{5}{17}$. **(Answer E)**

8. It is important to know angle rules for this one. For triangle ABE, we can discover ∠AEB is 65°, since all three angles add up to 180°. ∠AEB and ∠CED are vertical and are therefore both 65°. (The rule of alternate interior angles states that when two lines intersect each other, the alternate angles that are formed equal each other.) The angles of the triangle CDE need to add up to 180, which means angle ∠C is 85°. **(Answer C)**

9. This question can be solved with cross multiplication. $3(8+p) = 2(18+p)$ distributes to $24+3p = 36+2p$. Once simplified, $p = 12$. **(Answer E)**

10. Solving for x in the first equation will allow you to plug in x for the second one. Subtracting 24 from both sides gives $3x = -33, or\ x = -11$. When plugged into the second equation, $4(-11) + 12 = -32$. **(Answer B)**

11. This problem can be answered by converting the numerator and denominator into one fraction each.
    $7 = \frac{42}{6}$, and $4 = \frac{48}{12}$, so the expression becomes $\frac{\frac{42}{6}+\frac{5}{6}}{\frac{48}{12}-\frac{1}{12}}$, which becomes $\frac{\frac{47}{6}}{\frac{47}{12}}$. To divide by a fraction, you must multiply by its reciprocal. $\frac{47}{6}\ x\ \frac{12}{47}$ simplifies to $\frac{564}{282} = 2$. You can also cross-cancel the 47 to get $\frac{12}{6} = 2$ **(Answer C)**

12. This is an average, or arithmetic mean, problem. Since all of the barrels will equal the same amount of water at the end, then the water in them must be distributed equally. To find the average of the 3, add up the three values and divide by 3. First, you must get a common denominator. $\frac{11}{12} = \frac{22}{24}$, and $\frac{1}{6} = \frac{4}{24}$.
    $\frac{22}{24} + \frac{4}{24} + \frac{7}{24} = \frac{33}{24}$. When divided by three, the average is $\frac{11}{24}$. **(Answer D)**

13. The midpoint of a line falls exactly in the middle of the two endpoints, or the average of both ends. The x is $\frac{2-8}{2}$, or -3. The y is $\frac{-7+5}{2}$, or -1. Therefore, the midpoint is $(-3, -1)$. **(Answer D)**

14. This problem requires understanding scientific notation. Since the 10 is raised to a negative power, it means the value is a decimal, where $4.8 * 10^{-1} = 0.48$. (It has no zeros after the decimal point). $4.8 * 10^{-2} = 0.048$. (It has one zero after the decimal point.) Since each solution has one zero less than the number in its exponent, 10^{-84} will have 83 zeros after the decimal point. **(Answer A)**

15. Since the square and the triangle have the same area, we will solve for the square's area first. Since the area of a square is $side^2$, the area is 22^2, or 484. Now that we know the area of the triangle is 484, we can solve for the height. The area of a triangle is $\frac{1}{2} * base * height$. $\frac{1}{2} * 6 * height = 484$, or $3 * height = 484$. Therefore, the height will be $\frac{484}{3}$ or $161.\overline{33}$. **(Answer E)**

16. When solving percentages, use $\frac{\%}{100} = \frac{is}{of}$. Plugging in all of the values, $\frac{48}{100} = \frac{n}{73}$. **(Answer B)**

17. The first step is to solve the inequality for x. $x + 5 \leq 7 = x \leq 2$.
    Since x is less than **or** equal to 2, it will cover all values less than 2 **and** 2 itself, meaning the line will start at 2 with a filled-in dot, and go to the left. **(Answer D)**

18. To answer this problem, you have to solve for x.
    $6x + 6 = 3x - k$ => $6x = 3x - 6 - k$ => $3x = -6 - k$ => $x = \frac{-6-k}{3}$. **(Answer A)**

19. Since the two lines are not parallel, no comparisons can be drawn between the two sets of angles. This means that the comparisons have to be within the sets of angles. The rule about *vertical angles* is used, which states that when two lines intersect each other, the opposite angles equal each other. $\angle 1 \cong \angle 3$. **(Answer B)**

20. With a parallelogram, opposite sides are the same length. This means 2 of the 4 sides are each 22, and all of the sides equal 94. The other two sides equal 50 added together, so each one must be 25, since they must equal each other. The four sides are 22, 22, 25, 25. **(Answer D)**

21. To answer this question, plug in -3 for all x's. $5(-3)^2 - 4(-3) + 2 = 45 + 12 + 2 = 59$.
(Answer D)

22. This problem can be solved by subtracting one part from the sum to find the other part.
$(3x^3 + x^2 - 4x - 1) - (5x^3 - 2x^2 + x - 4) = (-2x^3 + 3x^2 - 5x + 3)$. Remember to keep the subtraction lined up with each part of the polynomial. **(Answer B)**

23. To begin this equation, we must solve for the length of $\overline{AB}$. Since the area is $\frac{1}{2} * base * height$, $96 = \frac{1}{2} * 12 * h$, or $h = 16$. However, we are solving for $\overline{AC}$. Using either knowledge of Pythagorean triples (this is a variation of the 3:4:5 triangle) or the Pythagorean formula, we find that $12^2 + 16^2 = 400$, so $\overline{AC}$ is 20. **(Answer D)**

24. Use Zone-F: Begin by attempting 0 in each of the functions, and see which ones give an answer of 17. This limits the options to A and C. Upon plugging in 1 for both equations, you find that C is the only viable answer. $y = 17t + 9$ **(Answer C)**

25. Right triangles always the Pythagorean theorem, so this problem can be solved either by knowing Pythagorean triples or by trying the Pythagorean formula $a^2 + b^2 = c^2$ with each of the pairs. 6, 8, and 10 are the only possible side lengths to form a right triangle. **(Answer E)**

26. If the first two hours averaged 55 miles, then 110 miles out of the total 412 were covered. This means the final 302 miles were covered in the last 6 hours of the trip. The average of 302/6 is 50.33, of which 50 is the closest. **(Answer D)**

27. It is important to recognize that the question asks for the *sum* of the two *solutions*. The two factors of $x^2 + x - 30$ are $(x - 5)(x + 6)$, which means the *solutions* are 5 and -6. Adding them together results in -1. **(Answer D)**

28. 60% of 1200 is 720. The problem says that **over 60%** must be obtained, so it must be greater than 720; it **cannot equal** 60% of 1200. Therefore x > 720. **(Answer A)**

29. First solve each side of the equation. $5x + 15 < 6x - 72$
This simplifies to $87 < x$.
"87 is smaller than x" can also be written as "x is bigger than 87". $x > 87$ **(Answer A)**

30. By plugging in both 77 and 95 to the formula to find their Celsius counterparts, we find that $77°F = 25°C$, and $95°F = 35°C$, so the range is $25° \leq C \leq 35°$. **(Answer D)**

31. The formula for circumference is $2\pi r$, or simply πd, so the circumference **in yards** is 32 π. However, the question asks for the answer in terms of feet, so the correct answer would be 32π x 3, or 96 π. **(Answer D)**

32. In order to compare these two mixed numbers, we need to write them as improper fractions with the same common denominators. The improper fractions would be $\frac{14}{3}$ and $\frac{28}{18}$. Upon multiplying the first fraction by 6, we can compare the two as $\frac{84}{18}$ and $\frac{28}{18}$. We can then just compare the numerators, finding that 28 of 84 is equal to $\frac{1}{3}$. Alternatively, we could simplify the $\frac{28}{18}$ fraction to $\frac{14}{9}$, and from there determine the ratio $\frac{14}{9}$ to $\frac{14}{3}$ to be equal to $\frac{1}{3}$. **(Answer B)**

33. Since the figure is a rectangle, we know that ∠CBE is a right angle, and therefore those three line segments form a right triangle. From here, we can use the Pythagorean theorem to determine what $\overline{BE}$ equals. $12^2 + \overline{BE}^2 = 20^2$, or $144 + \overline{BE}^2 = 400$. Therefore $\overline{BE}^2 = 256$, or 16. When we add this to $\overline{AE}$, the total length of $\overline{AB}$ is 28 centimeters. **(Answer C)**

34. Using SOHCAHTOA, we know the cosine value equals the adjacent over the hypotenuse. Coming from ∠B, the adjacent would be $\overline{BC}$, and the hypotenuse is $\overline{AC}$, so the cosine value would equal $\frac{BC}{AC}$. **(Answer D)**

35. The first step to solving this problem is to draw out where the mentioned lines and points would be. After doing so, we recognize that point C will be the same distance from point E that point B is from point F, and they intersect at the middle line. This means the intersection point is exactly halfway between points B and C, so the distance from that point to $\overline{AB}$ is half of the full length of the rectangle, or 6 centimeters. **(Answer B)**

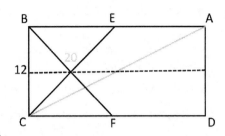

36. It is helpful to know the third side of the triangle. Use your knowledge of Pythagorean triplets (8-15-17) or calculate the third side the old-fashioned way: $8^2 + b^2 = 17^2$ to get b = 15. Now, use SOHCAHTOA to check which formula is right. The sin θ should be $\frac{15}{17}$. The cos θ should be $\frac{8}{17}$. The tan θ should be $\frac{15}{8}$. The cot θ should be $\frac{8}{15}$. Do not mix up answer C with the cos of θ. Only answer D is correct. **(Answer D)**

37. Since we are searching for the value t when h = 24 meters, we can plug 24 in for h and solve for t. $24 = -12t^2 + 36t$ The equation then simplifies to $2 = -t^2 + 3t$, or $-(t^2) + 3t - 2 = 0$ or $(x - 2)(x - 1) = 0$
The two solutions to this equation are $t = 1$ and $t = 2$. However, the question specifies the rocket's **ascent**, so we choose the earlier value of $t = 1$, as $t = 2$ would have occurred during the descent. **(Answer C)**

38. When working with any kind of regular polygon, the total of all interior angles will equal $(n - 2) * 180$, where n = the number of sides for the polygon. For a pentagon, therefore, we find that the total degrees of all interior angles will be $(5-2) * 180$, or 540. From here, we can subtract the known angle values to determine the remaining unknown value, which is 100°. **(Answer B)**

39. A line that is perpendicular should have a slope that is the opposite reciprocal of the original slope. We are therefore looking for a line that has the formula $y = -\frac{1}{3}x + b$.
At this point, it is quickly determined that answers A, B, C, and D are incorrect, although the various negative signs and fractions might confuse some students.
Checking answer E, we need to realize that a slope m can only be determined if the equation is written in the form $y = mx + b$.
We have to rewrite $-3y = x + 8$ to determine its slope.
Divide both sides by -3 to find $y = -\frac{1}{3}x - \frac{8}{3}$. The slope is perpendicular; the y-intercept does not matter. **(Answer E)**

40. The first step to solving this problem is to separate the numerators and denominators into two equations, where $2x - y = 7$, and $x + y = 8$. Using addition of the two equations, we find that $2x - y + x + y = 7 + 8$, or $3x = 15$. We now know that x = 5, and can solve for y in either equation, finding it to be 3. $\frac{x}{y}$, then, is $\frac{5}{3}$. **(Answer D)**

41. The quadratic formula is $x = \frac{-b \pm \sqrt{b^2 - 4ac}}{2a}$, where the equation is seen as $ax^2 + bx + c = 0$.

    In this case, $a = 1, b = -4$, and $c = 7$. Therefore, the formula for this particular equation becomes $x = \frac{-(-4) \pm \sqrt{(-4)^2 - 4(1)(7)}}{2(1)}$. When simplified, this becomes $x = \frac{4 \pm \sqrt{16 - 4(1)(7)}}{2(1)}$. **(Answer A)**

42. Since the student ratio is 4:3, we know that for every 4 sales at $45, there were 3 sales at $59. We can then find the average of these by taking 4 x $45 = $180, and 3 x $59 = $177, adding the two totals together to get $357, and then dividing by 7. The average then is $51. **(Answer D)**

43. There are many approaches to solving this problem, from looking at the answers to writing out all multiples of 7 and seeing which ones are also multiples of 6. Those numbers that fit both scenarios and have two digits are 42 and 84. The largest of those two numbers is 84. **(Answer C)**

44. If the difference between two numbers is the total distance between them, the average is meeting in the middle. Since n is the larger number, we need to subtract half of the total distance to reach the middle (or the average). Therefore, the appropriate expression would be $n - 9.5$. **(Answer E)**

45. The information given is in diameters, which we know is two times the radius. The radius of circle B therefore would be 1.5x, and the diameter of circle A remains 1x. The ratio then (of B to A) is 1.5:1, or 3:2. **(Answer D)**

46. The best way to solve this problem is to try each of the expressions in the answers until we reach one that is **always** an odd integer. If we plug in 1 to the first equation, we get 1, but if we plug in 2, we get 8, so it does not always produce an odd integer. If we plug in 1 to the second equation, we get 3, if we plug in 2, we get 9, and if we plug in 3 we get 27, so it seems to produce only odd integers. However, we should check all options to be certain. If we plug in 1 for the third equation, we get 3, but if we plug in 2 for the third equation, we get 6, so it does not always produce odd integers. For the fourth equation, plugging in 1 or 2 does not produce an odd integer. For the fifth equation, when we plug in 1, we get 4, so it does not always produce odd integers. Through process of elimination, we know that the only equation that fits the requirements is the second one. **(Answer B)**

47. Since we are looking for the length of all 8 sides of the pyramid, we will need to add up the 4 sides that make up the square base, along with the four sides that form the pyramid itself. Since it is a regular pyramid, we know that each of the four sides will be the same length. Using the Pythagorean theorem, we can determine the length of one of those sides, using half of the base length and the slant height as the other side lengths. $2^2 + (2\sqrt{3})^2 = c^2$ where c = the side length in question. This can be simplified to $4 + 12 = c^2$, or $16 = c^2$. C therefore is 4, bringing all of the sides making up the pyramid to a total of 16, and all of the sides forming the base to a total of 16, making the total of all 8 sides 32. **(Answer E)**

48. All of the potential answers have $4 \pm$ in their equation, so we know the discrepancy lies in the radicand. The square root of a negative number will include i, the square root of a^2 is a, and the square root of 16 is 4, so the correct answer must be $4 \pm 4ai$. **(Answer B)**

49. This logarithm can be rewritten as $k^{-4} = \frac{1}{256}$. This can then be rewritten again to remove the negative, making it $k^4 = 256$. From here, we can solve for k, finding it to be 4. **(Answer A)**

50. Underline what the question is asking for: <u>The amount of quarters</u>.

   Nickels = Pennies x 2   (He could have 5 or 10 pennies, resulting in 10 or 20 nickels)
   Nickels = Dimes – 2   (10 nickels result in 8 dimes, 20 nickels result in 18 dimes, etc.)
   Nickels = Quarters + 2   (10 nickels result in 12 quarters, 20 nickels result in 22 quarters etc.)

   The best strategy in this case is plugging the answers. As the answers are in ascending order, start with C (If it is too large, we will go to B or A. If it is too small, we will work on D and E.)

   18 quarters would result in 16 nickels and 8 pennies, However, the total of $16.50 indicates that there need to be five or ten pennies. Eliminate answer C.

   Since there need to be twice as many nickels as pennies, we know the number of nickels must be an even number, and from that the number of dimes and quarters must also be an equal number. This removes options B and D.

   6 quarters would result in 4 nickels and 2 pennies, and we can eliminate answer A since the total of $16.50 does not end in a 2 or a 7.

   Having eliminated all other options, we don't have to check Answer E. However, 42 quarters would result in 40 nickels, 20 pennies, and 38 dimes. All of these added together equal our total of $16.50. **(Answer E)**

51. It is important to note that the question states the values are all positive integers, so that when the segment is flipped over the y-axis, the line goes from being entirely in the first quadrant to entirely in the second quadrant, where all x's are negative, but all y's are still positive. This would change our x values to be $-a$ and $-c$, while our y values remain b and d. The correct answer then is $(-a, b)$ and $(-c, d)$. **(Answer A)**

52. We know the perimeter equation to be 2W + 2L = P. To get this in terms of length and perimeter, we can substitute (L−x) for the width, since it is x units shorter than the length. The equation now becomes $2(L - x) + 2L = P$, or $4L - 2x = P$. We can now solve for x, resulting in $-2x = P - 4L$, or $x = -\frac{P}{2} + 2L$. **(Answer B)**

53. The note tells us that the ratio between sides equals the ratio between their opposite angles, so to solve for $\overline{XZ}$, we can set up the equation as $\frac{\angle Y}{\angle X} = \frac{\overline{XZ}}{\overline{YZ}}$, or $\frac{\sin 82}{\sin 36} = \frac{\overline{XZ}}{14}$. This simplifies to $\frac{14 \sin 82}{\sin 36}$. **(Answer D)**

54. We can start simplifying the equation to $x^2 - 6 = \pm 3$, ➜ $x^2 = 6 + 3$ or $x^2 = 9$, ➜ $x^2 = 6 - 3$ or $x^2 = 3$. The answers to these two equations are $x = 3$ and $x = \sqrt{3}$, however the question specifies an **irrational** number, so we know the only correct answer is $\sqrt{3}$. **(Answer B)**

55. We can start by determining how much William paid for all of them, where 35 x $23.25 = $813.75 in total. For the end amount to be exactly $850 more, we need the total value to reach $1,663.75. Per bottle cap, this would be $\frac{\$1,663.75}{35}$, or approximately $47.55.
   From the reference point of $41.90 each, the average will need to increase by $5.65. **(Answer C)**

56. Logarithms with fractions can be rewritten as two different logs with subtraction, so for this case the equation becomes $\log_w w^3 - \log_w w^9$. The bases cancel, and the equation simply becomes $3 - 9 \ or \ -6$. Alternatively, we can simplify the fraction inside the initial log to $\log_w w^{-6}$, and when the bases cancel, the answer is -6. **(Answer A)**

57. When we have f(f(x)), we are essentially plugging in the entire f(x) equation into every "x" position inside the given function, in this case, f(x) itself. This becomes $4(4x + 7) + 7$, or $16x + 28 + 7$, which simplifies to $16x + 35$. **(Answer E)**

58. Whenever we have an absolute value inequality, whatever is in the absolute value is true, and the negative version of it is also true. In other words, $x - 4 < Z$, and $-(x - 4) < Z$, or $-x + 4 < Z$. The correct answers then are $x - 4 < Z$, and $4 - x < Z$. Alternatively, whenever we have $|x| < Z$, where x is any equation within absolute value, it can be written as $-Z < x < Z$, or for our purposes $-Z < x - 4 < Z$. Our two equations then are $x - 4 < Z$, and $x - 4 > -Z$, which, when multiplied by a negative on both sides, taking care to flip the sign, becomes $4 - x < Z$. **(Answer A)**

59. Since the specification is 6 parts of arsenic per 1 million parts of water, we have 6 in every 1 million, or 6 divided by 1 million. The correct answer is 6.0×10^{-6}. **(Answer B)**

60. For any regular polygon, all angles are the same, and the angle measurement is $\frac{(n-2) * 180}{n}$, where n equals the number of sides. For a nonagon, there are 9 sides, so the equation becomes $\frac{(9-2) * 180}{9}$. This simplifies to $\frac{1260}{9}$ or $140°$. **(Answer C)**

MATH TEST 2

60 minutes - 60 questions

Math Test 2

1. What is the perimeter, in feet, of a rectangle with a width of 8 feet and a length of 12 feet?

   A. 20 feet
   B. 24 feet
   C. 40 feet
   D. 48 feet
   E. 96 feet

2. A stapler has a regular price of $14.95 before tax. It is later marked down for clearance at 15% below the regular price. What is the new clearance price for the stapler before tax?

   A. $2.24
   B. $4.91
   C. $9.87
   D. $12.71
   E. $13.45

3. John, Diane, and Catherine each own shares of stock in Bill's Water Sports company. John owns 85 shares, Diane owns 60 shares, and Catherine owns 35 shares. If the current value of one share of stock is $5.20, what is the total value of John's, Diane's, and Catherine's shares of stock?

   A. $185.20
   B. $384
   C. $412
   D. $874
   E. $936

4. Susie is looking at a map to determine the distance between her house and the beach. If $\frac{1}{3}$ inch represents 25 miles, how many inches represent 575 miles?

   A. $2\frac{2}{3}$
   B. 5
   C. $6\frac{1}{3}$
   D. $7\frac{2}{3}$
   E. 23

5. A bag contains 7 yellow jellybeans, 4 blue jellybeans, 6 green jellybeans, and 4 red jellybeans, all the same shape and size. If 1 jellybean is randomly selected from the bag, what is the probability that it is yellow?

   A. $\frac{1}{7}$
   B. $\frac{1}{21}$
   C. $\frac{1}{3}$
   D. $\frac{1}{2}$
   E. $\frac{2}{3}$

6. $|5-2| - |2-9| = ?$

   A. -7
   B. -4
   C. 5
   D. 8
   E. 10

GO ON TO THE NEXT PAGE

7. In Rakeville, the daily low temperatures, in degrees Fahrenheit (°F), during a specific week in January were $-3, -8, 5, 12, -1, 6,$ and -2. To the nearest 1 °F, what was the mean daily low temperature for that week?

    A. -3 °F
    B. 1 °F
    C. 3 °F
    D. 4 °F
    E. 12 °F

8. If $7 + 3x = 64$, what is 4x?

    A. 9
    B. 19
    C. 36
    D. 52
    E. 76

9. The diagonal line $\overline{EG}$ divides quadrilateral EFGH into a right triangle and an equilateral triangle, as shown in the figure below. The given dimensions are in millimeters. How many millimeters long is $\overline{FG}$?

    A. $\sqrt{17}$
    B. 9
    C. 13
    D. 17
    E. 34

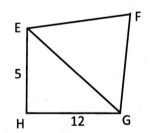

10. For $0 < k < 1$, then which of the following has the solution with the highest value?

    A. $\sqrt{k}$
    B. $\sqrt{k * k}$
    C. $k\sqrt{k}$
    D. $\sqrt{2k}$
    E. $k * k$

11. Which of the following expressions is equivalent to $(4x + 7)(3x - 5)$?

    A. $13x - 5$
    B. $13x + 2$
    C. $12x^2 - 35$
    D. $12x^2 + 7x + 2$
    E. $12x^2 + x - 35$

12. What is the slope intercept form of $3x - y + 2 = 0$?

    A. $y = 3x + 2$
    B. $y = -3x - 2$
    C. $y = -3x + 2$
    D. $y = 3x - 2$
    E. $y = x - \dfrac{2}{3}$

13. Which of the following equals

$$3\begin{bmatrix} 1 & 6 \\ 3 & 5 \end{bmatrix} + 2\begin{bmatrix} 5 & 3 \\ -2 & -1 \end{bmatrix}?$$

    A. $5\begin{bmatrix} 6 & 9 \\ 5 & 6 \end{bmatrix}$

    B. $\begin{bmatrix} 8 & 9 \\ 7 & 4 \end{bmatrix}$

    C. $\begin{bmatrix} 13 & 24 \\ -5 & -13 \end{bmatrix}$

    D. $\begin{bmatrix} 13 & 24 \\ 5 & 13 \end{bmatrix}$

    E. $\begin{bmatrix} 25 & 45 \\ 5 & 20 \end{bmatrix}$

GO ON TO THE NEXT PAGE

14. Ravi went on a road trip with friends that started and ended at his house. The entirety of his time was spent driving, eating, or resting. Ravi began his trip at 9:00 a.m. on Friday. During his time spent driving, he traveled 1,400 miles at an average speed of 50 miles per hour. The time spent driving was twice as long as the time spent resting, and the eating time was 20 hours. When did Ravi arrive back home?

   A. 1:00 p.m. on Saturday
   B. 7:00 p.m. on Saturday
   C. 3:00 a.m. on Sunday
   D. 9:00 a.m. on Sunday
   E. 11:00 pm on Sunday

15. To determine her students' overall test scores for the semester, Ms. Jackson drops the lowest test score and determines the average of the remaining test scores. Veronica took all 6 tests and earned the following test scores in Ms. Jackson's class this semester: 84, 81, 87, 93, 78, and 85. What overall test score did Veronica earn in Ms. Jackson's class this semester?

   A. 71.7
   B. 81.3
   C. 84.7
   D. 86
   E. 89.2

16. What is 130% of 478?

   A. 62.14
   B. 143.4
   C. 621.4
   D. 965.8
   E. 62,140

17. Which of the following graphs shows the solution set for the inequality $5x - 7 < 13$?

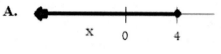

A.

B.

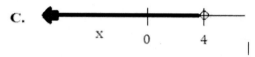

C.

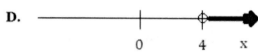

D.

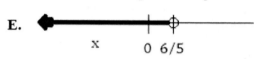

E.

18. Olivia bought several bags of grass seed, and each bag covers 2,000 square feet of lawn. She is planting grass on a lawn that is 25 feet wide. She starts with one bag and begins spreading the seed. Before she needs to open the next bag, Olivia can spread the seed in a rectangle that is the width of the lawn and how many feet long?

   A. 25 feet
   B. 40 feet
   C. 50 feet
   D. 80 feet
   E. 400 feet

19. A function is defined as $g(x) = -3x + 10$, and its domain is the set of numbers from 1 through 40, exclusive. For how many values of x is $g(x)$ negative?

   A. 36
   B. 37
   C. 38
   D. 39
   E. 40

GO ON TO THE NEXT PAGE

20. A formula often used to find the dollar value of an investment is $A = P(1 + r)^t$), where A is the total amount after t years, P is the initial amount invested, and r is the annual interest rate expressed as a decimal. According to this formula, which of the following is the closest to the dollar value of $2,500 invested for 9 months at a 6% annual interest rate?

   A. $2,555
   B. $2,610
   C. $4,225
   D. $6,130
   E. $171,800

21. The total cost, t dollars, for the Lakeville Drama Actors to perform at the local theater is determined by $t = r + 30a$, where r is the rent, in dollars, for the theater, and a is the number of actors who will participate. Thursday night's rental fee is $425, and there will be 50 actors contributing to the play. For the total price of exactly 250 tickets to equal the total cost of performing the play, how much should each ticket cost?

   A. $5.75
   B. $6.30
   C. $7.70
   D. $8.10
   E. $8.65

22. How many terms exist between 17 and 49, exclusive of 17 and 49, in the following arithmetic sequence?

   9, 13, 17 … 49

   A. 6
   B. 7
   C. 8
   D. 9
   E. 11

23. At Burkes' Sandwich Shop, Delilah spends $9.35 on the purchase of 3 cookies and 2 sandwiches, before tax is included. The price of each sandwich is s dollars. The price of each cookie is half the price of a sandwich. Which of the following systems of equations, when solved, gives the price, c dollars, of a cookie and the price, s dollars, of a sandwich at Burkes'?

   A. $\begin{cases} 3c + 2s = \$9.35 \\ 2s = c \end{cases}$
   B. $\begin{cases} 2c + 3s = \$9.35 \\ s = 2c \end{cases}$
   C. $\begin{cases} 3c + 2s = \$9.35 \\ s = 2c \end{cases}$
   D. $\begin{cases} 2c + 3s = \$9.35 \\ 2s = c \end{cases}$
   E. $\begin{cases} 2(c + s) = \$9.35 \\ 3c = 2s \end{cases}$

24. During a 6-year period, 1,225 houses were built in Smallville. The following graph shows how many houses were built in each of the 6 years. A certain percent of the 1,225 houses were built in 2004. Which of the following values is closest to that percent?

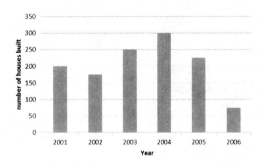

   A. 7.5%
   B. 10%
   C. 15%
   D. 25%
   E. 30%

GO ON TO THE NEXT PAGE

25. What is the result of the subtraction problem shown below?

$$(9x^2 - 5) - (-4x^2 + 3x - 6)$$

   A. $5x^2 - 2x - 6$
   B. $5x^2 + 3x - 11$
   C. $13x^2 + 3x - 11$
   D. $13x^2 - 8x - 6$
   E. $13x^2 - 3x + 1$

26. The expression $a^2 + 4a - 12$ is equivalent to:

   A. $(a + 4)(a - 3)$
   B. $(a - 12)(a + 4)$
   C. $(a + 6)(a - 2)$
   D. $(a - 4)(a + 3)$
   E. $(a - 6)(a + 2)$

27. The lengths of corresponding sides of two similar right triangles fit a ratio of 4:7. The hypotenuse of the larger triangle is 35 centimeters long. How long is the hypotenuse of the smaller triangle?

   A. 5 centimeters
   B. 9 centimeters
   C. 20 centimeters
   D. 28 centimeters
   E. $\frac{245}{4}$ centimeters

28. There are 360 runners registered for a marathon, and the runners are divided into 5 age categories, as shown below:

Age Category:	Under 18	18 - 30	30 - 40	40 - 50	Over 50
Number of Runners:	54	108	94	62	42

The prize committee has 40 prizes to award, and wants the prizes to be allocated to the different age categories proportionally. How many prizes should be allocated to the 18 - 30 age category?

   A. 6
   B. 8
   C. 10
   D. 12
   E. 15

29. In the standard (x,y) coordinate plane, a triangle with vertices $(-5, 2)$, $(-1, -1)$, and $(-3, -4)$. What will be the new coordinates of the vertices after the triangle has been shifted left 4 units?

   A. $(-5, -2), (-1, -5),$ and $(-3, -8)$
   B. $(-5, -2), (-1, 3),$ and $(-3, 1)$
   C. $(-9, 2), (-5, -1),$ and $(-7, -4)$
   D. $(-9, 2), (3, -1)$ and $(1, -4)$
   E. $(-1, 2), (3, -1)$ and $(-7, -4)$

30. Given $x > 0$, which of the following expressions is a factor of $x^2 - 4x - 60$?

   A. $x - 10$
   B. $x + 6$
   C. $x + 10$
   D. $x - 20$
   E. $x + 12$

GO ON TO THE NEXT PAGE

31. Computer monitor screen sizes are measured by the diagonal length of the rectangular screen. Grace recently changed from using a monitor with a 20" screen to a similar monitor with a 32" screen. If a picture appeared 9 inches long on the 20" screen, how long, to the nearest inch, will it appear on the 32" screen?

 A. 11
 B. 14
 C. 16
 D. 18
 E. 21

32. Which of the following inequalities orders the 4 following numbers from largest to smallest?

$$\sqrt{5}, 2.3, \frac{15}{7}, 2\frac{2}{9}$$

 A. $2.3 > 2\frac{2}{9} > \frac{15}{7} > \sqrt{5}$
 B. $\sqrt{5} > 2.3 > 2\frac{2}{9} > \frac{15}{7}$
 C. $2.3 > 2\frac{2}{9} > \sqrt{5} > \frac{15}{7}$
 D. $\frac{15}{7} > 2\frac{2}{9} > 2.3 > \sqrt{5}$
 E. $2.3 > \sqrt{5} > 2\frac{2}{9} > \frac{15}{7}$

33. In ΔXYZ shown below, $\sin Z = \frac{3}{5}$ and the length of $\overline{XY}$ is 12 inches. What is the length, in inches, of $\overline{XZ}$?

 A. 3
 B. 5
 C. 7.2
 D. 16
 E. 20

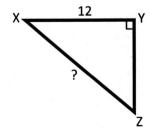

34. A square, shown below, has an area of 36 square inches. The circle inscribed in the square is tangent to the square at points J, K, L, and M. What is the area, in square inches, of the circle?

 A. 3π
 B. 9π
 C. 18π
 D. 36π
 E. 81π

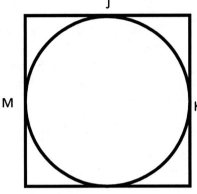

35. $\frac{5}{\sqrt{2}} + \frac{7}{\sqrt{3}} = ?$

 A. $\frac{(5\sqrt{3} + 7\sqrt{2})}{\sqrt{5}}$
 B. $\frac{(5\sqrt{3} + 7\sqrt{2})}{\sqrt{6}}$
 C. $\frac{12}{\sqrt{2} + \sqrt{3}}$
 D. $\frac{12}{\sqrt{5}}$
 E. $\frac{35}{\sqrt{6}}$

36. Jackson's Trampoline Emporium estimates its profit by subtracting its overhead costs from 60% of its net sales. Which of the following equations represents this relationship between estimated profit (P), net sales (S), and overhead costs (C) of Jackson's Trampoline Emporium?

 A. $P = \frac{60}{100}C - S$
 B. $P = \frac{60}{100}S - C$
 C. $P = S - \frac{60}{100}C$
 D. $P = 60C - S$
 E. $P = 60S - C$

GO ON TO THE NEXT PAGE

37. The sport field of our high school is divided into equal 3 rows. In the diagram provided, the top row has an area designated for Track equal to the area for Soccer. In the middle row, the four regions have equal areas, evenly divided for Soccer and Football activities. In the bottom row, the three regions have equal areas for Soccer, Track, and Football. What fraction of the field's area is designated for Track?

A. $\frac{1}{3}$

B. $\frac{5}{6}$

C. $\frac{5}{9}$

D. $\frac{18}{5}$

E. $\frac{5}{18}$

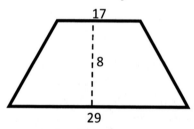

38. What is the perimeter, in inches, of the isosceles trapezoid shown below?

A. 46 inches
B. 54 inches
C. 62 inches
D. 66 inches
E. 74 inches

39. What is the amplitude of the function f(x) = $\frac{1}{3}$ sin(4x + Π)?

A. $\frac{1}{3}$

B. $\frac{1}{4}$

C. 3

D. 4

E. $\frac{4}{3}$

40. The Senior Class at Lakeridge High School held a sports-themed party. Each student who wore something sports-themed paid $3 for admission, and each student who did NOT wear something sports-themed paid $7 admission. A total amount of $710 was raised from the 150 students who attended. How much of the amount was raised from students who did NOT wear something sports themed?

A. $65
B. $140
C. $380
D. $455
E. $1050

41. Cans A and B are both right circular cylinders. The radius of the base of can A is 3 times the radius of the base of can B, and the height of can A is 7 times the height of can B. The volume of can A is how many times the volume of can B?

A. 10
B. 21
C. 42
D. 63
E. 147

GO ON TO THE NEXT PAGE

42. A bag contains 100 slips of paper. Written on each slip of paper, with no numbers repeated, is one of the following numbers: $\sqrt{1}, \sqrt{2}, \sqrt{3} \ldots \sqrt{100}$.
A slip of paper is drawn at random from the bag. What is the probability that the number on the piece of paper simplifies to a rational number?

    A. $\dfrac{0}{100}$

    B. $\dfrac{9}{100}$

    C. $\dfrac{10}{100}$

    D. $\dfrac{50}{100}$

    E. $\dfrac{74}{100}$

43. What are the real solutions to the equation $|x|^2 + 3|x| - 4 = 0$?

    A. ± 1
    B. ± 4
    C. 1 and 4
    D. -1 and -4
    E. ± 1 and ± 4

44. In the figure below, two nonadjacent sides of a regular hexagon are extended until they meet at point Z. What is the measure of $\angle Z$?

    A. $15°$
    B. $30°$
    C. $45°$
    D. $60°$
    E. $120°$

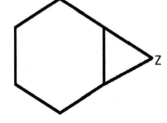

45. The expression $\sin^2 \theta - 3 + \cos^2 \theta = ?$

    A. -4
    B. -3
    C. -2
    D. 3
    E. 4

46. The fire station is located 6 miles north and 11 miles west of Dippersville. There is a fire 23 miles south and 5 miles east of Dippersville. Which of the following is the approximate distance, in miles, between the fire station and the fire?

    A. 18 miles
    B. 23 miles
    C. 33 miles
    D. 45 miles
    E. 52 miles

47. The slope of line z in the standard (x,y) coordinate plane is $\dfrac{4}{5}$. Which of the following equations is for a line perpendicular to line z?

    A. $4x + 5y = 12$
    B. $-5x + 4y = 9$
    C. $-4x + 5y = 9$
    D. $5x + 4y = 18$
    E. $4x - 5y = 12$

48. Two numbers are reciprocals if their product is equal to 1. If x and y are reciprocals and x is between 0 and 1, then y must be:

    A. Less than -1.
    B. Between -1 and 0.
    C. Equal to 0.
    D. Between 0 and 1.
    E. Greater than 1.

GO ON TO THE NEXT PAGE

49. A function is an odd function if and only if $f(-x) = -f(x)$ for every value of x in the domain of f. One of the functions graphed in the standard (x, y) coordinate plane below is an odd function. Which one?

A.

C.

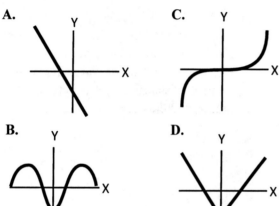

B.

D.

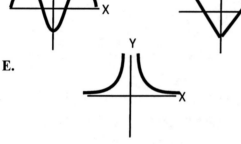

E.

50. For what value of x is $\log_{x+4} x^2 + 4 = 3$ true?

   A. -2
   B. -1
   C. 0
   D. 1
   E. 2

51. Let y be a positive odd integer. The expression yz^3 results in a negative even integer whenever z is any member of which of the following sets?

   A. All integers
   B. Positive even integers
   C. Positive odd integers
   D. Negative even integers
   E. Negative odd integers

52. An angle with measure θ such that $\cos \theta = -\frac{8}{17}$ is in standard position with its terminal side ending in Quadrant II, as shown in the standard (x,y) coordinate plane below. What is th

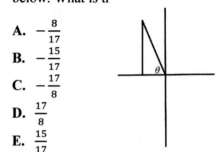

   A. $-\frac{8}{17}$
   B. $-\frac{15}{17}$
   C. $-\frac{17}{8}$
   D. $\frac{17}{8}$
   E. $\frac{15}{17}$

53. Tables of values for the functions f and g are given below. What is the value of $g(f(8))$?

x	$f(x)$		x	$g(x)$
-2	5		-7	3
3	8		-2	8
6	-3		4	-7
8	-7		8	6

   A. -7
   B. -3
   C. 3
   D. 5
   E. 6

GO ON TO THE NEXT PAGE

USE THE FOLLOWING INFORMATION TO ANSWER QUESTIONS 54-56.

In the figure shown, a larger circle with center D has a diameter that is 60 inches long. Point C lies on the larger circle in such a way that ∠ABC is 30°. The smaller circle intersects with center D.

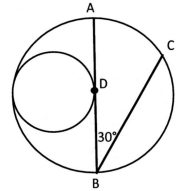

54. What is the area, in square inches, of the smaller circle?

A. 15π
B. 30π
C. 60π
D. 120π
E. 225π

55. What is the length, in inches, of arc $\overset{\frown}{AB}$?

A. 30π
B. 60
C. 60π
D. 75
E. 90π

56. The figure is placed in a standard (x, y) coordinate plane so that A has coordinates $(0, 15)$ and B has coordinates $(0, -15)$. What is the y-coordinate of C?

A. -5
B. 0
C. 5
D. 7.5
E. 10

57. Henry has a set of 3 numbers whose average is 35. When a fourth number, x, is added, the average becomes 50. What is the value of x?

A. 15
B. 42.5
C. 60
D. 85
E. 95

58. The solution set of which of the following equations is the set of real numbers that are 6 units away from -5?

A. $|x - 5| = 6$
B. $|x - 6| = 5$
C. $|x + 5| = 6$
D. $|x + 6| = 5$
E. $|x + 6| = -5$

59. In the figure below, parallel lines w and x intersect parallel lines y and z. If it can be determined from the information given, what is the sum of the degree measures of ∠A and ∠D?

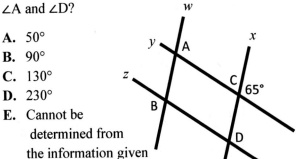

A. 50°
B. 90°
C. 130°
D. 230°
E. Cannot be determined from the information given

60. Which of the following complex numbers equals $(5 - 2i)(\pi + 4i)$?

A. $5\pi - 8i$
B. $5 + \pi - 2i$
C. $5 + \pi + 2i$
D. $(5\pi + 8) + (20 - 2\pi)i$
E. $(5\pi - 8) + (20 - 2\pi)i$

END OF THIS TEST
STOP! DO NOT TURN THE PAGE UNTIL TOLD TO DO SO.

Math Test 2 - Answer Key

1. C	21. C	41. D
2. D	22. B	42. C
3. E	23. C	43. A
4. D	24. D	44. D
5. C	25. E	45. C
6. B	26. C	46. C
7. B	27. C	47. D
8. E	28. D	48. E
9. C	29. C	49. C
10. D	30. A	50. A
11. E	31. B	51. D
12. A	32. E	52. E
13. D	33. E	53. C
14. E	34. B	54. E
15. D	35. B	55. A
16. C	36. B	56. D
17. C	37. E	57. E
18. D	38. D	58. C
19. A	39. A	59. C
20. B	40. D	60. D

Math Test 2

Name: _____   Date: _____

Mistakes: _____   ACT Score: _____

Essential Skills

Fractions	Percent	Average	Ratio	Irrational & Imaginary	Roots & Exponents	Sequence
32	2	7	4	60	35	22
37	16	15	27		42	
	20	57	28			
	24		31			
Page 168,	Page 170	Page 174	Page 182	Page 198	Page 194	Page 190

Number & Quantity

Algebra

Simple Equations	Quadratic Equation	Translation	Coordinates	Polygons	Circles	Triangles
6	11	3	29	1	41	9
8	25	14	46	18	54	59
43	26	21	56	34	55	
58	30	23		38		
		36		44		
		40				
Page 202	Page 206	Page 218	Page 252	Page 248	Page 240	Page 222

Geometry

Functions

Logic	Trig	Functions	Linear Equations	Tables & Graphs	Other	Probability
					Matrix	
10	33	19	12	17	13	5
48	39	53	47	49	Page 278	
51	45					
	52					
					Log	
					50	
Page 274	Page 262	Page 254	Page 258	Page 286	Page 290	Page 282

Stats and Probability

# of mistakes	ACT Score*
50-52	13
48-49	14
41-43	15
38-40	16
37-39	17
34-36	18
32-33	19
31	20
29-30	21
27-28	22
25-26	23
23-24	24
21-22	25
14-16	26
12-13	27
13-15	28
11-12	29
9-10	30
7-8	31
6	32
4-5	33
3	34
1-2	35
0	36

*approximate score

1) Mark your score on the right. Circle the questions you missed. **2)** Find your trends (categories with the most mistakes.) Set a goal: How many mastered categories will lead to a 3-point improvement? **3)** Study the pages in this book that will help you master the required skills. **4)** Review your missed questions.

Math Test 2 - Explanations

1. We know that the perimeter of a rectangle is 2W + 2L, or in this case, 2(8) + 2(12) = 16 + 24 = 40. **(Answer C)**

2. If the stapler was originally $14.95 and was marked down 15%, the new price is 85% of the original. 85% of $14.95 is $12.71. **(Answer D)**

3. All three groups of shares added together equal 180, so at $5.20 per share, their total value is $936. **(Answer E)**

4. This is a ratio problem; one-third of an inch relates to 25 miles as the unknown distance relates to 575 miles, or $\frac{\frac{1}{3}}{25} = \frac{x}{575}$. Cross multiplying and solving for x shows the answer to be $\frac{23}{3}$, or $7\frac{2}{3}$. **(Answer D)**

5. The number of jellybeans in the bag totals 21, so if 7 of those are yellow, there is a 1 in 3 chance that one chosen at random will be yellow. **(Answer C)**

6. The two absolute values should be solved first; the equation simplifies to 3 − 7, or −4. **(Answer B)**

7. The mean is the same as the average; when all seven temperatures are added up, the total is 9. When divided by 7 to find the average, the closest integer is 1. **(Answer B)**

8. When we solve for x, $3x = 57$ or $x = 19$. Therefore $4x = 76$. **(Answer E)**

9. We can use the Pythagorean theorem, or Pythagorean triples, to find that $\overline{EG}$ = 13 millimeters, and since ΔEFG is an equilateral triangle, we know all sides will be equal, and therefore $\overline{FG}$ will also equal 13. **(Answer C)**

10. This problem can be solved by choosing an easy value that fits the specifications, such as ½ . Once all 5 situations are tried, we find that $\sqrt{2k}$ produces the greatest value. **(Answer D)**

11. This is a FOIL problem, where the product is $12x^2 - 20x + 21x - 35$, which simplifies to $12x^2 + x - 35$. **(Answer E)**

12. To find the slope intercept form, we need to rearrange the equation so that it solves for y. Adding y to both sides leaves the equation as y = 3x + 2. **(Answer A)**

13. To solve this matrix problem, we have to first multiply the coefficients through to all different sections of each of the matrices, getting us to $\begin{bmatrix} 3 & 18 \\ 9 & 15 \end{bmatrix} + \begin{bmatrix} 10 & 6 \\ -4 & -2 \end{bmatrix}$. From here, we just add up each of the compartments, so we arrive at $\begin{bmatrix} 13 & 24 \\ 5 & 13 \end{bmatrix}$. **(Answer D)**

14. Ravi travelled 1,400 miles at an average speed of 50 miles per hour; thus he spent 28 hours driving. If driving was twice as long as resting, then resting was 14 hours, and eating was 20 hours, for a total of 62 hours spent on the road trip. Adding this total on to the starting time of 9:00 AM on Friday can be done several different ways; one such way is recognizing that 48 hours will jump ahead 2 full days, leaving 14 hours more after Sunday at 9:00 AM, which adds up to 11:00 PM on Sunday. **(Answer E)**

15. The question specifies that the lowest test score is dropped, so we only need to average the 5 highest test scores. These add up to 430, which, when divided by 5, determines an average of 86. **(Answer D)**

16. Another way to think of this problem is $478 * 1.3$, or 621.4. **(Answer C)**

17. The first step is to solve the inequality; we arrive at $x < 4$. Since x is less than, but not equal to, the domain of values will be going from 4 to the left, but not including 4, leaving it with a blank circle. **(Answer C)**

18. If one bag covers 2,000 square feet, and we already know width of the lawn to be 25 feet, we need to solve for the length it can cover. 2,000 divided by 25 is 80, the greatest length the grass seed bag can cover. **(Answer D)**

19. Since the question specifies exclusive, we are only working with 2 through 39 as the domain of answers; or a total of 38 options. This question is easier to solve as how many values are positive; plugging in 2 gives us an answer of 4, and plugging in 3 gives us an answer of 1. Beyond that point, all values are negative. Therefore, there are 36 values that give us a negative answer. **(Answer A)**

20. When we plug in the given information, the equation becomes $A = 2,500(1 + .06)^{3/4}$, since 6 percent is the same as .06 and 9 months is $\frac{9}{12}$ or $\frac{3}{4}$ of a year. This simplifies to $2,610. **(Answer B)**

21. The total cost will be $t = 425 + (30)(50)$ on that particular night, or $1,925. If 250 tickets will be sold, the price of each ticket needs to equal $7.70 to balance out the costs. **(Answer C)**

22. We can gain from the given information that the sequence adds 4 between each value. Therefore, when 17 and 49 are not included, the remaining values are 21, 25, 29, 33, 37, 41, and 45, for a total of 7 numbers. **(Answer B)**

23. $9.35 is the cost for 3 cookies and 2 sandwiches, so the first equation should be $3c + 2s = \$9.35$. If the price of a cookie is half that of a sandwich, then 2 cookies equals one sandwich, or $s = 2c$. **(Answer C)**

24. We need to look specifically at 2004 in reference to 1,225 houses. By looking at the graph, we find that 300 houses were built in 2004, which is $\frac{300}{1225} \approx 25\%$ of the total. **(Answer D)**

25. First, distribute the negative sign over all of elements of the second expression. Then add and subtract similar values.
$(9x^2 - 5) - (-4x^2 + 3x - 6) \rightarrow 9x^2 - 5 + 4x^2 - 3x + 6 \rightarrow 13x^2 - 3x + 1.$ **(Answer E)**

26. By looking at the initial expression, we know the two numerical values must multiply to equal -12 and add to equal 4. The only possible answer that fits these criteria is $(a + 6)(a - 2)$. **(Answer C)**

27. If the two triangles are similar, then their values follow a direct ratio between one another. The larger triangle's hypotenuse is 35 centimeters long, and the smaller triangle's hypotenuse is similar to it by a 4:7 ratio. The smaller triangle's hypotenuse, therefore, is 20 centimeters. Alternatively, cross multiply to get $\frac{x}{35} = \frac{4}{7} \rightarrow x = 20$ **(Answer C)**

28. There are 108 runners in the 18-30 category, or 30% of the total 360 runners competing. 30% of the 40 prizes should go to the 18-30 category, or 12 prizes.

    Alternatively, you can use cross-multiplication: $\frac{108}{360} = \frac{x}{40}$ ➜ $x = 12$. **(Answer D)**

29. Shifting left affects the x value negatively, and when coordinates are written as (x,y), that means the 4 should be subtracted from the original value to move the triangle's vertices left. The new vertex values are then $(-9, 2), (-5, -1)$, and $(-7, -4)$. **(Answer C)**

30. We know from the equation that the two values need to multiply to -60 and add up to -4. The two values that fit these criteria are $x - 10$ and $x + 6$. Since $x + 6$ is not a possible answer (given the criteria that $x > 0$) the correct factor must be $x - 10$. **(Answer A)**

31. If the monitor rectangles are similar, then the ratio between their diagonals will match the ratio between the horizontal images. We find the ratio to be 5:8 for the diagonals, so apply this ratio to a 9-inch-long image on the smaller screen to calculate a 14.4-inch-long image on the larger screen.

    Alternatively, cross-multiplication gives us $\frac{20}{32} = \frac{9}{x}$. ➜ $x = 14.4$. The closest value is 14.

    (Answer B)

32. Use your calculator to simplify the different values into their decimal form: 2.24, 2.3, 2.14, and 2.22. From here, we recognize that the second value is the largest, followed by the first, then the fourth, and then the third. Therefore, the inequality order should be $2.3 > \sqrt{5} > 2\frac{2}{9} > \frac{15}{7}$. **(Answer E)**

33. The sin of an angle equals the opposite side over the hypotenuse. Therefore, if the opposite side is 12, and the ratio is 3:5, the hypotenuse is 20. **(Answer E)**

34. The 1area of the square 36 square inches; therefore, the length of the square is 6, and the diameter of the inscribed circle is 6. The radius, then, is 3 inches; plugged in to $\pi r^2 = 9\pi$.

    (Answer B)

35. We need to get the denominator to be the same to add fractions; therefore, we can multiply the top and bottom of the first fraction by $\sqrt{3}$ and the top and bottom of the second fraction by $\sqrt{2}$. The equation now becomes $\frac{5\sqrt{3}}{\sqrt{6}} + \frac{7\sqrt{2}}{\sqrt{6}}$, which simplifies to $\frac{5\sqrt{3}+7\sqrt{2}}{\sqrt{6}}$. **(Answer B)**

36. If profit equals 60% of net sales minus overhead costs, the equation turns into $P = \frac{60}{100}S - C$.

    (Answer B)

37. If there are 3 rows of equal area, then each row is $\frac{1}{3}$ of the total area. Track, then, is $\frac{1}{2}$ of the top row, and $\frac{1}{3}$ of the bottom row, or $\left(\frac{1}{2} * \frac{1}{3}\right) + \left(\frac{1}{3} * \frac{1}{3}\right)$, which equals $\frac{1}{6} + \frac{1}{9}$, or $\frac{3}{18} + \frac{2}{18} = \frac{5}{18}$. **(Answer E)**

38. In order to determine the perimeter of the trapezoid, we need to determine the length of its two unknown sides. We can use the height and the difference between the two bases to form a right triangle with them; the height of the triangle would be 8 and the base would be half of the difference between the two bases, or 6, since the bottom base would be 6 inches longer on each side. From here, we can determine the length of the unknown side, using either the Pythagorean theorem or your knowledge of Pythagorean triples, to be 10. The perimeter, then, is $17 + 29 + 10 + 10$, or 66 inches. **(Answer D)**

39. The amplitude of a trigonometric function is the value by which the entire function is multiplied. In this case, it is $\frac{1}{3}$. **(Answer A)**

40. We can make a system of equations with this information; using s to refer to those who wore

$$s = 150 - n$$
$$3(150 - n) + 7n = 710$$
$$450 - 3n + 7n = 710$$
$$4n = 260$$
$$n = 65$$

something sports-themed and n to refer to those who did not, we find that $3s + 7n = 710$, and $s + n = 150$. From here, we can solve for either s or n and then plug in to the other equation to find that there were 65 students who did not wear something sports themed, raising \$455. **(Answer D)**

41. The formula for the volume of a circular cylinder is $\pi r^2 h$. If *can A* had a radius that is 3 times larger than *can B*, and a height that is 7 times larger than *can B*, the formula for its volume, in relation to *can B*, is $\pi(3r)^2(7h)$, or $63\pi r^2 h$. The volume for *can A* is 63 times larger than the volume for *can B*. **(Answer D)**

42. Radical values that will simplify to a rational number will only be those that are perfect squares; from the range of 1 to 100, those are $1, 4, 9, 16, 25, 36, 64, 81$, and 100: a total of 10 values. **(Answer C)**

43. Absolute values aside, we know the solutions to this equation to be $(x - 1)$ and $(x + 4)$, or $x = 1$ and $x = -4$. When the absolute value is factored in, we need to try both positive and negative values for both of these numbers; we find that only positive and negative 1 are answers to the equation. **(Answer A)**

44. The measure of $\angle Z$ must equal a total revolution, $360°$, divided by the number of sides. $360°$ divided by 6 sides, then, is $60°$. **(Answer D)**

45. One of the principles of trigonometry is that $\sin^2 \theta + \cos^2 \theta = 1$. The equation then simplifies to -2. **(Answer C)**

46. We need to use the distance formula for this equation. The distance from north to south is 29 miles, and from west to east is 16 miles. Plugging this in to the formula, we find $\sqrt{(16)^2 + (29)^2} = 33.12$ miles. **(Answer C)**

47. The perpendicular line needs to have a slope that is the opposite reciprocal of the slope of z. This problem can be solved by either transforming each answer into the slope-intercept form until one with a slope of $\frac{-5}{4}$ is found, or we can work backwards from the $\frac{4}{5}$ slope. Starting with slope intercept form, the equation would look like $y = \frac{-5}{4}x + c$, which then simplifies to $4y = -5x + c$, or $4y + 5x = c$. Only $5x + 4y = 18$ has this format. **(Answer D)**

48. Try several numbers between zero and one. The product needs to be equal to one, so if x is a fraction between zero and one, such as $\frac{1}{2}$, then y would need to be 2. If $x = \frac{1}{4}$, then y would need to be 4 etc. Therefore, in any scenario where x is less than one but greater than zero, y must be greater than 1. **(Answer E)**

49. By looking at the specifications of an odd function, we can determine that the y value of a positive x, such as 4, needs to be the negative equivalent of the negative x value, such as -4. In other words, if *when x is 4, y is 7*, then when x is -4, y should be -7. Using this information, we can determine that graph C is the only viable option. Alternatively, we can

use knowledge of odd functions to know they are reflected across the origin, in which case graph C is the only option. **(Answer C)**

50. This equation can be rewritten as $(x + 4)^3 = x^2 + 4$. From here, we can check the possible answers and discover that -2 solves the equation: $(2)^3 = 4 + 4$. **(Answer A)**

51. When a number is cubed, the cube is odd if the number is odd. The cube stays even when the original number is even. The cube stays positive when the original number is positive, and the cube is negative when the original number is negative. Therefore, if y is positive and odd, and the answer is negative and even, we need to multiply it by a negative and even number, such as $3 * -8 = -12$ You can try it out by plugging in random numbers. **(Answer D)**

52. The cosine gives us the adjacent and the hypotenuse. Using either Pythagorean theorem or Pythagorean triples, we find that the opposite side must be 15, (8-15-17 triangle). Since the sine function is "opposite over hypotenuse", the value is $\frac{15}{17}$. Use the rule "All Students Take Calculus" to determine that in the second quadrant the sine is positive. **(Answer E)**

53. To solve this function problem, we need to find what $f(8)$ equals, and then plug that value into the g function. $f(8) = -7$, and $g(-7) = 3$. **(Answer C)**

54. If the diameter of the large circle is 60 inches, and the small circle is half of its length, the diameter of the small circle is 30 inches, and the radius is 15 inches. Therefore, its area will be 225π. **(Answer E)**

55. Since points A and B are both on opposite sides of the circle, the arc that they form will be exactly half of the circumference. Therefore, since the circumference is $2\pi r = 60\pi$, the arc will be 30π. **(Answer A)**

56. Since point C comes at a 30° angle from point B, we can determine its equivalence in a coordinate plane: ∠BCD = 30°. ($\overline{DC}$ and $\overline{DB}$ are both radii of the same circle; therefore, the ΔDBC is isosceles. This is where the unit circle comes handy: the sine of a 30° angle is ½ or halfway 0 to 15, which is 7.5. **(Answer D)**

57. Draw average circles for clarity. If three numbers average 35, their TOTAL sum is 105. If a fourth number brings the average to 50, then their new TOTAL sum must be 200. The fourth number, x, must be the difference between these two totals. $200 - 105 = 95$. **(Answer E)**

58. First, cross of answer E: an absolute value can never be negative.

    We can gather from the question that the two real numbers we are looking for are 1 and -11. From here we can try all of the equations until we find one that has both 1, and -11 as an answer.

    Alternatively, plug in 1 and -11 into each equation and find out if BOTH answers equal 6. The only equation that fits those standards is $|x + 5| = 6$. **(Answer C)**

59. Using knowledge of angle relations, we can find that both ∠A and ∠D equal 65°, for a total of 130°. **(Answer C)**

60. When i is squared, it equals -1. Therefore, using FOIL, we arrive at
$(5 - 2i)(\pi + 4i)$ ➜ $5\pi + 20i - 2\pi i - 8i^2$ ➜ $5\pi + 20i - 2\pi i - 8(-1)$➜
$5\pi + 8 + 20i - 2\pi i$ ➜ $(5\pi + 8) + (20 - 2\pi)i$ **(Answer D)**

Reading

The Three Parts of the Reading Test

THE TEXT

I. Be an active reader!

- Underline important elements. Circle names. Draw arrows between contrasts and cause and effect passages.
- Each paragraph is a story in itself. Write a one-word or two-word summary in the margin.

THE QUESTIONS

II. Read the <u>questions</u> like a lawyer!

- Underline the most important element that needs to be answered.
- Be very precise and technical in your reasoning.

THE ANSWERS

III. Read the <u>answers</u> like a lawyer!

- Three answers must be 100% wrong. Find the word(s) that make them incorrect.
- Look for distractors:
    <u>F</u>ake ID's, <u>S</u>witches, <u>E</u>xtremes and <u>G</u>enerals.
- If you are left with two answers, reread the question.

READING
PART I - THE TEXT

Use the tips in this section to enhance your reading skills.

Enhance your reading speed if needed.

Read not just for information, but for precision.

Be an active reader:

> **Underline important elements.**
>
> **Circle names.**
>
> **Draw arrows between contrasts and cause-and-effect passages.**
>
> **Look for "trigger words."**
>
> **Stop after each paragraph and write a one-word or two-word summary in the margin.**

One-Minute Speed Reading Test

Read for exactly one minute. Mark your last word and add the words on that line to the number in the margin. **Name:**_____ **Speed:** _____ **Target: 350**

	Then a dog began to howl somewhere in a farmhouse far down the road—a
15	long, agonized wailing, as if from fear. The sound was taken up by another dog,
30	and then another and another, till, borne on the wind which now sighed softly
44	through the Pass, a wild howling began, which seemed to come from all over
58	the country, as far as the imagination could grasp it through the gloom of the
73	night.
74	At the first howl, the horses began to strain and rear, but the driver
87	spoke to them soothingly, and they quieted down, but shivered and sweated as
100	though after a runaway from sudden fright. Then, far off in the distance, from
114	the mountains on each side of us began a louder and a sharper howling—that of
129	wolves—which affected both the horses and myself in the same way—for I was
145	minded to jump from the *calèche* and run, whilst they reared again and plunged
158	madly, so that the driver had to use all his great strength to keep them from
175	bolting. In a few minutes, however, my own ears got accustomed to the sound,
188	and the horses so far became quiet that the driver was able to descend and to
204	stand before them. He petted and soothed them, and whispered something in
218	their ears, as I have heard of horse-tamers doing, and with extraordinary effect,
230	for under his caresses they became quite manageable again, though they still
241	trembled. The driver again took his seat, and shaking his reins, started off at a
256	great pace. This time, after going to the far side of the Pass, he suddenly turned
272	down a narrow roadway that ran sharply to the right.
283	Soon we were hemmed in with trees, which in places arched right over
295	the roadway until we passed as through a tunnel; and again great frowning rocks
309	guarded us boldly on either side. Though we were in shelter, we could hear the
324	rising wind, for it moaned and whistled through the rocks, and the branches of
338	the trees crashed together as we swept along. It grew colder and colder still, and
353	fine, powdery snow began to fall, so that soon we and all around us were
368	covered with a white blanket. The keen wind still carried the howling of the
383	dogs, though this grew fainter as we went on our way. The baying of the wolves
398	sounded nearer and nearer, as though they were closing round on us from every
412	side. I grew dreadfully afraid, and the horses shared my fear. The driver,
425	however, was not in the least disturbed; he kept turning his head to left and
440	right, but I could not see anything through the darkness.

FROM *DRACULA*, BY BRAM STOKER

Comprehension Questions:

1) **When did the horses begin to strain and rear?**
   A. When the first dogs howled
   B. When all the dogs started to howl
   C. When the first wolf howled
   D. When all the wolves started to howl

2) **What caused the horses to calm down after hearing the wolves?**
   A. The horses got accustomed to the sound.
   B. The driver talked to them soothingly.
   C. The driver took his seat again.
   D. The driver soothed and stroked the horses.

1) 90: first howl A   2) (not B: line 102!) 218 – 243: under his caress D

Top 10 Reading Strategies

1. Check your reading speed with our (or any) speed reading program. Your speed should be over 300 WPM, possibly 350 WPM.

2. Try to get a good overall picture of what the passage is about and where information is located in the passage. Underline 2-3 <u>main ideas and keywords in each paragraph.</u> If you don't spot any, <u>write a word or two in the margin</u> that indicates the paragraph's topic.

3. On average, spend 3-4 minutes rapidly reading and 4 minutes answering questions.

4. Skimming techniques:
   a) <u>Read the first sentence</u> of each paragraph at your normal pace. The first sentence is usually the main or topic sentence.
   b) Speed up your reading pace for the middle part of the paragraph.
   c) <u>Read the last sentence</u> of each paragraph at your normal pace. The last sentence is often a concluding or summary sentence.

5. For the **Prose Fiction** passage, do **not** focus on the first sentence in each paragraph. Focus on the characters, relationships, and emotions (underline these).

6. Skip words you don't know. Keep reading.
   If you must figure out an unknown word in order to answer a question, use context clues to figure out the meaning of the word. Cover the word and fill in the blank before you look at the answers.

7. During practice tests, write down the start time and end time for each story, including the questions, in order to get feedback about your timing. If you are taking more than 8½ minutes per section, you need to pick up the pace.

8. Infer … conclude .. indicate .. interpret …suggest. The answers to these types of questions are not directly stated in the passage, but you should look for evidence to draw a conclusion. Don't assume things that are not in the passage.

9. Cover up the answers to the questions when you read them. If you come up with the right answer to the question by yourself, you will be less fooled by the tricky answers that ACT writers like to include.

10. Look for distractors in the answers. (See page 365)

Reading Precisely

Johnny came home from school one day with a huge black eye. Tears rolled down his cheek when he explained to his mother how Douglas, a fifth grader, had picked a fight with him. "Douglas is a bully, Mom!" complained Johnny. "He is just plain mean!"

Johnny's mother immediately picked up the phone to call Douglas' home and speak to his mom. "Do you know what your son did today?" she asked immediately after she got a connection. During the response on the other line, her features softened. "I see," she said quietly. "Thank you very much." After she hung up the phone, she called Johnny over. "Son," she said, "I think we need to have a talk …."

It seems as if this is a straightforward story: *"Douglas, an older boy at school, is a bully. He hit Johnny in the eye. Johnny cried and told his mom what happened. After Johnny's mother talked to Douglas's mom, she does not believe her son's account of the story."* The end. We can infer that Johnny has been lying.

To get better in the ACT Reading section, examine each statement by analyzing it word by word. Look for evidence in the text. Consider if each statement is an actual fact (i.e., has a reference in the text.)

Fact 1: Douglas is a bully.
Incorrect. Although the text literally says so in line 2-3, this is not a fact. It is an opinion. The fact that Johnny says so does not make the statement true. A fact would be, "Johnny says that Douglas is a bully."

Fact 2: Douglas is older than Johnny.
Incorrect. There is no evidence for this. They might both be fifth graders, and Douglas might be younger, yet taller or stronger. We might take it for granted that older boys pick on younger boys, but sometimes age does not matter. There is no evidence in the text that suggests that Douglas is older than Johnny is.

Fact 3: Douglas hit Johnny in the eye.
Incorrect. There is evidence of the shiner, but does Johnny actually say that Douglas hit him? No. It appears that Johnny's mother believes that Douglas did; she called Douglas' mother to complain. However, the information that she believes her son's story still does not make it a fact.

Fact 4: Johnny cried and told his mom what happened.
Incorrect. Both aspects of this statement need to be true. Johnny might have told his mother a lie. He might have told only his side of the story. We cannot take his narrative for facts. (See fact number 1)

Fact 5: Johnny's mother talked to Douglas's mom.
Incorrect. Johnny's mother called Douglas' house. She wanted to talk to Douglas' mom, but the text never conforms that she did. Maybe she talked to Douglas, his father, or the babysitter.

Fact 6: Johnny's mother does not believe her son's account of the story.
Incorrect. She says, "We need to talk." This COULD mean she thinks the boy is lying, but you need to ask yourself if that is the ONLY possible explanation. Maybe everything Johnny says is true, but Douglas did end up with a broken bone. That could explain the story as well. If we stick to the information in the text, there is no evidence that helps us infer what the mother actually believes.

Inference 1: Johnny has been lying to his mom.
Incorrect. From the evidence, it appears that mom hears a different account from the person on the other end of the phone line. We can INFER that from words such as "her features softened" and "she said quietly" as well as from the way her demeanor changed from aggressive to friendly. That is evidence. However, consider alternative explanations. What if Douglas had lied to his mom? What if he was injured worse than Johnny? We can infer that the stories are different. We can infer that ONE of them could be incorrect, but we have no evidence that Johnny was the liar.

Reading Precisely - Quiz 1

Read the following paragraphs precisely. Be an active reader: underline words, circle names, and make notes if needed. Afterwards, check to see if the statements are true or false.
Try to read each paragraph only once, and cover it when you answer the questions.

1) My sister came bounding down the stairs, demanding her turn to watch television. I looked at my watch and reluctantly turned over the remote to her outstretched hand. As she started flipping through channels to watch her favorite show, my sister got a phone call from my friend Jenny about an invitation to go to lunch.

   A. My sister watched her favorite show.   TRUE / FALSE
   B. My sister talked on her cell phone.   TRUE / FALSE
   C. Jenny told my sister about the lunch invitation.   TRUE / FALSE
   D. Jenny wanted to go to lunch with my sister.   TRUE / FALSE
   E. Jenny and my sister are friends.   TRUE / FALSE
   F. Jenny was reluctant about going to lunch.   TRUE / FALSE

2) Liz had gotten to school early; it was the most anticipated school dance of the year. However, it seemed like everyone had a partner with whom to spend the evening, and, feeling disheartened, she went over to the tables where volunteer parents were serving water and other beverages. Nobody paid attention to her, but she noticed that Harold, her crush from her tennis team, had entered by himself as well. When Liz heard one of her favorite songs, she jumped up with new energy to join the crowd on the dance floor, only to trip over her chair and spill her Coke all over her dress.

   A. Liz wanted to dance with Harold on her favorite song.   TRUE / FALSE
   B. Liz was embarrassed by her fall.   TRUE / FALSE
   C. Liz spilled Coke all over her new dress.   TRUE / FALSE
   D. Harold has a crush on Liz.   TRUE / FALSE
   E. Liz's evening was ruined after she spilled her Coke.   TRUE / FALSE
   F. Harold did not have a partner at the dance.   TRUE / FALSE

Practice your logic with this one-line reading mystery. Only one answer solves the mystery.
3) What became of the haunted mansion on the top of the hill?
   A. The older couple who had lived there supposedly moved to another state.
   B. Nobody had lived in the mansion for at least 10 years.
   C. Everybody in the neighborhood had heard noises coming from the haunted mansion.
   D. The plot was bought by a realtor, and then sold to the state government.
   E. The house was bulldozed to make room for a parking lot.
   F. A new shopping center will open on top of the hill next year.

---

3) Only E answer the question.
2) All Statements are incorrect.
1) All Statements are incorrect.

Reading Precisely - Quiz 2

Read the following paragraphs precisely. Be an active reader: underline words, circle names, and make notes if needed. Afterwards, check to see if the statements are true or false.
Try to read each paragraph only once, and cover it when you answer the questions.

1) Jim and some of his friends had not gotten the grades they expected on a recent test, and while Jim's friends chose to talk to their teacher about the test, Jim decided to take matters into his own hands. He constructed a plan to get in to his teacher's office through the large window, make the necessary changes to the grades, and make his escape without anyone noticing. The first part of the plan went as intended, but before Jim could make it out of the teacher's office, the door began to open.

    A. Jim's teacher caught him cheating.   TRUE / FALSE

    B. Jim successfully changed his grades.   TRUE / FALSE

    C. Jim was unable to leave the office.   TRUE / FALSE

    D. Jim was a notorious cheater.   TRUE / FALSE

2) Margaret had been talking about the party on and off for the last ten minutes, and I was ready for her to get over it. I had been telling her that she should call to find out more information about it, rather than continually throw out questions that no one seemed to know the answer to. Finally, Margaret picked up the phone, and I watched as she called over to David's house. After she had stayed on the line for a few seconds, she suddenly turned pale and dropped the phone, causing me to jump to my feet.

    A. Margaret heard something horrible from David.   TRUE / FALSE

    B. Margaret wanted to attend the party.   TRUE / FALSE

    C. David was having a party at his house.   TRUE / FALSE

    D. Margaret heard something shocking on the phone.   TRUE / FALSE

    E. Margaret dropped the phone in front of me.   TRUE / FALSE

    F. I rushed to help Margaret before she fell.   TRUE / FALSE

Practice your logic with this one-line reading mystery. Only one answer solves the mystery.

3) What did the detective discover about the murder weapon?

    A. The victim had been involved in a long-lasting feud.

    B. The argument was about a disputed property line.

    C. The victim had no cuts or bullet wounds.

    D. Nobody had heard a gunshot or any loud noises.

    E. The baseball bat next to the victim belonged to his neighbor.

    F. The neighbor's son was found with blood on his hands.

    G. The son confessed to attacking the victim.

1) All Statements are incorrect.
2) D) correct E) correct
3) only E answers the question.

Reading Precisely - Quiz 3

Read the following paragraphs precisely. Be an active reader: underline words, circle names, and make notes if needed. Afterwards, check to see if the statements are true or false.
Try to read each paragraph only once, and cover it when you answer the questions.

1) We had been out fishing all day, looking for the big monster that supposedly inhabited the lake. We were about to give up when a fin appeared on the top of the water, not too far away. My friend Jane threw her line near the disturbance, and almost immediately her fishing pole bent over, twice as taut as with any fish we had encountered so far. The large fin began moving toward us, and I suddenly felt anxious. Jane, however, entirely in control of her emotions, reeled her line in and yelled, "We'll have a good dinner tonight!"

   A. We saw the monster towards the end of the day.   TRUE / FALSE
   B. Jake caught the monster almost immediately.   TRUE / FALSE
   C. I grew nervous when I saw the large fin.   TRUE / FALSE
   D. Jake and I ate the monster for dinner.   TRUE / FALSE
   E. We had caught many fish earlier in the day.   TRUE / FALSE
   F. Jake and I had hooked a huge fish on our poles.   TRUE / FALSE

2) I walked into the room and saw five pairs of eyes on me. I didn't think I was late to guitar practice, but I checked my phone to be sure. The screen lit up and said I was still early by two minutes, and I breathed a sigh of relief. Just as I was about to sit down, my phone rang. The caller ID said "Mom". Shortly after answering, I learned that I should go home immediately.

   A. I can play the guitar.   TRUE / FALSE
   B. The teacher had not yet begun my guitar practice.   TRUE / FALSE
   C. My mom was calling me.   TRUE / FALSE
   D. My mom told me I had to come home.   TRUE / FALSE
   E. I went home immediately.   TRUE / FALSE
   F. There was an accident at home.   TRUE / FALSE

Practice your logic with this one-line reading mystery. Only one answer solves the mystery.
3) Why was Carl missing after his class had visited the cathedral on the field trip?
   A. While inside the cathedral, Carl learned that he would be vacationing in Florida.
   B. Carl loved the ice cream from the shop across the street from the cathedral.
   C. Carl was fascinated with the colorful stained glass mosaics in the chapel.
   D. Carl got to spend time with his other friends in an experience outside of school.
   E. His teacher had given Carl several warnings to stay with the group.

---

3) Only C answers the question.
2) All Statements are incorrect.
1) All Statements are incorrect.

                               Copyright 2017 Winni van Gessel

Reading Precisely - Quiz 4

Read the following paragraphs precisely. Be an active reader: underline words, circle names, and make notes if needed. Afterwards, check to see if the statements are true or false.
Try to read each paragraph only once, and cover it when you answer the questions.

1) Lori woke up from a refreshing night's sleep, and a brief moment of panic left quickly as she realized it was still earlier than her usual wake-up time. She got up to go downstairs and fix herself breakfast, making a brief stop in the bathroom to brush her teeth and splash water on her face. As she made her way downstairs, she suddenly heard a loud crash.

   A. Lori panicked because she thought she had overslept.   TRUE / FALSE
   B. Lori used the bathroom and ate breakfast.   TRUE / FALSE
   C. Lori heard a loud crash downstairs after she brushed her teeth.   TRUE / FALSE
   D. Lori left her bedroom quickly to have breakfast downstairs. TRUE / FALSE
   E. Lori did not know what caused the crash.   TRUE / FALSE

2) There is quite a lot of discussion about the effects of cola on the human body that occur within minutes after consumption. Sources say that although the high sugar content stimulates many of the brain's pleasure sensors, the increasing sugar levels in the bloodstream cause the pancreas to produce more insulin, which aids the body by turning sugar into fat. Once the body has processed both the sugar and the caffeine from the sugary soda pop, blood pressure has increased, but so have the levels of dopamine, a neurotransmitter associated with pleasure. This association between cola and the "feel good" effect on dopamine levels is what makes humans consistently crave another can.

   A. Cola contains dopamine.   TRUE / FALSE
   B. The pancreas produces dopamine.   TRUE / FALSE
   C. Neurotransmitters help to turn sugar into fat.   TRUE / FALSE
   D. People with high insulin levels should not drink cola.   TRUE / FALSE
   E. The high sugar content stimulates the pancreas.   TRUE / FALSE
   F. The human body craves cola because of the drink's
      effect on some neurotransmitters.   TRUE / FALSE

Practice your logic with this one-line reading mystery. Only one answer solves the mystery.
3) What was the fact about the hotel that caused him to end his vacation?
   A. The beach was right outside our room, but it was filled with unsightly amounts of seaweed.
   B. There was a shuttle service to nearby restaurants, but they were all overpriced and noisy.
   C. The parking lot was back in the woods, and his wife was sprayed by a skunk.
   D. They stayed on the twelfth floor, the very top, because the owners were superstitious about the number thirteen and did not want a thirteenth floor.
   E. The place had only one elevator, and sometimes it took 20 minutes to get to his room.
   F. The manager at the front desk was outstanding, but only because he had tipped her.

[Answer box, printed upside-down:]

3) Only E answers the question.
2) E and F are correct
1) A is correct

Reading Precisely - Quiz 5

Read the following paragraphs precisely. Be an active reader: underline words, circle names, and make notes if needed. Afterwards, check to see if the statements are true or false.
Try to read each paragraph only once, and cover it when you answer the questions.

1) While the use of firearms rendered the use of archery outdated in warfare, the bow and arrow has never disappeared entirely in events leading up to modern times. In the 1700s, it was both a social and ceremonial sport; due to its popularity, archery societies were established complete with intricate costumes and identifying flags. The 1800s helped establish better rules and methods and even managed to include archery in the Olympics for the first time. After a small wane in the early 1900s, the sport was again revived by the United States which combined a pastime with science to create modern practices and the strategic bows, arrows, and techniques that we see today.

   A. The bow and arrow disappeared entirely in events leading up to modern times.
   B. In the 1700s warfare was a social and ceremonial sport.
   C. Archery societies were established due to popular costumes and identifying flags.
   D. Archery appeared for the first time in the Olympics in the year 1800.
   E. Archery lost some of its popularity in the beginning of last century.
   F. Science created modern practices and strategic bows.
   G. The sport is now the most popular in the USA, because of modern practices and strategic bows, arrows and techniques.

Practice your logic with this one-line reading mystery. Only one answer solves the mystery.
2) Why did the bride not show up at her wedding?
   A. The couple had had a big fight the day before the big event.
   B. The best venue in town had been booked, and the party was at vineyard way out of town.
   C. The bachelor party at the vineyard had gotten way out of hand the previous evening.
   D. The groom was waiting at the vineyard for his wife-to-be and had a huge hangover.
   E. The carriage that would drive her to the ceremony had broken an axle on the country roads.
   F. The bride's cell phone did not work because there were no cell towers near the vineyard
   G. Her mother-in-law was worried that the planning of the event had failed.
   H. Her father had predicted that she might never show up at the event.
   I. The bride had worried that the wedding would cost too much.

1) E is correct.
2) Only E answers the question.

Reading Precisely - Quiz 6

Family traditions have always been very important to me. When I was young, my parents would bring me breakfast in bed on my birthday. That event made me feel like a royal queen. On the first Friday of every month, all of my uncles, aunts, and cousins would come to our house to challenge each other in a charades competition. Every Easter, my mom would hide candy eggs around the house, and we would see
5 who could find the most. This led to a lot of laughter on Easter mornings. On Christmas, my sister and I were allowed to eat ice cream out of the carton, and my father would blast Christmas carols throughout the house. Today, I eat ice cream out of the carton all the time. I believe that these kinds of traditions help bring family members together. Those customs make holidays more personal and exciting - to have a special little secret the world does not know about. I want to make sure that when I have children, we have special family
10 traditions as well.

1. The author is considering **deleting** a sentence from the above paragraph. Which sentence can be omitted without affecting the elements that make the story coherent?
   A. That event made me feel like a royal queen.
   B. I believe that these kinds of traditions help bring family members together.
   C. This led to a lot of laughter on Easter mornings.
   D. Today, I eat ice cream out of the carton all the time.

2. The **tone** that the author uses to write about throughout the paragraph is
   A. melancholic, because she misses her family.
   B. reminiscent, since she is remembering her past.
   C. prideful, because her family has the best traditions.
   D. hopeful, because she wants to pass these on.

3. The author needs to change the sentence "That event made me feel like a royal queen." How can she **improve** her essay?
   A. Omit the word "royal".
   B. Add "who lives in a castle" after the "queen".
   C. Replace "It" with "This royal treatment".
   D. Replace the word "feel" with "act".

4. The **purpose** of this paragraph is
   A. to emphasize the importance of tradition.
   B. to reminisce about the author's childhood.
   C. to tell everyone to hide eggs on Easter.
   D. to give advice on how to better the holidays.

5. According to the text, it can be **inferred** that
   A. the author is good at charades.
   B. the author values tradition.
   C. Easter is the author's favorite holiday.
   D. the author has a very large family.

6. The word "secret" (line 9) **refers** to
   A. a tradition that nobody in the world knows about.
   B. the holidays in this story.
   C. the traditions in the author's family.
   D. memories that are personal and exciting.

7. Suppose the author wanted to write an essay about birthday traditions. Would this essay accomplish that **goal**?
   A. Yes, because she starts off with her birthday tradition.
   B. No, because she doesn't mention birthdays at all.
   C. No, because it includes other traditions as well.
   D. Yes, because she emphasizes how it made her feel.

1) D 2) B 3) C 4) A 5) B 6) C 7) C

READING
PART II - THE
QUESTIONS

Use the reading tips in this section to enhance your reading skills.

Read the question like a lawyer.

Underline the most important part of the question.

Become familiar with the types of questions in the ACT:

> **Reference**
> **Inference**
> **Except**
> **Vocab in Context**
> **Tone**
> **Purpose**

Types of Questions

There are several types of questions in the reading test
> Reference questions
> Inference questions
>> Assumptions
> Except questions
> Vocab in Context questions
> Tone questions
> Purpose questions
>> Detail
>> Summary (See English section as well)

 Tip: Read the questions like a lawyer.

 Tip: Don't look for just the right answer. ELIMINATE the incorrect choices.

Example: Why does Timmy need to stay after school?
- A. Timmy never finishes his homework on time.
- B. The teacher and Timmy are studying math each day after school at 3:30 PM.
- C. Het juiste antwoord is duidelijk te zien op deze regel.
- D. Timmy's high school is the most prestigious one in town.

Strategy: Look for words in the answers that make the statement wrong.
Answer A is incorrect because of the *extreme* adverb: <u>never</u>.
Answer B is incorrect because of the word "and": <u>the teacher</u> does not study math, Timmy does.
Answer C contains some difficult words. Let us skip it for now.
Answer D is a general statement, though it could be a correct one. However, it does not answer the question. We choose answer C, which, by the way, is the Dutch translation for "The correct answer is clearly visible on this line."

 Tip: If there are two or more "right" answers, re-read the question. There are often clues in the question that point precisely to one of the answers.

Tip: In order to make the activity above automatic and redundant, underline the key part of the question at the time that you read it. This way, you always make a straight connection between what is being asked and what is being answered.

Example: Which of the activities is an indication that Emily enjoys learning?
- A. Emily has straight A's in all her subjects.
- B. Emily speaks three languages fluently.
- C. Emily often plays new piano pieces with delight.
- D. Emily stays after school every day to work on her math.

Strategy: Underline the words: "<u>enjoys learning</u>"
Neither A, B, or D states anything about Emily enjoying the activity. Only option C answers the question. She plays new piano pieces (= learning) with delight (= joy).

Clarity

THIS PAGE ALSO APPEARS IN THE ENGLISH SECTION. (Page 104)
THE SKILL, HOWEVER, IS IMPORTANT IN THE READING SECTION AS WELL.

Many questions in the English ACT have four alternate options from which to choose.
About a third of all questions **start with a question**, after which the four answers are provided.
Often, the answer can be found by reading the question VERY PRECISELY.
Practicing this skill will help you throughout the ACT in English, Reading, Science, and even Math.

 Tip: Make it a habit to underline the most important part of the question.

Example: Based on the number of questions, which part of the ACT takes the most effort to complete?
    A. Math, because you have to read questions, memorize formulas, and calculate several steps to arrive to the answer.
    B. Reading, because there is a lot of information in the stories, and there is not enough time to process all the details.
    C. Science, because you have to understand the materials, the experiments, and the information in the tables and the graphs.
    D. English, because it has the most questions, and not everybody is a native speaker.

When you read the question for content, you might feel drawn to answer A, B, or C. However, if you read the question very precisely, there is an element in the way it is phrased that is only addressed by answer D.
Based on the number of questions, which part of the ACT takes the most effort to complete?
If you read the underlined portion carefully, the answer needs to show a reason that addresses the number of questions in the ACT sections. Only one answer does that. **(Answer D)**

 Tip: Read the questions like a lawyer! Every word adds a detail that needs to be considered.

Often, students skim the question and then bite their nails when more than one answer seems to be correct. You can save yourself a lot of time if you underline the essence of the question in the first place.

 Tip: If you end up with two (or more) answers that seem correct, re-read the question.

Example: What does Jolene always do at the end of her high-intensity exercises in the gym?
    A. She bows to her teacher to thank him and rolls up her new yoga mat.
    B. She slows down, closes her eyes, and takes a couple of breaths.
    C. She takes a shower, changes into her jeans and red blouse, and then goes straight home.
    D. She pays her monthly fees, so she can continue her membership.

If you followed the directions, you would have underlined the word "always" in the question and concluded that the second answer has to be the correct one. **(Answer B)**

 Tip: Often, students make mistakes when the question reads, "Which one is NOT correct," or "All statements are correct, EXCEPT which one?" The techniques on this page also help with those questions.

Clarity – Quiz 1

Eliminate the wrong answers to find the correct one.

1. The main purpose of this ACT book is
   A. to get better in math by memorizing formulas.
   B. to take the ACT as many times as you can.
   C. to internalize rules and strategies.
   D. to get a perfect score on the ACT.

2. At this point in the book, the author wants to add a detail that will help the reader increase his or her score. Which one should he mention?
   A. The average score on every ACT is 21.
   B. Purchase a speed reading software to help you with your reading speed. It will help you to finish the reading section on time and give you more time to analyze the answers.
   C. The author has taken numerous tests in order to analyze the ACT patterns. He knows what he is talking about.
   D. Don't worry if you have a bad day; you can take the ACT several times during the year and only your highest score counts.

3. How could one best describe the office in which the author wrote this book?
   A. The space is filled with a desk and two chairs, and overall it is quite messy.
   B. Lots of books are piled up in the office. Some books are dictionaries, while other ones are math and grammar books.
   C. The posters in his office are about colleges and universities.
   D. Outside the office is a staff of experienced writers and editors who helped to bring the book to its final production.

4. Which tone best describes the attitude of the students who use this book to study for their next ACT?
   A. Fearful, because the test score is the most important thing in their high school career.
   B. Curious, because they have never heard any of the tips or test strategies before.
   C. Cautious, because they are learning to apply new strategies while they are mindful about timing issues.
   D. Relieved, because they know they will score higher on their next ACT.

5. The book *Analyze your ACT* contains trendsheets. In this context, the word *trend* most nearly means
   A. tendency
   B. type of fashion
   C. certain style
   D. sheet with numbers

6. Why is the ACT so important?
   A. Without an ACT score, you cannot attend college.
   B. The ACT determines if you will get a scholarship or not.
   C. The ACT score often determines scholarship and admission standards.
   D. If you do not take the ACT again, you will not get a scholarship.

7. For the average student, which of the following statements is a typical experience when they take the ACT?
   A. Smart students typically get a high score on the ACT and feel confident about their skills.
   B. The average score for all students is a 21 for every part of the test.
   C. On average, a student takes the ACT test 2.3 times.
   D. A student does not know how to improve his or her ACT score because he or she lacks feedback about how to improve.

1) **C.** The main purpose is not to get a perfect score (extreme). Math is only one part of the book, and answer B does not answer the question. 2) **B.** Only B answers the question about increasing your score. 3) **A.** Only Answer A describes the office. (Not the posters or the books) 4) **C.** Watch for extremes in the answers: most important, never, they will. 5) **A.** Only the word *tendency* can be substituted in the original sentence. 6) **C.** Watch for extremes in the answers: cannot, you will. 7) **D.** Only answer D describes what an average student experiences.

Inference

Reference

A **reference** refers to a fact in the text. The ACT presents little stories that contain numerous facts. These facts can be used for references. Some questions ask, "the message in line 61 refers to …" The problem here is keeping track of all the details presented throughout the story. Be an active reader and underline important details.

Tip: Be careful not to mix up your facts.

> **Example 1**: "A young man spent the whole afternoon playing music in his room," Further on the text states, "The trumpet is his favorite instrument."
>
> Pay attention! The text never mentions that he spent the whole afternoon playing trumpet. (See the pages on distractors. Page 365)

Inference

An **inference** draws a conclusion <u>based on evidence</u> from the text.
When the ACT asks: "It can reasonably be inferred from the passage that …." there needs to be undisputable proof for the correct answer in the text.

Other phrases you might see are
"The text <u>suggests</u> .." and "The article <u>implies</u> .." "It could be <u>suggested</u> .."

Tip: Always ask, "Is there actual evidence in the text to back up this inference?"
Look for a reference in the story.

> **Example 2**: A text mentions that a man has a "very thick wallet".
> Can we infer that he is rich? No. His wallet can be full of credit cards or full of pennies and nickels. There is no proof that he has a lot of money.

Assumption

An **assumption** draws a conclusion <u>without proof</u>. Often, students assume things, while the question asks them to infer. Students are often not aware that they make these faulty assumptions.
Most people draw conclusions not based on evidence, but based on
- what they <u>think</u> might be a logical explanation,
- what they <u>believe</u> is a reasonable fact, or
- what they <u>take for granted</u>.

Tip: Always ask, "Is my conclusion foolproof? Are there other reasonable explanations?"
> **Example 3**: A boy in my math class gets D's on every test. Can we conclude that he must not be good in math?
> Answer: No. We often <u>assume</u> that his knowledge of math is the ONLY reason for getting low grades. (He might be good in math but struggle with reading word problems.) We assume that he does not understand the material. (He might be good in math but because of his job to support his family, he does not have time to study for the tests.) Another reason could be that he is depressed, anxious, etc.

Tip: Think like a lawyer! Stick to the text in a rigorous manner. Don't make stuff up. Question your conclusions. Be aware of your assumptions.

Inference - Quiz 1

An **assumption** draws a conclusion without proof. Most people draw conclusions based on what they <u>think</u> might be a logical explanation, what they <u>believe</u> is a reasonable fact, or what they <u>take for granted</u>. An **inference** draws a conclusion <u>based on evidence</u> from the text.

When the ACT asks: "It can reasonably be inferred from the passage that …." there needs to be undisputable proof for the correct answer in the text.

A father had an argument with his son in his living room. He refused to give him money because he was irresponsible and could not be trusted with more than a few dollar bills. While the meeting started with a quiet discussion, it ended with yelling and cursing and the man walked out of the room in frustration.

Indicate if the following statements are facts, inferences, or assumptions.

1. The son came to his father for money.   Fact   Assumption   Inference
2. The son was a teenager.   Fact   Assumption   Inference
3. The father refused to give the son money.   Fact   Assumption   Inference
4. The meeting did not go very well.   Fact   Assumption   Inference
5. The son was irresponsible.   Fact   Assumption   Inference
6. There were two people in the living room.   Fact   Assumption   Inference
7. The father yelled during the meeting.   Fact   Assumption   Inference
8. The son still lived at home.   Fact   Assumption   Inference
9. The father walked out of the room in frustration.   Fact   Assumption   Inference
10. Nobody received money during the meeting.   Fact   Assumption   Inference

---

Possible facts: The son is a well-to-do accountant. His father has Alzheimer's and is 86 years old. The family had asked the son to take care of the father's financial affairs and the son normally gives his dad some pocket money. During his latest visit, Dad got frustrated because the son gave him only $20.00, not the $1000.00 dollars he wanted. Read the story again. How many assumptions did you make the first time? Did you make up your own story about an irresponsible teenager?

Facts are stated in the text. <u>Inferences</u> are based on evidence in the text. You made <u>assumptions</u> if you made up your own story without considering reasonable alternatives.

1. The son came to his father for money. **Assumption.** It never stated who came to whom.
2. The son was a teenager. **Assumption.** No ages were given as evidence.
3. The father refused to give the son money. **Assumption.** "He" could refer to either father or son.
4. The meeting did not go very well. **Inference.** You can infer this from evidence! "*While the meeting started with a quiet discussion, it ended with yelling and cursing and the man walking out of the room in frustration.*"
5. The son was irresponsible. **Assumption.** "He" could refer to either father or son.
6. There were two people in the living room. **Assumption.** There is no evidence that nobody else was present.
7. The father yelled during the meeting. **Assumption.** It could have been the son who was doing all the yelling and screaming, or even a third person in the room.
8. The son still lived at home. **Assumption.** The story provides no evidence to back this up.
9. The father walked out of the room in frustration. **Assumption.** You have to make sure that there are no alternative explanations possible if you want to infer something. If both father and son were grownups, "the man" could refer to either father or son.
10. Nobody received money during the meeting. **Assumption.** There is no evidence for this statement.

Inference - Quiz 2

A student met with her professor one day. She needed help with a huge experiment that consisted of collecting data from thousands of participants in a poll. Years of experience enabled the expert to use certain algorithms in a custom-made computer program, and the data was successfully analyzed within days. A week later, she showed her gratitude by writing a letter in which she offered her appreciation for the program that had helped her complete the data analysis.

It can reasonably be inferred from the passage that

1. the student met with her professor because she needed help with her experiment.	Fact	Assumption	Inference
2. the student needed help collecting data.	Fact	Assumption	Inference
3. the professor helped the student with her experiment.	Fact	Assumption	Inference
4. the professor wrote a computer program.	Fact	Assumption	Inference
5. either the professor or the student analyzed the data.	Fact	Assumption	Inference
6. many polls were analyzed.	Fact	Assumption	Inference
7. the professor analyzed the data.	Fact	Assumption	Inference
8. the professor and the student conducted the experiment.	Fact	Assumption	Inference
9. the student was thankful that the experiment was completed successfully.	Fact	Assumption	Inference
10. the experiment was completed successfully.	Fact	Assumption	Inference

Possible facts: A Biology professor, Sylvia McAllister, was introduced to a graduate student, Maria, during a luncheon. The professor talked about her troubles with data analysis in her latest research grant. Maria, a computer science major, wrote a program for Dr. McAllister, who was grateful for the help she received.

Did you make up an equally believable story that is based on your assumptions? Stick with the facts.

1) The student met with her professor because she needed help with her experiment. **Assumption** The text does not state why they met. 2) The student needed help collecting data. **Assumption** "She" could refer to either the student or the professor. 3) The professor helped the student with her experiment. **Assumption** There is no reference in the text that the professor helped the student. 4) The professor wrote a computer program. **Assumption** There is no reference in the text that the professor wrote the program. 5) Either the professor or the student analyzed the data. **Assumption, Incorrect** There is no reference in the text. Other people could have helped with this. 6) Many polls were analyzed. **Incorrect Fact or Assumption** The text mentions only one poll. 7) The professor analyzed the data. **Assumption** There is no reference about his in the text. 8) The professor and the student conducted the experiment. **Assumption** There is no reference in the text to conclude indisputable who conducted the experiment. 9) The student was thankful that the experiment was completed successfully. **Assumption** It is equally possible that it was the professor who was grateful. 10) The experiment was completed successfully. **Assumption or Incorrect Fact.** The text states that the data analysis was successful, not the experiment.

Inference - Quiz 3

A family gathered at the bus station to welcome a soldier who was coming home from duty. He had not been home for three years and had seen many deaths and atrocities during his years of service. The mother, Emma Wilson, was worried about telling the traveler about the changes that had happened while the soldier had been gone. Her son, Peter, told her not to worry because the soldier had probably experienced worse things in the world. Mr. Wilson, meanwhile, stood away from his family, thinking about what to say to the soldier when he would finally arrive. He was not sure if he would even recognize him if there were many young men in uniform on the bus. The family grew quiet as the bus rolled into the station.

It can be inferred from the story that

1. the soldier had been away to war.	True	False
2. the war had been going on for three years.	True	False
3. the soldier had been on duty for three years.	True	False
4. the soldier had not seen his family for three years.	True	False
5. the soldier had not been in town for three years.	True	False
6. the family was going to give the soldier some unpleasant news.	True	False
7. the mother had not seen her son for a while.	True	False
8. the parents of the soldier were waiting at the bus station.	True	False
9. there were only three people waiting at the bus station.	True	False
10. there were several soldiers on the bus.	True	False
11. none of the Wilsons talked as they waited in the bus station.	True	False
12. the soldier had at least one brother.	True	False
13. the town had undergone some major changes while the soldier had been gone.	True	False
14. the dad was not sure what to say to the soldier when he arrived.	True	False
15. Mr. Wilson stood by himself, away from his family.	True	False

Possible facts: The Wilsons are the neighbors of the soldier and take care of his house when the soldier is gone. The Wilsons now have to deliver the news to the soldier that his home has burned down along with all his possessions.

It never states that they are the soldier's parents, nor that the soldier has been in a war. Were you assuming that your idea of the story was right? (Those are your assumptions.) To make an inference, there needs to be evidence in the story that you are right and that no reasonable alternative explanations are possible.

1) The soldier had been away to war and **2)** The war had been going on for three years. (There is no evidence of a war.) **3)** The soldier had been on duty for three years. (He had been gone for three years: only the last year could have been on duty.) **4)** The soldier had not seen his family for three years. (There is no evidence for this. If he had family, they could have visited him at his base, even if he had not been home for three years.) **5)** The soldier had not been in town for three years. (Not been home is not the same as not been in town.) **6)** The family was going to give the soldier some unpleasant news. (Correct, there is evidence about the unpleasant message: "Mrs. Wilson is…worried about telling the traveler about all the changes that had happened." Peter states, "…the soldier had probably experienced worse things in the world." (Evidence that the soldier is going to face something bad) Even the dad is "thinking about what to say to the soldier" (Evidence that it is not just a Mrs. Wilson thing.) **7)** The mother had not seen her son for a while. (It states that Mrs. Wilson just talked to her son, Peter, a minute ago!) **8)** The parents of the soldier were waiting at the bus station. (It never states that Mr. and Mrs. Wilson are the soldier's parents.) **9)** There were only three people waiting at the bus station. (There is no evidence that nobody else was there.) **10)** There were several soldiers on the bus. (No, Mr. Wilson is worried that there "might" be several soldiers on the bus.) **11)** None of the Wilsons talked as they waited in the bus station. (Incorrect, Mrs. Wilson definitely talked with Peter.) **12)** The soldier had at least one brother. (As Peter is his neighbor, there is no evidence for this.) **13)** The town had undergone some major changes while the soldier was gone. (A major change in the soldier's life does not necessarily mean a major change in the town.) **14)** The dad was not sure what to say to the soldier when he would arrive. (Do not mix up your facts: He was not sure if he would recognize the soldier.) **15)** Mr. Wilson stood by himself, away from his family. (In a crowded station, standing away from his family does not mean standing by himself.)

Inference Traps

Example: Clemens lives six minutes away from his office, but he was 30 minutes late for work this morning.

What can you infer?
- **A.** Something happened, and he left his house too late.
- **B.** Something happened between his house and the office.
- **C.** Something happened in his house or on his way to the office.
- **D.** Clemens was not on time this morning.

Often, we want to fill in the blanks in a story while, in fact, there are not enough details to support such a statement. This is when we "assume" things instead of "infer" things. Inferences are based on evidence in the text. Answers A and B are reasonable explanations, but they are not based on any evidence. Even answer C is based on the assumption that those two options are the only two possible explanations. Maybe Clemens came back from an overnight trip, or he went to the gym this morning and sprained his ankle. There is no evidence that rules out those alternative explanations. Therefore, we cannot determine what happened, and we cannot draw an inference to support any of the first three answers.

The problem is that answer D is not very satisfying. It does not explain anything. It does not solve the problem. It is very plain. However, we do not need attractive answers; we need **correct** answers, and answer D is 100% correct.

 Tip: Look for correct, indisputable answers.

Example: You are driving on the highway on your way to a very important interview in Louisville. To calm your nerves, you listen to some hard rock music. Suddenly, a police officer pulls you over.

It can be inferred from the story that the police officer pulled you over because
- **A.** you were speeding.
- **B.** your radio was playing too loud.
- **C.** you broke some type of law.
- **D.** he wants to talk to you about something.

 Tip: Ask yourself, "Is there is any evidence in the text to back up my inference?"

Answers A and B are not evident in the text at all. (Be careful! Do not confuse hard rock music with loud music; you can play hard rock music very quietly.)

Answer C looks great. When you break a law, an officer will pull you over. Before circling the answer though, ask yourself another question.

Tip: Ask yourself, "Is my explanation foolproof? Are there other reasonable explanations?"

The officer might stop random cars for alcohol screening. The officer might have noticed that you have an almost-flat tire. Your car might fit the description of an APB that went out after a recent bank robbery. All of these are explanations that do not involve breaking a law.

See? Answer D does not make a cool story. However, you can infer it from the text because there is evidence: the officer pulled you over. (It would be very unlikely that the officer pulled you over and then drove away again without saying something at all.) Answer D is the correct answer.

 Tip: Think like a lawyer. In the ACT, inference questions are based on <u>evidence</u> in the text.

Word Choice - Vocab in Context

Words can have different meanings depending on the sentence in which they appear.
Consider the word "set". They were working on the *set* (backdrop) for the play. The tennis player won the first *set* (part of a match). She had a *set* (collection) of matching antique vases. As you can quickly see, it is impossible to tell the meaning without the context.

Tip: When you face a question about the meaning of a word, do not look at the word. In fact, cross it out: xxxxx. Look at the rest of the sentence and find out what kind of word is missing. Draw your own conclusion before looking at the answers.

Tip: Reread the whole sentence again and substitute the four answers. Which makes most sense?

One day, a young student named Joey noticed many vacant seats in his English class. He asked the teacher, "Where are all of the other students at?" "Some of your classmates have gone to see a musical." Ms. Marshall replied with her usual xxxxx[1]. "However, it seems I need to repair[2] your grammar today, don't I, Joey?" she xxxx[3]. "Everyone please get out a sheet of notebook paper and begin to take notes for our English lesson." All of the students really enjoyed Ms. Marshall's English class, and even Joey wasn't upset because of the way she used to tailor[4] her model[5] sentences to a topic he enjoyed, such as ice cream or recess. Joey learned that he should not have used the word "at" in his question, as leaving it out would still result in the same function[6]. From now on, he intended to recycle[7] what he'd learned, so that he could become one of the best students ever.

1. As it is used in this sentence, "xxxxx" most nearly means
   A. index
   B. enroll
   C. formality
   D. sign up
2. Which of the following alternatives to the word "repair" would be least acceptable?
   A. fix
   B. mistake
   C. mend
   D. improve
3. As it is used in this sentence, "xxxx" most nearly means
   A. labeled
   B. touched
   C. flagged
   D. added
4. Which of the following alternatives to the word "tailor" would be least acceptable?
   A. customize

B. adapt
C. designer
D. mold

5. As it is used in this sentence, "model" most nearly means
   A. version
   B. textbook
   C. reproduction
   D. copy
6. Which of the following alternatives to the word "function" would be least acceptable?
   A. gathering
   B. purpose
   C. meaning
   D. use
7. As it is used in this sentence, "recycle" most nearly means
   A. use again
   B. convert into usable materials
   C. salvage
   D. separate from other materials

1) C The word was "register" 2) B 3) D the word was "tagged" 4) C 5) B 6) A 7) A

Copyright 2017 Winni van Gessel

Vocab in Context - Quiz 1

 Tip: When you see <u>three</u> words with the same meaning, and <u>one</u> word that stands out, that odd one out is often the correct answer. Look for a 3/1 split in the word choice answers. If one of the three similar ones is the correct answer, the other two should also be correct. Therefore, neither one can be the correct answer.

Today was Stacy's first day as a cadet at West Point Military Academy. While in line to register for classes she met another student, James, who seemed to know the <u>ropes</u>[1]. "Put your hair up in a bun," he told Stacy, "otherwise the <u>brass</u>[2] will give you a demerit. The army has a strict protocol, so you better learn how to <u>address</u>[3] your superiors before classes start." Stacy was grateful for any help she could get. She had heard rumors about what to expect: long hours to <u>cement</u>[4] knowledge of survival skills, obstacle courses so difficult they made the weakest cadets' knees <u>buckle</u>[5], and social events that were anything but a <u>riot</u>[6]. She was not worried about actually serving in the army, though; advances in military <u>technology</u>[7] meant it was unlikely that she would ever see combat.

1. As used in this sentence, the word "ropes" most nearly means
   A. strings
   B. procedures
   C. controls
   D. classes

2. As it is used in this sentence, "brass" most nearly means
   A. a shiny metal
   B. a category of musical instruments
   C. an officer
   D. brashness

3. Which of the following alternatives to the bolded portion would be least acceptable?
   A. listen to
   B. converse with
   C. speak to
   D. communicate with

4. As it is used in this sentence, "cement" most nearly means
   A. pour concrete
   B. learn something well
   C. constantly forget
   D. bind things together

5. Which of the following alternatives to the word "buckle" would be least acceptable?
   A. fold
   B. collapse
   C. crumple
   D. clasp

6. As it is used in this sentence, "riot" most nearly means
   A. a disturbance of the peace
   B. a fun time
   C. a type of military drill
   D. a protest

7. Which of the following alternatives to the word "technology" would be most acceptable?
   A. computers
   B. drones
   C. weaponry
   D. automation

1)B 2)C 3)A 4)B 5)D 6)B 7)A

Vocab in Context - Quiz 2

Bernie was a financier extraordinaire. He knew the markets, knew his clients, and had made millions selling and buying <u>futures</u>[1]. One day, his assistant Ted burst into his office; his face was pale and <u>grave</u>[2]. "Mr. Madoff," he said breathlessly, "There's a horrible problem. All the fishermen on the <u>channel</u>[3] are on strike, and they are <u>refraining</u> <u>from</u>[4] going to sea and catching bass." "The horror!", Bernie proclaimed. "How is the <u>market</u>[5] reacting?" The look on Ben's face said it all. Bernie knew that his impeccable reputation was on the line, and that he had <u>to cobble together</u>[6] a plan quickly. He started <u>to pitch</u>[7] his plan to Ted. "Now, Ted, we have to conduct a quick <u>operation</u>[8] to fix this problem. It may not be legal, per se, but it will be fine as long as no one else finds out. Ted smiled. He knew Bernie was too smart to ever get caught.

1. As it is used in this sentence, "futures" most nearly means
   A. time to come
   B. commodities
   C. tomorrows
   D. fortunes

2. As it is used in this sentence, "grave" most nearly means
   A. a rectangular hole in the ground
   B. death
   C. serious
   D. earthy

3. As it is used in this sentence, "channel" most nearly means
   A. a connecting body of water
   B. a part of a cable package
   C. a medium of communication
   D. a component of circuitry

4. Which of the following alternatives to the underlined portion would be least acceptable?
   A. warning against
   B. abstaining from
   C. refusing to
   D. ceasing from

5. As it is used in this sentence, "market" most nearly means
   A. bazaar
   B. advertising
   C. a system involving the selling and buying of shares
   D. a gathering of craftsmen

6. Which of the following alternatives to the underlined portion would be least acceptable?
   A. to put together
   B. to create
   C. to think of
   D. to repair

7. As it is used in this sentence, "to pitch" most nearly means
   A. to sing
   B. to tar
   C. to throw a ball
   D. to propose

8. Which of the following alternatives to the word "operation" would be least acceptable in this sentence?
   A. activity
   B. action
   C. surgery
   D. mission

1)B 2)C 3)A 4)A 5)C 6)D 7)D 8)C

TONE of Voice

Most words and sentences are <u>objective</u> or <u>neutral,</u> and a good scientific article or objective piece of writing should not reveal the writer's feelings or attitude towards the subject. Always check if the test states a fact or an opinion.

The grass is green.	(Neutral)
The classroom is quiet.	(Neutral)
I had a math test today.	(Neutral)
My uncle is coming tomorrow.	(Neutral)

However, many authors have a POINT OF VIEW (either positive or negative) or ATTITUDE towards a topic that they show through the use of particular words that are <u>subjective</u> or <u>biased</u>. Often, their attitude towards a topic is the reason why they wrote the article. They want to persuade the reader about their point of view. This property in literature is called TONE.

The grass is not green enough.	(Critical)
The classroom is suspiciously quiet.	(Distrust)
I don't think I passed my math test today.	(Disappointed)
My uncle is finally coming tomorrow.	(Joyful)

Tip: The TONE of an article can often be deduced from the author's use of adjectives and adverbs.

The great Republic of Mexico lies south of the United States.	(Pride)
The stupid referee called a penalty kick in the final minutes of the game.	(Upset)
This was, unfortunately, my last day in this office.	(Regretful)

Tip: You can infer the TONE from the use of verbs.

I soared through that psychology exam.	(Content)
That English course rocked!	(Enthusiastic)
I would like to be able to juggle someday.	(Hopeful)

Tip: The TONE of an article can be deduced from metaphors and analogies.

I thought that studying for Organic Chemistry would be a walk in the park.	(Cynical)
That guy looked like Hercules.	(Flattering)
You have the brain of a cheese sandwich!	(Condescending)

Tip: The TONE of an article is inferred from the text. (See page 353.) Therefore, if you think the author has a particular view, there should be <u>evidence</u> of that view in the text.

A typical ACT trick is to mention an answer that contains two tones, one of them very evident.

Tip: If the answer includes the word "<u>and</u>", both parts of the answer have to be correct.

Example: The tone of the information on this page was

A. questioning and informative	(There are no questions on this page.)
B. loving and persuasive	(No verbs or adjective indicate love.)
C. ecstatic and encouraging	(The word "ecstatic" is too extreme for this page.)
D. insightful and instructive	(Correct)

Tone of Voice - Exercise

Exercise 1: Create a sentence that has a certain tone of voice hidden in the message.
Use verbs, adjectives, adverbs, analogies, metaphors, etc.
Try several words from each row in the list below.

Exercise 2: Rewrite the sentences from Exercise 1 in an objective tone.

Example: 1. I worry that I cannot write that paper in time. (Nervous)
2. The paper may be submitted past the due date. (Neutral)

Example: 1. Those politicians don't know anything. (Exasperated)
2. Those politicians asked many questions. (Neutral)

Tone Of Voice Examples

angry	desperate	humorous	questioning
apathetic	disappointed	hurt	romantic
apologetic	disgusted	inquisitive	sad
appreciative	ecstatic	instructive	sarcastic
arrogant	encouraging	ironic	soothing
calm	enthusiastic	joyful	surprised
cheerful	excited	loud	sweet
condescending	fearful	loving	sympathetic
confused	friendly	nervous	tired
content	happy	persuasive	uninterested
contradictory	harsh	pleading	upset
cynical	humble	proud	wistful

How to Find the Main Idea

Summarize the Passage

Tip: To find the MAIN IDEA of a passage, look at the central topics of the paragraphs.
Each paragraph is a separate part of the story and has a central topic. This topic keeps a paragraph together. (If the writer wants to address a different topic, he or she would start a new paragraph)
The MAIN IDEA of the essay is the combination of the central topics of its paragraphs.
Before looking at the answers, summarize the <u>whole</u> passage in one sentence.
Questions look like this: "If the author had wanted to write about _____, would this essay do the job?"

Tip: A typical ACT trap is to claim the main idea is about one vivid detail that is not addressed in any of the other paragraphs.

Summarize Each Paragraph.

Tip: To summarize a paragraph, look for one or two ideas that all sentences have in common.
Before looking at the answers, summarize the whole paragraph in one or two words.
Then verify: Are all (or most) sentences about this main idea?
If a sentence in a paragraph focuses on another idea, it is often redundant.
This strategy comes handy in the English section: "At this point, the writer is considering adding _____".

Find Repetitive Themes or Ideas

Another way to look for the main idea is to look for a repetition of themes.

Tip: If you read through a paragraph and you have no idea how to summarize it because there is so much information, start looking for repeated words, phrases, ideas or similar ideas.

Watch out for Traps

Tip: The ACT likes to trap you by suggesting a main idea that is too limited.
The idea might be dominant in one paragraph, but not in ALL paragraphs.

Tip: The ACT likes to trap you by suggesting a main idea that is too broad.
If a story is about a student's graduation, the main idea is not "his life." If the story is about a student's math class, the main story is not about "her education."

Select your Final Answer

What should you do if two or more answers sound right?

Tip: Reread the question.
Frequently, a hint is given in the question that eliminates the last of your answer choices. Read the question word for word.

Tip: Reverse the main idea questions to check your answer.
If you wrote about the boy's life, would the essay just focus on his graduation?
If the essay was about the girl's education, why would the essay only talk about her math class?

Trigger Words

Trigger words are the steering wheel of each paragraph. They determine which way the story advances. Is the author going back and forth between two perspectives? Has the author given lots of examples to support a statement? Does the author jump back in time to show historical evidence?

 Tip: Mark trigger words so they stand out when you read a passage. Learn to recognize them.

Read the following words and determine how they influence the rest of the setnence. Do these words OPPOSE/CHANGE the first part of the sentence, or do they SUPPORT it?

Trigger word	Oppose/Support?	Trigger word	Oppose/Support?	
:		;		S-S/O
Accordingly		After all		S-S
Although		And		O-S
Anyhow		Additionally		S-S
As a result		Because		S-S
But		Besides		O-S
Despite		Consequently		O-S
Ergo		Due to		S-S
Furthermore		Even so		S-O
Hence		However		S-O
In fact		In conclusion		S-S
Ironically		In spite of		O-O
Moreover		Nevertheless		S-O
Nonetheless		Notwithstanding		O-O
On the contrary		On the other hand		O-O
Rather		Regardless		O-O
Since		So		S-S
Still		Therefore		O-S
Though		Thus		O-S
Unfortunately		While		O-O
When		Yet		S-O

See the answers on the right side of the page. O = Oppose; S = Support.

READING
PART III -
THE ANSWERS

Use the reading tips in this section to enhance your reading skills.

Don't read for information; read for precision.

Become familiar with the types of distractors in the ACT.

Fake Answers

Extreme Answers

Switched Answers

General Answers

After reading the question, formulate your own answer before you look at the multiple-choice options.

Cross off the answers that you can clearly eliminate.

If you are left with two answers, reread the question.

The Fake

Fake answers LOOK good, but if you check out the tiny details, you'll find that they are not the "real thing". The ACT is a test in which you have to pay attention to every word. Go over each answer with a fine-toothed comb and determine if <u>every part</u> of the sentence is correct. Don't let anyone sell you a fake; check every detail of a sentence: the beginning, the end, and especially suspicious words such as "and" and "of."

Tip: Mostly we read for **information**. *Practice so you learn to read for* **precision** *as well.*

Tip: Read like a lawyer!

AND

One word that is often neglected is the word "AND".

Tip: Split the answer into two separate statements, and verify if each one is independently correct.

Example: Albert Einstein was a nice and intelligent man, right? (We know he was intelligent, but where did it state that he was nice?)

Example: The capital of a state is the city that has the most people and that houses the government. (Only the last half is correct)

Example: Today, the teacher and the students were learning about Napoleon's wife, Josephine. (Was the teacher learning as well?)

OF

The ACT frequently uses the tiny word "OF" to deflect the meaning of an answer.
If the question asks about the final <u>will</u> OF an eccentric millionaire, make sure you pick the answer that talks about the millionaire's <u>will</u>, not about her nephew, the millionaire herself, her signature, or her family.

Tip: Underline the key word in the questions and the answers.

Example: What was the most interesting fact about the millionaire's <u>will</u>?
- **A.** Only her <u>nephew</u> knew beforehand that the millionaire had left a will.
- **B.** The <u>signature</u> of the will had to be verified by the accountant and an independent investigator.
- **C.** The <u>millionaire's family</u> had traveled from six different continents to hear about her will.
- **D.** The <u>document</u> caused consternation among the millionaire's family members.

(Underline the word <u>will</u> in the question. Only Answer D talks about the will.)

Small Changes

The ACT is very good in changing a fact from the text oh-so-slightly to make it 100% wrong.
Read carefully.

Example: Standing in the kitchen, my mother was covered in flour as she talked on the telephone with her travel agency because she wanted to book a flight to Italy.

FAKE Answers: My mother booked a trip to Italy. (No. She wanted to.)
The kitchen was covered in flour. (No. My mother was.)
My mother was in the kitchen with a book. (No. Book is a verb in the story, not a noun.)
My mother wanted to go to Italy. (No. The flight could have been for her daughter.)
The travel agency booked a flight to Italy for my mother. (No. We do not know that.)
My mother was covered in flowers. (No. Although the word "flower" sounds the same, it has a different meaning.)

Distractors - Quiz 1: The Fake

The actual instruction given to the children by the father would vary with his own education and at best be subject to all sorts of interruptions due to his private business or his public duties. We find that this embarrassment was appreciated in very early times, and that it was customary for a father who happened to have among his slaves one competent to give the needed instruction, to turn over to him the actual teaching of the children. It must be remembered that slaves taken in war were often much better educated than their Roman masters. Not all households, however, would include a competent teacher, and it would seem only natural for the fortunate owner of such a slave to receive into his house at fixed hours of the day the children of his friends and neighbors to be taught together with his own.

For this privilege, he might charge a fee for his own benefit, as we are told that Cato actually did, or he might allow the slave to retain as his property the little presents given him by his pupils in lieu of direct payment. The next step, one taken in times too early to be accurately fixed, was to select for the school a more convenient place than a private house, one that was central and easily accessible, and to receive as pupils all who could pay the modest fee that was demanded. To these schools, girls as well as boys were admitted, but girls came usually of families who preferred to educate their daughters in the privacy of their own homes and could afford to do so. The exceptions to this rule were so few, that from this point we may consider the education of boys alone.

FROM *THE PRIVATE LIFE OF THE ROMANS*, BY HAROLD WHETSTONE JOHNSTON

Make sure that every word in each answer is correct, not just the general meaning. Cross off the answers that are incorrect.

1. According to the passage
   A. slaves were competent teachers, and they might charge a fee for their own benefit.
   B. slaves taken in war were much better educated than their Roman masters.
   C. households included a competent slave, who could instruct the children, including the children of friends and neighbors.
   D. owners of educated slaves indirectly started the first school system in Rome.

2. According to the passage
   A. all Roman girls came from families who preferred to educate their daughters in the privacy of their own homes and could afford to do so.
   B. both girls and boys were taught in public schools, as long as they could pay the fee that was demanded.
   C. except for a few exceptions, girls were taught in public schools.
   D. except for a few exceptions, girls came usually of families who preferred to educate their daughters in the privacy of their own homes.

1) A) Wrong: ~~Some~~ slaves were competent teachers, b) wrong: ~~Often,~~ slaves taken in war were much better educated, c) wrong: ~~some~~ households included a competent slave, => D is correct

2) A) wrong: girls that went to school came usually from rich families, not all Roman girls; C) wrong: (switch) for a few exceptions, girls were taught in private circumstances. D) Read this literally. It states that most *girls* come from rich families, not girls *in roman schools* => B is correct

The Switch

A great way for the ACT to come up with wrong answers is switching items.

Switching People

Sometimes the answer mentions two people performing an action, while only one did it.
It is easy to mix up the people in a story that you read just once, especially if the names are unusual.
Because you do not have time to reread the article, you have to anticipate this distractor.

 *Tip: Make it a habit to **circle names**.*

Example: In front of the owner of the paper, Joshua Stuart, the editor-in-chief Josiah told the freelancer that the deadline had passed.

    A. The editor told Josiah that the deadline had passed.
    B. Joshua told the editor that the deadline had passed.
    C. Josiah heard from the freelancer that the deadline had passed.
    D. The freelancer heard from Josiah that the deadline had passed.

Switching the Order of Events

 Often, ACT answers use the exact words from the text, but not in the right order.
Tip: Watch out for words like before, earlier, already, previously, until that time, first, last, former, preceding, after, next, prior, later, etc.

Example: Until he discovered Lego blocks, my son's favorite toy was a red fire truck. It had eight wheels and an extension ladder. My son took it everywhere and parked it on the dining room table when he ate his meals. He wanted to be a fire-fighter in the future.

    What is the favorite toy of the author's son?
    A. A red firetruck   (Incorrect)
    B. Lego's   (Correct)

Example: Barack Obama was the president of the United States of America. Before that, he was an Illinois senator, and prior to that, he taught at the University of Chicago Law School.
Answer choice A: The article states that Obama first was a president, then he was a senator, and then he taught law at the University of Chicago. (Incorrect)

See how the answer mimics the text, but misconstrues the order of the events?

Switching Cause and Effect

Example: Because I ate only three Cheerios this morning, I was not very hungry.

Your brain makes a connection between the two events. After all, not being hungry and eating only three Cheerios go very well together. However, your brain does not always register HOW these two events are related. Therefore, you have to rephrase the sentence to verify: I ate only three Cheerios, and that resulted in my not being hungry? If I ate only three Cheerios, I should be hungry. Let's reverse the statement. Because I was not very hungry, I ate only three Cheerios. That makes a lot more sense.

 Tip: Be aware of cause and effect answers, and verify the logic between the two parts.

Distractors - Quiz 2: The Switch

The battle of Chancellorsville marked the zenith of Confederate good fortune. Immediately afterward, in June, 1863, Lee led the victorious army of Northern Virginia onward into Pennsylvania. The South was now the invader, not the invaded, and its heart beat proudly with hopes of success; however, these hopes went down in bloody wreck on July 4, when word was sent to the world that the high valor of Virginia had failed at last on the field of Gettysburg, and that, just before in the far West, Vicksburg had been taken by the army of the "silent soldier."

At Gettysburg, Lee had under him some seventy thousand men, and his opponent, Meade, about ninety thousand. Both armies were composed mainly of seasoned veterans, trained to the highest point by campaign after campaign and battle after battle; and there was nothing to choose between them as to the fighting power of the rank and file. The Union Army was the larger, yet most of the time it stood on the defensive; for the difference between the generals, Lee and Meade, was greater than could be bridged by twenty thousand men. For three days the battle raged. No other battle of recent time has been so obstinate and so bloody. The victorious Union army lost a greater percentage in killed and wounded than the allied armies of England, Germany, and the Netherlands lost at Waterloo the year before. Four of its seven corps suffered each a greater relative loss than befell the world-renowned British infantry on the day that saw the doom of the French emperor. The defeated Confederates at Gettysburg lost, relatively, as many men as the defeated French at Waterloo; but whereas the French army became a mere rabble, Lee withdrew his formidable soldiery with their courage unbroken, and their fighting power only diminished by their actual losses in the field.

FROM *HERO TALES FROM AMERICAN HISTORY*, BY HENRY CABOT LODGE AND THEODORE ROOSEVELT

1. The battle of Chancellorsville took place
   A. before June, 1863.
   B. in June, 1863.
   C. between June, 1863, and July 4, 1863.
   D. on July 4, 1863.

2. The article does not mention Lee's involvement in
   A. Vicksburg.
   B. Gettysburg.
   C. Chancellorsville.
   D. Pennsylvania.

3. The correct order of the battles is:
   A. Chancellorsville, Vicksburg, Waterloo, Gettysburg.
   B. Chancellorsville, Waterloo, Vicksburg, Gettysburg.
   C. Waterloo, Gettysburg, Chancellorsville, Vicksburg.
   D. Waterloo, Chancellorsville, Vicksburg, Gettysburg.

1) C 2) A 3) D

The Extreme

In our daily language, we often use words that are extremes, when we *technically* just want to indicate a general tendency. "Teenagers never shake hands anymore these days." "Why do you always have to argue with me?" "All of the kids in my school are smarter than I." "There is no food left in the house."

It is just easier to use this type of language rather than going into details or percentages. It has become so common, that we do not even notice when these words are used incorrectly in the ACT.

The ACT, however, is **very** precise in its use of language. It would never use extreme words unless they are backed up by the text. (*"Nobody has ever set foot on Mars before."*)

The ACT **does** use these words in the answer choices in order to make them 100% incorrect. If you miss any of your reference questions, you might have fallen for this trap.

👀 *Tip: Extremes in the answers are most always wrong, unless they can be backed up by the text. They are wrong because they are debatable. If you can think of ONE exception, that makes the answer incorrect.*

Examples: All students enjoy studying for the ACT.
You will never have a boring moment when you read this book.
No one can get a perfect score on this test.

Safe words to use:

- Might
- Could
- May
- Can

- Some
- Possible
- Usually
- Sometimes

- At least once
- Frequently

Words to avoid:

- Always
- Never
- At no time
- Positively

- All
- Absolutely
- Every
- Most

- Invariably so
- Completely
- Totally
- Perfect

Tone

👀 *Tip: You can spot extreme language by looking at the tone of the sentence.*
If you study your formulas, you will get a higher score on your ACT.
People who like to buy used cars, must also like to buy second-hand clothing.

Plurals

👀 *Tip: You can spot extreme language by looking for plurals.*
In 1968, the London Bridge was sold to an American entrepreneur. The bridge was taken apart and each piece was meticulously numbered. The bridge was then reconstructed over the Bridgewater Channel in Missouri. The London City Council received $ 2,460,000 from the proceeds of the bridge.

What was the topic of the paragraph above?
A. Bridges   (Incorrect. The article only talks about ONE bridge.)
B. A landmark   (Correct. Not my first choice, but not a wrong answer.)

Distractors - Quiz 3: The Extreme

Answers with extreme words are often easily proven wrong, unless they are backed up by the text. "All girls like chocolate." This statement is false if even one girl in the world does not like chocolate. "Nobody has ever set foot on Mars." This statement is correct as long as it can be backed up by science. Even non-negotiable statements like "if you read this book you will get a higher score on your next test" should be treated like an extreme: "you WILL get a higher score" is an unconditional statement.

Check the following answers for extremes that are NOT in the text.

The Civil War has left, as all wars of brother against brother must leave, terrible and heartrending memories; but there remains as an offset the glory which has accrued to the nation by the countless deeds of heroism performed by both sides in the struggle. The captains and the armies that, after long years of dreary campaigning and bloody, stubborn fighting, brought the war to a close, have left us more than a reunited realm. North and South, all Americans, now have a common fund of glorious memories. We are the richer for each grim campaign, for each hard-fought battle. We are the richer for valor displayed alike by those who fought so valiantly for the right, and by those who, no less valiantly, fought for what they deemed the right. We have in us nobler capacities for what is great and good because of the infinite woe and suffering, and because of the splendid ultimate triumph. We hold that it was vital to the welfare, not only of our people on this continent, but of the whole human race, that the Union should be preserved and slavery abolished; that one flag should fly from the Great Lakes to the Rio Grande; that we should all be free in fact as well as in name, and that the United States should stand as one nation—the greatest nation on the earth. But we recognize gladly that, South as well as North, when the fight was once on, the leaders of the armies, and the soldiers whom they led, displayed the same qualities of daring and steadfast courage, of disinterested loyalty and enthusiasm, and of high devotion to an ideal.

FROM *HERO TALES FROM AMERICAN HISTORY,* BY HENRY CABOT LODGE AND THEODORE ROOSEVELT

1. The author states in this article that
   A. all wars leave terrible and heartrending memories.
   B. all civil wars accrue countless deeds of heroism.
   C. all Americans have a common fund of glorious memories.
   D. all battles in the Civil War were hard-fought.

2. The author mentions that
   A. only one flag should fly across the United States.
   B. only the Civil War has left us terrible and heartrending memories.
   C. only bloody and stubborn fighting brought the war to close.
   D. only the leaders of the armies and the soldiers that they led displayed daring and steadfast courage.

3. The essay states that the United States is
   A. the country with the most courageous soldiers and leaders.
   B. the greatest nation on earth.
   C. the country with the most glorious history.
   D. the country with the most terrible memories.

1) C 2) A 3) B

The General

Each incorrect answer in the ACT must be 100% wrong. Still, many times we look at two or more answers and they all appear correct. Even when we check the information in the original text (a time-consuming procedure) we notice that several answers are still correct, which should be impossible on the ACT.

What should you do if more than one answer appear to be correct?
1) Read the <u>answers</u> word for word, to find small errors caused by extremes, fakes or switches.
2) Read the <u>question</u> word for word to find out what exactly the ACT is asking.
3) Be precise in your reasoning. Do not think about the **GENERAL** description, but the exact one.

Tip: Make it a habit to underline the key word in each question. It will save you time, avoid needless back-and-forth checking, and provide clarity in your process of eliminating wrong answers.

*Tip: Often, the ACT uses an answer that is straight from the text. In **GENERAL**, this is a correct statement, but it may not answer the question.*

Tip: The ACT frequently <u>paraphrases</u> the information from the text to hide the correct answer and uses <u>literal parts</u> from the text to make the wrong answers appear more attractive.

Sometimes, the ACT uses words to make you think that a **GENERAL** answer would be acceptable. However, you need to be precise in your language: ignore the parts in bold of the following statements:

The author would <u>most likely</u> agree with which of the following statements?

The first paragraph <u>primarily</u> serves to:

In line 20, 'dark' <u>most nearly</u> means:

Assumptions (See page 353)

The park was busy that day. Old people were on their daily stroll. A lady sat on a bench feeding a baby while a girl was jogging on the path in front of her. A family had a picnic on a blanket; the mom was pouring the drinks while the dad cut the vegetables for the little ones.

Because we like to make sense of the information in the text, we often fill in the gaps. We assume that the girl who jogs though the park enjoys it. **GENERALLY**, that could be true, but it could be that her mother, the team coach, makes her do it.

We assume that "the lady feeding the baby" is mother of the child, while there is no evidence that this is true. (It could be an aunt or a babysitter.) Be precise in your language. Be picky about your words

Feel-Good Answers

Wrong answers are often "feel-good, general answers" without direct evidence in the text, for example "the parents on the blanket loved their children." We assume this is true in **GENERAL**, but watch out! The questions in the ACT state "according to the passage," and it may not state in the text that the parents loved their children.

*Tip: It is a **reading** test. Be conscious of what part you actually read and what part of the story you filled in yourself.*

Distractors - Quiz 4: The General

General answers tend to quote the text almost word for word. They are correct statements but they do not answer the question. Make it a habit to underline the most important of each question to focus on the aspect that you are looking for in the answer.

Tasmania is an island rich in beautiful scenery — *extremely* beautiful all Australians tell you. Its mountain-ranges culminate in the lofty peaks of the Cradle Mountain, Ben Lomond, and Mount Humboldt. It is clothed with forests, in which the gum-trees attain to an extraordinary height. The climate is perfect, with a clear atmosphere and cool breeze, so that Tasmania has come to be the great sanatorium of Australia. When the heat of the summer declares itself in Melbourne and Sydney, there is a general exodus to Tasmania, and Hobart is vibrant during its season of three months. It seemed to me as if the Australians must be rather pushed to it for a watering-place if they make Hobart their principal one.

1. The writer gives the following description of Tasmania:
   A. In the heat of the summer, there is a general exodus from Melbourne and Sydney to Tasmania.
   B. Tasmania consists of the lofty peaks of the Cradle Mountain, Ben Lomond, and Mount Humboldt.
   C. Tasmania has become the great sanatorium of Australia.
   D. Hobart is vibrant during Tasmania's season of three months.

The hotel rooms are damp and cellar-like, with whitewashed walls, and the barest amount of furniture. Dressing is a lengthy process, when you have to divide your toilette between a brick-floored bath-room, and a dressing-room with one mirror and a chair, and a bedroom equally dismal. Moreover, they are built solely with regard to the heat, and in the cold nights and frosty mornings you suffer bitterly from the draught of air-traps from skylights in the roof, and doors and windows that refuse, and are never intended, to close tightly.

2. The author gives the following description of the hotel rooms:
   A. In the cold nights, you suffer from the bitter draughts of air-traps.
   B. They are draughty and built with regard to the heat.
   C. The bathroom floor is brick and the bedroom floor is equally dismal.
   D. The doors and the windows refuse to close tightly.

Mr. Lance, with his brother, has a 120,000-acre farm on which he runs 70,000 merino sheep. The sheep are managed by an overseer and six shepherds, all Highlanders. Except for the stud sheep, the flocks are rarely seen from one shearing-time to another, living out on the hills, on the tussock-grass, which gives them excellent pasture. The house was a small lodge, with an Italian fountain in front, which looked singularly out of place, facing towards the range called the Black Hills. There was a thick plantation of tall Scotch firs and eucalypti growing round the house as a shelter from the fierce winds that blow across these exposed plains.

3. The article gives the best description of the farm in which sentence?
   A. Mr. Lance ….. merino sheep.
   B. Except … pasture
   C. The house …. Black Hills
   D. There was ….. exposed plains.

FROM *FORTY THOUSAND MILES OVER LAND AND WATER* BY ETHEL VINCENT

1) C. Underline Tasmania in the question. Answer A talks about the exodus and answer D talks about Hobart. Answer B is incorrect; there is much more to Tasmania than these three mountain tops.

2) B. Underline hotel rooms in the question. Answer A talks about walls and the skylights. Answer C talks about the floor and D talks about the doors and the windows. 3) D

Reading Tips - What To Do

The Text

1. Time is of the essence! Always time yourself when your practice for the ACT. It will become a habit to monitor your time, and you will then be able to use this skill effectively on test day.
2. Read actively. Underline key points; it helps to draw your eyes to particular information in the text. Write one-word summaries next to the paragraph to impress the idea in your memory.
3. Do not skip the italicized introduction to the long passages. They contain important information that helps with the questions.
4. Focus on the main story line in the passages, not the details. Look for cause and effect, and contrasts. Look for trigger words ("therefore", "however", "since", "but".) Mark these elements by connecting them with arrows.
5. Mark where the author states an opinion, not a fact. Many questions pivot around the author's viewpoint.

The Questions

6. Underline the precise part of the question.
7. If a question is about a detail, it often states "According to the text" or "as stated in line 52". Just put your finger on the exact spot to see how it fits in the big picture. To better understand the context, make sure you read the sentence that comes before as well.
8. For vocabulary words, do not look at the answers! Look at the sentence in the text. Cover the answers and make up your own word that would best fill in the blank. THEN look at the answers to find the best match.
9. For main idea questions, make sure that your main idea is about the ALL of the paragraphs, not just about one or some of them.
10. For the purpose questions, make sure ALL of the sentences in the paragraph are about that purpose, not just one of them.
11. Inference questions, remember that "to infer" means to draw a conclusion based on evidence. Students often jump to unfounded conclusions.

Answers:

12. Stick to facts FROM THE TEXT ONLY. Do not let your personal knowledge interfere.
13. Evidence has to be presented in the text to support your inference.
14. Be very precise in your reasoning. You might not find the exact words in the text, but the answer has to fit the passage 100% without exception.
15. Find one exception to the argument in the answer to disprove a certain answer.
16. Watch out for distractors such as plurals, switches or extreme language.
17. Physically cross out all answers that you can disprove. If you have to look back, you might have time to look at two possible choices, not all four.
18. If in doubt between two answers, refer to the question and reread it for clues. ("According to the *last paragraph.*" "*Before* he went on his trip, the author wanted," etc.) Underlining helps.

READING TEST 1

35 minutes - 40 questions

4 passages:

Prose Fiction

Social Science

Humanities

Natural Science

Reading Passage Test 1-1 (Prose Fiction)

From <u>The Wizard's Son</u>
by Margaret Oliphant

When Walter seated himself beside Oona in the boat, and Hamish pushed off from the beach, there fell upon both these young people a sensation of quiet and relief for which one of
5   them at least found it very difficult to account. It had turned out a very still afternoon. The heavy rains were over, the clouds broken up and dispersing, with a sort of sullen stillness, like a defeated army making off in dull haste, yet not
10 without a stand here and there, behind the mountains. The loch was dark and still, all hushed after the sweeping blasts of rain, but black with the reflections of gloom from the sky. There was a sense of safety, of sudden quiet, of escape, in
15 that sensation of pushing off, away from all passion and agitation upon this still sea of calm. Why Oona, who feared no one, who had no painful thoughts or associations to flee from, should have felt this she could not tell. The sense
20 of interest in, and anxiety for, the young man by her side was altogether different. That was sympathetic and definable; but the sensation of relief was something more. She looked at him with a smile and sigh of ease as she gathered the
25 strings of the rudder into her hands.

"I feel," she said, "as if I were running away, and had got safe out of reach; though there is nobody pursuing me that I know of," she added, with a faint laugh of satisfaction.

30 The wind blew the end of the white wrapper round her throat towards her companion, and he caught it as she had caught the rudder ropes.

"It is I that am pursued," he said, "and
35 have escaped. I have a feeling that I am safe here. The kind water, and the daylight, and you—but how should you feel it? It must have gone from my mind to yours."

"The water does not look so very kind,"
40 said Oona, "except that it separates us from the annoyances that are on land—when there are annoyances."

She had never known any that were more than the troubles of a child before.

45 "There is this that makes it kind. If you were driven beyond bearing, a plunge down there and all would be over——"

"Lord Erradeen!"

"Oh, I don't mean to try. I have no
50 thought of trying; but look how peaceful, how deep, all liquid blackness! It might go down to the mystic center of the earth for anything one knows."

He leant over a little, looking down into
55 those depths profound which were so still that the boat seemed to cut through a surface which had solidity; and in doing this put the boat out of trim, and elicited a growl from Hamish.

It seemed to Oona, too, as if there was
60 something seductive in that profound liquid depth, concealing all that sought refuge there. She put out her hand and grasped his arm in the thrill of this thought.

"Oh, don't look down," she said. "I have
65 heard of people being caught, in spite of themselves, by some charm in it." The movement was quite involuntary and simple; but, on second thoughts, Oona drew away her hand, and blushed a little. "Besides, you put the boat out of trim,"
70 she said.

"If I should ever be in deadly danger," said Walter, with the seriousness which had been in his face all along, "will you put out your hand like that, without reflection, and save me?"

75 Oona tried to laugh again; but it was not easy; his seriousness gained upon her, in spite of herself.

"I think we are talking nonsense, and feeling nonsense; for it seems to me as if we had
80 escaped from something. Now Hamish is pleased; the boat is trimmed. Don't you think," she said, with an effort to turn off graver subjects, "that it is a pity those scientific people who can do everything should not tunnel down through
85 that center of the earth you were speaking of, straight through to the other side of the world? Then we might be dropped through to Australia without any trouble."

GO ON TO THE NEXT PAGE

1. The *defeated army* (line 9) refers to
   A. the rains.
   B. the clouds.
   C. the mountains.
   D. the sensation of quiet and relief.

2. The word *reflection* in line 74 nearly means
   A. image.
   B. likeness.
   C. thought.
   D. evidence.

3. It can be inferred from the text that
   A. both Oona and Walter escaped from something.
   B. Oona escaped from something, but both Oona and Walter felt they did.
   C. Walter escaped from something, but both Oona and Walter felt they did.
   D. Oona and Walter did not really escape from something, but they felt as if they did.

4. In line 49, with the words *"Oh, I don't mean to try"*, the young man in the boat is referring to
   A. swimming in the water.
   B. committing suicide.
   C. going to the center of the earth.
   D. going back to the troubles on the land.

5. It can be inferred from the text that there are how many people on the boat?
   A. 2
   B. 3
   C. 4
   D. More than 4

6. All of the following are mentioned in this story EXCEPT
   A. a feeling of relief.
   B. a feeling of safety.
   C. a feeling of shame.
   D. a feeling of nonsense.

7. The author uses the description of the loch, *"The loch was dark and still ... from the sky."* (lines 11 – 13) in order to draw a parallel to
   A. the feelings of safety and calmness of the main characters, while they remain aware of trouble ahead.
   B. Oona's sense of safety and her interest in the young man next to her.
   C. Walter's separation from his troubles on the land and his reflections on the gloom from the sky.
   D. the stillness of the people in the boat and how they both reflect on their dark pasts.

8. The passage states that Oona had
   A. grown up around the loch.
   B. had been pursued and recently escaped.
   C. grown up in a worry-free environment.
   D. wants to dig a tunnel through the center of the earth and move to Australia.

9. Walter's dialogue includes elements of
   A. wonder and relief.
   B. relief and annoyance.
   C. passion and wonder.
   D. feeling safe and falling in love.

10. The passage can be summarized as follows:
    A. All of the people in the boat are being pursued and the dialogue is about their feelings of relief and safety.
    B. The people in the boat are about to return to land where they will face an unnamed enemy, yet being together gives them comfort.
    C. Lord Erradeen is being pursued, while his subjects, Walter and Oona, exchange feelings of gloom and wonder.
    D. Oona and Walter both feel pursued and reflect on their feelings, which stem from being away on the water.

GO ON TO THE NEXT PAGE

Reading Passage Test 1-2 (Social Science)

Adapted from: <u>The Invention Of Printing</u>
by Theodore Low De Vinne

Engraving must be regarded as the first process in every method of printing. The impression of engraved forms on metal and wax, for the purpose of making coins and seals, is of great antiquity, having been practiced more than three thousand years ago, by people with a skill that cannot be surpassed in modern times. There are old Egyptian seals with faces of such minute delicacy that the fineness of the workmanship can be fully perceived only with the aid of a magnifying glass. There are coins from Macedonia that are stamped in a relief as bold as that of the best pieces of modern mints.

In Babylonia and Assyria, engraved forms were printed or stamped on clay that was specially prepared for this purpose. In the ruins of the ancient edifices of these primeval nations there is scarcely a stone or a kiln-burnt brick without an inscription or a stamp upon it. The inscriptions on stone appear to have been cut with a chisel, after the usual method of stonecutters; however, the stamps on the bricks were made from engravings on wood or by the separate impressions of some pointed instrument.

The characters on the Babylonian bricks are much more neatly executed than would seem necessary for inscriptions on so common a material as clay. But they are really coarse when compared with the inscriptions upon the small cylinders of clay which were used by the Assyrians for the preservation of their public documents. Historians have found a small six-sided Assyrian cylinder that contains sixty lines of minute characters which could be read only by the aid of a magnifying glass.

The clay was prepared for writing as well as for stamping. The Priests in Babylonia kept their astronomical observations on tiles that were subsequently baked in a furnace. Four large piles of tablets of unburned clay were found in the library or hall of records in the town of Assurbanipal. Some of the tablets are the grammars and primers of the language; some are records of agreements to sell property or slaves; some are filled with astronomical or astrological predictions. On one of them was inscribed the Assyrian version of the deluge.

The clay cylinders contained the memorials which were then considered as of most value, such as the proclamations of the king, or the laws of the empire. In the museum of the East India Company is the fragment of a clay cylinder which contains a portion of the decrees or annals of Nebuchadnezzar. For perpetuating records of this nature, the cylinders were admirably adapted. They were convenient for reference, and their legibility, after so long an exposure, shows that they were perfectly durable.

We do not know by what considerations Assyrian rulers were governed when about to choose between engraving or writing on clay; but it is not unreasonable to assume that the inscription was written or cut on the clay when one copy only of a record was wanted; if numerous copies were wanted, a die or an engraving on wood was manufactured, from which these copies were molded. No surer method of securing exact copies of an original could have been devised among a people that did not use ink and paper. These cylinders are examples of printing in its most elementary form.

This method of printing in clay was rude and imperfect, but, to some extent, it did the work of modern typography. Writings were published at small expense, and records were preserved for ages without the aid of ink or paper. The modern printer may wonder why this skill in printing was not further developed. The engraving that was used to impress clay could have been coated with ink and stamped on parchment. Simple as this application of the engraving may appear, it was never made. So far from receiving any improvement, the art of printing in clay gradually fell into disuse. It has been neglected for more than twenty-five centuries on the soil where it probably originated.

GO ON TO THE NEXT PAGE

11. The tone of the author throughout the article can best be described as
    A. agitated.
    B. wistful.
    C. awestruck.
    D. skeptical.

12. The word *edifices* as used in line 17 most nearly means
    A. nation states.
    B. constructions.
    C. inscriptions.
    D. boulders.

13. According to the fourth paragraph, (lines 36 – 47) tablets were used for all of the following EXCEPT
    A. legal transactions.
    B. proclamations of the king.
    C. predictions.
    D. educational materials.

14. Which of the following examples in the text can only be fully appreciated with a magnifying glass?
    A. Babylonian clay tablets
    B. Egyptian seals
    C. Macedonian coins
    D. Records in the town of Assurbanipal

15. Assyrians used cylinders
    A. to make it easier to keep records of agreements when selling slaves.
    B. to facilitate messages that were stamped on parchment.
    C. to ensure accurate replications.
    D. to preserve records of astronomical or astrological importance.

16. The word *die* in line 65 most nearly means
    A. a coloring substance.
    B. a deathly decease.
    C. a stamp.
    D. a cube used for gambling.

17. The last paragraph (line 72-86) mentions that cylinders
    A. could have been used with ink and paper.
    B. were always used with ink, but could never be used with paper.
    C. were always used with paper, but could never be used with ink.
    D. could never be used with ink or paper.

18. From the Babylonian records, it can be inferred that
    A. the priests were the only ones that practiced astrology.
    B. all Babylonians kept slaves.
    C. people consulted the central hall only for proclamations.
    D. a great importance was placed on the correctness of grammar.

19. The clay used by the Babylonians was created for
    A. writing only.
    B. stamping only.
    C. writing and stamping.
    D. writing, stamping, and dying.

20. Which of the following is true based on the passage?
    A. The inscriptions made by the Assyrians are coarse when compared to those of the Babylonians.
    B. The inscriptions made by the Babylonians are less fine when compared to those of the Assyrians.
    C. After many years, these inscriptions became unreadable.
    D. Engraving in clay is still a popular method of printing used today.

GO ON TO THE NEXT PAGE

Reading Passage Test 1-3 (Humanities)

From: <u>Navajo Silversmiths</u>
by Washington Matthews

Among the Navajo Indians there are many smiths who sometimes forge iron and brass, but who work chiefly in silver. When and how the art of working metals was introduced among
5 them I have not been able to determine; but there are many reasons for supposing that they have long possessed it; many believe that they are not indebted to the Europeans for it. Doubtless the tools obtained from American and Mexican
10 traders have influenced their art. Old white residents of the Navajo country tell me that the art has improved greatly within their recollection; that the ornaments made fifteen years ago do not compare favorably with those made at the present
15 time; and they attribute this change largely to the recent introduction of fine files and emery-paper.

At the time of the Conquest the so-called civilized tribes of Mexico had attained considerable skill in the working of metal, and it
20 has been inferred that in the same period the sedentary tribes of New Mexico also wrought at the forge. From either of these sources the first smiths among the Navajos may have learned their trade. However, those who have seen the
25 beautiful gold ornaments made by the rude Indians of British Columbia and Alaska, many of whom are allied in language to the Navajos, may doubt that the latter derived their art from a people higher in culture than themselves.

30 The appliances and processes of the smith are much the same among the Navajos as among the Pueblo Indians. But the Pueblo artisan, living in a spacious house, builds a permanent forge on a frame at such a height that he can work
35 standing, while his less fortunate Navajo confrère, dwelling in a low hut or shelter, which he may abandon any day, constructs a temporary forge on the ground in the manner hereafter described.

40 Notwithstanding the greater disadvantages under which the latter labors, the ornaments made by his hand are generally conceded to be equal or even superior to those made by the Pueblo Indian.

45 A large majority of these savage smiths make only such simple articles as buttons, rosettes, and bracelets; those who make the more elaborate articles, such as powder-chargers, round beads tobacco cases, belts, and bridle
50 ornaments are few. Tobacco cases, made in the shape of an army canteen, are made by only three or four men in the tribe, and the design is of very recent origin.

Their tools and materials are few and
55 simple. Rude as the results of their labor may appear, it is surprising that they do so well with such imperfect appliances, which usually consist of the following articles: a forge, a bellows, an anvil, crucibles, molds, tongs, scissors, pliers,
60 files, awls, cold-chisels, matrix and die for molding buttons, wooden implement used in grinding buttons, wooden stake, basin, charcoal, tools and materials for soldering (blow-pipe, braid of cotton rags soaked in grease, wire, and
65 borax), materials for polishing (sand-paper, emery-paper, powdered sandstone, sand, ashes, and solid stone), and materials for whitening (a native mineral substance—almogen—salt and water) represents the complete shop of a
70 silversmith, which was set up temporarily in a summer lodge, or hogan, near Fort Wingate. Fragments of boards, picked up around the fort, were used, in part, in the construction of the hogan, an old raisin-box was made to serve as the
75 curb or frame of the forge, and these things detracted somewhat from the aboriginal aspect of the place.

A forge built in an outhouse on my own premises by an Indian silversmith, whom I
80 employed to work where I could constantly observe him, was twenty-three inches long, sixteen inches broad, five inches in height to the edge of the fire-place, and the latter, which was bowl-shaped, was eight inches in diameter and
85 three inches deep. No other Navajo forge that I have seen differed materially in size or shape from this. The task of constructing this forge did not occupy more than an hour.

GO ON TO THE NEXT PAGE

21. According to the author, the Navajo Indians most likely gained their knowledge of working metals from
    A. the settlers of British Columbia.
    B. the Europeans.
    C. the American and Mexican traders.
    D. tribes from Mexico and New Mexico.

22. In the context of this passage, the word *rude* (line 25 and 55) most nearly means
    A. offensive.
    B. foul.
    C. uncivil.
    D. primitive.

23. The phrase *wrought at the forge* (line 21) implies that the tribes of New Mexico
    A. forged intricate metal swords.
    B. had the knowledge to make beautiful ornaments.
    C. worked with metal.
    D. had artists that worked with silver.

24. The purpose of the author's including the personal story of his own forge was
    A. to enhance his knowledge of Navajo traditions.
    B. to observe an Indian silversmith at work.
    C. to reveal that traditional methods are still employed today.
    D. to show that no Navajo forge is different in size or shape.

25. As used in line 37, the word *confrère* most nearly means
    A. dwelling or shelter.
    B. temporary forge.
    C. counterpart.
    D. competition.

26. The third paragraph (lines 40-44) implies
    A. the Pueblo Indians are superior, despite their disadvantages.
    B. the Navajo Indians are superior, despite their disadvantages.
    C. the superior ornaments are made by the Pueblo Indians, despite their disadvantages.
    D. the ornaments made by the Navajo Indians are not regarded as inferior, despite their disadvantages.

27. It can be inferred by the information in the fourth paragraph (line 45-53) that
    A. belts are not common in the Navajo society.
    B. belts are easier to make than tobacco cases.
    C. few Navajos wear belts.
    D. making belts requires more skill than making bracelets.

28. The Indians of British Columbia and Alaska
    A. were enemies of the Navajos.
    B. had the same appliances and processes as the Navajos.
    C. had excellent metal smiths.
    D. spoke the same language as the Pueblos.

29. According to the text, emery paper is used for
    A. polishing metal.
    B. constructing ornaments.
    C. adding color to the ornaments.
    D. The purpose is not mentioned in the article.

30. As used in line 74, a *hogan* is most likely
    A. a Navajo silversmith.
    B. the frame of a forge.
    C. an old raisin-box frame.
    D. a summer lodge.

GO ON TO THE NEXT PAGE

Reading Passage Test 1-4 (Natural Science)

Adapted from: <u>Textiles and Clothing</u>
by Kate Heintz Watson

Both the animal and vegetable kingdoms furnish materials for clothing as well as for all the textiles used in the home. The fleece of sheep, the hair of the goat and camel, silk, furs, and skins are
5 the chief animal products. The principal vegetable fibers are cotton, flax, ramie, jute, and hemp. Cotton, linen, wool, and silk have so far formed the foundation of all textiles and are the principal fibers used for clothing materials.

10 Cotton is the white downy covering of the seed of several species of the cotton plant. It is a native of many parts of the world. It was used in India and Pakistan 5000 years ago, and it was found by Columbus in the New World as well.

15 The value of cotton depends upon the strength and evenness of the fiber. In ordinary cotton, the individual fiber is about an inch in length. Very fine yarn can be spun from cotton because of the spiral character of the fibers. This
20 twist of the fibers is peculiar to cotton, being present in no other animal or vegetable fiber. Because of this twist, cotton cloths are much more elastic in character than those woven from linen, the fibers of which are stiff and straight.
25 Cotton does not take the darker dyes as well as animal fibers and for this reason, it does not combine satisfactorily with wool.

Wool is the most important animal fiber. Strictly speaking, the name applies only to the
30 hairy covering of sheep, but the hair of certain goats and of camels is generally classified under the same terms. Longer than a cotton fiber, the wool fiber is distinguished by its scale-like surface, which gives it its felting and spinning
35 properties. In contrast, hair has little or no scaly structure being in general a smooth filament with hardly any felting and spinning properties.

The great value of wool as a fiber lies in the fact that it is strong, elastic, soft, very susceptible
40 to dyes and, being woven, furnishes a great number of air spaces, rendering clothing made from it very warm and light.

Wool has the remarkable property of absorbing up to 30 percent or more of its weight
45 of water and yet does not feel perceptibly damp to the touch. This is called the hygroscopic moisture quality. Wool owes its superiority as a textile for winter garments and underclothing to this property.

50 Next to wool and cotton, flax is used most largely by textile manufacturers. The linen fiber consists of the cells of certain species of flax grown in Europe, Africa, and the United States. The flax plant is an annual plant and to obtain the
55 best fibers it must be gathered before it is fully ripe. Linen is one of the oldest textiles; it was used by the early Egyptians for the priests' garments and for the wrappings of mummies.

When freed from all impurities the chief
60 physical characteristics of flax are its snowy whiteness, silky luster and great tenacity. The individual fibers may be from ten to twelve inches in length; they are much greater in diameter than cotton. It is less pliant and elastic
65 than cotton and bleaches and dyes less readily. Linen cloth is a better conductor of heat than cotton and clothing made from it is cooler. When pure, it is, like cotton, nearly pure cellulose.

The silk fiber is the most perfect as well as
70 the most beautiful of all fibers. It is nearly faultless, fine and continuous, often measuring from 1000 to 4000 feet long, without a scale, joint, or a blemish. It is, however, not of the same diameter or fineness throughout its entire length,
75 as it becomes finer as the interior of the cocoon is approached. Silk differs from all other vegetable or animal fibers by being devoid of all cellular structure.

Silk, like wool, has the property of absorbing
80 considerable moisture without becoming perceptibly damp. Like wool and all the animal fibers, it is harmed by alkaline substances and solutions. The important physical properties of silk are its beautiful luster, strength, elasticity and
85 the readiness with which it takes dyes. Silk combines well with other fibers, animal and vegetable.

GO ON TO THE NEXT PAGE

31. One of the main ideas established by the passage is that
    A. the length of the fiber influences the property of the textile.
    B. silk has the longest fiber of all of the textiles discussed in the article.
    C. wool is the most popular animal fiber.
    D. plant fibers and animal fibers in the textile industry differ only in length.

32. The passage notes that cotton
    A. has fibers that are stiff and straight.
    B. is grown in every country of the world.
    C. was first discovered by Columbus in the New World.
    D. is more elastic than linen.

33. Which fact is not supported by the text?
    A. Wool is the most important animal fiber.
    B. Wool textiles are very warm.
    C. Wool is easily harmed by alkalis.
    D. Wool is devoid of all cellular structure.

34. The length of the fibers discussed in this article can be put in the following order:
    A. Silk, linen, cotton.
    B. Cotton, silk, wool.
    C. Linen, silk, cotton.
    D. Silk, cotton, linen.

35. In her comparison of wool and silk, the author states that
    A. they are the only textiles that can absorb moisture.
    B. they are both harmed by alkalis.
    C. silk has the property of absorbing water without ever becoming damp.
    D. wool is superior as a textile.

36. According to the text, the oldest plant fibers were first used by
    A. the Egyptians.
    B. people from India and Pakistan and the New World.
    C. people from Europe, Africa, and the United States.
    D. No reference to the usage of the oldest textile is made.

37. The text states that
    A. only wool has a hygroscopic moisture quality.
    B. both wool and silk have hygroscopic moisture qualities.
    C. all animal fibers have hygroscopic moisture quality.
    D. only animal fibers have hygroscopic moisture quality.

38. The author mentions goats and camels in order to
    A. emphasize that there are other animals than sheep that provide wool.
    B. illustrate that these animals are the second most important animals for the textile industry.
    C. demonstrate how they are the chief source of textile products where flax, cotton and silk are not locally grown.
    D. indicate that the fibers from these animals are used just as much as wool from sheep.

39. The characteristic of cotton that causes it to be elastic
    A. are its long fibers.
    B. is its capability to absorb moisture.
    C. is spiral character of its fibers.
    D. are the strength and evenness of its fibers.

40. The two fibers that combine the best in a textile are
    A. wool and silk.
    B. cotton and wool.
    C. linen and wool.
    D. ramie and jute.

END OF THIS TEST
STOP! DO NOT TURN THE
PAGE UNTIL TOLD TO DO SO.

Reading Test 1 - Answer Key

The Wizard's Son	The Invention of Printing	Navajo Silversmiths	Textiles and Clothing
1. **B**	11. **C**	21. **D**	31. **A**
2. **C**	12. **B**	22. **D**	32. **D**
3. **C**	13. **B**	23. **C**	33. **D**
4. **B**	14. **B**	24. **C**	34. **A**
5. **B**	15. **C**	25. **C**	35. **B**
6. **C**	16. **C**	26. **D**	36. **D**
7. **A**	17. **A**	27. **D**	37. **B**
8. **C**	18. **D**	28. **C**	38. **A**
9. **A**	19. **C**	29. **A**	39. **C**
10. **D**	20. **B**	30. **D**	40. **A**

Reading - Test 1

Analyze your ACT, Page 377

Name: _____ Date: _____

Mistakes: _____ ACT Score: _____

Prose Fiction			Time:		
Purpose	Reference	Vocab	Except	Infer	Tone / View
7	1	2	6	3	9
10	4			5	
	8				
Pg. 363	Pg. 342, 365	Pg. 358	-	Pg. 353	Pg. 361

Social Science			Time:		
Purpose	Reference	Vocab	Except	Infer	Tone / View
	14	12	13	18	11
	15	16			
	17				
	19 20				
Pg. 363	Pg. 342, 365	Pg. 358	-	Pg. 353	Pg. 361

Humanities			Time:		
Purpose	Reference	Vocab	Except	Infer	Tone / View
24	21	22		23	
	28	25		26	
	29	30		27	
Pg. 363	Pg. 342, 365	Pg. 358	-	Pg. 353	Pg. 361

Natural Science			Time:		
Purpose	Reference	Vocab	Except	Infer	Tone / View
31	32 .		33		
38	34 37				
	35 39				
	36 40				
Pg. 363	Pg. 342, 365	Pg. 358	-	Pg. 353	Pg. 361

# mistakes	ACT Score*
40	12
39	13
38	14
37	15
35-36	16
34	17
32-33	18
31	19
29-30	20
28	21
26-27	22
25	23
23-24	24
22	25
20-21	26
19	27
17-18	28
14-16	29
13-14	30
11-12	31
9-10	32
7-8	33
5-6	34
3-4	35
0-2	36

*approximate score

1) Mark your score on the right. Circle the questions you missed. **2)** Find your trends (categories with the most mistakes.) Set a goal: How many mastered categories will lead to a 3-point improvement? **3)** Study the pages in this book that will help you master the required skills. **4)** Review your missed questions.

Reading Test 1 - Explanations

PASSAGE 1-1. THE WIZARD'S SON

1. The phrase "defeated army" in line 9 refers to "the clouds" in line 7. The clouds are "taking off" with a stand here and there behind the mountains. **(Answer B)**

2. The word "reflection" in line 75 is referring to how Oona grasped Walter's arm in line 63, described as "involuntary" in line 68. She put her hand out without even thinking; reflection here most nearly means "thought." **(Answer C)**

3. By looking at the possible answers, we can tell the question is asking who *escaped*, versus who *felt* he or she had escaped. In lines 27-29, we find that Oona feels as if she escaped, but was not actually being chased. In lines 35-36, Walter notes that he is the one who actually escaped from pursuit. Therefore, only Walter escaped, but both Walter and Oona had the feeling that they did. **(Answer C)**

4. The phrase "Oh, I don't mean to try" can be inferred to reference the earlier statement in lines 46-48: "If you were driven beyond bearing, a plunge down there and all would be over". Jumping into water when you cannot stand your troubles any longer and ending it all most closely relate to suicide. **(Answer B)**

5. We can gather from the story that both Oona and Walter are in the boat, as they have a discussion during the passage. Hamish is also mentioned, having pushed off from the beach in lines 2 and 3 as well as in line 80. While a "Lord Erradeen" is mentioned, we can infer that is another name for Walter. There are three people in the boat. **(Answer B)**

6. The phrase "Sensation of relief" is mentioned in line 4, and the phrase "a sense of safety" is in line 14. Finally, Oona discusses how she and Walter "are talking nonsense" in line 79. The only feeling that isn't mentioned is shame. **(Answer C)**

7. The concept of "dark and still, all hushed after the sweeping blasts of rain" suggests everything is calm following some form of intensity and danger. Then, "but black with the reflections of gloom from the sky" suggests that not all of the danger has passed, or that more is yet to come. The best option that reflects both of these ideas is A, which provides a contrast between safety and apprehension. **(Answer A)**

8. There is no evidence to support that Oona grew up near the loch. She seems perhaps familiar with boating, as noted with the "sigh of ease as she gathered the strings of the rudder into her hands", but this does not mean she lives near this particular loch. We can gather she was not actually pursued, but merely had the feeling she had been, which is noted in lines 27-29. It is very likely that she DID grow up in a worry-free environment, as alluded to in lines 44-45. Lastly, she mentions that scientists should dig through the center of the earth to reach Australia faster, but does not suggest she wants to do so herself. The only fully correct answer, confirmed by the passage, is that she grew up in a worry-free environment. **(Answer C)**

9. We must consider all of Walter's quotations when answering this question. The first time Walter speaks, lines 34-38, he mentions how he has escaped and now feels safe, suggesting a feeling of relief. Then in lines 45-53, he wonders about the depth of the lake and the center of the earth and how it could relate to the loch. Later, in line 71-75, he is serious about her touch in the context of danger. He is never specifically passionate or annoyed, nor does he fall in love within his dialogue. **(Answer A)**

10. The first answer is incorrect because the passage states that Walter has escaped and now feels safe. The second answer is incorrect because no enemy is mentioned; the passage does not mention whom or what Walter is escaping. The third answer is incorrect, because it is inferred that Lord Erradeen and Walter are the same person. The fourth answer then must be correct, as both feel a sense of being pursued, and talk about how it feels to be out on the loch. **(Answer D)**

PASSAGE 1-2. THE INVENTION OF PRINTING

11. It can be inferred that the author is awestruck, mentioning how impression was "practiced more than three thousand years ago, by people with a skill that cannot be surpassed in modern times." (lines 5-7) He also talks about how an Assyrian cylinder "contains sixty lines of minute characters which could be read only by the aid of a magnifying glass." (lines 33-35) **(Answer C)**

12. The word "edifice" is found in the context of "In the ruins of the ancient edifices of these primeval nations there is scarcely a stone or kiln-burnt brick without an inscription or a stamp upon it" in lines 16-19. From this we can tell that edifice does not mean a nation state, an inscription, or a boulder, as there cannot be ruins of boulders or inscriptions. **(Answer B)**

13. The fourth paragraph talks about tablets in lines 41-48. Here we see mention of legal agreements of transaction, astronomical predictions, grammars and primers of the language, etc. The text does NOT mention the proclamations of the king; those were inscribed on cylinders (line 50), not tablets. **(Answer B)**

14. There are two places in the passage where the use of a magnifying glass is mentioned, line 11 and line 36. The first inclusion refers to old Egyptian seals, whereas the second one refers to Assyrian cylinders of clay. The latter is not an option in the answers. **(Answer B)**

15. Lines 68-73 mention that using cylinders provided a sure method of making exact copies of the original, similar to printing. **(Answer C)**

16. Lines 65-68 say that a die would be manufactured, and copies would be made from it. We can infer that a die would serve a similar purpose to an engraving on wood. A die, then, is not a coloring substance or a deathly decease. Gambling is never mentioned in the text. A stamp, then, is more correct than a cube, as copies can easily be made from a manufactured stamp. **(Answer C)**

17. While the text mentions that those who used the cylinders did not have access to ink and paper, it also states "the engraving that was used to impress clay *could* have been coated with ink and stamped on parchment" (lines 78-80). Therefore, while the materials were not available, they were well suited nonetheless. The word "never" in the other answers point to extreme statements. **(Answer A)**

18. The first three possible answers are all assumptions made from the text that do not have any actual backing. While priests did practice astrology, there is no proof they were the **only** ones; while slave trade is recorded, there is no proof **all** Babylonians owned them. The tablets were "found in the library or hall of records" (line 41) but that does not mean that the hall was commonly visited, or **only** for proclamations. The only reasonable inference is that grammar was given high value, hence it appears on the tablets. **(Answer D)**

19. The passage states, "The clay was prepared for writing as well as stamping" in lines 36-37, which rules out options A and B. Nowhere in the passage is the process of dyeing mentioned, so the two uses were writing and stamping. **(Answer C)**

20. The author discusses many times how the inscriptions are still remarkably readable, and laments how "the art of printing in clay gradually fell into disuse" (lines 83-84), which leaves us with option A or B. Paragraph three draws a comparison between Babylonian and Assyrian inscriptions; the phrase "they are really coarse when compared with the inscriptions… used by the Assyrians" shows that the Babylonian inscriptions were less fine than those of the Assyrians. **(Answer B)**

PASSAGE 1-3. NAVAJO SILVERSMITHS

21. The sentence "From either of these sources the first smiths among the Navajos may have learned their trade" (lines 22-24) is referring to the tribes of Mexico and the sedentary tribes of New Mexico. **(Answer D)**

22. The first example of rude, line 25, could be any of the options, although it does not seem like the author is insulting the Indians, when he also praises their art. In line 55, we can deduce that the correct answer is *primitive* because results of labor cannot be offensive, foul, or uncivil. **(Answer D)**

23. From looking at the text, we know beautiful ornaments are not directly attributed to the tribes of New Mexico, but to the Indians of British Columbia, so answer B must be incorrect. *Wrought at the forge* in particular is an action that relates to silversmith work; the only parallel answer is "worked with metal". **(Answer C)**

24. The author didn't include the story to enhance his knowledge or to observe an Indian silversmith. Both of those answers explain why he obtained a personal forge, but not why he included this story. Including the personal story was not necessary to enforce that **all** Navajo forges are the same size, so the answer must be "to reveal that traditional methods are still applicable". **(Answer C)**

25. The sentence states that the Pueblo artisan builds a permanent forge, whereas his less fortunate Navajo *"confrère"* constructs a temporary forge on the ground. The confrère, then, in relation to the Pueblo artisan, must be his counterpart. **(Answer C)**

26. We can gather from the paragraph that the author is not implying either group of people is superior to the other, so options A and B are incorrect. He instead suggests that "the ornaments made by his hand are generally conceded to be equal or even superior to those made by the Pueblo Indian" (lines 42-45), and we can see from the past paragraph that "his hand" refers to the Navajo Indian. Therefore, the ornaments of the Navajo are either equal or superior and are therefore not regarded as inferior. **(Answer D)**

27. We can gather from the paragraph that "those who make the more elaborate articles" such as belts, "are few" (lines 50-53). This does not imply that there are fewer belts or that few Navajos wear belts. While tobacco cases are discussed in detail, it does not necessarily mean that they are harder to make than belts. The only answer that is confirmed in the text is that belts fall under the "more elaborate articles" category, whereas bracelets are simple articles. **(Answer D)**

28. The passage referring to the Indians of British Columbia and Alaska (lines 26-27) says they were allied through language, but not necessarily actual allies or enemies; they merely shared a similar language, not necessarily the same. Nowhere does it mention similar appliances or processes to the Navajos; the author only compliments their skill with ornaments, suggesting they had well-trained metalsmiths. **(Answer C)**

29. While emery-paper is first mentioned in line 17, its actual purpose is noted in lines 66-67 as polishing. **(Answer A)**

30. The passage states that a *hogan* (line 71 and 74) is another word for a summer lodge where a Navajo silversmith might set up temporarily. It is therefore not the workshop of the silversmith, nor the forge, nor the raisin-box frame. **(Answer D)**

PASSAGE 1-4. TEXTILES AND CLOTHING

31. The first answer is the only one that is both true and represents a main idea. The second answer is true, but is not the main idea of the passage. The third answer is incorrect as animal textiles can also include silk. The fourth answer is incorrect, as plant and animal fibers have a variety of differences between them; length is only one of many discrepancies. **(Answer A)**

32. Cotton is noted as more elastic than linen (lines 23-24). **(Answer D)**

33. The passage states wool is the most important animal fiber in line 29. In line 43 it says clothing made from wool is warm and light. Finally, in lines 85-87, the passage notes that wool is harmed by alkaline substances. The only fact not mentioned is that it is devoid of cellular structure. **(Answer D)**

34. Silk is described as 1000 to 4000 feet long (line 76), cotton is about an inch in length (lines 18-19) and linen is ten to twelve inches in length (lines 65-66). The correct order then, from largest to smallest, is silk, linen, cotton. **(Answer A)**

35. The comparison states, "Like wool … it is harmed by alkaline substances and solutions" (lines 86-87) when referring to silk. **(Answer B)**

36. While the passage talks about **how old** some of the discussed fibers are, it never states which fiber is **the oldest**, or which people used the first fibers. **(Answer D)**

37. The passage discusses that the hygroscopic quality is being able to absorb a large percent of the textile's weight in water and not feel damp (line 44-50), in regards to wool. Later in the passage (lines 83-85) it states that silk also displays the same property. **(Answer B)**

38. While the passage includes goat and camel hair alongside the fleece of sheep, it never says they are used just as often, or are second most important. The inclusion serves the role of emphasizing the range of animals that are used for producing textiles. **(Answer A)**

39. The passage states in lines 19-25 that the spiral character of the fibers allows for a twist of fibers that creates greater elasticity. **(Answer C)**

40. The passage states that "Cotton… does not combine satisfactorily with wool" (lines 26-28) due to its inability to take darker dyes. The same then applies to linen, which "dyes less readily" (line 68) than cotton. The two textiles that combine the best then are silk, which "combines well with other fibers, animal and vegetable" (lines 90-91) and wool. **(Answer A)**

READING TEST 2

35 minutes - 40 questions

4 passages:
Prose Fiction
Social Science
Humanities
Natural Science

Reading Passage Test 2-1 (Prose Fiction)

Adapted from <u>War and Peace</u>
by Leo Tolstoy

"Well, Prince, so Genoa and Lucca are now just family estates of the Buonapartes. But I warn you, if you don't tell me that this means war, if you still try to defend the infamies and horrors
5 perpetrated by that Antichrist—I really believe he is Antichrist—I will have nothing more to do with you and you are no longer my friend, no longer my 'faithful slave,' as you call yourself! But how do you do? I see I have frightened you—sit down
10 and tell me all the news."

It was in July, 1805, and the speaker was the well-known Anna Pávlovna Schérer, maid of honor and favorite of the Empress Márya Fëdorovna. With these words she greeted Prince
15 Vasíli Kurágin, a man of high rank and importance, who was the first to arrive at her reception. Anna Pávlovna had had a cough for some days. She was, as she said, suffering from *la grippe; grippe* being then a new word in St.
20 Petersburg, used only by the elite.

All her invitations without exception, written in French, and delivered by a scarlet-liveried footman that morning, ran as follows:

"If you have nothing better to do, Count (or
25 Prince), and if the prospect of spending an evening with a poor invalid is not too terrible, I shall be very charmed to see you tonight between 7 and 10—Annette Schérer."

"Heavens! what a malicious attack!" replied
30 the prince, not in the least disconcerted by this reception. He had just entered, wearing an embroidered court uniform, knee breeches, and shoes, and had stars on his breast and a serene expression on his flat face. He spoke in that
35 refined French in which our grandfathers not only spoke but thought, and with the gentle, patronizing intonation natural to a man of importance who had grown old in society and at court. He went up to Anna Pávlovna, kissed her
40 hand, presenting to her his bald, scented, and shining head, and complacently seated himself on the sofa.

"First of all, dear friend, tell me how you are. Set your friend's mind at rest," said he without
45 altering his tone, beneath the politeness and affected sympathy of which indifference and even irony could be discerned.

"Can one be well while suffering morally? Can one be calm in times like these if one has any
50 feeling?" said Anna Pávlovna. "You are staying the whole evening, I hope?"

"And the gala at the English ambassador's? Today is Wednesday. I must put in an appearance there," said the prince. "My daughter is coming
55 for me to take me there."

"I thought today's gala had been canceled. I confess all these festivities and fireworks are becoming wearisome."

"If they had known that you wished it, the
60 entertainment would have been put off," said the prince, who, like a wound-up clock, by force of habit said things he did not even wish to be believed.

"Don't tease! Well, and what has been decided
65 about Novosíltsev's dispatch? You know everything."

"What can one say about it?" replied the prince in a cold, listless tone. "What has been decided? They have decided that Buonaparte has burnt his
70 boats, and I believe that we are ready to burn ours."

Prince Vasíli always spoke languidly, like an actor repeating a stale part. Anna Pávlovna Schérer on the contrary, despite her forty years,
75 overflowed with animation and impulsiveness. To be an enthusiast had become her social talent and, sometimes even when she did not feel like it, she became enthusiastic in order not to disappoint the expectations of those who knew her. The
80 subdued smile which, though it did not suit her faded features, always played round her lips expressed, as in a spoiled child, a continual consciousness of her charming defect, which she neither wished, nor could, nor considered it
85 necessary, to correct.

GO ON TO THE NEXT PAGE

1. In the first paragraph, Anna is trying to encourage the Prince to
   A. declare war.
   B. provide updates about military matters.
   C. defend infamies and horrors.
   D. break their friendship.

2. It can be inferred from Anna's rank in society that
   A. she was a chamber maid who had climbed in rank.
   B. she was trying to marry a prince.
   C. she held social events for princes and counts.
   D. she spent the evenings with the empress.

3. The relationship between Anna and the Prince can be described as
   A. snobbish and superior.
   B. civilized and intimate.
   C. respectful and gracious.
   D. argumentative and hostile.

4. The words *malicious attack* (line 29) refer to
   A. the first part of the princess' greeting. (line 1-8)
   B. the events of the war. (line 3)
   C. the coughing spell of the hostess. (line 17-20)
   D. the words in the invitation. (line 24-28)

5. The passage is organized as
   A. a chronological description of the prince's visit.
   B. a disagreement that goes back and forth between Anna and the Prince.
   C. a flashback of events that influenced Anna's party.
   D. a dialogue between two people, with sporadic observations from the author.

6. From the discussion about the English ambassador's gala, all the following can be inferred, EXCEPT
   A. Anna has forgotten about the date.
   B. The prince intends to go to the event.
   C. The festivities are tonight.
   D. Anna is weary of parties.

7. The word *languidly* (line 72) most nearly means
   A. dreamily.
   B. methodically.
   C. animatedly.
   D. coldly.

8. The words "wound up clock" (line 61) are most likely used to convey that the Prince
   A. was constrained by time during his visit.
   B. was agitated during the visit.
   C. never believes a word he says.
   D. felt compelled to make a certain comment.

9. The passage suggests that
   A. the French of the past was more sophisticated than today.
   B. French was used to portray an elevated status.
   C. the author's grandfathers only spoke and thought in French.
   D. French has a gentle, patronizing intonation.

10. The *continual consciousness* (line 82-83) refers to
    A. the subdued smile.
    B. a spoiled child.
    C. her charming defect.
    D. her faded features.

GO ON TO THE NEXT PAGE

Reading Passage Test 2-2 (Social Science)

From: Kings, Queens and Pawns
by Mary Roberts Rinehart

I started for the Continent on a bright day early in January. I was searched by a woman from Scotland Yard before being allowed on the platform. The pockets of my fur coat were
5 examined; my one piece of baggage, a suitcase, was inspected; my letters of introduction were opened and read.

"Now, Mrs. Rinehart," she said, straightening, "just why are you going?"
10 I told her exactly half of why I was going. I had a shrewd idea that the question in itself meant nothing. But it gave her a good chance to look at me. She was a very clever woman.

And so, having been discovered to be
15 carrying neither weapons nor seditious documents, and having an open and honest eye, I was allowed to go through the straight and narrow way that led to possible destruction. Once or twice, later on, I blamed that woman for letting
20 me through. I blamed myself for telling only half of my reasons for going. Had I told her all, she would have detained me safely in England, where hostile airplanes overhead with bombs and unpleasant little steel darts were not always
25 between one's eyes and heaven. She let me through, and I went out on the platform.

The leaving of the one-o'clock train from Victoria Station, London, is an event and a tragedy. Wounded who have recovered are going
30 back; soldiers who have been having their week at home are returning to that mysterious region across the Channel: the front.

Not the least of the British achievements had been to transport, during the deadlock of the
35 first winter of the war, almost the entire army, in relays, back to England for a week's rest. It had been done without the loss of a man, across a channel swarming with hostile submarines. They came in thousands, covered with mud, weary,
40 eager, their eyes searching the waiting crowd for some beloved face. And those who waited and watched as the cars emptied sometimes wept with joy and sometimes turned and went away alone.

Their week over, rested, tidy, eyes still
45 eager but now turned toward France, the station platform beside the one-o'clock train was filled with soldiers going back. There were few to see them off. There were not many tears. Nothing is more typical of the courage and patriotism of the
50 British women than that platform beside the one-o'clock train at Victoria. And out on the platform, saying little because words are so feeble, pacing back and forth slowly, went these silent couples. They did not even touch hands. One felt that all
55 the unselfish stoicism and restraint would crumble under the familiar touch.

The platform filled. Sir Purtab Singh, an Indian prince, with his suite, was going back to the English lines. I had been a neighbor of his at
60 Claridge's Hotel in London. I caught his eye. It was filled with cold suspicion. It said quite plainly that I could put nothing over on him. But whether he suspected me of being a newspaper writer or a spy I do not know.
65 Somehow, considering that the train was carrying a suspicious and turbaned Indian prince, any number of impatient officers and soldiers, and an American woman who was carefully avoiding the war office and trying to look like a
70 buyer crossing the Channel for hats, the whistle for starting sounded rather inadequate. It was not martial. It was thin, effeminate, absurd. And so we were off, moving slowly past that line on the platform where no one smiled. Grief and tragedy,
75 in that one revealing moment, were written deep. I shall never forget the faces of the women as the train crept by.

And now the train was well under way. The car was very quiet. The memory of those
80 faces on the platform was too fresh. There was a brown and weary officer across from me. He sat very still, looking straight ahead.

I drew a long breath, and ordered luncheon. I was off to the war. I might be turned
85 back at Folkstone. There was more than a chance that I might not get beyond Calais, which was under military law. But at least I had made a start.

GO ON TO THE NEXT PAGE

11. The author portrays the feelings of the couples who are waiting on the platform as
    A. courageous and patriotic.
    B. said little, because words were feeble.
    C. pacing back and forth.
    D. stoic and restrained.

12. The author gives a detailed description of the starting whistle in order to
    A. represent the start of the war.
    B. contrast the silence of the couples.
    C. parallel the hesitant start of the author's journey.
    D. represent the chaos of the platform.

13. The author describes the soldiers as all of the following EXCEPT
    A. courageous and patriotic.
    B. rested and tidy.
    C. weary and dirty.
    D. eager and impatient.

14. We can infer from the passage that the Indian prince
    A. was going back to England.
    B. was the only one there whom the author mentions by name.
    C. was the only one there who had stayed in the Claridge's hotel.
    D. was wearing a turban and royal clothes.

15. As used in line 15, the word *seditious* most nearly means
    A. disloyal.
    B. peaceful.
    C. tempting.
    D. hidden.

16. The author uses which of the following tones to portray the women in this passage?
    A. Detached and knowledgeable
    B. Passionate and observing
    C. Stoic and restrained
    D. Emotional and brokenhearted

17. The author uses which of the following points of view throughout the paragraphs of this passage?
    A. First person perspective
    B. Second person perspective
    C. Third person perspective
    D. Multiple perspectives

18. It can be inferred from the passage that the woman from Scotland Yard let Mrs. Rinehart through to the platform because
    A. neither her behavior nor her possessions were suspicious.
    B. the author told her only half the truth.
    C. the author had papers of introduction.
    D. the author told her she was a spy.

19. This passage is an example of a type of historical document that is called
    A. a primary source.
    B. biographical science fiction.
    C. an objective document.
    D. an example of oral history.

20. In line 31, the region across the Channel is called mysterious because
    A. the soldiers have not been there yet.
    B. nobody knows where he or she is going.
    C. it is both an event and a tragedy.
    D. the front is an undefined place that shifts over time.

GO ON TO THE NEXT PAGE

Reading Passage Test 2-3 (Humanities)

Adapted from: <u>Great Artists</u>
by Jennie Ellis Keysor

Often in examining the lives of great men we are compelled to pass over some events which, to say the least, are not praiseworthy. Of Raphael this was not true. He was gifted with all
5 admirable qualities, and so many-sided was his genius that, while we think of him first as a painter, we must not forget that he also carved statues, wrote poems, played musical instruments, and planned great buildings.

10 So much was he adored by his pupils that, after he grew to be famous, he never went on the streets unless he was followed by an admiring throng of these students, ever ready to do his bidding or to defend his art from any possible
15 attack by malicious critics. He lived at a time when artists were fiercely jealous of each other, and yet wherever he went, harmony, like a good angel, walked unseen beside him, making whatever assembly he entered the abode of peace
20 and good-will.

Raphael was born in the small mountain town of Webmo in Umbria, a secluded region east of Florence. Hardly fifty miles away was the village of Assisi, where Saint Francis had lived
25 and labored. The inhabitants of Umbria led simple, religious lives. From these two causes arose what is called the Umbrian school of painting. All painters belonging to this school made pictures very beautiful and full of fine
30 religious feeling. No wonder that, in Raphael's time when this spirit was fresh and strong, it gave a character of piety and sweetness to the works of all the painters of Umbria.

Now, the greatest of all the Umbrian
35 painters, before Raphael, was a queer little miserly man named Perugino. Although he was of mean appearance and ignoble character, he had an unmistakable power in painting mild-eyed Madonnas and spotless saints against delicate
40 landscape backgrounds. People disliked the man, but they could not help seeing the beauty of his art, and so his studio was crowded. When Perugino noted the lad and some of his work, he said, "Let him be my pupil: he will soon become

45 my master." As nearly as we can learn, Raphael remained in this studio from 1495 to 1504.

Perugino's style of painting greatly pleased Raphael. He was naturally teachable and this, with his admiration for Perugino's pictures,
50 made his first work in the studio very much like his master's. Indeed, it is almost impossible to tell some of his earliest pictures from those of his teacher.

To Raphael, with his love of the
55 beautiful, with his zeal to learn, Florence was a city like no other. Within her walls Leonardo da Vinci was painting, Michelangelo carving, and Savonarola preaching. During his time in Florence, Raphael painted many of his best-
60 known pictures. It is said that he painted a hundred of Madonnas there, so much did he love the subject, and so successful was he in representing the child Jesus and the lovely mother.

65 Now while Raphael was painting these drooping-eyed, mild-faced Madonnas and learning great lessons from the masters of Florence, a wonderful honor came to him. He was called to Rome by the Pope and given some of the
70 apartments of the Vatican to decorate in any way he wished. With the painting of these walls Raphael and his pupils were more or less busy during the remainder of the artist's short life.

Raphael's works seem almost perfect
75 even from the beginning, yet he was always studying to get the great points in the work of others and to perfect his own. Perhaps this is the best lesson we may learn from his intellectual life—the lesson of unending study and
80 assimilation.

Judged by the moral standard of his time, Raphael was absolutely spotless. Seldom, in any man, have all good qualities joined with a versatile genius to the extent that they did in
85 Raphael. No wonder that his friends caused to be inscribed on his tomb these words - *"This is that Raphael by whom Nature feared to be conquered while he lived, and to die when he died."*

GO ON TO THE NEXT PAGE

21. The tone of the passage is mostly
    A. idolizing and informative.
    B. critical and comparative.
    C. unbiased and educational.
    D. detailed and thorough.

22. Which of the following brings about an *abode of peace and good will* (line 19-20)?
    A. artists
    B. the assembly
    C. harmony
    D. students

23. The paintings from the Umbrian school can be best characterized as
    A. simple and spotless.
    B. fresh and strong.
    C. virtuous and charming.
    D. secluded and pious.

24. The author paints Perugino's appearance in a negative image in order to
    A. show contrast with the beauty of Raphael.
    B. show that Raphael could soon be his master.
    C. illustrate the humble beginnings of Raphael.
    D. contrast his personality with his expertise.

25. It can be inferred from the fifth paragraph (lines 48-54) that
    A. some of Raphael's work might be attributed to Perugino.
    B. Perugino took credit for some of Raphael's work.
    C. Raphael copied Perugino's works.
    D. Raphael admired all of Perugino's painting.

26. All of the following were used to describe Raphael EXCEPT
    A. versatile genius.
    B. possessing unmistakable power.
    C. teachable and zealous.
    D. admirable and honored.

27. Leonardo da Vinci and Michelangelo are mentioned in order to
    A. compare Raphael with his contemporaries.
    B. exemplify the importance of Florence.
    C. explain why Raphael painted his first pictures in Florence.
    D. show how other artists shared his love of the beautiful and zeal to learn.

28. According to the text:
    A. Raphael became the Pope's favorite painter.
    B. the Pope gave Raphael permission to decorate the Vatican any way he wished.
    C. the Pope gave Raphael some of his apartments as a reward for decorating the Vatican.
    D. one of Raphael's last major works was commissioned by the Pope himself.

29. The inscription on Raphael's tomb most nearly means
    A. nobody captured the "secrets" of Nature like Raphael.
    B. Raphael conquered Nature until he died.
    C. Raphael had a dominating personality, which was apparent in all of his Nature paintings.
    D. Raphael struggled against Nature, but in the end, Nature conquers all.

30. According to the author, one of the downfalls of Raphael was
    A. his fierce jealousy.
    B. his study and assimilation.
    C. his focus on Madonnas.
    D. the author did not mention any downfalls.

GO ON TO THE NEXT PAGE

Reading Passage Test 2-4 (Natural Science)

From: <u>An Introduction to the History of Science</u> by Walter Libby

Medicine, which is almost certain to develop in the early history of a people in response to their urgent needs, has been justly called the foster-mother of many sciences. In the records of Egyptian medical practice can be traced the origin of chemistry, anatomy, physiology, and botany.

The first physician of whom history has preserved the name, I-em-hetep (He-who-cometh-in-peace), lived about 4500 B.C. Recent researches have also brought to light, near Memphis, pictures, not later than 2500 B.C., of surgical operations. They were found sculptured on the doorposts at the entrance to the tomb of a high official of one of the Pharaohs. The patients in the illustration, are suffering pain, and, according to the inscription, one cries out, "Do this [and] let me go," and the other, "Don't hurt me so!"

Our most satisfactory data in reference to Egyptian medicine are derived, however, from the Ebers papyrus. This document displays some little knowledge of the pulse in different parts of the body, of a relation between the heart and the other organs, and of the passage of the breath to the lungs (and heart). It contains a list of diseases. In the main it is a collection of prescriptions for the eyes, ears, stomach, to reduce tumors, affect purgation, etc. There is no evidence of a tendency to homeopathy, but mental healing seems to have been called into play by the use of numerous spells and incantations. Each prescription, as in medical practice to-day, contains as a rule several ingredients. Among the seven hundred recognized remedies are to be noted poppy, castor-oil, gentian, colchicum, squills, and many other familiar medicinal plants, as well as bicarbonate of soda, antimony, and salts of lead and copper. The fat of the lion, hippopotamus, crocodile, goose, serpent, and wild goat, in equal parts, served as a prescription for baldness. In the interests of his art, the medical practitioner ransacked the resources of organic and inorganic nature. The Ebers papyrus shows that precision in the use of medicaments weights of very small denominations were employed.

The Egyptian embalmers relied on the preservative properties of common salt, wine, aromatics, myrrh, cassia, etc. By the use of linen smeared with gum they excluded all putrefactive agencies. They understood the virtue of extreme dryness in the exercise of their antiseptic art. Some knowledge of anatomy was involved in the removal of the viscera, and much more in a particular method they followed in removing the brain.

Across the Mediterranean, the Babylonians attained some celebrity with a university that is now believed to have been a school of medicine. Modern research has uncovered letters by a physician, addressed to an Assyrian king in the seventh century B.C., referring to the king's chief physician giving directions for the treatment of a bleeding from the nose from which a friend of the prince was suffering, and reporting the probable recovery of a poor fellow whose eyes were diseased. Other letters from the same general period mention the presence of physicians at court. We have even recovered the name (Ilu-bani) of a physician who lived in southern Babylonia about 2700 B.C. The most interesting information, however, in reference to Babylonian medicine dates from the time of Hammurabi. It appears from the code drawn up in the reign of that monarch that the Babylonian surgeons operated in cases of cataract. They were entitled to twenty silver shekels (equivalent to seven or eight dollars) for a successful operation. If the patient lost his life or his sight as the result of an unsuccessful operation, the surgeon was condemned to have his hands amputated.

The Babylonian records of medicine like those of astronomy reveal the prevalence of many superstitious beliefs. The spirits of evil bring maladies upon us; the gods heal the diseases that afflict us. The Babylonian books of medicine contained strange interminglings of prescription and incantation. The priests studied the livers of sacrificial animals in order to divine the thoughts of the gods—a practice which stimulated the study of anatomy.

GO ON TO THE NEXT PAGE

31. The purpose of the passage as a whole would best be described as
    A. to tell about the first people in history who used medicine.
    B. to highlight the first two physicians in history and their environments.
    C. to compare and contrast the Egyptian and Babylonian cultures.
    D. to show early historical evidence of medicinal procedures.

32. The author mentions the pictures of surgical operations at the tomb's entrance
    A. to show how they were found.
    B. to illustrate that medicine was not working at all.
    C. to demonstrate the failures of the first procedures.
    D. to highlight the beginnings of scientific experimentation.

33. Which of the following topics were mentioned in the Ebers papyrus?
    A. Tumors, embalming, and a cure for baldness.
    B. Nosebleeds, spells, and incantations.
    C. Medicinal dosage, surgery, and prescriptions.
    D. Diseases, medicinal ingredients, and anatomy.

34. It can be inferred from the text that *antimony* (line 38) is most likely
    A. a medicinal plant.
    B. an incantation.
    C. an element.
    D. an animal fat.

35. The word *denominations* in line 46 most nearly means
    A. currencies.
    B. values.
    C. classifications.
    D. religions.

36. The author mentions the process of embalming in order to
    A. illustrate the Egyptians' knowledge of anatomy.
    B. explain the virtue of extreme dryness.
    C. show the Egyptian's reliance on preservative properties.
    D. show why the embalmers removed the brain.

37. The passage contains all of the following facts EXCEPT
    A. I-em-hetep performed surgical operations.
    B. the Assyrian king had physicians at court.
    C. Babylonian surgeons were regulated by law.
    D. incantations were used by Egyptians and Babylonians.

38. The text mentions that the nosebleed was
    A. related to an eye disease.
    B. a common occurrence in seventh century B.C.
    C. suffered by a friend of the king.
    D. a documented Babylonian incident.

39. It can be inferred from the fifth paragraph (lines 57 – 82) that
    A. the Babylonians had advancements over the Egyptians.
    B. there were rules that regulated the practice of medicine.
    C. all Babylonian kings had chief physicians.
    D. surgeons had a secret code that they lived by.

40. Medicine is called the *foster-mother* in line 4 because
    A. it gave birth to all other sciences.
    B. it predated all other sciences.
    C. it influenced many other sciences.
    D. it can be traced to the origin of all other sciences.

END OF THIS TEST

STOP! DO NOT TURN THE PAGE UNTIL TOLD TO DO SO.

Reading Test 2 - Answer Key

War and Peace	Kings, Queens, and Pawns	Great Artists	An Introduction to the History of Science
1. **B**	11. **D**	21. **A**	31. **D**
2. **C**	12. **C**	22. **C**	32. **D**
3. **C**	13. **A**	23. **C**	33. **D**
4. **A**	14. **B**	24. **D**	34. **C**
5. **D**	15. **A**	25. **A**	35. **B**
6. **A**	16. **B**	26. **B**	36. **A**
7. **B**	17. **D**	27. **B**	37. **A**
8. **D**	18. **A**	28. **D**	38. **D**
9. **B**	19. **A**	29. **A**	39. **B**
10. **C**	20. **D**	30. **D**	40. **C**

Reading - Test 2

Analyze your ACT, Page 393

Name: _____ Date: _____

Mistakes: _____ ACT Score: _____

Prose Fiction			Time:		
Purpose	Reference	Vocab	Except	Infer	Tone / View
8	1	7	6	2	5
	4			3	
	10			9	
Pg. 363	Pg. 342, 365	Pg. 358	-	Pg. 353	Pg. 361

Social Science			Time:		
Purpose	Reference	Vocab	Except	Infer	Tone / View
12	11	15	13	14	16
19				18	17
				20	
Pg. 363	Pg. 342, 365	Pg. 358	-	Pg. 353	Pg. 361

Humanities			Time:		
Purpose	Reference	Vocab	Except	Infer	Tone / View
24	22		26	25	21
27	23		30	29	
	28				
Pg. 363	Pg. 342, 365	Pg. 358	-	Pg. 353	Pg. 361

Natural Science			Time:		
Purpose	Reference	Vocab	Except	Infer	Tone / View
31	33	35	37	34	
32	38			39	
36	40				
Pg. 363	Pg. 342, 365	Pg. 358	-	Pg. 353	Pg. 361

# mistakes	ACT Score*
38	11
36-37	12
35	13
33-34	14
32	15
30-31	16
29	17
27-28	18
26	19
24-25	20
23	21
21-22	22
20	23
18-19	24
17	25
15-16	26
14	27
12-13	28
11	29
9-10	30
7-8	31
6	32
4-5	34
2-3	35
0-1	36

*approximate score

1) Mark your score on the right. Circle the questions you missed. **2)** Find your trends (categories with the most mistakes.) Set a goal: How many mastered categories will lead to a 3-point improvement? **3)** Study the pages in this book that will help you master the required skills. **4)** Review your missed questions.

Copyright 2017 Winni van Gessel

Reading Test 2 - Explanations

PASSAGE 2-1. WAR AND PEACE

1. In the first paragraph, Anna is not trying to get the Prince to formally declare war, but admit that the military is taking the threat seriously. She tells him NOT to defend the infamies and horrors, and only threatens to break their friendship; she does not ask him to. The only remaining answer is that she desires knowledge of foreign affairs. **(Answer B)**

2. Anna was not a maid, but a maid of honor (lines 13-14). The fact she is acquainted with the Prince implies she is not attempting to be elite, but already is. While the passage states she is a favorite of the Empress (line 14), it never suggests that she spent her evenings there. The remaining answer is that she often holds social events, which can be inferred from the fact she has invited several Counts and the Prince. **(Answer C)**

3. A relationship can hardly be described as snobbish or superior (though people's attitudes can be), and while their relationship is civilized, it is certainly not intimate. The tone of their conversation is more bickering than argumentative, and while the Prince calls Anna's greeting venomous, their relationship is not hostile. (He kissed her hand, etc.) The only correct answer for the relationship is respectful and gracious. **(Answer C)**

4. The rest of that sentence says the Prince was "not in the least disconcerted by this reception" (lines 31-32). From this we can infer he is referring to Anna's bombardment of questions when he first arrived. **(Answer A)**

5. The passage certainly is not a chronological description; it contains a large amount of dialogue and does not directly follow chronology. There is more to the passage than just dialogue, however, and the two are certainly not disagreeing back and forth. There is no evidence in the passage to suggest it is a flashback, or that the events that are discussed would influence Anna's party. The only remaining answer is a dialogue with sporadic observations from the author, who fills in information about those conversing. **(Answer D)**

6. The passage never suggests that Anna forgot about the date; she thought it had been cancelled, but didn't forget when it was originally supposed to be. **(Answer A)**

7. The phrase "like an actor repeating a stale part" (lines 73-74) can be used to determine the meaning. It is certainly not animated, and while he uses a "cold, listless tone" (line 69) earlier in the passage, that's not what is being described this time around. The Prince does not speak dreamily, seeming more uninterested than absentminded. Methodically is the only correct option. **(Answer B)**

8. The phrase "wound-up clock" (line 62) refers to the fact that the Prince says things out of habit without really meaning what he says. While he may not have believed **everything** he said, it is too much of a stretch to suggest he did not believe **a single word**. Therefore, it is implied that he felt compelled to say something. **(Answer D)**

9. The passage discusses the use of French twice, both in the context of being refined and proper. When it mentions the French of the past, it does not suggest it was more sophisticated, or that the grandfathers spoke solely French. The "general patronizing intonation" (line 37-38) is said to be because of his presence in society, not because of the French language. Therefore, French was used to portray an elevated status. **(Answer B)**

10. The "continual consciousness" (line 84) refers to her charming defect. Without the interruptions and other details, the sentence reads as follows: "Her smile expressed a continual consciousness of her charming defect, which she did not want to correct." In other words, she was conscious of her charming defect. **(Answer C)**

PASSAGE 2-2. KINGS, QUEENS, AND PAWNS

11. The feelings of the couples are described as possessing "unselfish stoicism and restraint" in line 55. Courageous and patriotic describes only British women, and the other two options do not describe their feelings. **(Answer D)**

12. We can gather from the passage that the war has already begun; hence the soldiers are returning for a break before going back out to the front. If it was contrasting the silence of the couples, it would be loud and strong, but it is described as sounding "rather inadequate. It was not martial. It was thin, effeminate, absurd." (lines 76-78) In the same way, it does not represent the chaos of the platform, on which there seemed to be little. The only viable answer is to parallel the start of the author's journey: high-pitched and nervous whereas both of them (the author and the whistle) should have been strong and in control. **(Answer C)**

13. The phrase involving "courage and patriotism" is referring to the British women (line 49) not the soldiers. **(Answer A)**

14. It states that the prince was turbaned, but the text does not describe his clothes. from the words, "I had been a neighbor of his at Claridge's Hotel in London", it is clear that both the writer and the prince stayed there; he was not the only one. The text states that the prince is going back to the English *lines*, not to England, as the train station is located in London. The one thing that is clear from the passage is that the author mentioned only the prince by name. **(Answer B)**

15. Since the word *seditious* is referring to documents being taken out of England during a war, it is unlikely that it means tempting. Peaceful or hidden documents would not be something of importance. The security check was instead looking for treasonous, or disloyal, documents. **(Answer A)**

16. The question asks about the *tone* of the passage, not about the women in the story. The author is undoubtedly involved in the scene that she is describing, so the word detached does not apply. She describes the *women* as stoic and restrained, but does not use those *tones* herself. While she gives great reason for the women to be emotional and brokenhearted, she is not very emotional in her own choice of words. Instead, she clearly appreciates their support of the war effort, and observes small details regarding their behavior. **(Answer B)**

17. While the author stays primarily in first person, almost half the paragraphs are written from a different perspective, not using the first person even once in those paragraphs. (Paragraph 2, 5, 6, 7, and 10) The author shows knowledge of things beyond her own perception, and uses the subject "one" on occasion, in place of "I". Therefore, she is using multiple perspectives. **(Answer D)**

18. Lines 15-17 discuss how she was not regarded as suspicious; otherwise, she would have been stopped by security. The other options do not give good reason as to why she would be let through. **(Answer A)**

19. Since the author is herself part of the story, she can be considered a primary source. Science fiction is not historical, and an objective document would have no opinions in it. Since more is included in the passage than speaking, it is not oral history. **(Answer A)**

20. This section is included in lines 31-33, and says the soldiers are "returning", and therefore have been there before and although many of them might be assigned to a new position, it is unlikely that *nobody* knows where he or she is going. C is incorrect because "the leaving of the train is an event and a tragedy," not the front. The passage states that **the front** is mysterious, and only answer D gives a reasonable explanation for that. **(Answer D)**

PASSAGE 2-3. GREAT ARTISTS

21. Throughout the article, the author shows great admiration for Raphael, saying that he has "no events that should be passed over" (lines 2-3), his works "seem almost perfect even from the beginning" (lines 74), and that morally "Raphael was absolutely spotless" (line 82). She is certainly not critical or unbiased, and detailed and thorough are more adjectives for her writing style, not for her tone, which is idolizing. **(Answer A)**

22. Looking back at line 17, we can see it was "harmony" that walked alongside Raphael and made any assembly "the abode of peace and good-will" (lines 19-20). **(Answer C)**

23. The Umbrian school's paintings in particular are described as "very beautiful and full of fine religious feeling" (lines 29-30). It is also mentioned that they possessed "a character of piety and sweetness" (line 32). The correct characteristics then, for the paintings, are virtuous and charming. **(Answer C)**

24. The sentence states, "Although he was of mean appearance and ignoble character, he had an unmistakable power in painting..." (lines 36-38); drawing a direct contrast between personality and skill. **(Answer D)**

25. The fifth paragraph says that due to great similarity, it is difficult to ascribe some works to either Raphael or Perugino. It never says that Perugino himself took credit or that Raphael produced exact copies. While Raphael certainly admired Perugino's work, it never suggested he admired ALL of it. The correct inference is due to the similarities, there might have been a potential error in attribution. **(Answer A)**

26. The phrase "possessing unmistakable power" is referring to Perugino in line 38. **(Answer B)**

27. When Leonardo da Vinci and Michael Angelo are included, they are not compared against one another, nor mentioned as motivation for Raphael to work in Florence. While the passage states Raphael had a "love of the beautiful" (lines 55-56) and a "zeal to learn" (line 56), it never implies the other artists shared the same feeling. Their inclusion is to amplify the greatness of Florence, and its role in the art world. **(Answer B)**

28. The passage states that Raphael "was called to Rome by the Pope and given some of the apartments of the Vatican to decorate in any way he wished" (lines 70-72). It does not say that Raphael was the Pope's favorite, or that Raphael could decorate **all** of the Vatican. (Extremes) Furthermore, Raphael was given the apartments to decorate, not as a reward. At the end of the paragraph, however, it says that "Raphael and his pupils were more or less busy during the remainder of the artist's short life" (lines 73-75) suggesting that the apartments were indeed the last great work he accomplished. **(Answer D)**

29. The inscription in lines 86-88 suggest Raphael had some form of power over Nature that no one else had possessed, nor would be able to possess again. When putting this in terms of painting, it suggests that Raphael was able to capture the essence of Nature in his works better than anyone else. **(Answer A)**

30. The phrase "fierce jealousy" (line 16) is attributed to other artists, and noted that he did not display the same personality. The author considers Raphael's focus on study and assimilation to be the best thing to learn from him, and while the focus on Madonnas is highlighted, it is never considered a downfall. Therefore, the author attributes no downfalls to Raphael in the passage. **(Answer D)**

PASSAGE 2-4. AN INTRODUCTION TO THE HISTORY OF SCIENCE

31. The passage talks about the first **documented** people to use medicine, but does not necessarily tell of the first people who used it ever. While it does mention two physicians, they are not the main focus of the passage. In the same way, parts of Egyptian and Babylonian cultures are mentioned, but they are not entirely documented to provide an accurate comparison. The purpose then is to show early evidence of medicinal practice. **(Answer D)**

32. The author did not mention the pictures to show how they were found, and the pictures themselves show that medicine was having some success. He would not need to include the pictures to demonstrate shortcomings of early procedures, so they must have been included to highlight the beginnings of experimentation. **(Answer D)**

33. Tumors and a cure for baldness were mentioned in the papyrus, but not embalming. Spells and incantations were included, but not nosebleeds. Medicinal dosage and prescriptions are mentioned, but not surgical procedures. The only answer that includes all topics is diseases, medicinal ingredients, and anatomy. **(Answer D)**

34. Antimony is not described in the list of medicinal plants, so it must not be one itself. It is mentioned prior to animal fats, but not listed among those either. Incantations would not be part of a prescription, so the only remaining answer is that antimony must be an element; it is mentioned alongside copper and salt. **(Answer C)**

35. The phrase containing denominations says "precision in the use of medicaments weights of very small denominations were employed." (lines 45-47). The only option that satisfies this sentence is values, as weights using small values would allow for precision. **(Answer B)**

36. The discussion of embalming includes "Some knowledge of anatomy was involved" (line 54). The other options do not accurately portray why the process would be mentioned. **(Answer A)**

37. The passage never says that I-em-hetep performed surgical operations; he is only identified as "the first physician of whom history has preserved the name" (lines 8-9). **(Answer A)**

38. The text says the letter gave directions for a nosebleed and "reported the probable recovery of a poor fellow whose eyes were diseased." It did not say they were suffered by the same person. The treatment was for a friend of the prince, not a friend of the king (lines 65-66). It never implies nosebleeds were a common occurrence, but only shows it as a documented incident. **(Answer D)**

39. The passage states that, according to a code drawn up by a monarch, "the Babylonian surgeons operated in cases of cataract" (lines 76-78) and they would also have their hands amputated in case of failure (lines 80-83). Together these facts show that medicine was regulated by rules. **(Answer B)**

40. The first paragraph shows how *some* of the other sciences trace their origin through the need for medicine, not *all* of the sciences, as A, B and D suggest. **(Answer C)**

Science

TABLES

Spending 10 seconds longer scrutinizing at a table will save you time and points in the end. Don't just look at the data; understand the significance.

Look for patterns, irregularities, comparisons, and conclusions.

Don't be too cocky! When you see a connection, write it down. When you think something is important, circle it! Don't do everything in your head.

Use your left index finger to mark a place in a table when a question asks you for specific data.

When you see two tables that look alike, jot down what is different. The explanation is often in the text.

Watch for units, percentages, and for the number 0.

Tables

Do not look at the tables as a mere illustration. **"Read" the tables**! Understand the story that the data tells you. A few seconds of studying the data will pay off when you get to the questions.

Dog	Weight of the dog	Lbs. of food eaten
1	20	2
2	40	4
3	8	0.8
4	4	0.4
	Table 1	

Data tables are great tools to gather and organize data. They may not be in the right order. Sometimes you have to put them in the right order to see a relationship.

A typical ACT trick is matching the data in Table 1 with a graph. Although the numbers in the columns go up and down, the relationship is linear.

Number of Families	Number of Children
5	0
8	1
12	2
7	3
2	4
2	5
	Table 2

Tip: Look for patterns.
Before you start answering questions, **look for patterns** between the two columns. Look for a relationship between the rows: Table 1 shows a linear relationship; Table 2 shows a bell curve.

Tip: Draw conclusions from the data.
Before you start answering questions, **draw conclusions** from the information in the table. Table 3 shows that most flowers in the spring are sold in February (Valentine's Day?) and the most popular flower is the red rose. Mark these conclusions when you see them. It helps to understand the information in the tables.

	February	March	April	May
Tulips sold	213	45	61	112
Red Roses	450	62	73	194
Pink Roses	390	51	68	150
		Table 3		

Month	Sold Cars
Jan	6
Feb	10
March	8
April	15
May	10
June	9
Table 4 – Percent of cars sold (out of 400) in 2015	

Tip: Look for irregularities at the beginning and patterns and the end of the tables.
See Table 5 and 6. Is the data for each result always increasing?*
If yes, is it a linear relationship?**

Tip: Read the units!
"16" could mean "16 million people," "16 percent," or "16 nanoseconds." Don't fall for visual appearances.
Quick! In Table 4, how many cars were sold in February?***

If a table shows percentages, make sure you link it to the actual number. If the table **only** shows percentages, be aware that you **cannot** make any conclusions about the numbers.

Trial	Result
1	2.715
2	3.694
3	4.498
4	7.789
5	8.951
6	10.445
7	11.689
8	11.689
9	13.531
10	16.058
Table 5	

Trial	Result
A	1
B	3
C	6
D	9
E	12
F	15
G	18
H	21
I	24
J	27
Table 6	

*** Table 4 shows that 40 cars were sold in February, not 10!
** No. In Table 6, all results increase in threes, except the first pair.
* No. In Table 5, trials 7 and 8 show the same results.

Tables - Quiz 1: Football 　　　**2 minutes**

A student who was interested in the physics of the game of football asked the coach why footballs are not inflated with gases that are less dense than air. In order to find out, she decided to test the performance of footballs that were filled with different gases. In addition, she wanted to find out if the pressure of those gases affected the kick distance. (The average football is inflated anywhere from 12.5 to 13.5 PSI). In order to test the effects of these variables, she gathered three common gases - nitrogen, oxygen, and helium - and compared their densities to air under normal atmospheric pressure. (See Table 1)

Air Density (Kg/m^3)	He Density (Kg/m^3)	N_2 Density (Kg/m^3)	O_2 Density (Kg/m^3)
1.225	0.1664	1.165	1.331

Table 1

The coach then recruited a kicker from the team to kick footballs filled with different gases five times each from a tee. The average of the distances in yards, rounded to the nearest whole number, are displayed in Table 2.

Inflation (PSI)	Air Kick Distance (yds.)	He Kick Distance (yds.)	N_2 Kick Distance (yds.)	O_2 Kick Distance (yds.)
13	60	66	61	59
12	57	64	59	56
11	50	59	51	49
10	40	52	42	40

Table 2

1. Which of these changes to the experiment would most improve its validity?
   A. Using more types of gases.
   B. Using more levels of inflation.
   C. Kicking the ball more times in each trial.
   D. Punting the ball instead of kicking from a tee.

2. Which gas had the smallest range in distance for the different pressures?
   A. Air
   B. N_2
   C. O_2
   D. He

3. Does the density of the gas affect the distance that the football traveled?
   A. Yes, the less-dense gases tended to make the football travel farther.
   B. Yes, the denser gases tended to make the football travel farther.
   C. No, while some less-dense gases made the football travel farther, others did not.
   D. No, there was no direct correlation between the density of the gas and the distance the football traveled.

1)C 2)D 3)A

Tables - Quiz 1: Football   (Answers)

Tip: Use your fingers as much as possible, especially on questions with tables. It will help you keep track of what part of the table the question is referring to.

1. Which of these changes to the experiment would most improve its validity?

There are a few simple ways to improve the validity of an experiment. One of the major ways is to increase the number of trials or to increase the repetition of each test, which would increase the validity because it makes the results more accurate. The more tests that are run, the more accurate the results will be. **(Answer C)**

2. Which gas had the least variability in distance for the different pressures?

Inflation (PSI)	Air Kick Distance (yds)	He Kick Distance (yds)	N₂ Kick Distance (yds)	O₂ Kick Distance (yds)
13	60	66	61	59
12	57	64	59	56
11	5	59	51	49
10	4	52	42	40

Use your fingers to find the highest and lowest distance traveled for each gas used. The gas with the smallest difference in the two numbers is the gas with the smallest range, in distance. Helium has the smallest range: $66 - 52 = 14$. The other gases had a range as follows:
Air $60 - 40 = 20$;
Nitrogen $61 - 42 = 19$; and
Oxygen $59 - 40 = 19$ **(Answer D)**

3. Does the density of the gas affect the distance that the football traveled?

Table 1 shows the density of each gas. Note that they are not in order of density.

Tip: If items in a list are out of order, number them in order.

Table 2 shows the distance traveled for each gas. By comparing the density to the distance traveled, we can see that there is a trend. As the density of the gas increases, the distance traveled by the football decreases. **(Answer A)**

Air Density (Kg/m³)	He Density (Kg/m³)	N₂ Density (Kg/m³)	O₂ Density (Kg/m³)
1.22	.1664	1.165	1.331
3	1	2	4

Inflation (PSI)	Air Kick Distance (yds)	He Kick Distance (yds)	N₂ Kick Distance (yds)	O₂ Kick Distance (yds)
13	60	66	61	59
12	57	64	59	56
11	50	59	51	49
10	40	52	42	40
	3	1	2	4

Tables - Quiz 2: Solubility

2 minutes

Temperature of Solvent (°C)	Rate of Solubility (g/sec)
-20	0
-10	0
0	0
10	0
20	0
30	0
40	0
50	26.5
60	33.5
70	44
80	44
Table 1	

1. Based on Table 1, scientists can conclude that the rate of solubility starts
   A. at -20° C.
   B. at 40° C.
   C. between 40 and 50° C.
   D. at 50° C.

2. Based on Table 1, scientists predict that the rate of Solubility at 100° C will be
   A. more than 44 g/sec, because the table shows increasing data as the temperature increases.
   B. more than 44 g/sec, because the measurement at 80 degrees °C is obviously not correct and should be higher.
   C. 44 g/sec, because it is likely that the solubility has reached a maximum rate.
   D. around 55 g/sec, because from 60° to 80° the solubility increased about 11 g/sec. Therefore, between 80° and 100° the solubility will also increase with about 11 g/sec.

3. The best conclusion that can be drawn from this experiment is
   A. As the temperature goes up in the solution, the rate of solubility in the solvent also goes up.
   B. As the solvent temperature increases, the rate of solubility in the solvent increases.
   C. The rate of solubility increases between 40 and 80 degrees °C, and is constant in temperatures above and below that range.
   D. The rate of solubility increases between 40 and 70 degrees °C, and is constant in temperatures above and below that range.

4. Which graph cannot be drawn from the partial results of this experiment?

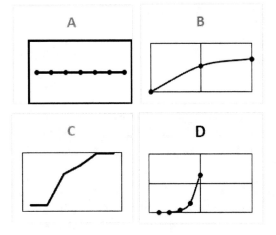

   A. Table A
   B. Table B
   C. Table C
   D. Table D

Tables Quiz 2: Solubility (Answers)

1. **Based on Table 1**, scientists can conclude that the rate of Solubility <u>starts</u>:

Underline the word <u>starts.</u>

20	0
30	0
40	0
50	5
60	5

At 40° C, nothing is happening.
At 50 ° C, the solvent has a solubility rate of 26. Solubility must have started somewhere between 40 and 50° C. **(Answer C)**

2. **Based on Table 1**, scientists predict that the rate of solubility at 100° C will be

50	26.5
60	33.5
70	44
80	44
90	
100	

 Tip: Draw the new data in the table. Sometimes it will take TWO steps to get there. This is a popular disratction by the ACT.

In the first part of the experiment, the solubility stopped at 44° C. It is possible that it might go up again, and it is possible that it might go down. It is even possible that the measurement at 80° C is incorrect. However, there is no **evidence** for any of these hypotheses. We have to rely on the presented data, so the only scientific conclusion that is supported by the data is that the maximum rate of 44 g/sec is reached. **(Answer C)**

3. The best **conclusion** of this experiment is
Below 40 degrees and between 70 and 80 degrees, the solubility does not change. Answer A and B are incorrect.

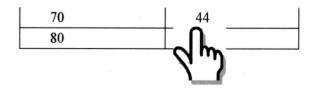

70	44
80	

The rate of solubility is constant between 70 and 80 degrees. Answer C is incorrect.
(Answer D)

4. Which graph **cannot** be drawn from the results of this experiment?

Tip: Check the data points of each graph and match them up with the table.

Graph A represents solubility points from -20° C to 40° C.
Graph B represents solubility points from 50° C to 70° C.
Graph C represents solubility points from 30° C to 80° C.
Graph D does **not** represent any data series from Table 1. **(Answer D)**

Tables - Quiz 3:Air Conditioning **2 minutes**

With fuel prices rising and summer approaching, a group of thrifty scientists wanted to find out whether opening the windows or using the air conditioner was the more fuel efficient way to cool down a car. To test this, the scientists used a common mid-sized sedan and filled it with two gallons of fuel. They took the car to a track and allowed the car to run until it was the fuel tank was empty. For a control test, they ran it once without either the windows down or air conditioning. They then ran three more tests, one with the air conditioning on, one with the windows lowered completely, and one with both the windows lowered and the air conditioning on. Below are their results.

Test Parameters	Miles Traveled	Fuel Efficiency (MPG)
Windows Up and no Air Conditioning	60	30
Windows Down	52.2	26.1
Air Conditioning On	53	26.5
Windows Down and Air Conditioning On	46	23

1. Using the results of this experiment, which is the most fuel-efficient way to stay cool during the summer in a car?
    A. Air Conditioning on.
    B. Windows down.
    C. Both windows down and Air Conditioning on.
    D. Having neither windows down or the Air Conditioning on.

2. Which of these changes to the experiment would add the most validity to the results?
    A. Measuring the fuel efficiency with only one window down.
    B. Measuring the temperature inside and outside the car to see which method keeps the driver the coolest.
    C. Using more fuel in each trial.
    D. Using multiple types of cars to account for aerodynamic variables of car models.

3. Which of these is the dependent variable in the experiment?
    A. The method for cooling the car.
    B. The amount of fuel used.
    C. The fuel efficiency of the car in each trial.
    D. The type of car used.

4. Of these aspects of the experiment, which one was NOT a controlled variable?
    A. The amount of fuel used.
    B. The type of car used.
    C. The location of the tests.
    D. None of these.

5. How are the miles traveled and fuel efficiency related in this experiment?
    A. They are directly related.
    B. They are inversely related.
    C. They are indirectly related.
    D. They have no relationship.

1) A 2) D 3) C 4) D 5) A

Tables - Quiz 3:Air Conditioning (Answers)

1. Using the results of this experiment, which is the most fuel-efficient way to <u>stay cool</u> during the summer in a car?

The key to this question is finding the most fuel-efficient way to <u>stay cool</u>. This automatically eliminates the trial with no air conditioning and the windows not rolled down. From the three

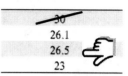

Fuel Efficiency (MPG)

30
26.1
26.5
23

tests remaining, we must now find the most fuel-efficient way to stay cool. To find this, you must look at the fuel efficiency miles per gallon (mpg) for each of the three remaining tests and pick the highest one. The highest fuel efficiency of the remaining three options is 26.5 mpg. **(Answer A)**

2. Which of these changes to the experiment would add the most validity to the results?

Adding validity to an experiment means increasing the accuracy of the results. One of the major ways to add validity to results is to do multiple trials for each test. On the ACT, many of the options will give you ways to expand the experiment, but will not make the results more accurate. The only option that gives a way to improve the accuracy of the results is using multiple types of cars. Although this also expands on the experiment, it will help answer the overall question of which method provides the best fuel efficiency while staying cool in a moving car. **(Answer D)**

3. Which of these is the dependent variable in the experiment?

Tip: As soon as you see a graph, write IV over the independent variable and DV over the dependent variable.

The dependent variable is the variable that the experiment is testing for. It is the variable that the researchers will examine and use to draw conclusions. In this experiment the researchers are comparing the fuel efficiencies of different ways to lower the temperatures in a car. That means that the fuel efficiency is the dependent variable. **(Answer C)**

4. Of these aspects of the experiment, which one was <u>not</u> a controlled variable?

A controlled variable is a variable that is held constant for all trails and tests in an experiment. By reading the section above the table, you are able to tell that each trial had the same amount of fuel in the tank, each test was conducted using the same car, and each test was conducted at the same location. All of the possible solutions are controlled variables. **(Answer D)**

5. How are the miles traveled and fuel efficiency related in this experiment?

To find the answer to this question, you must compare the results between the miles traveled and the fuel efficiency for each test. Since an increase in the miles traveled also indicates an increase in the fuel efficiency, there is a direct relationship between the two. **(Answer A)**

Tables - Quiz 4: Soda and Candy **3 minutes**

Two students combined soda and a type of candy that causes the CO_2 in the soda to expand rapidly. They observed that the pressure that caused the soda to shoot out of a bottle was large enough to lift the bottle if it was placed upside down. They wondered whether the type of soda or the brand affected how high the soda would propel the bottle. They gathered five different soda flavors of two different brands in 2 liter bottles. Following precise procedures, they dropped candies in each bottle and recorded the results in Table 1. They repeated the experiment with a different brand and recorded those results in Table 2.

Flavor	# of Candies	Height Reached (ft.)
Cola	5	10
Cola	10	14
Cherry	5	8
Cherry	10	13
Orange	5	12
Orange	10	17
Diet Cola	5	15
Diet Cola	10	19
Lemon Lime	5	10
Lemon Lime	10	11

Table 1. Performance with Soda Brand 1

Flavor	# of Candies	Height Reached (ft.)
Cola	5	11
Cola	10	12
Cherry	5	13
Cherry	10	16
Orange	5	9
Orange	10	12
Diet Cola	5	14
Diet Cola	10	18
Lemon Lime	5	10
Lemon Lime	10	11

Table 2. Performance with Soda Brand 2

1. Which was a dependent variable and which was an independent variable in this test?

	Dependent	Independent
A.	Flavor of Soda	Height reached
B.	Brand of Soda	Height reached
C.	Flavor of soda	Brand of Soda
D.	Height reached	Brand of Soda

2. Which of these would improve the validity of the students' results?
   A. Using more flavors of soda.
   B. Repeating the whole experiment
   C. Using a third brand of soda.
   D. Changing the amount of candy dropped in each soda.

3. When only five candies were dropped, which flavor performed worst on average?
   A. Cherry
   B. Lemon Lime
   C. Orange
   D. Cola

4. Increasing the candies from 5 to 10 per bottle resulted in the largest difference in performance for which flavor and brand?
   A. Cherry of Brand 2
   B. Diet Cola of Brand 1
   C. Orange of Brand 1
   D. Diet Cola of Brand 2

1) D 2) B 3) B 4) C

Tables - Quiz 4: Soda and Candy (Answers)

1. Which was a dependent and which was an independent variable in this test?

Tip: As soon as you see a table, write IV over the independent variable and DV over the dependent variable.

The <u>independent</u> variable is manipulated by the experimenter. The <u>dependent</u> variable shows the results of the experiment due to the manipulation of the independent variable. In this case, the brand of soda, the flavor, and the amount of candies are independent variables. The experimenter changes these variables to find out what happens. The dependent variable is the height reached because it depends on the brand of soda, on the flavor, and on the amount of candies. **(Answer D)**

2. Which of these would improve the validity of the student's results?

The ACT is concerned about the <u>scientific method</u>: keep everything constant, change one variable, and measure the outcome precisely. One of the main ways to improve the validity of an experiment is to do more trials. The only option that offers a suggestion of more trials is to redo the whole experiment. All of the other options offer ways to expand the experiment, not improve the accuracy of the results. **(Answer B)**

3. When only five candies were dropped, which flavor performed worst on average?

For this question, only look at the data that tells you when five candies were dropped. Find the data that shows the lowest height reached for both Table 1 and Table 2. Now, average the two numbers of the two results (Tables 1 and 2). With two results of 10ft, Lemon Lime reached the smallest <u>average</u> height. **(Answer B)**

4. Increasing the candies from 5 to 10 per bottle resulted in the largest difference in performance for which flavor?

In this question, it is key that you use your fingers to guide your thinking to the correct answer. Go through each of the four options and subtract the height reached with 5 candies from the height reached with 10 candies. Place one finger on the brand number to make sure you have that correct, and one finger on the flavor of soda.

Flavor	# of Candies	Height Reached (ft.)
Cola	5	10
Cola	10	14
Cherry	5	8
Cherry	10	13
Orange	5	12
Orange	10	17
Diet Cola	5	15
Diet Cola	10	19
Lemon Lime	5	10
Lemon Lime	10	11

Table 1. Performance with Brand 1

In Brand 1, the orange flavor had an increase of 5 ft. when the number of candies increased from 5 to 10. **(Answer C)**

Tables - Quiz 5: Approval Rates   **3 minutes**

A company in Lexington, Kentucky, has several divisions that produce multiple products. One of the most important ways to check customer satisfaction with these products is to compare approval rates.

If the approval rate is increasing, the company knows that the brand is doing well. If the approval rate is decreasing, the company knows that the brand needs to be reevaluated, and will most likely change aspects of the product.

Figure 1 shows the approval ratings from 2012-2014 for the only five brands that are produced by one of the divisions.

Approval Ratings			
	2012	2013	2014
Brand A	96	100	50
Brand B	20	22	26
Brand C	46	50	52
Brand D	4	5	12
Brand E	70	80	86

Figure 1

1. Which brand had the largest percent increase in approval rates from 2012-2013?
   - **A.** Brand A
   - **B.** Brand B
   - **C.** Brand C
   - **D.** Brand D

2. Which brand needs to be reevaluated by the company?
   - **A.** Brand A
   - **B.** Brand C
   - **C.** Brand D
   - **D.** None of the above

3. If each brand was ranked based on approval rating in 2013, how many brands would have a different ranking in 2014?
   - **A.** 1
   - **B.** 2
   - **C.** 3
   - **D.** 4

4. What proportion of brands in this division is doing well for the company?
   - **A.** 5/5
   - **B.** 4/5
   - **C.** 3/5
   - **D.** 1/5

1) D 2) A 3) C 4) B

Tables - Quiz 5: Approval rates (Answers)

 Tip: If a question seems confusing because it is not directly stated in the table, READ the section that explains the table. Look for key words.

1. **Which brand had the largest percent increase in approval rates from 2012-2013?**

   Just because a <u>number</u> is large does not mean the <u>percent increase</u> is large. You cannot use a calculator, so try to ballpark your numbers. Your percent increase can be found by $\frac{change}{original}$.

   A. from 96 to 100 is a difference of 4. $\frac{4}{96} =$ about 4% increase

   B. from 20 to 22 is a difference of 2. $\frac{2}{20} =$ 10% increase

   C. from 46 to 50 is a difference of 5. $\frac{4}{46} =$ about 9% increase

   D. from 4 to 5 is a difference of 1. $\frac{1}{4} =$ 25% increase

   Even if you are a few percentages off, clearly the 25 % is the biggest increase. **(Answer D)**

Tip: An improvement of a few points for low numbers is more significant that an improvement of a few points for large numbers.

2. **Which brand needs to be reevaluated by the company?**

   The explanation of the table states that if an approval rate decreases, the company needs to reevaluate that specific brand. By looking at the table, only one brand decreases in approval rating. This happened to Brand A between 2013-2014. **(Answer A)**

3. **If each brand was ranked based on approval rating in 2013, how many brands would have a different ranking in 2014?**

   In 2013, the rankings for approval ratings are:

1 – Brand A	100
2 – Brand E	80
3 – Brand C	52
4 – Brand B	22
5 – Brand D	5

   In 2014, the rankings for approval ratings are:

1 – Brand E	86
2 – Brand C	52
3 – Brand A	50
4 – Brand B	26
5 – Brand D	12

   You can mark these rankings right on the table. Think on Paper! Only the top three brands (E, C, and A) have changed ranking from 2013 to 2014. **(Answer C)**

4. **What proportion of brands in this division is doing well for the company?**

   According to the passage next to the graph, if a brand's approval rating is increasing, it is "doing well" for the company. Brand A is the only brand that decreases. The other 4 out of 5 are doing well. **(Answer B)**

Tables - Quiz 6: Bouncy Balls   **2 minutes**

A company that manufactures rubber bouncy balls is attempting to create the bounciest ball in the world. The engineers of the company decide that the best way to accomplish this would be to experiment with different varieties of rubber to see how the composition of the ball affects its bounciness.

The experiment included four different varieties of rubber often used in bouncy balls. Balls made of the different materials were each bounced with a force of two Newtons four times from various heights to see how high they would bounce. The company uses one of the varieties in this experiment (Rubber B) currently in its production of bouncy balls. This variety was used as a control. Below are the results.

Rubber A

Drop Height (m)	Height of First Bounce (m)
1	2.5
2	5
3	7.5
4	10

Rubber B

Drop Height (m)	Height of First Bounce (m)
1	2
2	4
3	6
4	8

Rubber C

Drop Height (m)	Height of First Bounce (m)
1	3
2	6
3	9
4	12

Rubber D

Drop Height (m)	Height of First Bounce (m)
1	1.5
2	3
3	4.5
4	6

1. Which variety of rubber should the engineers choose in order to achieve their goal?
   A. Rubber A
   B. Rubber B
   C. Rubber C
   D. Rubber D

2. Which of the following would improve the validity of these results?
   A. Using a stronger force to bounce each ball.
   B. Using more types of rubber.
   C. Dropping each ball from only one height.
   D. Dropping each ball multiple times from each height.

3. Which of the following is the independent variable in this experiment?
   A. The company that manufactures bouncy balls.
   B. The height of the first bounce of each ball.
   C. The type of rubber used in each ball.
   D. Rubber B, because it was used as a control.

4. Which of the following would be an expected result if the number of Newtons increased?
   A. A decrease in bounce height.
   B. An increase in bounce height.
   C. No change in bounce height.
   D. No reliable trend to be found.

1)C 2)D 3)C 4)B

Tables - Quiz 6: Bouncy Balls   (Answers)

 Tip: As soon as you look at a table or graph, mark the independent variable with "IV" and the dependent variable with "DV."

 Tip: If a question asks about anything other than the data in the table or graph, read the entire passage above/below the figure.

1.   Which variety of rubber should the engineers choose in order to achieve their goal?

The section above the tables says that the company's goal is to create the bounciest ball in the world. This can be achieved by creating balls that bounce higher than others. To find the ball that bounces the highest, you need to look at all four tables. The table that has the highest bouncing ball for all drop heights is the bounciest ball. **(Answer C)**

Rubber A

Drop Height (m)	Height of First Bounce (m)
1	2.5
2	5
3	7.5
4	10

2.   Which of these would <u>improve</u> the <u>validity</u> of these results?

The validity of an experiment is the accuracy of the results. One of the main ways to increase the accuracy of an experiment is to do multiple trials and average the results. The other options would not improve the validity of the results because they offer ways to expand on the experiment, not ways to increase the accuracy of the experiment. **(Answer D)**

3.   Which of these is the <u>independent variable</u> in this experiment?

The independent variable in an experiment is the variable that is manipulated by the researchers. The independent variable is NOT the variable the experiment is testing for. In this experiment, the independent variables are the drop height and the type of rubber ball. Only one of these is an option
In order to answer question 3, start by finding the variables. There are three variables present in this table: two independent variables and a dependent variable. If you follow the rules from the first tip, you should label Rubber A and Drop Height as the independent variables and the height of the first bounce as the dependent variable. This should make answering the question more straightforward. **(Answer C)**

4.   Which of the following would be an expected result if the number of Newtons increased?

The section above the tables states that the force exerted on the ball was held constant throughout the entire experiment. It can be assumed that the harder the ball is thrown downward, the higher it will bounce. **(Answer B)**

Tables - Quiz 7: Treadmill   **4 minutes**

A fitness program measured the calories burned by a 200-pound male, jogging on a treadmill at a constant speed of 6 miles per hour at different inclinations between 0^0 and 10^0.
Measurements in the table below are the *additional calories burned* versus jogging the same distance at 0^0 inclination.

Minutes	Degrees incline	Additional calories burned
10	1	5.9
10	3	17.8
10	5	29.6
10	10	58.8
20	1	11.9
20	3	35.5
20	5	59.1
20	10	117.5
30	1	17.9
30	3	53.3
30	5	88.7
30	10	176.3
50	1	29.8
50	3	88.8
50	5	147.8
50	10	293.8
100	1	59.6
100	3	177.5
100	5	295.5
100	10	587.6

1. Approximately how many more calories does this person burn in 30 minutes if he raises the treadmill from 1 degree to 5 degrees?
   A. 24
   B. 35
   C. 71
   D. 118

2. When jogging for 20 minutes, raising the treadmill an additional 2 degrees will burn
   A. 11.9 more calories.
   B. 23.6 more calories.
   C. 35.4 more calories.
   D. 59.1 more calories.

3. Additional calories burned are constant at about
   A. $\dfrac{5.9 \text{ cal} * \text{degrees inclination}}{\text{minute run}}$
   B. $\dfrac{0.59 \text{ cal} * \text{degrees inclination}}{\text{minute run}}$
   C. 5.9 cal * minutes run * degrees inclination
   D. 0.59 cal * minutes run * degrees inclination

4. If the treadmill is set on an inclination of 8 degrees, the runner will burn an additional
   A. 4.8 calories in 10 minutes.
   B. 47.2 calories in 20 minutes.
   C. 236 calories in 30 minutes.
   D. 188.8 calories in 40 minutes.

5. Raising the inclination of the treadmill burns more calories because of
   A. effort against the force of gravity.
   B. effort because of increasing friction.
   C. effort because of increasing amount of energy.
   D. effort because of increasing speed and time.

1) C 2) B 3) A 4) A 5) D

Tables - Quiz 7: Treadmill (Answers)

1. Approximately how many <u>more</u> calories does this person burn in 30 minutes if he raises the treadmill from 1 degrees to 5 degrees?

Underline the word "more". Put your index finger on the 30-minute part of the table.

20	10	117.5
30	1	17.9
30	3	53.3
30	5	88.7
30	10	176.3
50	1	29.8

Strategy: Mark the values of 1 degree (17.9) and 5 degrees (88.7). Reread the question. You need the find the difference between these two values: 71 more calories.
(Answer C)

2. When jogging for 20 minutes, raising the treadmill an <u>additional 2 degrees</u> will burn …

Underline "additional 2 degrees". Then, put your left index finger on the 20-minute part of the table.

10	10	58.8
20	1	11.9
20	3	35.5
20	5	59.1
20	10	117.5
30	1	17.9

Strategy: From 1 degree, an additional 2 degrees will make 3 degrees. Mark the values of 1 degree (about 12) and 3 degrees (about 35). Reread the question. You need the find the difference between these two values: 23.6 more calories. **(Answer B)**

Alternatively, you could have used the values of 3 and 5 degrees, which also indicates an "additional 2 degree" raise. 59.1 – 35.5 = 23.6 more calories.

3. Additional calories burned are constant at about

When asking about graphs or relationships, <u>any</u> point in the table should be able to pinpoint the right answer. Therefore, pick an easy number to do the math.
Pick the number 10 or 100 for minutes and pick the number 1 for degree incline.
Then, plug these numbers into the formula.
Answer A is correct $\frac{5.9\,\text{cal} * 1}{10} = \frac{59\,\text{cal} * 1}{100} = 0.59$
Answer B uses the correct constant (0.59) in the formula but divides it by time.
Answers C and D get larger and larger and therefore would not be constant. **(Answer A)**

4. If the treadmill is set on an inclination of 8 degrees, the runner will burn an additional …

This data needs to sit in the table right between the 5-degree and 10-degree notation.
Answer A (4.8 calories in 10 minutes) is incorrect because it is not between 29.6 and 58.8
Answer B is incorrect (47.2 calories in 20 minutes) because it is not between 59.1 and 117.1
Answer C (236 calories in 30 minutes) is incorrect because it is not between 88.7 and 176.3
Answer D is correct (188.8 calories in 40 minutes) **(Answer D)**

5. Raising the inclination of the treadmill burns more calories because of …

If you walk uphill (or on an inclined treadmill), you need to move forward with each step <u>and</u> you need to move up, away from the gravitational force of the earth. **(Answer A)**

Tables - Quiz 8: Crop Rotation   **2 minutes**

In agriculture, it has long been the tradition to rotate crops in fields. This practice produced more crops overall, but farmers never knew exactly why. It was only recently proven that specific plants absorb certain elements while they introduce other elements back into the earth. By rotating crops, farmers allow the soil to achieve a balanced composition.

Recently, a scientist decided to test how to rotate corn and soybeans in eight greenhouses in order to control all outside factors that might have altered the results of previous experiments. One group of four greenhouses kept the same corn or soybean crops for six years, while the other four rotated the crops every two years.

Time	Soybeans (lbs.)	Corn (lbs.)
Year 1	624	435
Year 2	616	426
Year 3	628	432
Year 4	602	417
Year 5	634	428
Year 6	629	421

Table 1. Greenhouses in Group 1

Time	Soybeans (lbs.)	Corn (lbs.)
Year 1	632	426
Year 2	617	418
Year 3	563	387
Year 4	430	321
Year 5	380	269
Year 6	312	240

Table 2. Greenhouses in Group 2

1. In which year and group did the scientist collect the largest amount of corn?
   A. Group 2, Year 1
   B. Group 2, Year 6
   C. Group 1, Year 3
   D. Group 1, Year 1

2. In which year was the difference in soybean yield the greatest?
   A. Year 4
   B. Year 3
   C. Year 1
   D. Year 6

3. The validity of this experiment would improve if the researchers
   A. vary the temperature in the greenhouses.
   B. compare the crops inside the greenhouses with crops in the field.
   C. continue testing for a longer stretch of time.
   D. use crops other than soybeans and corn.

4. Do these results prove the usefulness of crop rotation?
   A. Yes, the greenhouses where crops were rotated yielded more lbs. of soybeans each year, so the rotation is useful.
   B. No, the greenhouses yielded less lbs. of produce when the crops were rotated, so the rotation was not useful.
   C. No, the difference in lbs. of produce during the first two years was not significant, so the rotation was not useful.
   D. Yes, because the greenhouses yielded more lbs. of corn in the sixth year when the crops were rotated.

1)D 2)D 3)C 4)D

Tables - Quiz 8: Crop Rotation   (Answers)

1. In which year and group did the scientist collect the largest amount of corn?

Underline "largest amount of corn". Use your fingers to indicate the corn part of the table. This question is about the corn column from both Tables 1 and 2. Look for the largest amount of corn produced in a given year. This happens in Table 1 in the first year. 435 lbs. No other year, even in Group 2, produced more corn. **(Answer D)**

2. In which year was the difference in soybean yield the greatest?

Use your fingers to go down the soybean column in Group 1 and Group 2. Compare the soybean yield in Group 1 to the soybean yield in Group 2. The largest difference between the two groups happens in Year 6: 629 lbs. – 312 lbs. = 317 lbs. **(Answer D)**

Time	Soy Beans (lbs.)	Corn (lbs.)	Time	Soy Beans (lbs.)	Corn (lbs
Year 1	624	435	Year 1	632	426
Year 2	616	426	Year 2	617	418
Year 3	628	432	Year 3	563	387
Year 4	602	417	Year 4	430	321
Year 5	634	428	Year 5	380	269
Year 6	629	421	Year 6	312	240
Table 1. Greenhouses in Group 1			**Table 2. Greenhouses in Group 2**		

3. What would improve the validity of this experiment?

This is a typical ACT trick. All of the options appear to better the experiment, but only one improves the validity. Improving the validity of the experiment means improving the accuracy of the results. Think about how you can improve on the scientific method. The ACT will always give you options that expand on the experiment, but not improve the accuracy. To make an experiment more valid, you do not want to add or change the independent or dependent variables. Instead, you want to find a way to add data to the current experiment. In this experiment, you could increase the amount of time that the experiment is being conducted. **(Answer C)**

4. Do these results prove the usefulness of crop rotation?

In the section above the tables, it is stated that crop rotation produced more crops. Based on this information, you can conclude that the group in Table 1 has its crops rotated because every two years there is a small spike of crop production. In Table 2, the production of soybeans and corn decreases year after year. The information explains this difference by mentioning that "specific plants absorb certain elements while they introduce other elements back into the earth". If you compare the numbers after six years of harvest, you can see that Group 1 outperforms Group 2 and you can conclude that crop rotation is useful. **(Answer D)**

GRAPHS

Because of the time restriction, many test takers merely glance at the "pictures" instead of scrutinizing the graphs for scientific details.

Read the Y-axes. (Tilt your head if you need to!) The ACT loves to hide information here.

Find the connections between the X and Y axes: patterns, irregularities, comparisons, and conclusions.

Spending 10 seconds longer looking at a graph will save you time and points in the end.

Don't be too cocky! When you see a connection, write it down. When you think something is important, circle it! Don't do everything in your head.

Graphs are data, too; write numbers on the highs and lows of a graph. Circle the units.

When you see two graphs that look alike, make a note how they are different.

Graphs - Overview

Graphs and tables are different ways of presenting <u>the same data</u>. (See Table 1 and Graph 1.)

Lost socks	
Week 1	2
Week 2	1
Week 3	4
Week 4	2
Week 5	5
Week 6	0

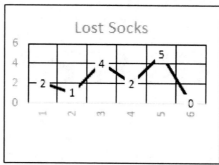

Table 1 ← Same Story! → Graph 1

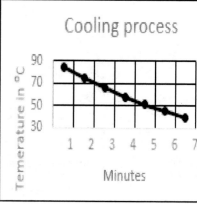

Graph 2

 Tip: *Verify with <u>one single point</u> in the table which graph is incorrect.*

Some graphs have continuing data between each data point, some do not.
  Graph 1: After 4½ weeks, I did **not** lose 3½ socks.
  Graph 2: At 4½ minutes, I **can** infer that the temp. was 50°C.

Each graph tells a visual story of the relationship between the X and the Y-axis.
Do not answer any questions until you understand this relationship.

 Tip: *Summarize the story of the graph to yourself and make notes along the way.*

Even if the graph goes UP, it may mean that the values go down! Be aware of visual distractions in the ACT.

 Tip: *Double check what the graph actually measures. Don't fall for the visual distractors.*

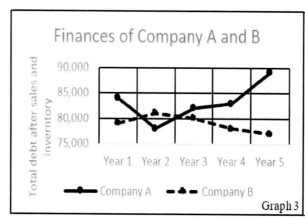

Graph 3

1. According to Graph 3, the company that was financially better off in year 5 was
A. company A
B. company B
C. both companies
D. neither company

Some graphs have two different Y-axes. They will be labeled for different sets of data. Be careful: your eyes will automatically be drawn to the values on the nearest axis, which could be for a different value.

 Tip: *Circle the units. Mention the units again in your answer to make sure you are looking at the right numbers.*

1) B: Higher debt does not mean more money!)

Graphs - Test-taking Skills

The science test will be the last part of your ACT. Most likely, you will be less alert than you were when you started. Work through the exercises in this book to practice your skills and habits that will help you to avoid simple mistakes.

Draw on your graphs to create visual clues.

Tip: If there are two lines, <u>label the lines</u> to avoid confusion and to save time by eliminating the key.

Tip: Information in the Y-axis is often overlooked because it is printed vertically. Make it a habit to <u>circle the units</u>, and <u>mark the peaks and valleys</u>.

Check the scale on the graph. Each part of the line represents certain data.
Connect the X and Y values of a data point with swift lines of your <u>pencil</u>, not with your eyes.
Complicated graphs are simply three or four stories in the same graph. Rather than being intimidated and continue straight to the questions, "read" the graph, and separate the individual stories.
Take it one step at a time. Make quick notes for each bar, line, or relationship on the graph

Tip: If a graph has an abbreviation, stop!
Find out in the text what the abbreviation stands for so that you can understand the story in the graph.

Two Graphs

Read the graphs to <u>spot the difference</u>. (Is the scale the same? What about the Y-axis, the title, the year?)
Read the text to find out <u>what caused the difference</u>. (A different ingredient? A different time or method?)
Example: How do substance A and B in Graph 1 and Graph 2 differ when it comes to temperature and time?

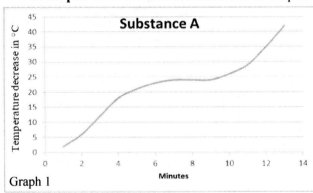

Graph 1

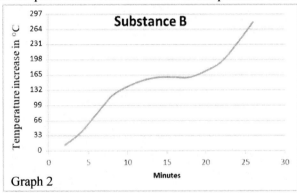

Graph 2

"What if" Questions

Tip: Don't rely on your eyes only.
Draw the data on the graph! Looks can be deceiving.

Example: According to Graph 3, how much would the volume be with a side length of 4 cm?
What about a side length of 5 cm?

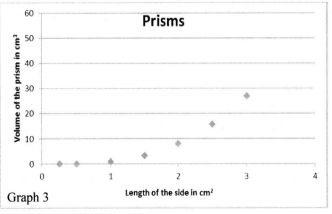

Graph 3

Volume = S^3
Understanding the graph tell you the relationship:
The line curves exponentially. Side length 5 has a volume of 125.
Example 2. Side length 4 corresponds with a volume of 64.
Did you spot the increase / decrease in the Y-axis?
Example 1. Graph 1 and 2 have different Y and X axes.

Graphs - Quiz 1: Elephant Tusks **2 minutes**

The Indian elephant has long been revered for its valuable ivory tusks. While the poaching of elephants is illegal, ivory is so valuable that in many places hunters still hunt elephants. The following graph shows the trend of the mean tusk length of Indian elephants from 1975-2005.

The dramatic decrease in tusk length for these elephants is wholly due to predation and natural selection. Because the elephants with the longest tusks were hunted more frequently by poachers, those with shorter tusks were able to breed more often, allowing for the genes for shorter tusks to be passed down.

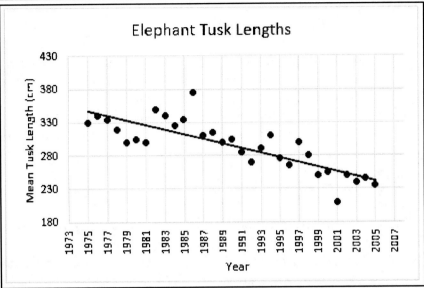

Figure 1

1. Which statement is true about the years from 1978-1986:
    A. The mean tusk length during these years decreased at a steady rate.
    B. The mean tusk length during these years increased at a steady rate.
    C. The mean tusk length during these years decreased at the beginning and increased at the end.
    D. The data within this set has no trend that is observable.

2. What can we infer from the data in Figure 1?
    A. The mean tusk length of Indian elephants has dropped an equal amount every year from 1975-2005.
    B. The number of Indian elephants has steadily decreased from 1975-2005.
    C. Poachers have started removing small parts of the tusks of elephants, rather than the entire tusk, which lowers the average tusk length from 1975-2005.
    D. While there is variability in the individual means for each year, the overall trend of the mean tusk length is negative from 1975-2005.

3. Which table represents the data collected for the mean tusk length (cm)?

Year	Mean Tusk Length
1980	235
1986	275
1995	375
2005	305

Table A

Year	Mean Tusk Length
2005	235
1995	275
1986	375
1980	305

Table B

Year	Mean Tusk Length
2005	305
1995	375
1986	275
1980	235

Table C

Year	Mean Tusk Length
1980	330
1986	310
1995	280
2005	240

Table D

1) C 2) D 3) B

Graphs - Quiz 1: Elephant Tusks (Answers)

1. Which statement is true about the years from 1978-1986

In this case, you cannot put your index finger on one data point, so circle the region that pertains to the question. Also underline in the text that the graph shows the <u>trend of the mean tusk length</u>. In other words, each dot is the mean tusk length of that given year. The mean tusk length varies from year to year although a *line of best fit* shows that there is a gradual decline of tusk lengths over the years.

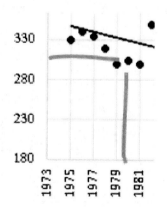

 Tip: Do not look at the line of best fit when the question asks about actual data.

 Tip: When a question asks for a true statement, three answers must be false.

Even though the line of best fit shows a decrease in mean tusk length, the actual data points shows a decrease at the beginning and an increase at the end. **(Answer C)**

2. What can we <u>infer</u> from the data in figure 1?

The question asks you to refer to Figure 1. Figure 1 only refers to the mean tusk lengths (not the number of elephants as in Answer B) from 1975-2005. The figure gives no explanation for the decrease of the trend line (as in Answer C.) Figure 1 shows a line of best fit that decreases over time, but there are individual data points both above and below the trend line. Therefore, Answer A is incorrect. A slope that decreases over the horizontal axis is a negative trend. **(Answer D)**

3. Which table represents <u>the data collected</u> for the mean tusk length (cm)?

This question is similar to question 1 and 2 because it is asking for the actual data instead of the *line of best fit*. You must look at each possible answer and match the correct years to the correct mean tusk lengths.

 Tip: Graphs and tables are two different ways of presenting <u>the same data</u>. You can often verify with <u>one single point</u> in the table which graph is incorrect.

The first data point in Table A is 1980. Draw two lines on the graph to determine that in 1980 the average tusk length was about 300 cm. Only Answer B reflects this same value.

Note: Many students will choose D because the data in the chart matches the line of best fit, but that is not what the question is asking. The question is asking for which table matches the <u>data collected</u>, not the line of best fit. **(Answer B)**

Graphs - Quiz 2: Immigration 1 **2 minutes**

Hundreds of thousands of immigrants enter the United States every year. There are spikes of immigration when more people enter the country than usual, and there are dips of immigration when fewer people enter than usual. Figure 1 shows a chart about the origin of immigrants to Kentucky from 1990 to 1998.
Each segment of the graph represents the percentage of immigrants of different nationalities.

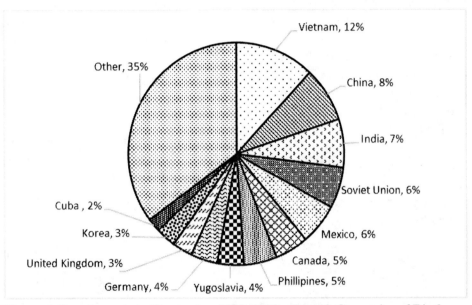

Figure 1. Immigrants to Kentucky, 1990-1998. Top 12 Countries of Birth

1. From 1990 to 1998, immigrants to Kentucky came mostly from which country?
   A. Mexico
   B. The United States of America
   C. Vietnam
   D. Other

2. Which two countries combined represent more than 10% of all immigrants to Kentucky from 1990 to 1998?
   A. Mexico and Cuba
   B. The United Kingdom and Korea
   C. Soviet Union and Germany
   D. The Philippines and Mexico

3. From 1990 to 1998, the least number of immigrants came from which country?
   A. Other
   B. Cuba
   C. Vietnam
   D. Unknown

4. Which country had more immigrants to Kentucky than Yugoslavia, but less immigrants than India?
   A. Germany
   B. Mexico
   C. Other
   D. China

1) C 2) D 3) D 4) B

Graphs - Quiz 2: Immigration 1 (Answers)

1. From 1990 to 1998, immigrants to Kentucky came mostly from which country?

Many people would want to say "other." However, the top 12 countries are already given by name. The section of "other" could actually represent over 100 different countries. Although a large part of the graph, it is insignificant data. Vietnam was the country with the most immigrants to the Kentucky. **(Answer C)**

2. Which two countries combined represented together more than 10% of all immigrants to Kentucky from 1990 to 1998?

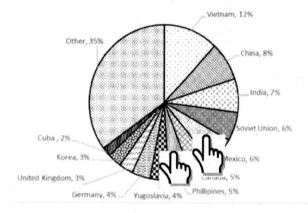

Go through each of the four options and find the one where more than 10% of all immigrants is shown. Use one finger to find the first country, and the second finger to find the second country. The Philippines and Mexico add up to more than 10% of the immigrant population. **(Answer D)**

3. From 1990 to 1998, the least number of immigrants came from which country?

Because the "other" section could mean hundreds of countries where only a miniscule number of immigrants came from, it is impossible to know which country the least number of immigrants came from. **(Answer D)**

4. Which country had more immigrants than Yugoslavia, but less immigrants than India?

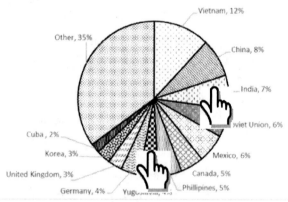

Place one finger on Yugoslavia and one finger on India. Of the four countries listed as possible answers, find the one that is between your two fingers (because the percentages are in order). The country between Yugoslavia and India that is listed as a possible answer is Mexico. **(Answer B)**

Graphs - Quiz 3: Pitching Speed   **2 minutes**

A high school baseball coach wanted to know whether the speed at which the team's pitcher threw the ball had a strong impact on the average hit percentage of the opposing team. The coach hypothesized that the faster a pitch is, the less likely the batter is to hit the ball.

The coach analyzed the last 20 games in which the team played and graphed the results by comparing the speed of a pitch to the percentage of those pitches that were missed. The coach then graphed the results of the analysis below. The data also showed that the average pitch speed was 78 mph, and the average hit percentage of pitches was 63.7 percent.

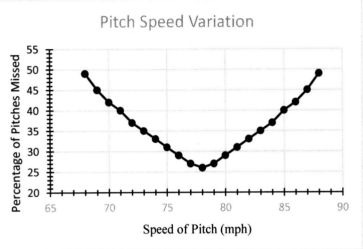

1. According to the graph, was the coach's hypothesis correct?
   A. Yes, the higher speed pitches have a lower likelihood of being hit than those that were slower.
   B. Yes, the pitches that were hit most were not the fastest pitches.
   C. No, the pitches that were hit most often were those that were the fastest.
   D. No, the pitches that were hit most often were those in-between the fastest and the slowest

2. According to the data, which pitch speed would be most likely to be hit by the team?
   A. 88 mph
   B. 85 mph
   C. 76 mph
   D. 63.7 mph

3. Assuming the coach's data is accurate, which of these explanations would best describe why this correlation exists?
   A. Because the average pitch is 78mph, the players are more used to hitting at that speed, which accounts for the higher hit percentage at that speed.
   B. The highest and lowest speed pitches allow players who might swing the bat earlier or later than average to hit these pitches more often.
   C. Because the slowest pitches are the easiest to react to, they have the highest hit percentage.
   D. Because players want to hit the faster balls more often, the hit percentage for the fastest pitches is highest.

1) D 2) C 3) A

Graphs - Quiz 3: Pitching Speed   (Answers)

1. According to the graph, was the coach's hypothesis correct?

This question requires you to read the section before studying the graph. Without this information, it is impossible to know the coach's hypothesis. According to explanation, the coach hypothesized that players are less likely to hit the ball if it is thrown faster.

The second step of answering this question is to look at the graph to see what happened during the 20 games. A key part of the graph is that the vertical axis is "percentage of pitches missed" not "percentage of pitches hit". Many students will miss this important fact if they just look at the <u>image</u> of Pitch Speed Variation, rather than studying the <u>data</u> in the graph. As the pitch speed increases, the percentage of balls missed increases.

We are looking for the overall trend in the data to find when players are more and less likely to hit the baseball. Because the graph changes directions when the speed is in the middle of the graph, we know that this is a crucial point. Since the vertical axis states that this is measuring the percentage of balls missed, the lowest point on the graph represents the speed that players are most likely to hit the ball. This shows that pitches in the middle are more likely to be hit which contradicts the hypothesis given by the coach. **(Answer D)**

2. From this data, which pitch speed would be most likely to be hit by the team?

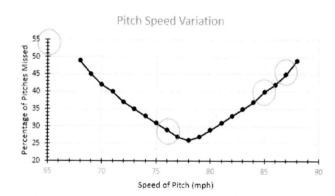

To find the speed that is most likely to be hit by the team, you must recognize that the vertical axis is labeled "percentage of pitches missed" (not "percentage of pitches hit".) This is a crucial step in figuring out the speed that is most likely to be hit. A low percentage of being missed is the same as a high percentage of being hit. That means that we are looking for the lowest point on the graph based on the four possible choices. The lowest point on the graph given the four possible choices is at 76 mph.

(Answer C)

3. Assuming the coach's data is accurate, which of these explanations would best describe why this correlation exist?

This question is asking why most players are able to hit pitches thrown at a medium speed rather than pitches thrown very slow or very fast. Answers C and D are both incorrect because their explanations do not reflect the data in the graph: neither the fastest or slowest pitches were hit at a high percentage.

Answers A and B both explain the current situation, but only one gives a possible answer as to why the data looks the way it does. Answer B is suggesting that players who prefer to swing early or late have a greater chance to hit the ball if the ball is thrown faster or slower. Although this may be true, it does not explain the trend in the data. It only explains why some of the slow and fast pitches were hit. Answer A gives a possible explanation because more players are hitting the ball at a medium speed. **(Answer A)**

Graphs - Quiz 4: Weather   **2 minutes**

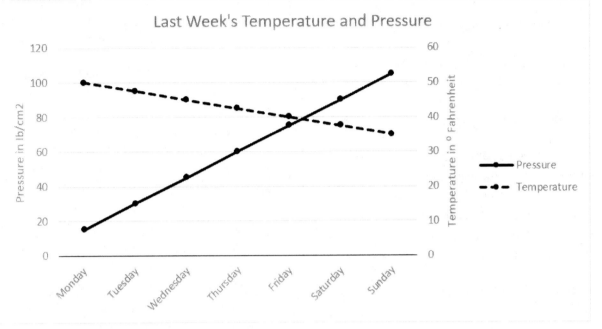

Last Week's Temperature and Pressure

1) What was the temperature on Tuesday?
   A. 30° F
   B. 35° C
   C. 48° F
   D. 95° F

2) On which day did the temperature (in Fahrenheit) measure the same value as the pressure (in pounds per centimeter squared)?
   A. Monday
   B. Wednesday
   C. Friday
   D. Sunday

3) Which set of data gives the correct temperature range and pressure range?

	Temperature	Pressure
A.	35 - 100	15 - 55
B.	15 - 55	100 - 35
C.	35 - 55	15 - 100
D.	35 - 50	15 - 105

1) C 2) B 3) D

439   Copyright 2017 Winni van Gessel

Graphs - Quiz 4: Weather   (Answers)

 Tip: Read and understand the entire graph before you answer any questions pertaining to it.

 Tip: If a graph has two vertical axes, label both lines on the graph carefully.

1. What was the temperature on Tuesday?

This graph contains two sets of data. Each set is represented on a different vertical axis. Pressure is represented on the left vertical axis while temperature is represented on the right vertical axis. To find temperature, you must find the correct line and corresponding vertical axis.

The most common mistake is to let your eyes do the job. It is easy to spot Tuesday on the X-axis, and it is not difficult to determine that the dotted line is the temperature. However, your eyes will look for the closest data reference, which is <u>on the left!</u>

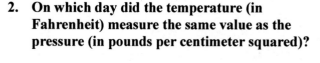

 Tip: Circle the units and use them in your answer.
"What is the temperature?"
 "90."
"90 what?"
"90 pounds per square centimeter." ???
The dotted line and the vertical axis <u>on the right</u> are the ones that represents temperature in this graph. The answer is about 48 degrees Fahrenheit. **(Answer C)**

2. On which day did the temperature (in Fahrenheit) measure the same value as the pressure (in pounds per centimeter squared)?

This question can be tricky because most people will read this question and see the key word "same" and see the lines intersect. They assume that this is the answer solely because the lines intersect. This is incorrect because at the intersection, the pressure is equal to 80 lb/cm^2 and the temperature is equal to 40°F. The fact that they cross is purely a visual coincidence. This question is asking for the day in which the temperature is equal to the pressure. To do this, go through each of the four possible answers and compare the temperature to the pressure. The only day where temperature is equal to pressure is Wednesday when the temperature is 45°F and the pressure is 45 lb/cm^2. **(Answer B)**

3. Which set of data gives the correct temperature range and pressure range?
This problem is asking for the correct <u>range</u> for both the temperature and pressure in the graph. To answer the question, you must associate each line with the correct vertical axis. The pressure line corresponds with the left vertical axis while the temperature line corresponds with the right vertical axis.

 Tip: Write numbers down as you go.

The temperature line shows a range in the data from 35-50 and the pressure line shows a range in the data from 15-105. **(Answer D)**

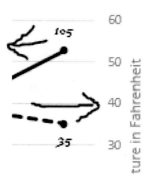

Graphs - Quiz 5: Immigration 2   **3 minutes**

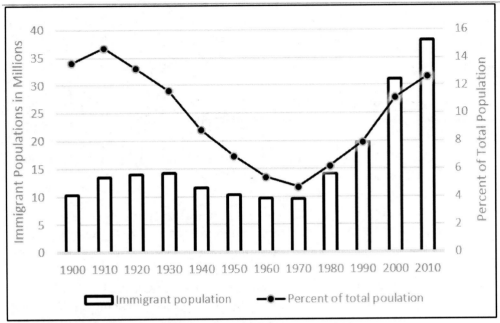

Figure 1, U.S. Immigrant Population, 1900 – 2010

1. According to Figure 1, what was the range (in millions) of the immigrant population between 1900 to 2010?
   A. 10-13
   B. 10-15
   C. 13-38
   D. 10-38

2. According to the graph, what percentage of the U.S. population consisted of immigrants in 1940?
   A. 11.6
   B. 8.8
   C. 23
   D. Unknown

3. According to the graph, how many millions of immigrants lived in the U.S.A. in 2010?
   A. 12.6
   B. 15
   C. 38.1
   D. Unknown

4. In what year was the number of immigrants identical to the percentage of the rest of the population living in the US?
   A. 1990
   B. 2000
   C. 2010
   D. None of these years

5. What year saw the biggest decrease in immigrants as a percentage of the total population?
   A. From 1910 to 1920
   B. From 1930 to 1940
   C. From 1960 to 1970
   D. From 1990 to 2000

6. The two parts of the graph
   A. are directly related to each other.
   B. measure the same quantity but are unrelated.
   C. measure similar quantities in different relationships.
   D. have no relationship with each other.

1) D 2) B 3) C 4) C 5) D 6) C

Graphs - Quiz 5: Immigration 2   (Answers)

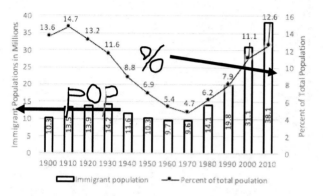

Immigrant population   ▬ Percent of total poulation

Tip: If a graph has 2 vertical axes, draw a line towards the line/bar that each side represents and label each part clearly.

1. **According to Figure 1, what was the range (in millions) of the immigrant population between 1900 to 2010?**

    Draw a line from the bars to the left vertical axis because they both represent the immigrant population in millions. The lowest value is 10, The highest value is 38. **(Answer D)**

2. **According to the graph, what percentage of the U.S. population consisted of immigrants in 1940?**

    The <u>percentage</u> of the US population is represented by the line above the bars on the graph. Find the year 1940 on the X-axis and follow it up until you hit the line. The corresponding vertical axis on the right tells you that the percent of total population at in 1940 is a little over 8%.
    (Answer B)

3. **According to the graph, how many millions of immigrants lived in the U.S. in 2010?**

    Make sure you follow the tip above. Draw a line from the bars to the left vertical axis because they both represent the immigrant population in millions. If you go to 2010 on the X-axis and follow the bar to the top, you will see that the immigration population is 38.1 million.
    (Answer C)

4. **In what year was the number of immigrants identical to the percentage of the rest of the population in the USA?**

    Just because the bar graph and line graph touch each other does not mean that the results are identical. There are two separate axes that represent different data. If you follow the tip above, you will notice the difference in the data. There is no point on the graph where the number of immigrants is equal to the percentage of the rest of the population living in the USA.
    (Answer D)

5. **What year saw the biggest decrease in immigrants as a percentage of the total population?**

    This question refers to the line graph, not the bar graph. You know this because it deals with percentages, not the actual population. The biggest fall in the line graph occurs from 1930-1940. **(Answer B)**

6. **The two parts of the graph**

    Both parts of the graph represent the immigrants in the U.S.A. but focus on different measures. The bar graph shows the immigrant population in millions, and the line graph shows the immigrants as a percent of the total population of the United States. **(Answer C)**

Graphs - Quiz 6: Invasive Species **2 minutes**

An invasive species is a species that has been introduced to an area in which it would normally not be found. A prolific example is the European Starling, a mostly *insectivorous* bird that was introduced to North America in the mid-20th century. Below is a graph that demonstrates the effect of this invasive species on a 15-square-mile region of North America where in 2003 a few European Starlings were introduced to an otherwise stable ecosystem.

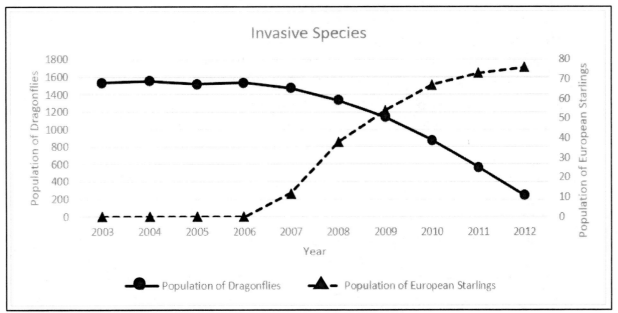

Figure 1

1. In which year are the dragonfly and European Starling populations closest to each other?
   A. 2003
   B. 2008
   C. 2009
   D. 2012

2. How many dragonflies were in the area of study in 2011?
   A. Approximately 30
   B. Approximately 70
   C. Approximately 550
   D. Approximately 1600

3. What is the most likely explanation of the data in Figure 1?
   A. When the starlings were introduced, they disrupted the ecosystem and caused the dragonflies to migrate to a new location.
   B. The starlings that were introduced disrupted the food chain because the birds consumed dragonflies at a greater rate than the insects could repopulate.
   C. The starlings ate all the dragonflies, which allowed the population of starlings to grow rapidly.
   D. The dragonflies were able to grow rapidly in population because the starlings competed with the insects' main predator.

1) D 2) C 3) B

Graphs - Quiz 6: Invasive Species (Answers)

1. In which year are the dragonfly and European Starling populations closest to each other?

The key to this question is to look at the values on both vertical axes. In Figure 1, each horizontal line represents different populations for starlings and dragonflies. In 2009, the same horizontal line represents 50 European Starlings (on the right) and 1200 dragonflies (on the left.) Draw arrows and circle your y-axis to form a habit of reading accurate data.

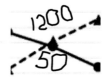

This question asks when the populations are closest to one another. Since the European Starlings never reach a population above 75 and the dragonflies never reach a population less than 250, we already know that the two populations are never equal to one another, but they come closer and closer each year.

The highest value on the graph for the European Starlings population and the lowest value on the graph for the dragonfly population happen in the same year: 2012. **(Answer D)**

 Tip: When two lines cross but represent data on two different axes with two different scales, the intersection has no meaning at all. It is only a visual distraction.

2. How many <u>dragonflies</u> were in the area of study in 2011?

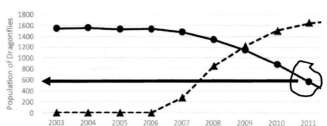

To find the population of dragonflies you must use the correct set of data. The solid line and the left vertical axis represent the population of dragonflies. The population of dragonflies was slightly less than 600. **(Answer C)**

The most common mistake is to let your eyes do the job. It is easy to spot 2011 on the X-axis, and it is not difficult to determine that the solid line represents the dragonflies. However, your eyes will look for the closest data reference, which is <u>on the right</u>, but wrongly tells you how many starlings were observed in 2011.

3. What is the most likely explanation of the data in Figure 1?

Answer C states that the starlings ate <u>all</u> the dragonflies, which is incorrect.
Answer D states that the dragonfly population increased, which is not true based on the graph.

That leaves only Answer A and Answer B. Both answers are possible explanations for the decrease in the dragonflies' population, but Answer A does not give a reason for the increase in the starling population.
On the other hand, Answer B uses information from the text (The starlings are insectivorous, which means they eat insects) to explain why there was a decrease in the dragonflies, while in the meantime the starlings thrived. Note how the slope is flattening out due to the decreased food supply in 2011 and 2012. **(Answer B)**

RESEARCH SUMMARIES (Experiments)

The questions are all about understanding the data.

90 % of the information falls into place when you understand the connection between the dependent and the independent variable: patterns, irregularities, comparisons, and conclusions.

The text often talks about the independent variable. Underline it when you read it. The tables and graphs show the results of the dependent variable.

Spending 10 seconds longer looking at a setup of an experiment will save you time and points in the end.

Don't be too cocky! When you see a connection, write it down. When you think something is important, circle it! Don't do everything in your head.

When you **read** about different stages in an experiment (repetitions under different circumstances or the addition of new variables) **take notes** and jot down what elements changed!

Follow the Scientific Method in all your reasoning.

Research Summaries (Experiments)

Tip: Start with the graphs and the data. 90% of the important information is located right there. Read quickly through the rest of the information.

Tip: DO NOT answer any questions unless you understand the setup and the purpose of the experiment. Many students go to the questions before fully understanding the research. This is not rocket science; this is the ACT. Even when the data looks complicated, all the information you need is provided on the page.

Tip: Always take note of the italicized words in the text. They are central to understanding the information and the questions later on.

Often, an experiment in the ACT has several stages. First the researcher changed, this, then that, and then one more detail. Pay attention to these changes.

Tip: Identify the independent and the dependent variables for every table, graph, and change in the experiment.

Variables

The <u>independent variable</u> tells you what the researcher is changing.
The <u>dependent variable</u> is the data that the researcher is gathering.

A researcher kept growth record of plants in the lab. She added some salt to the soil of a plant. After two weeks, she measured the plant at 4.5 inches (A). To find out if the salt had affected the plant's growth she checked the lab records. Looking at the logs, she learned that the week before the plant had measured 4.8 inches (B). At the time that the salt had been added to the soil, according to the record, the plant had measured 5.0 inches.

The Scientific Method

A good researcher keeps all variables the same, changes <u>one</u> aspect, records the data accurately, repeats the trials several times, and calculates the averages.

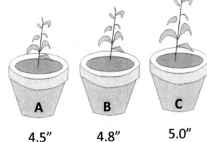

4.5"   4.8"   5.0"

Figure 1.

Tip: Take note of the order in the steps of the experiments.

Tip: Mark on your paper if you see inconsistencies. They might have slipped your mind by the time you are answering questions later.

Example 1: The researcher recorded that the plant in Figure 1
A. had grown 0.2 inches during the experiment.
B. had grown 0.3 inches during the experiment.
C. had grown 0.5 inches during the experiment.
D. had not grown at all.

1) D. The plants lost 0.5 inches in height.
Scientifically, this approach is sound; however, the ACT loves a more confusing approach like this one.

Experiments - Quiz 1: Bouncy Balls **3 minutes**

Jackson and Joel wanted to determine which of their favorite bouncy balls bounced higher. They ran three different tests to determine which brand was superior in bounce height.

For their first experiment, they dropped each ball four times from a height of 5 meters. They recorded the results in Table 1.

Table 1		
Trial	Distance bounced (meters)	
	Super Bouncer	Power Bouncer
1	4.6	4.2
2	4.0	4.4
3	4.4	4.2
4	4.6	4.9
Average.	4.4	4.4

For their second experiment, Jackson and Joel dropped each ball from varying heights. They recorded the results in Table 2.

Table 2		
Height (meters)	Distance bounced (meters)	
	Super Bouncer	Power Bouncer
5	4.7	4.4
10	9.2	8.9
15	13.9	13.1
20	18.3	17.7
Average.	11.5	11.0

For their third experiment, Jackson and Joel dropped each ball once and measured the distance bounced on four consecutive bounces. They recorded the results in Table 3.

Table 3		
Bounce	Average distance bounced (meters)	
	Super Bouncer	Power Bouncer
1	9.2	8.8
2	8.6	8.0
3	7.8	7.0
4	7.0	5.6

1. Based on the data from these experiments, when each ball was dropped from a height of 5 meters we can conclude that
   A. the Super Bouncer is superior with a bounce that is 0.3 m. higher on average.
   B. the Super Bouncer and the Power Bouncer perform equally well.
   C. the Super Bouncer performs the worst, because its lowest bounce was 4.0 m.
   D. the Power bouncer outperforms the Super Bouncer every time with a best bounce of 4.9 m.

2. Based on Tables 2 and 3, the bouncy balls in the third experiment were dropped from approximately which distance?
   A. 1 meter
   B. 5 meters
   C. 10 meters
   D. Cannot be determined

3. After dropping a ball and letting it bounce four times, the Power Bouncer measured
   A. 0.4 m. lower than the Super Bouncer.
   B. 0.8 m. higher than its first bounce.
   C. 1.4 m. lower than its first bounce.
   D. 3.2 m. lower than its first bounce.
   E. 13.3 meters higher than its first bounce.

4. Conclusive data to determine which ball performs the best can be found in
   A. Table 1 only.
   B. Table 1 and 2.
   C. Table 2 and 3.
   D. Table 3 only.

1) B 2) C 3) D 4) C

Experiments - Quiz 1: Bouncy Balls (Answers)

Strategy: When you read something in the text that relates to the graphs or tables, make a connection with <u>arrows or writing</u>. You may think you will remember it, but this is the science part of the ACT, about 3 hours into the test!

For their first experiment, they dropped each ball four times from a <u>height of 5 meters</u>. The results are recorded in table 1.

Start at 5 meters

Table 1

| Trial | Distance bounced (meters) | |
	Super Bouncer	Power Bouncer
1	4.6	4.2
2	4.0	4.4
3	4.4	4.2
4	4.6	4.9
Ave.	4.4	4.4

1. Based on the data from these experiments, when each ball was dropped from a height of 5 meters we can conclude that

Answer A is incorrect: Although it does bounce 0.3 m. higher at trial 3 and once in table 2, the Super Bouncer does not bounce 0.3 m. higher <u>on average</u>. Answer C is incorrect: Scientific conclusions come from multiple tries, not a single measurement. Answer D is incorrect because the Power bouncer does not outperform the Super Bouncer <u>every time</u>.
The Super Bouncer and the Power Bouncer perform equally well if you look at the averages. On individual trials, they might vary, but good scientific conclusions are based on the averages of several trials. **(Answer B)**

2. Based on Tables 2 and 3, the bouncy balls in the third experiment were dropped from approximately which distance?

Table 2

| Height (meters) | Distance bounced (meters) | |
	Super Bouncer	Power Bouncer
5	4.7	4.4
10	9.2	8.9
15	13.9	13.1
20	18.3	17.7
Ave.	11.5	11.0

For their third experiment, Jackson and Joel dropped each ball once and measured the distance on four consecutive bounces. They recorded the results in table 3.

Table 3

| Bounce | Average distance bounced (meters) | |
	Super Bouncer	Power Bouncer
1	9.2	8.8
2	8.6	8.0
3	7.8	7.0
4	7.0	5.6

How are the two tables similar? What do they have in common? Only the first bounce in Table 3 is similar to the data in Table 2. The data in Table 3 is very close to the 10-meter drop in the previous two tables. **(Answer C)**

3. After dropping a ball and letting it bounce four times, the Power Bouncer measured

Use your finger to find the right spot in the table. (Table 3, multiple bounces; right side, Power Bouncer)
8.8 - 5.6 = 3.2 meters.
(Answer D)

Table 3

| e distance bounced (meters) | |
Bouncer	Power Bouncer
.2	8.8
.6	8.0
.8	7.0
.0	5.6

4. Conclusive data to determine which ball performs the best can be found in

A good experiment is repeated several times and the averages can support a conclusion. In Table 1, the averages were identical and did not prove one ball superior to the other. Both Tables 2 and 3 show the average bounce of the Super Bouncer to be higher than the Power Bouncer. **(Answer C)**

Experiments - Quiz 2: Tire Pressure **3 minutes**

When left untreated, a small hole in a tire can progressively influence the tire pressure over time. A researcher took two identical tires and measured the Tire Pressure Loss (TPL) over a period of two weeks. For verification purposes, each tire was monitored for an initial period of two weeks to make sure it held pressure. Neither tire showed any loss of pressure: Tire A retained a constant of 32 lb/in^2 (32 PSI) while Tire B retained a constant of 34 lb/in^2 (34 PSI). Then the researcher deliberately drilled an identical small hole in each tire and noted how the pressure evolved over 14 consecutive days.
The data for both tires is displayed in Graph 1.

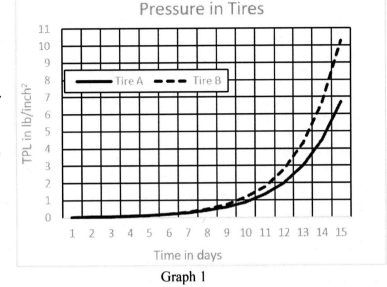

Graph 1

1) At the end of day 14, what was the approximate tire pressure of Tire A?
   A. 6   lb/in^2
   B. 8   lb/in^2
   C. 26 lb/in^2
   D. 38 lb/in^2

2) At the end of day 13, the pressure in Tire B was approximately how much more than in Tire A?
   A. 2 lb/in^2
   B. 4 lb/in^2
   C. −2 lb/in^2
   D. They have approximately the same amount of pressure.

3) The tire pressure in both tires
   A. was higher in week 2 than in week 1.
   B. was lower in week 2 than in week 1.
   C. was equal in both weeks.
   D. cannot be determined because it changes continuously.

4) From the data in Graph 1, we can establish that the researcher drilled a hole in the tire
   A. two weeks before Day 1.
   B. at the beginning of Day 1.
   C. during Day 7.
   D. during Day 14.

1) C 2) D 3) B 4) B

Experiments - Quiz 2: Tire Pressure (Answers)

Tip: Whenever you see an <u>abbreviation</u>, make sure you know what it stands for. What is TPL?

Tip: Watch out for data presented <u>backwards</u>. The line in Graph 1 goes up, but the pressure goes down.

Tip: The ACT loves to combine the two tips above into one table or one graph.

Did you make any mistakes? Be aware of mistakes that you can avoid if you are diligent.
  A. Circle abbreviations.
  B. Write on your graphs.
  C. Understand the experiment.
If you understand the tips above, looking up the data is fairly easy.

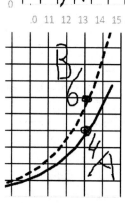

1. At the end of day 14, what was the approximate tire pressure of Tire A?

Eliminate the keys and write on the graph. Put your finger on the right spot and be precise about what the point on the graph indicates. At the end of day 14, the TPL (Tire Pressure <u>Loss</u>) is 6 PSI. The question asks for the <u>pressure</u> in tire A. 32 − 6 = 26 PSI. **(Answer C)**

2. At the end of day 13, the pressure in Tire B was approximately how much higher than in Tire A?

Write on your graph. Mark the data: B lost 6 PSI and A lost 4 PSI. B's pressure is now 34 − 6 = 28 PSI and A's pressure is now 32 − 4 = 28 PSI. After 13 days, the pressure is the same. **(Answer D)**

3. The tire pressure in both tires was

Science experiments depend on your understanding the concept. Do not answer any questions until you know what is going on. If there is a hole in the tire, what happens to the pressure? It goes down. Watch out for data that is presented backwards. The graph goes <u>up</u>, but the pressure goes <u>down</u>. **(Answer B)**

4. From the data in Graph 1, we can establish that the researcher drilled a hole in the tire

This information is in the text. The data sits in the graph, but the procedure can be found in the description.

"For verification purposes, each tire was <u>monitored for an initial period of two weeks</u> to make sure it held pressure. Neither tire showed any loss of pressure: Tire A kept a constant of 32 lb/in^2 (32 PSI,) while Tire B kept a constant of 34 lb/in^2 (34 PSI.) <u>Then, the researcher deliberately drilled a similar small hole</u> in each tire and noted how the pressure evolved over <u>14 consecutive days</u>. The data for both tires is displayed in Graph 1." **(Answer B)**

Experiments - Quiz 3: Acidity   **3 minutes**

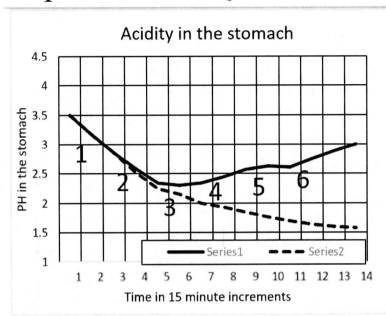

Acidity in the stomach

PH in the stomach

Time in 15 minute increments

Series1 — — Series2

When people eat food, the stomach's parietal cells produce hydrochloric acid to help break down food. In some individuals, this can cause heartburn, which feels like a burning sensation in the chest and is caused by acid regurgitation into the esophagus. *Antacids* often help to neutralize the acid and reduce the effect of heartburn.

Each 15 minutes, the patient ate 50 grams of highly fatty foods to keep the amount of food in the stomach constant during the whole test period. Scientists then tested five different remedies to reduce the acidity of the stomach lining. These antacids were administered during regular intervals. The acidity of the stomach was measured each 15 minutes in PH. (PH stands for "power of hydrogen." It is a logarithmic scale of the molar concentration of hydrogen ions.) The results of the first trial are displayed in the graph as Series 1. A day later, the experiment was repeated under the same circumstances, but without antacids. This experiment was recorded as Series 2.

1) Exactly 1.5 hours after the start of the first trial, the PH in the stomach was
   A. between 1.5 and 2.
   B. between 2 and 2.5.
   C. between 2.5 and 3.
   D. between 3 and 3.5.

2) The scientists dismissed two antacids because they did not seem to have an effect on reducing the stomach acidity. These antacids were
   A. antacid 1 and 2.
   B. antacid 2 and 3.
   C. antacid 1 and 5.
   D. antacid 3 and 5.

3) Compared to Series 1, the acidity in the stomach during the control test was
   A. generally higher than in Series 1.
   B. generally lower than in Series 1
   C. the same in the first three hours and then the PH was higher.
   D. the same in the first three hours and then it was lower.

4) During Day 2 (Series 2), how did the acidity at the end of the eighth 15-minute interval compare to the acidity at the end of the second 15-minute interval?
   A. 1 times stronger
   B. 1.5 times stronger
   C. 2 times stronger
   D. 10 times stronger

1) B 2) C 3) A 4) D

Copyright 2017 Winni van Gessel

Experiments - Quiz 3: Acidity   (Answers)

1) **Exactly 1.5 hours after the start of the first trial, the PH in the stomach was**

Since this question is asking for information about the first trial, the only important data points are in Series 1 (the non-dashed line). One and a half hours of data is <u>six</u> time increments (each time increment is 15 minutes). After 1.5 hours, Series 1 is between PH 2 and 2.5. **(Answer B)**

2) **The scientists dismissed two antacids because they did not seem to have an effect on reducing the stomach acidity. These antacids were**

The section next to the graph states that Series 2 was the control group (no antacids were taken) and Series 1 was the experimental group (antacids were taken). The first antacid had obviously no effect. (Both the control and the antacid produced the same results.) Antacid 2 had a small impact on the stomach acidity by slowing the process down. Antacid 3 was able to bring the PH up again, and so did 4 and 6. (look at the effect these last three antacids had by observing what happened in the 15 minutes afterwards. Antacid 1 and 5 did not have the desired result. **(Answer C)**

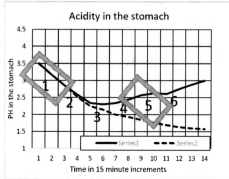

3) **Compared to Study 1, the acidity in the stomach during the control test was**

Watch out for graphs with inverse values. Underline the question: Does it ask about the PH, or the Acidity? Does the answer talk about the first three hours, or the first three 15-minute intervals? According to the text, Series 1 (experimental group) is the non-dashed line and Series 2 (control group) is the dashed line. This question is asking to compare the two days of study. The PH scale ranges from 0-14. Any PH lower than 7 is considered to be acidic. When acidity rises (away from 0), the PH gets lower (closer to 0). The control group always has a higher or equal acidity (lower or equal PH) as the experimental group. Therefore, the acidity in the control test was generally higher than in Day 1 (Series 1). **(Answer A)**

4) **During Day 2 (Series 2), how did the acidity at the end of the seventh 15-minute interval compare to the acidity at the end of the second 15-minute interval?**

Use you pencil or your index finger. Check the dotted line. After seven 15-minutes intervals, the PH was 2; after two 15-minutes intervals, the PH was 3.
The PH scale is logarithmic. (Yes, there are a few scientific facts that the ACT expects you to remember from class.) Therefore, the acidity was 10 times stronger after almost 2 hours. **(Answer D)**

CONFLICTING VIEWPOINTS

Scrutinize the viewpoints for scientific differences and similarities.

Make a T-table to save time. Making notes often provides you with better understanding and insights.

Don't be too cocky! When you see a connection, write it down. When you think something is important, circle it! Don't do everything in your head.

Because of time restrictions, you can choose to keep this passage (traditionally, there is only one) until the end.

Conflicting Viewpoints

The section with conflicting viewpoints is traditionally one of the longer sections of the ACT and the one in which students make a lot of mistakes. Because every question weighs equally, consider saving this section for the end. (Timewise, you might be better off if you complete six questions in the next experiment.) If you have only minutes to spare, you can even do half of the conflicting viewpoints by reading only the information and the questions about Scientist 1.

Tip: Skip this section and come back to it at the end of the test.

T-Tables

A lot of information in the text has to do with how the two scientists agree with each other and where they disagree. The best way to do this is to put them side by side. (See model below)

Tip: Draw a T-Table.
- For Scientist 1, write the most important elements in the table on the left.
  - Use abbreviations, drawings, and diagrams.
- For Scientist 2, write similar elements next to those of Scientist 1 on the other side of the T.
  - Draw opposing arrows where the theories contrast.
  - Write an equal sign where the scientists agree on a fact.
  - If one scientist has a theory that the other does not address, leave the space on the other side of the table blank

Types of Questions

Detail: These questions ask about specific information. Which of the scientists said….?
→Refer to the T-table.

Inference: These questions ask you to make an inference. Who would agree with ….?
Make inferences based on only the presented elements in the text.
→ Refer to the T-table.

Comparison: These questions analyze similarities and differences between arguments.
Who supports the claim that …..? Scientist 1, Scientist 2, both scientists, or neither of them.
→Refer to the T-table.

Tip: The time it will take to make a T-table will be offset by the time you save because you will not have to re-read the text over and over again for pertinent details.

Tip: Rather than reading, make a T-table to help you understand each scientist's argument clearly. The act of writing things down helps you to internalize the information.

Let's practice. In the T-table below, you can see how ideas (here represented by letters) compare.

Scientist 1	Scientist 2
A	A
B-	B+
C	
	D

Viewpoints - Quiz 1: Noises   **3 minutes**

For many people, specific noises – like nails on a chalkboard or scratching glass with a knife – can cause a strong negative reaction. While it is agreed that the sensitivity to these noises is widespread, the cause of this reaction is still debated.

Scientist 1
The cringe-inducing noises to which most humans respond negatively have a solely evolutionary basis. The reason humans find these noises uncomfortable is due to a vestigial reflex in response to a source of danger. In Macaque monkeys, for example, warning calls for danger mimic the frequencies of these unpleasant sounds. In other words, the negative response to these sounds exists because humans used to have similarly unpleasant-sounding calls to warn of danger.

Scientist 2
While evolution might play a role in this phenomenon, the reason that humans find these noises uncomfortable is not a vestigial reflex. The reaction is due to the fact that these sounds cause harm to humans. Each of these uncomfortable noises lie between 2000 and 5000 Hertz, which is in the highest range of sound that humans can hear. Long-time exposure to these noises is harmful to the human ear. The brain responds negatively as a protective response. This accounts for the fact that humans find these sounds unpleasant.

1. Which of these claims would most harm Scientist 1's argument?
   A. Human ancestors relied heavily on warning cries to alert for threats of danger.
   B. Men and women have different responses to these sounds.
   C. The frequency range of warning calls in primates tends to favor the range of 800 to 1500 Hz.
   D. The brain does not respond to the threat of auditory harm.

2. Evolution can explain many of the processes and reflexes in the body. Which of the scientists bases his or her theories on the fact that evolution plays a role in the way humans react to uncomfortable noises?
   A. Scientist 1
   B. Scientist 2
   C. Both scientists
   D. Neither scientist

3. A study found that humans become uncomfortable when presented with images of the actions that might cause these noises. Which scientist's theory does this most support?
   A. Scientist 1, because if he argues that it is a vestigial reflex, seeing the picture would also trigger a danger response.
   B. Scientist 1, because he argues that the response to these sounds is not solely auditory.
   C. Scientist 2, because she argues that the body is uncomfortable due to the harm these sounds cause in the long run, so pictures of the same situation trigger the same response from the brain.
   D. Scientist 2, because she argues that the frequency is the only reason humans become uncomfortable when they hear these sounds.

1) C 2) C 3) C

Viewpoints - Quiz 1: Noises (Answers)

Tip: Whenever you see the conflicting viewpoints passage, make a T-chart. It takes a little time, but it makes answering each question much easier. Most of the questions compare the main points of each scientist, and you do <u>not</u> have time to reread the passage for each question.

Scientist 1	Scientist 2
All evolution	Maybe evolution
Vestigial reflex (danger)	NOT vestigial reflex
Monkeys – warning calls	sounds can harm us.
similar frequency	
Humans used to use same warning calls	high range of hearable sound (2000-5000 Hertz)

1. **Which of these claims would most <u>harm</u> Scientist 1's argument?**

   Scientist 1 argues that the vestigial reflex is the reason humans find these noises uncomfortable. The scientist argues that the unpleasant sounds mimic the sounds created during warning calls for animals.

   The only option that opposes the views of Scientist 1 is the one that states the frequency range of warning calls is different than the range of the unpleasant sounds. According to the T-chart you just made, the range for an unpleasant sound is 2000-5000 Hertz. If the range of warning calls is found to be much lower than the range for an unpleasant sound, then Scientist 1's argument would be greatly hurt. **(Answer C)**

2. **Evolution can explain many of the processes and reflexes in the body. Which of the scientists bases his or her theories on the fact that evolution plays a role in the way humans react to uncomfortable noises?**

   Both scientists state that evolution plays a role in their theories. **(Answer C)**

3. **A study found that humans become uncomfortable when presented with images of the actions that might cause these noises. Which scientist's theory does this most support?**

   According to the chart you just made, Scientist 2's main argument is that humans consider these sounds to be uncomfortable because their frequencies might be harmful. Scientist 1's argument is that the sound resembles a warning call from other animals and past generations of humans.

   Being shown images would <u>not</u> support Scientist 1 because the picture is not comparable to warning calls. However, being shown images would support Scientist 2 because the pictures show the same threat of danger as the noises. **(Answer C)**

Viewpoints - Quiz 2: Diets   **3 minutes**

Recently, vegetarian diets have become much more popular than they have been in the past. Below, two scientists state their ideas on the health benefits of a vegetarian lifestyle.

Student 1

A vegetarian lifestyle is much healthier than the omnivorous lifestyle that most people pursue. By increasing the number of vegetables in the diet, the amount of vitamins and minerals absorbed by the body increases drastically. Further, because meat products account for more than half of people's saturated fat intake, cutting it out can only decrease the amount of saturated fats ingested, leading to an overall healthier body.

Student 2

While eating fruits and vegetables is important, they cannot account for the entirety of one's diet for ideal health to be achieved. Meat is the main source of protein that people consume, which is necessary for muscle growth, development, and maintenance. Further, while meat can be a major source of saturated fat, there are lean options that reduce fat intake by a large margin. While saturated fat is not good for the body, the benefit of protein outweighs the cost of a slightly higher fat intake.

1. If a study were to find that the amount of protein one can process from nuts and beans was equivalent to the amount of protein in meat, whose argument would be most harmed?
   A. Student 1, because the protein in beans and nuts does not address the issue of saturated fat in meat.
   B. Student 1, because the protein in meat is better than the protein in nuts and beans.
   C. Student 2, because Student 2's main argument for eating meat is the protein it provides; finding an alternate source for that protein invalidates his point.
   D. Student 2, because protein in nuts and beans is even better than protein in meat.

2. Do the two students disagree on the negative effects of saturated fats?
   A. No, because both students acknowledge that saturated fat is bad.
   B. No, because neither student argues that saturated fat is bad for the body.
   C. Yes, because Student 1 argues that saturated fat is bad for the body while student 2 argues that it is not.
   D. Yes, because Student 2 argues that saturated fat is bad for the body, but student 1 does not.

3. Student 2's argument would be best supported if which of these were found to be true:
   A. Vegetables account for 80% of humans' vitamin and mineral intake.
   B. Saturated fats are good for the body when accompanied by large amounts of protein.
   C. The protein found in vegetables is equivalent to meat protein in its ability to grow, develop, and maintain muscle.
   D. The minerals found in vegetables can cause negative health effects.

1) C 2) A 3) B

Viewpoints - Quiz 2: Diets (Answers)

Tip: Whenever you see the conflicting viewpoints passage, make a T-chart. It takes a little time, but it makes answering each question much easier. Most of the questions compare the main points of each student, and you do <u>not</u> have time to reread the passage for each question.

Student 1	Student 2
Vegetarian lifestyle is better	Fruits/vegetables important, but need meat
Veggies = more minerals absorbed	Meat = protein for muscles
Meat = saturated fat	Lean options for meat

1. **If a study were to find that the amount of protein one can process from nuts and beans was equivalent to the amount of protein in meat, whose argument would be most harmed?**

Student 2's main argument is that we need meat for protein. Since this information suggests that we can get a good source of protein from items other than meat, her answer is harmed the most by this statement. **(Answer C)**

2. **Do the two students disagree on the negative effects of saturated fats?**

Both of the students agree that saturated fat is bad for the body. Student 1's main argument is that the saturated fats in meat is unnecessary because you can get proper nutrition without eating meat. Student 2 takes this point further and suggests that the protein benefits outweigh the negative side of saturated fats. **(Answer A)**

3. **Student 2's argument would be best supported if which of these were found to be true:**

Although both students agree that saturated fats are bad for the body, Student 2 suggests that we should still eat meat containing it. He states that the benefits from consuming protein from meat outweigh the health risks of eating saturated fat in meat. If it was found that saturated fats are actually good for the body, Student 2's argument would benefit greatly: we would get the good source of protein without the negative effects of saturated fat. **(Answer B)**

Viewpoints - Quiz 3: Dementia   **3 minutes**

Ever since the discovery of dementia, scientists have been working to find ways to stop its progress or to reduce the likelihood of humans developing it. Recently, there have been studies showing that mentally challenging games help to reduce the likelihood of developing dementia. Two scientists debate the validity of these games in role of reducing the progress of dementia.

Scientist 1

During growth, the brain has the ability – known as neuroplasticity – to develop and adapt. Neuroplasticity accounts for the neurons in the brain to be malleable and change in order to adapt to new situations. These mentally challenging games attempt to exercise the brain in order to increase neuroplasticity, just as people would exercise in order to keep their muscles healthy. Because these games cause the brain to work hard at simple tasks, they increase the neuroplasticity of the brain, and thus delay the onset of dementia.

Scientist 2

Although the aforementioned games are helpful to increase one's skill at certain exercises, do not increase neuroplasticity and therefore do not stop the progress of dementia. Neuroplasticity is at its highest during early childhood development and significant at this stage. The issue with these games is that they treat the brain like a muscle when it isn't a muscle at all. While working repeatedly on a task has been proven to increase certain skills relayed to that particular task, the same skill has not been proven to increase skill in other, unrelated areas. While these games allow the user to become better at the games themselves, they do not "exercise" the brain as they claim because the brain can't be "exercised" at all.

1) Scientist 1's argument would be most improved if which of the following observations were made?
   A. The neuroplasticity of the brain can increase with repeated stimulation.
   B. Chimps who participated in brain training showed signs of dementia.
   C. Dementia is a communicable disease.
   D. The cause of dementia is related to diet.

2) One study found that the human brain has high neuroplasticity during childhood, but that the levels of neuroplasticity plummet to almost zero at about 20 years of age. Which scientist's argument is helped by this claim?
   A. Scientist 1, because Scientist 1's brain games can help raise the neuroplasticity after it has decreased.
   B. Scientist 1, because Scientist 1 believes that neuroplasticity can be increased over time with training.
   C. Scientist 2, because Scientist 2 argues that neuroplasticity cannot be improved and that it decreases over time.
   D. Scientist 2, because Scientist 2's argument hinges on the idea that the brain's neuroplasticity level can increase.

1. A 2. C

Viewpoints - Quiz 3: Dementia   (Answers)

Tip: Whenever you see the conflicting viewpoints passage, make a T-chart. It takes a little time, but it makes answering each question much easier. Most of the questions compare the main points of each scientist, and you do not have time to reread the passage for each question.

Scientist 1	Scientist 2
Neuroplasticity – develop and adapt	Games do not increase neuroplasticity
– neurons adapt to new situations	Games increase skill, but not unrelated skills
– increased by games	Games treat brain like a muscle when it is not

1. **Scientist 1's argument would be most improved if which of the following observations were made?**

Scientist 1 argues that neuroplasticity is increased when we play certain types of games. The more games we play, the more our we increase our neuroplasticity. If a repeated stimulation can increase neuroplasticity, then a repetition of challenging games should do the same. **(Answer A)**

2. **One study found that the human brain has high neuroplasticity during childhood, but that the levels of neuroplasticity plummet to almost zero at about 20 years of age. Which scientist's argument is helped by this claim?**

Scientist 2 directly states that neuroplasticity is at its highest during childhood and therefore it must be at decreased levels as time goes on. Scientist 1 makes no claim about the decrease in neuroplasticity as a person ages. **(Answer C)**

Viewpoints - Quiz 4: Mpemba   **3 minutes**

The Mpemba Effect describes the tendency of hot water to freeze more quickly than cold water. Below, two scientists debate the validity of the Mpemba Effect and its possible causes.

Scientist 1

The Mpemba Effect is an easy-to-test phenomenon that can be seen in everyday life. When water is heated, evaporation occurs on its surface. Because of this, the water cools more quickly because evaporation is endothermic, meaning it absorbs energy from its surroundings. Furthermore, because hot water evaporates, there is simply less of it to freeze, so it freezes more quickly than water at a cooler temperature. Therefore, the Mpemba Effect is a valid theory.

Scientist 2

The Mpemba Effect is invalid for several reasons. First of all, testing on the Mpemba Effect has been inconclusive. While many scientists around the world have attempted to prove or disprove the effect, none has been successful in replicating any results. The counterargument of this phenomenon can be explained very simply. When two containers of water are placed in the same freezer, one of them will always freeze first because of the slight variation of impurities in the water. In other words, the reason that one container freezes first is not its temperature, but its composition. Because the composition of water is so difficult to discern, it is impossible to replicate the reliability of the Mpemba Effect.

1. Scientist 1's argument would be most improved if which of the following observations were made?
   A. Warm water releases dissolved gases more quickly than cold water, which allows it to freeze more quickly.
   B. The atoms in warm water move much more quickly than the atoms in cold water.
   C. Cold milk tends to freeze more quickly than warm milk.
   D. Carbonated water freezes at a slower rate than distilled water.

2. A recent study found that distilled water at various temperatures froze in the same amount of time when placed in a freezer. Which scientist's claim is most harmed by this study?
   A. Scientist 1, because she argues that the Mpemba effect is caused by evaporation, which cannot happen to distilled water.
   B. Scientist 1, because she argues that warm water will always freeze before cold water.
   C. Scientist 2, because he argues that when two containers of water are placed in a freezer, one will always freeze first.
   D. Scientist 2, because he argues that the temperature of water does not affect the rate at which it freezes.

1) A 2) B

Viewpoints - Quiz 4: Mpemba (Answers)

Tip: Whenever you see the conflicting viewpoints passage, make a T-chart. It takes a little time, but it makes answering each question much easier. Most of the questions compare the main points of each scientist, and you do NOT have time to reread the passage for each question.

Scientist 1	Scientist 2
Mpemba Effect works	Mpemba Effect is invalid, inconclusive
Heated water, evaporation on surface	due to composition
evaporation is endothermic	variations in water
less water to freeze	impossible to replicate exactly

1. **Scientist 1's argument would be most improved if which of the following observations were made?**

According to the chart, Scientist 1 is claiming that the effect is valid due to heated water evaporating out of the container. Because the container is filled with less water, it is then easier to freeze. Therefore, Scientist 1 claims that warm water will freeze quicker than cold water. The only option that displays a result where warm water freezes faster than cold water is: warm water releases dissolved gases more quickly than cold water, which allows it to freeze more quickly. **(Answer A)**

2. **A recent study found that <u>distilled water</u> of various temperatures each froze in the same amount of time when placed in a freezer. Which scientist's claim is most <u>harmed</u> by this study?**

According to the chart, Scientist 1 claims that warm water freezes faster than cold water. Scientist 2 claims that this is not necessarily true because of the inconsistencies in the composition of water. The results from when distilled water is used support the argument of Scientist 2 more than the argument of Scientist 1, because the composition of distilled water is always the same. Since the warm water did not freeze faster when distilled water was used, Scientist 1's argument is harmed because she argues that warm water will always freeze before cold water. **(Answer B)**

SCIENCE TEST 1

35 Minutes - 40 Questions

Science Test 1 - Passage 1

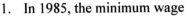

In 1938, the United States instituted a minimum wage for all workers at $0.25 per hour. Since then, the government has changed it frequently, but not every year, to keep up with the economy. (See Figure 1)

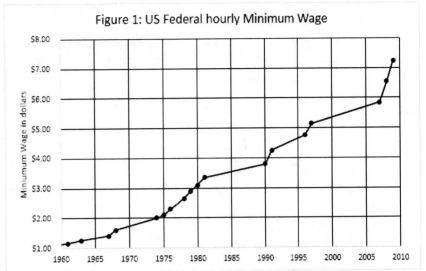

Figure 1: US Federal hourly Minimum Wage

1. In 1985, the minimum wage
   - **A.** deceased.
   - **B.** increased.
   - **C.** stayed the same.
   - **D.** was absent. There was no minimum wage that year.

2. Between 1960 and 1980 the minimum wage in the US rose
   - **A.** approximately 1 dollar.
   - **B.** approximately 2 dollars.
   - **C.** approximately 3 dollars.
   - **D.** approximately 4 dollars.

3. In 2005, the minimum wage in the US was approximately
   - **A.** $5.15.
   - **B.** $5.70.
   - **C.** $5.85.
   - **D.** There was no minimum wage that year.

4. If the changes in minimum wage during the last 50 years follow a linear trend, it is possible to predict that the minimum wage in 2015 will be approximately
   - **A.** $10.00.
   - **B.** $8.50.
   - **C.** $7.25.
   - **D.** It cannot be determined from this graph when the next change will happen.

5. If two line segments in Figure 1 have the same slope, that would mean that
   - **A.** a similar percentage increase in the hourly wage.
   - **B.** a similar increase in the hourly wage.
   - **C.** a similar frequency of changes in the minimum wage.
   - **D.** an increase similar to the line of best fit.

6. It can be deduced from the graph that in the State of Utah, the minimum wage in 2009
   - **A.** had to be $7.25, because each state has to follow federal regulations.
   - **B.** could have been lower or similar to $7.25, because each state can set its own regulations about wages.
   - **C.** could have been higher or similar to $7.25, because each state can set its own regulations about wages.
   - **D.** could have been higher or lower than $7.25, because each state can set its own regulations about wages.

7. According to the graph, multiple increases in the minimum wage during a short timespan indicate
   - **A.** an unstable political arena.
   - **B.** a healthy economy.
   - **C.** a trend that follows a long time of stability.
   - **D.** none of the answers above.

GO ON TO THE NEXT PAGE

Science Test 1 - Passage 2

Wakeboarding is a relatively new water-sport that requires special equipment. In 2010, Matt opened a water-sport store, Matt's Aquatics, to sell wake-boards every day of the week. The records below show his sales through May 31, 2016. The introduction of wakeboard rentals in 2012 affected the sales numbers, but on December 31st, 2015, Matt celebrated the fact that the store had sold a total of 2500 wakeboards since opening day.

Year	Wakeboards Sold	Percent of Wakeboards Sold
2010	525	21
2011	575	23
2012	250	10
2013	350	14
2014	375	15
2015	425	17
Table 1 – Wakeboards sold (out of 2500)		

In the first five months of 2016, Matt's Aquatics has sold a total of 100 wakeboards. Table 2 shows how many wakeboards were sold each month in 2016 as of May 31st.

Month	Wakeboards
January	14
February	17
March	22
April	24
May	23
Table 2 – Wakeboards sold in 2016	

Matt realized that many people just wanted to rent a wakeboard for a few hours instead of buying them permanently. In 2012, Matt's Aquatics introduced daily rentals of wakeboards and they have continued to rent them out every day since.

Year	Wakeboards
2010	0
2011	0
2012	10
2013	17
2014	22
2015	24
Table 3 – Average daily wakeboard rental by year	

8. The number 17 in Table 1 represents the fact that
   A. 17 wakeboards were sold in 2015.
   B. 17 out of 2500 wakeboards were sold in 2015.
   C. 17% of 2500 wakeboards were sold in 2015.
   D. 17% of 425 wakeboards were sold in 2015.

9. The number 22 in Table 3 means
   A. 22 wakeboards were rented each day in 2014.
   B. 22 wakeboards were rented on average each day in 2014.
   C. 22% of wakeboards were rented each day in 2014.
   D. 22% of wakeboards were rented on average each day in 2014.

10. How did the introduction of wakeboard rentals affect the number of wakeboards sold?
   A. Wakeboard rentals reduced the number of wakeboards sold.
   B. Wakeboard rentals increased the number of wakeboards sold.
   C. Wakeboard rentals did not affect the number of wakeboards sold.
   D. It cannot be determined because wakeboard rentals did not start until 2012.

GO ON TO THE NEXT PAGE

11. How do the sales numbers of 2016 compare to the sales numbers in 2015?
    A. By May 2016, the sales numbers have already exceeded the sales numbers of 2015.
    B. In February 2016, the sales were identical as in 2015.
    C. A comparison cannot be made until month-to-month sales numbers in 2015 are provided.
    D. A comparison cannot be made because there is no information about wakeboard rentals in 2016.

12. How many physical wakeboards did Matt's Aquatics need to have available for rent in 2015?
    A. Between 1-24
    B. Between 22 and 24
    C. 24
    D. At least 24

13. It can be concluded from the data that
    A. less people have bought wakeboards in 2016 than by this time in 2015.
    B. on average, Matt rented more wakeboards each day than he sold each day in 2015.
    C. there was a 2% increase in wakeboards sold from 2014 to 2015.
    D. wakeboard sales have increased for every month in 2016.

GO ON TO THE NEXT PAGE

Science Test 1 - Passage 3

A group of electric engineers was interested in finding out which metal would be the best fit for use in electrical wiring. They needed more insight on conductivity, resistivity, density, and melting points. The engineers collected data about common metals at 20 $^{\circ}$C and plotted this data in Table 1 in order to compare them. The *Electrical Conductivity* (EC) indicates a material's ability to conduct electricity. It is measured in Siemens/meter. The *Electrical Resistivity* (ER) of a material is its quality to oppose the flow of electric current. The ER is measured in Ohm.meter.

Metal	Electrical Conductivity (10^6 Siemens/m)	Electrical Resistivity (10^{-8} Ohm.m)	Density (g/cm^3)	Melting Point (°C)
Aluminum	36.9	2.7	2.7	660
Brass	15.9	6.3	8.5	900
Carbon steel	5.9	16.9	7.7	1400
Copper	58.5	1.7	8.9	1083
Gold	44.2	2.3	19.4	1064
Iron	10.1	9.9	7.9	1528
Lead	4.7	21.3	11.3	327
Palladium	9.5	10.5	12	1555
Platinum	9.3	10.8	21.4	1772
Silver	62.1	1.6	10.5	961
Tin	8.7	11.5	7.3	232
Titanium	2.4	41.7	4.5	1668
Tungsten	8.9	11.2	19.3	3422
Zinc	16.6	6	7.1	419

Table 1

14. Which of the following metals in Table 1 is the most conductive?
    A. Copper
    B. Mercury
    C. Silver
    D. Gold

15. Which metal with a density of less than 10g/cm^3 has the lowest melting point?
    A. Lead
    B. Tin
    C. Silver
    D. Gold

16. Mercury has a density of 13.5 g/cm^3 and is liquid at room temperature. Which of the following metals would float if placed in a pool of mercury?
    A. Platinum
    B. Gold
    C. Titanium
    D. Tungsten

17. The relationship between electric conductivity and electric resistivity is
    A. $ER = 100 - EC$.
    B. $ER = 100/EC$.
    C. $EC = ER$.
    D. $EC = 1/ER$.

GO ON TO THE NEXT PAGE

18. Early scientists had a theory that the density of the material was fairly consistent with the ability of that material to resist electricity. Were they correct?

    A. No. Although it is true for all other metals, copper, gold, and silver do not have a low resistivity despite their low density.
    B. No. There is no relationship between density and resistivity.
    C. Yes. Materials with a higher density also show a higher ability to conduct electricity.
    D. Yes. Materials such as aluminum, iron, palladium and zinc have very close measurements for density and resistivity.

19. Bronze is an alloy of copper and tin (and a small quantity of other metals.) It has the following properties:

	Electrical Resistivity	Density (g/cm^3)
Bronze	13.5	8.8

Table 2

According to the data in Table 1 and Table 2, we can conclude that

    A. bronze has a higher EC than copper, but lower than tin.
    B. bronze has a higher EC than copper and tin.
    C. bronze has a lower EC than copper and tin.
    D. bronze has a lower EC than copper but higher than tin.

20. In order to compare the electrical conductivity between metal wires, which setup would give the best experimental data?

    A. Change the length of the wires but keep the metal the same.
    B. Change the types of metal and the diameter of the wire.
    C. Keep all aspects of the test identical, except for the type of metal.
    D. Keep the type of metal the same, but change the temperature in each trial.

GO ON TO THE NEXT PAGE

Science Test 1 - Passage 4

Alleles are alternative forms of the same gene. Pea plants have two different alleles for the gene that determines texture: the dominant allele *R* for smooth and the recessive allele *r* for wrinkled. Pea plants also have two different alleles for the gene that determines color: the dominant allele *Y* for yellow and the recessive allele *y* for green. *Homozygous* pea plants have two identical alleles that are either dominant or recessive. *Heterozygous* plants have one each of two different alleles. A recessive trait can only be observed when the dominant form of that allele is absent.

	RY	Ry	rY	ry
RY	RRYY	RRYy	RrYY	RrYy
Ry	RRYy	RRyy	RrYy	Rryy
rY	RrYY	RrYy	rrYY	rrYy
ry	RrYy	Rryy	rrYy	rryy

Table 1, Punnett Square of Pea Plants

The results of breeding two heterozygous pea plants are shown within the Punnett square of Table 1. (*Punnett squares* are used to predict the probability of specific traits in the offspring.)

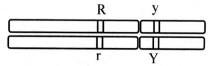

Figure 1, an example of a pea plant that is a heterozygous for both texture and color.

21. Assuming the scientists were attempting to breed pea plants to get a smooth, green pea, how many results from the square allow for that outcome?
    A. 9
    B. 3
    C. 1
    D. 2

22. What is the result of crossing two peas with alleles **rY** and **ry**?
    A. **rrYy**, because dominance does not matter.
    B. **rrYY**, because the **Y** allele is dominant
    C. **rryy**, because the **y** allele is recessive
    D. The result is not certain, because there are several possible combinations.

23. If one of the two original pea plants had the genes **RRYY**, all of the plants would be
    A. green and wrinkled.
    B. green and smooth.
    C. yellow and wrinkled.
    D. yellow and smooth.

24. How many of the results were homozygous for at least one gene?
    A. 4
    B. 8
    C. 9
    D. 12

25. What portion of the plants in the offspring are wrinkled?
    A. 1/2
    B. 1/4
    C. 1/8
    D. 1/16

26. If numerous pairs of yellow wrinkled peas are crossed, their offspring will be
    A. all yellow and all wrinkled.
    B. some yellow, some green, but all wrinkled.
    C. some wrinkled, some smooth, but all green.
    D. all green and all smooth.

GO ON TO THE NEXT PAGE

27. Based on their appearance, a farmer only selects all the green smooth peas to breed next year, in order to weed out the wrinkled ones. Will he be successful?
    A. Yes, because the alleles for green and smooth appearance are dominant.
    B. Yes, because the green and smooth peas do not have any alleles that make a pea yellow or wrinkled.
    C. No, because the allele for wrinkled is dominant.
    D. No, because some of the selected peas are heterozygous.

GO ON TO THE NEXT PAGE

Science Test 1 - Passage 5

The debate about the behavior of light has been passionate since the emergence of scientific study. Light can be observed in different colors and different intensities, based on wavelengths and frequency. The properties of light more recently have become a keystone in understanding the universe. There are different schools of thought that seek to explain the impact of these properties.

Scientist 1

Light acts wholly as a particle. It is emitted by a source and travels in a straight line and interacts with anything that comes in its way. The reflection of light at angles proves this, as particles can be deflected and continue moving, though they lose energy. When a particle of light strikes a detector, it can be observed to give off a set amount of energy. Energy transmitted by waves increases as the intensity of the source increases.

Scientist 2

Light is not a particle; it is a wave. Waves, similar to particles, are able to be reflected off of surfaces and continue to move onward in a new direction. Further, refraction—the act of light bending when it encounters matter with different density than air—can only be achieved with waves, as waves are able to move through transparent or translucent objects of differing densities. Light also causes interference in radio waves, which can only be achieved by another wave.

Scientist 3

Light is both a particle and a wave. Light travels as particles called photons in the form of waves, which allows for both to be true. Because of this, light is able to be refracted. It does not impart more energy based on the strength of the light, as it would if it were solely a wave. Light seemingly moves as a wave until it comes into contact with something, in which case it seems to take on the properties of a particle.

28. Light traveled from Point A to Point B. The energy in the photons at Point B was measured to be less than at Point A. This observation supports
    A. Scientist 1 only.
    B. Scientists 1 and 2.
    C. Scientist 2 only.
    D. Scientists 1 and 3.

29. Scientist 1's argument would be best supported if which of these were observed:
    A. Photons transmit more energy when their light source is stronger.
    B. Ultraviolet light acts solely as a wave.
    C. Refraction can occur to particles as well as waves.
    D. Waves can be reflected in the same way particles can.

30. The fact that light travels in waves is supported by
    A. all scientists.
    B. Scientists 1 and 2.
    C. Scientist 2 only.
    D. Scientists 2 and 3.

31. The statement, "Light can bend in different directions," would be mostly supported by
    A. all scientists.
    B. Scientists 1 and 2.
    C. Scientist 2 only.
    D. Scientists 2 and 3.

GO ON TO THE NEXT PAGE

32. If a study were to find that particles could cause interference in radio waves, which scientist's theory would be most harmed?

   A. Scientist 2, because one of Scientist 2's main points is that only waves can cause radio interference.

   B. Scientist 1, because the ability of particles to cause interference would strengthen the idea that light is a particle.

   C. Scientist 1, because Scientist 1's theory hinges on particles and waves having different properties.

   D. Scientist 3, because Scientist 3's argument would only account for light being a particle, rather than both a particle and a wave.

33. Lasers are a form of light, and they follow the curvature of the earth. This information harms the foundation of the theory of all the scientists, EXCEPT

   A. Scientist 1.

   B. Scientists 1 and 2.

   C. Scientist 2 only.

   D. Scientists 2 and 3.

GO ON TO THE NEXT PAGE

Science Test 1 - Passage 6

A local architect decided to test the strengths of various glues to see which glue is the strongest type to use in her small-scale models. She tested five kinds of glue for this comparison: hot glue, white craft glue, super glue (cyanoacrylate), a two-part epoxy, and wood glue.

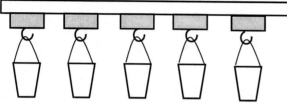

The glues were used to adhere large plastic blocks to the bottom of a tall platform. The blocks were clamped and the adhesives were left to set for a while before being tested. In order to test the strengths of these glues, the architect hung buckets from hooks in the blocks and placed weights of half a kilogram each into the buckets until the block released from the platform. The results are displayed in Table 1.

Type of glue	Maximum weight (kg)
Wood	0.5
White	0.5
Super	2.0
Epoxy	2.0
Hot	0.5
Table 1	

34. A colleague worried about the accuracy of the test. Do the numbers gathered in this experiment accurately reflect the strengths of these glues?
    A. Yes, because these strengths reflect exactly what weight the glues could hold.
    B. Yes, because it does not matter what unit of measurement she uses to be accurate.
    C. No, because the units of measurement were too imprecise.
    D. No, because the weight of the bucket was not accounted for.

35. Which of these changes to the experiment would most improve its validity?
    A. Repeating the whole experiment two more times.
    B. Using larger blocks for more precise measurement.
    C. Using different quantities of glue.
    D. Measuring in grams instead of kilograms.

After evaluating the critique of her colleague, the architect decided to repeat her first experiment, this time waiting exactly 2 hours before she put weights in the bucket. (See Table 2)

Type of glue	Maximum weight (kg)
Wood	5.5
White	3.0
Super	7.0
Epoxy	15.0
Hot	3.5
Table 2	

36. If the architect had used 100-gram weights instead, what would have happened to the data in Table 2?
    A. The unit digit will be the same, but the tenth digit will go up to show more precise results.
    B. The unit digit might go up or down, but the tenth digit will provide additional information to show more precise results.
    C. The unit digit will go down, and the tenth digit will provide additional information to show more precise results.
    D. The unit digit will stay the same or go down, and the tenth digit might provide additional information to show more precise results.

GO ON TO THE NEXT PAGE

Type of glue	Maximum weight (kg)
Wood	14.0
White	3.5
Super	7.5
Epoxy	13.0
Hot	4.0
Table 3	

37. The architect decided to run another experiment just like the last, this time using a wooden block instead of a plastic one. The results of that test are displayed in Table 3. Which of these explanations best describes why the results changed in this test?
   A. The changes were due to a natural variability in glue strength.
   B. The use of a wooden block allowed some glues to perform better than with plastic.
   C. The weight of the wood block was heavier than the plastic block, causing the glues to fail at lower weights.
   D. The wooden block allowed the glues to hold tighter to the bottom of the platform.

38. By comparing Tables 2 and 3, we can infer that
   A. the glues performed better between two wooden surfaces than between plastic and wood.
   B. the glues performed worse between two wooden surfaces than between plastic and wood.
   C. only wood glue performed better between two wooden surfaces than between plastic and wood; the others performed worse.
   D. some glues perform better between two wooden surfaces while others perform better between plastic and wood.

39. How could the architect have made improvements to more accurately control her dependent variable?
   A. Because the test results depend on the weight of the blocks, using small amounts of water that can be weighted to the nearest gram would help to provide more accurate results.
   B. Because the test results depend on the time that the blocks are clamped, adding various times would provide more accurate results.
   C. Because the test results are distorted by the weight of the bucket, hanging various weights directly on the hooks would provide more accurate results.
   D. Because the tests depend on the type of glue, adding additional glues to the experiment would provide more accurate results.

40. A nearby handyman was interested in the results of this experiment. He repeated the exact same experiment with an unknown glue. He kept a block clamped for two hours and measured that it took 3500 grams before the block came down.

   If the measurements in both experiments are reliable, which of the following statements can be supported by the test results?
   A. He used a wooden block with hot glue.
   B. He used a plastic block with wood glue.
   C. He used a plastic block with hot glue.
   D. He used a wooden block with super glue.

END OF THIS TEST
STOP! DO NOT TURN THE PAGE UNTIL TOLD TO DO SO

Science Test 1 - Answer Key

1. **C**	11. **C**	21. **B**	31. **D**
2. **B**	12. **D**	22. **A**	32. **A**
3. **A**	13. **B**	23. **D**	33. **D**
4. **C**	14. **C**	24. **D**	34. **C**
5. **B**	15. **B**	25. **B**	35. **A**
6. **C**	16. **C**	26. **B**	36. **D**
7. **D**	17. **B**	27. **D**	37. **B**
8. **C**	18. **B**	28. **A**	38. **D**
9. **B**	19. **C**	29. **C**	39. **C**
10. **A**	20. **C**	30. **D**	40. **C**

Science Test 1

Name: _____ Date: _____

Mistakes: _____ ACT Score: _____

Charts and Graphs

	Lookup		What if?		Why?	
Graph	1　　2	3	4	6	5	7
Table	8　9　11	14　15	12　　16	19	10　　13	17　18　20
Other						
	Tables: Page 412　　Graphs: Page 430					

Experiments

	Lookup		What if?		Why?	
Graph						
Table	21　　22	23　24　25	26　36　40		27　34　35	37　38　39
Other						
	Tables: Page 412　　Graphs: Page 430　　Experiments: Page 446					

Opposing Viewpoints

	Lookup		What if?		Why?	
Graph						
Table						
Other	1　　31　30　28		29　33　32			
	Conflicting Viewpoints: Page 454					

# Mistakes	ACT Score*
32	12
31	13
30	14
29	15
28	16
27	17
26	18
25	19
24	20
22-23	21
20-21	22
19	23
17-18	24
15-16	25
13-14	26
12	27
11	28
10	29
9	30
7-8	31
4-6	33
3-4	34
1-2	35
0	36

*approximate score

1) Mark your score on the right. Circle the questions you missed. **2)** Find your trends (categories with the most mistakes.) Set a goal: How many mastered categories will lead to a 3-point improvement? **3)** Study the pages in this book that will help you master the required skills. **4)** Review your missed questions.

Science Test 1 - Explanations

MINIMUM WAGE

1) What do the four dots around 1980 mean? They mean that the minimum wage increased almost every year. What does the long line to 1990 mean? This indicates that the minimum wage did not change from 1980 to 1990. Some lines are about continuums (e.g. when measuring temperature) while others record individual data points (e.g. when graphing stock market prices) in which case the line in between the points is just a visual connector. In 1985, there was no new dot. Hence, there was no change in the minimum wage; it stayed the same. **(Answer C)**

2) Be precise in your look-up questions: Put your left finger on the data and mark your numbers. The difference between 3 dollars and about 1 dollar is more or less 2 dollars. **(Answer B)**

3) In 2005, there was no new dot. Therefore, there was no change in the minimum wage; it stayed the same as in 1997 at $5.15. **(Answer C)**

4) When working with new data in a graph, use your pencil! Draw a straight line that follows the data closely. Your eye might tell you the answer is $8.50, but the pencil will tell you differently. **(Answer C)**

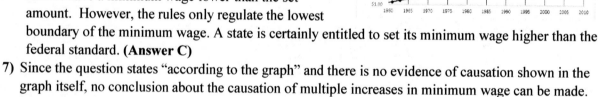

5) An increase of 50 cents on the left is the same as an increase of 50 cents on the right. **(Answer B)**

6) A state has to follow federal regulations, and therefore cannot have a minimum wage lower than the set amount. However, the rules only regulate the lowest boundary of the minimum wage. A state is certainly entitled to set its minimum wage higher than the federal standard. **(Answer C)**

7) Since the question states "according to the graph" and there is no evidence of causation shown in the graph itself, no conclusion about the causation of multiple increases in minimum wage can be made. **(Answer D)**

WAKEBOARDS

8) The number 17 is located in the column labeled Percent of wakeboards Sold and in the row labeled 2015. The title of the table states "Wakeboards sold (out of 2500)" Therefore, the number 17 means that 17 percent of 2500 wakeboards were sold in 2015. **(Answer C)**

9) The number 22 is located in the column labeled Wakeboards Rented in the row labeled 2014. The title of the table states that all of the numbers represent the average number of wakeboards rented per day. Therefore, the number 22 means that on average there were 22 wakeboards rented every day in 2014. **(Answer B)**

10) It is stated in the passage above Table 3 that the introduction of wakeboard rentals "affected the sales numbers". Both the passage and Table 3 show that Matt's Aquatics started renting wakeboards in 2012. According to Table 1, the number of wakeboards sold decreased from 575 wakeboards in 2011 to 250 wakeboards in 2012. Therefore, the introduction of wakeboard rentals reduced the number of wakeboards sold. **(Answer A)**

11) A and B are wrong. Although the tables look similar, you cannot look at the numbers from a single month in table 2 and compare them to the sales of a whole year in table 1. Answer D is not valid because we do not have to have information about the rentals to compare the sales numbers to.

However, Answer C is valid. We cannot compare the results of a few months with the sales of the whole year before, unless month-to-month sales numbers in 2015 are provided. **(Answer C)**

12) The table states that Matt rented 24 wakeboards <u>on average</u> each day. This means that some days he rented out less than 24 wakeboards, and some days he rented out more than 24 wakeboards. To be ready for those busy days, he needs at least 24 wakeboards available for rent **(Answer D)**

13) Answer A is wrong; it is impossible to tell if Matt's Aquatics had sold more in 2016 by May 31st than in during the same time period in 2015 because that information is not given. Answer C is wrong because to find the percent increase, you do not look at the difference in percentages of the total number of wakeboards sold. Instead you subtract the 375 wakeboards (2014) from the 425 wakeboards (2015) (=50) and divide this number by 375. The percent increase was 13.3% (much larger than 2%). Answer D is wrong because there was a decrease in the number of wakeboards sold between April and May in 2016. Therefore, the only answer left must be correct. Answer B states that on average there are more wakeboards rented than bought. If you divide the sales numbers from table 1 by 365, the numbers show that each day, Matt sells between 1 and 2 wakeboards on average. Table 3 shows the average wakeboard rentals per day which averages between 10 and 20 per day. **(Answer B.)**

CONDUCTIVITY

14) Silver has the highest Siemens/meter (62.1 x 106) and is therefore the most conductive of the metals. **(Answer C)**

15) Go through the density column and make a mark by the metals that have a density less than $10g/cm^3$. Of these metals, find the one with the lowest melting point. In this case, tin has a density of $7.3g/cm^3$, which is lower than $10g/cm^3$, and the lowest melting point of $232C°$. **(Answer B)**

16) Materials with lower densities float in liquids of higher density. To determine which metal would float in mercury, go through the four metals given as options and look for the one with a density lower than $13.5g/cm^3$. The answer that has a density lower than $13.5g/cm^3$ is titanium. **(Answer C)**

17) Even though Table 1 does not show the relationship between electric conductivity and electric resistivity, you can use deductive reasoning to find the correct answer. To figure out the correct answer, you can pick any of the metals and plug them into the possible relationship formula. A is incorrect because if you subtract the electrical conductivity from 100, it will not give you the electrical resistivity. C is incorrect; when you look at the two columns (electrical conductivity and electrical resistivity) you can see that they are not equal to each other. D is incorrect because 1 divided by a number larger than 1 will always give a decimal between 0 and 1. No metal has an electrical conductivity less than 1. Therefore, B must be the correct answer. **(Answer B)**

18) You are looking to see if there is a pattern between the density and electrical resistivity of the metals. By comparing the two tables, it is clear that there is no pattern between the two. Some densities are much smaller than the electrical resistivity, some are much larger than the electrical resistivity, and some are around the same value. Therefore, early scientists were not correct because there is no relationship between density and resistivity. **(Answer B)**

19) By looking at the pattern between electrical conductivity and electrical resistivity, we can conclude that as electrical conductivity increases, electrical resistivity decreases. Bronze has a higher electrical resistivity than copper and tin, which means that it also has a lower electrical conductivity than copper and tin. **(Answer C)**

20) This test seeks to compare different types of metal wires to find the difference in electrical conductivity. That means that the independent variable is the type of metal used in the wire. The size

and length of the wire needs to be same in all trials. The only variable that needs to be changed is the type of metal in the wire. **(Answer C)**

ALLELES

21) In order to get a smooth pea, the pea must have at least one *R*, since it is a dominant allele. In order to get a green pea, the pea must have two *y*'s, since it is a recessive allele. The only results from the square that have that outcome are ***RRyy, Rryy,*** and ***Rryy.*** **(Answer B)**

22) According to the Punnett square, you will always end up with a combination of the two alleles. *rrYy*, whether one is dominant or not. The *trait* can only be observed when the dominant form of that allele is absent, but the *alleles* always combine consistently. **(Answer A)**

23) Both *R* and *Y* are dominant alleles. Since one of the original pea plants has no recessive alleles present, all of the pea plants bred from this plant would show the same dominant genes. In this case, all of the plants would be yellow and smooth. **(Answer D)**

24) Homozygous pea plants have at least two alleles that are identical. Go through the Punnett square and mark all of the results that have any homozygous alleles (***RR, YY, rr,*** and *yy*). This Punnett square has 12 results that were homozygous for at least one gene. **(Answer D)**

25) For a pea plant to be wrinkled, it must have the two recessive alleles for the gene that determines texture. Go through the Punnett square and mark any results that contain ***rr***. In this Punnett square, there are only 4 results that contain the alleles ***rr***. Since there are 16 total results, the proportion of wrinkled pea plant offspring is ¼. **(Answer B)**

26) For a pea to be wrinkled, it must have two recessive alleles for the gene that determines texture. If two wrinkled peas are crossed, they will both have ***rr*** alleles and therefore make only more wrinkled peas. For a pea to be yellow, it only needs one dominant allele for the gene that determines color. Since a yellow pea could have the alleles *Yy* or *YY* there can be some variation in color when yellow peas are crossed. **(Answer B)**

27) Although smooth peas have a dominant allele, they can also contain the recessive allele for the wrinkled gene. The green smooth peas could be either homozygous, with the alleles ***RR***, or heterozygous, with the alleles ***Rr***. Since some of the peas being crossed could be heterozygous and contain recessive alleles, it is not guaranteed that there will be no wrinkled offspring. **(Answer D)**

LIGHT

28) Scientist 1 is the only scientist who states that energy is lost when it travels from one point to another. Scientists 2 and 3 do not mention a loss of energy. **(Answer A)**

29) Even though Scientist 1 mentions nothing about refraction, she makes the argument that light is a particle, not a wave. If refraction can occur to a particle as well as a wave, it would greatly help her argument that light is a particle. **(Answer C)**

30) Both Scientists 2 and 3 state that light travels in waves. Scientist 2 states that light is a wave while Scientist 3 states that light is both a particle and a wave. However, they both agree that light travels in waves. **(Answer D)**

31) Scientist 2 proposes that light can be refracted; it can bend when it encounters matter with different density than air. Scientist 3 also supports refraction, but Scientist 1 does not. **(Answer D)**

32) Scientist 2's statement reads, "Light also causes interference in radio waves, which can <u>only</u> be achieved by another wave." When new evidence shows that particles can also interfere with radio waves, it harms Scientist 2's position most.

33) Scientist 1 is the only scientist who states that light travels in a straight line. The other two scientists mention refraction and how light can change directions. Because the lasers are following the curvature of the earth, they would not be going in a straight line. Therefore, this would hurt the argument of Scientist 1. **(Answer D)**

GLUE

34) According to Table 1, there were only two maximum weights that the glues could reach. These were 0.5kg and 2.0kg. This test did not accurately reflect the strength of the glues because the measurements were too imprecise. **(Answer C)**

35) To increase the validity, the tests should be made as accurate as possible. This can be done by improving the controls and variables of a flawed experiment or by adding additional trials. In this case, repeating the experiment two more times would help the validity. **(Answer A)**

36) If the architect had used 100-gram blocks instead of half-kilogram blocks, the test would have been more accurate. The weight would not have increased (i.e. five 100-gram blocks would still weigh the same as one half-kilo block.). However, the buckets could have held slightly less weight than originally described because the architect recorded the results when the buckets fell. The buckets might have fallen at a more specific weight rather than the half-kilogram increment used. **(Answer D)**

37) Some of the maximum weights in Table 3 increased while others decreased. This means that some glues functioned better when connected to the wooden block instead of to the plastic one. **(Answer B)**

38) Use your finger to compare the results when each type of glue was used with the plastic blocks to the results collected when each type was connecting the wooden blocks. Most of the maximum weights increased when wood was used for the blocks, but not all of them. This means that some types of glue work better for wood on wood and some work better for plastic on wood. **(Answer D)**

39) The dependent variable in the experiment is the maximum weight of the glues. The use of the bucket is not necessary for this experiment. If the architect had used the weights directly, the true maximum weights could be found. This would provide more accurate results. **(Answer C)**

40) Note: 3500 grams is the same as 3.5 kilograms. The two possible options that showed this result were the plastic block with hot glue and the wooden block with white glue. The latter is not an option in the answer, leaving plastic block with hot glue as an answer **(Answer C)**

SCIENCE TEST 2

35 Minutes - 40 Questions

Science Test 2 - Passage 1

Climographs are used in meteorology to plot the rainfall and temperatures of an area during a specific time frame. The data in the graph represents the temperatures and rainfall for Lexington, KY.

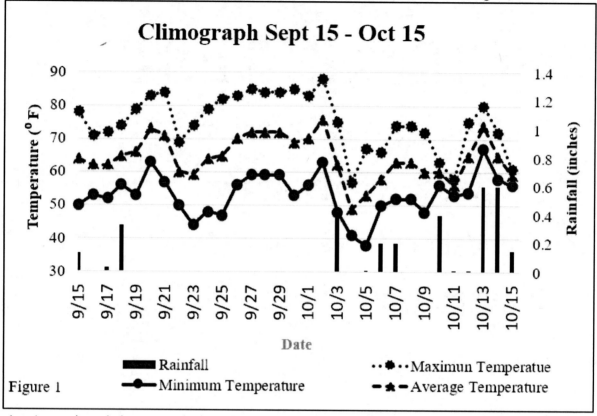

Figure 1

1. Approximately how many inches of rain fell on 9/18?
    A. Between 0 and 20
    B. Between 20 and 40
    C. Between 40 and 60
    D. More than 60

2. On which day was there the least variety in temperature?
    A. 9/23
    B. 9/15
    C. 10/11
    D. 10/7

3. On which day was the highest minimum temperature measured?
    A. 10/1
    B. 10/13
    C. 10/14
    D. 9/20

4. If the scale of the temperature in Figure 1 were changed to degrees Celsius, what would happen to the graph?
    A. The temperatures would be colder overall, because in this range the readings in Celsius are lower than the readings in Fahrenheit.
    B. The temperatures would be warmer overall, because in this range the readings in Celsius are higher than the readings in Fahrenheit.
    C. While the numbers on the graph would change, the lines would be identical because the actual temperatures would not change.
    D. The lines on the graph would have a different relationship to each other and would not mirror the current graph.

GO ON TO THE NEXT PAGE

5. According to Figure 1, the total rainfall measured is
   A. higher in October than in September.
   B. higher in the first week of October than in the first week of September.
   C. higher in the second week of October than in the first week of October.
   D. higher in September than in the second week of October.

6. Certain days have a wide range of temperatures, while others have a small gradient. Which of the following explanations is supported by the graph?
   A. As the year progresses, the days get shorter, which causes less variation in temperatures.
   B. On rainy days, the temperatures drop drastically.
   C. On days with the most rain, the cloud cover prevents large temperature fluctuations.
   D. During days without rain, the average temperature is fairly constant.

GO ON TO THE NEXT PAGE

Science Test 2 - Passage 2

A group of students wanted to see if the density of a metal had any significant effect on its melting point. They gathered data from various metals and plotted them in Figure 1.

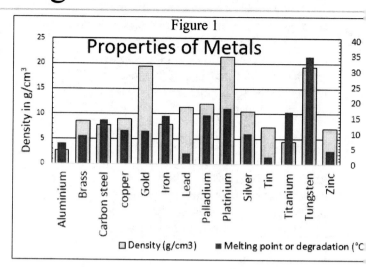

Figure 1

7. Which metal has the highest melting point?
   A. Platinum
   B. Tungsten
   C. Gold
   D. Titanium

8. What is the density of Titanium?
   A. 4.5 g/cm3
   B. 8 g/cm3
   C. 16 g/cm3
   D. 1600 g/cm3

9. Which of these metals has the largest difference between the values of its melting point and its density?
   A. Tungsten
   B. Platinum
   C. Lead
   D. Gold

10. What is the range of densities (in g/cm^3) and melting points (in °C) in this graph?

	Density	Melting Point
A.	3 – 21	2 – 34
B.	3 – 34	3 – 3400
C.	3 – 21	200 – 3400
D.	3 – 34	2 – 34

11. Which of the following tables matches the data on Figure 1?
   A. Table 1
   B. Table 2
   C. Table 3
   D. Table 4

Metal	Density	Melting Point
Copper	10.8	1243
Gold	19.4	1064
Iron	15.2	790

Table 1

Metal	Density	Melting Point
Copper	8.9	1083
Gold	19.4	1064
Iron	7.9	1528

Table 2

Metal	Density	Melting Point
Copper	10.8	890
Gold	10.6	1940
Iron	15.2	790

Table 3

Metal	Density	Melting Point
Copper	8.9	1083
Gold	10.6	1940
Iron	7.9	1528

Table 4

GO ON TO THE NEXT PAGE

486

12. Mixing copper and iron creates bronze, an alloy stronger than its components. Bronze has a melting point of approximately 925 °C, a density of 83 g/cm^3. We can deduce from the graph that
    A. the melting point of bronze is lower than each of its ingredients, while its density is fairly similar.
    B. the density of bronze is lower than each of its ingredients, while its melting point is fairly similar.
    C. the melting point of bronze is higher than each of its ingredients, while its density is fairly similar.
    D. the density of bronze is higher than each of its ingredients, while its melting point is fairly similar.

13. Crates filled with equal weights of a single metal have different volumes. According to the information provided in Graph 1, the largest crate will have the metal with the
    A. lowest density because density is proportional with volume.
    B. highest density because density is proportional with volume.
    C. lowest density because density is inversely proportional with volume.
    D. highest density because density is inversely proportional with volume.

GO ON TO THE NEXT PAGE

Science Test 2 - Passage 3

Attempt	Time to complete maze (seconds)			Average	Time to complete maze (seconds)			Average
	Rat 1	Rat 2	Rat 3		Mouse 1	Mouse 2	Mouse 3	
1	29	28	30	29	27	25	23	25
2	28	24	29	27	25	23	21	23
3	23	24	27	25	21	19	19	20
4	20	22	24	22	19	18	17	18
5	17	19	21	19	17	16	15	16
6	17	19	19	18	16	16	14	15
7	16	17	17	17	15	14	14	14
8	15	16	17	16	14	13	12	13
9	14	16	17	16	14	13	11	13
10	14	14	15	14	13	13	11	12
Table 1								

14. How much longer did it take Rat 2 to finish the maze on his second attempt than it took Mouse 3 to finish on his sixth attempt?
    A. 8 seconds
    B. 10 seconds
    C. 14 seconds
    D. 24 seconds

15. What was the difference in time between the slowest mouse and the quickest rat on ther fourth attempt?
    A. 1 second
    B. 2 seconds
    C. 7 seconds
    D. 12 seconds

16. What was the difference in the average time of the six animals between their first attempt and their tenth attempt?
    A. 15 seconds
    B. 14 seconds
    C. 13 seconds
    D. 12 seconds

17. The graph that represents the fastest mouse is

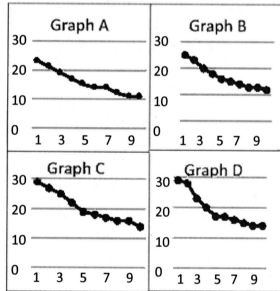

A. Graph A.
B. Graph B.
C. Graph C.
D. Graph D.

GO ON TO THE NEXT PAGE

18. As the animals completed their ten tries through the maze, their speeds
    A. increased all the time.
    B. decreased all the time.
    C. increased some times.
    D. decreased some times.

19. The researchers decided to continue the experiment for another ten trials, numbered trials 11-20. Based on the data in Table 1, the most likely prediction is
    A. the times of the animals will continue to decrease most of the time.
    B. the times of the animals will approximate 0 at the end of the trials.
    C. the times of the animals will decrease at first, then increase as the animals tire.
    D. the times of the animals will stay fairly close to their times in attempt 10.

20. The goal of the experiment was to study learning behavior so that the researchers could apply this knowledge to humans. What is the most likely reason that the researchers did not perform this experiment with humans?
    A. Humans are smarter than rodents and would be able to predict the results.
    B. There is too great a variety between humans to make this test valid.
    C. The cost to run this experiment with humans would be too high.
    D. Humans have free will and would not be willing to run through a maze to help with the experiment.

GO ON TO THE NEXT PAGE

Science Test 2 - Passage 4

Students in a physics class were tasked with finding the best projectile to use with a small catapult that their teacher had constructed the day before. Their goal was to find a projectile that would go the farthest when thrown. They were given three balls of different sizes that would work with the catapult, as well as metal beads that could be inserted into the balls to increase their weight. Below are their findings.

Table 1 - Trials with 1" Ball

Weight (g)	10	20	30	40	50	60	70	80	90	100
Distance Traveled (m)	3	3.5	4	4.7	5	5.2	4.8	4.3	3.8	3.2

Table 2 - Trials with 1.5" Ball

Weight (g)	10	20	30	40	50	60	70	80	90	100
Distance Traveled (m)	2.4	3	3.6	4	4.5	4.7	4.3	3.7	3.1	2.6

Table 3 - Trials with 2" Ball

Weight (g)	10	20	30	40	50	60	70	80	90	100
Distance Traveled (m)	1.8	2.6	3	3.8	4.2	4.3	3.9	3.1	2.6	2.1

Each ball was fired once from the catapult at each weight increment. Every trial was completed in the same space. The only differences in the trials were the size of the balls and the weight of the beads that were inside of the balls.

21. Which of these is the independent variable within the first trial?
    A. The size of the ball.
    B. The distance the ball traveled.
    C. The catapult.
    D. The weight of each ball.

22. If the trend shown in these trials continues with the use of balls of a greater diameter, what distances would we expect with a 3" ball?
    A. There would be an overall increase in the distance traveled for the 3" ball as compared to each of the other trials.
    B. With a 3" ball, the distance traveled with lower weights would be much lower, but would increase with more weight.
    C. There would be an overall decrease in the distance traveled for the 3" ball as compared to other trials.
    D. The distances traveled using a 3" ball are impossible to predict using only the data shown here.

23. Which change to the experiment would add the most validity to the results?
    A. Using a larger number of balls of different diameters.
    B. Using smaller increments of weight change for the trials.
    C. Firing each ball from the catapult multiple times and using the averages of the distances traveled for their data.
    D. Using larger balls with less weight.

24. Which graph most closely mirrors the test results with the 1" ball?

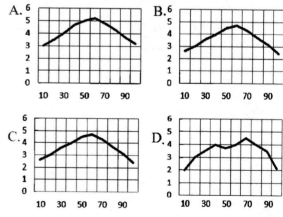

GO ON TO THE NEXT PAGE

25. The 90-gram, 1" ball travels the same distance as the 40-gram, 2" ball. A logical conclusion, supported by the data from Tables 1-3, would be
    A. the trajectories of the balls overlap.
    B. both balls reached the same height.
    C. both balls had the same resistance.
    D. the two balls are identical in their average between weight and size.

26. Considering all the data from Trials 1 through 3, the optimum weight and size to load on this catapult is
    A. 60 grams, depending on the size of the ball.
    B. 60 grams, regardless of the size of the ball.
    C. 1 inch, regardless of the weight of the ball.
    D. 1 inch, depending on the size of the ball.

27. The students repeated the whole experiment, this time increasing the angle of the catapult by 10%. Based on the results of Trials 1 - 3, it can be inferred that the balls in Trials 4 - 6
    A. will travel higher and farther.
    B. will travel higher, but not farther.
    C. will travel farther but not higher.
    D. can show either improvement or decline in their height or distance.

GO ON TO THE NEXT PAGE

Science Test 2 - Passage 5

While sleep has always been a necessary part of human life, the scientific community is torn as to why humans need sleep and exactly how much sleep is necessary for normal human function. Two scientists propose their models for understanding sleep and its necessity for humans.

Scientist 1

The most important merits of sleep for humans are two-fold. Sleep allows humans to rest their bodies, allowing for increased cellular regeneration, which increases the rate at which injuries heal. Sleep also allows the body to digest food more readily, as it is able to focus the majority of its energy on digestion instead of movement. Because the merits of sleep are purely physical, being in a resting state is just as helpful as deep sleep. In order to fully heal and allow for adequate digestion, the body needs to be in a resting or sleeping state for at least one-third of the day.

Scientist 2

The primary function of sleep is to allow the body to devote all of its energy to other tasks that would normally not be a priority in an awake state. While sleep does allow greater energy to be used for digestion and healing, that is not its only benefit. The most important of these tasks is transferring short-term memories into long-term storage within the brain, which can only occur during Rapid Eye Movement (REM) sleep. REM only occurs during specific cycles of deep sleep and is necessary for humans to process memory as well as regain energy that is lost during the day. In order to fully utilize REM sleep, humans must be asleep for at least 7 hours without interruption each day.

28. Scientist 2's argument would be most improved if which of the following observations were made?
    A. More REM sleep leads to increased forgetfulness.
    B. Large amounts of rest and no sleep allows for humans to be equally productive.
    C. Less sleep leads to longer recovery times of wounds.
    D. Increased REM sleep allows for better memory.

29. Scientist 1's argument would be best supported by which of these observations?
    A. Long periods of lying down during the day aid in faster recovery from injuries.
    B. Dolphins rest half of their brains at a time, instead of sleeping for long periods like humans.
    C. Continuous sleep for 5 hours allows for students to score better on tests.
    D. The majority of digestion occurs while moving.

30. Scientist 1 argues that
    A. REM cycles are necessary.
    B. sleep is necessary because it allows the body to put energy toward cellular regeneration.
    C. because the benefits of sleep are physical, a resting state is equally as beneficial as sleep.
    D. the main merit of sleep is moving memories from short-term to long-term storage.

GO ON TO THE NEXT PAGE

31. A third scientist found that short naps throughout the day allow for humans to function normally. Which scientist's argument does this weaken most?
    A. Scientist 1, because according to him, either a sleeping or resting state is equally helpful for normal function.
    B. Scientist 1, because according to him, the body needs to be in a resting or sleeping state for one-third of the day.
    C. Scientist 2, because according to her, REM sleep is most effective when broken up by large gaps of wakefulness.
    D. Scientist 2, because according to her, REM sleep is most effective when utilized for a continuous 7 hours.

32. All of the following are "other tasks" as referred to by Scientist 2 EXCEPT
    A. cellular regeneration.
    B. digestion.
    C. REM sleep.
    D. memory transfer.

33. After more than 24 hours without sleep, human behavior starts to resemble that of a person with increased blood-alcohol concentration: incoherent speech, reduced recollection, and sluggishness. This observation mostly supports the viewpoint of
    A. Scientist 1, because he states that merits of sleep are purely physical.
    B. Scientist 2, because she states that humans must sleep for at least 7 hours without interruption each day.
    C. Scientist 1, because he states that humans devote all of its energy to other tasks during sleep.
    D. Scientist 2, because she states that sleep is necessary to process memory as well as regain energy.

34. A fourth scientist argues that sleep is necessary for healing, resting, memory processes, and digestion. This position directly conflicts with the viewpoints of
    A. Scientist 1 only.
    B. Scientist 2 only.
    C. Scientists 1 and 2.
    D. neither one of the scientists.

GO ON TO THE NEXT PAGE

Science Test 2 - Passage 6

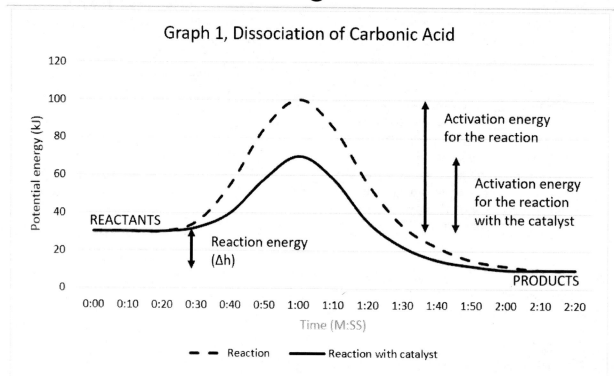

Graph 1, Dissociation of Carbonic Acid

A chemistry student is studying the effect of a catalyst on a chemical reaction. A *catalyst* is a substance that reduces the necessary energy required to start a reaction (the *activation energy*), without altering the total change of energy (Δh) of the whole reaction. The catalyst reduces the amount of energy needed at the *transition state,* the highest amount of potential energy measured in each reaction.

The student dissociates 1 mole of carbonic acid, which becomes carbon dioxide and water. She tracks the dissociating acid in a beaker and measures the mass of the water that is produced after the reaction has completed. From these measurements, she can deduct the progress of the experiment and the amount of reactants (in this case carbonic acid) used.

She runs the reaction again, this time adding carbonic anhydrase as a catalyst. She graphs the potential energy, in kilojoules, as a function of time, which is calculated after measuring changes in temperature.

35. Which is the correct formula of the chemical reaction without the catalyst??
    A. $H_2 + CO_3 => CO_2 + H_2O$.
    B. $CO_2 + H_2O => H_2 + CO_3$
    C. $CO_2 + H_2O => H_2CO_3$
    D. $H_2CO_3 => CO_2 + H_2O$

36. Which of the following statements is true of the graph above?
    A. The addition of the catalyst had no effect on the potential energy of the entire reaction.
    B. The potential energy of the reaction was lowest during the transition state.
    C. The addition of the catalyst lowered the potential energy after the completion of the reaction.
    D. The potential energy of the reactants was less than that of the products.

GO ON TO THE NEXT PAGE

37. How would the reaction change if the student were to dissociate 2 moles of carbonic acid?
    A. The disparity between the catalyzed and standard reactions' potential energy would increase.
    B. The mass of the products produced would double.
    C. The mass of the products produced would be reduced by half.
    D. The activation energy of the reactants would decrease.

38. The chemistry student measured the amount of water that was produced to draw conclusions about the number of kilojoules produced. Instead of water, she could also have measured the production of:
    A. H_2O.
    B. carbonic acid.
    C. carbonic anhydrase.
    D. CO_2.

39. As defined in the text, a catalyst reduces the necessary energy required for a reaction. Which of the following choices explains how a catalyst works in an everyday example?
    A. Enzymes in some laundry detergent speed up cleaning by breaking down certain compounds.
    B. A catalytic converter in a car uses platinum and rhodium to convert toxic gases.
    C. Increasing the heat of a cup of tea helps to speed up the time in which sugar dissolves in the liquid.
    D. To produce ammonia in fertilizers, iron is used to facilitate this process at a lower temperature.

40. After adding a second catalyst, the same process will be completed with
    A. less reaction energy and similar reactants.
    B. more product in less time.
    C. more efficiency and similar time.
    D. less reaction energy and similar time.

END OF THIS TEST
STOP! DO NOT TURN THE PAGE
UNTIL TOLD TO DO SO

Science Test 2 - Answer Key

1. **A**	11. **B**	21. **D**	31. **D**
2. **C**	12. **A**	22. **C**	32. **C**
3. **B**	13. **C**	23. **C**	33. **D**
4. **C**	14. **B**	24. **A**	34. **D**
5. **C**	15. **A**	25. **A**	35. **D**
6. **C**	16. **B**	26. **A**	36. **A**
7. **B**	17. **A**	27. **D**	37. **B**
8. **A**	18. **C**	28. **D**	38. **D**
9. **A**	19. **D**	29. **A**	39. **C**
10. **C**	20. **C**	30. **C**	40. **C**

Science Test 2

Analyze your ACT, Page 483

Name: _____ Date: _____

\# Mistakes: _____ ACT Score: _____

Charts and Graphs

	Lookup	What if?	Why?
Graph	1 5 2 7 8 3 9 10	12	4 13 6
Table	11 15 14 18	16 19 17	20
Other			
	Tables: Page 412 Graphs: Page 430		

Experiments

	Lookup	What if?	Why?
Graph	24 36	37	
Table	26	22 27	21 25 23
Other	35 39	38 40	
	Tables: Page 412 Graphs: Page 430 Experiments: Page 446		

Opposing Viewpoints

	Lookup	What if?	Why?
Graph			
Table			
Other	30 32	28 33 29 31 34	
	Conflicting Viewpoints: Page 454		

# Mistakes	ACT Score*
33	13
32	14
31	15
30	16
29	17
28	18
27	19
25-26	20
24	21
22-23	22
20-21	23
19	24
17-18	25
15-16	26
13-14	27
12	28
10-11	29
9	30
7-8	31
6	32
4-5	33
3	34
1-2	35
0	36

*approximate score

1) Mark your score on the right. Circle the questions you missed. **2)** Find your trends (categories with the most mistakes.) Set a goal: How many mastered categories will lead to a 3-point improvement? **3)** Study the pages in this book that will help you master the required skills. **4)** Review your missed questions.

Science Test 2 - Explanations

KENTUCKY WEATHER

1) According to the legend, the bars at the bottom of the graph represent rainfall. The next step is to find the correct vertical axis that corresponds with rainfall. In this graph, the right vertical axis represents rainfall. **(Answer A)**

2) The day with the least variety in temperature will occur when the minimum and maximum temperatures are closest together. The day when the minimum and maximum temperatures are closest to one another occurs on 10/11. **(Answer C)**

3) This question requires you to look at the correct line to identify the highest point. The question can be difficult because it has the two key words "highest" and "minimum." However, the word "minimum" is referring to the data set while "highest" is referring to the actual temperature. The minimum temperature is portrayed by the completely filled line. Once you have located the correct line, the question is asking for the highest point on this line. This occurs on 10/13. **(Answer B)**

4) Occasionally, the ACT will test your general knowledge of science, rather than simply your interpretation of graphs. To answer this question correctly, you must have a clear understanding of the relationship between Celsius and Fahrenheit. Both measure temperature, but they do it on different scales. Using a different scale would not change the difference in temperature from day to day. These differences are represented by the graph. The only thing that would change are the numbers that *represent* the temperature on the left Y-axis. **(Answer C)**

5) The rainfall increased as the month of October continued. The second week of October (10/8 to 10/14) had more rainfall than the first week of October (10/1 to 10/7). The bars in the first week equal a larger amount than the bars in the second week. **(Answer C)**

6) According to the graph, the temperature is colder on the days that it is raining. The question is asking about fluctuations in temperature, not about high and low temperatures. The only explanation that can be based on information *from the graph* is that on days with the most rain, there will be more cloud coverage which might prevent large temperature fluctuations. **(Answer C)**

MELTING METALS

7) The melting point is represented by the smaller, darker bar in the graph. The bar that shows the highest melting point is tungsten. **(Answer B)**

8) Density is represented by the larger, lighter bar in the graph (e.g. the bar that shows the lowest density is aluminum. The values for density can be found on the left Y-axis. The value for titanium is slightly less than 5. **(Answer A)**

9) There are two vertical axes on this graph. Each one has a vastly different range of data. The melting point increases at a much higher rate than the density scale. All density values are between 3 and 21, while the melting points differ from each other by hundreds of degrees. Therefore, a metal that has a very high melting point will have the greatest difference between that and density. The metal with the highest melting point is tungsten (3400 degrees!) That means that tungsten must have the greatest difference between melting point and density. (3400 – 19) **(Answer A)**

10) Since there are two vertical axes, you need to pay attention to which graph means which variable. The light grey bars correspond with density on the left vertical axis. The dark bars correspond with melting point on the right vertical axis. The density ranges from 3-21 g/cm^3 while the melting point ranges from 200-3400°C (or 2-34 on the graph since melting point is shown in 100°C). **(Answer C)**

11) Since there are two vertical axes, you need to make sure you are looking at the right one. The melting point is represented by the dark bar on the right vertical axis. The density is represented by the light bar on the left vertical axis. Use your fingers to match up the density and melting point of the possible answers until they are what is depicted in the table. These tables each has six numbers to analyze. As

soon as you find one that is wrong, move on to the next table. All six melting points/densities have to be correct, but if you find three tables that are incorrect, the last one must be correct. Table 2 has all six melting points/densities correct as displayed on the graph. **(Answer B)**

12) Write the information given from the question next to the graph. If you compare the melting point and density of bronze to iron and copper, you will notice that the melting point is much lower. However, the density is very similar to both copper and iron. **(Answer A)**

13) Because the crates have equal weights, it will take more of a lighter metal to equal the same weight of a heavier metal. For example, a pound of feathers requires a lot more feathers than a pound of nails. Therefore, the box of a lighter metal would be larger than a heavier metal. Density and volume are inversely proportional because the larger the density, the smaller the volume it will take up in the box. **(Answer C)**

RATS AND MICE

14) Make it a habit to put your left index finger on the data. Use your pencil to circle the numbers if needed. Rat 2 took 24 seconds and mouse 3 took 14 seconds. 24-14 is 10 seconds. **(Answer B)**

15) The slowest mouse took 19 seconds on attempt #4. The quickest rat took 20 seconds on attempt #4. 20-19 is 1 second. **(Answer A)**

16) The average of all six animals in their first attempt was (25+29)/2 = 27. The average of all six animals in their last attempt was (12+14)/2 = 13. 27 – 13 = 14 seconds. **(Answer B)**

17) The fastest mouse is mouse 3. Graph C and D start around 30 seconds and end around 15 seconds. Mouse 3's final scores are 14, 14, 12, 11, and 11. Only Graph A shows this data: look for two scores that are the same in the table as well as the graph. **(Answer A)**

18) The question is about their <u>speed</u>; however, the table shows the <u>times</u> of the rats. Speed increased as time decreased. The speeds did not always increase because sometimes the times were the same between trials. **(Answer C)**

19) At the beginning, the animals decreased times almost every trial. The last few trials show that the animals are starting to get as quick as possible at the maze. You can tell this because their times are beginning to even out. This means that their times will most likely stay the same in the trials 11-20. **(Answer D)**

20) In order to create this experiment for humans, the maze would have to be much larger. This would cause an unnecessary cost. Rats and mice are small enough that a reasonable maze can be made without too much cost. Since the brains of rodents and humans are similar, researchers can compare the results of this experiment to humans. **(Answer C)**

CATAPULT

21) Any variable that is manipulated by the researcher is called the independent variable. In this case, the weight of the ball is the variable that is being manipulated, and therefore is the independent variable. **(Answer D)**

22) This question requires you to look at all three tables and compare similar weights. According to the tables, as the diameter of the ball increases, the distance traveled decreases for balls of the same weight. **(Answer C)**

23) Adding other weights, balls, or diameters is a good idea to expand the results, but these additions do not make the current results more valid. The only flaw in the design of this experiment is that each ball was only catapulted once from each distance. Conducting several trials with the same balls and the same distance to obtain averages would increase the accuracy of the study. **(Answer C)**

24) Graphs and tables are two different ways of presenting the same data. You can often pick one single point in the table and test this point quickly on each graph to eliminate the wrong answers. For example, take the 40-gram weight. The graph should show a 4.7-meter distance. The only graph that does this is Graph A. **(Answer A)**

25) Since these balls are thrown from the same catapult, the initial position and initial angle is the same for every ball. Therefore, if two balls traveled the same distance, they must have done so by following the same trajectory. **(Answer A)**

26) On all three trials of this experiment, the largest distance traveled happened when the weight of the ball was 60 grams. However, the distance traveled differed depending on the size of the ball. The smaller the ball, the further it traveled when it was 60 grams. Therefore, the optimum weight is 60 grams depending on the size of the ball. **(Answer A)**

27) Catapults hurl projectiles through the air in an arc. One angle attains the maximum height and another angle reaches the maximum distance. Because we do not know the original angle, we do not know if we move towards or away from those defined angles. **(Answer D)**

SLEEP

28) Scientist 2 thinks that REM sleep is a crucial part of our sleep cycle. She argues that REM sleep is the major reason why we need sleep. Scientist 2 also mentions the REM stage is necessary for converting short term memories into long term memories during sleep. **(Answer D)**

29) Scientist 1 mentions that sleeping aids in the healing of injuries. Since he believes that resting and sleeping have the same benefits, resting would also help heal injuries. **(Answer A)**

30) Scientist 1 directly states that a resting state and a sleeping state are equally helpful. **(Answer C)**

31) Scientist 1 believes that sleep needs to occur for at least one third of the day. Scientist 2 believes that sleep needs to occur for 7 hours with no interruption. Having short naps spread out throughout the day would hurt Scientist 2's argument more because Scientist 1 claims nothing about sleep needing to be consecutive. **(Answer D)**

32) Scientist 2 states that tasks that are not a priority when awake are considered "other tasks". According to Scientist 2, these include digestion and healing, short term memory transfer, and the regeneration of energy (cellular regeneration). The only task that is not mentioned as an "other task" is REM sleep. **(Answer C)**

33) A high blood-alcohol concentration would affect memory transfer as well as amount of energy in the body. Scientist 2 states that both the transfer from short-term memory to long-term memory and the regeneration of energy are two major functions of sleep. Because of this, this observation would mostly support the viewpoint of Scientist 2. **(Answer D)**

34) Scientist 4 brings up four major reasons why sleep is necessary. However, even when scientists say different things, that does not mean that they directly oppose one another. Scientist 1 and scientist 2 oppose each other; they disagree about the notion that rest and sleep have the same function. Although scientist 1 and scientist 2 have different opinions, neither one would directly oppose the findings of scientist 4. **(Answer D)**

ACTIVATION ENERGY

35) While this question seems like you need to know chemical formulas for acids off the top of your head, there's an easier way to solve this problem. The answer to this is clearly found in the text. "She dissociates 1 mole of carbonic acid, which becomes carbon dioxide and water." In other words, the correct equation has to produce water (H_2O) and something else. In light of this fact, only A and D can be correct. In order to decide the correct answer, you should then look at the left side of the equation. The text mentions that the scientist only start with one substance (carbonic acid), while answer A stars off with two substances (including hydrogen). **(Answer D)**

36) You can get to the right answer by making some inferences. B is incorrect just by looking at the graph; the energy rises during the transition state for both reactions. C is incorrect because both reactions have the same energy after they have completed. D is incorrect because it is clear on the graph that the reactants have higher potential energy than the products. So, even without knowing much about reactions and catalysts, B, C, and D can be ruled out. A is correct because, while it

appears that the catalyst lowered the potential energy of the reaction overall, it only lowered the potential energy of the transition state. The potential energy of the entire reaction is really measured by the change of energy between the reactants and products, and you can see that the potential energy in the beginning and in the end of the graph are equal for both reactions. **(Answer A)**

37) This question requires some prior knowledge of how ratios in chemical reactions work. The amount of acid originally dissociated was 1 mole, as is stated in the text. Because the ratio of amount of reactants to products is constant in chemical reactions, the amount of product would change at the same rate as the amount of reactant. In other words, if you start with twice as much, you end up with twice as much. **(Answer B)**

38) The two products of the reaction are water and carbon dioxide. So, if she already measured water, only carbon dioxide is left to collect. **(Answer D)**

39) Out of the given options, you are looking for one that does not change the reactants or the products, yet lowers the amount of (potential) energy needed to make the process happen. A and C both talk about the speed of the process, not the potential energy. Read the question carefully; this is not the answer we are looking for. Adding heat actually increases the amount of energy needed to complete the process. Answer B is wrong because it states that a process takes place, but it does not give an explanation. The question specifically asks for an explanation. In answer D, the reactants and the products are the same, but by adding iron, the process takes place at a lower temperature (in other words, at a lower energy level.) **(Answer C)**

40) The time that it took the reaction to occur in the original experiment was the same with or without the catalyst. Adding a new catalyst will therefore not affect the time. The original catalyst decreased the amount of potential energy needed to make the reaction happen. Adding a new catalyst will further decrease the amount of potential energy needed for the reaction to occur. This would increase the efficiency of the reaction. **(Answer C)**

TEST 1- English: Date: Goal: Score:

1. Ⓐ Ⓑ Ⓒ Ⓓ	16. Ⓐ Ⓑ Ⓒ Ⓓ	31. Ⓐ Ⓑ Ⓒ Ⓓ	46. Ⓐ Ⓑ Ⓒ Ⓓ	61. Ⓐ Ⓑ Ⓒ Ⓓ
2. Ⓐ Ⓑ Ⓒ Ⓓ	17. Ⓐ Ⓑ Ⓒ Ⓓ	32. Ⓐ Ⓑ Ⓒ Ⓓ	47. Ⓐ Ⓑ Ⓒ Ⓓ	62. Ⓐ Ⓑ Ⓒ Ⓓ
3. Ⓐ Ⓑ Ⓒ Ⓓ	18. Ⓐ Ⓑ Ⓒ Ⓓ	33. Ⓐ Ⓑ Ⓒ Ⓓ	48. Ⓐ Ⓑ Ⓒ Ⓓ	63. Ⓐ Ⓑ Ⓒ Ⓓ
4. Ⓐ Ⓑ Ⓒ Ⓓ	19. Ⓐ Ⓑ Ⓒ Ⓓ	34. Ⓐ Ⓑ Ⓒ Ⓓ	49. Ⓐ Ⓑ Ⓒ Ⓓ	64. Ⓐ Ⓑ Ⓒ Ⓓ
5. Ⓐ Ⓑ Ⓒ Ⓓ	20. Ⓐ Ⓑ Ⓒ Ⓓ	35. Ⓐ Ⓑ Ⓒ Ⓓ	50. Ⓐ Ⓑ Ⓒ Ⓓ	65. Ⓐ Ⓑ Ⓒ Ⓓ
6. Ⓐ Ⓑ Ⓒ Ⓓ	21. Ⓐ Ⓑ Ⓒ Ⓓ	36. Ⓐ Ⓑ Ⓒ Ⓓ	51. Ⓐ Ⓑ Ⓒ Ⓓ	66. Ⓐ Ⓑ Ⓒ Ⓓ
7. Ⓐ Ⓑ Ⓒ Ⓓ	22. Ⓐ Ⓑ Ⓒ Ⓓ	37. Ⓐ Ⓑ Ⓒ Ⓓ	52. Ⓐ Ⓑ Ⓒ Ⓓ	67. Ⓐ Ⓑ Ⓒ Ⓓ
8. Ⓐ Ⓑ Ⓒ Ⓓ	23. Ⓐ Ⓑ Ⓒ Ⓓ	38. Ⓐ Ⓑ Ⓒ Ⓓ	53. Ⓐ Ⓑ Ⓒ Ⓓ	68. Ⓐ Ⓑ Ⓒ Ⓓ
9. Ⓐ Ⓑ Ⓒ Ⓓ	24. Ⓐ Ⓑ Ⓒ Ⓓ	39. Ⓐ Ⓑ Ⓒ Ⓓ	54. Ⓐ Ⓑ Ⓒ Ⓓ	69. Ⓐ Ⓑ Ⓒ Ⓓ
10. Ⓐ Ⓑ Ⓒ Ⓓ	25. Ⓐ Ⓑ Ⓒ Ⓓ	40. Ⓐ Ⓑ Ⓒ Ⓓ	55. Ⓐ Ⓑ Ⓒ Ⓓ	70. Ⓐ Ⓑ Ⓒ Ⓓ
11. Ⓐ Ⓑ Ⓒ Ⓓ	26. Ⓐ Ⓑ Ⓒ Ⓓ	41. Ⓐ Ⓑ Ⓒ Ⓓ	56. Ⓐ Ⓑ Ⓒ Ⓓ	71. Ⓐ Ⓑ Ⓒ Ⓓ
12. Ⓐ Ⓑ Ⓒ Ⓓ	27. Ⓐ Ⓑ Ⓒ Ⓓ	42. Ⓐ Ⓑ Ⓒ Ⓓ	57. Ⓐ Ⓑ Ⓒ Ⓓ	72. Ⓐ Ⓑ Ⓒ Ⓓ
13. Ⓐ Ⓑ Ⓒ Ⓓ	28. Ⓐ Ⓑ Ⓒ Ⓓ	43. Ⓐ Ⓑ Ⓒ Ⓓ	58. Ⓐ Ⓑ Ⓒ Ⓓ	73. Ⓐ Ⓑ Ⓒ Ⓓ
14. Ⓐ Ⓑ Ⓒ Ⓓ	29. Ⓐ Ⓑ Ⓒ Ⓓ	44. Ⓐ Ⓑ Ⓒ Ⓓ	59. Ⓐ Ⓑ Ⓒ Ⓓ	74. Ⓐ Ⓑ Ⓒ Ⓓ
15. Ⓐ Ⓑ Ⓒ Ⓓ	30. Ⓐ Ⓑ Ⓒ Ⓓ	45. Ⓐ Ⓑ Ⓒ Ⓓ	60. Ⓐ Ⓑ Ⓒ Ⓓ	75. Ⓐ Ⓑ Ⓒ Ⓓ

TEST 1- Math: Date: Goal: Score:

1. Ⓐ Ⓑ Ⓒ Ⓓ Ⓔ	16. Ⓐ Ⓑ Ⓒ Ⓓ Ⓔ	31. Ⓐ Ⓑ Ⓒ Ⓓ Ⓔ	46. Ⓐ Ⓑ Ⓒ Ⓓ Ⓔ
2. Ⓐ Ⓑ Ⓒ Ⓓ Ⓔ	17. Ⓐ Ⓑ Ⓒ Ⓓ Ⓔ	32. Ⓐ Ⓑ Ⓒ Ⓓ Ⓔ	47. Ⓐ Ⓑ Ⓒ Ⓓ Ⓔ
3. Ⓐ Ⓑ Ⓒ Ⓓ Ⓔ	18. Ⓐ Ⓑ Ⓒ Ⓓ Ⓔ	33. Ⓐ Ⓑ Ⓒ Ⓓ Ⓔ	48. Ⓐ Ⓑ Ⓒ Ⓓ Ⓔ
4. Ⓐ Ⓑ Ⓒ Ⓓ Ⓔ	19. Ⓐ Ⓑ Ⓒ Ⓓ Ⓔ	34. Ⓐ Ⓑ Ⓒ Ⓓ Ⓔ	49. Ⓐ Ⓑ Ⓒ Ⓓ Ⓔ
5. Ⓐ Ⓑ Ⓒ Ⓓ Ⓔ	20. Ⓐ Ⓑ Ⓒ Ⓓ Ⓔ	35. Ⓐ Ⓑ Ⓒ Ⓓ Ⓔ	50. Ⓐ Ⓑ Ⓒ Ⓓ Ⓔ
6. Ⓐ Ⓑ Ⓒ Ⓓ Ⓔ	21. Ⓐ Ⓑ Ⓒ Ⓓ Ⓔ	36. Ⓐ Ⓑ Ⓒ Ⓓ Ⓔ	51. Ⓐ Ⓑ Ⓒ Ⓓ Ⓔ
7. Ⓐ Ⓑ Ⓒ Ⓓ Ⓔ	22. Ⓐ Ⓑ Ⓒ Ⓓ Ⓔ	37. Ⓐ Ⓑ Ⓒ Ⓓ Ⓔ	52. Ⓐ Ⓑ Ⓒ Ⓓ Ⓔ
8. Ⓐ Ⓑ Ⓒ Ⓓ Ⓔ	23. Ⓐ Ⓑ Ⓒ Ⓓ Ⓔ	38. Ⓐ Ⓑ Ⓒ Ⓓ Ⓔ	53. Ⓐ Ⓑ Ⓒ Ⓓ Ⓔ
9. Ⓐ Ⓑ Ⓒ Ⓓ Ⓔ	24. Ⓐ Ⓑ Ⓒ Ⓓ Ⓔ	39. Ⓐ Ⓑ Ⓒ Ⓓ Ⓔ	54. Ⓐ Ⓑ Ⓒ Ⓓ Ⓔ
10. Ⓐ Ⓑ Ⓒ Ⓓ Ⓔ	25. Ⓐ Ⓑ Ⓒ Ⓓ Ⓔ	40. Ⓐ Ⓑ Ⓒ Ⓓ Ⓔ	55. Ⓐ Ⓑ Ⓒ Ⓓ Ⓔ
11. Ⓐ Ⓑ Ⓒ Ⓓ Ⓔ	26. Ⓐ Ⓑ Ⓒ Ⓓ Ⓔ	41. Ⓐ Ⓑ Ⓒ Ⓓ Ⓔ	56. Ⓐ Ⓑ Ⓒ Ⓓ Ⓔ
12. Ⓐ Ⓑ Ⓒ Ⓓ Ⓔ	27. Ⓐ Ⓑ Ⓒ Ⓓ Ⓔ	42. Ⓐ Ⓑ Ⓒ Ⓓ Ⓔ	57. Ⓐ Ⓑ Ⓒ Ⓓ Ⓔ
13. Ⓐ Ⓑ Ⓒ Ⓓ Ⓔ	28. Ⓐ Ⓑ Ⓒ Ⓓ Ⓔ	43. Ⓐ Ⓑ Ⓒ Ⓓ Ⓔ	58. Ⓐ Ⓑ Ⓒ Ⓓ Ⓔ
14. Ⓐ Ⓑ Ⓒ Ⓓ Ⓔ	29. Ⓐ Ⓑ Ⓒ Ⓓ Ⓔ	44. Ⓐ Ⓑ Ⓒ Ⓓ Ⓔ	59. Ⓐ Ⓑ Ⓒ Ⓓ Ⓔ
15. Ⓐ Ⓑ Ⓒ Ⓓ Ⓔ	30. Ⓐ Ⓑ Ⓒ Ⓓ Ⓔ	45. Ⓐ Ⓑ Ⓒ Ⓓ Ⓔ	60. Ⓐ Ⓑ Ⓒ Ⓓ Ⓔ

1. **TEST 1- Reading:**   Date: Goal: Score:

2. Ⓐ Ⓑ Ⓒ Ⓓ	12. Ⓐ Ⓑ Ⓒ Ⓓ	22. Ⓐ Ⓑ Ⓒ Ⓓ	32. Ⓐ Ⓑ Ⓒ Ⓓ
3. Ⓐ Ⓑ Ⓒ Ⓓ	13. Ⓐ Ⓑ Ⓒ Ⓓ	23. Ⓐ Ⓑ Ⓒ Ⓓ	33. Ⓐ Ⓑ Ⓒ Ⓓ
4. Ⓐ Ⓑ Ⓒ Ⓓ	14. Ⓐ Ⓑ Ⓒ Ⓓ	24. Ⓐ Ⓑ Ⓒ Ⓓ	34. Ⓐ Ⓑ Ⓒ Ⓓ
5. Ⓐ Ⓑ Ⓒ Ⓓ	15. Ⓐ Ⓑ Ⓒ Ⓓ	25. Ⓐ Ⓑ Ⓒ Ⓓ	35. Ⓐ Ⓑ Ⓒ Ⓓ
6. Ⓐ Ⓑ Ⓒ Ⓓ	16. Ⓐ Ⓑ Ⓒ Ⓓ	26. Ⓐ Ⓑ Ⓒ Ⓓ	36. Ⓐ Ⓑ Ⓒ Ⓓ
7. Ⓐ Ⓑ Ⓒ Ⓓ	17. Ⓐ Ⓑ Ⓒ Ⓓ	27. Ⓐ Ⓑ Ⓒ Ⓓ	37. Ⓐ Ⓑ Ⓒ Ⓓ
8. Ⓐ Ⓑ Ⓒ Ⓓ	18. Ⓐ Ⓑ Ⓒ Ⓓ	28. Ⓐ Ⓑ Ⓒ Ⓓ	38. Ⓐ Ⓑ Ⓒ Ⓓ
9. Ⓐ Ⓑ Ⓒ Ⓓ	19. Ⓐ Ⓑ Ⓒ Ⓓ	29. Ⓐ Ⓑ Ⓒ Ⓓ	39. Ⓐ Ⓑ Ⓒ Ⓓ
10. Ⓐ Ⓑ Ⓒ Ⓓ	20. Ⓐ Ⓑ Ⓒ Ⓓ	30. Ⓐ Ⓑ Ⓒ Ⓓ	40. Ⓐ Ⓑ Ⓒ Ⓓ
11. Ⓐ Ⓑ Ⓒ Ⓓ	21. Ⓐ Ⓑ Ⓒ Ⓓ	31. Ⓐ Ⓑ Ⓒ Ⓓ	41. Ⓐ Ⓑ Ⓒ Ⓓ

TEST 1- Science: Date: Goal: Score:

1. Ⓐ Ⓑ Ⓒ Ⓓ	11. Ⓐ Ⓑ Ⓒ Ⓓ	21. Ⓐ Ⓑ Ⓒ Ⓓ	31. Ⓐ Ⓑ Ⓒ Ⓓ
2. Ⓐ Ⓑ Ⓒ Ⓓ	12. Ⓐ Ⓑ Ⓒ Ⓓ	22. Ⓐ Ⓑ Ⓒ Ⓓ	32. Ⓐ Ⓑ Ⓒ Ⓓ
3. Ⓐ Ⓑ Ⓒ Ⓓ	13. Ⓐ Ⓑ Ⓒ Ⓓ	23. Ⓐ Ⓑ Ⓒ Ⓓ	33. Ⓐ Ⓑ Ⓒ Ⓓ
4. Ⓐ Ⓑ Ⓒ Ⓓ	14. Ⓐ Ⓑ Ⓒ Ⓓ	24. Ⓐ Ⓑ Ⓒ Ⓓ	34. Ⓐ Ⓑ Ⓒ Ⓓ
5. Ⓐ Ⓑ Ⓒ Ⓓ	15. Ⓐ Ⓑ Ⓒ Ⓓ	25. Ⓐ Ⓑ Ⓒ Ⓓ	35. Ⓐ Ⓑ Ⓒ Ⓓ
6. Ⓐ Ⓑ Ⓒ Ⓓ	16. Ⓐ Ⓑ Ⓒ Ⓓ	26. Ⓐ Ⓑ Ⓒ Ⓓ	36. Ⓐ Ⓑ Ⓒ Ⓓ
7. Ⓐ Ⓑ Ⓒ Ⓓ	17. Ⓐ Ⓑ Ⓒ Ⓓ	27. Ⓐ Ⓑ Ⓒ Ⓓ	37. Ⓐ Ⓑ Ⓒ Ⓓ
8. Ⓐ Ⓑ Ⓒ Ⓓ	18. Ⓐ Ⓑ Ⓒ Ⓓ	28. Ⓐ Ⓑ Ⓒ Ⓓ	38. Ⓐ Ⓑ Ⓒ Ⓓ
9. Ⓐ Ⓑ Ⓒ Ⓓ	19. Ⓐ Ⓑ Ⓒ Ⓓ	29. Ⓐ Ⓑ Ⓒ Ⓓ	39. Ⓐ Ⓑ Ⓒ Ⓓ
10. Ⓐ Ⓑ Ⓒ Ⓓ	20. Ⓐ Ⓑ Ⓒ Ⓓ	30. Ⓐ Ⓑ Ⓒ Ⓓ	40. Ⓐ Ⓑ Ⓒ Ⓓ

TEST 2- English: Date: Goal: Score:

1. ABCD	16. ABCD	31. ABCD	46. ABCD	61. ABCD
2. ABCD	17. ABCD	32. ABCD	47. ABCD	62. ABCD
3. ABCD	18. ABCD	33. ABCD	48. ABCD	63. ABCD
4. ABCD	19. ABCD	34. ABCD	49. ABCD	64. ABCD
5. ABCD	20. ABCD	35. ABCD	50. ABCD	65. ABCD
6. ABCD	21. ABCD	36. ABCD	51. ABCD	66. ABCD
7. ABCD	22. ABCD	37. ABCD	52. ABCD	67. ABCD
8. ABCD	23. ABCD	38. ABCD	53. ABCD	68. ABCD
9. ABCD	24. ABCD	39. ABCD	54. ABCD	69. ABCD
10. ABCD	25. ABCD	40. ABCD	55. ABCD	70. ABCD
11. ABCD	26. ABCD	41. ABCD	56. ABCD	71. ABCD
12. ABCD	27. ABCD	42. ABCD	57. ABCD	72. ABCD
13. ABCD	28. ABCD	43. ABCD	58. ABCD	73. ABCD
14. ABCD	29. ABCD	44. ABCD	59. ABCD	74. ABCD
15. ABCD	30. ABCD	45. ABCD	60. ABCD	75. ABCD

TEST 2- Math: Date: Goal: Score:

1. ABCDE	16. ABCDE	31. ABCDE	46. ABCDE
2. ABCDE	17. ABCDE	32. ABCDE	47. ABCDE
3. ABCDE	18. ABCDE	33. ABCDE	48. ABCDE
4. ABCDE	19. ABCDE	34. ABCDE	49. ABCDE
5. ABCDE	20. ABCDE	35. ABCDE	50. ABCDE
6. ABCDE	21. ABCDE	36. ABCDE	51. ABCDE
7. ABCDE	22. ABCDE	37. ABCDE	52. ABCDE
8. ABCDE	23. ABCDE	38. ABCDE	53. ABCDE
9. ABCDE	24. ABCDE	39. ABCDE	54. ABCDE
10. ABCDE	25. ABCDE	40. ABCDE	55. ABCDE
11. ABCDE	26. ABCDE	41. ABCDE	56. ABCDE
12. ABCDE	27. ABCDE	42. ABCDE	57. ABCDE
13. ABCDE	28. ABCDE	43. ABCDE	58. ABCDE
14. ABCDE	29. ABCDE	44. ABCDE	59. ABCDE
15. ABCDE	30. ABCDE	45. ABCDE	60. ABCDE

TEST 2- Reading: Date: Goal: Score:

1. ABCD
2. ABCD
3. ABCD
4. ABCD
5. ABCD
6. ABCD
7. ABCD
8. ABCD
9. ABCD
10. ABCD

11. ABCD
12. ABCD
13. ABCD
14. ABCD
15. ABCD
16. ABCD
17. ABCD
18. ABCD
19. ABCD
20. ABCD

21. ABCD
22. ABCD
23. ABCD
24. ABCD
25. ABCD
26. ABCD
27. ABCD
28. ABCD
29. ABCD
30. ABCD

31. ABCD
32. ABCD
33. ABCD
34. ABCD
35. ABCD
36. ABCD
37. ABCD
38. ABCD
39. ABCD
40. ABCD

TEST 2- Science: Date: Goal: Score:

1. ABCD
2. ABCD
3. ABCD
4. ABCD
5. ABCD
6. ABCD
7. ABCD
8. ABCD
9. ABCD
10. ABCD

11. ABCD
12. ABCD
13. ABCD
14. ABCD
15. ABCD
16. ABCD
17. ABCD
18. ABCD
19. ABCD
20. ABCD

21. ABCD
22. ABCD
23. ABCD
24. ABCD
25. ABCD
26. ABCD
27. ABCD
28. ABCD
29. ABCD
30. ABCD

31. ABCD
32. ABCD
33. ABCD
34. ABCD
35. ABCD
36. ABCD
37. ABCD
38. ABCD
39. ABCD
40. ABCD

NOTES

It is never too soon to start planning for college.

- College List Development
- ACT/SAT Prep Classes
- Career & Major Help
- Athletic Recruiting
- Financial Aid
- Scholarships
- Grades

We help make college more affordable.

CPSIA information can be obtained
at www.ICGtesting.com
Printed in the USA
FSOW02n2151160717
36246FS

9 780692 892220